ISBN 978-1-5282-4262-2
PIBN 10923211

1 MONTH OF
FREE
READING

at

www.ForgottenBooks.com

By purchasing this book you are eligible for one month membership to ForgottenBooks.com, giving you unlimited access to our entire collection of over 1,000,000 titles via our web site and mobile apps.

To claim your free month visit:

www.forgottenbooks.com/free923211

English
Français
Deutsche
Italiano
Español
Português

www.forgottenbooks.com

Mythology Photography **Fiction**
Fishing Christianity **Art** Cooking
Essays Buddhism Freemasonry
Medicine **Biology** Music **Ancient**
Egypt Evolution Carpentry Physics
Dance Geology **Mathematics** Fitness
Shakespeare **Folklore** Yoga Marketing
Confidence Immortality Biographies
Poetry **Psychology** Witchcraft
Electronics Chemistry History **Law**
Accounting **Philosophy** Anthropology
Alchemy Drama Quantum Mechanics
Atheism Sexual Health **Ancient History**
Entrepreneurship Languages Sport
Paleontology Needlework Islam
Metaphysics Investment Archaeology
Parenting Statistics Criminology
Motivational

LAWS

OF THE

STATE OF NEW YORK,

PASSED AT THE

EIGHTY-FIFTH SESSION

OF THE

LEGISLATURE,

BEGUN JANUARY SEVENTH, AND ENDED APRIL TWENTY-THIRD, 1862, IN THE
CITY OF ALBANY.

ALBANY:
WEARE C. LITTLE, 525 BROADWAY,
1862.

~~signature~~

CERTIFICATE.

———◆◆◆———

STATE OF NEW YORK,
      SECRETARY'S OFFICE,
         Albany May 23d, 1862.

Pursuant to the directions of the act entitled "An act relative to the publication of the Laws," passed April 12, 1843, I hereby certify that the following volume of the Laws of this State, was printed under my direction.

                    HORATIO BALLARD, Secretary of State.

In this volume, "every act which received the assent of three-fifths of all the Members elected to either House of the Legislature," pursuant to Section 14, of Article 7, of the Constitution of this State, is designated under its title by the words ."Three-fifths being present." [See Laws of 1847, Vol. 1, Chap. 253.]

And every "act which received the assent of two-thirds of all the Members elected to each branch of the Legislature," pursuant to Section 9, of Article 1, of the Constitution, is designated under its title by the words "By a two-third vote." [See Laws of 1842, Chap. 306.]

LIST OF OFFICERS.

"§ 4. There shall be prefixed to each volume of the Session Laws, hereafter published, the names and residence of the Governor, Lieutenant-Governor, Senators and Members of Assembly, and presiding officers of both Houses in office at the time of the passage of the Laws contained in such volumes."—*Laws of 1847, Chap. 458, Sec. 4.*

NAMES AND RESIDENCES

Of the Governor, Lieutenant-Governor, Senators, Members of Assembly, and presiding officers of both Houses in office at the time of the passage of the Laws contained in this volume.

NAME.	OFFICE.	RESIDENCE.	
		COUNTY.	NEAREST POST OFFICE.
Edwin D. Morgan,	Governor,	Albany,	Albany.
Robert Campbell,	Lt.-Governor,	Steuben,	Bath
Monroe Henderson,	Senator	Queens,	Jamaica
Jesse C. Smith,	do	Kings,	Brooklyn
Henry C. Murphy,	do	Kings,	Brooklyn
Christian B. Woodruff,	do	New York,	New York.
Charles G. Cornell,	do	New York,	New York.
John J. Bradley,	do	New York,	New York.
Richard B. Connolly,	do	New York,	New York.
Hezekiah D. Robertson,	do	Westchester,	Bedford.
Henry R. Low,	do	Sullivan,	Monticello.
Jacob S. Freer,	do	Ulster,	Ellenville.
William H. Tobey,	do	Columbia,	Kinderhook.
Ralph Richards,	do	Washington,	Hampton.
John V. L. Pruyn,	do	Albany,	Albany.
Joseph H. Ramsey,	do	Schoharie	Lawyersville.
John Willard,	do	Saratoga,	Saratoga Springs
Russell M. Little,	do	Warren,	Glens Falls.
Charles C. Montgomery,	do	St. Lawr'ce,	Waddington.
James A. Bell,	do	Jefferson	Dexter.
Alexander H. Bailey,	do	Oneida,	Rome.
George A. Hardin,	do	Herkimer,	Little Falls.
Richard K. Sanford,	do	Oswego	Fulton.
Allen Munroe,	do	Onondaga,	Syracuse.
Henry A. Clark,	do	Chenango,	Bainbridge.
Lyman Truman,	do	Tioga,	Owego.
Chauncey M. Abbott,	do	Cayuga,	Niles.
Charles J. Folger,	do	Ontario,	Geneva.

NAME.	OFFICE.	RESIDENCE.	
		COUNTY.	NEAREST POST OFFICE.
Charles Cook, ...	Senator, ...	Schuyler.....	Havana.
Lysander Farrar, ...	do	Monroe......	Rochester.
Almanzor Hutchinson, ...	do	Orleans......	Gaines.
Wilkes Angel, ...	do	Allegany	Angelica
John Ganson, ...	do	Erie	Buffalo.
Horace C. Young, ...	do	Cattaraugus .	New Albion.
Jonathan M. Ackley,..........	Assemblyman, .	Jefferson ...	Worthville.
Hndrew L. Allen,..............	do	Cattaraugus..	Machias,
Samuel M. Alley,.............	do	Steuben.	Hornellsville.
Thomas G. Alvord,............	do	Onondaga....	Salina
Albert Andrus,...............	do	Franklin	Malone.
Smith Anthony, ...	do	Cayuga	Fleming.
Eli Avery,...................	do	Oneida.	Clayville
A. Bleecker Banks, ...	do	Albany	Albany.
Thomas Barry, ...	do	Cortland....	Marathon.
George Bartlett,..............	do	Broome......	Binghamton.
Tracy Beadle,................	do	Chemung. ...	Elmira.
Charles L. Benedict,...........	do	Kings.......	New York City.
Jesse F. Bookstaver,..........	do	Ulster......	Saugerties.
Leroy E. Bowe, ...	do	Otsego	Middlefield.
Benjamin E. Bowen, ...	do	Oswego	Mexico.
William H. Brand, ...	do	Madison.	Leonardsville
Daniel B. Bryan,.............	do	Steuben.	Sonora.
James H. Burr,..............	do	Fult. & Ham.,	Gloversville.
James W. Bush,..............	do	New York,..	New York.
John Callahan, ...	do	New York,..	New York.
John A. Case, ...	do	Erie, ...	Holland
Noah A. Childs,..............	do	New York, ..	New York.
Cornelius A. Church,..........	do	Otsego.	Morris.
David S. Coddington,..........	do	New York, ..	New York.
William J. Coey,.............	do	New York, ..	New York,
Isaac Coles,.................	do	Queens, ...	Glen Cove.
Almerin J. Cornell,...........	do	Albany	Rensselaerville
Ezra Cornell,................	do	Tompkins....	Ithaca.
Jonathan B. Cowles, ...	do	Greene	Durham
Alvah E. Cruttenden,..........	do	Allegany. ...	Canaseraga.
James Darcy,................	do	Kings.......	Brooklyn.
Nicholas E. Darrow,..........	do	Orleans......	Clarendon.
Emry Davis,.................	do	Chautauqua..	Busti.
John C. Davis, ...	do	Suffolk......	River Head.
Chauncey M. Depew,..........	do	Westchester..	Peekskill
William Dewey,..............	do	Jefferson ...	Three Mile Bay.
William Doyle, ...	do	Albany	Albany
John B. Dutcher,.............	do	Dutchess, ...	Pawling
Smith Ely,..................	do	Richmond....	New Brighton.
Francis B. Fisher,............	do	Chenango ...	Greene.
Benjamin H. Fletcher,.........	do	Niagara, ...	Lockport.
John Fulton,................	do	Saratoga	Waterford.
R. Nelson Gere,..............	do	Onondaga....	Geddes.
Ezra P. Goslin,..............	do	Erie	Akron.
Thomas S. Gray, ...	do	Warren, ...	Warrensburgh.
Edmund Green, ...	do	Dutchess....	Tivoli
Henry D. Hall, ...	do	Queens	Jamaica

NAME.	OFFICE.	RESIDENCE.	
		COUNTY.	NEAREST POST OFFICE.
William A. Halsey, ...	Assemblyman, .	Cayuga......	Port Byron.
Newberry D. Halsted,*........	do	Westchester.	Rye.
James S. Haring, ...	do .	Rockland, ...	Orangeburg.
Alvin O. Hause, ...	do	Schuyler, ...	Weston.
John S. Havens, ...	do	Suffolk, ...	Patchogue
Palmer E. Havens, ...	do	Essex, ...	Essex.
George W. Hazelton, ...	do	Jefferson, ...	Black River.
Nathaniel M. Houghton,......	do	Saratoga	South Corinth.
Daniel R. Hudson, ...	do	Orange, ...	Blooming Grove.
Calvin T. Hulburd, ...	do	St. Lawrence.	Brasher Falls
Willard Johnson, ...	do	Oswego, ...	Fulton.
Edward Jones, ...	do	New York..	New York.
William J. C. Kenny, ...	do	New York, ..	New York.
Henry C. Lake, ...	do	Chautauqua, .	Charlotte Centre.
Richard J. Laler, ...	do	Kings, ...	Brooklyn
William Lamont, ...	do	Schoharie, ..	Charlotteville.
Daniel Leamy, ...	do	New York, ..	New York.
George L. Loutrel, ...	do	New York, ..	New York.
Edward D. Loveridge, ...	do	Allegany, ...	Cuba.
Benjamin L. Ludington, ...	do	Sullivan, ...	Monticello.
Frederick A. Lyman, ...	do	Onondaga, ...	Marcellus.
Dennis McCabe, ...	do	New York, ..	New York.
George E. McGonegal, ...	do	Monroe, ...	Rochester.
Alexander McLeod, ...	do	New York, ..	New York.
Edgar McMullen, ...	do	Kings, ...	Brooklyn.
Samuel T. Maddox, ...	do	Kings, ...	Williamsburgh.
Francis O. Mason, ...	do	Ontario	Canandaigua
David G. Maxon, ...	do	Rensselaer ..	Petersburgh.
Orson Moore, ...	do	Herkimer, ...	Russia
John W. Murphy, ...	do	Erie, ...	Buffalo.
Philip H. Neher, ...	do	Washington .	West Pawlet, Vt.
Nicholas Newkirk, ...	do	Montgomery	Fort Hunter.
Daniel M. O'Brien, ...	do	New York, ..	New York.
Darius A. Ogden, ...	do	Yates, ...	Penn Yan.
William G. Olvany, ...	do	New York, ..	New York.
David B. Parce, ...	do	Chenango ...	South Otselic
Lucius Peck, ...	do	Wyoming, ..	Java.
Thomas D. Penfield, ...	do	Oneida, ...	Camden.
Royal Phelps, ...	do	New York, ..	New York.
David Pickett, ...	do	Ontario, ...	Gorham
George T. Pierce, ...	do	Ulster, ...	Esopus.
Peter A. Porter, ...	do	Niagara, ...	Niagara Falls.
Benjamin Pringle, ...	do	Genesee, ...	Batavia.
Andrew J. Provost, ...	do	Kings, ...	Williamsburgh.
Abram Pryne, ...	do	Wayne, ...	Williamson.
Albert G. Purdy, ...	do	Madison, ...	Oneida.
Thomas H. Reed, ...	do	Putnam, ...	Brewster's Station.
James Redington, ...	do	St. Lawrence.	Waddington.
Addison G. Rice, ...	do	Cattaraugus .	Ellicottville
Elias Root, ...	do	Oswego, ...	Oswego.
Charles J. Saxe, ...	do	Rensselaer, ..	Troy.
Simon J. Schermerhorn, ...	do	Schenectady .	Schenectady.
Charles M. Scholefield, ...	do	Oneida......	Whitestown.

*Deceased.

NAME.	OFFICE.	RESIDENCE.	
		COUNTY.	NEAREST POST OFFICE.
* Willett Searles,..............	Assemblyman,	Albany	Coeymans.
Horatio Seymour,..............	do	Erie	Buffalo.
Henry Sherwood,..............	do	Steuben	Addison.
Samuel Skinner,..............	do	Livingston, ..	Nunda
Andrew Smith,..............	do	New York..	New York.
Henry D. H. Snyder, Jr., ...	do	Lewis, ...	Port Leyden.
George Springer, ...	do	Herkimer, ..	Starkville.
Lemuel Stetson, ...	do	Clinton, ...	Plattsburgh.
Jeremiah Sweet,..............	do	Oneida, ...	Utica.
Pierre C. Talman,..............	do	Westchester,.	Morrisania.
George H. Taylor,..............	do	Washington,.	Fort Edward.
Jacob Ten Broeck,..............	do	Columbia, ...	Hudson.
Eron N. Thomas, ...	do	Wayne, ...	Rose
William M. Thomas, ...	do	Kings, ...	Brooklyn
Elias F. Townsley,..............	do	St. Lawrence,	De Kalb.
Benjamin F. Tracy, ...	do	Tioga, ...	Owego.
Eliphaz Trimmer,..............	do	Monroe,.....	Rochester.
John Van Etten, Jr,..............	do	Orange, ...	Huguenot.
Peter J. Van Vleet,..........	do	Seneca, ...	Ovid.
Alexander Ward,..............	do	New York, ..	New York.
Daniel Waterbury,..............	do	Delaware, ...	Margaretville.
Sylvester Waterbury, ...	do	Rensselaer, ..	Nassau.
Benjamin R. Wells, ...	do	Monroe	North Chili.
Ebenezer Westbrook,..............	do	Ulster,......	Accord.
Nelson K. Wheeler,..............	do	Delaware, ...	Deposit.
Matthew Wiard, ...	do	Livingston, ..	East Avon.
Samuel Wilbor,..............	do	Columbia, ...	Chatham.

* Elected to fill vacancy occasioned by the death of John Vanderzee.

PRESIDING OFFICERS AND CLERKS.

NAME.	OFFICE.	RESIDENCE.	
		COUNTY.	NEAREST POST OFFICE.
Robert Campbell,.............	President of the Senate, ...	Steuben, ...	Bath.
Henry J. Raymond,..........	Speaker of the Assembly,..	New York, .	New York City.
James Terwilliger,..........	Clerk of the Senate,.....	Onondaga,..	Syracuse.
Joseph B. Cushman, ...	Clerk of the Assembly,..	Oneida, ...	Utica.

LAWS

OF THE

STATE OF NEW YORK,

PASSED AT THE

EIGHTY-FIFTH REGULAR SESSION OF THE LEGISLATURE, BEGUN
THE SEVENTH DAY OF JANUARY, AND ENDED THE
TWENTY-THIRD DAY OF APRIL, 1862,
AT THE CITY OF ALBANY.

Chap. 344.*

AN ACT to revive and extend "An act respecting the appropriation of the waters of the Black River for the use of the Black River Canal and Erie Canal feeder," passed April third, eighteen hundred and fifty-seven.

Passed June 29, 1861; three-fifths being present.

The People of the State of New York, represented in Senate and Assembly, do enact as follows:

SECTION 1. An act of the legislature of the State of New York, passed April third, eighteen hundred and fifty-seven, entitled "An act respecting the appropriation of the waters of the Black river for the use of the Black River canal and Erie canal feeder," is hereby revived and its provisions extended to one year from the passage of this act, so far as the same relates to the heirs of the

* This bill was not signed by the Governor in time to be bound with laws of 1861.

2

late Edmund Kirby, John Bradley, Charles E. Clarke, Merrill Coburn, Peter S. Howk, John O. Dougherty, J. C. Lepper, Moulton and Symonds, Edmund Rawson, William Wilson the heirs of Maria Babcock, William V. Morgan, and the heirs of the late Adriel Ely.

§ 2. This act shall take effect immediately.

Chap. 1.

AN ACT to authorize the Board of Supervisors of the county of Kings to provide for the relief of the families of volunteers.

Passed February, 1, 1862; by a two-third vote.

The People of the State of New York, represented in Senate and Assembly, do enact as follows:

Amount of money, rate of interest, &c.

SECTION 1. The treasurer of the county of Kings is authorized under the direction of the board of supervisors of said county, to borrow on the credit of said county, such sum of money as has been or may be expended, or may be required by said county, for the relief of families of volunteers from said county, in the military service of the United States, or the State of New York, to an amount not exceeding two hundred thousand dollars, and to give his official bonds for the payment of the same, in such form as the said board may prescribe, with interest at a rate not exceeding seven per cent per annum, payable as the board may direct; the money so borrowed and the bonds so issued, and the proceeds thereof, shall be appropriated for such relief of volunteers' families as aforesaid, and the repayment of money borrowed for such purpose and required therefor, and for no other purpose whatever.

Tax to be levied &c.

§ 2. The said board of supervisors shall cause to be levied and collected, and paid annually, such sums as may be necessary to pay the interest on the money so borrowed, and to pay the principal in installments as the same becomes due; the number and times of such installments shall be determined by the said board of supervisors and the treasurer shall apply the money so collected and paid to him towards the interest and principal of the money so borrowed.

§ 3. This act shall take effect immediately.

Chap. 2.

AN ACT to legalize certain ordinances of the corporation of the city of New York.

Passed February 1, 1862; three-fifths being present.

The People of the State of New York, represented in Senate and Assembly, do enact as follows:

SECTION 1. The following three ordinances of the mayor, aldermen and commonalty of the city of New York, to-wit:

1st. An ordinance entitled "An ordinance making an appropriation in aid of the defence of the national union, and authorizing the borrowing of money for that purpose," passed April twenty-third, eighteen hundred and sixty-one. *To legalize ordinance of April 23, 1861.*

2d. An ordinance entitled "An ordinance making an appropriation in aid of the families of volunteers from this city serving in the defence of the national union," passed July seventeenth, eighteen hundred sixty-one. *Legalize ordinance passed July 17, 1861.*

3d. An ordinance entitled "An ordinance making an appropriation in aid of the families of volunteers from this city serving in the defence of the national union," passed December sixteenth, eighteen hundred sixty-one, are hereby severally declared to be lawful and of binding force. *Legalize ordinance passed December 16, 1861.*

§ 2. This act shall take effect immediately.

Chap. 3.

AN ACT for the relief of certain of the town collectors of taxes in the county of Allegany.

Passed February 4, 1862; three-fifths being present.

The People of the State of New York, represented in Senate and Assembly, do enact as follows:

To extend time on renewal of securities.

SECTION 1. If the collectors of taxes of the several towns in the county of Allegany whose tax warrants are now returnable on the first of February, eighteen hundred and sixty-two, shall on or before the tenth day of February, eighteen hundred and sixty-two, pay over all moneys by them collected, and shall respectively renew their securities, to the satisfaction of the supervisors of said towns respectively, the time for collecting and making the final returns of taxes in said towns, shall be extended to the first day of March next, and the said collectors are hereby authorized and empowered to levy and collect said taxes at any time before the last named day the same as they are now authorized by law to levy and collect the same.

§ 2. This act shall take effect immediately.

Chap. 4.

AN ACT to secure the better application of funds to relieve the poor in the town of Little Falls, Herkimer county.

Passed February 7, 1862; three-fifths being present.

The People of the State of New York, represented in Senate and Assembly, do enact as follows :

Construction of the board of alms.

SECTION 1. The supervisor of the town of Little Falls, and the president of the village of Little Falls, together with a commissioner of alms, to be elected annually at the town meeting in the town of Little Falls, shall together constitute a board of alms for the town of Little

Falls. No person shall be eligible as such commissioner for any two years in succession.

§ 2. The said board of alms shall have the control of the funds applicable to the relief of the poor in said town and the dispensation of the same. Two of said board shall constitute a quorum to do business, and in case of a vacancy in said board the other members may fill such vacancy by appointment, until the same shall be filled by election or other legal appointment. *Control of the funds.*

§ 3. The board of alms for said town shall have power to procure, by rent, suitable ground and buildings for an alms house, for a term not exceeding three years. It may also, when specially authorized by a vote of the electors at an annual town meeting, procure by purchase, in the name of the town, suitable ground and buildings for a town alms house, at a cost not exceeding five thousand dollars. *To rent or purchase grounds for alms house.*

§ 4. The board of alms of said town shall appoint an overseer of alms for said town, who shall hold his office during the pleasure of said board, and said board shall determine his compensation, which compensation shall not exceed three hundred dollars per annum. It shall also appoint a treasurer of the poor fund of said town, and take such security for the faithful performance of his duties, and to account for and pay over the funds entrusted to him, as they may deem adequate, and shall also determine his compensation, which shall not exceed thirty dollars per annum. The said board shall keep a record of all its proceedings, and shall adopt needful rules as to their own meetings, and as to the management and dispensation of the funds for the relief of the poor under their control, and for the government of the treasurer and overseer of alms. *To appoint an overseer.* *Also a treasurer.* *The board to keep a record.*

§ 5. All moneys appropriated to the relief of the poor of said town, shall be paid over to the treasurer of the poor fund of said town, and all payments and disbursements shall be made by him in cash, upon the order of the overseer of alms, or such other person as the board of alms may direct, and said treasurer shall not loan any moneys that may come into his hands, nor shall he use them for any other purpose than is provided for by this act. Any interest which shall accrue on said funds shall be credited to said town. *Duties of treasurer.*

§ 6. The board may cause to be purchased all or any needful supplies for the relief of the poor, in such quantities as they may deem best; but not to exceed a supply for one year; and they may contract for such supplies, including medical and surgical services, to be delivered or rendered from time to time as the same may be required or called for; but such contracts shall not extend beyond thirty days after the annual town meeting next ensuing the time when such contracts shall be made. Said board may also furnish relief to the poor chargeable to the county or to any other town, and receive compensation therefor.

§ 7. The duties of the office of overseer of the poor of the town of Little Falls, are hereby transferred to the overseer of alms of said town, to be administered under the direction of said board of alms; to take effect as soon as said board shall notify in writing the overseer of poor of said town, that the overseer of alms has been appointed and is ready to enter upon his duties. The said overseer of alms shall, from that time perform all the duties heretofore devolved upon the overseers of poor, subject, however, to the direction of the board of alms, and shall keep the vouchers, registers, accounts and charges required by law of overseers of poor. He shall report to the board as often as they may direct, and shall prepare, annually, a statement to be read at the annual town meeting, showing the names of all persons or families who have received relief, and the amount to each person or family.

§ 8. The board of alms shall audit and allow all charges and expenses incurred under their direction, for the relief of the poor, including expenses and the compensation of officers, and shall report the same through the supervisor, to the board of supervisors of the county, who shall thereupon apportion the same to the town and county respectively, in the ratio of the amount expended for the relief of the poor chargeable to the town and county respectively, and shall cause the same to be inserted in the tax lists and raised as town and county charges. The board of alms shall audit and allow all charges and expenses incurred under their direction for the relief of the poor chargeable to the town, including expenses and the compensation of officers, and shall report the same through the supervi-

Board to purchase supplies.

Duties of overseer of alms.

Board of alms to audit all charges and report to board of supervisors.

sor, to the board of supervisors of the county, who shall, after auditing the expenses chargeable to the county, apportion the expenses so audited to the town and county respectively, and shall cause the same to be inserted in the tax lists and received as town and county charges.

§ 9. The said board of alms may audit and allow, for their own services, a sum not exceeding one hundred dollars per annum, to be apportioned among them as the majority may direct, to be deemed expenses of administering the poor fund, and raised as provided in the last preceding section. *Remuneration of board.*

§ 10. Nothing contained in this act shall be so construed as in any way to interfere with the powers of the board of supervisors in relation to the auditing of the poor accounts of the county.

§ 11. This act shall take effect immediately.

Chap. 5.

AN ACT to authorize the board of supervisors of the county of Ulster to defray certain expenses of board, transportation and so forth of the twentieth regiment of the New York Militia.

Passed February 13, 1862 ; three-fifths being present.

The People of the State of New York, represented in Senate and Assembly, do enact as follows :

SECTION 1. The board of Supervisors of the county of Ulster, at their next annual session are hereby authorized and required to levy the sum of four thousand three hundred dollars upon the taxable property of said county, to defray certain expenses of board, transportation and so forth of the twentieth regiment of New York Militia, as the same were audited by said board at its annual meeting in December, eighteen hundred and sixty-one ; said amount to be levied, collected and paid into the treasury of said county in the same manner as other taxes, and to be paid out on like certificate as any other charge against the county. *To levy tax of $4,300.*

§ 2. This act shall take effect immediately.

Chap. 6.

AN ACT to amend the act entitled "An act to provide for the incorporation of Fire Insurance Companies," passed June twenty-fifth, eighteen hundred and fifty-three.

Passed February 15, 1862.

The People of the State of New York, represented in Senate and Assembly, do enact as follows :

Sec. 23, of chap 466, laws of 1853, amended. SECTION 1. Section twenty-three of the act entitled "An act to provide for the incorporation of fire insurance companies," passed June twenty-fifth, eighteen hundred and fifty-three, is hereby amended by adding thereto at the end thereof, the following words : " The provisions of this section shall apply to all foreign companies, partnerships, associations and individuals, whether incorporated or not incorporated.

Chap. 7.

AN ACT to authorize the supervisors of Tompkins county to re-imburse certain expenses to Frederick H. Miller, of Lansing.

Passed February 15, 1862 ; three-fifths being present.

The People of the State of New York, represented in Senate and Assembly, do enact as follows:

To pay expenses incurred on account of lunatic son. SECTION 1. The board of supervisors of the county of Tompkins are hereby authorized to examine the claim of Frederick H. Miller of the town of Lansing in said county, for expenses incurred by him on account of his son Palmer Miller, a lunatic, in the years eighteen hundred and fifty-nine, eighteen hundred and sixty, and eighteen hundred and sixty-one, in conveying said Palmer Miller to and from the State Lunatic Asylum, at Utica, and for expenses incurred by him for said Palmer

Miller while at said asylum; and the said board of supervisors are hereby empowered to pay the said Frederick H. Miller such sum as they shall find to be just and equitable, the same to be paid as other county charges.

§ 2. This act shall take effect immediately.

Chap. 8.

AN ACT to amend an act entitled "An act making appropriations for the support of government for the fiscal year, commencing first day of October, in the year eighteen hundred and sixty-one," passed April thirteenth, eighteen hundred and sixty-one.

Passed February 18, 1862; three-fifths being present.

The People of the State of New York, represented in Senate and Assembly, do enact as follows:

SECTION 1. The act entitled "An act making appropriations for the support of government for the fiscal year commencing on the first day of October, in the year one thousand eight hundred and sixty-one" is hereby amended by striking out from the clause of said act making an appropriation for refunding money to purchasers for the redemption of lands sold for taxes, the words "twenty-five" and insert in lieu thereof the words "one hundred and twenty" so that the said clause will read as follows: For refunding money to purchasers for the redemption of lands sold for taxes, *one* hundred and twenty thousand dollars.

§ 2. This act shall take effect immediately.

"Twenty-five" stricken out and "one hundred and twenty" inserted.

3

Chap. 9.

AN ACT to facilitate the construction of a portion of the Erie Canal Enlargement.

Passed February 19, 1862; three-fifths being present.

The People of the State of New York, represented in Senate and Assembly, do enact as follows:

Five days notice only given in letting certain sections.

SECTION 1. Public notice of the time and place for the reception of sealed proposals for entering into contracts for the completion of work remaining to be done on sections three hundred and twenty-five, three hundred and twenty-six, three hundred and twenty-seven, three hundred and twenty-eight, three hundred and twenty-nine, three hundred and thirty, three hundred and thirty-one, three hundred and thirty-two, three hundred and thirty-three, three hundred and thirty-four, three hundred and thirty-five, three hundred and thirty-six, and three hundred and thirty-seven Erie Canal Enlargement, may be published for five days in the state paper, and in such newspapers in the vicinity of the work as the contracting board shall direct; and such contracting board, for the purposes of this act, shall have the same powers and perform the same duties and be subject to all the conditions and restrictions provided by law previous to the tenth day of July, eighteen hundred and fifty-one, in respect to contracts by canal commissioners for work or materials upon the canals of this state.

§ 2. This act shall take effect immediately.

Chap. 10.

AN ACT to empower the court of general sessions of the peace in and for the city and county of New York to extend its terms and to authorize its adjournments.

Passed February 19th, 1862; three-fifths being present.

The People of the State of New York, represented in Senate and Assembly, do enact as follows :

SECTION 1. The court of general sessions of the peace in and for the city and county of New York, is hereby empowered to extend any of its terms, and to make any adjournments of the said court within its discretion by any order or orders to said effect duly entered in its minutes. To extend the time of its terms and make adjournments

§ 2. This act shall take effect immediately.

Chap. 11.

AN ACT to consolidate the two election districts in the town of Danby and erect one election district therein.

Passed February 19, 1862; three-fifths being present.

The People of the State of New York, represented in Senate and Assembly do enact as follows:

SECTION 1. The supervisor, assessors, and town clerk, of the town of Danby, in the county of Tompkins, are hereby constituted a board with full powers to consolidate the two election districts of said town, and erect one election district therein. They shall make a certificate of such alteration, exhibiting the district as altered, which certificate shall be filed in the office of the town clerk, and copies thereof shall be posted in said town as provided in sections fifteen and sixteen, title three, article three, chapter six, of the Revised Statutes. Make and file certificate of alteration.

§ 2. This act shall take effect immediately.

.Chap. 12.

AN ACT to amend chapter three hundred and thirteen of the Laws of eighteen hundred and sixty-one, entitled "An act giving the consent of the State of New York to the purchase by and ceding jurisdiction to the United States over certain lands within this State to be occupied as sites of light houses, keeper's dwellings and fortifications and their appurtances," passed April eighteenth, eighteen hundred and sixty-one.

Passed February 20, 1862; by a two-third vote.

The People of the State of New York, represented in Senate and Assembly do enact as follows :

For building forts, batteries, magazines, wharfs. &c., adjacent to Fort Hamilton and Tompkins.
SECTION 1. The last paragraph of the seventh section of the act entitled "An act giving the consent of the state of New York to the purchase by and ceding jurisdiction to the United States over certain lands within this state to be occupied as sites of light houses, keeper's dwellings and fortifications, and their appurtenances," passed April eighteenth, eighteen hundred and sixty-one, is hereby amended so as to read as follows : For the purpose of building and maintaining thereon batteries, forts, magazines, wharfs and other necessary structures, with their appendages, adjacent to Fort Hamilton, Kings county, Long Island, and adjacent to Fort Tompkins in the town of Southfield, county of Richmond, Staten Island.

How U. S. may acquire title in certain cases.
§ 2. The eight* section of the said act shall be amended so as to read as follows : In case the United States shall desire to purchase any land selected in pursuance of the first and seventh sections of said act or either of said sections, and shall be unable to agree for the purchase of the same, it shall have the right to acquire title to the same in the manner hereinafter prescribed, provided however, that a due regard be had to the improvements and buildings on the same, the damage, if any, to the adjacent lands now belonging to the same

*So in original.

owners, and that the title be acquired before the first day of January, eighteen hundred and sixty-three.

§ 3. Section twelve of said act is hereby amended so as to read as follows: The commissioners of appraisal appointed in pursuance of this act shall be entitled each to one hundred dollars compensation for their services, provided however that they make their report within thirty days after their appointment and before receiving said compensation. Said commissioners shall be residents of the county in which the said lands respectively are situated, or of the city and county of New York. In case any such commissioner shall die, decline, resign, or for any other reason be unable to serve, the court designated in said act, shall appoint another in his place.

§ 4. This act shall take effect immediately.

Chap. 13.

AN ACT to authorize the trustees of the village of Yonkers to raise money by tax.

Passed February 22, 1862; three-fifths being present.

The People of the State of New York, represented in Senate and Assembly, do enact as follows:

SECTION 1. The trustees of the village of Yonkers, in addition to the powers now vested in them by law, are hereby authorized and empowered to raise at any time during the year one thousand eight hundred and sixty-two, a further sum of money, not exceeding six thousand dollars, by tax to be assessed upon the estate, real and personal, within the bounds of said village, and to be collected from the several owners and occupants thereof, for the purpose of affording assistance and relief to the families of volunteers from said village who have enlisted in the service of the United States.

§ 2. Such moneys shall be assessed, levied, raised, collected and paid over to the treasurer of said village in the same manner as is now provided by law for the raising of money to defray the ordinary and contingent expenses of said corporation, and all the provisions of law now applicable to the assessing, levying, raising,

collecting and paying over taxes for ordinary and contingent expenses of such corporation, are hereby made
applicable, so far as may be, to the moneys authorized
to be raised by this act.

To be appli-
ed to the re-
lief of fami-
lies of vol-
unteers.
§ 3. All moneys raised and collected under the powers
granted by this act shall be applied and appropriated to
the assistance and relief of such of the families of volunteers from said village now enlisted in the service of the
United States, as shall, in the judgment of said trustees,
require such assistance and relief, and to the re-payment
of such sums of money as may have been or may hereafter be temporarily advanced to such trustees or to the
committee on relief of families of volunteers, for such
purpose by any citizen or citizens or committee of citizens or bank in such village, over and above the amounts
voluntarily subscribed and paid for the purposes aforesaid.

Trustees
have power
to appoint a
person to
distribute
funds.
§ 4. The said trustees shall have power to delegate
the distribution of such moneys, or of any part thereof,
to any officer or persons whom they may designate, and
to direct the treasurer of said village to pay over to
such officer or persons, upon a draft or drafts to be
drawn in the manner now provided by law, such sum
or sums of money raised under the provisions of this
act, as they may by resolution determine ; but no officer
or person to whom such distribution shall be delegated,
shall receive any pay or compensation for his services
in making such distribution.

To pass or-
dinances to
carry law in-
to effect.
§ 5. The trustees of said village are hereby authorized
and empowered to pass such ordinances and resolutions
as shall be necessary to carry into effect the object and
purposes of this act.

No private
subscrip-
tion to be
paid out of
funds raised
§ 6. The money to be raised by this act shall be applied to the purpose aforesaid and to no other. And no
part thereof shall either directly or indirectly be used
or applied to repay to any person or persons any private
or individual subscription made for the purpose of raising money for aid or relief to the families of volunteers.

§ 7. This act shall take effect immediately.

Chap. 14.

AN ACT to authorize the Common Council of
the city of Buffalo to borrow money.

Passed February 22, 1862 ; three-fifths being present.

*The People of the State of New York, represented in
Senate and Assembly do enact as follows:*

SECTION 1. The resolution of the Common Council of the city of Buffalo adopted on the twenty-second day of April, one thousand eight hundred and sixty-one, whereby the said Common Council determined to borrow from the contingent fund of said city the sum of fifty thousand dollars to be used in aiding to furnish board, clothing and other necessary supplies to all who should volunteer to enter the military service of the country and in aiding and assisting the families of such as should need material aid during their absence in the service of their country, and the borrowing of said sum of money by said council from said contingent fund, for the purpose aforesaid, and all the acts of said council in relation to the application and distribution of said sum of fifty thousand dollars, are hereby confirmed. And for the purpose of repaying and reimbursing to said contingent fund the said last named sum. The Common Council of the city of Buffalo is hereby authorized and empowered to borrow upon the credit of said city the sum of fifty thousand dollars, and for that purpose the said Common Council may in its discretion, issue the bonds of the city of Buffalo for a sum not exceeding fifty thousand dollars, payable with interest at the rate of seven per centum per annum, in such sums, at such times respectively, not exceeding twenty years from the date thereof, and at such place or places within this state as the said Common Council shall determine. And the said council shall add to the amount of the general tax of said city of each year a sum sufficient to pay so much and such part of said bonds, and the interest thereon as may become due the following year, the payment of which shall not be otherwise provided for.

Confirming resolution of common council passed April 22, 1861.

To borrow $50,000.

To issue bonds bearing interest.

Annual tax for the payment of bonds and interest.

§ 2. The said Common Council of the city of Buffalo is hereby authorized and empowered in its discretion,

To issue bonds for $37,000.

to issue the bonds of said city for a sum not exceeding thirty-seven thousand dollars payable in the same manner as the bonds mentioned in the first section of this act, for the purpose of paying and cancelling certain bonds of said city, issued on the twentieth day of October, one thousand eight hundred and fifty-two, known

Payment of "ship canal bonds" and other indebtedness of city. as "the ship canal bonds," upon which there is now past due the sum of eleven thousand dollars; and certain other bonds of said city issued on the first day of June, one thousand eight hundred and fifty-two, being a part of the funded debt of said city, upon which there will be due on the first day of June, one thousand eight hundred and sixty-two, the sum of fifteen thousand dollars and certain other bonds of said city issued on the first day of June, one thousand eight hundred and fifty-four, to pay the indebtedness of the old city of Buffalo upon which there will be due on the first day of June one thousand eight hundred and sixty-two, the sum of

Annual tax to be levied to pay debt and interest eleven thousand dollars and the said Common Council shall add to the amount of the general tax of said city of each year, a sufficient sum to pay so much and such part of said bonds mentioned in this section and the interest thereon, as may become due in the following year, the payment of which shall not be otherwise provided for, such addition to said general tax to be assessed upon the taxable property within the limits of the old city of Buffalo.

No part of money to be raised for any other purpose. § 3. No part of the moneys authorized by this act to be borrowed, and no part of the proceeds of the bonds herein authorized to be issued, shall be paid or appropriated for any purpose whatever other than that herein expressed as the purpose for which said money is to be borrowed and said bonds issued. And nothing in this act contained shall be so construed as to prevent the said Common Council from borrowing any part of said fifty thousand dollars, for the purpose aforesaid, or from issuing the bonds herein authorized, for such sums as may be necessary to pay and cancel any part of the said bonds heretofore issued by the said city of Buffalo.

§ 4. This act shall take effect immediately.

Chap. 15.

AN ACT to amend the charter of the village of Saratoga Springs.

Passed February 28, 1862; three-fifths being present.

The People of the State of New York, represented in Senate and Assembly, do enact as follows:

SECTION 1. All that territory lying within two paral- Boundary of village. lel lines, one of which is three-fourths of a mile east and the other three-fourths of a mile west of the centre line of Broadway or Broad street, as its course now runs through the village of Saratoga Springs and extending from the north line of the town of Saratoga Springs, as far south as the present south line of said village in such centre line shall be included within and constitute the village of Saratoga Springs.

§ 2. The office of overseer of highways in the village Overseer of highways of Saratoga Springs, is hereby abolished, and the person abolished. appointed to the office of general superintendent of said village, shall possess all the powers and perform all the duties pertaining to the office of such overseer, and shall receive the same compensation as overseers, not to exceed two hundred dollars in any one year.

§ 3. This act shall take effect immediately.

Chap. 16.

AN ACT to authorize the Commissioners of Highways to construct a bridge in the town of Olive, county of Ulster across the Esopus creek, and to borrow money for that purpose.

Passed February 28, 1862; three-fifths being present.

The People of the State of New York, represented in Senate and Assembly, do enact as follows:

SECTION 1. The commissioners of highways in the Commis- sioners of town of Olive, Ulster county. are hereby authorized to highways to borrow proceed forthwith to the construction of a bridge across $2,500.

·4

the Esopus creek, at Shokan, in the town of Olive, upon the site of the former bridge lately carried away by the flood, and are further authorized, for such purpose, to borrow a sum of money sufficient to enable them to build such bridge, provided the sum does not exceed the sum of two thousand five hundred dollars.

To give their bonds for the same

§ 2. The said commissioners are hereby authorized to execute their official bond for the payment of the money so to be borrowed, with interest, in three equal annual installments, the one installment to be payable on the tenth day of February, eighteen hundred and sixty-three; the next installment on the tenth day of February eighteen hundred and sixty-four, and the last installment on the tenth day of February eighteen hundred and sixty-five; such bonds and the money secured thereby shall become a legal charge against the said town of Olive, and the board of supervisors of the county of Ulster are hereby

Tax to be levied to pay debt and interest

directed to levy upon the town of Olive, and include in the tax rolls of said town, for the year eighteen hundred and sixty-two, for the year eighteen hundred and sixty-three and for the year eighteen hundred and sixty-four such sums as may be necessary to pay the interest on said sum, and to pay said installments as they respectively become due.

To be let to lowest bidder.

§ 3. The said commissioners shall let the job of building said bridge to the lowest responsible bidder, and to be built according to the plan and specification of said commissioners.

§ 4. This act shall take effect immediately.

Chap. 17.

AN ACT making appropriations for the canal debt and the maintenance of the canals, for the fiscal year commencing on the first day of October eighteen hundred and sixty-two.

Passed February 28th, 1862; three-fifths being present.

The People of the State of New York, represented in Senate and Assembly, do enact as follows:

$800,000 appropriated for expenses of canals

SECTION 1. The following sums are hereby appropriated out of the canal revenues of the state canals, for the fiscal year commencing on the first day of October, eighteen hundred and sixty-two, for the expense of the collection of tolls, superintendence and ordinary repairs of the public works, salaries of the canal commissioners, state engineer and surveyor, auditor of the canal department, clerk hire and incidental expenses of the canal department, and canal appraisers, the sum of eight hundred thousand dollars, or so much thereof as may be necessary.

To pay the interest and reimburse the principle of the canal debt as it existed on the first day of June, one thousand eight hundred and forty-six, the sum of one million seven hundred thousand dollars. ^{$1,700,000 to pay interest and principal of canal debt.}

For payment toward the sinking fund for the extinguishment of the general fund debt, the sum of three hundred and fifty thousand dollars. ^{General fund debt $350,000.}

For the payment of the interest on loans made under the constitution for the enlargement and completion of the canals the sum of seven hundred and ten thousand dollars, or so much thereof as may be necessary. ^{To pay interest on loans for enlargement, $710,000.}

To constitute a sinking fund for the extinguishment of the principle of the loans made under section three of article seven of the constitution, the sum of four hundred and six thousand two hundred and forty-three dollars, but no investment in such fund shall be made except from the surplus revenues of the canals received during the year, after paying the interest on the debt contracted under section three of article seven of the constitution. ^{For sinking fund to extinguish debt created by Art. 7. of the Constitution. $406,243.}

To pay the general fund to defray the necessary expenses of the state, the sum of two hundred thousand dollars. ^{Necessary expenses of the state $200,000.}

§ 2. The following sums are hereby appropriated out of the proceeds of any tax to be levied and collected under the provisions of the act, chapter two hundred and seventy-one, of the laws of eighteen hundred and fifty-nine, to pay the interest and redeem the principal of the loan of two million five hundred thousand dollars, to provide for the payment of the floating debt of the state. ^{To be appropriated out of any tax that may be levied for payment of debt created by chap. 200, Laws of 1859.}

To pay the interest on said loan for the fiscal year commencing on the first day of October next, one hundred and fifty thousand dollars. ^{For interest $150,000.}

For sinking fund to pay principal $188,888.

To provide for the sinking fund to pay the principal of said loan, one hundred and thirty-eight thousand eight hundred eighty-eight dollars, being for one year's contribution to said fund, as provided for by the act aforesaid.

To reimburse contractors $30,000.

§ 3. The sum of thirty thousand dollars or so much thereof as may be necessary, is hereby appropriated and shall be paid out of the " Repair Trust Fund " to reimburse to the several contractors of canal repairs whose contracts shall have been completed during the present or the next fiscal year, the sums deposited by them as security for the performance of their contracts, together with such interest as may have been paid into the treasury thereon, which sums shall be paid by the treasurer, on the warrant of the auditor of the canal department, based upon the draft or certificate of a canal commissioner, showing that the repair contractor in whose favor such draft may be made or to whom such certificate may be given, is entitled to have the deposit refunded.

§ 4. This act shall take effect immediately.

Chap. 18.

AN ACT to revise the charter of the city of Utica.

Passed February 28, 1862; three-fifths being present.

The People of the State of New York, represented in Senate and Assembly, do enact as follows :

' TITLE I.

OF THE BOUNDARIES AND CIVIL DIVISIONS OF THE CITY.

Boundary of city.

SECTION 1. The district of country contained within the following boundaries, to wit : Begining at the point in the middle of the Mohawk river where the division line between lots numbered one hundred and one and one hundred and two, in Crosby's manor, intersects it, and thence running southerly on said division line to the centre of the road leading from Utica to the Burr Stone Mills (so called ;) thence easterly in the centre of said road to the line between lots numbered one hundred, and one hundred one, in Crosby's manor; thence southerly along said last mentioned line to the line between the farms owned by Samuel S Thorn and John Butterfield; thence easterly along the last mentioned line to the centre of the old Seneca turnpike; thence easterly along the centre of the Slayton's bush-road (so called) to its intersection with the centre of the road leading northerly through the farm formerly owned by Robert McBride; thence northerly in the centre of said last mentioned road to the present southerly bounds of the city of Utica; thence easterly along the present bounds of the city of Utica to the easterly bounds of Oneida county; thence northerly oh the easterly bounds of Oneida county to the centre of the Mohawk river, and thence westerly up the middle of the Mohawk river to the place of beginning, shall hereafter constitute and be known as " the City of Utica."

§ 2. The inhabitants of said city shall be a corporation by the name of " the city of Utica," and may sue and be sued, complain and defend in any court, make and use a common seal, and alter it at pleasure, and may receive by gift, grant, devise, bequest, or purchase, and hold and convey such real and personal estate as the purposes of the corporation may require. Corporate name and privileges.

§ 3. The said city shall be divided into seven wards as follows : The part thereof lying northerly of the Erie canal, and easterly of the middle of Genesee street, shall be the first ward. The part thereof . lying northerly of the Erie canal, and westerly of the middle of Genesee street, shall be the second ward. The part thereof lying southerly of the Erie canal and westerly of the middle of Genesee street, and easterly of the Chénango canal, shall be the third ward. The part thereof lying southerly of the Erie canal, easterly of the middle of Genesee street, westerly of a line running from the Erie canal southerly through the middle of First and Dudley streets, to the middle of South street and northerly of a line commencing at the intersection of South and Dudley streets, and running westerly through the middle of South, George and Rebecca streets, to the middle of Genesee street, shall be the fourth ward. The part thereof lying southerly of the Erie canal, easterly of the fourth ward, and northerly of a line commencing at the intersection of South and Dudley streets, and running easterly Boundary of wards.

through the middle of South street, to its termination, and thence easterly in a straight line to the city line, shall be the fifth ward. That part thereof lying southerly of the Erie canal, and westerly of the third ward, shall be the sixth ward. That part thereof lying easterly of the middle of Genesee street, and southerly of the fourth and fifth wards, shall be the seventh ward.

TITLE 2.

OF THE OFFICERS OF THE CITY, THEIR ELECTION, APPOINTMENT, AND TERM OF OFFICE.

Denomination and enumeration of officers.

§ 4. The officers of the city shall be denominated city officers and ward officers. The city officers shall be a mayor, a recorder, a treasurer, a city attorney, an overseer of the poor, and four justices of the peace, who shall be elected by ballot by the electors of the city; and a clerk, a city surveyor, a street commissioner, a chief engineer, and twelve policemen, who shall be appointed by the common council; and such other officers as the common council may appoint under the provisions of this act. The ward officers shall be, in each ward, a supervisor, two aldermen, one assessor, one collector, one constable, and so many inspectors of election as shall be required by the law relative to elections. The ward officers shall be elected by ballot by the electors of the respective wards

Qualifications necessary for officers.

§ 5. No person shall be eligible or appointed to any office created by this act, unless he shall be at the time of his election or appointment, an elector and resident of said city; and no person shall be eligible or appointed to any ward office, unless he shall be, at the time of his election or appointment, an elector and resident of the ward for which he shall be elected or appointed. Whenever any city officer shall cease to be a resident of said city, or any ward officer shall cease to be a resident of the ward for which he was elected or appointed, his office shall thereby become vacant.

Election of officers other than recorder.

§ 6. An election for officers of the city, except the recorder to be called the city election, shall be held annually on the first Tuesday in March, at such places as the common council shall from time to time appoint. Such election and all special elections held under the provisions of this act, shall be conducted in all respects in the manner general elections in cities are by law required to be conducted, and all the provisions of law ·relative to such elections shall be applicable to the city elections, except that the polls shall be opened at eight o'clock in the forenoon and be closed at five o'clock in the afternoon. The recorder shall be elected at the time and in the manner provided by the " act to provide for the election of recorders in cities," .passed June eighteenth, eighteen hundred and fifty-one.

§ 7. The electors at the city election shall vote for *Form of ballot.* city officers to be elected, upon a ballot endorsed " city," and for ward officers to be voted for in the ward wherein the electors reside, upon a ballot endorsed " ward." Each ballot shall designate the office to which each person voted for is intended to be chosen. The ballots may be printed or written, or partly printed and partly written. They shall be deposited by the inspectors of election in separate boxes; one to contain those endorsed " city," and one those endorsed " ward."

§ 8. If there be one or more vacancies to be supplied *Vacancies to be filled* in any office where the full term of the office shall be *at the city election,* more than one year, such vacancy or vacancies shall be *where term* filled at the city election, and if there be more than one *is longer than one* vacancy in any office, the ballot shall designate for which *year.* term the person voted for is intended to be chosen.

§ 9. Upon the canvass of the votes in each election *Inspectors · cause statement of canvass to be filed with city clerk.* district being completed, the inspectors thereof shall cause a statement thereof to be made and signed by them and shall on the same day or next day thereafter, file the same with the clerk of the city. The clerk shall present the statement to the common council at a meeting to be held for the purpose on the Friday succeeding the election. The common council shall thereupon determine who by a plurality of votes, are elected to fill the offices voted for, and make and subscribe a certificate thereof in the book of records of its proceedings. The clerk shall thereupon serve upon each person elected to an office, either personally or at his place of residence, a notice of his election. In case of a failure to elect any officer by reason of a tie vote or otherwise, the office shall be deemed vacant, and the common council, to be composed of the members thereof whose terms shall not have expired, and the members thereof who shall have been elected at the election in which such failure

shall occur, shall appoint a person to fill the vacancy
for the remainder of the current civil year, if it is one
which the common council is authorized to fill, or order
a new election to fill it if it is not.

Time of commencement of official term, and termination of the same.
§ 10. All officers elected by the electors of the city
shall enter upon the duties of their offices on the Tuesday succeeding their election, and continue in office
until the Tuesday succeeding the next annual city election, excepting the recorder, justice of the peace, aldermen and assessors. The recorder and justices of the
peace shall enter upon the duties of their office on the
first day of January succeeding their election, and continue in office four years from that day, unless elected
to fill vacancies in the term of a former incumbent, when
they shall enter upon the duties of their offices as soon
as qualified, and discharge them for the unexpired term
of such former incumbent. Aldermen and assessors
shall enter upon the duties of their offices on the Tuesday succeeding their election, and except as hereinafter
provided, shall continue in office until the Tuesday succeeding the second annual city election thereafter.
Three of the assessors elected at the first city election
after this act takes effect shall continue in office but one
year. At the first meeting of the common council after
such election shall have been held, it shall be determined
by lot which of the assessors shall continue in office for
one and which for two years. An alderman or assessor
elected to fill a vacancy in the term of a former incumbent, shall hold his office during such term.

To hold until successors are elected or appointed.
§ 11. All officers of said city shall continue in office
until their successors are elected or appointed, and have
taken their oaths of office and become qualified to serve
therein. All officers heretofore elected in said city,
whose term of office has not expired, shall continue in
office for the term for which they were elected

Certain officers to file their bonds with city clerk.
§ 12. The treasurer, city attorney, overseer of the
poor, clerk, street commissioner, policemen and collectors, shall severally, before they enter upon the duties
of their offices, file with the clerk, a bond to the city of
Utica, in such penalty and with such sureties as the common council shall direct, the sureties to be approved by the
common council, conditioned that they shall faithfully
perform the duties of their respective offices, and account
for and pay over all moneys to be received by them by

virtue thereof. The common council may at any time, by ordinance or resolution, require any other officers or servants of the corporation to file such bond.

§ 13. Every person elected justice of the peace, or constable, in said city, shall, before he enters upon the duties of his office, with two or more sureties, to be approved by the common council, execute in the presence of the clerk, an instrument in writing by which such justice or constable and his sureties shall jointly and severally agree to pay to each and every person who may be entitled thereto, all such sums of money as the said justice or constable may become liable to pay them by reason or on account of any moneys which justice or constable may collect or receive by virtue of his office, or on account of any official default; the clerk shall certify under the corporate seal of the city, the fact of the instrument having been executed before him, and a copy thereof duly authenticated by the clerk shall be presumptive evidence of the execution thereof by the officer and his sureties in all courts. Actions may be brought upon such instruments in the name of any person or persons entitled to the money or damages sought to be collected by virtue thereof at any time, but the same must be brought during the term for which the justice or constable making them was elected, or within two years after its expiration. *(Board of justice and constable.)*

§ 14. The common council shall examine into the sufficiency of the proposed sureties of any officer or person from whom a bond or instrument in writing with sureties may be required under the provisions of this act, and may require such sureties to be examined on oath as to their property and liabilities. The oath may be administered by any member of the common council. The deposition of the surety shall be reduced to writing and subscribed by him, certified by the officer administering the oath, and annexed to and filed with the bond or instrument. Any person swearing falsely under the provisions of this section, shall upon coviction be deemed guilty of perjury. *(Common council to examine sufficiency of sureties.)*

§ 15. Within ten days after any person who shall have been elected or appointed to any office in the city, shall have received from the clerk notice of his election or appointment as herein provided, he shall take and file with the clerk, the constitutional oath, and shall file with *(Officers to take official oath within ten days after notified.)*

him any bond or instrument with sureties required by
the provisions of this act. If he shall neglect to do so,
the common council may declare the office to which he
was elected or appointed vacant, and appoint a person to
fill the vacancy, if it is one which the common council
is authorized to fill, or order a new election to fill it if it
is not.

Resigna-
tions to be
made to
common
council.
§ 16. Resignations of any office held under the provisions of this act, may be made to the common council.
The common council may fill vacancies in any offices
provided for by this act for the remainder of the current
civil year, excepting in the case of aldermen.

TITLE 3.

OF THE OFFICERS OF THE CITY, THEIR POWERS AND DUTIES.

Powers and
duties of the
mayor.
§ 17. The mayor shall be a member of the common
council, and when present its presiding officer. It shall
be his duty to see that the laws of the state and the ordinances of the city are faithfully executed therein, and to
recommend to the common council such measures as he
may deem necessary or expedient for its welfare. As the
head of the police of the city he shall maintain peace and
good order therein. He shall possess the same powers
and authority in criminal cases with which justices of the
peace in towns are invested. In addition to the powers
now vested in him by law, he shall have power to administer any oath or affirmation required or authorized
by law, and may take affidavits in all cases where justices
of the peace are required or authorized to take the same
and with like force and effect. He shall also have power
to appoint special policemen, who shall possess the same
powers and be subject to the same liabilities as ordinary
policemen, for the benefit of any person, society, or corporation, for proper purposes, at the expense of the person, society or corporation desiring such appointment, but
without any expense or liability whatever on the part of
the city.

Of recorder.
§ 18. The recorder shall possess the powers and perform the duties now possessed and performed by the
recorder of the said city. The act to establish a recorder's court in the city of Utica and for other purposes
passed May seventh, eighteen hundred and forty-four as
amended by subsequent acts, shall remain in force, ex-

cepting that but one term of said court shall be held in said city in each year. Such term shall be held on the third Tuesday in March.

§ 19. The treasurer shall receive all moneys belonging Treasurer. to the city, and keep an accurate account of all receipts and expenditures, so as to exhibit the amount paid under each particular class of purposes for which money shall be raised. He shall deposit and keep all moneys belonging to the city, or that shall come to his hands, in such one of the banks in said city as will pay the highest rate of interest, not exceeding seven per cent, for such deposits, for the use of the city, and will give security for the payment of such deposits to be approved by the common council, and will also agree to loan to the city all such sums as the common council may be authorized to borrow, under the provisions of this act. All moneys shall be drawn from him in pursuance of a resolution of the common council, by warrants specifying for what purpose they are drawn, signed by the clerk and countersigned by the mayor. He shall, fifteen days before the annual city election in each year, present to the common council and file with the clerk an account of all his receipts and disbursements since the date of the last report, and a statement of the financial condition of the city, a copy of which shall be published in the official newspapers, at least ten days before such election. He shall perform such other duties as this act may require, and such as the common council may prescribe.

§ 20. The city attorney shall have the managment and City attorney. charge of all the law business of the corporation, in which the city is interested, unless the common council otherwise direct. He shall keep a record of all suits and proceedings which, as city attorney, he shall have in charge. In case of his sickness or absence he shall have power to authorize any attorney to appear for and on behalf of the city, in any suite or proceeding. He shall when required by the common council, prepare all legal papers for the city, and shall when so required, be the legal adviser of the common council and of the several departments of the corporation. He shall, when desired by the common council, see that all proceedings in relation to improvements and the opening of streets are regularly conducted, and he shall perform such other duties as are required of him by this act and such as the council may prescribe. But this section shall not be construed to substitute the city attorney as attorney in any action or proceeding the prosecution or defence of which was commenced by a predecessor.

§ 21. The overseer of the poor shall, subject to the *Overseer of* direction of the common council, possess all the powers *the poor.* conferred by law upon the overseers of the poor of the several towns of Oneida county, and be subject to the same duties, liabilities and obligations.

§ 22. The justices of the peace in said city shall possess *Justices of* the same jurisdiction in civil cases which is vested in *the peace.* justices of the peace in towns. In the absence of the recorder from the city, or in case of a vacancy in the office, or his inability, to perform the duties of his office they may exercise jurisdiction in criminal cases, but not otherwise. They shall possess the same powers which are possessed by commissioners of deeds in other cities.

§ 23. The clerk, supervisors, assessors, collectors, con- *Clerk of su-* stables, and inspectors of elections shall possess the same *pervisors,* *assessors* powers and perform the same duties, and be subject to *and others.* the same liabilities respectively as like officers in towns in the county of Oneida, excepting as provided for in this act.

Special § 24. The clerk shall keep the corporate seal, and all *duties of* *clerk.* papers belonging to the city, and shall attend the meetings of the common council and make a record of its proceedings, and perform such other duties as are required of him by this act, and such as he will be charged with by the common council. He shall keep an accurate account of all warrants issued, in a book to be provided for that purpose. Copies of all papers filed in his office, and transcripts from the record of the proceedings of the common council, duly certified by him under the corporate seal, shall be evidence *of all courts, in like manner as if the originals were produced and proven.

City sur- § 25. The city surveyor shall prepare plans, specifica- *veyor.* tions and estimates, when thereto directed by the common council, of proposed public improvements, and shall superintend the opening of streets, and the preservation of the true lines thereof, and perform such other duties as he may be charged with by the common council.

Street com- § 26. The street commissioner shall superintend the *missioner.* making of public improvements ordered by the common

*So in the original.

council, and make contracts for work and labor which may be necessary, and discharge such other duties as the common council may require. He shall keep accurate accounts of all expenditures incurred by him in the performance of his duties, accompanied with statements of the cause of the expenditure, and shall render the same to the common council when thereto requested. No contract or agreement made by him on the part of the city shall be binding, until the same is ratified by the common council, but when so ratified it shall have the same effect as if executed under the corporate seal.

§ 27. The chief engineer shall have the superintendence of the fire department. It shall be his duty to see that the apparatus for extinguishing fires belonging to the city is kept in proper order, and from time to time to report to the common council any necessary reparation or measure to render the condition of the department efficient. He shall appoint a first and second assistant engineer, who shall under his direction perform any services and exercise any control which he could in the operations of the department. In the absence of the chief engineer the first assistant engineer shall possess his powers and exercise his duties in the superintendence of the department, and in the absence of the chief engineer and first assistant, the second assistant engineer shall possess his powers and exercise his duties. They shall perform such other duties as the common council may prescribe. *Chief engineer.*

§ 28. The chief of police shall under the direction of the mayor, be the chief police officer of the city, and shall have the same power and authority in criminal cases that the sheriff of Oneida county, or any constable thereof possesses, and within the city of Utica the same power and authority in civil cases which a constable possesses. It shall be his duty to see that the laws of the state and the ordinances of the city for the preservation of peace, morality and good order, are faithfully observed and enforced in the city, and he shall discharge such other duties as are required of him by this act, and such as the common council may prescribe. *Chief of police.*

§ 29. The aldermen of the city shall be members of the common council. Every member of the common council shall have the power, and it shall be his duty without warrant to arrest or cause to be arrested any persons en- *Aldermen.*

gaged in his presence in disturbing the public peace, or violating any law of the state, or ordinance of the city for the preservation thereof, or of good order, or morality, and to bring or cause such persons to be brought before the mayor, recorder, or a justice of the peace for trial.

§ 30. The other officers in said city shall discharge the duties required of them by this act, and such other duties as the common council may require.

§ 31. There shall be appointed in the manner now prescribed by law, seven commissioners of deeds in and for said city, on or before the first day of April next. Said commissioners shall hold their office till the first day of January, A. D., one thousand eight hundred and sixty-three. And the said common council of said city shall, on or before the said first day of January, one thousand eight hundred and sixty-three, by resolution of the board, determine and limit the number of commissioners of deeds to be thereafter appointed in and for said city ; and from the time of the passage of said resolution, all existing provisions of law relative to limiting and determining the number of commissioners of deeds in cities of this state, their appointment and terms of office, shall apply to said city, such commissioners before entering upon the duties of said office shall take and subscribe the constitutional oath of office before the clerk of the county of Oneida.

§ 32. The mayor and aldermen shall constitute the common council of said city The common council shall hold stated meetings at times to be determined by it, from time to time, and special meetings whenever called by the mayor, or by any two aldermen, by notice to each member thereof, to be served personally, or by leaving the same at his place of abode. A majority of its members shall constitute a quorum for the transaction of business ; but in case from any cause at any time there shall be in office a less number of aldermen than shall or may be necessary to make such quorum, then a majority of the aldermen in office acting in council, or the mayor, shall have power to and shall order special elections to fill the vacancies in the office of aldermen, to be held in the manner prescribed in this act. When present the mayor shall preside at all meetings of the common council. In case of his absence from the city, or his inability

to perform the duties of his office, or during a vacancy
in the office, the common council shall appoint one of the
aldermen its chairman. and such chairman shall be vested
with the power and execute the duties of the mayor, and
continue such chairman for such time not exceeding the
continuance of such absence, inability or vacancy, as the
council may desire.

§ 33. The common council shall determine the rules of *Judge of the qualifica-*
its own proceedings, and be the judge of the election *tions of its*
and qualifications of its own members, and have power *own mem-*
bers.
to compel their attendance ; and shall have power to
prescribe the duties of all the officers and persons appointed by them to any office or place whatever, subject
to the provisions of this act.

§ 34. The common council shall appoint the clerk, the *Shall ap-*
point cer-
city surveyor, the street commissioner, the chief engi- *tain officers.*
neer, and policemen, and so many fence viewers, clerks
of markets, sextons'te have charge of the burial grounds
belonging to the city, and messengers to attend upon its
meetings, as it may deem necessary. Such officers shall .
hold their offices during the pleasure of the common
council.

§ 35. The common council shall have the care, manage- *To have*
manage-
ment and control of the property of the city and its *ment and*
control of
finances ; it shall have power to ordain, alter, modify, *city and its*
and repeal ordinances not repugnant to the constitution *finances.*
and laws of this state, such as it shall deem expedient
for the good government of the city, the preservation of
peace and good order, the suppresion of vice and immorality, the benefit of trade and commerce, and the health
of the inhabitants thereof, and such other ordinances,
rules and regulations as may be necessary to carry such
power into effect. It is also particularly authorized to
enact ordinances for the following purposes :

First. To preserve peace and good order, and to re- *Preserve*
order.
strain, prevent, detect, and punish vice, immorality, and
every kind of fraudulent device and practice.

Second To restrain and prevent and to suppress dis- *Suppress*
disorderly
orderly and gaming houses, billiard tables, and all in- *houses.*
struments and devices for gaming.

Third. To restrain and punish vagrants, mendicants, *Punish*
vagrants
street beggars and persons soliciting alms, keepers of *and others.*
houses of ill fame, common prostitutes, bawds, and disorderly persons, and to prevent and punish drunkenness

and disorderly or immoral conduct in public places and streets.

Punish disturbance in the street.   *Fourth.* To prevent any riot, noise, or public disturbance, and all disorderly assemblies.

Auction and peddling.   *Fifth.* To regulate auction sales, and to prohibit hawking and peddling in the streets.

Regulate sale of intoxicating liquors.   *Sixth.* To prevent the selling or giving away with intent to evade the excise laws, any strong or spirituous liquors by any storekeeper, trader, or grocer, to be drank in any shop, store, grocery, house, outhouse, yard, or garden, owned, occupied, or controlled by the person selling or giving away the same, except by persons duly licensed thereto, and to prohibit the selling or giving away of any strong or spirituous liquors to any child, apprentice, or servant, without the consent of his or her parent, guardian, master or mistress.

Regulate keeping of gunpowder &c.   *Seventh.* To regulate the keeping and conveying of gunpowder and other combustible and dangerous materials, and the use of candles and lights in barns and stables.

Sale of wood, hay and coal.   *Eighth.* To regulate the places of exposing for sale wood, coal, hay and lime, in the streets of the city.

Soliciting passengers and ringing of bells.   *Ninth.* To restrain and regulate the soliciting of passengers for any means of public conveyance, and of guests for taverns or public boarding houses, and the ringing of bells.

License cartmen and hackmen.   *Tenth.* To license and regulate cartmen, porters, and drivers of hackney carriages and baggage or other wagons or vehicles used to carry passengers or baggage for hire, and to limit their compensation.

Exhibitions.   *Eleventh.* To restrain and regulate all exhibitions of natural or artificial curiosities or animals, all theatrical or other shows, exhibitions, or performances for money.

Sealer.   *Twelfth.* To appoint a sealer and examiner of weights and measures in the city.

Burial of dead.   *Thirteenth.* To regulate the burial of the dead, and to direct and require the keeping and returning of bills of mortality, and to impose penalties on physicians, sextons, and others, for any default in or violation of any ordinance passed under this subdivision.

Dogs.   *Fourteenth.* To regulate or prevent the running at large of dogs, and to destroy them, and to impose a tax upon the owners or possessors of dogs.

Fifteenth. To restrain the running at large of cattle, horses, sheep, swine, and geese in said city, and to cause such as may be found running at large to be impounded and sold to discharge the penalty for the violation of the ordinance and the expenses of impounding and sale. Cattle, horses &c.

Sixteenth. To establish and regulate public pounds, and to appoint masters thereof from time to time Pounds.

Seventeenth. To determine what are nuisances, and to prevent, abate, and remove them. Nuisances.

Eighteenth. To prevent and punish horse racing and immoderating riding or driving in the streets or highways, and every game, practice or amusement in the streets or elsewhere, having a tendency to frighten teams or horses, or to annoy persons passing in or along the streets and highways, or to endanger property. Horse racing.

Nineteenth. To prevent and punish the discharge of firearms, rockets, gunpowder, and fireworks in the streets of the city, or in the vicinity of any building. Discharge of firearms, rockets &c.

Twentieth. To light the streets of the city.

Twenty-first. To establish, make, and regulate public wells, acqueducts, and reservoirs of water for the convenience of the inhabitants of the city and its protection against fires, and to prevent the unnecessary waste of water. Wells and reservoirs.

Twenty-second. To regulate and prescribe what shall be a sufficient and lawful division fence. Division fence.

Twenty-third. To compell all persons to remove the snow, ice, and dirt from the sidewalks in front of the premises occupied or owned by them, and to keep the streets swept in front of such premises, and to punish the encumbering of streets and sidewalks with carriages, carts, sleds, sleighs, wheelbarrows, boxes, wood, lumber, timber, or other substance or material whatsoever. Cleaning sidewalks.

Twenty-fourth. To ascertain, establish, and settle the boundaries of the city and all streets, alleys, and highways therein, and to remove and prevent all encroachments thereon. Establish city boundaries.

Twenty-fifth. To prescribe the duties of the policemen, chief engineer, and the members of the fire department, and the duties of citizens upon occasions of fires. To regulate the powers and duties of the chief of police and policemen, to require them at their own expense to furnish and wear, while on duty, a suitable uniform; and to adopt such measures as they shall deem expedient for Duties of policemen, chief engineer and members of fire department.

the purpose of carrying out the duties of the police department, and of securing promptness, vigilance, and efficiency therein.

Fire buckets.

Twenty-sixth. To require the occupants of buildings to provide themselves with fire buckets, and to prescribe the manner in which they shall be marked and kept, and to regulate their use at fires.

Public markets.

Twenty-seventh. To establish and regulate public markets, and to restrain and regulate the sale of fresh meat and vegetables in the city, and to license butchers, and for cause shown to revoke their licenses.

Chimneys.

Twenty-eighth. To regulate the construction of chimneys, and to compel their sweeping and cleaning.

Fireplaces, stovepipes, &c.

Twenty-ninth. To prevent the dangerous construction or condition of chimneys, fireplaces, hearths, stoves, stovepipes, ovens, boilers, and apparatus used in any building or manufactory, and to cause the same to be removed or placed in a safe and secure condition, and to direct and regulate the manner of keeping ashes.

Dangerous manufactories.

Thirtieth. To regulate and prevent the carrying on of manufactories dangerous in causing or promoting fires, or producing disagreeable or unwholesome odors.

Scuttles.

Thirty-first. To compel the owners or occupants of buildings to have scuttles in their roofs, and stairs or ladders leading to them.

Idle and suspicious persons.

Thirty-second. To authorize the mayor, aldermen fire wardens, and other officers of the city to keep away from the vicinity of any fire all idle and suspicious persons, and to compel all persons in said city to aid in the extinguishment of fires and the protection and preservation of property thereat.

Safety of building.

Thirty-third. To authorize and require the policemen and other officers to enter all buildings and inclosures at proper times to ascertain whether their arrangements for fire or the preservation of ashes are dangerous, and to cause such as are dangerous to be put in a safe condition.

Board of health.

Thirty-fourth. To organize a board of health, to consist of seven members in addition to the mayor, who shall be its president, and to provide measures for the preservation of the health of the inhabitants, and to prevent the spread of infectious or pestilential diseases.

§ 36. The common council shall have power by resolution,

First. To compel the owner or occupant of any grocery Remove nuisances. cellar, chandler's shop, soap factory, tannery, stable, slaughter house, barn, privy, sewer, or other unwholesome or nauseous building or place, to. cleanse, remove, or abate the same, whenever and as often as it shall deem it necessary for the health, comfort, and convenience of the inhabitants of the city; and in case such owner or occupant will not proceed as directed, to cleanse. remove, or abate the same, to cause it to be done at the expense of such owner or occupant, and to sue for and recover the expense thereof in a civil action.

Second. To compel the owner or occupant of any build- Ruinous buildings and walls. ing or wall in the said city; which may be in a ruinous or unsafe condition, to render the same safe, or to remove it; and in case he will not proceed as directed, either to render it safe or remove it, to cause the same to be done at the expense of such owner or occupant, and to sue for and recover the expense thereof in a civil action.

Third. To require the removal or destruction of any Dead carcasses. dead carcass or other unwholesome or offensive substance, or substance likely to become unwholesome or offensive, from any street, lot, or building, by the owner or occupant thereof, and in case such owner or occupant will not proceed as required to remove or destroy the same, then to cause the same to be done at the expense of such owner or occupant, and to sue for and recover the expense thereof in a civil action. But no dead carcass shall be thrown or deposited in the Mohawk river or on its banks within the limits of said city, under such penalties for each offence, not exceeding ten dollars, as the common council by ordinance shall prescribe.

Fourth. To take such measures as it shall deem Prevent the spread of disease. necessary to prevent the introduction into the city, or the spreading therein, of any pestilential or infectious disease, and to cause any persons, not residents of the city, infected with any such disease, to be removed to some suitable and proper house or hospital within the city, to be nursed and treated for such disease.

Fifth. To require any building, fence or other erection, which may be placed within or erected upon the line of any street or highway in the city, to be removed therefrom by the owner or occupant, and in case of his neglect to remove the same, to cause it to be removed at the expense of such owner or occupant, and to sue for and recover the expense thereof in a civil action.

Pass laws
and regula-
tions.

§ 37. The common council may enforce observance of all ordinances, by-laws, regulations and resolutions which it is permitted to pass in order to carry into effect the powers vested in it, by the imposition of penalties on the persons violating the same, not exceeding fifty dollars for one violation, to be recovered in a civil action in any court having cognizance thereof.

Publication
of ordinan-
ces.

§ 38. Every ordinance imposing a penalty or forfeiture for a violation of its provisions, shall, after the passage thereof, be published for three weeks successively at least once in each week, in the official newspapers. The affidavits of the printer or publisher of such newspapers or of their foreman of the publication thereof, taken before any officer authorized to administer oaths, and filed with the clerk, or a copy of such affidavits certified by the clerk under the corporate seal, shall be conclusive proof of such publication in all courts and places; until such publication, the ordinance shall not become operative.

Manner of
service of
resolution.

§ 39. A copy of any resolution of the common council, passed pursuant to the thirty-sixth section of this act, certified by the clerk under the corporate seal of the city, may be served upon any person to be affected thereby, personally, or in case such person cannot be found at his or her residence or usual place of business therein, then by leaving it at such residence, with a person of suitable age and discretion. The resolution shall thereupon, so far as such person is concerned, have the same effect as an ordinance duly made and published by the common council In case the person to be affected by the resolution is a non-resident, no service of a copy thereof shall be necessary, unless he or she has an authorized agent in the city, when the service shall be made upon such agent in the manner in this section provided.

Actions to
be brought
in corporate
name of the
city.

§ 40. All actions brought to recover any penalty or forfeiture incurred under this act, or the ordinances, resolutions, by-laws or police regulations made in pursuance of it, shall be brought in the corporate name of the city ; and in such action it shall be lawful and sufficient to allege in the complaint, that the defendant is indebted to the said city in a sum, stating the penalty, and referring to the section of this act or to the ordinance, resolution, or by-law under which the penalty is claimed, and under such complaint to give the special matter in evidence; and the defendant may answer by a denial, general or specific, and give the special matter in evidence. The first process in any such action brought in a justice's court may be by warrant, and execution upon any judgment rendered therein may require that in case nothing shall be found of which the amount can be collected, the defendant shall be taken and imprisoned in the jail of Oneida county for thirty days. Female defendants may be imprisoned under the execution provided for in this section, in the same manner as male defendants. *Female defendants may be imprisoned.*

§ 41. The common council may, by a vote of two-thirds of all the members elected, and on the payment of all costs, and saving the city harmless from all expenses, remit penalties or forfeitures imposed by virtue of this act. But in case the defendant omits for the space of ten days after the passage of the resolution remitting such penalty to pay such costs and expenses, the resolution remitting such penalty shall cease to be operative. And the officer before whom such penalty shall have been recovered, shall, at any time, on the demand of the city attorney or any policeman, or any member of the common council, issue execution on the judgment of such penalty and costs, and such execution shall be enforced for the whole amount of such judgment, the same as if such resolution had not been passed. *May remit penalties.*

§ 42 All penalties, forfeitures, claims or costs, due to the city, when paid to any justice of the peace, shall be paid by him to the treasurer within one week after their receipt by him. Whenever execution shall be issued by a justice of the peace upon any judgment in favor of the city, the same shall be returned by the officer receiving the same, to the justice who issued it, on or before the return day thereof; and if such officer neglects to return the same for twenty days after the return day thereof, the justice who issued it shall report the fact to the treasurer, who shall cause a suit to be brought against the officer for the default. No officer of the city shall receive any penalty or forfeiture due to the city for the violation of any ordinance, or any claim arising under the thirty fifth or thirty-sixth section of this act, except the treasurer of the city, a justice of the peace before whom an action has been instituted therefor, or an officer having power by execution to collect it. *All penalties, claims, forfeitures and costs to be paid to the treasurer.*

Designate
papers to
publish pro
ceedings.

§ 43. The common council shall, at the first meeting
held, on or after the second Tuesday in March in each
year, designate three daily newspapers published in the
city, in which a copy of the record of its proceedings
and all notices and documents required to be published
by this act shall be printed for the ensuing year. They
shall be called the official newspapers The compensation of such official newspapers, for publishing the record
of proceedings, shall be fixed by the common council ;
and their aggregate compensation for publishing all
notices and documents required to be published by this
act, shall be the compensation allowed by statute, or by
the provisions of this act, for two newspapers, which
amount shall be divided equally between the official
newspapers so designated. In case there shall be but
two daily newspapers published in the city, or in case
but two daily newspapers will make such publication at
the rates herein provided, the publication in two daily
official newspapers of any notice, proceeding or document
required to be published by this act, shall be deemed
sufficient publication under the provisions of this act.

May remove
from office
certain offi-
cers.

§ 44. The common council may remove from office the
treasurer, city attorney, overseer of the poor, assessors,
collectors or constables. No such officer shall be removed except for cause. and not until he shall have
notice in writing of the character of the charges made
against him, and an opportunity be given him of being
heard in his defence. The cause of such removal shall
be assigned in writing and entered in the records of the
proceedings of the common council

Salaries of
certain offi
cers.

§ 45. The common council shall pay to the mayor an
annual salary not exceeding two hundred and fifty dollars ; and to the treasurer an annual salary not exceeding six hundred dollars, whose salary shall be in lieu of
all commissions or other compensation whatever ; and
to the city attorney an annual salary not exceeding seven
hundred dollars, which shall be in lieu of all fees, commissions or compensation whatever, which salaries shall
be paid quarterly. The several officers appointed by the
common council under the provisions of this act, whose
compensation is not otherwise provided for, shall be
allowed and paid for their respective services such compensation as the common council shall deem reasonable ;
and the inspectors and poll clerks of all elections held in

any ward of the city shall be allowed and paid the same compensation that is allowed by law to like officers in the towns for their services at general elections.

§ 46. If any person having been an officer in said city shall not within ten days after notification and request, deliver to his successor in office all the property, papers and effects of every description in his possession or under his control, belonging to said city, or appertaining to the office he held, he shall forfeit and pay for the use of the city fifty dollars, to be recovered in a civil action in the name of the city, besides all damages caused by his neglect or refusal so to deliver. *(margin: Forfeitures for failure to deliver papers to successors in office.)*

TITLE 5.*

OF THE IMPOSITION AND COLLECTION OF TAXES FOR CITY PURPOSES, AND THE FUNDS, REVENUE AND EXPENDITURES OF THE CITY.

§ 47 The common council shall have power in each year to raise by tax sixteen thousand dollars, exclusive of the expense of its collection. and of the poll tax hereinafter authorized, to provide for the following purposes: *(margin: Common council have power to raise by tax in each year $16,000.)*

1st. Defraying the expenses of the police department.

2d. Making and repairing streets, highways and bridges.

3d. Providing necessary apparatus and means for the prevention and extinguishment of fires

4th. Defraying the contingent expenses of the city.

5th. Defraying the expenses of public improvements proper to be done by the city.

The common council shall also have power to raise by tax upon real and personal property liable to taxation in each ward, such sum as shall be determined by the common council to be necessary, to defray the expense of lighting the streets in the several wards; which sums so assessed upon the several wards shall be in addition to the tax in this section above provided for, and shall be collected therewith; and all moneys raised for this purpose upon the real and personal property of each ward shall be kept by the treasurer as a separate fund for such ward, and shall be drawn from the treasury only by orders specifying that the same were drawn to meet the expenditure for which they were raised. *(margin: Also for lighting streets.)*

*So numbered in the original.

Poll tax.

§ 48. In raising the tax provided in the preceeding section of this title, the common council shall first cause a roll of all persons in each ward who would be liable to be assessed for work on highways if the city were a town, except such persons as are assessed upon some of the assessment rolls of the city as the owners of real or personal estate, to be made by the assessors, and shall then impose upon each of such persons a tax of not less than sixty-two and a half cents, nor more than two dollars and fifty cents, as a poll tax for the making and repairing of streets, highways and bridges, and which shall be in addition to the tax provided in such section. The common council shall then cause two copies to be made of the last assessment roll made by the assessors for each of the wards in the city, with columns prepared for the insertion of the poll tax and for taxes upon real and personal estate ; they shall then cause to be inserted in the copies for each ward respectively, the poll tax to be imposed upon the persons resident in such ward ; they shall then impose upon the persons and property assessed in the assessment rolls of all the wards of the city, the amount of tax to be raised under the provisions of said section, and also the amount of any other tax, or tax for extraordinary purposes which may be required or authorized by law. The amount to be paid by each person and each property shall be entered in appropriate columns, and when the taxes shall be entered therein and properly corrected, the rolls shall be signed by the mayor and clerk, and one copy of each of the said rolls for each ward shall be immediately filed with the clerk and the other delivered to the treasurer. They shall thereafter be called the tax lists.

Tax list to be evidence of imposition of tax.

§ 49. The tax lists filed with the clerk, or delivered to the treasurer, shall in all courts and places be evidence of the imposition of the taxes therein contained, and the taxes therein assessed upon or in respect to any real estate shall be liens thereon for two years from the time the tax lists are filed with the clerk.

Notice to be published in official newspaper.

§ 50. Upon receiving the tax lists the treasurer shall cause notice to be published in the official newspapers once in each week for three successive weeks that they have been left with him, and that he will be ready at his office between nine and twelve o'clock in the forenoon and two and five o'clock in the afternoon of each day, except Sunday, for one month ensuing the first publication of such notice, to receive payment of the taxes thereon, and that persons paying their taxes within that period will be charged no commission for the collection thereof. The treasurer shall for one month after the first publication of such notice attend daily at his office from nine o'clock to twelve o'clock in the forenoon and from two o'clock to five o'clock in the afternoon, excepting Sundays, to receive taxes on such list, and no commissions for collections shall be charged on taxes paid within that period. Upon receiving any tax the treasurer shall write paid opposite to it, in a column prepared for the purpose, and shall give the person paying a receipt therefor, and keep a check list of all receipts so given. *Treasurer to receive taxes.*

§ 51. At the expiration of the month mentioned in the preceding section, the treasurer shall deliver the tax lists in his hands of each ward to the collector of such ward, with a warrant under his hand thereto annexed, directing and requiring him to collect all taxes thereon not marked paid, within sixty days thereafter, and to return the said list together with the moneys collected, to him at the expiration of such sixty days. The collectors of the wards shall then proceed to collect the uncollected taxes upon the tax lists so delivered to them respectively, in the same manner and with the same powers and duties as a town collector in the collection of taxes imposed by the board of supervisors. They shall be permitted in addition to the taxes on the tax lists to collect from each tax-payer a commission not to exceed five cents for any amount of tax less than one dollar, nor the rate of five per cent. upon any tax exceeding one dollar. But no collector shall receive any commission on the taxes not collected by him. Each collector shall pay over all moneys in his hands to the city treasurer from time to time as the common council shall direct. The common council shall have no power to renew the collectors' warrants, or to extend the time for the collection of taxes. *Collectors of the wards*

§ 52. If any collector shall neglect or refuse to pay over to the treasurer any moneys by him collected, or shall be guilty of any default in the performance of his duties, the common council may cause an action to be brought against him and his sureties upon his official bond, without further proceedings prior thereto. *Default or neglect of collector.*

7

§ 53. If any of the taxes mentioned in the tax lists shall remain unpaid, and the collector shall be unable to collect the same, he shall deliver to the treasurer an account of the taxes so remaining due ; and upon making oath before him that the sums mentioned in such account remain unpaid, and that he has not been able upon diligent inquiry to discover any goods or chattels belonging to or in possession of the persons charged with or liable to pay such sums, whereon he could levy the same, he shall be credited by the treasurer with the amount thereof. The treasurer shall thereupon deliver such return to the clerk, who shall lay the same before the common council at its next meeting, and such return shall be filed with the city clerk. In case any tax or assessment shall be returned to the city treasurer as unpaid by any one of the collectors of the said city, there shall be charged thereon, for the benefit of the city, the sum of five per cent. on each dollar of the tax or assessment so returned, and one per cent. per month thereafter for each month the same shall remain unpaid from the time of such return until the payment thereof, and all the provisions of this act in regard to the collection of such taxes or assessments shall apply to the collection of said sums so charged.

List of un-
paid taxes
to be pub-
lished in
official
newspaper.

§ 54. Upon the return of any unpaid taxes or assessments to the treasurer, or at such time thereafter as the common council shall determine, the common council shall cause a copy of so much of the tax lists as contain them to be published in the official newspapers once in each week for eight successive weeks, with a notice that if the same are not paid to the treasurer within such eight weeks, the lands, if any, upon which or in respect to which they are imposed, will be sold at a time and place therein specified at public auction to the person who shall take the same for the shortest period and pay the taxes, with the expense incurred thereon, and of the sale. At the time and place specified, or at the time and place to which the sale may be postponed, the treasurer shall sell the same at public auction to the person or corporation who will take the same for the shortest period and pay the tax, percentage, and expense incurred thereon ; but no real estate shall for any city tax or assessment be sold for a period exceeding twenty years, exclusive of the time allowed for redemption. Each parcel of real estate shall be sold separately.

§ 55 Upon making any sale of real estate under the provisions of the last preceding section, the treasurer shall execute two certificates of the fact, containing the name and residence of the purchaser, a description of the property sold, the time when and the term for which it was sold, and stating the particular tax or assessment, and the amount thereof, together with the percentage and expenses, for which the sale was made, and providing that if the owner thereof, or some one on his or her behalf, shall not within fifteen months after such sale redeem the same from the effect of the sale by the payment for the purchaser's use to the treasurer of the city of the money paid thereon, with interest at the rate of one per cent. per month until paid, the purchaser, his legal representatives, or assigns, will be entitled to a deed thereof. One of such certificates the treasurer shall file with the clerk of the city and the other deliver to the purchaser. Such certificate shall be presumptive evidence of the facts therein contained.

Certificate of treasurer on sale of real estate.

§ 56. At any time during such fifteen months any owner or claimant of real estate so sold, or of any specific part or undivided interest therein, or any one in his or her behalf may redeem the same from the effect of the sale by paying the treasurer for the use of the purchaser, his representatives or assigns, the sum of money paid therefor, with interest thereon at the rate of one per cent per month until paid, or he may redeem any undivided part thereof by paying its proper proportion of such moneys and interest, or any part thereof which belongs to him and which by accident or mistake was assessed and taxed as parcel of other real estate, by paying its proper proportion of such moneys and interest, and on such payment being made the title acquired by such sale shall cease and determine. At least sixty days before the expiration of the time for redemption, the purchaser, his representatives or assigns, shall give notice to the owner, requiring him to redeem the premises by making the payment above mentioned on or before the day when the time for such redemption will expire, which day shall be specified in such notice. If such owner be a resident of the city, the notice shall be served on him personally or by leaving the same at his residence with some person of suitable age and discretion; if he be not a resident of the city, then by leaving such notice

Redemption of tax sales.

with his agent, if he have one in the city, personally, or by leaving it at the residence of such agent in the city, with some suitable person ; and if he have no such agent, then by serving such notice on the person in possession of the premises, personally, or by leaving the same with some suitable person in his family, and if there be no person in possession, then by mailing such notice to the owner at his reputed place of residence if it can be ascertained, or by publishing such notice for three successive days in the official newspapers. In case the owner is unknown, or cannot, after a reasonable diligence, be found, the publication of such notice, as above provided in this section, shall be sufficient service. If the owner, his representatives or assigns, shall not redeem the premises in the manner required by this act, on or before the expiration of said fifteen months, his or their right of redemption shall thenceforth be divested. The affidavits of any such service or publication, taken before any officer authorized to take affidavits to be read in courts of record, and filed with the treasurer in the office of the city clerk, shall be presumptive evidence of the facts therein contained. The treasurer shall execute no deed, unless upon the production and filing with him of an affidavit of such service.

Mortgagor or judgment debtor may defeat sale. § 57. Any person having a mortgage, judgment, or decree which shall be a lien on the premises so sold, at the time of, or at any time after such sale, or within fifteen months thereafter, may defeat the sale thereof at any time within fifteen months after the sale, in the same manner and with the same effect as the owner or claimant of said premises may do, and shall thenceforward have a further lien on said premises for the amount paid by him to defeat the sale thereof, with interest, which may be added to his mortgage, judgment or decree, and enjoyed and enforced by him in the same manner as though it formed a part thereof. The receipt of the treasurer, acknowledged or proven in due form of law to entitle conveyances of real estate to be recorded, shall be evidence of such payment.

Treasurer to deed lands if not redeemed. § 58. In case the real estate so sold, or any part thereof, shall not be redeemed as provided for by this act, after the expiration of fifteen months from the time of making the sale, and upon proof of the service of such notice as hereinbefore provided, the treasurer shall exe-cate to the purchaser or purchasers, his or their legal representatives or assigns, a deed or deeds thereof, or of the parts unredeemed for the period for which it shall have been purchased, containing a description of the premises, of the fact of assessment, advertisement, and sale, the date of the sale, the price for which the premises were sold, and the time of the service of notice to redeem, which deed or deeds may be recorded as a lease of real estate, and shall be presumptive evidence in all courts and places that such tax and assessment was legally imposed, and that the proceedings to authorize such sale were duly taken, and in all respects correct ; and such grantee may obtain possession thereof in the manner prescribed by law in relation to persons holding over demised premises, after the expiration of their terms without the consent of the landlord, and shall have, hold, and enjoy the said premises so sold during the term for which the same were granted, to be computed from the expiration of fifteen months after the day of sale thereof, free and clear from all liens, claims, and demands of any other owner or occupant of the same, and subject to the lien of all taxes and assessments that may have been charged or levied thereon at the time of such sale or at any time thereafter, and at the expiration of such time, such grantee, his heirs or assigns, may remove any building or fixture that may have been erected on the premises during the said term. The city treasurer shall keep a register of all certificates and deeds of sale granted under this act, in a book to be provided for that purpose, and preserve all certificates of sale to, and all assignments thereof required to be produced canceled and filed upon his executing a deed, and shall also preserve all affidavits of service of notice to redeem, and all canceled certificates, and file such affidavits and certificates in the city clerk's office.

§ 59. For the expenses attending the advertisement, sale, and conveyance of real estate for unpaid taxes or assessments by virtue of this act, the said city shall be entitled to charge and collect the following fees: For advertising. fifty cents each parcel for each official newspaper in which the sale shall be published ; treasurer's fee for attending sale and giving certificate, fifty cents, and for giving deed to the purchaser, fifty cents ; and five per cent upon the amount of the tax, to be paid to

Fees for expenses, sale, &c., of real estate for taxes.

the treasurer for the use of the city, in addition to the per centage authorized to be charged by section fifty-three.

Infants may redeem. § 60. In case the real estate sold for any tax or assessment shall belong to any person under the age of twenty-one years, such person on attaining the age of twenty-one years, or within fifteen months thereafter, may redeem the same from the purchaser, his heirs or assigns, by depositing with the treasurer for his, her, or their use, the amount for which the same was sold, with fifteen per cent thereon.

Removing buildings from premises purchased and redeemed. § 61. The purchaser of any real estate sold for a tax or assessment pursuant to the provisions of this act, or his heirs or assigns, may, within a reasonable time, not exceeding ninety days after any redemption made pursuant to the last preceding section of this act, remove any buildings or improvements erected by him, her, or them thereon, but in so doing shall commit no unnecessary damage to the same.

Must be redeemed within two years. § 62. No real estate shall be sold under the provisions of this act for any tax or assessment, excepting within two years from the time the same was filed with the clerk.

Commence action for taxes. § 63. The common council shall have power to collect by civil action any tax imposed pursuant to the provisions of this act against any person, which shall be returned by a collector as unpaid, in whole or in part; but such action must be commenced within two years after such return by the collector.

§ 64. All the provisions of this act as to ordinary taxes shall apply to every assessment under this act, for whatever purpose imposed.

May re-assess. § 65. In case any tax shall be returned by the collector unpaid, which, by reason of the non-residence of the person bound to pay the same, or for any other cause, cannot be collected, the common council may re-assess and collect in the succeeding year the amount thereof on the property upon which any such tax was imposed, or may add the amount thereof to the moneys authorized by the provisions of this act to be raised by tax in the succeeding year.

Collectors of county taxes in city § 66. The collectors of county taxes in said city shall, upon receiving the tax lists, cause a notice to be published in the official papers of the city, once in each week, for three successive weeks, that they will be ready at some convenient place in said city, between nine and twelve o'clock in the forenoon, and two and five o'clock in the afternoon of each day, except Sunday, for one month ensuing the first publication of such notice, to receive payment of the taxes on the lists in their hands, and all persons paying their taxes within the said month shall only be charged a commission of one per cent thereon.

§ 67. After the expiration of said period, the collectors of the county taxes shall be permitted to collect from each tax payer a commission not to exceed five cents for any amount of tax less than one dollar, nor the rate of five per cent upon any tax exceeding one dollar.

§ 68. The common council is prohibited from bor- rowing any money or contracting any pecuniary obliga- tion whatever, on the part of the city, excepting as fol- lows: It may make temporary loans to anticipate not exceeding two-thirds of the ordinary tax of the current fiscal year, and to be paid before the first day of February within such fiscal year.

§ 69. The common council shall contract no debt on the part of the city, excepting as herein otherwise pro- vided, which shall not be payable within the fiscal year in which it is contracted, and which cannot be discharged from the income of such year. In case any alderman of the said city shall vote for any appropriation, or for the expenditure of any moneys not authorized by the charter of said city, or by some law, or in violation of any of the provisions of law, every such alderman shall be liable to a penalty of one hundred dollars, to be sued for and recovered in any court, with costs, by and in the name of any citizen of said city. And in case the com- mon council of said city shall contract any debt after the first Tuesday of March in any year, and before the first Tuesday of March thereafter, which shall remain unpaid for one month after the last mentioned day for want of sufficient funds in the treasury to pay the same; or in case the common council shall authorize any expen- diture for any purpose in such year, exceeding the amount which the said council are authorized by law to raise for such purposes, the alderman voting for the con- tracting of any such debt, or to authorize any such ex- penditure, shall be personally liable to each and every party entitled to payment; and the city of Utica shall not be liable to pay the same, or shall the common council audit or pay any debt so contracted or expenditure so made.

TITLE 6.

OF THE POLICE OF THE CITY.

Appointment of policemen.

§ 70. The common council shall appoint twelve policemen, to hold office during its pleasure, who shall constitute the police of the city. The common council shall designate and select one of them as chief of police, and another of them as assistant chief of police. The common council may, by a vote of three-fourths of the members elected, increase the number of policemen. The mayor may, also, appoint in extraordinary emergencies an additional number of policemen, to continue in office until the next meeting of the council, if the mayor shall deem their continuance until that time necessary. The policemen appointed under this section shall have the same power and authority in criminal cases as constables possess by law, and they shall also have the same power and authority in civil cases or proceedings, which a constable possesses, to serve and execute all process and papers on behalf of the city, but not otherwise. They shall be subject to the same liabilities and perform the same duties as such constables, except as herein otherwise provided.

Duties of police.

§ 71. The policemen of said city shall execute the orders and commitments of the recorder and of the justices of the peace, and of all courts held by him or them, and shall convey all persons sentenced by him or them to jail, or house of refuge; and they shall serve and execute all civil process or proceedings issued or directed by any officer or court in favor of the city, or in which the city shall be a party.

No fees for arrests.

§ 72. No fees or compensation other than as herein provided, shall be charged or received by any policemen for the arrest, confinement, or discharge of any person, or for mileage, or for serving any process or warrant, or for discharging any other duty required by this act to be performed by him.

No present or reward for services.

§ 73. No policeman shall receive any present or reward for services rendered or to be rendered, unless with the approbation of the mayor; such approbation to be given in writing and filed in the city clerk's office. Any policeman who shall receive any fee, present or reward in violation of this section, shall forfeit his office.

§ 74. It shall be the duty of the chief of police, under the direction of the mayor, to superintend the police department, of which he shall be the chief executive officer. He shall keep a record, in a book to be provided for that purpose, of all cases and legal proceedings in the police department and of all services performed by him and the several policemen in each case, and of such fees as are allowed to constables of towns for like services. He shall, at least every month, report to the common council the state of the department, and particularly of such fees, and whether any members are delinquent in their duties. The assistant chief of police shall, under the direction of the chief of police, perform any services and exercise any control which he could in the management and operations of the department. In the absence or during the inability of the chief of police, he shall possess his powers and execute his duties.

§ 75. The common council of said city of Utica is hereby authorized to charge to the county of Oneida, or to said city as one of the towns thereof, or to any town therein, for services performed by the policemen in criminal proceedings, such fees as are allowed to constables of towns for like services, and chargeable to said county, city, or towns; and the same shall be audited and allowed by the board of supervisors of said county, or by the boards of town auditors of such towns, to and for the benefit of said city of Utica. In cases arising under the ordinances or police laws or regulations of such city, where judgment shall be rendered in favor of said city, or where the city would be entitled to judgment, the same fees for the services of such policemen as constables would be entitled to for like services, shall be included in such judgment and charged for the benefit of said city, and when paid or collected shall be paid to the city treasurer within five days after the receipt thereof.

§ 76. The constables elected in said city, or in the different towns of Oneida county, shall not, as such, be compelled to serve within the city of Utica any summons, warrant, subpœna, commitment, order, notice,

Duties of chief of police.

Charge county of Oneida for certain services of police.

County and town officers not to be compelled to

8

serve cer-
tain proces-
ses. paper or process whatever, of any name or nature, issued or directed by the recorder, or any justices of the peace of said city, in the execution of the laws of the state for the prevention of crime and the punishment of criminal offenders, or of the police laws or regulations of the state, or of the ordinances, police laws or regulations of the said city, or in any proceedings collateral to or connected with the execution of such general laws or police laws or regulations or ordinances; nor shall the county of Oneida, or any of the towns therein, or the city of Utica, be chargeable with or in any way liable to pay any such constable any fees or disbursements whatever, for services rendered, or disbursements paid or incurred, under or by virtue of such summons, warrant, subpœna, commitment, order, notice, paper or process whatever.

Police to
obey order
of mayor. § 77. It shall be the duty of all the policemen to obey the orders of the mayor, recorder, aldermen, or justices of the peace, for enforcing the laws of the state and the city ordinances.

Work
house. § 78. The common council shall have power to occupy and maintain as a city workhouse the building and premises in said city, known as the city hospital; to appoint keepers thereof, and overseers of the persons confined therein or required to labor as hereinafter mentioned, and to prescribe all necessary regulations for the government of such workhouse and the officers thereof. The common council shall have power to require and compel all persons who shall be committed to jail by the recorder, under the seventeenth section of an act entitled " An act to suppress intemperance, and to regulate the sale of intoxicating liquors," passed April 16, 1857, or under either of the acts entitled " Of beggars and vagrants," or " Of disordily* persons," or by any justice of the peace of said city, during the absence or inability of the recorder, or a vacancy in his office; and all persons who shall be committed to jail for any violation of the ordinances or police laws or regulations of said city, to be confined at hard labor in such workhouse, or to labor in the streets or elsewhere in said city. And in case such person shall refuse to perform such labor, the common council shall have the power to inflict such reasonable punishment as shall be necessary to secure obedience and submission. The city shall have the bene-

*So in the original.

fit of the labor of such persons; and in case where such persons shall labor upon public improvements authorized by the common council, under the provisions of this act, the reasonable value of such labor, to be determined by the common council, may be included in the costs and expenses of such improvement, and assessed upon the property benefited, in cases where such assessment is authorized by the provisions of this act.

TITLE 7.

OF THE POWERS OF THE COMMON COUNCIL IN RELATION TO STREETS AND PUBLIC IMPROVEMENTS.

§ 79. The common council shall have the powers, perform the duties, and be subject to the liabilities of commissioners of highways in towns, with the exceptions and modifications contained in this act. It shall also have power:

1st. To lay out, open, make, amend, repair, alter, extend, widen, contract and discontinue streets, lanes and highways, walks, bridges, drains and sewers in the city, with all necessary wells, grates and other things requisite and proper for the use of such drains and sewers, or for carrying off the surface water from such streets and highways. *Streets, bridges, drains and sewers.*

2nd. To clean the same, and to pass ordinances requiring the same to be kept clean and in proper order, and free from encroachment, incumbrance or injury. *Clean the same.*

3rd. To require, direct and regulate the planting, rearing and preserving of ornamental trees, in the streets and public grounds of the city. *Trees.*

4th. To lay out, improve and ornament public parks and pleasure grounds, and to pass ordinances and regulations concerning their preservation and use. *Public park.*

§ 80. But the common council shall not lay out any street, lane, alley, square, pleasure ground, park, highway or walk, or alter any such as may already be laid out or used, so as to extend or run across or over the site of any dwelling house at the time actually erected, without the written consent of the owner of such dwelling house, unless it shall have at first purchased the same; provided, however, that such dwelling house shall have been erected in good faith upon said site, before the commencement of the proceedings to make such improvement. *Consent of owner in certain cases.*

Surveyed
and record-
ed.
§ 81. The common council shall cause all streets, alleys, lanes, highways, side and crosswalks, public parks and pleasure grounds, and all drains and sewers in said city, to be surveyed, described and recorded in a book to be kept by the clerk for that purpose, and to cause maps thereof to be made and filed with the clerk. Such record and map shall be prima facie evidence of the facts therein described and portrayed, in all actions between the city and other persons touching their location.

Notice to
lay out
street to be
published.
§ 82. Whenever the common council shall intend to lay out, extend, open, contract, widen or discontinue any street, lane or highway, it shall cause a notice of such intention to be published for eight days in the official newspapers, stating the day upon which it will act thereupon ; which day shall be at least eight days subsequent to the first publication of the notice.

§ 83. In case it shall not be necessary to appropriate for the purpose contemplated in section eighty-two, any real estate which shall not belong to said city, or which shall not be given to the city for the purpose, the common council, upon the day fixed in the notice, may proceed to lay out, extend, open, widen or discontinue such street, lane or highway mentioned in the notice.

Description
of property
appropri-
ated.
§ 84. In case it shall be necessary to appropriate for any street, lane or highway, or any square, park or pleasure ground, any real estate not belonging to the city, or which the city may not be permitted by the owner freely to appropriate, the common council, before it shall determine to make such improvement, shall make an order directing some officer or officers of the city, to be designated in such order, to ascertain and report a description of the real estate required to be appropriated, with the names of the owners ; what the whole expense of the improvement would amount to ; whether any, and if any, what part thereof ought to be borne by the city, and whether any, and if any, what real estate would be benefited by the improvement requiring the appropriation of such real estate, specifying the same in parcels, described with certainty, with the names of the owners, if they can be ascertained. It shall cause a notice to be
Notice of
proposed
improve-
ment to be
published in the official papers for one week, specifying the proposed improvement, the estimated expense thereof, and the portion or part of the city to be assessed therefor,

and shall require all persons interested in the subject matter of such improvement, to attend the common council at a time and place in such notice to be stated. At the time and place so stated, the common council shall proceed to hear the allegations of the owners and occupants of houses and lots situated within the portions or parts of the city so specified as aforesaid, and, after hearing the same, shall make such further order in respect to such improvement as it shall deem proper.

published in official paper.

§ 85. If the common council shall, after hearing the parties interested as aforesaid, determine to make any of the improvements in this title specified, and that the lands of any person will be necessary for that purpose, it shall enter in its minutes a resolution declaring such determination and containing a brief and general description of the lands so deemed necessary, and also of that part or portion of the city which it shall deem benefited by such improvement.

Common council to enter its determination.

§ 86. The common council may purchase the land so deemed necessary of the owner or owners thereof, upon such terms and for such compensation as it shall judge reasonable, and thereupon receive a conveyance or conveyances thereof to the city. If such purchase be made, the common council may authorize and direct all or any portion of the costs and expenses of such improvement to be assessed and collected on the real estate benefited thereby. Whenever the common council shall purchase the land so deemed necessary, and pay for the same without any assessment on the property benefited, no other proceedings shall be necessary than such as are required by section eighty-two. But if the common council shall determine that the whole or any part of the purchase price, or of such costs and expenses, should be assessed upon the property benefited, the common counsel* shall appoint not less than three, nor more than five disinterested freeholders of the city, to apportion and assess the same upon the property benefited. Such freeholders shall proceed in the making such apportionment and assessment in the same manner as in that respect required of the commissioners hereinafter mentioned. If such freeholders, or any of them shall decline to or be unable to serve, by reason of sickness or from any other cause, the common council may appoint other qualified freeholders in their places.

Common council may purchase lands necessary for improvements.

*So in the original.

To file map
of improve-
ment if una-
ble to pur-
chase.

§ 87. In case no agreement for such purchase can be made, the common council sha'l cause a copy of such resolution, toge.her with a map of the proposed improvement to be made, designating on such map the lots, tracts and parcels of land which are deemed necessary to be taken, and showing the commencement and termination of the proposed improvement, and also the part or portion of the city deemed to be benefited thereby, to be filed in the city clerk's office.

Notice of
application
to the courts
to be pub-
lished.

§ 88. The common council shall cause to be published for at least eight days in the official papers, a notice specifying and briefly describing the land necessary for such public improvement, and the portion of the city deemed to be benefited by the making thereof, and stating that an application will be made to the supreme court, the county court of the county of Oneida, or the recorder's court of the city of Utica, which courts shall always be deemed to be opened for that purpose, at a time and place in said notice to be specified, for the appointment of commissioners to ascertain and determine what damages and compensation the owner or owners or occupants of such land to be taken will be entitled to for the same, and to apportion and assess the damages and expenses attending such improvement upon the real estate benefited thereby. The common council shall, also, at least five days before the time named for such application, cause a copy of such notice to be served upon each of the owners and occupants of the premises to be taken. Such notice shall be served personally upon persons residing in the city, or by leaving the same at their places of abode, with some person of suitable age and discretion. Upon non-residents it may be served personally, or upon their agent residing in the city, if there be one, or by mailing it, addressed to them at their reputed places of abode. In case the owners are unknown, or after due diligence cannot be found, or their places of abode cannot be ascertained, the publication of the notice in the official newspapers shall be equivalent to personal service.

Application
may be
made in
term or in
vacancy.

§ 89. The application specified in the eighty-eighth, ninetieth, and ninety-third sections of this act, may be made either in term or in vacation, and for the purpose of hearing and deciding such applications, the said courts shall be always open.

§ 90. At the time and place in said notice specified, or Court to appoint commissioners. at such other time and place as the court shall appoint, and upon filing proof by affidavit to the satisfaction of the court, of the publication and service of such notice as above provided, and upon hearing the city by its attorney or cousel,* and the parties interested if desired, the said court shall appoint not less than three nor more than five commissioners, who shall be freeholders and residents of the city of Utica, not interested in any of the land to be taken or assessed, nor of kin to any owner or occupant thereof, to ascertain and determine, as hereinafter mentioned, the damages which the owners or occupants of such land to be taken will be entitled to, and to apportion and assess, as hereinafter mentioned, such damages, together with all expenses of such improvement (except such portion thereof, if any, as the common council shall have determined ought to be borne by the city) upon the real estate benefited thereby. If the commissioners or any of them, shall decline to, or be unable to serve from sickness or any other cause, other commissioners may be appointed in their places by the court to which the first application was made, upon giving two days notice to the persons interested who appeared at the first application, of the time and place at which such appointment will be made. The qualifications of the commissioners appointed under this section shall not be questioned by any person interested, except such as shall have appeared at the time of their appointment and specified their objections in writing to the court.

§ 91. The commissioners so appointed shall, before Commissioners to be sworn. they enter upon the duties of their office, be sworn faithfully to discharge their duties, according to the best of their ability, and to make report of their proceedings according to the provisions of this act, without favor or partiality. They shall give public notice by a notice published in the official papers of said city for six days, of the time when, and the place where, they will first meet to enter upon their duties ; and at the time appointed, or at any time to which they may adjourn, they shall proceed to view the lands and premises proposed to be taken, and may then, or at any other time to which they may adjourn, hear such proofs and allegations of

*So in original.

the parties interested, as they, in their discretion, may deem proper; and may issue subpœnas for the attendance of witnesses, and may examine witnesses on oath, to be administered by either of them. They, may, if deemed necessary, adjourn from time to time, not exceeding the time in which they are required to report, but the granting or refusing of any adjournment shall in all cases, be in their discretion; and they shall keep minutes of the testimony and all proceedings taken by or before them. They shall determine and award to the owner, or owners and occupants, if there be any occupants who are not owners, such damages as in their opinion they will severally sustain for the lands to be taken for such improvements, after making due allowance for any benefit such owner, or owners, or occupants may derive from such improvement. They shall also assess and apportion the whole amount of damages, together with all costs and expenses of such improvement (except such portion thereof, if any, as the common council shall have determined ought to borne by the city,) upon the real estate benefited thereby, as described in the report of the officer or officers mentioned in section eighty-four of this act, as nearly as may be in proportion to the benefits each shall be deemed to receive from said improvement.

To report within sixty days.

§ 92 The said commissioners shall, with all convenient speed, and within sixty days after their appointment, unless the common council shall, by resolution, extend the time, and then, within the time so extended, make their report, signed by them, or a majority of. them, to the common council of said city, in which they shall describe, with all practicable certainty, the several pieces and parcels of land or premises to be taken for such improvement; the name and residence of the owners or occupants thereof, respectively, if known; the rights of such owners or occupants so far as can be ascertained, and the amount of damages which should be paid to each of said owners or occupants   They shall also annex to their report, as a part thereof, an assessment in the form of an assessment list, in which they shall specify and set down in seperate columns an accurate description of each parcel of real estate assessed; the name of the owner or occupant, if known; the amount assessed upon each parcel, and the amount to be collected upon each.

If there be any building on any land taken for such improvement, the value thereof to remove shall be ascertained by the commissioners, and stated in their report, and the owner thereof may remove the same in ten days, or such other time as the common council shall allow, after the confirmation of the report of the commissioners; if he shall so remove it, the value thereof so ascertained shall be deducted from the damages awarded to him; if it be not so removed the common council may sell it at private sale, or at public sale, on ten days public notice in the official newspapers, to the highest bidder. The amount realized for such building, in either case, shall be deducted from the assessment made under this section, pro rata among the several parcels of real estate assessed. The assessment list shall be made to resemble in form, as nearly as practicable, the tax lists, and be provided with a column in which payments can be entered by the treasurer. They shall also return the minutes of the proceedings and evidence, if any be taken by them, to the common council, at the time of making their report, and their report, together with the minutes, shall be filed in the office of the city clerk. They shall be entitled to the sum of two dollars each, as their compensation, for each day actually and necessarily spent by them in discharging their duties as such commissioners.

§ 93. On the coming in of the said report, the common council shall cause to be published in the official newspapers, a daily notice, that at a time therein fixed, and which shall be at least six days after the first publication thereof, it will act upon the same, and during which time the report will be left at the office of the city clerk, where all persons interested may examine the same; and that, unless objections are made and filed by some person interested, said report will be confirmed. Prior to such day, any person interested objecting to the matters contained in the report, shall file with the clerk his objections in writing. If no such objections are so made as aforesaid, the common council may confirm the said report; and if objections are made as aforesaid, any person interested may be heard before the common council touching the matter, on the day specified in the notice, or on such other day or days as the common council shall appoint, before action is had

Common council to publish notice of time when they will act on report.

9

, thereupon. The common council may then confirm said report, and authorize and direct the appropriation of the real estate and the making of the improvement, or set the same aside, and refer the same back to the same commissioners, or new commissioners. to be appointed as herein mentioned. If the reference be to new commissioners, they shall be appointed in the manner hereinbefore provided for the appointment of the first commissioners, except that the notice required to be published need only state the time and place at which they will be appointed, and the purpose for, and the improvement with reference to which they will be appointed ; and excepting that no notices of such application need be served, but the publication of such notice shall be sufficient service.   The commissioners shall proceed in all things in the making and return of the second report as though it were the first report.   The second report shall be final and conclusive, without further confirmation, subject, nevertheless, to the right of any of the parties interested, to appeal to the supreme court, as hereinafter provided.

Appeal may
be taken.   § 94. Any person interested therein may, within twenty days after the confirmation by the common council of the first report of the commissioners, or after filing the second report, appeal from the council to the supreme court.   The only grounds of appeal shall be a want of the conformity of the proceedings to the provisions of this act; the propriety or utility of the improvement, or the equity of the award for damages, or of the assessment, shall not be questioned on such appeal.   The appeal shall be made by producing to some judge of the supreme court, or the county judge of Oneida county, an affidavit showing the irregularity complained of, and a bond to the city in the penalty of two hundred and fifty dollars, executed by two free-holders of the city, conditioned for the payment, if an appeal should be allowed, of all costs that may be awarded by the court against the appellant, in ten days after the decision of the appeal, and by procuring the approval of the judge of the bond and his allowance of the appeal, to be endorsed by him on the bond and affidavit respectively, and filing the affidavit and allow-ance, and the bond and approval, with the county clerk, and serving a copy thereof on, and delivering the same

to, the mayor or clerk of the city. Such appeal shall operate as a stay of proceedings until the decision of the court. The common council shall return, under the city seal, copies of all the proceedings in the matter, and file the same with the county clerk within thirty days after service of the notice of appeal. The papers used on such appeal shall be the affidavit and allowance, and the bond and approval, and the return herein required, together with such other papers as the appellant shall serve on the mayor or clerk, ten days before the next term of the court at which such appeal shall be heard, and whatever papers the city may desire to use on the hearing of such appeal in answer thereto. No notice of the time and place of hearing shall be necessary. The court shall, at the first special term after such appeal, or at such other special term as may be agreed upon, or as the court shall direct, summarily hear and decide the appeal, and award costs to the successful party. If the appellant shall fail to bring such appeal to a hearing at such special term, the appeal shall be dismissed with costs, the decision of the court shall be final and conclusive, and judgment may be entered with costs upon such dismissal, or on the decision of the court, and execution issue thereon.

§ 95. Upon the confirmation of the first report of the commissioners or upon the filing of the second report, two copies of the assessment list annexed thereto, shall be made and signed by the mayor and clerk, one of which shall be filed in the city clerk's office, and the other delivered to the treasurer. *Two copies of report to be signed and filed in city clerk's office.*

§ 96. The assessment filed with the clerk and delivered to the treasurer, shall, in all courts and places, be evidence of the assessments therein specified; and all sums of money assessed therein, upon or in respect to any real estate, shall be liens thereon for two years from the time the assessment lists are filed with the clerk. *Evidence of the assessment.*

§ 97. Upon receiving the assessment lists, the treasurer shall cause to be published in the official newspapers, a notice similar to the one required upon receiving the tax lists, and the treasurer shall proceed thereon to collect the moneys upon the same in the same manner as upon a tax list, and at the expiration of the month during which he shall receive payments thereon, he shall deliver it to the collector of the ward in which the *Treasurer to proceed to collect the money.*

moneys, or the greater part thereof, on the said list are to be collected; and such collector shall proceed thereon to collect the money due thereon in the same manner that he is required to collect taxes upon the tax lists, and to make return in like manner ; and all the provisions of this act relative to the collection of city taxes, shall apply to such assessments.

Certain expenses to be borne by the city. § 98. In case it shall appear by the report mentioned in section eighty-four of this act, that any portion of the * of such improvement ought to be borne by the city, 'the same shall be a charge upon the city treasury, and shall be paid from the current revenue of the city.

Common council to grade and pave streets. § 99. The common council shall have power to cause any street, highway, lane or alley in said city, to be graded, leveled, paved or repaved, and to cause such crosswalks, sidewalks, drains and sewers to be made therein as it shall deem necessary, and the same to be repaired, amended or relaid as it shall deem necessary. Prior to the passage of any ordinance for such purpose, it shall cause a plan and accurate specification of the work proposed to be constructed to be prepared and filed with the city clerk. It shall then cause to be published in the official newspapers, the said specification, with a notice that on a certain day. at least eight days from the first publication thereof, the common council will act in relation to its construction, and **Proposals to be received.** in the meantime sealed proposals for constructing the work, with bonds for the faithful performance thereof, will be received by the mayor. Upon the day mentioned in the notice, the mayor shall, in the presence of the common council, open the sealed proposals for constructing the work. In case the whole expense of any improvement under this section, in the opinion of the common council, will not exceed the sum of thirty dollars, no specification or notice need be published, except the publication in the official proceedings of the action of the common council in relation thereto, at least eight days before final action shall be taken **To be accompanied with bond.** thereon. No proposal shall be considered, which shall not be accompanied by a bond with sureties, and in a penalty, both to be approved by the common council, conditioned that if the proposal be accepted, the person proposing will construct the work at the price and upon

*So in the original.

the terms proposed, according to the plans filed with the clerk and the specifications published, and subject to the supervision and approval of such person as the common council may designate for the purpose, and that such person will erect and maintain suitable guards and lights to prevent injuries to such work, or to persons or property, by or in consequence of the prudent and careful use of such street, highway, lane, alley, side or crosswalk, during the progress of such work, and will save the city harmless and indemnified against all loss, damage or expense that may arise by or through any neglect of such person or those in his employ, to erect or maintain such guards and lights, or either of them. The common council shall then determine whose is the most favorable proposal. It may then, by a vote of a majority of all its members, authorize and direct the construction of the proposed work, accept the most favorable proposal, and direct the expense thereof to be assessed in the manner hereinafter stated, unless at the next meeting of the common council, one or more of the persons liable to be assessed for said work, shall propose (and tender bonds therefor as aforesaid) to do the work at an expense at least fifteen per cent less than the proposal deemed the most favorable, in which case the work shall be let to the person or persons last proposing ; provided however, that all of said propositions are not deemed unreasonable.

To determine the expense of paving and grading streets to be assessed on property adjoining.

1st. In case the work shall be the grading, leveling or paving a street, lane or alley, whether with or without crosswalks, cellar drains or sewers, at one operation, or the grading, leveling or paving a street, lane or alley, the city surveyor shall ascertain the aggregate front length of lots upon both sides thereof, and the front length of each lot or parcel with a correct description thereof, and the name of the owner so far as it can be ascertained. The common council shall then determine the expense of the whole work, including the expenses of surveying, advertising and preparing the assessment lists, and cause the average expense upon each foot front of the lots or parcels of land on both sides of the said street, lane or alley, excluding cross streets from the computation, to be ascertained, and each lot or parcel of real estate to be assessed with its portion of the expense, by multiplying its number of feet front into the average expense per foot.

2nd. In case the work shall be the constructing of any crosswalk in a street, or any drain or sewer separate from any other work, if the expense thereof shall not exceed one hundred dollars, such expense together with surveyor's fees, expense of advertising, and two dollars for the expenses of such assessment, shall be assessed by the street commissioner and city surveyor, without notice, upon the real estate which they shall deem benefited thereby, as near as may be in proportion to the amount of its benefits. The fees of such officers for making such assessment shall be one dollar each. If the expense thereof shall exceed one hundred dollars, the common council shall appoint three disinterested freeholders of the city to assess the expense of its construction, including expenses of surveying, advertising, and fees of the freeholders, which shall in no case exceed the sum of one dollar and fifty cents each per day, upon such real estate as they shall deem benefited thereby, in proportion to the amount of its benefits. If the sewer or drain is the continuation or extension of one previously existing, the said officers or freeholders, in making their assessments, shall take into consideration such sums as have theretofore been assessed upon the real estate benefited, in order, so far as practicable, to render the assessment equal upon each lot or parcel, considering the whole drain or sewer, as continued or extended, a single work.

3rd. In case the work shall be the constructing a sidewalk, each lot or parcel of land fronting thereon, shall be assessed with the expense of its construction in front thereof, by the city surveyor and common council, in the manner provided in subdivision one of this section.

4th. In case the work shall be the repairing of any street, or the regrading of any paved street for the purpose of repairing, the expense thereof shall be paid out of the moneys mentioned in section forty-seven of this act.

May form
street into
plank road.   § 100. Upon a petition of the owners, or the authorized agents of the owners, of more than one-half of the land fronting upon any street or highway which shall not have been paved, that the same may be formed into a plank road, the common council shall have power to form it into a plank road as follows: A notice shall be published in the official newspapers for eight days, that

until a certain day, at least eight days after the first publication thereof, sealed proposals will be received by the mayor for constructing a plank road thereon, according to the specifications in the notice contained. Upon the day mentioned in the notice, the mayor shall, in the presence of the common council, open such sealed proposals. No proposal shall be considered which shall not be accompanied by a bond, such as is provided in section ninety-nine of this act. The common council may then, if the most favorable proposal is deemed a reasonable one, accept the same and direct the expense thereof to be assessed in the manner provided in subdivision one, section ninety-nine, unless at the next meeting of the common council, one or more of the persons liable to be assessed for work, shall propose (and tender bonds therefor as aforesaid) to do the work at an expense at least fifteen per cent less than the proposal deemed the most favorable, in which case the work shall be let to the person or persons last proposing; provided, however, that all of said propositions are not deemed unreasonable.

§ 101. The notice required by sections ninety-nine and one hundred may be first published at least eight days before the time therein specified for opening and acting upon the proposals to be received under it, and in case the common council do not meet on the day mentioned in such notice, the proposals received by the mayor pursuant thereto, shall be opened at the next subsequent meeting of the common council. After opening proposals received pursuant to notice published according to said sections, and determining whose is the most favorable, or that the most favorable one is deemed reasonable, the common council may postpone further action upon the construction of the proposed work, and the acceptance of the proposals, from time to time, not to exceed one month from the day specified in the notice for opening the proposals. Notice to be published eight days. May postpone further action.

§ 102. Whenever all the proposals received pursuant to such notice, are deemed by the common council to be unreasonable, they may make a contract for the work to be done according to the published specifications by such persons as they may think proper, at a specified price, which price shall not exceed the lowest sum proposed, and assess the expense thereof, including survey- May reject proposals.

ing and advertising, in the manner provided in said sections ninety-nine and one hundred.

Gaslight posts.

§ 103. The common council may order and direct the erection of gas light posts, in any of the streets in said city. The work shall be done in the manner provided in section ninety-nine, and the expense thereof assessed in the manner provided in subdivision number two of said section.

Ornamenting public squares.

§ 104. The common council shall have power to order the pitching, paving, graveling. raising, enclosing, ornamenting, and protecting any public square, area, or pleasure ground, now or hereafter laid out in the city, to improve the same by the construction of walks and rearing and protecting ornamental trees therein, and to cause such part of the expense thereof as it shall deem just, to be assessed upon and collected of the real estate benefited thereby, in the manner provided in the second sub-division of section ninety-nine of this act.

Plan of improvement need not be published in certain cases.

§ 105. No plan of any crosswalk, sidewalk, paving, plank road, or gas light posts, need be published under said sections ninety-nine and one hundred ; but where a plan of any work is required, it shall be sufficient publication thereof to file the same with the clerk, and refer thereto intelligibly in the published notice

Separate works may be constructed at the same time.

§ 106. Where practicable, several separate works may be noticed, ordered and constructed at the same time, and assessed by the same officers or freeholders, under subdivision number two of said section ninety-nine, and for the purposes of all expenses of advertising and assessment, be considered as one work   Where such expenses are paid in common by more than one work, each work shall be assessed with its just portion thereof.

Appeal to common council.

§ 107. Any person considering himself aggrieved by any assessment made pursuant to the provisions of section ninety-nine, may appeal therefrom to the common council ; such appeal shall be in writing, and shall be delivered to the clerk or presiding officer of the common council within twenty days after the filing of such assessment with the clerk. In case of appeal to the common council, the common council shall appoint a time within eight days after receiving such appeal for hearing those interested, and may adjourn said hearing as may be necessary ; they shall have power in their discretion to confirm said assessment, or to annul the same and direct a new assessment to be made by three other freeholders or officers, in the manner provided in said subdivision number two of section ninety-nine, which reassessment shall provide for the expenses of both assessments. and shall be final and conclusive. *

§ 108. The common council may direct the repair of any drain, sidewalk, or sewer, where it shall be necessary, and when, in its opinion, its repair cannot be judiciously let upon contract, and when the same shall be completed, cause the expense thereof to be assessed and collected in the same manner that the expense of constructing a drain, sidewalk, or sewer, is assessed and collected. *Repair drains, sidewalks and sewers without entering into contract.*

§ 109. Upon the assessment being made as provided in this title, an assessment list shall be made to resemble, as nearly as practicable, the tax list in its form, and be provided with a column in which payments can be entered by the treasurer. Two copies thereof shall be made by the clerk and signed by the mayor and clerk, one of which shall be filed with the clerk and the other delivered to the treasurer. All the provisions of this act relative to the tax lists mentioned in section fortyeight of this act, to the assessments therein, and to the collection and payment of the moneys thereon, shall be applicable to the assessment lists provided in this title. The clerk's fees for making such copies shall be one dollar each. *Assessment list to be made out.*

§ 110. All moneys received by the treasurer upon any assessment list made pursuant to the provisions of this act, shall be kept by him distinct from all other moneys, and shall be drawn from him only by orders expressly directing their application to the payment of the expenses for which the assessment was made. *Moneys received on, to be kept separate.*

§ 111. No moneys belonging to the city shall be paid out by the treasurer upon orders drawn against moneys to be raised upon an assessment list.

§ 112. In case the common council shall at any time ascertain that the expense of any public improvement cannot be defrayed by the moneys raised upon the assessment list provided therefor, it may cause the deficiency to be assessed upon the real estate described therein. in sums proportioned to the former assessment. All the provisions of this act relative to the assessment lists, heretofore mentioned, to the assessments therein, and the *May assess deficiency in any assessment.*

10

collection and payment of the moneys thereon, shall be applicable to the second assessment list in this section provided.

Length of notice for building sidewalk. § 113. In all cases where a sidewalk is directed to be constructed, not less than sixty day's time in case of a stone sidewalk, and thirty days in all other cases, shall be given to the owners of real estate fronting thereon, to construct the same under the direction of the street commissioner.

No real estate to be taken unless paid for or tender made. § 114. No real estate shall be taken or appropriated for the opening, widening, or altering any street, lane, or alley, in the city, without the leave of the owner, until the recompense reported by the commissioners to be proper therefor, be paid or tendered to the owner, or deposited to his or her use in one of the banks in the city, to be designated by the common council for that purpose. Upon such payment, tender, or deposit being made, the same may* appropriated for that purpose.

Case of infant owners. § 115. When any owner of such real estate shall be known to be an infant 'under the age of twenty-one years, any officer authorized by law to appoint guardians of infants, may, on the application of the infant or of the common council, appoint a guardian for such infant, taking from him adequate security for the faithful performance of his duties as such; and all notices required to be served upon the infant shall be served upon such guardian, who shall see to the protection of the rights of such infants.

TITLE 8.

OF THE POWERS OF THE COMMON COUNCIL FOR THE PREVENTION AND EXTINGUISHMENT OF FIRES.

Roofs. § 116. The common council shall have the power by ordinances to prescribe limits within which no building shall hereafter be constructed, except of brick or stone, with slate or metalic roofs, and to impose a penalty for the violation of such ordinances of one hundred dollars for each offence, and twenty-five dollars for each week's continuance of the prohibited building. Such penalties shall be collectable of the person offending, in a civil action in any court of competent jurisdiction.

Fire engines and fire companies. § 117. The common council shall procure fire engines and other necessary and convenient apparatus for the

*So in the original.

prevention and extinguishment of fires, and provide safe
and convenient places for keeping the same. It shall
have power to organize fire companies, and to appoint
a competent number of able bodied and reputable
inhabitants of the city firemen to belong to such companies, and prescribe their duties and make rules and
regulations for their government, and to impose reasonable penalties and forfeitures for a violation thereof.
Such companies shall have the care and management of
the apparatus for extinguishing fires, under the .rules
provided by the common council and the control of the
chief engineer and his assistants and the fire wardens.
The common council shall have power to remove firemen
in its discretion.

§ 118. The members of the common council shall be **Fire ward-ens.**
firewardens, and shall have power to appoint such other
persons fire wardens as may be necessary, and such
persons shall perform such duties as the common council
may prescribe.

§ 119. Firemen appointed by the common council **Exemptions of firemen.**
shall, during the term of their service, be exempt from
serving upon juries in courts of record, and in the militia,
except in case of war, invasion or insurrection. The
name of each fireman shall be registered with the clerk
of the city, and evidence to entitle him to the exemption
provided, shall be the certificate of the clerk made
within one year from the time when the exemption is
claimed. Such certificate shall not be granted until the
fireman shall make and file with the clerk an affidavit
that during the preceding year he has actually been
present and acted with the company to which he is
attached at two-thirds of the number of fires at which
the apparatus was present during the preceding year,
unless prevented by absence from the city, illness, or
other unavoidable circumstance.

§ 120. Every fireman who shall have faithfully served **Term of service.**
as such in the city of Utica, or in the former village of
Utica, or both, for the term of five years, shall thereafter
.be exempt from serving on juries in courts of record, or
in the militia, except in cases of war, invasion, or insurrection. The evidence to entitle such person to the
exemption provided in this section, shall be a certificate
under the corporate seal signed by the mayor and clerk.
No such certificate shall hereafter be given until the

applicant shall have made and filed with the clerk an affidavit that for five years preceding he has actually and habitually been present with his company at fires in the city, when not detained therefrom by absence from the city, illness, or other unavoidable circumstance.

TITLE 9.

OF THE AUDITING OF CLAIMS AGAINST THE CITY.

Accounts to be verified.   § 121. All claims and accounts against the city shall be audited by the common council upon days to be designated for the purpose, at least as often as once in three months. The common council, or any member thereof, may require any account against said city to be verified by the affidavit of the person presenting it, or to whom it is due, in the same manner that town accounts are required to be verified, and such verification may be made before any member of the common *Must be in writing.* council. All claims must be presented in writing. They shall be numbered and filed with the clerk, and a brief entry of the name of the claimant, number, nature and amount of the claim made by the clerk, in a book kept by him for the purpose, prepared with appropriate letters and columns, so that the entry shall serve as an alphabetical index to the claim. The book shall be provided with a column in which shall be entered, after the claim, the date when it is audited, and the amount, if any, allowed thereon. The claims shall be audited and the amounts allowed without unreasonable delay. In case the common council shall disallow any claim, or any part thereof, its decision shall be a bar to the claim disallowed or the part not allowed, unless an action shall be commenced against the city thereon within six months from the time the same was allowed.

Cannot be withdrawn from the file.   § 122 No claim against the city which has been presented to the common council to be audited, shall be withdrawn from the files. No claim or demand against the city which has not been audited, or which has not been liquidated by the common council, shall bear interest.

No costs be recorded against the city in certain cases.   § 123. No costs shall be recovered against the city in any action brought against it for any unliquidated claim which has not been presented to the common council to be audited; nor shall costs be recovered against the city in any action upon any unliquidated claim which shall have been allowed in part by the common council, unless the recovery be for a greater sum than the amount allowed by the common council, with the interest thereon from the time it was allowed.

TITLE 10.

OF COMMON SCHOOLS.

§ 124. The act entitled "An act in relation to common schools in the city of Utica," passed April seventh, eighteen hundred and forty-two, and the several acts amending the same, shall continue in force, excepting where their provisions are herein expressly amended, anything herein contained to the contrary notwithstanding.

TITLE 11.

OF THE BOARD OF TOWN AUDITORS.

§ 125. The city shall be regarded as one of the towns of Oneida county under the provisions of article fifth, chapter eleven of part one of the Revised Statutes, and the supervisors and clerk thereof shall constitute its board of town auditors for the purpose of auditing and allowing town charges and claims.

§ 126. The said board of town auditors shall meet on the Tuesday succeeding their election for the purpose of organization. The city clerk shall be the clerk of said board. The said board shall then elect from their own number a chairman and a treasurer. Said treasurer shall receive all moneys raised by said board of town auditors, under the provisions of any law, or for any purpose, and pay out the same according to law, keeping an accurate account of his receipts and expenditures, so as to exhibit the amount paid under each particular class of purposes for which money shall be raised. He shall, at the last meeting of said board, before the annual city election, present to the board of town auditors and file with the clerk an account of all his receipts and disbursements, since the date of the last report. He shall, within ten days after his appointment, and before assuming his duties as such treasurer, file with the clerk a bond to the town of Utica, in such penalty and with

Time of meeting and organization.

such sureties as the board of town auditors may direct,
the sureties to be approved by said board, conditioned
that he shall faithfully perform the duties of treasurer,
and account for and pay over all moneys to be received
by him by virtue of such office. The board shall meet
at the call of the chairman or clerk, on written notice
served on each member, for the purpose of approving
such bond. In case such treasurer shall not furnish a
satisfactory bond within the time required by this
section, the office shall be deemed vacant, and the board
shall meet again as soon as practicable, on like call and
notice as heretofore provided, and appoint another
member its treasurer, under the same provisions and
conditions. The treasurer shall receive for his services
the compensation now provided by law to be received
by supervisors for similar services.

Business of.

§ 127. The said board of town auditors shall meet for
the purpose of auditing and allowing town charges and
claims, on the day succeeding the annual general election.
No account shall be audited by said board unless the
same is presented or filed with the clerk within three
days after their first meeting under the provisions of this
section The clerk shall publish reasonable notice of
such meeting, and of the time within which claims must
be presented.

TITLE 12.

MISCELLANEOUS PROVISIONS.

Who may administer oaths.

§ 128. The mayor or the chairman of any committee
or special committee of the common council, shall have
power to administer any oath, or take any affidavit in
respect to any matter pending before the common
council or such committee.

False swearing.

§ 129. Any person who may be required to take any
oath or affirmation, or to take any affidavit or statement
under oath or affirmation, under or by virtue of any
provision of this act, who shall, under such oath or
affirmation, in any such statement or affidavit, or otherwise, wilfully swear falsely as to any material fact or
matter, shall be guilty of perjury.

Interested parties.

§ 130. No person shall be an incompetent judge,
justice, juror, or witness in any action in which the city
is a party, or is interested, by reason of his being an
inhabitant or owner of real or personal estate therein.

§ 131. Every person now or hereafter elected or appointed under this act to any office, who shall be sued for any act done or omitted to be done, under such election or appointment, and any person who shall be sued for having done any act or thing by the command of any such officer, if any final judgment shall be rendered in his behalf, or by which he shall be entitled to costs, such officer or person shall be entitled to double costs, under the provisions of the Revised Statutes. *Double costs in certain cases.*

§ 132. Whenever the common council shall, by reason of the absence of a quorum, or from any other cause, fail to meet, it shall be lawful for the common council to transact any business under any notice required to be published by this act, or in any proceedings or matter whatever, at its next regular meeting, with the same force and effect as if such business had been transacted at the time fixed therefor. *Want of quorum.*

§ 133. The common council may from time to time require the city surveyor to prepare and furnish to any of the assessors brief but certain descriptions of any real estate, to enable him to prepare the assessment roll of his ward or require the city surveyor to prepare a roll for such assessor containing the description of the real estate in the ward, with blanks for valuation and for the names of persons owning personal estate, and such other blanks as are required in assessment rolls, and the descriptions or rolls thus prepared shall be followed by the assessors in making their rolls. The services of the city surveyor, under this section, shall be audited and paid in the same manner as the assessors are paid, and he shall be allowed a reasonable compensation for his services. *Certain services of city surveyor.*

§ 134. After the assessors of the city shall have completed their assessment in the manner provided by law, and made a separate roll for each ward of the city, they shall file the same with the clerk of the city, who shall correct any clerical errors therein, and make exact copies of each of them, which copies he shall certify to be correct, and deliver the same to one of the supervisors of the city on or before the first day of November, to be by him presented to the board of supervisors as the assessment rolls for the several wards of the city. *Assessment when complete to be filed with city clerk.*

§ 135. The several wards of the city shall be considered towns for the purposes of the provisions of the *In regard to juries.*

Revised Statutes entitled " Of the return and summoning of juries," in respect to the return of jurors ; and the
supervisor and assessor elected in the respective wards
shall execute the duties therein enjoined upon the
supervisor, assessors and town clerks of the several towns
in the state, except that a duplicate of the returns of
jurors made by them shall be filed in the office of the
clerk of the city.

Annual town and county tax. § 136. The city of Utica shall be regarded as one of
the towns of Oneida county, for the purpose of raising
and collecting the annual town, county and state taxes,
and the same provisions of law which shall apply to the
assessment and collection of taxes in the towns of the
state, and the duty of all officers concerned therein or
connected therewith, excepting as the same are modified
and altered by this act, shall be applicable thereto ; but
in assessing and laying the town, county and state taxes
therein, the same shall be assessed and laid upon the
assessment rolls, prepared as herein provided for each
of the wards of the city, which shall be delivered to the
collectors of the respective wards for collection, in the
manner provided by law.

§ 137 The city of Utica for all purposes except those
provided for in this act shall be regarded as one of the
towns of Oneida county.

Supply of water. § 138. The sum heretofore fixed as the annual sum to
be paid to the Utica water works company for a supply
of water for the purpose of extinguishing fires shall be
added in each year to the tax authorized to be raised by
the forty-seventh section of this act, and shall be collected therewith, and by the same power and authority,
and the sixtieth section of the act to incorporate the
Utica water works company, passed March thirty-first,
one thousand eight hundred and forty-eight, so far as it
conflicts with the provisions of this section, is hereby
repealed.

Map of streets le-galized. § 139. The streets of the city of Utica, as laid down on
Lorenzo M. Taylor's map of eighteen hundred and fifty,
which map is lithographed, shall be and are hereby declared to be legally opened streets, subject to such control of the common council of said city, as is provided in
the act hereby amended, excepting Bright street, those
parts of Catherine, Jay, Elizabeth, Mary, Blandina, Lansing and Rutger streets, that lie between Third and

Mohawk streets; and changing the name Ann street to Eagle street, and that part of Broadway street lying between its intersection with Court street and Genesee street to Court street; and excepting such other changes in regard to the streets of the city as have been made by the common council since the twenty-ninth of June, eighteen hundred and fifty-three.

§ 140. The fiscal year under the provisions of this act Fiscal year. shall commence on Thursday of the second week before the annual city election. The civil year shall commence on the second Tuesday in March in each year.

§ 141. All acts or parts of acts inconsistent with or repugnant to the provisions of this act are hereby repealed. But this repeal, or anything contained in this act, shall not be construed to take away, impair or affect any right or remedy acquired or given by the acts hereby repealed; and all existing suits or proceedings may be continued and completed, and all offences committed, or penalties or forfeitures incurred, and all the existing ordinances of said city, shall continue and remain in force, with the same effect as though this act had not been passed.

§ 142. The legislature may at any time alter, amend, or repeal this act.

§ 143. This act shall take effect immediately.

Chap. 19.

AN ACT to enable the town of Galen to raise money to complete and furnish the town house and lock-up erected in the village of Clyde in said town.

Passed March 1, 1862; three-fifths being present.

The People of the State of New York, represented in Senate and Assembly, do enact as follows:

SECTION 1. The inhabitants of the town of Galen, in To vote a the county of Wayne, in this state, entitled to vote for tax at the annual town town officers, may, at their next annual town meeting, meeting. vote to raise by tax a sum of money sufficient, in addi-

11

tion to the sum already voted and raised, to pay for completing and furnishing the town house and lock-up, erected in the village of Clyde, in said town.

§ 2. If a majority of such electors present and voting thereon shall vote in favor of raising such additional sum, the board of supervisors shall at their next annual session require the sum so voted to be collected with the other expenses of said town.

§ 3. The village of Clyde, in said town, may convey to said town of Galen an equal undivided half of the lot of ground on which said town house and lock-up is now erected, and hereafter the said building and lot shall be owned and occupied by said corporations in common, and shall be under the joint superintendence of the board of trustees of said village, and the supervisor of said town, and their successors in office.

§ 4. This act shall take effect immediately.

Chap. 20.

AN ACT to authorize the commissioners of highways of the town of Fishkill, in the county of Dutchess, and the towns of Rosendale and Malboro,* in the county of Ulster, to appoint overseers of highways in said towns.

Passed March 1, 1862 ; three-fifths being present.

The People of the State of New York, represented in Senate and Assembly, do enact as follows :

SECTION 1. Instead of the mode now authorized by law of electing overseers of highways in the town of Fishkill, in the county of Dutchess, and the towns of Rosendale and Marlboro, in the county of Ulster, the commissioners of highways or a majority of them shall, within fifteen days succeeding each annual town meeting, appoint some suitable person in each road district in said town as overseer of highways in said district

§ 2. The persons so appointed shall be overseers of highways for the ensuing year, and shall have all the

* So in the original.

powers and be subject to the same responsibilities as such officers now are by law.

§ 3. The commissioners, or a majority of them, shall have power at any time to fill any vacancies that may occur by death or otherwise, in the office of overseer of highways in any district in said towns.

§ 4. This act shall take effect immediately, and all acts and parts of acts contrary thereto are hereby repealed.

Chap. 21.

AN ACT providing for the distribution of Soldiers' Allotments.

Passed March 6, 1862; three-fifths being present.

The People of the State of New York, represented in Senate and Assembly, do enact as follows :

SECTION 1. It shall be the duty of the treasurer of this state to receive from the paymaster general of the United States army, or from the secretary of the treasury of the United States, such sum or sums as may have been or may hereafter be assigned by volunteers in the service of the United States for the benefit of their families or others, in conformity with orders of the war department and to give the necessary receipts therefor.

§ 2. The treasurer of this state, as often as once in every three months shall cause to be made a list of all persons to whom moneys are assigned, classified by counties, and shall mail to the county treasurer of each county the list of assignees residing in such county.

§ 3. It shall be the duty of the county treasurer immediately, on receiving the list from the treasurer of the state to give notice thereof to the assignees and to ascertain if it be their desire to receive the moneys assigned to them, through the county treasurers. In all cases where such is their desire, it shall be the duty of the county treasurers to procure a written request to that effect, which shall accompany their drafts upon the treasurer of the state, and no moneys shall be drawn

Moneys to be drawn on draft and written request of assignee.

from the treasurer of the state unless it be upon such draft and upon the written request of the said assignee, the identity of whom shall be duly certified by the supervisor or a justice of the peace of the town or ward where the assignee resides, but the request when once made shall remain in force until finally revoked in writing.

County treasurer to keep record.

§ 4. County treasurers shall enter the names, rank, pay per month, amount to be reserved, name and address of assignees on a list prepared for that purpose, which shall be preserved as a permanent record of his office and shall require the signature of the assignee or his or her order in writing, in receipting from time to time for the amount assigned.

Comptroller to draw his warrant on treasurer.

§ 5. The comptroller shall draw his warrant upon the treasurer in favor of county treasurers upon their complying with the provisions of this act. All moneys uncalled for and remaining in the hands of county treasurers for the period of one year, shall be repaid by them to the treasurer of the state. The aggregate of the sums hereby authorized to be paid over to county treasurers, is hereby appropriated payable as aforesaid and for the purposes named. No fee or charge shall be made or received by any officer under this act.

§ 6. This act shall take effect immediately.

Chap. 22.

AN ACT to amend an act entitled "An act to reorganize and regulate the common schools and the board of education in the city of Brooklyn," passed April fourth, eighteen hundred and fifty.

Passed March 7, 1862; three-fifths being present.

The People of the State of New York, represented in Senate and Assembly, do enact as follows :

SECTION 1. The act entitled "An act to reorganize and regulate the common schools and the board of education in the city of Brooklyn," passed April fourth, eighteen hundred and fifty, is hereby amended as follows: On or after the first Monday of February, in the year one thousand eight hundred and sixty-two, and in each year thereafter, the mayor of the city of Brooklyn shall nominate and with the approval of a majority of all the members elected to the common council thereof, appoint competent and suitable persons residents of said city, to fill the vacancies in said board of education occasioned by the expiration of the term of office of members of said board. *Common council on nomination of mayor to fill vacancies in board of education.*

The term of office of such persons shall be three years; and in making such appointments care shall be taken to preserve the representation in said board of at least one member from each school district, as now or may be hereafter determined. The persons so appointed shall hold office until their successors shall be appointed. *Term of office to be three years.*

§ 2. In case the said mayor shall not so nominate, or the said common council shall not on or before the first day of March in each year, approve such nominations, or any of them, or such others as the said mayor may make, then the members of said board of education whose term of office shall then have expired, and whose successors shall not have been appointed, as aforesaid, shall continue to hold their said offices until the first Monday of February then next ensuing, and until their successors are appointed. *If not appointed before the first day of March, to hold over until February next ensuing.*

§ 3. Hereafter all vacancies in said board, occasioned otherwise than by expiration of the term of office, shall be filled on the nomination of the mayor with the approval of the common council, as aforesaid. *All vacancies hereafter to be filled by mayor and common council,*

§ 4. All acts and parts of acts inconsistent with this act are hereby repealed.

§ 5. This act shall take effect immediately.

Chap. 23.

AN ACT to amend an act entitled "An Act to incorporate the White Plains Fire Department,"
passed April tenth eighteen hundred and fifty-
seven.

Passed March 7, 1862; three-fifths being present.

*The People of the State of New York, represented in
Senate and Assembly, do enact as follows:*

SECTION 1. Section one of an An act entitled "An act to
incorporate the White Plains fire department," passed
April tenth eighteen hundred and fifty-seven, is hereby
amended so as to read as follows: All that portion of the
towns of White Plains and Greenburgh, in the county of
Westchester, which is embraced in the following limits,
to wit: Commencing at the centre of the Bridge over
the Bronx river on the road leading from the old Methodist meeting house in White Plains, to Greenburgh;
running thence southerly by and along said Bronx river
till it comes to the junction of a small brook with said
Bronx river, a little to the northward of the residence
of William Roberts, in said town of Greenburgh; thence
running northwesterly, westerly and northerly, by and
along said brook, with its various windings and turnings,
until it comes to the northerly side of the highway which
runs westerly from the westerly side of Tarrytown road
to Hart's corners; thence westerly by and along the
northerly side of said road, which leads to Hart's corners,
until it comes to a bend in said last mentioned road,
opposite the southeasterly corner of the residence of
Daniel Burtnett; thence running southerly by and along
the westerly side of said road which leads to Hart's
corners, until it comes to the southerly side of the road
which leads from White Plains over Chatterton's hill,
where it joins the said road which leads to Hart's corners,
nearly opposite the residence of John Hart; thence running in a straight line southeasterly to the town line
dividing the town of White Plains from the town of
Scarsdale; thence southeasterly by said town line to the
highway leading to New York; thence northeasterly in

Bounds of
department.

a straight line to the southeasterly side of the lane of
Robert Buckhout ; thence northeasterly in a straight line
to a point opposite to the centre of the road leading from
North street to the house of Nathaniel Hyatt ; thence
northeasterly by and along the centre of said road to the
west branch of the Mamaroneck river ; thence northwesterly by and along the west branch of Mamaroneck
river to the gate or waste way at the foot of St. Mary's
Lake ; thence westerly in a straight line to the bridge
over the brook crossing the highway between the house
of John Fisher and the house of Ann Fisher ; thence
westerly by and along the centre of said highway to the
centre of the highway leading from North Castle to
White Plains ; thence northerly by and along the centre
of said highway to a point opposite to the centre of a
road hereinbefore mentioned ; thence westerly and by
and with the centre of said road to the place of beginning
is hereby declared to be the corporate limits of the
White Plains fire district."

§ 2. Section eight of said act is hereby amended so as
to read as follows :

" § 8 The trustees shall, as often as any sum or sums
of money shall be voted for any of the purposes aforesaid,
and within ten days thereafter, make out a tax list and
assessment roll, to be based upon the last assessment
rolls of the towns of White Plains and Greenburgh, as
far as the same shall apply to property embraced within
said fire district, and also make out a warrant for the
collection of said tax so voted as aforesaid, returnable at
the expiration of thirty days from the delivery of the
same to the collector, and to deliver the same to the
collector of the said town of White Plains, within fifteen
days from the time of such vote, and it shall be the duty
of any public officers of said towns of White Plains and
Greenburgh in whose possession the assessment rolls of
said towns may be, to permit the said trustees upon
demand to take and use the said assessment rolls of the
said towns for the purpose of preparing the assessment
roll and tax list in this section directed to be prepared
by them ; and it shall be the duty of the collector of the
said town of White Plains to collect said tax from the
taxable inhabitants of said fire district, in the same manner as the taxes in said town of White Plains are now
by law authorized to be collected by him. and said col-

Compensa-
tion of col-
lector.

lector may receive and collect, in addition to the sum authorized to be collected by him as aforesaid, the sum of five cents on each dollar so.collected by him under the warrant of said trustees, as and for his fees. The acts herein directed to be performed by the trustees of said fire district may be performed by a majority of said trustees."

§ 3. This act shall take effect immediately.

Chap. 24.

AN ACT to appropriate the proceeds of the State tax for the support of Common Schools.

Passed March 7, 1862 ; three-fifths being present.

The People of the State of New York, represented in Senate and Assembly, do enact as follows :

Appropri-
ated $1,081,-
325.57 for
support of
common
schools.

SECTION 1. The sum of one million and eighty-one thousand three hundred and twenty-five dollars and fifty-seven cents, being the amount of the tax of three-fourths of a mill on each dollar of the aggregate assessed valuation of the real and personal property of this state, for the support of common schools, is hereby appropriated for the support of common schools during the current fiscal year, to be apportioned and distributed according to law.

§ 2. This act shall take effect immediately.

Chap. 25.

AN ACT to provide for the more speedy payment of the volunteers from this state, mustered into the service of the United States, and within this state, on the first day of March, eighteen hundred and sixty-two.

Passed March 8, 1862; three-fifths being present.

The People of the State of New York, represented in Senate, and Assembly do enact as follows:

SECTION 1. The comptroller of this state is hereby authorized, upon the credit of the state. to borrow such sum or sums of money, not to exceed the sum of three hundred and fifty thousand dollars, as may be necessary for the purposes of this act. Comptroller to borrow $350,000.

§ 2 From the sum or sums so borrowed, or from any money in the treasury of the state not otherwise appropriated, he shall from time to time, pay to the paymaster general of the United States, on his requisition, to be approved by the governor of this state, so much money as shall be necessary to pay and discharge all arrears of monthly pay, due and payable according to the rules and regulations of the United States military service on the first day of January, eighteen hundred and sixty-two, to any officer or private of the volunteers of this state, who shall have been mustered into the military service of the United States, and shall have been within this state on the first day of March, eighteen hundred and sixty-two. To pay all volunteers in the state on March 1st, 1862.

§ 3. But no money shall be borrowed or paid out by virtue of the provisions of this act unless the comptroller shall first receive from the secretary of the treasury of the United States, satisfactory assurances to the effect that the moneys advanced under the provisions of this act shall be applied as herein contemplated, and that such moneys shall be repaid to this state in not more than ninety days from the date of the advance thereof, or shall be credited to this state on account of the direct tax which it has assumed pursuant to the act of Congress of August fifth, eighteen hundred and sixty-one. Consent of the treasurer of the U. S. to be obtained to foregoing provisions.

§ 4. This act shall take effect immediately.

12

Chap. 26.

AN ACT to extend the time for the collection of taxes in the town of New Scotland.

Passed March 8, 1862; three-fifths being present.

The People of the State of New York, represented in Senate and Assembly, do enact as follows:

Collector to pay over moneys collected and renew securities.

SECTION 1. If the collector of the town of New Scotland, in the county of Albany, shall, within the time now appointed by law, pay over all moneys by him collected, and shall renew his securities to the satisfaction of the supervisor of said town of New Scotland, the time for the collecting and making the final returns of the taxes in said town shall extend to the first day of April next.

§ 2. This act shall take effect immediately.

Chap. 27.

AN ACT to amend the charter of the Republic Fire Insurance Company.

Passed March 8, 1862.

The People of the State of New York, represented in Senate and Assembly, do enact as follows:

SECTION 1. Section thirteen of the charter of the Republic Fire Insurance Company is hereby amended to

Surplus to be applied to redemption of certificates.

read as follows: Whenever the accumulation of the net profits, together with the capital stock, shall exceed five hundred thousand dollars, the board of trustees may apply the excess, after the payment of dividends and interest, as herein above provided, annually thereafter, towards the redemption, in whole or in part of the certificates, commencing with those of the oldest date, and whenever funds shall be provided to redeem certificates, no interest shall be paid to holders of the same, after notice shall have been given to them that funds are provided for the redemption thereof; such notice shall be given by publishing the same daily for ten days, in two newspapers printed in the city of New York.

§ 2. This act shall take effect immediately.

Chap. 28.

AN ACT to release the Interest of the People of the State of New York in certain land, to William Bircury.

Passed March 8, 1862; by a two-thirds vote.

The People of the State of New York, represented in Senate and Assembly, do enact as follows :

SECTION 1. The interest of the people of the state of New York in that piece of land situate in the town of New Windsor, in the county of Orange and State of New York, which is described as follows : bounded eastwardly by Water street, northwardly by Clinton street, westwardly by Front street, and southwardly by the half lot once belonging to Daniel Gautly as will appear by reference to a map made by Charles Clinton, deceased, is hereby released to William Bircury, subject however to the payment of a mortgage thereon, made by Henry Moore the younger, to Patrick Mullin, which mortgage the said William Bircury assumes to pay. But no right of action shall accrue hereby to the said William Bircury, against any person for any money paid by him as purchase money for the said land.

§ 2. This act shall take effect immediately.

Chap. 29.

AN ACT to amend An Act entitled "An Act to provide for the more speedy payment of the volunteers from this State mustered into the service of the United States and within this State on the first day of March eighteen hundred and sixty-two," passed March eighth eighteen hundred and sixty-two.

Passed March 12, 1862; three-fifths being present.

The People of the State of New York, represented in Senate and Assembly do enact as follows:

SECTION 1. The third section of the act entitled "An act to provide for the more speedy payment of the volunteers from this state mustered into the service of the United States and within this state on the first day of March eighteen hundred and sixty-two," passed March eighth eighteen hundred and sixty-two, is hereby amended by adding at the end of the said third section the following words, viz:

To pay volunteers in certain cases without requisition of paymaster-general.

"In case the assurances from secretary of the treasury and the requisition from the paymaster general contemplated by this section shall not be received before any of the regiments of the said volunteers now in this state shall be required to move forward the comptroller shall be authorized to draw his warrant immediately in favor of any paymaster in the service of the United States for an amount sufficient to pay such regiments as contemplated by this act."

§ 2. This act shall take effect immediately.

Chap. 30.

AN ACT to extend the time for the collection of taxes in the town of Queensbury, in the county of Warren.

Passed March 14, 1862 ; three-fifths being present.

The People of the State of New York, represented in Senate and Assembly, do enact as follows :

SECTION 1. The time for the collection of the taxes now raised and uncollected in the town of Queensbury, in the county of Warren, may be extended to a period not later than the first Monday of April next, in the manner and according to, and on complying with the terms and provisions of the act entitled "An act authorizing the extension of the time for the collection of taxes in the several towns and cities of this state," passed January thirty-first, eighteen hundred and fifty-seven.

§ 2. This act shall take effect immediately.

Chap. 31.

AN ACT to legalize the levy and collection of a tax in the county of Tioga to defray the expenses of enrolling, organizing, mustering and subsisting volunteers for the military service in the United States, and for aid to their families.

Passed March 15, 1862 ; three-fifths being present.

The People of the State of New York, represented in Senate and Assembly, do enact as follows :

SECTION 1. The levy by tax upon the taxable property of the county of Tioga, of the sum of six thousand five hundred dollars contained in the general tax levy, by the supervisors of the county of Tioga, at their last annual meeting, for the purpose of defraying the expenses during the spring, summer and fall of eighteen hundred and sixty-one, of enrolling, organizing and subsisting

To legalize the tax laid by supervisors for organizing, &c., volunteers.

volunteers in the county of Tioga, preparatory to their
being mustered into the service of the United States, and
for aid to the families of such volunteers and the collection thereof, are hereby legalized and declared to be
valid in law.

§ 2. This act shall take effect immediately.

Chap. 32.

AN ACT to legalize and confirm an appropriation
of ten thousand dollars made by the common
council of the city of Syracuse.

Passed March 15, 1862 ; three-fifths being present.

*The People of the State of New York, represented in
Senate and Assembly, do enact as follows :*

SECTION 1. The appropriation made by the common
council of the city of Syracuse, of the sum of ten thousand
dollars, for the support of the families of volunteers, by
resolution passed April twenty-third, eighteen hundred
and sixty-one, is hereby legalized and confirmed.

§ 2. This act shall take effect immediately.

Chap. 33.

AN ACT to amend the several acts incorporating
the village of Fulton, in the county of Oswego.

Passed March 17, 1862; three-fifths being present.

*The People of the State of New York, represented in
Senate and Assembly, do enact as follows :*

SECTION 1 The act to incorporate the village of Fulton, in the county of Oswego, passed April twenty-ninth,
eighteen hundred and thirty-five, and the acts amendatory thereof, passed April thirteenth, eighteen hundred
and thirty-seven, and July first, eighteen hundred and
fifty-one, are hereby revised and amended so as to read
as follows :   •

§ 2. That part of the town of Volney, in the county of Oswego, contained within the boundaries hereinafter described, shall be a village by the name of Fulton, and the citizens of the state, from time to time inhabitants within said boundaries, shall be a corporation by the name of " The village of Fulton;" and in addition to the powers hereinafter specially granted, shall possess all the general powers, and be subject to the restrictions, contained in the third title of the eighteenth chapter of the first part of the Revised Statutes, except the fifth and sixth subdivisions of the first section, and the fifth, ninth and tenth sections of the same title, which are hereby declared inapplicable to the corporation hereby created; and the said corporation shall also possess the powers conferred on similar corporations by the second section of an act entitled " An act authorizing certain trusts," passed May fourteenth, eighteen hundred and forty.

§ 3. The territory within the following boundaries Boundaries. shall constitute the village of Fulton, to wit: Commencing at the northwest corner of G. Newkirk's location, thence easterly along the northerly line of said location to the northeast corner thereof; thence southerly along the easterly line of said location, until said line intersects the stream of water known as the Burdick creek; thence up the said creek, along the centre thereof, until the same intersects the highway known as the Fay road; thence westerly along the centre of said road to the easterly bounds of said village, as fixed by an act of the legislature, entitled " An act to amend an act entitled 'An act to incorporate the village of Fulton, passed April twenty-ninth, eighteen hundred and thirty-five,' passed April thirteenth, eighteen hundred and thirty-seven;" thence southerly and westerly along the last mentioned bounds to the centre of the Oswego river; thence down the said river, along the centre thereof, to the place of beginning.

§ 4. The officers of the village shall consist of: A pre- Officers. sident, six trustees, a police justice, three assessors, a collector, a clerk, a treasurer, a street commissioner, one or more policemen, a jailor, and such subordinate officers as are authorized by this act, or by general laws.

§ 5. The clerk, street commissioner, policemen and Certain officers to be jailor shall be appointed by the trustees, and hold their

appointed by trustees. offices during their pleasure. All other officers, hereinbefore enumerated, shall be elected at elections to be held as hereinafter prescribed; and, except the police justice and assessors, shall hold their office for one year, and until others are elected and qualified. The assessors shall hold their office for three years, one to be elected in each year; and the police justice shall hold his office for four years.

Annual meeting. § 6. The annual meeting for the election of officers, and the transaction of other business, shall be held in said village on the last Tuesday in March of each year; and, at each annual election, the place for holding the next election must be determined by the electors; or, if they fail to do so, the trustees, by resolution, must designate the place. If the trustees omit to designate the place, the election must be held at the same place where the last annual election was held. A notice of the annual meeting and election shall be published in all the newspapers of the village, for at least two weeks before the election.

Qualification of voters. § 7. Every resident of said village, qualified to vote for a member of assembly, and who shall have been a resident of said village for thirty days next preceding any village meeting, may vote at such village meeting; but no person shall vote upon a proposition to raise money by taxation, unless he shall have resided in said village for six months next preceding the time he offers to vote, and shall be a bona fide tax-payer in said village, and have been assessed on the last assessment roll of the village, for property therein.

Annual reports to be made to town meeting. § 8. At the annual meeting before the polls are opened for the election of officers, the reports hereinafter required to be made, must be presented and read to the meeting. The president of the village, or in his absence, a president for the time being, to be chosen by the trustees, must preside. The election of officers must be by ballot, with all the names voted for on one ballot, designating the office of each. Poll lists must be kept by the clerk of the village and some other person designated by the president. The president and trustees shall constitute the inspectors of such election; if either be absent the trustees may appoint a person in his place. The vote upon any proposition shall be taken by ballot, if before such voting commences, at least one-third of all persons present qualified to vote on such proposition requires it. The polls of the election shall be opened at nine o'clock in the forenoon, and continue open until four o'clock in the afternoon. The qualifications of voters on any question of raising money by tax shall be determined by the inspectors, who may have recourse to the last assessment roll of the village for that purpose, and may also examine on oath, to be administered by one of them, any person offering to vote, in respect to his qualifications. The inspectors shall publicly canvass the votes before adjournment, and shall certify the same upon the records of the village, together with any resolution adopted by the meeting.

§ 9. The several officers elected must each, before entering upon the duties of his office, take the oath of office prescribed by the constitution. The president and trustees shall render service without compensation. The assessors shall be paid such compensation as the trustees may prescribe, not to exceed the per diem allowance paid to town assessors for similar services. The compensation of the treasurer, street commissioner and clerk shall be determined by the trustees, and paid out of the general fund. The omission of any officer to take the oath of office, or when security is required, to give the security, and file such oath or security with the clerk, within eight days after an election or appointment, shall be deemed a refusal to take the office. *Oath of office.*

§ 10. A vacancy in any office may be filled by the trustees, by the appointment of a person to the office, if the office be elective, to hold until the next annual meeting; if it be any other office, to hold during the pleasure of the trustees. *Vacancies filled by trustees.*

FINANCIAL REGULATIONS AND RESTRICTIONS.

§ 11. The annual meeting in addition to the election of officers, may pass such resolutions as it may deem proper, instructing the trustees in the discharge of their duties; and they shall be bound by such instruction, so far as they are within the powers by this act conferred on such meeting, or on the trustees. The meeting shall also determine the sum to be raised by general tax upon the taxable property in the village, for the ordinary expenses of the village. The failure of such meeting to deter- *Annual meeting may instruct trustees.*

13

mine the sum, shall be deemed the adoption of the sum which was so raised for that purpose the last preceding year.

§ 12 The following items, only, are included in the ordinary expenses of the village :

1. The compensation of those officers of the village to whom compensation is expressly allowed by law.

2. For publishing the charter and by-laws of the village; the proceedings of the trustees; notices of annual and special meetings, and all other notices and papers required or authorized by this act to be published.

3. For defraying the expenses of necessary surveys and maps of the village, and of the streets, public squares, and cemeteries.

4. For procuring the necessary blank books and blank forms, papers, book-cases, for the use of the clerk and other village officers, and for rent of a room and furniture, fuel and lights for the meetings of the trustees, and for the annual and special meetings of the electors

5. For prosecuting and defending actions in which the village is a party, or bound to indemnify a party, and for other services requiring legal skill.

6. For constructing and repairing crosswalks, and for paying any damages lawfully ascertained or assessed, upon laying out, opening, altering or discontinuing any street in said village.

7. For the necessary advances for making sidewalks, removing snow and ice therefrom; abating nuisances, and for doing any other act they are authorized to do, after such proceedings have been had, as to make such expenses a lien upon real property upon failure of the owners to comply with the directions of the trustees in relation thereto.

8. For maintaining and keeping in repair and serviceable condition fire engines, hooks and ladders, and other necessary apparatus for extinguishing fires The number of fire engines not to exceed one for the first two thousand inhabitants, and one additional engine for every one thousand additional inhabitants.

9. For maintaining and keeping in repair and in good order for use, an engine house for each engine and its apparatus, or for hiring suitable places for those purposes.

10. For keeping in repair the public force-pumps and

reservoirs which now are, or hereafter may be constructed, and the water pipes and fixtures connected therewith.

11. For making and maintaining sidewalks and fences about and in front of the public grounds of said village, set apart and dedicated to public use and for planting and securing trees in and about such grounds, and for paying taxes and assessments lawfully assessed on such public grounds, or any property of the village.

12. For precautionary measures for guarding the public health in times of pestilence, and to guard against the small pox, or other infectious or pestilential diseases when they appear in the village, by providing suitable places for the temporary removal of such persons from populous parts of the village, and defraying the expenses incident to such removal.

13. To maintain light in such of the streets of the village as they may deem proper. *Also by tax for special purposes.*

14. For the necessary expenses of doing any act expressly required or authorized by law.

§ 13 Such meeting may, by resolution, also direct the trustees to cause to be raised, by a general tax upon the taxable property of the village, a specific sum of money for special purposes, in addition to the ordinary expenses of the village, in the cases and manner, and under the restrictions, hereinafter prescribed; it must be for one or more of the following objects:

1. To purchase fire engines to supply the place of those worn out or unfit for use, or for a new fire company, as prescribed in subdivision eight of last section.

2. To purchase a site and build a suitable fire engine house thereon, when necessary for an additional engine.

3. For the construction of public force-pumps and reservoirs, procuring grounds for the same, for supplying the same with water, and the necessary fixtures therefor, for extinguishing fires.

4. For improving the public grounds in the village, and enclosing the reservoirs thereon by iron fences.

5. For purchasing a site, and erecting thereon a suitable building for village purposes.

6. For procuring and erecting necessary fixtures for lighting the streets of the village.

7. For paying any lawful judgment against the village.

§ 14. Before any tax for a special purpose, or to *Notice to be published.*

increase the amount for the ordinary expenses of the village for the current year, can be voted, notice thereof must be published, for at least two weeks next before such meeting, in all the newspapers published weekly, or oftener, in said village, subscribed by the president and a majority of the trustees, stating that the meeting will be called upon to vote for a special tax, or to increase the ordinary expenses of the village, specifying the object, stating the sum proposed to be raised and an estimate by items of the whole cost of the proposed object. A resolution to raise money by special tax can embrace but one special purpose, and must be voted on seperately. But no resolution authorizing such tax, can be adopted within three months next preceding the time appointed for the next annual meeting, except it be to pay a lawful judgment recovered against the village. A resolution to raise money by tax for a special purpose, or which necessarily requires a special tax for its accomplishment, adopted in violation of this section, is void.

To be kept in a separate account.

§ 15. The money so raised for a special purpose must be applied to such special purpose only, and must be kept a distinct fund in a separate account on the treasurer's books; except that its purpose and objects may be changed to any other object, by a subsequent resolution of another meeting, adopted after notice in the same manner as herein provided for the resolution directing such tax, when such change can be made without violating a contract.

When not over $1,000 to be raised, warrant must be issued within the year.

§ 16. When the entire estimated expense of completing any special object, for which a tax shall have been voted, as provided in section thirteen, or when the aggregate estimated expense of all such special purposes shall not exceed one thousand dollars, the whole amount thereof must be assessed, and the warrant for the collection thereof must be issued within the year in which the resolution is adopted. If the whole amount required exceed one thousand dollars, the excess over that sum, and not exceeding four thousand dollars more, must be assessed and collected, one thousand dollars in the second year, one thousand dollars in the third year, one thousand dollars in the fourth year, and one thousand dollars in the fifth year, until the sum of five thousand dollars shall have been collected. The aggregate amount for all such special objects and purposes required at any one meeting, or in any one year, cannot exceed five thousand dollars, exclusive of interest thereon, until the same can be paid by five annual collections, as in this section provided; and when once ordered, no subsequent action of a meeting shall be necessary to enable the trustees to collect the sum of one thousand dollars in each year, as herein provided.

§ 17. Money cannot be borrowed on the credit of, nor can any debt be created in behalf of the village, payable at a future time; nor can any debt or liability be incurred by the village, except for the ordinary expenses of the village, within the income of the current year, applicable to that purpose; nor can any money or property of the village be appropriated or applied for any purpose except as authorized by this act, except that when the raising of money for a special purpose shall be ordered, as provided in this act, the amount may be borrowed, or a liability by contract, for the special purpose, may be incurred, not exceeding the expense ordered, until the amount can be raised by tax as before provided. *In regard to borrowing money.*

§ 18. Any officer or person who shall assume to create a debt or incur a liability, or appropriate any money or property of the village, contrary to the provisions of this act, or shall assent thereto, shall be personally liable for such debt or liability, and to the village for such money or property; and each of the trustees present when such violation shall have been enacted, shall be deemed to have assented thereto, unless his dissent be expressed and entered upon the journal. Any wilful violation of the last section shall also be a misdemeanor. *Personal liability of officers.*

§ 19. Whenever a vote by ballot, authorizing a special tax shall be required, as provided in section eight, such vote shall be taken in the following manner, viz: One or more resolutions shall be offered, substantially in the following form:

"*Resolved*, That the sum of (naming the sum) be raised by a tax for the purpose of (stating concisely the purpose of raising the proposed tax.)" *Form of ballot for special tax.*

If more than one resolution be proposed, they shall be numbered. The ballot shall have on the inside the words "For the resolution," or "Against the resolution," and be deposited in a separate box, to be labelled "village tax;" and when more than one resolution is submitted, the ballot shall have the words " for the first resolution," or "against the first resolution," and so as to each resolution submitted.

§ 20. The electors may at any meeting authorize the trustees to dispose of any property belonging to the village, subject to such terms as to the conditions of sale, and the price, as the said meeting shall prescribe ; provided notice of such meeting and its objects shall have been given as is required in section fourteen, for raising a special tax.

Electors may authorize trustees to dispose property.

POWERS AND DUTIES OF THE PRESIDENT.

§ 21. The president shall be the chief executive officer of the village, and shall preside at all annual and special meetings of the electors, and at the meetings of the trustees, but has no vote, except a casting vote when there is a tie. He may submit propositions for the action of the trustees. It is his duty to see that the provisions of this act and the village by-laws and ordinances are faithfully executed, and to institute prosecutions for violation thereof. He has the power, and it is his duty, to suspend until after the next annual election, the operation of any resolution or ordinance of the trustees, by his order, to be entered upon the records of the village, with his reasons therefor, when in his judgment it is in violation of this act, or of any law of this state, or appropriates money, or involves expenditures improvidently. If adopted by the next board of trustees, it shall not be so suspended. The president in behalf of the village, must execute all leases, contracts, licenses, and other papers to be executed, as the act of the village, when so authorized by the trustees.

§ 22. The president shall have power, and it shall be his duty, to suppress riots, and to order and compel all tumultuous assemblages to disperse, and he shall have the same power for this purpose as is given by the law to sheriffs in case of resistance to the execution of process.

To suppress riots.

§ 23. The president may, when in his judgment the safety of person or property, or the good order of the village demands it, designate one or more persons, by appointment in writing. to act as special policemen for such time, not extending beyond the next meeting of the trustees, as he shall deem necessary, when he shall report to such meeting the appointments so made, and his reasons therefor

Appoint special policemen.

§ 24. The president shall submit to the annual meeting a report of the financial transactions of the village for the year, showing: *Make an annual report.*

1. All moneys raised or received, and from what sources, distinguishing also the purposes to which they were devoted.

2. All payments, specifying each item, and out of what fund, and showing whether any items, and if any stating them, have been allowed and disallowed by the trustees, and to whom paid.

3. The entire indebtedness of the village, if any, distinguishing the funds indebted, and stating the payments thereon, and when made. The president must also submit an estimate of the amount required to be raised by tax for the ensuing year for ordinary village expenses, specifying in detail as far as practicable. It may also contain such statements as the president may deem useful for the information of the meeting.

§ 25. The president's report shall be submitted to a meeting of the trustees at least ten days before the annual meeting, and so much at least thereof as shows the receipts and expenditures for the year, and the estimates for the ensuing year, shall be published in the official paper of the village at least five days before the annual meeting. *To be submitted to trustees.*

POWERS AND DUTIES OF THE TRUSTEES.

§ 26. The trustees can only transact business as a board sitting in public, at least four trustees or three trustees and the president being present, and all their acts shall be entered upon the journal of the village. The concurrence of four trustees is required to pass any ordinance or resolution which necessarily involves the payment of any money, or the appropriation of any money or property of the village, or for any assessment upon lots for sidewalks or streets, or laying out or altering a street, or declaring a nuisance and directing its removal or abatement. The concurrence of a majority of the members of the board present is sufficient for any other act. *Number required to vote for an appropriation.*

§ 27. Meetings of the trustees shall be held pursuant to adjournment, or upon a call by the president or any four trustees. The board shall have power to declare the absence of any member from three consecutive meet- *Meetings of trustees.*

ings thereof, except in case of sickness, absence from the village, or other disability, a resignation of office. It shall be the duty of the president or trustees calling a meeting to cause to be notified all the trustees who are in the village at the time. If the president be absent at a meeting, the trustees may appoint a president for the time being from their own number, who shall not thereby lose his right to vote as trustee, but when he votes as trustee he shall have no casting vote on a tie.

§ 28. It shall be the duty of the trustees, and they shall have the power:

To appoint certain officers and fill vacancies.
1. To appoint the several officers, whose offices are held by appointment under them, and to fill vacancies therein, and to fill any vacancy which may occur, in any other office, by appointment of a suitable person to hold until the person elected to such office at the next annual election shall have duly qualified. Persons appointed to office by the trustees, unless sooner removed, shall hold until their successors shall be appointed by the succeeding board of trustees, and shall have duly qualified.

To declare vacancies.
2. To declare vacant any office in consequence of the insanity, removal from the village, or the conviction of an infamous crime of the incumbent thereof.

Public property.
3. To provide for the care, custody, and preservation of public property, records and papers of the village.

To remove for official misconduct.
4. To see that the officers of the village perform their duties faithfully, and to remove, for official misconduct or neglect of duty, officers holding under their appointment. Before any action shall be had as herein provided, the officer charged with official misconduct or neglect of duty shall be entitled to one week's notice in writing, specifying the charges made, and appointing a time and place for the hearing thereof.

Call special meetings.
5. To call special meetings of the electors when, in their judgment, the interests of the village shall require it.

6. To give notice, in the manner prescribed by this act, of the annual and special meetings of the electors.

7. To carry into effect every resolution of instruction lawfully adopted at any meeting of the electors.

Examine accounts and claims.
8. To examine all accounts and claims against the village, and allow such as are just and legal.

Fix compensation of certain officers.
9. To fix the compensation of the assessors, treasurer, street commissioner and clerk.

10. To issue warrants for the collection of taxes, and *Issue warrants for taxes.* of all the assessments authorized by this act to be made. The warrant shall require the moneys therein mentioned to be paid to the treasurer, and shall be returnable in sixty days from the time of issuing the same; and, if not wholly collected, to renew the same, returnable in thirty days.

11. To order real property to be leased to satisfy tax- *To lease real proper- ty for pay- ment of taxes.* es, expenses or assessments charged thereon, and not paid or collected.

12. To prevent the dangerous construction and condi- tion of chimneys, fire-places, hearth-stones, stove pipes, *Regulations to prevent fires.* ovens, boilers and apparatus used in any building or manufactory, and to cause the same to be removed or placed in a safe condition, when considered dangerous, and to prevent the deposit of ashes in unsafe vessels and places; to authorize the fire wardens, or other officers of the village, to keep away from the vicinity of any fire, all idle or suspicious persons, and to require all persons to aid in extinguishing fires, and the preservation of pro- perty exposed to danger thereat; and generally to es- tablish such regulations for preventing and extinguishing fires as they may deem expedient.

13. To appoint fire wardens and to prescribe their *Appoint fire wardens.* powers and duties. The trustees shall also be fire war- dens of said village.

14. To regulate, permit or prohibit any natural or ar- *Shows and exhibitions.* tificial curiosity, caravans of animals, circuses or thea- trical and other shows, exhibitions or performances for gain or profit, within the bounds of the corporation. The trustees may license any such exhibition or perform- ance on payment, for the benefit of the corporation, of such sum as they may determine; any person or persons who shall exhibit or perform as before mentioned, with- out such license, shall each forfeit and pay the sum of twenty-five dollars for every such performance or exhi- bition. But nothing in this subdivision shall be con- strued to prevent the delivery of literary, historical and scientific lectures in said village, and the use and exhibi- tion of apparatus illustrating the same, and receiving money therefor.

15. To direct the manner, determine the material to *Crosswalks.* be used in, and superintend the construction and repair- ing of side-walks and cross-walks in said village.

14

Streets.

16. To exercise exclusive jurisdiction over all the streets in said village ; to discontinue, to grade and im, prove streets or parts of streets not already graded ; lay out new streets, and to extend streets, or to widen those which are less than three rods wide, and grade and improve such new streets or parts thereof according to the provisions of this act ; and to cause the damages and expenses, when not collected by a general tax, to be assessed, collected and paid in the manner hereinafter provided   Sections seventy-two and seventy-three of chapter sixteen, article four, title first, part first (fifth edition) of the Revised Statutes, shall not be deemed to restrict the powers of the trustees in laying out, opening, or extending streets in said village.

Trustees to be commissioners of highways.

17. To exercise the powers and duties of commissioners of highways of towns within the limits of the village, except the assessment of highway labor, so far as those powers and duties are consistent with other parts of this act, and are applicable to the village ; to direct the application of highway labor to the improvement of the highways in such places within the village as they may deem best ; also to direct the application of a part thereof, not exceeding ten per cent, in any year, to the grading of the public grounds, and to planting and protecting trees thereon.

Riots and disturbances.

18. To prevent any riot or noise, disturbances or disorderly assemblages ; to suppress and restrain disorderly houses, groceries, houses of ill fame, billiard tables, ball alleys, gaming tables, or any other instruments or devices for gaming.

Ringing of bells and fireworks.

19. To prevent or regulate the ringing or tolling of bells, blowing of horns, crying of goods and wares, firing of guns, pistols, crackers, rockets and squibs ; the throwing or playing with fire-balls, or any other fire works charged with gunpowder, or any other explosive or highly inflammable material ; and the building of fires in any of the public streets of the village.

In regard to public health.

20. To compel the owners or occupants of any grocery, tannery, cellar, stable, barn, privy, sewer, sink or any other unwholesome house or place, to cleanse or abate the same, from time to time, as often as may be necessary for the health, comfort or convenience of the inhabitants of said village ; to prevent the depositing, leaving, or keeping of any unwholesome or nauseous substance in any

street in said village; and to prevent and regulate bathing in the rivers, canals or ponds within the village.

21. To prescribe regulations as to the location of Drains. private drains, water-logs, and discharging posts, water pipes and gas pipes in the streets, and for the prevention of injury or obstruction to the streets thereby.

22. To make such regulations in respect to keeping Dogs. and confining dogs as they may see fit.

23. To prevent injury to the cemeteries and burying Cemeteries. grounds in said village, not otherwise provided for by law; and defacing, injuring, displacing, destroying, cutting, or marring any tomb, grave, tomb-stone, monument, or any memento, and the trees, shrubs, plants and flowers therein.

24. To provide for the building and preservation of Public fences around the public grounds; the preservation of grounds. shade and ornamental trees on such grounds and in the streets of said village, and to prevent injury to the same.

25. To designate a newspaper published within the Newspaper village, to publish the by-laws, ordinances and proceed- ing Lotles. ings of the trustees, notices of the annual and special meetings, and all other notices and papers required or authorized by this act to be published.

26 To make such by-laws. not inconsistent with the By-laws. laws of this state, or of the United States, as they shall deem proper ; to carry into effect the provisions of this act, and of other laws applicable to the village, and the powers vested in any officer thereof, and to prescribe penalties, not exceeding fifty dollars for each violation of any such by-law ; but no such by-law shall take effect until two days after it shall have been published in the official paper of the village, of which publication affidavit must be made and filed with the village clerk.

27. To perform all the duties imposed on them by this act, or any other law of this state.

§ 29. The trustees have the power in their discretion : To restrain cattle, &c.

1 To restrain cattle, horses, sheep, swine and geese from going at large in the streets, under a penalty not exceeding five dollars for each animal. Animals so going at large shall be liable to be distrained, impounded and sold, as may be provided by the by-laws, and the owner of every such animal shall be liable to the penalty.

2. To prohibit the incumbering of the streets, side- Incumber-

ing streets and walks.

walks and crosswalks of said village with teams, carriages, lumber, timber, firewood or any other substance or material. To cause buildings and other structures encroaching upon the street to be removed at the expense of the owners thereof; to permit building materials to be deposited on the streets in front of any lot, to any extent, and for any such time as they may prescribe.

Clear the sidewalks.

3. To compel the removal, by the occupant or owner of any lot, of snow and ice from the sidewalk in front thereof, within such time after verbal notice as they may direct.

Gunpowder.

4. To limit the quantity of gunpowder or other explosive or combustible material which may be kept in any store or building within any specified part of the village.

Nuisances.

5. To determine the existence of a public nuisance in any part of the village, and to compel its removal or abatement, in the manner prescibed in this act.

Wooden buildings.

6. To prohibit the erection of wooden buildings within or in the vicinity of the compact parts of the village to be specified.

Immoderate driving.

7. To prohibit the flying of kites, playing of ball, rolling of hoops, sliding down hill, or immoderate driving of horses in any of the streets or parts of the village.

Pounds.

8. To establish and regulate public pounds, appoint keepers thereof, and prescribe their compensation and fees.

Examiner of weights and measures.

9. To appoint examiners of weights and measures, and scales for such village; such examiner shall have the power, at all reasonable and proper times, within business hours, to inspect and examine the weights, measures, and scales used in said corporate limits, and shall have the right to enter any store, building, or the place where the same shall be used, for the purpose of such inspection and examination; their compensation to be prescribed by the trustees, and to be paid out of the general fund of the village.

Unsafe buildings and walls.

10. To compel the owners or occupants of any wall or building within the village which may be in a ruinous or unsafe condition, to render the same safe, take down or remove the same, and to prohibit such erections.

Hay market.

11. To regulate places for marketing hay and wood, and to designate a place to be occupied by the carmen of the village when not employed.

Pedling

12. To prohibit any person from retailing meat from

wagons, **sleighs,** or other vehicles, in said village, without meat with-out license.
license; **such** license may be granted with or without
charge in the discretion of the trustees.

13. To give names to streets, and numbers to tenements Name streets.
and blocks, and to change the same; to cause a map of
the village to be made, and lithographed or engraved, and
to sell the same to defray the expense thereof.

14. To cause prosecution upon any contract or liability To prose-cute.
in which the village is interested, or for fines and penalties imposed by this act, or by any by-law or ordinance
of the village, and to enforce the collection thereof, or
to remit the same or any part thereof.

15. To employ attorneys in the prosecution or defence Employ attorneys.
of any action by or against the village; for the transaction of any business of the village requiring professional
skill.

16. To do any act necessary to carry into effect any
resolution, ordinance or other proceeding, which by this
act they are authorized to adopt.

LAYING OUT, EXTENDING, WIDENING, GRADING AND DISCON-TINUING STREETS.

§ 30. Before a street or part of a street can be ordered Notice to be published.
by the trustees to be laid out, opened, extended, widen-
ed, graded, improved or discontinued, by means of an
assessment as hereinafter provided, a notice of the application, subscribed by the president of the village, stating
the time and place when the same will be considered,
must be published in the official paper of the village for
at least two successive weeks before the time appointed
therefor, requesting all persons who may be interested
to appear and show cause, if any they have, against the
application. The application or petition shall be filed
with the clerk of the village.

§ 31. Upon application of any person liable to be as- May direct street to be opened.
sessed as hereinafter provided, residing upon a street or
part of a street not heretofore opened or worked, the
trustees may by ordinance direct such street or part of
a street to be opened, graded and improved.

§ 32. The trustees, upon application of a majority of Widen or discontinue streets.
the persons who own lots fronting on a proposed street,
such applicants being also the owners of more than half
the land to be taken for such proposed street, may lay
out and establish any new street within the village, or

upon application of such majority of the owners of lots fronting on any street, may discontinue or extend such street, or if it be less than three rods wide, may increase its width to a width not exceeding sixty-six feet.

Estimated expenses assessed on lots. § 33. The ordinance for improving or grading a street, or part of a street, must direct the expenses of the improvement to be estimated and assessed upon the lots fronting upon such street or part of street, or upon the owners thereof, in proportion to the benefit which the owners respectively shall be deemed to have received thereby.

§ 34. The ordinance to lay out, extend, discontinue or widen a street, when the consent of all the owners of property taken, or persons damaged thereby, expressly waiving claims for damages, be not first obtained and filed with the clerk of the village, must direct the damages sustained by the owner of any lot injured by such laying out, discontinuing, widening, or extending such street, who has not waived his claim for damages, to be estimated and assessed on all the lots, or on the owners of lots, in the vicinity manifestly benefited by such laying out, widening, extending or discontinuing of such street, and in proportion to the benefit which the owners respectively shall be deemed to receive thereby.

Damage to be assessed by the commissioners. § 35. When an assessment shall be directed by the trustees for improving or grading a street, or when a new street shall be laid out, or a street extended, widened or discontinued, and the persons claiming to have been damaged thereby shall not have waived their claims for damages, the estimate of damages and the assessment thereof shall be made by three commissioners, residents of the village, to be appointed by the county judge of Oswego county, on application of the trustees. If either of such commissioners refuse or neglect to serve, others may be appointed in his place in the same manner from time to time, and as often as necessary. Such commissioners shall be freeholders within said village, not of kin to the applicants for or the persons damaged by the laying out, widening, extending or discontinuing such street, nor interested in any land to be assessed, taken or affected thereby.

Survey and maps to be made. § 36. The trustees must cause the proper surveys and maps to be made, and when land is taken for a street, or a street discontinued, the names of the owner, with a description of the parcels belonging to each, shall be exhibited thereon. They shall also appoint time and place for the meeting of the commissioners, and cause at least five days' notice thereof to be served on all such owners.

§ 37. The commissioners shall, before they enter on the performance of their duties, take and subscribe an oath, faithfully to execute their duty according to the best of their ability, such oath to be filed with the clerk of the village. At the time and place appointed, the commissioners shall meet and examine the locality of the street to be laid out, widened, extended or discontinued. They shall hear the persons interested, and proofs, if any are offered, of the value of the property, and of any other facts affecting the question; but not the opinion of witnesses, as to the amount to be assessed, or the damages to be awarded. They may take into consideration any benefit to be derived from the proposed improvement. A majority of such commisoners may decide, and if it be to improve and grade a street, they shall estimate the expense thereof; if a new street be laid out, or a street discontinued, widened or extended, they shall assess the damages to the owners of the lands taken, or the persons injured thereby. They shall assess the expense or damages upon all lots subject to be assessed therefor, and upon the owners of such lots, in proportion, as near as practicable, to the benefits which the respective owners shall be deemed to have received, and shall certify the same to the trustees, within ten days after the first meeting of such commissioners; said report to be immediately filed with the village clerk. An assessment so made shall be final and conclusive, and thereby become a lien upon the lots, and a demand against the owners thereof, unless within ten days after the filing of the report an appeal be brought as in the next section provided.

Commissioners to be sworn.

§ 38. Any person considering himself aggrieved by such report, or in case the village shall have assumed the payment of all or any portion of the damages estimated as hereinafter provided, such person, or the trustees of the village, may within ten days after the filing of the same, appeal to the county court of the county, by filing with the village clerk, and serving on each of the commissioners, a notice of appeal, stating the grounds thereof. The appellant shall, at the same time, pay to each of the

Persons aggrieved may appeal.

commissioners two dollars for their return. The commissioners, or a majority of them, shall, within ten days, return to the county court, and file with the clerk thereof a full return of all the evidence and proceedings taken

Manner of appeal. before them, and the reasons for their decision. Such commissioners may be compelled to make or amend their returns in the same manner as the returns of justices in appeal cases, at any time within ten days after the filing thereof. On a notice, by either party, of five days, the appeal may be brought on to argument, on the commissioners' report, the return of the commissioners and the notice of appeal. The county court may, in deciding such appeal affirm, modify or disapprove such report, as said court may deem proper, without reference to technical objections. If the court shall modify or disapprove the said report, it may refer it back, with instructions to the commissioners, for correction or the court may appoint three other commissioners to assess anew the damages, who shall proceed in all respects as the commissioners making the first assessment are required to proceed; and the determination of such court or commissioners shall be final; and all assessments made in pursuance thereof shall be a lien upon the lots so assessed, and a demand against the owners thereof. The county court shall always be open for the transaction of any business under this section.

Compensation of commissioners. § 39. The commissioners shall be entitled to receive two dollars each, for each and every day necessarily employed in the business; these fees, and other necessary expenses of the village attending the business, are included in the ordinary expenses of the village; the commissioners are authorized to administer oaths when necessary in discharge of their duties.

In case of infants. § 40. When there are infants, or other incompetent persons, owners, whose property is affected by any such improvement, the county or supreme court shall appoint guardians *ad litem* to protect their interests and prosecute appeals.

Call special meeting of inhabitants in certain cases. § 41. The trustees, whenever an application is made to them, to lay out, extend, widen, or discontinue a street, as provided in this act, may, if in their judgment the interests of the village demand, at the next annual meeting, or at a special meeting called in the manner prescribed in section fourteen, submit to such meeting the question of paying the damages in laying out, extending, widening or discontinuing any street by a general tax. The vote on such question may be taken by ballot, and the qualifications of voters thereon shall be such as are prescribed in section seven of this act. The meeting may direct that all or a part of the expense or damage thereof be paid by a general tax; if a part only shall be directed to be paid by such tax, such part shall be deducted by the commissioners from the aggregate expense or damages, and a balance assessed upon the lots and owners as before specified.

SIDEWALKS.

§ 42. Whenever the trustees shall direct a sidewalk in front of any lot to be made, they shall direct the grade, width, form of construction, and may prescribe the materials, or direct it to be covered with flagging, stone, hard brick, or plank, with such curbing as they may deem proper. When required to be covered with flagging or brick, at least sixty days' notice shall be given to the owner, his agent or occupant of the lot; in all other cases thirty days' notice must be given. Whenever they shall direct a sidewalk to be repaired only, ten days' notice of such requirement shall be given.

NUISANCES.

§ 43. When a nuisance shall be declared to exist in any part of the village and required to be removed or abated, such reasonable notice requiring the removal or abatement thereof, as the trustees may direct, shall be served upon the person liable to remove or abate the same.

§ 44. All expenses incurred by the village in the enforcement of any ordinance requiring the making, grading, or repairing any sidewalk, the removing snow and ice or other obstructions therefrom, the removal or abatement of a nuisance, or the doing of any other act they are authorized to do, the person or persons required to do the same, having neglected or refused, may be collected by warrant to be issued by the trustees, by action or by lease of lots, as hereinafter prescribed. All such expenses are hereby declared to be a lien upon the lots affected by such act or improvement, and an indebt-

Provision for meeting certain expenses incurred.

15

edness against the owner thereof or person or persons liable to pay the same.

ASSESSMENT OF TAXES.

Trustees to direct assessors. § 45. The trustees shall, within sixty days after the annual meeting, direct the assessors to assess upon the taxable inhabitants and property liable to assessment and taxation in the village, such sum as they may deem necessary, besides funds received and estimated to be received from other sources, to defray the ordinary expenses of the village for the current year, not to exceed the amount allowed for that purpose by the annual meeting; also the sum required by this act and applied toward the payment of the debt of the village; also any sum directed to be raised for a special purpose and which, under the provision of this act, can be raised in that year. They shall, also, in addition, determine the number of days of highway labor to be assessed for every one thousand dollars valuation on the assessment roll, and which shall not be less than two nor more than four days, for every one thousand dollars.

Time of making assessment. § 46. It shall be the duty of the assessors, within sixty days after the annual election, to prepare an assessment roll and valuation of property subject to taxation in the village, and to complete the same, in all respects, as nearly as practicable, in the manner prescribed by law in respect to town assessors; and the village assessors are hereby invested with the same powers in respect to assessment as town assessors have, including the power to administer oaths, and to correct the valuation, on the application of persons interested; but the notice of the time and place of meeting to hear applications to correct the valuation, shall be published at least two weeks next preceding the time appointed, in the official paper of the village, and also posted in three public places in the village.

In certain cases not to be deemed a part of village. § 47. Farms and parts of farms situated within the boundaries of the village, occupied as such, and not adjoining the towing-path of the canal, or any regular street of the village, or when so adjoining, the parts thereof lying more than three hundred feet from such street or canal, are not for the purpose of taxation, except the assessment of highway labor, to be deemed a part of such village, but for that purpose to be subject to the officers of the towns in which they are situated in the same manner as if they were not included in the boundaries of the village.

§ 48. Upon the completion of the assessment roll of valuation, and upon receiving from the trustees their direction, stating the several sums to be raised by general tax for the current year, authorized by this act, the assessors shall apportion the amount required to be raised according to the valuation, and set the several sums so apportioned opposite the valuation in the same manner as required for town and county tax lists. *(Assessors to apportion the amount to be raised.)*

§ 49. When a tax for a special purpose shall be ordered by a special meeting, after the annual tax list is completed, the assessors shall assess the same upon the valuation prepared for the annual tax for that year.

ASSESSMENT OF HIGHWAY LABOR.

§ 50. The assessors shall also perform the duty, and they are hereby vested with the powers of commissioners of highways of a town, in assessing highway labor upon the persons and property in the village subject to assessment therefor, such assessment upon property must be made from the valuation in the last assessment roll of the village, except the farm lands, which are to be assessed from the town assessment within which the property is situated, and when completed, shall be certified and delivered to the trustees, and be filed and kept with the clerk of the village. *(Valuation taken from last assessment roll.)*

§ 51. Upon the return of the assessment of highway labor, the trustees shall cause a copy thereof to be delivered to the street commissioner, with a direction subscribed by them thereon, to cause the same to be expended in improving the highways in the village, and otherwise, as he may be directed by the trustees, under the provisions of this act. *(Street commissioner to cause the money to be expended.)*

STREET COMMISSIONER'S DUTIES.

§ 52. The street commissioner, upon the receipt of the assessment roll, has the power, and is charged with the same duties in respect to the persons and property assessed, and for the collection of the assessment and the expenditure thereof, within the village as is vested by law in the overseer of a highway in a town within his road district, except that any person may commute by *(Commutation fee.)*

paying fifty cents for each day's labor assessed to him or upon his property, upon being notified of his assessment.

To keep in order the highways. § 53. It shall be the duty of the street commissioner to enforce, collect and apply all the highway labor assessed, and to keep in good condition all the highways within the boundaries of the village, subject to the direction of the trustees, as herein provided, and to superintend personally the work done; to make return on oath to the trustees as often as required, and at least once a month, showing by items, the amount of money collected and paid out, to whom, and for what purpose; the amount of work, the kind of improvement, and when and on what street or place expended, and at least two weeks before the annual meeting, to return their assessment rolls, with all the money or work collected noted thereon, and showing all arrearages uncollected, and to render a full account on oath, stating the amount received and applied, and the balance, if any, which has been collected and not expended, and to pay over any such balance to the treasurer, to be expended by his successor.

Unpaid assessment to be added to next year. § 54. If the highway assessment of any person or property shall be returned by the street commissioners unpaid, the assessors for the ensuing year shall add the amount thereof to the assessment of the same person or property for that year. If any property owned by a person not a resident of the village, shall be insufficiently described, either upon the general assessment roll, or for highway labor, to enable a sale thereof to be made, the assessors who made the same may alter and correct such description at any time before the final return thereof to the trustees. All taxes on real property of persons not resident in the village, including highway labor, to be estimated at the rate of fifty cents a day, are liens on the lots assessed when sufficiently described.

Compensation of street commissioner. § 55. The compensation of the street commissioner shall be determined by the trustees at a specified sum for each day actually spent in the discharge of his duties, to be stated by him on oath with his monthly returns, and shall be allowed by the trustees, and audited in the same manner as other claims against the village. When so allowed, and not otherwise, he may retain his compensation out of the collections of commutations for highway labor.

§ 56. Before entering upon his official duties, the street commissioner shall execute a bond to the corporation, in such penalty, and with such sureties as the president shall approve, conditioned that he will faithfully perform the duties of his office.

COLLECTOR'S POWERS AND DUTIES.

§ 57. All taxes and assessments, except for highway labor, made under this act, may be collected under a warrant for that purpose, to be issued by the trustees, to be returned by them within sixty days after the receipt thereof by the collector, with his certificate showing his collections thereon. The collector shall be vested with the same powers, and shall be entitled to the same compensation in respect thereto, and before entering upon his official duties, shall execute a like bond to be approved by the president of the village, as collector of taxes in the town, and must proceed in the same manner, except as herein otherwise provided, and except that the notice of times and places at which he will receive taxes required to be posted, shall also be published in the official paper of the village; and he must, within the time fixed for the return of his warrant, pay over to the treasurer all moneys collected by him. If any shall remain uncollected the warrant may be renewed once and again, for thirty days.

TREASURER'S DUTIES.

§ 58. The treasurer must receive, keep and disburse the funds of the village. He shall keep proper accounts of all moneys received and paid out, referring to his entries of payments to the vouchers by number, and stating the name of the person to whom the payment was made, and if to an assignee, the name of the person in whose favor the claim was allowed. A separate account must be kept of all moneys raised for the ordinary expenses of the village by tax, including in the same all receipts from licenses, and other sources not raised for a special purpose, and of the disbursement thereof. This shall be known as the general fund. A separate account shall also be kept of the receipts from taxes and assessments for any special purpose, and the disbursement thereof.

To prepare an annual statement. § 59. The treasurer's books shall at all times be subject to be examined by any elector, and he must prepare, and one week before the annual meeting, present to the trustees a statement showing the condition of every fund, showing the receipts on account of the same, and the disbursements thereof, when and to whom paid. It is his duty to pay on presentation all claims allowed as provided in this act, out of the proper fund, and if there be no fund out of which it can be paid, to make an entry upon the claim, stating presentment and non-payment, and reason therefor. He must also pay over to his successor in office, after he shall have taken the oath and given the security required by this act, and not before, all balances of money received but not legally disbursed, and deliver to him the books and papers of his office.

Pay over to successor all balance of money.

Give a bond. § 60. Before entering upon the duties of his office, the treasurer shall execute a bond to the corporation, in such penalty and with such sureties as the president shall approve, conditioned that he will faithfully perform the duties of his office.

CLERK'S DUTIES, RECORDS AND PAPERS.

§ 61. The clerk shall attend the meetings of the trustees, and the annual and special meetings of the electors, and record in a book, known as the journal of the village, all resolutions, ordinances, directions, and other determinations adopted at such meetings, including the election of officers, with their oaths of office. He shall also enter in a book, to be known as the clerk's minutes, a memorandum of all notices served by him, stating the time and manner of service, with any other minutes directed by this act to be kept by him. He shall serve all notices and file all papers required by the trustees, or by this act, make copies of assessment rolls, tax lists, and other papers required by the trustees or president, and keep in good order the books and papers pertaining to his office.

In regard to notices.

Evidence in certain cases. § 62. The entries in the journal, or sworn copies thereof, are sufficient evidence of acts lawfully entered; the entries in the clerk's minutes shall be presumptive evidence of the facts therein stated; and when a notice is required by this act, or by the trustees, to be served or published, an affidavit of such service by the clerk, made and filed within ten days thereafter, or if published in a newspaper, an affidavit of the publisher or his foreman, made and filed within ten days after the last publication, is sufficient evidence of the facts therein stated; but this section shall not prevent the truth and correctness of such entries from being controverted or countervailed by other proofs, in an action brought within one year after the entries are made or papers filed to vacate the same, in which action their truth or correctness shall be expressly called in question by the pleadings. The clerk's books and papers shall, at all times, be subject to examination by any elector.

POLICE JUSTICE.

§ 63. The police justice shall be elected at the annual election of officers of said village, and shall hold his office for four years, and until another is elected and qualified. Before entering upon the duties of his office, **Take oath of office.** he shall take and subscribe the usual oath of office, and file the same in the clerk's office of Oswego county, at which office his election shall be certified by the president and clerk of said village. He shall possess the same powers, and be subject to the same duties and liabilities in criminal cases, as justices of the peace of the several towns in the state; and is hereby authorized and empowered to inflict punishment by fine not exceeding one hundred dollars, or imprisonment not exceeding one year, or both; and may, in his discretion, when the sentence of any person shall be for a time not less than three months, commit such person to the penitentiary of the county of Onondaga, providing the agreement authorized by section seven of chapter three hundred and thirty-eight of the laws of eighteen hundred and fifty shall have been made by the board of supervisors of the county of Oswego.

§ 64. The police justice is hereby authorized to charge **Fees.** and receive for the use of the town of Volney, in any criminal proceedings, such fees as are now allowed by law to justices of the peace for like services; and all fees and charges for services performed by such police justice, and which are chargeable upon the county of Oswego or any town therein, as hereinafter provided, shall be audited and allowed by the board of supervisors of Oswego county, or the board of town auditors of such towns respectively, to and for the benefit of said town of Volney; the orders therefor to be made payable to the supervisor of the said town of Volney.

Charge against town where offence committed.

§ 65. All services rendered by the police justice, in the examination, trial, and punishment of any person charged with any offence committed in any town in Oswego county, which, if tried therein, would be chargeable to such town, shall be a charge against such town.

Residence and juris-diction.

§ 66. The police justice shall reside in the village, and shall keep his office in some convenient place therein. He shall have exclusive jurisdiction in all criminal cases arising in the village, and which are cognizable in courts of justices of the peace in this state. He shall not receive, for his own use, any fees for services performed by him, but shall receive an annual salary of five hundred dollars, to be paid by the town of Volney as other town charges.

Keeps book of entries.

§ 67. The police justice shall keep a book, in which he shall enter all business done by him, and shall make accounts thereof together with all fines, costs and fees received by him in any case, in the same manner as accounts of justices of the peace in like cases, in which he shall charge the same fees as are allowed by law to justices of the peace, and which shall be duly verified by him, which accounts shall be audited as hereinbefore

Make an annual report.

provided. He shall report to the board of town auditors, annually, all moneys received by him from all sources, and the same shall be audited by said board, and deducted from his salary, and the balance collected as hereinbefore provided.

Office hours of.

§ 68. The police justice shall attend at his office from nine to eleven o'clock in the forenoon of every day, and as much longer as the duties of his office may require, and hear all complaints, hold courts of special sessions, and conduct all other proceedings required by law.

In case of sickness or absence from vil-lage.

§ 69. When the police justice is incapacitated to act, by reason of sickness or absence from the village, or in case of a vacancy in his office, any justice of peace of the town of Volney, residing in said village, shall have the same powers, and be subject to the same duties and liabilities, as such police justice, and shall receive for all services in criminal cases the same fees as are now allowed by law to justices of the peace. All warrants issued by any justice of the peace residing in the village, except as provided in this section, shall be made returnable before the police justice.

POLICEMEN.

§ 70. The policemen shall have the same powers, and be subject to the same duties and liabilities in criminal cases, and shall receive the same fees, to be audited in the same manner, as the constables of the several towns in this state. The town constables of the town of Volney shall receive no compensation for any criminal business done by them arising in the village of Fulton.

§ 71. It shall be the special duty of the policemen to *Arrest all persons guilty of offences.* arrest any and all persons guilty of any crime, misdemeanor or offence against the peace and good order of society They shall execute all processes issued by the police justice, including commitments to the penitentiary. They have power without process to arrest and bring before the police justice persons guilty in their presence of violating the public peace, or any village ordinance for preserving good order and decorum. They shall discharge all duties required of them by the laws of this state.

§ 72. The said policemen shall be subject to the control of the president and trustees in the discharge of all *Under the control of the president.* duties relating to the municipal rules and regulations of said village. And whenever, in their opinion, the good order and safety of the village demand they may detail one or more of said policemen for any special duty, and they may require any policemen to do duty at any time of the day or night. The services of the policemen rendered under the direction of the president and trustees shall be audited and paid out of the general fund of the village. The trustees may prescribe the dress or uniform to be worn by such policemen.

MANNER OF AUDITING CLAIMS.

§ 73. Claims against the village can only be paid when presented, allowed and certified, as follows:

1. The claim must be in writing, showing the nature *Must be in writing and verified.* thereof, and when comprising several items, specifying them, and must be verified by affidavit thereon of the claimant, or of some other person, to the effect that the services were rendered or the disbursements made, or

16

otherwise proving the facts constituting the claim, and that no payment has been made thereon, or if any; how much. The president, or any trustee, may administer the oath.

2. The claim must be presented to the board of trustees and allowed by resolution, entered in the journal for such sum, if any, as the trustees shall be satisfied is justly and legally due from the village thereon, stating the fund out of which it is payable.

3. The allowance of the claim, with the date when allowed and specifying the fund out of which it is payable, must be entered on or attached thereto by the clerk, and a registry thereof made by him, referring to a number marked thereon.

4. When allowed and certified, it must be paid by the treasurer out of the proper funds and no other, and then filed in his office, and the proper entry thereof made at the time by him.

MANNER OF SERVING NOTICES.

§ 74. When notice is required by this act to be given to the owners of property, it shall be served, unless otherwise provided, by delivery of a copy personally to the owner, or if. he be absent from home, by leaving such copy at his residence with a person of suitable age and discretion. When an owner resides out of the village, notice to him may be served on his tenant in possession, or when the premises are unoccupied, on his agent. If neither owner nor agent reside in the village, such notice may be served by mail, addressed to such owner or agent at his last place of residence. When verbal notice is authorized by this act, such notice may be served upon the owner, agent or occupant of the premises. An affidavit by the clerk, stating the service of such notice and specifying the manner thereof, filed in his office within ten days after the service, with a memorandum thereof made in his book of minutes, shall be presumptive evidence of such service. Notice to the owner is, in all cases, to be deemed notice to the incumbrancers, so far as their interests are involved in the proceedings.

When owner res des. out of .he village.

LEASE OF LOTS FOR ASSESSMENTS.

§ 75. When a tax or assessment, which is a lien upon a lot, shall be returned by the collector unsatisfied, or when a lien upon a lot shall arise from default of the owner to make or repair a sidewalk, or remove snow and ice or other obstruction therefrom, or remove or abate any nuisance, it may be enforced by an order of the trustees, directing the lot to be leased for a time sufficient to pay the lien, and interest and costs. The order must describe the lot, and the trustees must estimate therein according to their best judgment, the length of time for which the use of the lot will be worth the amount required to be raised, with interest and costs.

Order must describe the lot.

§ 76. Upon such order the president shall cause a notice to be published for three successive weeks in the official paper of the village, stating the amount required, including interest to the time of the first publication, and designating the time and place when the lot will be leased at public auction to pay the same. After such notice, payment thereof, with interest and cost of advertising may be made at any time before the property is struck off. If payment is not made, the president must cause the property to be leased to the person and to his assigns, who will take the same for the shortest term, and will pay therefor the amount required, with interest and costs. But the time which may elapse after such leasing before possession is obtained—reasonable diligence for that purpose being used—shall constitute no part of the term. Such lessee shall have the same remedies to obtain possession, if withheld, as a purchaser under an execution on a sheriff's sale after title is perfected.

Notice of leasing to be published.

§ 77. An affidavit of the president, or of any person who may under his direction, act as an auctioneer, stating the fact of such leasing, specifying the time and place thereof, the amount raised, and the length of time for which the property was leased, must be made and filed in the office of the clerk, and a note thereof made in the clerk's book of entries.

Affidavit of auctioneer.

§ 78. After any lot shall have been leased, notice thereof shall be given by the clerk to the owner, stating the length of time for which the same was let, and the sum for which it was let; stating that unless it be redeemed by payment thereof, and ten per cent. in addition to the treasurer, for the benefit of the lessee, within thirty days after service of such notice, a lease will be executed by the president to the lessee. After thirty

Notice to be given to the owner of property leased.

days from the service of the last mentioned notice a
lease may be executed of the property, to the person to
whom it was struck off, or his assigns, for the term for
which it was struck off, briefly referring to the non-payment of the tax, assessment or lien. The lease shall be
presumptive evidence that all the proceedings creating
a lien, and for the enforcement thereof, to and including
the lease, have been regular and according to law.

VILLAGE JAIL.

§ 79. It shall be lawful for the board of trustees of
said village to rent suitable rooms for a jail therein, and
pay an annual sum for the use thereof. The said board
of trustees shall also have power to appoint a keeper of
said jail, and to provide for the necessities of those confined therein. The said jailer shall possess the same
powers and shall be entitled to the same fees as other
keepers of the common jail of Oswego county, and shall
be paid in like manner. Any court or officer having
jurisdiction may commit persons charged or convicted
of crime to the said village jail, in the same cases in
which such court or officer might be authorized by law
to commit such person to the common jail of the county
aforesaid, except that no person shall be committed to
such village jail to await the action of the grand jury
upon his case. In cases when such court or officer may
commit such offender to said village jail upon conviction,
they may be sentenced to hard labor, and for that purpose the village jail shall be a workhouse or penitentiary,
and all persons sentenced thereto at hard labor may be
taken out and compelled to work on the streets, sidewalks and public grounds of said village, under the
direction of the board of trustees thereof, or of any
person appointed by said board for the purpose. The
expenses incident to such village jail shall be audited
and paid by the county of Oswego, except such as shall
be incurred under the ordinances of said village, or in
the working of the persons aforesaid, in which cases the
same shall be paid by said village.

*What sen-
tence to
hard labor
may be
worked on
the streets.*

AUCTIONS.

*Must have a
license.*

§ 80. It shall not be lawful for any person or persons,
or the agent of any person or persons, to sell at public
auction within the said village, any goods, wares or

merchandise, the owner of which shall be a non-resident of said village, or which wares and merchandise shall have been brought into said village, for the purpose of selling the same at public auction, without first procuring a license therefor, which shall be granted by the president, under the regulations to be established by the board of trustees, and for which said board may fix the price, not to exceed fifty dollars for each and every week said sale shall continue.

§ 81. Any person violating any of the provisions of the preceding section shall forfeit to said village one hundred dollars for each violation, to be sued for and recovered in the name of the trustees of the village; provided, however, that nothing in this or in the preceding section shall apply to any officer of the county of Oswego, or constable selling at public vendue any goods, wares, or merchandise by him seized or taken on execution, or other legal process, or which it is his duty under any state law to sell at public auction, or to any assignee or receiver appointed by any court or officer in proceedings at law, or under any state statute, when said goods, wares or merchandise, at the time of the said assignment, shall be in said village, or when the debtor, assignee or receiver shall be resident of said village, at the time of the appointment of said assignee or receiver. *$100 forfeiture for violation.*

MISCELLANEOUS PROVISIONS.

§ 82. Leases, contracts, and other instruments may be executed, when proper, by the president of the village, substantially as follows :

The Village of Fulton,
by A—— B——, *President.*
By direction of the trustees.

Proof of the hand-writing of the president, and that he was such at the time the paper bears date, is presumptive evidence of the due execution thereof. Notices and licenses may be subscribed by the officers authorized to give them, by their proper signatures, adding thereto their designation of office. *Presumptive evidence.*

§ 83. Actions may be maintained by and against the village in the same manner as by and against other corporations. Actions for penalties may be brought before a justice of the peace in the village, and the first process *Of actions by and against the village.*

in any such action may be by summons or warrant, and it is not a valid objection against said justice or juror in any action, that he is a resident of the village, or subject to taxation therein.

Public highways.   § 84. All the public streets in said village laid down on the several maps thereof, heretofore laid out or dedicated to public use, are hereby declared public highways.

All officers to be resident.   § 85. All officers elected or appointed under this act shall be residents of the village of Fulton, and the removal of any officer therefrom shall vacate his office. All resignations of officers under this act shall be made to the trustees, subject to their acceptance.

§ 86. All ordinances or by-laws passed under this act, unless otherwise provided, shall continue in full force until revoked by the trustees.

Loaning of the village funds a misdemeanor.   § 87. Any officer of the village who, by the provisions of this act, may receive any money raised or collected pursuant to its provisions, or under color or pretence thereof, and who shall loan the same, or otherwise appropriate the same to his own use or that of another, in violation of his duty, or shall refuse upon demand to deliver to his successor in office any money, books, papers or other property belonging to the village, shall be deemed guilty of a misdemeanor, and may be punished by fine and imprisonment.

Former acts repealed.   § 88. All former acts and parts of acts, relative to the incorporation of the village of Fulton, are hereby respectively repealed; but such repeal shall not affect any act done, privilege granted, right vested or established, institution located, or any proceeding, suit or prosecution had or commenced, previous to the time when such repeal shall take effect; nor shall the term of office or the compensation of the present police justice and assessors of said village be affected thereby; and the corporation hereby created succeeds to all the property, rights and duties of the corporation for which this is substituted, subject to the provisions of this act.

§ 89. This act is hereby declared a public act.

§ 90. This act shall take effect on the last Tuesday of March, one thousand eight hundred and sixty-two.

Chap. 34.

AN ACT to extend the time for the collection of taxes in certain towns in the county of Westchester, and the town of Walkill in the county of Orange.

Passed March 20, 1862; three-fifths being present.

The People of the State of New York, represented in Senate and Assembly, do enact as follows :

SECTION 1. The time for the collection of annual taxes in the towns of Morrisania, West Farms, Ossinning and Westchester, in the county of Westchester, and the town of Walkill in the county of Orange, may be extended by the several supervisors thereof, to the first day of May, eighteen hundred and sixty-two. *Supervisors authorized to extend the time.*

§ 2. Such supervisors, may give such extension and renew the warrants of the several collectors of said towns, upon the collectors executing and delivering proper bonds with sureties to the satisfaction of the supervisor for the amount of taxes uncollected by said collectors respectively. The bonds so taken shall be filed, and be a lien in the same manner as is now provided by law in the case of collectors bonds. *Collectors to execute new securities.*

§ 3. This act shall take effect immediately.

Chap. 35.

AN ACT for the relief of the inhabitants of the village of Clyde, in the county of Wayne.

Passed March 20, 1862; three-fifths being present.

The People of the State of New York, represented in Senate and Assembly, do enact as follows :

SECTION 1. The Canal Commissioners are hereby authorized and required to enquire into and examine the complaint of the inhabitants of Clyde in the county of Wayne, in relation to the existence of a pool of stag- *Canal commissioners to abate nuisances.*

nant water at or near the site of the former lock on the Erie Canal, in said village, and if it shall appear that a pool of stagnant water or nuisance has been occasioned by the construction of said canal, or by the non-construction or filling up of a culvert under said canal, or by any other cause for which the state is justly responsible, then said commissioners are hereby directed and required to abate such nuisance in such manner as seems to them in accordance with the best interests of the state, and adequate to allow the escape of said water.

§ 2. This act shall take effect immediately.

Chap. 36.

AN ACT to enable the electors of the town of Johnstown to vote by districts for town officers.

Passed March 21, 1862; three-fifths being present.

The People of the State of New York, represented in Senate and Assembly, do enact as follows:

To be divided into two districts.
SECTION 1. The town of Johnstown shall be divided as hereinafter provided into two election districts, for the election of all town officers required by law to be elected by ballot.

District No. 1.
§ 2. District number one shall comprise the present election districts number one and three, in said town, and shall hold its elections in the village of Johnstown.

District No. 2.
§ 3. District number two shall comprise the present election district number two in said town, and shall hold its elections in the village of Gloversville.

Inspectors of election.
§ 4. The board of town auditors of the town of Johnstown shall be inspectors of annual and special town elections, held in said town for the election of all town officers required by law to be elected by ballot.

To designate place of holding elections.
§ 5. The board of town auditors aforesaid, at their annual meeting of the Tuesday preceding the annual town meeting, in the year eighteen hundred and sixty-two, and in each year thereafter, shall designate the house in each of the villages of Johnstown and Gloversville at which town elections shall be held during the year, and they shall thereupon give notice, written or

printed, of the annual town elections in said district,
together with a list of all such town officers as are to
be elected by ballot at such elections, to be posted in
five public places in each district, at least five days
before the holding of such annual town elections, which
election shall be the same day on which the annual town
meeting is or shall be hereafter held.

§ 6. The said board of town auditors shall also, at the Manner of appointing inspectors of election.
meeting on the Tuesday preceding the annual town
meeting, and in each succeeding year thereafter, assign
and designate three of their number for each district
to hold the election therein, and who shall be allowed to
vote in the district where they shall be respectively
assigned; a certificate specifying the officers thus
assigned and designated for each district, shall be signed
by the board and filed in the office of the town clerk
immediately.

§ 7. In case of a vacancy in the board of inspectors Manner of filling vacancy.
in any election district in said town, or of the absence
or inability of any town officer, assigned and designated
as aforesaid, to act as inspector at any election, the
inspector or inspectors who may be present are hereby
authorized to fill all such vacancies by appointment from
among the electors of such district for the time being
who shall take the oath of office as hereinafter provided.

§ 8. The inspectors assigned and designated, or ap- Compensation of inspectors.
pointed as hereinafter provided, shall receive the same
compensation provided by law for inspectors of elections
in towns and wards.

§ 9. If a special election shall be called to fill a vacancy Notice for special election, how given.
in any town office, the town clerk shall give the like no-
tice as provided in section five, together with a list of
such town officers as are to be elected at such election,
and the justices of the peace in said town, shall meet at
the place of holding the poll in district number one, on
the succeeding day and proceed to complete the canvass
and declare the result as hereinafter provided for annual
town elections.

§ 10. The inspectors of each election district shall Organization of board of inspectors.
meet at the time and place where an election shall have
been appointed to be held therein, and shall proceed to
organize themselves as a board for the purpose of presiding at and conducting said election,

17

§ 11. The inspectors shall appoint one of their number chairman of the board, who shall administer to the other inspectors the oath of office as prescribed by the constitution and the same oath shall then be administered to the chairman by one of the other inspectors.

§ 12. The inspectors, or a majority of them, shall then appoint a clerk, who shall take the constitutional oath of office, which shall be administered to him by the chairman, who shall keep a poll list and make such other minutes as may be required.

Proclamation of opening of poll.

§ 13. Before the electors shall proceed to vote for any town officer, proclamation shall be made of the opening of the poll and when the poll will close.

To preserve order.

§ 14. The inspectors shall have the same authority to preserve order as is possessed by the board of inspectors at a general election, and shall proceed in the same manner and be governed by the same rules as is provided for the election of town officers in title three, article one of the Revised Statutes.

Manner of canvassing votes.

§ 15. As soon as the poll of an election shall have been finally closed, the inspectors in their several districts shall proceed to canvass the votes. Such canvass shall be public and shall not be adjourned or postponed until it shall have been finally completed.

Statement to be given.

§ 16 When the canvass shall have been completed and the result ascertained, a statement of all the votes taken, the number received by each candidate shall be made in writing, and certified by the inspectors of such district, with one ballot of each kind found to have been given for the officers to be chosen at such election, securely attached to such statement

§ 17. The inspectors in each district shall designate one of their number who shall deliver such statement so made and certified to, to the board of the annual town meeting, which shall be held on the succeeding day, at the place of holding the poll in district number one, on or before ten o'clock in the forenoon of said day.

Board of town meeting to complete statement.

§ 18. The board of such annual town meeting shall then proceed to complete the canvass by adding all the statements from the several districts together and declare the result the same as though such votes had been polled at such annual town meeting and the persons having the greatest number of votes shall be declared elected to the offices for which they have been designated respectively.

§ 19. The commissioners of highways of said town shall, on the last Tuesday in January, eighteen hundred and sixty-two, and in each year thereafter, make a list of all the highway districts in said town election district number one ; and also a list of all the highway districts in said town election district two, and deliver said lists, each one certified by them, to the town clerk of said town on or before the Tuesday preceding the annual town election of said town. *Commissioners of highways to make list of highways.*

§ 20. The town clerk of said town shall on the Tuesday preceding the annual town election in said town, deliver a certified copy of the said list of highway districts in said town election district number one, to the inspectors of elections of said district. designated in pursuance of section sixth of this act. He shall at the same time, also deliver a certified copy of the said list of highway districts in said town election district number two, to the inspectors of elections of said district designated as aforesaid. *Clerk to deliver them to inspectors of election.*

§ 21. At the annual town election held in said election district number one, there shall be elected in the manner now provided by law, overseers of highways for the highway districts enumerated in said list for said election district number one and at the annual town election held in said election district number two, there shall be elected in the manner now provided by law, overseers of highways for the highway districts enumerated in said list for said election district number two. *Manner of electing overseers of highways.*

§ 22. The clerks of said election districts shall make a list of said overseers of highways so elected in each of their said districts and return and file the same in the town clerk's office of said town during the day following said election. *Clerk to file list of overseers.*

§ 23. All such business as is usually done at the annual town meeting, other than the election of town officers, and not herein provided for, shall hereafter be done in the presence of, and under direction of the said town board, of the annual town meeting at their meeting on the day succeeding the annual town election, immediately after completing the canvass of the vote, as herein provided. It shall be done in public and every elector of said town who shall be present shall be entitled to vote on all questions there decided. *Other business not provided for.*

§ 24. This act shall take effect immediately.

Chap. 37.

AN ACT authorizing the board of supervisors of the county of New York to borrow money in anticipation of the collection of the annual taxes in said county and to issue county revenue bonds therefor.

Passed March 21, 1862; three-fifths being present.

The People of the State of New York, represented in Senate and Assembly, do enact as follows:

To borrow to meet necessary charges and appropriations.

SECTION 1. It shall and may be lawful for the board of supervisors of the county of New York to borrow from time to time upon the faith and credit of said county, in anticipation of the collection of the annual taxes of said county, such sum or sums of money as may be necessary to pay the ordinary charges and expenses, under appropriations made by said board of supervisors for the support of the county government including the metropolitan police within said county, and to pledge and appropriate as security for the payment of the money so borrowed and the interest thereon, an equal amount of said taxes; provided that the amount so borrowed shall at no time exceed the sum which the said board may, by then existing laws, be authorized to impose and raise by taxation during the year in which such moneys may be borrowed.

Not to exceed the amount authorized by law.

To be placed with the treasurer.

§ 2. The moneys so borrowed shall be deposited by the parties lending the same in the county treasury, and it shall be the duty of the county treasurer to give proper receipts therefor.

Comptroller to issue certificates of indebtedness.

§ 3 Upon the presentation of the receipts of the county treasurer for such sums of money as aforesaid at the office of the comptroller, it shall be the duty of the comptroller to prepare and deliver in exchange therefor, bonds or certificates of indebtedness for an equal amount which shall be known and distinguished as "County revenue bonds of the county of New York," and be made payable within one year from the date when the said money was so borrowed and deposited.

§ 4. The said county revenue bonds shall bear interest at a rate not exceeding seven per cent per annum and shall be signed by the comptroller, countersigned by the mayor and sealed with the common seal of said board of supervisors attested by their clerk. *Bonds to bear 7 per cent interest.*

§ 5. The amount required to meet the interest upon such bonds shall be included in the annual estimates of the said comptroller of the expenses of said county, and the same shall be levied and collected as a part of the general tax of said city and county, in the same manner as other taxes for county and city purposes are by law levied and collected. *Interest to be raised as part of the general tax.*

§ 6. Nothing in this act contained shall be construed to authorize the said board of supervisors to incur expenses or to contract debts for any purpose or purposes not expressly authorized by law.

§ 7. This act shall take effect immediately.

Chap. 38.

AN ACT to authorize the county treasurer of the county of Westchester to issue bonds upon the credit of said county, for the relief of the families of volunteers, and for the payment thereof.

Passed March 21, 1862; three-fifths being present.

The People of the State of New York, represented in Senate and Assembly, do enact as follows :

SECTION 1. The county treasurer of the county of Westchester is hereby directed to issue bonds upon the credit of the county of Westchester, in sums not less than one hundred dollars each, and bearing interest thereon, at the rate of seven per cent per annum, to an amount not exceeding fifty thousand dollars, and to apportion such bonds among the respective towns in the said county, in proportion to the assessed valuation of the taxable property, real and personal therein, to be estimated according to the last corrected assessment rolls of the respective towns in said county, and the said treasurer shall deliver to the supervisor of the respective *County treasurer to issue bonds to the amount of $50,000.* *To apportion the same among the several towns.*

towns the bonds which shall be apportioned to each town respectively.

Supervisors to convert into money. § 2. The respective supervisors shall convert the bonds so delivered to them into money and hold the proceeds thereof subject to the direction of the board of town auditors in their respective towns, and the money so held by them shall be designated the relief fund

Town auditors to determine upon the applications for relief. § 3. The board of town auditors, of the several towns in the said county, shall meet at some convenient place, to be designated by the supervisor immediately after the passage of this act, to receive and determine upon applications for the relief of the families of volunteers residing in such town, and they shall make a list of the families requiring aid, and determine upon the amount to be paid to each family, and furnish the supervisor **Supervisors to pay the warrants drawn by town board.** with a copy of such list, and shall draw their warrants upon the supervisor from time to time, in favor of and deliver the same to the person or family requiring aid, and the supervisor shall pay the amount of such warrants out of the relief fund, so as aforesaid to be held by him, and in all cases take a receipt for the amount paid from the person in whose favor such warrant shall be drawn. The board of town auditors may at any time correct, alter or modify such list.

Inhabitants to dispose by vote of any portion not used. § 4 In case no part of such moneys or only a part thereof shall be expended by the respective towns in relieving the families of volunteers, then the electors of said towns, at their annual town meetings, may, by vote, appropriate said moneys, or any portion thereof, to any purpose for which said towns are now authorized by law to levy a tax, or such towns may. by vote, appropriate said moneys, or any part thereof, in such amounts as they may deem proper, to any other town or towns in said county for the relief of the families of volunteers residing in such other town or towns, or, the said electors, at such meeting, may, by vote, reimburse any person or persons any moneys already advanced by him or them to the credit of such town or towns for the relief of such families out of said fund.

Supervisors to report annually amount of moneys expended. § 5. The supervisors of the respective towns shall report, upon oath, at the next annual town meeting of their respective towns, and thereafter annually, the amount of moneys received pursuant to the provisions of this act. And if he has paid or disposed of the same, or any part thereof, and how disposed of, and for what purpose, and the balance, if any, on hand.

§ 6. The board of supervisors of the county of Westchester shall appropriate the sum of ten thousand dollars annually for the purpose of paying said bonds, until the whole amount thereof shall be paid, and they shall also appropriate an annual amount sufficient to pay the interest thereon. *Board of supervisors to appropriate $10,000 annually for payment of bonds.*

§ 7. The services required to be performed by any officer under this act shall be rendered without any fee or reward therefor, except that the actual expenses incurred may be audited by the board of supervisors, and by them directed to be paid. *No fees for services.*

§ 8. The several supervisors shall give a bond to the county treasurer in a penalty double the amount received by them respectively, with sufficient sureties, to be approved by such treasurer, conditioned for the faithful performance of their respective duties under this act, before said treasurer shall deliver said bonds. *Supervisors to give bonds for performance of this act.*

§ 9. This act shall take effect immediately.

Chap. 39.

AN ACT in relation to Vassar Female College.

Passed March 22, 1862; three-fifths being present.

The People of the State of New York, represented in Senate and Assembly do enact as follows:

SECTION 1. The real and personal property of Vassar Female College, to the exent it is by its act of incorporation authorized to hold the same, is hereby exempted from taxation.

§ 2. This act shall take effect immediately.

Chap. 40.

AN ACT to legalize the official acts of Nathan T. Young as justice of the peace.

Passed March 22, 1862.

The People of the State of New York, represented in Senate and Assembly, do enact as follows:

SECTION 1. All the official acts of Nathan T. Young, as a justice of the peace of the town of Rathbonè in the county of Steuben, are hereby declared to be as valid and effectual for all purposes as if said Nathan T. Young had been duly elected and qualified as a justice of the peace, according to law.

§ 2. This act shall take effect immediately.

Chap. 41.

AN ACT in relation to the corporation called the Baptist Missionary Convention of the State of New York.

Passed March 22, 1862.

The People of the State of New York, represented in Senate, and Assembly do enact as follows:

Time of existence continued.
SECTION 1. The corporation called the Baptist Missionary Convention of the State of New York, is hereby continued for the term of twenty-five years from and after the twenty-eighth day of March, eighteen hundred and sixty-two, with the same powers which it now possesses, and subject to the same liabilities and restrictions to which it is now subject.

Power to hold by gift, devise, &c.
§ 2. The corporation shall have authority to take and hold by gift, bequest, devise or grant any real or personal property, subject to the provisions of law relating to bequests and devises to religious societies, and to use and dispose of the same; and all real or personal property heretofore bequeathed and devised to said corporation, shall be deemed and become vested in said corpo-

ration, which is hereby authorized to take and hold the same subject to the provisions of law relating to bequests and devises to religious societies. But the whole amount of the real property held by the said corporation shall not exceed the yearly income of five thousand dollars.

§ 3. The legislature may at any time annul or repeal this act.

§ 4. This act shall take effect immediately.

Chap. 42.

AN ACT to authorize the city of Poughkeepsie to borrow money to pay the debt incurred for the relief of the families of soldiers, to pay the floating debt of said city, and for other specified purposes.

Passed March 22, 1862; three-fifths being present.

The People of the State of New York, represented in Senate and Assembly, do enact as follows:

SECTION 1. The common council of the city of Poughkeepsie is hereby authorized to borrow on the credit of said city, the sum of four thousand one hundred dollars, to be applied to the debt already incurred by said city for the relief of the families of soldiers, and also such further sums as from time to time may be needed for the relief of soldiers from said city who have heretofore enlisted in the service of the United States, not exceeding however ten thousand dollars in the whole, including the debt aforesaid.

$4,000 to be borrowed for relief of families of volunteers.

§ 2. The common council of said city is also hereby authorized to borrow on the credit of the said city the further sum of twenty-three thousand five hundred and ninety-seven dollars and seventy cents, to be applied as follows: Five thousand two hundred dollars thereof to the payment of the floating debt of said city (including a note given on its behalf by the mayor for five thousand dollars and interest,) and eighteen thousand three hundred and ninety-seven dollars and seventy cents thereof to the payment of the contingent expenses of said city

To borrow $28,000 to pay floating and other debts of the city.

18

during the current fiscal year, and the interest and installments of its funded debt falling due within the same period.

To issue certificates of indebtedness, payable annually with interest. § 3. For the moneys borrowed pursuant to the first section of this act the said common council is hereby authorized to issue bonds or certificates of indebtedness in the name and under the seal of said city. and signed by the mayor and chamberlain, in sums of five hundred dollars each payable on the first days of March in each year hereafter, with interest semi-annually on the first days of March and September, but if there be any fractional part less than five hundred dollars of the amount so borrowed, a like bond or certificate, drawing interest semi-annually as above, shall be issued therefor payable one year after the last of the others issued for the same purpose shall fall due.

§ 4 For the moneys borrowed pursuant to the second section of this act, the said common council is hereby authorized to issue bonds or certificates of indebtedness in the name and under the seal of the said city, and signed by the mayor and chamberlain, in sums of one thousand dollars each, payable one on the first day of March in each year hereafter, with interest semi-annually on the first days of March and September : but for the fractional sum of three hundred and ninety-seven dollars and seventy cents, part of the last said moneys so borrowed, a like bond or certificate shall be issued payable one year after the last of the others issued for the same purpose shall fall due.

Tax to be levied for payment of principal and interest. § 5. Due provision by tax shall be made in each year by the said common council for the payment of the interest and principal falling due on all said bonds or certificates during the next ensuing fiscal year, and such interest and principal shall be assessed, levied and raised in the same manner as any other public or general tax of said city and in conjunction with the general taxes of said city.

§ 6. This act shall take effect immediately.

Chap. 43.

AN ACT to authorize attorneys of the Supreme Court of this State residing in adjoining States, to practice in the Courts of this State.

Passed March 22, 1862.

The People of the State of New York, represented in Senate and Assembly, do enact as follows :

SECTION 1. Any regularly admitted and licensed attorney of the Supreme Court of this State, and whose only office for the transaction of law business is within this state, may practice as such attorney in any of the courts of this State notwithstanding he may reside in a state adjoining the state of New York, provided that this act shall extend only to attorneys who have been heretofore admitted to practice in the Courts of this State, and who reside out of the State of New York, and that service of papers which might according to the practice of the Courts of this State, be made upon said attorney at his residence, if the same were within the state of New York, shall be sufficient if made upon him by depositing the same in the post office in the city or town wherein his said office is located, directed to said attorney at his office, and paying the postage thereon ; and such service shall be equivalent to personal service at the office of such attorney.

§ 2. This act shall take effect immediately.

Chap. 44.

AN ACT to amend an act entitled "An act to amend an act entitled 'An act for the better regulation of the firemen in the city of New York,' passed March second eighteen hundred sixty-one."

Passed March 22, 1862 ; three-fifths being present.

The 'People of the State of New York, represented in Senate and Assembly, do enact as follows :

SECTION 1. Section four of the " Act to amend, an act entitled an act for the better regulation of the firemen in the city of New York, passed March second eighteen hundred and sixty-one " is hereby amended so as to read as follows :

Extending powers of commissioners.

" Section eleven of said act shall read as follows: The said commissioners shall have cognizance of all complaints against volunteer firemen for riotous or disorderly conduct at fires, or alarms of fire or for violation of any of the state or city laws, respecting the firemen of the city of New York ; they shall diligently enquire into the same, and if the parties so charged shall be proved guilty the said commissioners are hereby empowered to suspend expel or disband such firemen and the said commissioners or a majority thereof shall have power to alter or change the entry of expulsion on the firemen's register to " resignation," and also to alter, change or modify any judgment or decree of suspension subject to the approval of the board of appeals or a majority thereof.

§ 2. All acts or parts of acts inconsistent with this act are hereby repealed.

§ 3 . This act shall take effect immediately.

Chap. 45.

AN ACT to amend an act entitled "An act for
the more effectual draining of certain swamps
and low lands in the towns of Pine Plains and
Stanford in the county of Dutchess," passed
April fourteenth, eighteen hundred and fifty-
nine.

Passed March 22, 1862; three-fifths being present.

*The People of the State of New York, represented in
Senate and Assembly, do enact as follows :*

SECTION 1. The whole amount to be assessed by the provisions of the act entitled "An act for the more effectual draining of certain swamp and low lands in the towns of Pine Plains and Stanford in the county of Dutchess, passed April fourteenth, eighteen hundred and fifty nine," shall not exceed the sum of two thousand dollars, unless by the direction and consent of two thirds of the persons owning land subject to assessment, at a special meeting called for that purpose or at the regular annual meeting, when a further sum, not exeeding five hundred dollars may be raised. *Not to exceed $2,000 to be assessed, unless by a special meeting.*

§ 2. The assessment heretofore made by the commissioners shall be given up and cancelled, and in the place thereof, the commissioners shall make a re-assessment and before making the same, shall cause a survey to be made of the lands subject to assessment, and shall cause notices to be posted up in three public places, in the vicinity where the persons interested reside, at least six days previous thereto, of the time and place of making such re-assessment, all persons who shall have paid any portion of the former assessment shall be credited for such sum in the collection of the re-assessment. *New assessment to be made.*

§ 3. That a tax be raised and levied upon all the proprietors of such lands, to be taxed for the purpose of blasting and cleaning out the rocks in the lower part of the ditch, and that each person have the right at his election in lowering and cleaning out the ditch on his own land, in the time and manner directed by the commissioners and that those persons whose lands do not *Persons may perform the labor on their own lands.*

adjoin said ditch may work out their assessment upon such part as shall be directed by the commissioners, and in case any person shall refuse or neglect to work out his assessment, then the same shall be collected in money, the same as any other assessment.

Qualifica-
tions of
those enti-
tled to vote. § 4. That the qualifications of voters at all future meetings shall be regulated according to the lands owned by them subject to taxation, as appears by the last assessment of the commissioners, each person holding two acres of said land, to have one vote, and one vote in addition for every two acres held by such person, but no person to be entitled to more than twenty-five votes at any election ; and all that portion of section eight of said act as follows : "Every person owning lands bene-fitted by said act shall be entitled to one vote, in case the person so offering to vote shall be challenged, he shall swear he does own such lands," is hereby repealed.

Commis-
sioners to
report annu-
ally. § 5. That the commissioners annually elected shall render an account of their proceedings to the proprietors at each annual election, and shall then deliver the moneys and their accounts and papers in relation to their trust, to the commissioners who shall be elected to succeed them.

§ 6. This act shall take effect immediately.

Chap. 46.

AN ACT to improve the Central Park in the city of New York.

Passed March 25, 1862 ; three-fifths being present.

The People of the State of New York, represented in Senate and Assembly, do enact as follows :

Appropri-
ating N. Y.
State Arse-
nal building
for museum
and gallery. SECTION 1. The commissioners of the Central Park in the city of New York are hereby authorized to set apart and appropriate to the New York Historical Society the building within said Park heretofore known as the New York State Arsenal, together with such grounds adjoining the same as the said commissioners may de-termine to be necessary and proper for the purpose of establishing and maintaining therein by the said Society

a museum of antiquities and science and a gallery of art.

§ 2. The expense of arranging and fitting up of the said arsenal building for the use and purpose aforesaid shall be borne by the said New York Historical Society, and the said society shall have the right, at its own expense, to add to, enlarge, or if need be to take down the present building, and erect another on the ground so set apart, and appropriated ; the plan of such addition or new building having been first submitted to and approved by the commissioners of the said park. Power to alter the buildings.

§ 3. The museum and gallery contemplated in the first section of this act, when so established, shall be accessible to the public under proper regulations, to be adopted by the said society, approved by the said commissioners, and not inconsistent with the proper administration and management of the said park. Gallery to be accessible to the public.

§ 4. The evidence of setting apart and appropriation of the said arsenal building and grounds within the said park to the said New York Historical Society for the purpose aforesaid shall be a resolution to that effect adopted by the board of said commissioners, duly acknowledged by its president and recorded in the office of the register of the city and county of New York. Evidence of appropriation.

§ 5. If the said New York Historical Society shall so establish their said museum of antiquities and science and gallery of art, then so long as they shall continue there to maintain the same, they shall occupy and enjoy the said building and grounds thus set apart and appropriated to them for the purpose aforesaid free from any rent, assessment, or charge, whatever therefor, and if the said society shall at any time hereafter for any cause, discontinue their said museum of antiquities and science and gallery of art in the said arsenal building or on the said grounds, then the said arsenal building and any building whatever erected under the provision of this act, and the said grounds before set apart and appropriated, shall revert to the said Central Park, for the general purposes thereof; but the said society shall in such case be permitted to remove therefrom the said museum of antiquities and science and gallery of art, and all its other property. Buildings to revert to the Central Park.

§ 6. The Legislature may at any time alter, repeal or amend this act.

§ 7. This act shall take effect immediately.

Chap. 47.

AN ACT to amend the charter of the village of Albion.

Passed March 26, 1862; three-fifths being present.

The People of the State of New York, represented in Senate and Assembly, do enact as follows:

SECTION 1. Subdivision twenty-seven of section forty-one of An act entitled "An act to condense and amend the several acts relating to the village of Albion," passed April first eighteen hundred and forty-two is hereby amended so as to read as follows:

Three commissioners of the cemetery to be appointed by trustees.

§ 27. Relative to burying grounds and cemeteries and the manner of burying the dead in said village and in burying grounds that may be procured for that purpose by said village; the trustees shall have power to appoint three commissioners of the cemetery, one to hold his office for one year, one for two years, and one for three years, to be designated by the said trustees, and on the expiration of the term of office of each of such commissioners, to appoint some suitable person in his place, who shall hold his office for three years, excepting as hereinafter provided; the term of office of the first commissioners to be appointed to commence on the first Monday in May next, and in case of the death, resignation or removal from the village of any such commissioner or in case of his neglect or refusal to serve, the said trustees may appoint some other person in his place and fill any vacancy that may occur; the said commissioners

To have management of cemetery grounds.

shall have the supervision and management of the cemetery grounds belonging to said village; they shall also have power to employ a keeper and such assistants as may be necessary, to improve and keep in order the said grounds, to sell cemetery lots, collect pay therefor, and do all such other acts and things in relation to said grounds, as may be deemed proper, subject, however, to such rules and regulations as may be adopted by the trustees of the village. The compensation of such commissioners, keeper, or other employees on said grounds, to be determined by the said trustees.

§ 2. Subdivision twenty-eight of the same section of said act is hereby amended so as to read as follows:

§ 28. To provide for grading and leveling any public squares or grounds in said village, and for setting and protecting ornamental and shade trees. The trustees shall have power to let by contract to the lowest responsible bidder, any such improvements, and any work or labor upon the streets, lanes and alleys in said village, as they may deem for the advantage of said village; such improvements as the trustees shall not let by contract, as aforesaid, to be done under the supervision of the street commissioners, subject to the control and direction of the trustees.

§ 3. This act shall take effect immediately.

Trustees to let by contract the labor done on streets.

Chap. 48.

AN ACT to amend the act entitled "An act to provide for the incorporation of villages," passed December seventh, eighteen hundred and forty-seven, so far as relates to the village of Boonville in the county of Oneida.

Passed March 26, 1862; three-fifths being present.

The People of the State of New York, represented in Senate and Assembly, do enact as follows :

TITLE I.

SECTION 1. The corporation of the village of Boonville in the county of Oneida is hereby deemed and declared a valid corporation, and the trustees of said corporation elected March, eighteen hundred and sixty-one, are deemed and declared the trustees of said corporation, and their acts from the time of their election are hereby legalized.

Legalizing acts of trustees.

§ 2. All that part of the village of Boonville included within the bounds of the said village of Boonville is hereby declared a separate road district, and the trustees of said village shall possess and exercise all the power, and be subject to all the duties and liabilities of commissioners and overseers of highways in like cases.

A separate road district.

19

TITLE II.

OF VILLAGE OFFICERS—THEIR ELECTION AND APPOINTMENT

List of officers. § 1. There shall be elected hereafter, by ballot, within and for said village, by the electors residing therein, the following officers : A president of said village, five trustees, three assessors, a police justice, a collector, a treasurer, and a clerk. The persons so elected shall be inhabitants and electors of said village.

Annual election. § 2. The annual election for village officers shall be held on the last Tuesday in February in each year, at such place within said village as the trustees shall appoint, and the polls of every such election shall remain open from one to four o'clock of the same day. The trustees for the time being shall preside at and be inspectors of all elections in and for said village, and certify the result thereof. The provisions of the act entitled "An act respecting elections other than for military and town officers," passed April fifth, eighteen hundred and forty-two, with the amendments and additions thereto, shall be applicable to the elections held under this act, except so far as they are inconsistent with the provisions of this act.

Canvass of votes. § 3. Upon the canvass of the votes taken at any such election being completed, the inspectors thereof shall thereon determine who, by a plurality of votes, are elected to fill the offices voted for, and shall make and subscribe a certificate thereof on the village records. In case there shall be a tie in the vote for any elective office, the trustees shall appoint a special election, to be held not less than three nor more than eight days thereafter, for the election of such officer, and the clerk of said village shall give immediate notice thereof, and of the time and place of such election, by posting written or printed notices thereof in at least five of the most public places in the said village.

Present officers to hold over. § 4. The present officers of said village shall hold their offices until the first board of trustees elected under this act shall become organized, and all officers elected under this act shall enter on the duties of their offices on the Tuesday next following their election, and shall continue in office until the Tuesday following the next annual election of officers, and until their successors are elected and qualified. It shall be the duty of the clerk of the village to give notice of each annual election, and of the place at which the same is appointed to be held, by posting in a conspicuous place a notice thereof in five public places in said village, at least ten days before the election. But the first election under this act shall be held on the first Tuesday of May, one thousand eight hundred and sixty-two, and all subsequent elections shall be held on the last Tuesday of February in each year. At any meeting of the electors of said village to elect village officers, or at any other meeting of such electors legally called and held, the electors attending such meeting may, by resolution, direct the trustees to cause to be raised by general tax on the taxable property liable to be assessed for taxes in said village, any sum not exceeding the sum of fifteen hundred dollars. And the electors attending any such meeting may also by resolution, direct the trustees to cause sidewalks to be made or repaired on any public street or road in said village, or any part of any such street or road; and in every such resolution such street or road, or part of such street or road, and the materials with which such sidewalk shall be made or repaired shall be specified.

§ 5. The trustees shall annually appoint a street commissioner, a chief engineer of the fire department, and two assistant engineers, who shall respectively hold their offices during the pleasure of the trustees. Resignation of office may be made to the trustees The removal of any village officer from the village shall vacate his office. A vacancy in any elective office caused by removal, death, resignation or otherwise, may be filled by the trustees by appointment, and the person so appointed shall hold the office until the Tuesday succeeding the next annual election.

§ 6. The clerk of the village shall, immediately after any election or appointment to office as aforesaid, notify in writing every person so elected or appointed of his election or appointment. The several persons so elected or appointed shall, within six days thereafter and before entering on the duties of their respective offices, take the oath of office prescribed by the constitution of this state, and file the same with the clerk. Any person elected or appointed to any office, except that of collector, treasurer. street commissioner, or police justice, who shall neglect so to do, shall forfeit for the use of the village, the sum of ten dollars, and his office shall be deemed to be vacant. The treasurer, collector, and street commissioner shall, before entering on the duties of their respective offices, each execute and file with the village clerk a bond in such penalty as the trustees shall require, and with such sureties as shall be approved by the president, conditioned that he will faithfully execute the duties of his office, and will duly pay over or account for all moneys received by him in his official capacity; and a neglect to file such bond within ten days after being required so to do by the trustees, shall be deemed to vacate the office of the person so neglecting.

§ 7. The president, trustees, treasurer, chief engineer and assistants, shall receive no compensation for their services; the compensation of the clerk, street commissioner, and assessors, shall be determined by the trustees; and the compensation of the street commissioner shall not exceed two dollars for each day's actual service by him.

TITLE III.

OF THE POWERS AND DUTIES OF THE PRESIDENT.

§ 1. The president shall be the chief executive officer of the village; he shall preside at the meetings of the trustees; he shall only vote when there is a tie, but he may submit propositions for the action of the trustees; and he shall see that the provisions of this act and the by-laws of the village are faithfully executed, and shall receive complaints and institute prosecutions for their violation; he shall have power, and it shall be his duty to suspend, until the next meeting of the board of trustees, the operation of any resolution or ordinance of the trustees, by his orders to be entered on the journal, with his reasons therefor, when it is, in his judgment, in violation of law, or appropriates money, or involves expenditures improvidently, but if, at such next or any subsequent meeting within sixty days thereafter, on reconsideration of such resolution or ordinance, a majority of all the trustees elected shall agree to pass the same, it shall take effect as a resolution or ordinance of the village; in all such cases the votes shall be determined by the yeas and nays, and the names of the persons voting for and against the passage of the measure shall be entered on the journal. The president, on behalf of the village, shall execute all laws, licenses, contracts, and other papers to be executed as the act of the village, when so authorized by the trustees.

§ 2. The president shall annually, ten days before the annual election, prepare a report of the financial transactions of the village for the previous year, showing:

1. All moneys received, and from what sources.

2. All payments, specifying each item.

3. The entire indebtedness of the village, and for what purpose contracted.

§ 3. The president's report shall be submitted to a meeting of the trustees, at least ten days before the annual election.

§ 4. The president may administer oaths required by this act to be taken.

§ 5. The president shall have power, and it shall be his duty, to suppress riots, and to order and compel tumultuous assemblies to disperse. And he shall have the same power for the purpose, as is given by law to sheriffs, in cases to resistance to process.

TITLE IV.

OF THE POWERS AND DUTIES OF THE TRUSTEES.

§ 1. The board of trustees shall hold meetings pursuant to adjournment, or upon a call by the president or any three trustees; and it shall be the duty of the president or trustees calling a meeting to cause to be notified, all the trustees, by serving the same on the trustees personally, or by leaving the same at their residence with some person of mature age on the premises. Votes upon any question shall be taken by ayes and nays whenever required by the president or by any trustee.

§ 2. In the absence of the president, any one of the trustees may be appointed chairman for the time. A majority of the board shall constitute a quorum for the transaction of business.

§ 3. It shall be the duty of the trustees, and they shall have the power:

1. To appoint a police constable, and such other subordinate officers as they shall deem necessary, and they shall have the power to remove such officers at pleasure.

Care of public property.   2. To provide for the care, custody and preservation of the public property, records and papers of the village.

Fire department.   3. To organize and keep under good and efficient organization, a fire department.

Audit accounts.   4. To examine all accounts and claims against the village, and allow such as are just and legal.

Examine clerk's and treasurer's accounts.   5. To prescribe the manner in which the treasurer shall keep the accounts and vouchers of his office, and also the manner in which the clerk shall keep the records and papers of the village, and to examine such accounts, vouchers and records from time to time, in order to detect errors therein.

For prevention of fires.   6. To prevent use of any unsafe fireplaces, stoves, chimneys, stove pipes, smoke houses, or repository of ashes, and to compel the same to be put in safe condition, and to direct and authorize the engineers from time to time to inspect in the day time every house and lot in the village, in relation to its security against fire.

Exercise powers of commissioners of highways.   7. To exercise the powers and duties of commissioners of highways of towns within the limits of the village, so far as those duties are consistent with other parts of this act and are applicable to the village, and to direct the application of the highway tax and labor assessed on the persons and property within the village, to the grading, planking, draining, and otherwise improving the highways in such places within the village or leading to it, as they may deem best, and also direct the application of a part thereof to the grading of any public grounds, and the planting and securing trees thereon, and the construction and repairing of sewers.

Suppress houses of ill fame and gambling.   8. To suppress disorderly houses, and houses of ill fame.

   9. To restrain and prevent and suppress gaming houses, billiard tables, and all instruments and devices for gaming.

Slaughter houses.   10. To direct and control the location of all slaughter-houses, markets, or shops for the selling of meat, houses

Gunpowder. for storing gunpowder and other combustible and explosive substances, and to regulate the keeping selling, or conveying thereof.

Unwholesome or nauseous substances.   11. To prohibit the depositing, and prevent the keeping of any unwholesome or nauseous substance, and to compel the cleaning of any filthy place or dwelling.

Racing in the streets.   12. To prohibit horse racing and immoderate driving in the streets; to prevent the incumbering of the streets, crosswalks and sidewalks in said village, and to compel every person to clear the dirt and obstructions from off ^{Obstructing sidewalks.} the sidewalk in front of the premises owned or occupied in whole or in part by such person, and to provide for the cleaning off the snow from off the crosswalks and sidewalks at such places and in such manner as they shall deem best.

13. To prevent and regulate the ringing or tolling of ^{Tolling of bells and improper noises.} bells, except those of railroad engines, blowing of horns or crying of goods and wares, firing of guns, gunpowder or other explosive compounds, and the making of any improper noise which may tend to disturb the peace of the village, and to regulate the sale or exposure to sale of fire crackers, rockets, squibs, or other explosive compounds.

14. To restrain and punish vagrants, mendicants, and ^{Punish vagrants and others.} persons soliciting alms; keepers of houses of ill fame, common prostitutes and disorderly persons, and to prevent and punish drunkenness and disorderly or immoral conduct in public streets and places.

15. To regulate and determine the places of bathing in ^{Bathing.} the river, canal, or other waters within the village.

16. To regulate the burial of the dead and protect the ^{Burial of dead.} public cemeteries.

17. To perform all the duties imposed upon them by this act, or by any law of the state.

§ 4. The trustees shall have power in their discretion:

1. To establish and regulate a public pound, and appoint and define the duties of a pound-master, so that ^{Establish a pound.} the same be not inconsistent with the laws of this state.

2. To restrain horses, cattle, sheep and swine from ^{Restrain horses and cattle.} going at large in the streets, under a penalty not exceeding five dollars for each animal, and to cause any such animals to be impounded or sold, as may be provided by the by-laws to prevent them from going at large, and to satisfy such penalty and the · expenses, the owner or owners of any such animals shall be liable for such penalty.

3. To cause buildings and other structures encroaching on the streets, to be removed at the expense of the ^{Remove encroachments} owners or occupants thereof, and to issue their warrant against any such owner or occupant to collect the necessary expense of such removal.

4. To permit building material to be deposited on the street in front of any lot, to such extent and for such a time as they may prescribe.

Nuisances. 5. To determine the existence of a public nuisance in any part of the village, and to compel its removal or abatement, and if not done within such time as the trustees may allow, to cause the same to be removed or abated at the expense of the village, and to declare such expense to be a lien on the lot whence the nuisance was removed or whereon it was abated, and to enforce the collection thereof by leasing or selling the premises in the manner prescribed in this act for the collection of taxes, or by action against the owner or occupant of the lot, or against any person who may have caused or maintained such nuisance.

6. To prohibit the flying of kites, playing ball, rolling hoops, or sliding down hill in any specified street or parts of said village.

Appoint firemen. 7. To appoint and dismiss firemen, including members of fire engines and hook and ladder and hose companies, and to make regulations for their conduct and government.

Name streets. 8. To give names to the streets, and numbers to the lots and tenements, and to change the same.

Prosecute. 9. To cause prosecutions upon any contract or liability in which the village is interested, or for fines and penalties imposed by this act, or by any by-law of the village, and to enforce the collection thereof, or to remit the same or any part thereof.

Employ attorneys. 10. To employ attorneys in the prosecution or defence of any action by or against the village, or for the transaction of any business of the village requiring professional skill.

Public wells. 11. To establish and regulate public wells, pumps, aqueducts and reservoirs.

Lighting streets. 12. To provide for lighting the streets of said village, and to protect the public lamps.

Dogs. 13. To make regulations for taxing and confining dogs, and for destroying such as may be found running at large, contrary to any ordinance.

Shows. 14. To prohibit all exhibitions of any natural or artificial curiosity, caravans, circuses, theatrical and other shows or exhibitions or performances for money, within the bounds of the village; and if the trustees shall deem advisable, to license the same on payment of such sum as they shall specify on granting such license.

15. To do any act necessary to carry into effect any resolution, ordinance, or other proceeding which they are authorized to adopt by this act or by any statute.

§ 5. The trustees may make, amend and repeal all such by-laws, ordinances, and police regulations, not contrary to the laws of this state, as may be necessary or proper to carry into effect the provisions of this act, and of any other laws applicable to said village, and to the power vested in any officer thereof; and may prescribe penalties not exceeding twenty-five dollars, for the violation of any such by-law or ordinance. Every such by-law or ordinance shall be published at least three weeks by posting the same in a conspicuous place in five public places in said village, or by publishing the same two weeks successively, once in each week, in the newspapers printed in the village of Boonville, and shall not take effect until after such publication. Proof of such publication, by the affidavit of the printer of such paper, his foreman, or clerk, or of the person who posted the same, shall be filed with the clerk of the village, and shall be prima facie evidence of such publication or posting. *Make by-laws.*

§ 6. The trustees shall have power, from time to time, to prescribe the duties of the several officers appointed by them, subject to the provisions of this act. *Prescribe duties of officers.*

§ 7. No trustee shall be appointed to any office by the board of trustees, nor shall the president or any trustee be interested in any contract made with the corporation, and any contract made in violation of this provision shall be void. *Not be interested in contracts.*

§ 8. The trustees shall have power to apply any and all moneys raised by any tax in said village, to the purchasing of any personal property for the use of said village, and to the defraying the necessary expenses of the corporation, and also to the leasing or purchasing of so much land as may be necessary for the erection of engine houses, a house for the confinement of criminal or disorderly persons and vagrants, a public pound, public hay scales, and to the building and keeping in repair public wells, cisterns and reservoirs within said village, and the water pipes and fixtures connected therewith, and to the making and maintaining crosswalks and light- *Necessary expenses.*

20

ing the streets in said village, and to such other purposes as the trustees in their discretion shall deem necessary and for the interest of the said village.

Grade walks and streets. § 9. The said trustees shall likewise have power to cause the sidewalks, streets and highways within said village to be leveled, raised, graveled, planked and repaired, and the sidewalks ornamented with trees, and to compel the owners and occupants of any lands or lots adjoining such sidewalk, to make such improvement upon the sidewalk as aforesaid in front of said land or lot, to determine and prescribe the manner of doing the same, and the materials to be used therein, and the quality of such materials; and in case the owner or owners, occupant or occupants of any such land or lot should neglect or refuse to complete the said required improvements to the sidewalks within such reasonable time as shall be required by the trustees, the said trustees may cause such improvements to such sidewalks to be made or completed, and the expense thereof may be by them assessed on such owner or owners, occupant or occupants so neglecting or refusing, and be collected by warrant to be issued by the president and trustees, in the same manner as other taxes are directed to be collected by this act; and in case such tax or assessment shall not be paid or collected the trustees may cause such real estate to be leased or sold for payment and collection of such assessment and expenses of sale, in the same manner and with the effect and subject to the provisions of sections thirty-five, thirty-six, thirty-seven, thirty-eight, thirty-nine.

May levy a tax for certain purposes. § 10. The trustees shall have discretionary power to raise, levy and collect from the taxable property in said village, any sum not exceeding three hundred dollars, in any one year, which they shall deem necessary for any of the purposes mentioned in section twenty-one of this act, the same to be assessed and collected in the same manner prescribed for the assessment and collection of other taxes directed or authorized to be raised, levied, assessed and collected, by and under this act.

TITLE V.

DUTIES OF THE TREASURER AND CLERK.

Treasurer. § 1. The treasurer shall receive all moneys belonging to the village, and shall pay out the same on the order of the president countersigned by the clerk. No such order shall be given except in pursuance of a resolution of the board of trustees, duly entered on the village records, specifying the amount for which such order is directed to be issued, to whom, and what for.

§ 2. The treasurer shall, twenty days before each annual election, present to the president a statement showing the state of the treasury, and the several sums received and paid out during the year, and when received and paid, and from and to whom. He shall deliver to his successor in office, on receiving six days' notice to that effect, all moneys, books, vouchers and papers appertaining to the office. Report annually.

§ 3. The clerk shall attend and act as clerk at all the meetings of the trustees, and record in the proper journals of the village all resolutions, ordinances, directions and determinations adopted at such meetings. He shall also enter in a book, to be called the clerk's minutes, a memorandum of the service of all notices by him, stating the time and manner of service, and of any other acts pertaining to the duties of his office which the trustees may require him to enter. He shall serve all notices and file all papers required by the trustees or by this act to be served or filed, make copies of such assessment rolls and other papers as may be required by the trustees or president, and shall keep in good order the books, records and papers appertaining to his office. When requested by the president or by any trustee, he shall enter in the journals the names of the trustees voting on each side on any question. Within three days after any meeting of the electors of said village shall have voted any tax, he shall furnish to the trustees and treasurer, a certified copy of the resolution or vote raising such tax. Duties of clerk.

§ 4. The entries in the journals and clerk's minutes, or sworn copies thereof, shall for every purpose be presumptive evidence of the facts therein stated.

TITLE VI.

OF THE ENGINEERS AND FIREMEN.

§ 1. The chief engineer of the fire department shall, under the direction of the trustees, have the general superintendence and custody of the fire engines, engine houses, hooks, ladders, hose, public cisterns, and other Duties of chief engineer, conveniences for the prevention and extinguishment of fires. It shall be his duty to see that the same are kept in proper order, and to make detailed reports to the president of the village of the state of that department, one week before each annual meeting, and to make like reports to the trustees as often as they may require.

§ 2. It shall be the duty of the chief engineer to be present at fires and take command of the fire companies, hose companies, and hook and ladder companies, and have the general control of the apparatus for extinguishing fires.

Of assistant engineer.

§ 3. The assistant engineer shall aid the chief engineer at all fires; and in case of the absence of the chief engineer, the duties and powers of the office shall be exercised by the first assistant engineer, or, in his absence, by the second assistant engineer.

May require bystanders to assist at fires.

§ 4. The president or any engineer or trustee may keep all idle or suspicious persons away from the vicinity of any fire, and may require the inhabitants of said village, or any bystanders to form ranks or lines to carry water for the extinguishing of any fires in said village, and to aid the firemen in working their engines, hooks and ladders and hose, and to aid in removing or protecting any property thereat; and any person refusing to obey such order shall be subject to a fine of three dollars, to be sued for and recovered in the name of the corporation and paid to such fire company as the chief engineer may direct.

Fire buckets.

§ 5. The trustees shall require the inhabitants of said village to keep a certain number of fire buckets, and in such manner as they shall prescribe, and regulate the use of them in case of fire.

Firemen.

§ 6. The present firemen of the village of Boonville shall continue firemen of said village, subject to removal by the trustees. The firemen of said village shall, during the term of service, be exempted from serving on juries and in the militia, except in cases of war, insurrection, or invasion.

Exempt from jury duty.

Evidence of term of service.

§ 7. The name of each fireman, with the date of his appointment, and term of service, shall be registered with the clerk of the village, in a book to be kept for that purpose; and the only evidence necessary to entitle a fireman to his exemption, shall be the certificate of the president and clerk of the village, under the seal of the village, which shall be given without fee.

TITLE VII.

OF THE ASSESSMENT AND COLLECTION OF TAXES.

§ 1. It shall be the duty of the assessors, in each year, *Prepare an assessment roll.* to prepare an assessment roll of the property liable to taxation in said village, and to complete the same, in all respects, as nearly as practicable, in the manner prescribed by law in relation to town assessors, and to deliver the same to the clerk of the village, within thirty days after the election; and the assessors are hereby vested with the same powers, in respect to assessment, as town assessors, including the power to administer oaths, and to correct valuations, on the application of persons interested. The valuations of taxable property, included in any such assessment roll, shall be ascertained, as far as possible, from the last assessment roll of the town of Boonville, and no person shall be entitled to any reduction in the valuation of such property, as so ascertained, unless he shall give notice of his claim to such reduction to the assessors, before the tax roll shall be made out.

§ 2. When the trustees shall have received from the clerk a certified copy of the resolution or vote of the electors of said village, at any meeting legally held by them, directing any tax to be raised, they shall make out a roll under their hands, apportioning the sum of money to be raised for the taxable property within the village, according to the assessment roll made by the assessors, and the trustees shall, by warrant, authorize *Trustees issue warrant for collection of tax.* the collector, under the hands of the president and trustees, to collect the said tax, together with the percentage thereon, allowed by law for his fees, and to pay the said tax to the treasurer of the village, within thirty days from the date of said warrant. The tax roll shall then be delivered by the president of the village to the collector, who shall immediately post notices thereof in at least ten public places in said village, which notices shall state that any person who shall pay his tax within fifteen days from the date of said notices, shall be charged with one per cent collector's fees thereon only, and that *Collectors' fees.* the collector will attend at a place in said village (to be specified), on two days (to be specified), within the fifteen days for the purpose of receiving payment of taxes, and he shall attend at such time and place accordingly;

and any person or corporation paying the amount of his
or its tax within fifteen days, shall be charged with one
per cent. thereon, for the fees of the collector, and no
more. After the expiration of the fifteen days, the collector shall proceed to collect the unpaid taxes in said
roll specified, with five per cent. thereon for his fees, in
the same manner as is now provided by law for the collection of town and county taxes, and with the like
power and authority as collectors of towns, and shall
pay the said tax to the treasurer, at the time specified
in his warrant.

Trustees
may renew
warrants.

§ 3. The trustees may, from time to time, renew any
warrant issued for the collection of any tax or assessment, whenever any tax or assessment shall be returned
uncollected, or issue a new warrant for the collection
thereof, and in such renewal or new warrant, specify the
time when said warrant shall be returned.

Proceeding
in case of
non-pay-
ment of tax.

§ 4. Whenever any person or corporation, upon whose
real estate a tax or assessment shall be imposed or
assessed in pursuance of this act, shall refuse or neglect
to pay the same within the life of the warrant issued for
the collection thereof, and there shall be no sufficient
personal property of such person or corporation found
within the limits of said village, whereof the same can
be levied and collected, the collector holding such warrant shall make return thereof, under oath, subscribed
by him to the trustees; who are, thereupon, hereby
authorized to cause the real estate on which such tax or
assessment was imposed or assessed, to be sold at public
auction, for a term of time, for the payment of such tax
or assessment, giving six weeks notice of such sale in a
newspaper, published in the village of Boonville, having
the largest circulation in said village, and serving personal notice on the owner of such real estate, if he be a
resident of said village, and if not a resident, then serving notice by mail on such owner, if his place of residence be known to said trustees; and the said real estate
shall be sold to the person who will offer to take the
same for the shortest term for the payment of such tax
and assessment, with interest thereon, from the date of
the warrant, and the expenses of the said publication,
notice and sale, which shall be the same as provided by
law in cases of foreclosure of mortgage by advertisement. But the owner, his agent, or his assigns, may,

within three years after such sale, redeem the same by paying or tendering to the purchaser, or his legal representatives, or to the treasurer of the village the amount of the bid at such sale, with interest at the rate of ten per cent per annum. And all the provisions of the act entitled "An act authorizing mortgagees to redeem real estate sold for taxes and assessments," passed May fourteenth, eighteen hundred and forty, shall apply to any such sale, and any mortgagee of the premises, or any part thereof, shall have the benefit of said act, and the notice required to be given by the second section of said act, shall not be given until after the time limited for the owner or his assigns to redeem.

§ 5. When any real estate shall be sold for the collection of any tax or assessment, and the owner thereof, his agents, heirs or assigns shall not within three years thereafter have paid or tendered to the purchaser thereof, or his legal representatives, or to the treasurer of the village the amount of the bid on such sale, and the same shall not have been redeemed by any mortgagee of such real estate within three months after the expiration of three years, as above provided, with interest at the rate of ten per cent. per annum from and after the time of such sale, the trustees shall deliver to the purchaser or his assigns, a certificate of such sale under the seal of the village, and signed by the president and clerk, the execution whereof may be proved and acknowledged in the same manner as a deed, and which may in like manner and with like effect be recorded as other conveyances of real estate. *(margin: Trustees to give certificate of sale.)*

§ 6. The purchaser at any such sale, on receiving such certificate, or his executor, administrator or assigns, may immediately enter into the possession of such real estate, and hold, occupy and enjoy during the time for which it was sold as aforesaid ; and such certificate shall in all courts and places be held presumptive evidence of the right of such purchaser, his heirs or assigns, to the possession of such premises during the time, as against the owner, or those claiming under them ; and all buildings put on the premises during such term by the purchaser, his heirs or assigns, may be removed at or before the expiration thereof. *(margin: Rights of purchaser under the certificate.)*

§ 7. Highway taxes shall be levied and collected in said village as follows :

Highway taxes.

1. The street commissioner, within thirty days after his appointment, shall deliver to the clerk of the village, a list subscribed by him containing the names of all the inhabitants of said village liable to work on the highways.

2. Within forty days after the annual election of officers of said village in each year, the trustees shall ascertain the amount of highway taxes for the ensuing year.

3. Every male inhabitant of said village, being above the age of twenty-one years, (excepting ministers of the gospel, priests of every denomination, paupers, idiots and lunatics,) shall be assessed for one day's labor, reckoning the value of the same at fifty cents.

Assessment of.

4. The trustees shall apportion and assess the residue of said highway taxes reckoning to the value of each day's labor at fifty cents, upon the estate, real and personal of said village, and of corporations and owners of non-resident land therein, as the same shall appear from the last assessment roll of said village.

Collection of.

5. The highway taxes assessed as aforesaid upon property in said village, and against corporations therein, and against individuals whose names are upon said assessment roll, shall be collected in money in the same manner as ordinary taxes within said village, and when collected, the same shall be applied by the trustees as directed in subdivision seven of section sixteen of this act.

Duty of street commissioner.

6. The trustees shall make out and deliver to the street commissioner of said village a list of all persons assessed for highway labor therein, whose names are not on the last assessment roll of said village, and he shall proceed to notify said persons to work out their assessments on the streets and highways within said village, in the same manner as overseers of highways are directed to proceed by the provisions contained in article third, title first, chapter sixteen of the first part of the Revised Statutes. And every person when so notified shall work out his assessment under the direction of the said commissioner, or he may commute for the same at the rate of fifty cents per day, to be paid to the said street commissioner, and to be applied and expended by him under the direction of the trustees, in the improvement of the streets, sidewalks, roads and highways within said village. If any person shall neglect or refuse to labor or commute as aforesaid, he shall be liable to the same penalties, and

to be enforced by the street commissioner in the same manner, as is provided in the article of the Revised Statutes above referred to.

§ 8. The street commissioner shall keep an accurate account of all moneys received by him for commutations or penalties, stating the persons from whom and when received, and the expenditures of such moneys, and shall report the same to the trustees when requested by them, and he shall in all cases, by the first day of January in each year, render and file with the clerk of the village an account in writing and verified by his oath, and showing:

1. The names of all persons contained in the aforesaid list, delivered by him to the trustees.

2. The names of all those who have actually worked on the highways, under his direction, in payment of their poll tax.

3. The names of all those who have been fined, and the sums in which they have been fined.

4. The names of all those who have commuted, the amount received for commutations, and the manner in which the moneys received from fines and commutations have been expended.

TITLE VIII.

OF THE POLICE DEPARTMENT.

§ 1. The police justice shall have the same power and jurisdiction, and be subject to the same duties and liabilities as the justices of the peace in the town of Boonville, and his judgments and proceedings may be reviewed in the same manner as is or may be provided in cases of judgments and proceedings of justices of the peace.

§ 2. Such police justice shall keep an office within said village, and hear all complaints, hold courts, and courts of special sessions, and conduct all other criminal business that may by law be done by a justice of the peace.

§ 3. No justice of the peace of the town of Boonville shall be bound to render any service, or be entitled to receive any fees in criminal cases arising in said village, or in cases for fines or penalties imposed by this act, or the by-laws and regulations of the said village, except during a vacancy in the office of police justice, and except

21

that in case a complainant shall, by his own oath, or that of any other person, prove to such justice of the peace that said police justice is absent from the village, or is sick, or otherwise unable to attend to such application ; then the justice of the peace to whom such application is made shall hear the complaint, and may issue the warrant to apprehend the person charged with the commission of the offence, and shall be entitled to receive therefor the fees allowed by law ; but such warrant shall be made returnable before the said police justice.

Duties of
constables. § 4. It shall be the duty of every constable arresting any person on a criminal warrant, issued by any justice of the peace in said village, to take such prisoner before the said police justice, unless it shall appear by the warrant that the offence charged was committed out of the village of Boonville, and the police justice shall proceed therein as though the warrant was issued by or returnable before him ; and in case the police justice is absent from the town, or by reason of sickness, or other cause is unable to hear the case, then the constable shall take the prisoner arrested before one of the justices of the peace of the town of Boonville, who shall proceed therein, and be entitled to fees for his services.

Police jus-
tice to issue
subpœnas. § 5. It shall be the duty of the police justice, whenever requested by the president or any trustee of said village, to issue subpœnas requiring any person appearing before him to give evidence upon a complaint for an offence committed in said village, upon the return of such subpœna the police justice shall examine the witness or witnesses on oath in relation to the offence supposed to have been committed, and if it shall appear that any such offence has been committed, he shall proceed thereon in the same manner as though such witness had voluntarily made such complaint before him.

Exclusive
jurisdiction
in cases of
fines and
penalties
&c. § 6. The said police justice shall have exclusive jurisdiction in all cases brought to recover a fine, forfeiture, or penalty, for the violation of this act, and of the by-laws, ordinances, rules or regulations of said village, and for the recovery of taxes and assessments, imposed or assessed pursuant to the village charter. Every such action brought in the police justice's court shall be in the name of the corporation, and may be commenced by summons or by warrant. If judgment be given against

the defendant in such action, execution may be issued
thereon immediately, unless it is for a tax or assessment,
and shall require, if the officer to whom it is issued
cannot find goods or chattels of the defendant whereof
the judgment can be collected, that the defendant may
be imprisoned in close custody, in one of the county
jails, in the county of Oneida, for a term not exceeding
thirty days.

§ 7. He shall keep a book, in which he shall enter all _{Keep account of all}
business done by him, and shall make out his accounts of _{business.}
all business done by him, which may be a town or county
charge, against the town of Boonville, or county of
Oneida, in the same manner as bills of the justice of
the peace in like cases; and in which he shall charge
the fees as allowed by law to justices of the peace, and
which shall be duly verified by him, and be audited by
the town auditors of said town, or board of supervisors
of said county, as the case may require, and the amount
audited shall be levied as other town and county charges,
and paid over to the treasurer of the village.

§ 8. In all cases where said police justice shall decide _{Costs.}
or give judgment in favor of any party, it shall be with
costs of the action or proceeding, including witnesses'
or officers' fees; and whenever any plaintiff or complainant, or defendant, in any action or proceeding, shall
be adjudged to pay costs, the said police justice shall
tax for his services such fees as are allowed by law to _{Fees.}
justices of the peace, which costs and fees shall be collected according to law. And all fines, penalties, and
forfeitures, imposed by or recovered before said police
justice, for criminal offences, or for a violation of this
act, or of any by-law, ordinance, rule or regulation of
said village, shall be received by him from the person
who shall collect the same, and paid over to the treasurer of the village.

§ 9. Such police justice shall quarterly, or oftener if _{Render an account under oath.}
required by the president or trustees, render an account,
on oath, to the trustees of the village in writing, in which
shall be specifically stated the amount of fines, penalties,
and forfeitures, received by him in every case, and all
fees or other moneys received by him belonging to the
corporation, and shall forthwith pay over the same to
the treasurer of the village.

§ 10. The police constable shall have the same powers, _{Police constable.}

and be subject to the same duties, in criminal and in civil cases, cognizable by the police justice, as constables in the town of Boonville, and shall give his security in the same manner, but to be approved by the president, and filed with the clerk of the village.

Duties of.

§ 11. It shall be his especial duty to arrest any and all persons in the village, guilty of any crime, misdemeanor, or offence against the peace or good order of society, and take them before the police justice to be dealt with according to law. The police constable shall also be bound to take strict notice of any unnecessary noise or disturbance in the streets, or other places in the village, particularly in the night time; to admonish offenders, and if the offence be of sufficient magnitude, to arrest them and take them before the police justice to answer for the offence. He shall also act as watchman in the night, whenever the trustees require it.

TITLE IX.

MISCELLANEOUS PROVISIONS.

§ 1. No person shall be an incompetent judge, justice, witness or juror, by reason of his being an inhabitant of the village of Boonville, or liable to taxation therein, in any action or proceeding in which the said village is interested.

No arrests during the holding of election.

§ 2. No person entitled to a vote at any election, held under this act, shall be arrested on any civil process within said village during the time of holding such election.

Double costs in certain cases.

§ 3. Every person elected or appointed to any office under this act, who shall be sued for any act done or omitted to be done by him in virtue of his office, and who shall have final judgment rendered in his favor whereby he shall be entitled to costs, shall recover double costs as defined in the Revised Statutes.

Persons may be sued in the name of the village.

§ 4. Whenever any person or corporation shall refuse or neglect to pay any tax or assessment duly assessed against any such person or corporation, the trustees may collect the same by action in the corporate name of said village against any such person or corporation, but such action shall not operate to release any lien upon property for such tax, until the judgment rendered in such suit shall have been fully satisfied.

§ 5. Whenever any real estate in said village shall be owned by two or more persons jointly, or as tenants in common, a notice served on one of such persons shall be sufficient notice to all for any purposes requiring notice under this act, unless one of such persons or tenants in common shall be a non-resident, in which case notice shall be mailed to said non-resident, directed to his place of residence, or in case said residence is not known, said notice shall be published for two successive weeks, once in each week, in a state paper. *Service of notices on joint tenants.*

§ 6. The trustees may take precautionary measures to guard the public health in times of pestilence, and to provide against infectious and pestilential diseases when they appear in the village, by providing suitable places for the temporary removal of persons having such diseases from the populous parts of the village, and defray the expenses incident to such removal. *Public health.*

§ 7. All former acts and parts of acts relative to the village of Boonville, are hereby respectively repealed, but such appeal shall not affect any act done, privilege granted, right vested or established, institution located, or any suit, proceeding or prosecution had or commenced previous to the time when such repeal shall take effect; all taxes and assessments levied and assessed, and not collected or directed to be levied and assessed, and not levied and assessed prior to this act taking effect, shall be levied, assessed and collected in the manner prescribed in this act for the collection of taxes and assessments. All officers elected or appointed under or by virtue of any act or acts hereby repealed, shall continue in office until the first board of trustees elected under this act shall become organized. *Repeal of former charter.*

§ 8. All acts and parts of acts inconsistent with this act are hereby repealed.

§ 9. This act shall take effect immediately.

Chap. 49.

AN ACT to amend an act entitled "An act to make the village of Summit Four Corners a seperate road district," passed June fourth, eighteen hundred and fifty-three.

Passed March 26, 1862 ; three-fifths being present.

The People of the State of New York, represented in Senate and Assembly, do enact as follows :

SECTION 1. Section one of the act entitled "An act to make the village of Summit Four Corners, in the town of Summit in the county of Schoharie, a separate road district, passed June fourth, eighteen hundred and fifty-three," is hereby amended so as to read as follows : The village of Summit Four Corners, in the town of Summit and county of Schoharie, is hereby declared and constituted a separate road district within the limits hereinafter stated, to-wit: commencing at the Methodist Episcopal Church, and running thence an easterly direction through said village to the highway leading from said village to Jefferson, and thence along the said Jefferson highway in a southerly direction through said village to the south bounds of a certain lot of land owned by Thomas Ferguson, and now occupied by Joseph Lamoreau.

§ 2. This act shall take effect immediately.

Chap. 50.

AN ACT for the relief of families of volunteers in the service of the United States, from the town of German Flats in the county of Herkimer.

Passed March 26, 1862 ; three-fifths being present.

The People of the State of New York, represented in Senate and Assembly, do enact as follows :

To raise $1,000.

SECTION 1. The board of supervisors of the county of Herkimer, at their regular annual meeting to be held for the year eighteen hundred and sixty-two, are hereby authorized and required to raise by tax to be levied upon the taxable property of the town of German Flats, in said county, in the same manner as other town charges are levied and raised, one thousand dollars, for the purpose of refunding moneys and interest expended, and to provide a fund for the support of families of volunteers in the service of the United States. But no moneys to be raised by virtue of the provisions of this act, shall be paid out to any person hereafter volunteering or enlisting; nor to any relative of his; nor to any member of his family; nor to any person for any money voluntarily paid or subscribed, or article voluntarily furnished to any volunteer, or relative, or family of such volunteer, or to any volunteer.

§ 2. The money raised by virtue of this act when collected, shall be paid over to Josiah Shull, Samuel E. Coe, D. D. Devoe, the volunteer relief committee of the town of German Flats, by the treasurer of Herkimer county, and said committee shall apply so much thereof as may be needed therefor, to the payment of a certain note of one thousand dollars and interest, now held by the Mohawk Valley bank. After paying the amount and interest due to the said bank for the amount drawn from the said bank by said committee, the remainder, if any, shall be applied for the relief of families of such volunteers by said committee. If, after paying all the demands on said fund, there shall be any moneys remaining in the hands of such committee, it shall be refunded to the town for the support of the poor therein.

§ 3. The said relief committee shall account for the moneys which shall come into their hands by virtue of this act, to the supervisor of the town, at such time as he may direct.

§ 4. This act shall take effect immediately.

Chap. 51.

AN ACT to repeal chapter two hundred and seventeen of the laws of eighteen hundred and sixty, entitled "An act to authorize the town of Hannibal, in the county of Oswego, to purchase a farm and erect thereon a town poor house."

Passed March 26, 1862; three-fifths being present.

The People of the State of New York, represented in Senate and Assembly, do enact as follows :

SECTION 1. The act entitled "An act to authorize the town of Hannibal, in the county of Oswego, to purchase a farm and erect thereon a town poor house," passed April tenth, eighteen hundred and sixty, is hereby repealed.

§ 2. All moneys heretofore collected under and by virtue of said chapter two hundred and seventeen of the laws of eighteen hundred and sixty, shall be applicable to the payment of any town expenses, upon a vote of the electors of the town, at any regular town meeting, and in the absence of any vote of the electors of the town in reference to the disposition of the funds so collected, they shall be applicable to the support of the paupers chargeable to said town, and shall be held and disbursed in the same manner as other funds raised for the aid or support of the poor of said town.

§ 3. This act shall take effect immediately.

Chap. 52.

AN ACT to incorporate Zephyr Hose Company Number Four of Port Richmond.

Passed March 26, 1862; three-fifths being present.

The People of the State of New York, represented in Senate and Assembly, do enact as follows :

SECTION 1. William F. Disosway, Theodore W. Edwards, Edgar H. Morris, Samuel F. Barker, Vincent Fountain,

Jr., Sidney E. Smith, Caleb Mott, Cornelius D. Disosway, Theodore Simonson, William H. Fountain, Clement Disosway, Joseph G. Drew, are hereby constituted a body corporate by the name and description of "Zephyr Hose Company No. Four of Richmond county," and by that name they and their successors shall and may have perpetual succession; and by that name they and their successors shall be, in law, capable of purchasing any real estate necessary for the erection of buildings, the preservation of hose carriages, and apparatus and other uses and purposes connected with the affairs and management of their company, and may purchase and hold any hose carriages and apparatus, tools, implements or other personal estate necessary for use at fires or in carrying on the affairs of the company to the amount, for both said real and personal property, of five thousand dollars; and said company or their successors shall have power to sell, convey and dispose of the said real and personal estate owned by them. *Purchase real estate and erect buildings.*

§ 2. The said corporation shall have full power to make and establish such by-laws, rules and regulations as they from time to time, shall think proper, as to their officers, the time, place and manner of electing them, and the period of their continuance in office and as to their powers and duties, and as to the election of members and as to the government of the persons appointed by them as firemen and with respect to the purposes for which this corporation is constituted. *To make by-laws.*

§ 3. The said corporation shall have full power and authority to nominate and appoint a sufficient number of firemen not exceeding forty, to have the care, management, working and using of the hose carriage and apparatus, and all the implements belonging to said corporation, and who shall be ready at all times in extinguishing fires; and further that the said corporation or a majority thereof shall have power from time to time, to remove any fireman so to be appointed when, and as often as they shall think proper, and to appoint others to fill the vacancies occasioned by removal or otherwise. *Appoint firemen.*

§ 4. Each of the said persons so to be appointed firemen as aforesaid, who shall serve as such firemen for five years, shall be during such service exempted from serving as a juror in any of the courts of this *Exemption from jury duty.*

22

state, and shall also during such service, be exempted from all militia duty, except in case where the militia are ordered into actual service.

§ 5. This act shall take effect immediately.

Chap. 53.

AN ACT to amend an act entitled "An act in relation to courts in Kings County," passed April fifteenth, eighteen hundred and fifty-two.

Passed March 26, 1862; three-fifths being present.

The People of the State of New York, represented in Senate and Assembly, do enact as follows:

SECTION 1. Section one of an act entitled "An act in relation to courts in Kings county," passed April fifteenth, eighteen hundred and fifty-two, is hereby amended by adding thereto as follows :

No person shall be permitted to appear before any justice or justices of the peace or before the police justice in said city, in any suit, action, matter or proceeding, either civil or criminal, as the attorney or representative of any party or parties to such suit, action or proceeding, unless such person is an attorney and counsellor at law of the supreme court of this state, and any violation of this provision is hereby declared a misdemeanor on the part of the justice knowingly permitting the same.

§ 2. This act shall take effect immediately.

Chap. 54.

AN ACT to amend an act entitled "An act to incorporate the International Bridge Company" passed April seventeenth eighteen hundred and fifty-seven, and the several acts amendatory thereof.

Passed March 26, 1862.

The People of the State of New York, represented in Senate and Assembly, do enact as follows :

SECTION 1. The twenty-first section of the act entitled An act to amend an act entitled 'An act to incorporate the International Bridge Company' passed April seventeenth eighteen hundred and fifty-seven and the several acts amendatory thereof, is hereby amended so as to read as follows :

§ 21. If the said bridge shall not be commenced within five years from the first day of April, eighteen hundred and sixty-two, and completed within ten years thereafter, said corporation shall from thenceforth cease. To be completed in ten years.

§ 2. This act shall take effect immediately.

Chap. 55.

AN ACT to repeal section one of chapter forty-eight of laws of eighteen hundred and fifty-one, and chapter four hundred and fifteen of laws of eighteen hundred and fifty-three.

Passed March 26, 1862.

The People of the State of New York, represented in Senate and Assembly, do enact as follows :

SECTION 1. Section one of chapter forty-eight of the laws of eighteen hundred and fifty-one, and chapter four hundred and fifteen of the laws of eighteen hundred and fifty-three, are hereby repealed ; provided, however, that all roads and streets now in use within the corporation line of the village of Dundee, in the county of Yates, shall continue to be deemed public highways, and as such shall be and remain under the control and authority of the commissioners of highways of the town of Starkey in said county.

§ 2. This act shall take effect immediately.

Chap. 56.

AN ACT to authorize the city of Troy to raise money by tax and to borrow money.

Passed March 26, 1856; three-fifths being present.

The People of the State of New York, represented in Senate and Assembly, do enact as follows :

To borrow $40,000.

SECTION 1. The mayor, recorder, aldermen and commonalty of the city of Troy, are hereby authorized to borrow upon the bonds to be issued under the corporate seal of said city and the signature of the mayor thereof, a sum of money not exceeding forty thousand dollars, for the purpose of paying any claims and demands now existing and outstanding against said city, and for the payment of which no other provision is made. Such bonds shall be made payable at such times as the common council of said city shall fix for that purpose, and shall bear interest at not exceeding seven per cent per annum, payable semi-annually, but nothing in this act contained shall authorize said city to dispose of said bonds at less than their par value, and the amount so borrowed shall be applied to the purposes specified in this section and not otherwise.

Raise by tax yearly, the interest.

§ 2. It shall be lawful for the common council of said city to raise by tax, in the same manner as the tax for contingent expenses shall be laid on the freeholders and inhabitants of said city and taxable property therein liable to taxation, such sums of money as shall be necessary from year to year to pay the interest accruing yearly on the bonds to be issued by virtue of this act, and such moneys when collected shall be applied to that purpose only.

§ 3. The common council shall in the manner provided Provide for payment of bonds by tax. in the second section hereof, raise by tax in each year, when the bonds which are authorized to be issued under this act shall become due and payable, a sufficient sum of money to pay the bond or bonds becoming due in that year and such money when collected shall be applied to that purpose only.

§ 4. The said mayor, recorder, aldermen and com- Borrow $30,000. monalty of the city of Troy, are also hereby authorized to borrow upon the bonds to be issued under the corporate seal of said city and the signature of the mayor thereof, the sum of thirty thousand dollars for the purpose of paying the bonds of said city for that amount, issued under and by virtue of the act of the legislature, passed April thirteenth, eighteen hundred and fifty-nine, and payable on the first day of April, eighteen hundred and sixty-two. Such bonds shall be made payable at such times as the common council of said city shall fix for that purpose, and shall bear interest at not exceeding seven per cent per annum, payable semi-annually; but nothing in this act contained shall authorize said city to dispose of said bonds at less than their par value, and the amount so borrowed shall be applied to the purpose specified in this section and not otherwise.

§ 5. The common council shall in the manner provided Raise yearly by tax the interest. in the second section hereof, raise by tax such sums of money as shall be necessary from year to year, to pay the interest accruing yearly on the bonds to be issued by virtue of the fourth section of this act, and such moneys when collected shall be applied to that purpose only.

§ 6. The common council shall in the manner provided Provide for payment of bonds. in the second section hereof, raise by tax in each year when the bonds that are authorized to be issued under the fourth section of this act shall become due and payable, a sufficient sum of money to pay the bond or bonds becoming due in that year, and such money when collected shall be applied to that purpose only.

§ 7. This act shall take effect immediately.

Chap. 57.

AN ACT to amend an act entitled "An act to amend 'An act to provide for the incorporation of villages,' passed December seventh, eighteen hundred and forty-seven, so far as relates to the village of Niagara Falls," passed March twenty-seventh, eighteen hundred and fifty-five.

Passed March 26, 1862; three-fifths being present.

The People of the State of New York, represented in Senate and Assembly, do enact as follows:

SECTION 1. Subdivision four of section one of chapter ninety-eight of session laws of eighteen hundred and fifty-five, is hereby amended so as to read as follows:

To licence and regulate drivers and runners.

To license and regulate carmen, truckmen, porters, and drivers of cabs, carriages, omnibuses, stage coaches of every description, and baggage and other wagons used for hire, and to limit their charges and compensation, for services to be rendered within five miles of the outskirts of said village, in any direction; to restrain and prohibit all runners, solicitors, or guides for boats, carriages, railroads, public houses, places of resort or for any other place or purpose whatsoever; to license, regulate, and restrain all guides, and to limit their compensation for any services to be rendered within five miles from the outskirts of said village, in any direction.

§ 2. Subdivision seven of said section shall read as follows:

Watch house.

To rent and fit up a suitable building, or to rent a suitable room, or to lease or purchase sufficient land, and to erect thereon a suitable building for a watch-house, or place of confinement of all persons charged with any offence against the laws of the state, or the by-laws or ordinances of said village, while awaiting trial or examination; and any constable of the town of Niagara, or any police constable of said village, may arrest with or without process, drunken or disorderly persons, or vagrants, and guilty in the presence of such officer, or police constable, of violating the public peace, or any village

Duty of police constable.

by-law or ordinance, for preserving the public order or
decorum ; and if it be in the night time, to confine the
person or persons so arrested in said watch-house until
nine o'clock on the following morning, when such per-
son or persons shall be brought before a justice of the *Of justices.*
peace, for trial or examination ; and any justice of the
peace in said village may order persons charged with
offences as aforesaid, to be confined in said watch-house,
from time to time, as may be necessary while awaiting
trial or examination, or until the final termination of the
case before such justice ; and said trustees shall make
all necessary rules and regulations for the control and
government of the said watch-house, shall appoint a
keeper of the same, and regulate his compensation, and
remove him at pleasure, and have generally all the necessary powers to render the same efficient for the purposes intended, by the establishment of such watch-
house ; and the trustees shall have power, and it shall
be lawful for them, to assess and raise by tax upon the
taxable property, in said village, such sum of money as
they may deem necessary for the erection and mainten-
ance of lamps, lamp-posts, gas pipes, and fixtures in any *Lamp posts and gas pipes.*
of the streets, alleys, or parks of said village, and to sup-
ply and pay for gas to illuminate the streets and public
places in said village ; provided that no such tax shall
be levied and raised for the purpose of lighting said
streets and places as aforesaid, unless the electors of said
village, entitled to vote to raise taxes therein, shall, at
any meeting of the electors, duly notified according to
law, by resolution, direct such tax to be raised for lighting the streets and public places as aforesaid, in the
same manner as other general taxes are to be raised in
said village.

§ 3. Section three of said chapter is hereby amended
so as to read as follows :

All actions brought to recover any penalty for the *Actions in the name of*
violation of any ordinance passed by virtue of this act, *the corpora-*
or the acts hereby amended, shall be brought in the cor- *tion.*
porate name of said village, and the first process which is
issued in said action shall be a summons or warrant ;
such summons shall issue without endorsement, in the
same manner as a summons in a civil action upon contract,
or a warrant may be issued upon the oath of the complainant, setting forth that a cause of action has accrued

to said village, against the defendant, for a violation
of an ordinance of said village, as the complainant verily
believes, and judgment may be rendered in any such
action for the amount of the penalty sought to be
recovered, with costs of prosecution; and if the defendant, in any such action, has no goods or chattels, lands
or tenements, whereof the judgment can be collected,
the execution shall require·him to be imprisoned in the
county jail of Niagara county for a term not exceeding
thirty days, or until such judgment be paid, and such
imprisonment not to exceed one day for each dollar of
said judgment; and no person shall be an incompetent
judge, justice, constable, juror, or witness, in any action
in which the said village is a.party, or is interested, by
reason of his being an inhabitant or owner of personal
or real estate therein, or holding an appointment to office
in said village from the board of trustees thereof; all
penalties and forfeitures, and all moneys received for
licenses, shall be paid to the village treasurer, and shall
be appropriated by the trustees as they may deem necessary, for the benefit of said village.

§ 4. Section five of said chapter is hereby amended so
as to read as follows:

Duties of
village
clerk.

The village clerk shall make and sign an entry or
record, in the books provided for that purpose, of every
ordinance enacted by the said trustees, and of the time
and manner of its first publication, and such entry or
record, or a copy thereof, authenticated by the president
of the board of trustees, under the village seal, shall be
presumptive evidence in all courts and places of the due
passage of such ordinance, of its having been duly published, and of the time of its first publication; and the
proceedings for the incorporation of the village of
Niagara Falls, in the county of Niagara, under and in
pursuance of an act of the legislature of the state of
New York, entitled "An act to provide for the incorporation of villages," passed December seventh, eighteen
hundred and forty-seven, as filed and recorded in the
office of the clerk of said county, and in the records of
said village, are hereby declared to be regular and valid,
and the district described within the survey map and
boundaries of said village, so filed and recorded as
aforesaid, shall be a village by the name of the village
of Niagara Falls, and the citizens of this state from time

to time inhabitants within the said boundaries shall be a corporation by the name of " The village of Niagara Falls," and hereafter it shall not be necessary in any action, suit or proceeding, in any court or before any magistrate of this state, to prove the incorporation of said village, or produce any evidence in relation thereto.

§ 5. All fines imposed by any justice or court of Fires. special sessions in said village, under chapter ninety-eight of session laws of eighteen hundred and fifty-five, and amendments thereto, and all money that comes into his hands as such justice, or as a court of special sessions, by fines shall be paid over to the treasurer of said village within thirty days after the same comes into his hands.

§ 6. Section fourteen of said chapter is hereby amended so as to read as follows :

In addition to those persons described in section one, Riotous and title five, chapter twenty of the Revised Statutes, all other disorderly persons, or persons found fighting or quarreling sons. in any alley, street or lane, or in any public place, or in view from any public place, street, lane, or alley, in said village ; any person who shall make an indecent exposure of his person in public view; all persons who shall make a noise and disturbance of the public peace ; all and every person within said village, who shall take, seize, carry away, or attempt to seize, take, or carry away, or control any baggage, box, parcel, package, or any goods or chattels of any kind whatever, without the consent of the owner thereof, or the person having the same in charge, or by due process of law, within said village, or on territory lying between the village of Niagara Falls and the village of Niagara city; all persons who shall follow with intent to solicit, annoy, or solicit any person or persons for any carriage, railroad, public house, tavern, places of resort, or any other place or places, or for any purpose whatever, within said village of Niagara Falls, shall be deemed disorderly persons, and may be proceeded against and punished according to the provision of this act and of the acts hereby amended.

§ 7. This act is hereby declared to be a public act, and shall take effect immediately.

23

Chap. 58.

AN ACT to authorize the common council of the city of Rochester to raise money for the purpose of building a new bridge, in conjunction with the supervisors of Monroe county, over the Genesee river at Clarissa street, in said city.

Passed March 27, 1862; three-fifths being present.

The People of the State of New York, represented in Senate and Assembly, do enact as follows :

May borrow $15,000. SECTION 1. It shall be lawful for the common council of the city of Rochester to borrow, on the faith and credit of said city, any sum of money not exceeding fifteen thousand dollars, for a term not less than twenty years, at a rate of interest not exceeding seven per cent per annum, such interest to be paid semi-annually, and to issue the bonds of the said city therefor, under the corporate seal of said city, and the signature of the mayor or such other officer as the common council may direct to sign the same. The bonds so executed may be in such sums and payable at such place as the common council may designate, and may be payable to the holder or bearer thereof, and in such case shall be transferable by delivery.

May sell bonds and apply money to building bridge. § 2. The common council of said city may dispose of such bonds to such persons or corporations, and upon such terms as they shall deem most advantageous to said city, but for not less than par ; and the money which shall be so borrowed and raised, shall, together with a sufficient additional amount to be raised and appropriated by the supervisors of Monroe county, be used and applied to the purpose of constructing a new bridge over the Genesee river at Clarissa street in said city, and of constructing the piers, abutments and appurtenances necessary thereto, and to no other purpose whatever.

Shall raise the interest annually by tax. § 3. The said common council, in addition to such other moneys as it is or shall be authorized to raise by tax, shall, in each and every year after the issuing of said bonds or obligations, until they shall be paid, raise by a tax upon all the taxable property within said city, and in the manner now or hereafter prescribed by law for raising taxes therein, sufficient money to pay the interest on the said bonds or obligations for such year, as it shall become due, which shall be exclusively applied to that purpose.

§ 4. This act shall take effect immediately.

Chap. 59.

AN ACT to authorize the city of Troy to borrow money to pay such amount of the bonds of said city issued to the Troy Union Railroad Company, due first of January, eighteen hundred and sixty-three, as shall not be covered by money on hand for that purpose.

Passed March 27, 1862; three-fifths being present.

The People of the State of New York, represented in Senate and Assembly, do enact as follows:

SECTION 1. The mayor, recorder, aldermen and commonalty of the city of Troy are hereby authorized to borrow, upon bonds to be issued under the common seal of said city, and the signature of the mayor thereof, such sum of money, as with the money then on hand applicable to that purpose, shall be sufficient to pay the bonds of said city, issued to the Troy Union Railroad Company, payable on the first day of January, eighteen hundred and sixty-three, amounting to one hundred thousand dollars. Such bonds shall be made payable at such times as the common council of said city shall designate for that purpose, and shall bear interest at, not exceeding, seven per cent per annum, payable semi-annually, but shall not be disposed of at less than their par value; and the amount so borrowed shall be applied to the purpose specified in this section and not otherwise.

§ 2. The interest on the bonds authorized by the first section of this act, shall be paid in the manner provided by section one of "An act to authorize the city of Troy

to raise money by tax, and to borrow money," passed
April, thirteenth eighteen hundred and fifty-nine.

§ 3. The principal of such bonds shall be paid out of
moneys to be received by said city of Troy from the
Troy Union Railroad Company, or the several railroad
corporations composing the same, on account of principal under the compromise made in eighteen hundred
and fifty-eight, and such moneys shall be applied to the
payment of the bonds to be issued under the first section
of this act, and the bonds issued by said city to the said
Troy Union Railroad Company, and to no other purpose.

Chap. 60.

AN ACT to amend an act entitled "An act to
perpetuate the evidence of the deaths of Nicholaas Van Staphorst and others," passed May thirteenth, eighteen hundred and forty-six, and to
relieve parties from procuring the attendance of
certain witnesses whose testimony has been
heretofore perpetuated.

Passed March 27, 1862.

*The People of the State of New York, represented in
Senate and Assembly, do enact as follows :*

SECTION 1. The third section of the act entitled "An
act to perpetuate the evidence of the death of Nicholaas
Van Staphorst and others," passed May thirteenth, one
thousand eight hundred and forty-six; is hereby amended
so that the same shall read as follows :

Copies of said deposition or depositions, with the
certificate of said justice, when duly certified by the
secretary of state, shall be prima facie evidence in all
courts and places within this state, of the facts certified
by the said justice as having been satisfactorily proved
to him ; and such copies with such certificate, when so
certified by the secretary of state, may be recorded in
any of the counties of this state, and when so recorded,
the record thereof and duly certified copies of such
record or records, may be read in evidence in all courts

and places, to the same extent and with like effect as records of deeds and certified copies of such records.

§ 2. This act shall take effect immediately.

Chap. 61.

. AN ACT to release the interest of the State of New York in lands acquired by escheat, to Solomon Myers.

Passed March 27, 1861 ; by a two-thirds vote.

The People of the State of New York, represented in Senate and Assembly, do enact as follows :

SECTION 1. All the right, title and interest which the people of this state have in and to certain real estate in the town of Moreau, Saratoga county, State of New York, heretofore conveyed to Solomon Myers by Garret C. Norris, are hereby released to the said Solomon Myers.

§ 2. This act shall take effect immediately.

Chap. 62.

AN ACT to authorize the incorporated banks of the state to take and hold any stock of the United States or of the State of New York.

Passed March 27, 1862.

The People of the State of New York, represented in Senate and Assembly, do enact as follows :

SECTION 1. That it shall and may be lawful for any bank incorporated by any act of the legislature of the State of New York, or any banking association, or individual bankers to take and to become the owner of any stock of the United States or of the State of New York.

§ 2. That so much of the several acts incorporating such banks or authorizing the business of banking and the acts amendatory thereof as is inconsistent with the foregoing section be and the same is hereby repealed.

§ 3. This act shall take effect immediately.

Chap. 63.

AN ACT to amend an act entitled "An act to consolidate the cities of Brooklyn and Williamsburgh and the town of Bushwick into one municipal government, and to incorporate the same," passed April seventeenth, eighteen hundred and fifty-four, and the several acts amendatory thereof and supplemental thereto, or affecting the same.

Passed March 27, 1862; three-fifths being present.

The People of the State of New York, represented in Senate and Assembly, do enact as follows :

SECTION 1. Section four of title two of the act entitled "An act to consolidate the cities of Brooklyn and Williamsburgh and the town of Bushwick, and to incorporate the same," passed April seventeenth, eighteen hundred and fifty-four, is hereby amended so as to read as follows:

Relating to the election of aldermen.

§ 4. There shall be chosen by the electors of the several wards respectively herein mentioned, at the general state elections to be held in the year one thousand eight hundred and sixty-two, and every two years thereafter, one alderman from each of the second, fourth, sixth, eighth, tenth, twelfth, fourteenth, sixteenth and eighteenth wards of the said city; and in the year one thousand eight hundred and sixty-three, and every two years thereafter, one alderman from each of the first, third, fifth, seventh, ninth, eleventh, thirteenth, fifteenth, seventeenth and nineteenth wards of the said city. The aldermen so chosen shall be entitled to take their seats on the first day of January next succeeding their election; and the terms of office of the present aldermen of the said wards respectively, shall continue until their successors shall be chosen as above provided, and shall have qualified.

§ 2. Section twelve of said title two is hereby amended so as to read as follows:

Time of holding stated meetings.

§ 12. The common council shall hold stated meetings, commencing on the first Monday of January in each

year, unless the said first Monday happen on the first
day of the year, in which case such stated meetings shall
commence on the second Monday of January; but the
mayor, or in his absence any three aldermen, may call
special meetings of the common council by notice to
each alderman, served upon him personally or left at his
usual place of residence. The common council may at
any regular meeting, by resolution, order a special meeting, and such resolution shall not require the approval
of the mayor.

§ 3. Section thirteen of said title two is hereby amended so as to add after the word "by-laws," in the first
clause thereof, the words "subject to the provisions of
this act and not inconsistently therewith."

§ 4. Subdivision thirty-three of section thirteen of said
title two is hereby repealed.

§ 5. Section twenty-one of title two of said act of incorporation, is hereby amended so as to read as follows:

§ 21. The mayor and comptroller of said city shall an- *Annual statement of the amount to be raised by tax.*
nually, on or before the first Monday of June, present to
the common council, and the supervisors of the city, in
joint meeting, a statement in writing of the several sums
of money which they shall deem necessary to be raised
by tax for the various purposes contemplated by this
act and otherwise by law for the year commencing on
the first day of January next thereafter.

§ 6. Section twenty-two of said title two is hereby
amended so as to read as follows:

§ 22. The common council and the supervisors of the *Meeting of common council and supervisors in joint board.*
city, shall meet in joint board on the first Monday of
June, in each year, and then, or as soon thereafter as
practicable, proceed to determine, by a majority of at
least two-thirds of the members present, what sums will
be necessary to defray the expenses of said city for the
year to commence on the first day of January next thereafter, not exceeding in the aggregate the total amount
estimated by the mayor and comptroller in their statement to the said joint board, and also the interest due,
or to become due in that year, on the public debt of the
city, and any installments due, or to become due thereon, in that year, together with such sums as by this act
are authorised for the use and benefit of the public
schools of said city, and as are, or shall be required by
law to be paid into the sinking fund of the city, and as

shall be necessary to pay any judgments recovered against the city. It shall not be lawful for the said joint board to determine for the expenses or purposes for any one year of the fire department, including all salaries therefor, any greater sum than fifty thousand dollars; and no greater sum shall be levied or raised for such expenses or purposes in the taxes of any one year.

§ 7. Section three of title three of the said act of incorporation is hereby amended so as to read as follows:

Election of officers to be on the day of the state election.

§ 3. Elections for mayor and such other officers as are by the provisions of this act to be elected, shall be held by the electors of the said city on the day of the general state election, at the same time and places, and in such manner and under such regulations as or shall be prescribed by law in regard to state elections; the comptroller, treasurer, auditor, collector of taxes and assessments and commissioner of taxes shall be elected at such election in the year one thousand eight hundred and sixty-two; the mayor and street commissioner shall be elected at such election in the year one thousand eight hundred and sixty-three. The present incumbents of the respective offices aforesaid, except the collector of taxes and assessments, shall continue in office until the first day of January after the election of their respective successors as herein provided, and until such successors shall have qualified. The present collector of taxes and assessments shall continue in office until the first day of July, eighteen hundred and sixty-three, and until his successor shall have qualified.

§ 8. Section four of said title three is hereby amended so as to read as follows:

Judiciary to be on a separate ballot.

§ 4. At the said elections the city judge, police justice and justices of the peace, or such of them as are required to be chosen at any election, shall be voted for on a separate ballot endorsed "judiciary;" the mayor, comptroller, auditor, city treasurer, street commissioner, collector of taxes and assessments, commissioner of taxes, or such of them as shall require to be chosen at any election, shall be voted for on a separate ballot to be endorsed "city officers," and the aldermen, supervisors and other ward officers, to be elected by the wards respectively, shall be voted for on a separate ballot endorsed "ward officers." Such ballots shall be deposited by the inspectors of the different election districts in separate boxes to be provided by the city.

§ 9. Section twenty-three of said title three is hereby amended so as to read as follows:

§ 23. The official term of the several persons who shall be elected in pursuance of this act, shall commence on the first day of January next after their election, except that of the collector of taxes and assessments, whose term shall commence on the first day of July next after his election; and the official terms of all persons who shall be appointed to any office or place in pursuance of this act shall commence as follows:

1. Such as are required to give security for the performance of their duties from the time such security shall be given and approved.

2. Such as are not required to give security from the time they shall have taken and filed the oath of office hereinafter mentioned.

§ 10. Section twenty-four of said title three is hereby amended so as to read as follows:

§ 24. The common council shall, at their first meeting thereof in January in each year, or as soon thereafter as practicable, by ballot appoint a city clerk, a health officer, a keeper of the city hall, a messenger of the common council and two inspectors of pavements, and by ballot or otherwise, so many pound masters, clerks of markets, surveyors, sealers of weights and measures and clerks of departments as they shall deem it expedient to appoint, but no such appointment shall be lawful unless the compensation for such officers respectively shall have been previously provided for by tax. All persons so appointed shall hold their respective offices until the first day of January next after their appointment, and until their successors shall have been appointed and shall have qualified. The present incumbents of the offices mentioned in this section shall hold their places until the first day of January, one thousand eight hundred and sixty-three, and their successors shall have qualified. The office of inspectors of meats is hereby abolished. The common council shall, at their first meeting in January in the year one thousand eight hundred and sixty-three, and at their first meeting in every second year thereafter, or as soon after that day in such years as may be practicable, appoint the attorney and counsel

24

for the corporation in this title before mentioned. The present attorney and counsellor shall continue in office until a successor shall have been appointed as aforesaid and shall have qualified.

§ 11. Section twenty-nine of said title three is hereby amended so as to read as follows:

Payment of salaries.

§ 29. The common council shall grant and pay to the mayor, comptroller, auditor, street commissioner, collector of taxes and assessment, commissioner of repairs and supplies, commissioner of taxes, attorney and counsellor, treasurer, assessors, and all other officers, clerks, or other persons elected or appointed under, or in pursuance of this act, except to aldermen and supervisors, such stated salaries as it may from time to time, deem proper; but such salaries shall be, instead of all fees and perquisites whatever, for services to be performed by such officers; and all such fees and perquisites shall be collected and paid to the treasurer of the city, for the use of the city, by every such officer and clerk, monthly, under oath, to be filed with the comptroller, before he shall be entitled to receive any such salary; but no officer's salary shall be increased after his election and during his continuance in office, nor shall it be diminished without a vote of two-thirds of the members elected to the common council, in favor of such diminution.

§ 12. Section thirty-four of said title three is hereby amended so as to read as follows:

Concerning the election of supervisors.

§ 34. There shall be elected at the general election, to be held in the year one thousand eight hundred and sixty-two, and at such election every two years thereafter, by the electors respectively of the first, third, fifth, seventh, ninth, eleventh, thirteenth, fifteenth, seventeenth, and nineteenth wards of the said city, one supervisor for each of said wards; and there shall be elected at the said general elections in the year one thousand eight hundred and sixty-two, and again in the year one thousand eight hundred and sixty-three and at such elections every two years after the said election in the year one thousand eight hundred and sixty-three, by the electors respectively of the second, fourth, sixth, eighth, tenth, twelfth, fourteenth, sixteenth and eighteenth wards of said city, one supervisor for each of the said last mentioned wards. The supervisors so chosen shall be entitled to take their seats on the first day of January succeeding their election, and shall hold their offices until their successors shall be chosen as above provided and shall have qualified. The terms of office of the present supervisors shall continue until their successors, as above provided, shall be chosen and shall be qualified. The supervisors to be chosen, as by this section provided, shall possess the powers and be entitled to the compensation, respectively, of supervisors of the county of Kings.

§ 13. There shall be a commissioner of taxes chosen by the voters of the city at large, at the election to be held in the year one thousand eight hundred and sixty-two, and at such election every third year thereafter. He shall keep, in suitable books to be provided for that purpose, a record of all information which he may be able to obtain in respect to the taxable property and persons liable to taxation in the city of Brooklyn, and all changes in the ownership of real estate in said city, of which he can obtain information. He shall appoint a suitable person in said office, whose business it shall be, under his direction, to take charge of the ward maps, to amend and correct the same, and also the record of the property in the office of the commissioner of taxes, both as regards the proprietorship and extent of such property, by a daily examination of the conveyances which shall be left for record in the office of the register of the county of Kings, which examination he shall be entitled to make free of all charges whatsoever during office hours; to make all the necessary surveys for the purpose of such correction, and to prepare all maps which shall be necessary for the use of the board of assessors. *(Commissioner of taxes.)*

§ 14. Section three of title four of said act of corporation is hereby amended so as to read as follows:

§ 3. Whenever a petition for opening or widening any street, road, avenue, park or square in said city, signed by a majority of the persons owning land on the line of the same, shall be presented to the common council of said city, the common council shall cause a notice to be published in the corporation newspapers, that such application has been made, and of the time (which shall not be less than twenty days after the first publication of such notice) when they will proceed on said petition, which notice shall be published daily, in the newspapers *(In relation to opening or widening streets.)*

employed by the corporation, for two weeks successively; and unless a remonstrance, signed by a majority of the persons to be assessed for the expenses thereof, shall be presented to them on or before the day specified in said notice, and if they shall deem the application proper they may, on the day specified in said notice, or as soon thereafter as may be, by a resolution, decide that such improvement be made. Before giving notice of the pendency of such application, the common council shall fix the limit or district of assessment, beyond which the assessment shall not extend, and a description of such limit or district shall be inserted in and form a part of such notice. If the common council shall deem it proper to permit such improvements to be made, they shall cause application to be made to the supreme court, in the second district, at a general term thereof, for the appointment of three persons as commissioners to estimate the expense of the said improvement, and the amount of damages to be sustained therefrom, by the owners of lands and buildings, and all other persons interested in the premises, who may be affected thereby. The persons so appointed shall not be interested in the improvement. The said court may also appoint another, or others, to act in the place of any one or more of such commissioners who may die, decline serving, remove from the city, be or become interested in the improvement, or from any cause may be disabled from serving.

§ 15. Section five of said title four is hereby amended so as to read as follows:

Map of premises to be made.

§ 5. The common council shall cause a map to be made by a competent surveyor, on which map shall be designated by feet and inches, as near as may be, the several pieces of land, buildings necessary to be taken for the improvement, and of any residue of lots or pieces of land within the district of assessment, of which lots or pieces of land only a part will be required of the same for the purpose of said improvement; which said lots or pieces of land to be taken, and residues of lots or pieces of land, shall be numbered in figures from one upwards; and the map aforesaid, shall form and constitute a part of the reports of the said commissioners of estimate, and of the board of assessors in relation to said improvement, and shall be deposited with said reports respectively, for examination, in the office of the clerk of the county of Kings, and in the office of the commissioner of taxes, with said reports respectively, as hereinafter provided. In case there shall be no ward maps showing the lots or pieces of land within the district of assessment, the map to be made as aforesaid, shall also show the several pieces of land within the district of assessment.

§ 16. Section seven of said title four shall be amended so as to read as follows:

§ 7. The report of said commissioners shall be made **Report of commissioners.** in a tabular form, with columns in which shall be distinctly given the whole expense of the proposed improvement and the several items of such expense, the number on the map of the pieces of land required for the improvement, and of any residues within the district of assessment of lots or pieces of land of which only a part will be required for the same, the names of persons interested in the property taken for the improvement, and the nature of their interest, and the amount awarded to the different parties, and so many and such other different columns and tabular statements as may be necessary to state the true interests of the parties in the lands and premises, and their liabilities in relation thereto.

§ 17. Section fifteen of title four of said act of incorporation, is hereby amended so as to read as follows:

§ 15. Upon the confirmation of the report of the com- **Duties of assessors.** missioners of estimate of the expense of the improvement, it shall, together with the map, be delivered to the board of assessors of said city, whose duty it shall be to apportion and assess the expenses of the improvement as determined by the report of the said commissioners, upon the lands and premises benefited or intended to be benefited, by the improvement within the district of assessment, in proportion to the benefit derived by such lands and premises respectively thereby. The said board of assessors shall make their apportionment and assessment in a report or list in tabular form, with columns, giving the numbers, according to the ward map or maps, of the pieces of land assessed for benefit; or when there are no ward maps, according to the map made by order of the common council for the purposes of the improvement as aforesaid, the names of the owners or occupants thereof respectively, the amount assessed on each piece of land and on the different in-

terests therein, the balance of awards to be received by
the different parties over their assessments, the assessment to be paid by the owners of the pieces of land
assessed respectively, and by other persons interested
therein, the balance of assessment to be paid by any
such owners or persons over any awards made to them
respectively, and such other statements as they may
deem necessary to make. And upon the completion of
the report of the said board of assessors, the same proceedings shall be had in relation thereto in all respects,
until the confirmation thereof by the supreme court, as
are required in relation to the report of the commissioners of the estimate of the expense of the improvement
by sections twelve, thirteen and fourteen of this title;
and all the provisions of said sections for review, appeal,
revision, correction and confirmation thereof, shall
apply thereto, except that the said report shall be filed
in the office of the commissioner of taxes for examination, and that, if the court shall send the same back for
revision and correction, it shall be sent back to the board
of assessors. Upon the confirmation of the report or
assessment list of the said board of assessors, and not
until then, the rights of the owners or other parties interested in the lands taken to the awards made to them
respectively shall become fixed, and the common council
shall be thereupon authorized to cause such improvement to be made. In case any such assessment list or
report of the board of assessors shall be afterwards set
aside or declared void for irregularity or other cause,
which shall not affect the validity of the awards made in
the same improvement, it shall be the duty of the board
of assessors to make out a new assessment list or report
in the manner herein provided, which further report and
the assessment therein, shall be subject in all respects to
the provisions in this section and otherwise in this act
provided in relation to the original reports and the
assessments thereby made. If the said board of assessors shall, instead of making out an assessment list as
aforesaid, merely report that the lands and premises
within the assessment district are not benefited to the
amount estimated by the said commissioners for the expenses of the improvement, as the said board of assessors
may and shall do, if in their judgment, such be the fact,
the court shall, upon the presentation of such report for

confirmation, order the proceedings for said improvement to be discontinued, and thereupon all proceedings had in relation thereto, shall be null and void, and the city of Brooklyn shall in no case be liable in relation thereto. It shall be sufficient in making the awards and assessments for damages or benefits under this act, or any special or other act relating to laying out. opening, widening or extending any street, avenue, boulevard, park or square, in the said city, for the commissioners appointed or to be appointed to make the same, and for the board of assessors to state in their reports respectively, the name or names of the parties interested in each piece or parcel of land and buildings or other property taken, and the name or names of the owners or occupants of each piece of land assessed for benefit as said names may appear in the office of the commissioner of taxes; and all assessments for benefit and taxes so made, shall be liens upon the land in regard to which they shall be made, notwithstanding any error in the name of the parties interested, owner, or owners or occupant, the same as if such name were correct; and it shall not be lawful for the said commissioners in any proceeding pending or to be commenced for the purposes aforesaid, in pursuance of this act or any special or other act in relation to streets, avenues, boulevards or parks, to include or allow any sum whatever in the assessment of the expenses of the improvement for searches or abstracts of title. And if in any case such searches shall be necessary, it shall be the duty of the attorney and counsellor of the city to make them, by virtue of his office as by this act provided, and in such case the statutory fees of the register of the county of Kings therein, may be allowed and no more.

§ 18. Section seventeen of said title four is hereby amended so as to read as follows:

§ 17. The commissioners of estimate and assessment, to be appointed as aforesaid, shall be allowed three dollars each for each and every day actually and necessarily employed about their duties, not exceeding for the three commissioners collectively, the sum of two hundred dollars; and such compensation and the expense of said map, and the costs and fees of the attorney and counsellor, as hereinafter provided, with the disbursements paid to the register of the county of Kings for his fees as fixed by law, and the fees of the clerks of the court for

Compensation of commissioners.

any services required by the provisions of this title, shall
be estimated as a part of the expenses of the improvement, and no other expenses besides the amount awarded
for damages than those herein specified, shall be included
in any assessment.

§ 19. Section twenty-eight of said title four is hereby
amended so as to read as follows:

§ 28. The mayor shall nominate and by and with the
consent of two-thirds of all the city supervisors convened in meeting duly notified, appoint on or before the
tenth day of January, one thousand eight hundred and
sixty-three, and every third year thereafter, five assessors, no two of whom shall be residents of any one ward,
and at least two of whom shall be residents of the eastern
district of said city, who shall perform, under the direction and supervision of the said commissioner of taxes,
the duties heretofore performed by the assessors of the
several wards of said city, and by this or any other act
required of them; and shall have all the powers of assessors of the different towns of this state. The assessors
first appointed under this act shall hold their office for
the term of one, two, three, four and five years respectively. All subsequent appointments shall be for the
term of five years, except where vacancies occur by
death, resignation or inability to serve, and such appointments shall be for the balance of the unexpired term.
The commissioner of taxes shall for the purpose of determining which of the persons first appointed shall serve
for such terms respectively, shall within ten days after
their appointment notify them to attend at his office,
and in the presence of the persons so appointed who
shall attend, proceed to choose by lot, and in that manner
determine which of said assessors shall serve for the
terms aforesaid respectively. He shall within twenty-
four hours thereafter file in the office of the county clerk
a certified statement of such fact. The said assessors
shall, together, constitute a board of assessors. Should
such assessors or any of them, by reason of sickness or
other inability, be unable to perform the duties required
of them by this act, the mayor by and with the consent
of two-thirds of all the city supervisors convened as
aforesaid, shall appoint other persons in their stead, who
shall hold their offices for the balance of the term of the
persons so superseded. The terms of the assessors now

in office shall continue till the first day of January, one thousand eight hundred and sixty-three, and all of them shall then expire.

§ 20. Section thirty of said title four is hereby amended so as to read as follows:

§ 30. All assessments of lands for taxes for general purposes, or for benefit from local improvements shall refer to the ward maps, when they shall exist, and where a portion of any lot or piece of land shall be taken for any improvement, the residue thereof shall be deemed to be held for any assessment previously laid thereon remaining unpaid. In case ward maps do not exist for any ward or wards, the common council shall as soon as in their judgment it is advisable, direct the same to be made.

§ 21. Section thirty-one of said title four is hereby amended by adding thereto as follows:

It shall be the duty of the said assessors to attend during such examination and review and correct said rolls as may be just and proper. The commissioner of taxes shall cause copies of such corrected rolls of each ward of said city respectively, to be made out, and after being duly sworn to by at least two of the assessors, according to the oath provided by law in regard to assessment rolls in the different towns of this state, and further to the effect that they have together personally examined within the year past, each and every lot or parcel of land, house, building or other assessable property within the ward, to be delivered to the board of supervisors of the county of Kings, which board shall proceed thereon in the manner required by law for the laying and collecting of taxes.

§ 22. The commissioner of taxes shall have power to apportion between the different owners of any piece or parcel of land, any tax or assessment for benefit remaining unpaid thereon, upon receiving an affidavit showing the true limits and extent of each interest; but such apportionment shall not be effectual unless the same be certified to the collector of taxes and assessments, and a minute thereof duly entered on the original tax or assessment lists, and if returned as unpaid; also on the account of unpaid taxes in his office. The amounts so apportioned shall be liens upon the pieces of land and property to which they shall be apportioned respective-

25

ly, the same as if they had been originally so taxed or assessed

§ 23. The commissioner of taxes shall have power to rectify any errors committed in the laying of any tax or assessment, as well for the general purposes of said city as for any local improvement therein, in the following cases:

Errors and mistakes.

1. When the error is entirely clerical.
2. When the mistake is in the name of the party taxed or assessed.
3. When the quantity of the real estate or nature of the buildings thereon shall be erroneously given.
4. When the personal estate shall be over-estimated, and the party assessed shall have been absent from the city for the thirty days the books shall have been open for examination and correction. Such power can be exercised only upon the application of the aggrieved party or his agent, supported by an affidavit setting forth the facts, and no correction shall be valid until it shall be certified to the collector of taxes and assessments, and duly entered on the original tax or assessment list in his office.

Persons erroneously taxed.

§ 24. Any person who shall, by reason of being erroneously taxed or assessed, pay a tax or assessment for benefit upon real estate in said city, belonging to another person or persons, shall be entitled to receive the same back from the collector of taxes and assessments, at any time before the expiration of the warrant of such collector, provided no change shall have been made in the title or ownership of such real estate subsequently to the levying of such tax or assessment for benefit; and in case of such repayment, the collector shall correct the tax or assessment list, noting the facts therein, and such corrected tax or assessment shall be a valid lien upon the land, the same as if it had not been erroneously paid. After the expiration of the time of the warrant of the collector without repayment by him, or in case of any change of title or ownership, as aforesaid, the person so erroneously paying a tax or assessment as aforesaid, shall have a right of action to recover, in any court having jurisdiction of the amount, from the party owning the real estate at the time of levying such tax or assessment, the sum which he shall have paid erroneously as aforesaid.

§ 25. **Section** six of title five of said act of incorpo- Duty of collector.
ration is hereby amended by adding the following thereto:

It shall not be necessary for the collector to call upon
the persons taxed, in the annual tax rolls, or at their place
of residence, and demand the taxes, in cases where such
taxes are for real estate; nor shall it be necessary for
him to levy any such tax upon real estate by distress
and sale of the goods and chattels of the persons who
ought to pay the same; but he shall, upon receiving
such annual tax rolls, cause a notice to be published for
thirty days in all the public newspapers of the said city,
that the said tax rolls have been completed and delivered
to him for the purpose of collecting the taxes mentioned
therein, and that all taxed persons are required to pay
their taxes at his office, in the city hall, without delay,
under the penalties of the law. He shall annex to such
notice and publish therewith, a copy of the fourteenth
section of this title.

§ 26. Section eight of said title five, is hereby amended Percentage.
by inserting "three" instead of "five" as the percentage
to be added and included in every tax and assessment,
for benefit for the expense of collection.

§ 27. Section fifteen of said title five is hereby amended
so as to read as follows:

§ 15. If any of the taxes mentioned in the assessment Collector to make return of unpaid taxes to county treasurer.
rolls annexed to the warrants from the board of super-
visors shall remain unpaid at the expiration of one hundred and eighty days from the time said assessment
rolls shall be delivered to the collector, and he shall not
be able to collect the same, he shall deliver to the county
treasurer an account of the taxes so remaining due, with
an affidavit that the same is a true account of the taxes
remaining unpaid, and that he has not been able, upon
diligent enquiry, to discover any goods and chattels
belonging to, or in possession of the persons charged in
said rolls for personal taxes, whereon to levy the amount
of such personal taxes; he shall be credited by the
county treasurer with the amount thereof, and if any of
the assessments, mentioned in the assessment rolls annexed to the warrants from the common council, for
the collection of assessments for benefit, shall remain
unpaid at the expiration of the said one hundred and
twenty days, and he shall not be able to collect the same,
he shall deliver to the comptroller of said city an

account of the assessments so remaining due, with an affidavit as hereinafter mentioned.

§ 28. Section twenty-six of said title five is hereby amend so as to read as follows:

To sell pro-perty at public auc-tion for taxes. § 26. If any such tax for general purposes or assessment for benefit for local improvements shall remain unpaid on the day specified in said notice, the collector shall proceed to sell by public auction, at the city hall of said city, the property on which said tax or assessment for benefit shall have been imposed, for the lowest term of years for which any person will take the same, and pay the amount of such tax or assessment for benefit, with the interest and expenses, and he shall continue the sale from time to time until all such lands shall be sold. The collector shall make it an absolute condition with all persons purchasing at such sale, that payment **Time of payment.** be made (within forty-eight hours) after the close of the sale each day, and it will not be sufficient for him to receive any sum or sums in part, but all moneys received by him must be in full payment of the tax or assessment for benefit together with the interest and expenses which shall have accrued thereon at the date of sale. Any neglect, failure or refusal on the part of any purchaser or purchasers to comply with this condition (which shall be read by the collector at the time of commencing the sale each day,) shall render such sale void and of no **Re-sold next day if not paid.** effect ; and it shall be the duty of the collector, on the first day to which the sale shall have been adjourned, to re-sell the same for the lowest term of years for which any person will take the same and pay the amount of such tax or assessment for benefit, with the interest and expenses thereon, and until such re-sale has been effected any person owning such property shall have the right to redeem the same as though no sale had been made. Any collector who shall, knowingly, for any purpose whatever, make or cause to be made, any false record in relation to the terms of sale, or any false record of the transactions at such sales or shall refuse to allow the person or persons entitled to redeem any property so sold, to redeem the same as herein provided, shall in addition to the forfeiture of office be deemed guilty of a **Certificate of sale.** misdemeanor. The collector shall deliver to the purchaser complying with the terms of any such sale a certificate of such sale, and note the same on the account of unpaid taxes or assessments for benefit, as the case may be transmitted to him by the county treasurer or comptroller, and also on the original tax or assessment rolls, and on the abstracts hereinbefore directed to be kept in his office; such certificate of sale shall be recorded in the collector's office, in proper books kept for that purpose, and shall constitute a lien upon the lands and premises therein described, after the same shall have been so recorded; and no assignment of any certificate given on the sale of lands shall have any effect until notice of the same, with the name and residence of the assignee, shall be filed in the office of the collector of taxes and assessments.

§ 29. Section twenty-seven of said title five is hereby amended so as to read as follows:

§ 27. No owner whose deed, or in case he holds such property by descent or devise, the deed of his ancestor or devisor shall have been duly recorded in the office of the register of the county of Kings, before the sale thereof for any tax or assessment for benefit, and no mortgagee, lessee or assignee of either, whose mortgage, lease or assignment shall have been so recorded, shall be divested of his rights in such property by reason of such sale, unless six months notice in writing of such sale shall have been given by the purchaser or those claiming under him to such owner, mortgagee, lessee or assignee personally, if a resident in the county of Kings or a county adjoining thereto; or if such owner, mortgagee, or lessee be not such resident, then by depositing such notice in one of the postoffices of said city directed to the owner, mortgagee, lessee or assignee, at his place of residence as stated in the deed, lease, mortgage or assignment of such mortgage or lease. *Rights of owners and parties interested.*

§ 30. Section twenty-nine of said title five is hereby amended so as to read as follows:

§ 29. The owner, mortgagee or other person interested in such land, may at any time within two years after the sale thereof, for any unpaid tax or assessment for benefit, and before the expiration of the notice mentioned in section twenty-seven of this title, redeem said lands by paying to the collector of taxes and assessments for the use of the purchaser thereof, or his assigns, the said purchase money, together with any subsequent assessment for benefit or tax, which the said purchaser may have *Privilege of redemption.*

paid, chargeable on said land, and which he is hereby authorized to pay, provided a notice of such payment shall have been filed in the office of the collector of taxes and assessments, with interest at the rate of fifteen per cent. per annum in addition thereto, and also two dollars for each notice given to any owner, mortgagee or lessee of a longer term than three years, provided due proof of such service shall have been filed in said office. The certificate of such collector acknowledging the payment and showing what land, and on account of what tax or assessment for benefit such payment is intended to redeem, shall be evidence of such redemption. Such redemption shall discharge the land described in said certificate from the lien created by the assessment for benefit or tax, in respect of which such sale shall have been made, or by such sale or certificate.

§ 31. Section thirty-two of said title five is hereby amended so as to read as follows:

Certain accounts to be kept by the collector of taxes. § 32. The said collector shall note on the account of unpaid taxes, and also upon the original tax or assessment roll, or copy thereof in his office, all payments made to him after any account of unpaid taxes or assessments for benefit, shall be sent back to him by the county treasurer or comptroller as aforesaid; and if any sale shall be made he shall also, in like manner, note that fact; and also, any redemption or assignment of which he shall receive the notice hereinbefore required, and the memorandum of payment on any return of unpaid taxes, or abstract of assessments for benefit, or copy thereof, in the office of the collector, shall be sufficient evidence of such payment. He shall also forthwith, upon receiving the same, render to the treasurer of the city, an account of the proceeds of any sale for unpaid assessments for benefit, and of any moneys received or collected by him that may be paid to such treasurer, and at the same time pay over the said moneys received by him. And the said collector shall also render to the treasurer of the county an account of the proceeds of any sale for unpaid taxes, and of moneys received or collected by him that may be paid to such treasurer, and at the same time pay over said moneys received by him.

§ 32. Section thirty-three of said title five is hereby amended so as to read as follows:

§ 36 The collector shall execute to the purchaser, or his assigns, pursuant to the terms of sale, when the lands sold for any tax or assessment for benefit shall not have been redeemed as by this act provided, a proper conveyance of the lands so sold by him. Said conveyance shall contain a brief statement of the proceeding had for the sale of said land, and shall be evidence that such sale and other proceedings have been regularly made, and had according to the provisions of this act. He shall, also, forthwith, note the same on the account of unpaid taxes, or abstract of assessments for benefit, or copy thereof kept at his office. The grantee named in said conveyance, his representative and assigns, shall be entitled as against all persons whomsoever to the possession of said premises, and to the rents, issues and profits thereof, pursuant to the terms of his or her conveyance, and shall be entitled to obtain possession of the lands described in such conveyance, by summary proceedings, in the same manner as if provided by law for the removal of persons who hold over or continue in possession of real estate sold by virtue of and execution against them.

To convey the lands sold.

§ 33. In place of the provisions of title six of said act of incorporation in regard to " the day and night police department," the said title six shall hereafter read as follows :

OF CONTRACTS.

1. The mayor, comptroller, street commissioner, collector of taxes and assessments, and when elected as by this act provided, the commissioner of taxes, shall constitute a board to be known as the board of contracts of said city. A majority of such officers present at any meeting regularly called, according to the by-laws to be adopted by said board, shall constitute a quorum for the transaction of business. The mayor, or in his absence such member of the board as the members present at any meeting thereof shall appoint, shall preside thereat. The said board shall keep a record of all its acts and proceedings, and for that purpose the city clerk shall be the clerk thereof.

Board of contracts.

2 All acts, orders, resolutions, ordinances, or other proceedings of the common council, involving any expenditures of money or any liability on the part of the

Powers an duties of.

city to pay money, except for salaries, or for its own
use, as hereinafter mentioned, shall be sent to the said
board of contracts for execution, and it shall not be lawful for the common council to expend other than for
salaries out of moneys previously raised by tax and in
the treasury for such purpose, or to authorize or empower any member or committee of its own body, or any
body or person whatsoever, other than the said board of
contracts, to expend any moneys in the treasury, except
such sum, if any, as may be previously raised by tax and
in the treasury for the specific use of the common council. Nor shall the common council be able to bind or
render liable the city to pay any moneys other than for
salaries, and its own use as aforesaid, except through
the board of contracts, as by this title provided.

3. All contracts, agreements, or liabilities, in the
nature of contracts, by which the city shall be held liable
to pay money, whether for the general expenses of the
city or for local improvements, or otherwise, however,
except for salaries and the purposes of any specific fund
of the common council as aforesaid, shall be made by the
board of contracts, in pursuance of resolutions, orders or
ordinances of the common council, or provision of law
(except as in the next section of this title provided)
directing the work, labor, services, materials, supplies,
repairs, buildings, fire engines, hose carriages, or other
articles to be done, obtained, or constructed, or the title
in fee, use or occupation of any real estate to be had, as
the case may be ; and all proposals for such work, labor,
services, materials, supplies, repairs, buildings, fire
engine, hose carriages, or other articles, title in fee, use
or occupation of real estate, shall be made to, and determined by the said board of contracts. All contracts for
work, labor, materials, repairs or supplies, involving an
expense of more than one hundred dollars, shall be entered into with the lowest responsible bidder, after publication for proposals therefor, for ten days, unless the
exigency of the case require a shorter time, in the corporation newspapers. It shall not be lawful for the said
board of contracts to enter into any contract or agreement, or to incur any liability on the part of the city,
unless the money shall have been previously appropriated and raised therefor, and in the treasury, except for

(margin note:) Contracts to be made with the lowest responsible bidder.

local improvements and for objects the expense of which
is to be raised by local assessments.

4. All contracts and agreements for blank books and *Blank books stationery, &c.* stationery, fuel and other supplies of a consumable and
indispensable character for the public offices, courts,
station houses, engine houses, and other public buildings, may be made by the said board of contracts without any order of the common council, as the public exigencies shall require, under the restrictions in the preceding section of this title provided.

5. No contract for supplies of any kind shall be made
for a longer period than one year.

6. The provisions of this title shall not apply to the
water and sewerage department.

7. All repairs of public buildings, wharves and piers *Repairs.*
belonging to the city, and of streets, fire engines and
other property of the city, may be ordered by the board
of contracts without the order or resolution of the common council, in cases where the entire expense of such
repairs for any one object shall not exceed fifty dollars;
but in no case whatsoever, unless the money to pay
therefor shall have been appropriated and in the treasury, and the nature and cost of such repairs shall be
first submitted to said board. Repairs of fire engines,
hose carriages, engine houses and other property appropriated to the use of the fire department, shall be super-
intended by the chief engineers of such department for
their respective districts, under the direction of the said
board of contracts, in pursuance of resolutions of the
common council, where the cost of such repairs shall
exceed fifty dollars, and of the order of said board of
contracts in cases not exceeding that amount as aforesaid.

§ 34. Section twenty of title six of said act is hereby
kept in force, and shall form section eighteen of title
eleven of said act of incorporation.

§ 35. Section nine of an act entitled "An act relative
to local improvements in the city of Brooklyn," passed
April eleventh, eighteen hundred and sixty-one, is hereby amended by adding thereto the following words: but
no such bond shall be issued for any certificate or certificates issued upon any illegal or irregular assessment
which has been or may be declared invalid or which is
in contest.

26

§ 36. Section two of title ten of said act of incorporation is hereby amended so as to read as follows :

§ 2. The said accounts shall be distributed in four
distinct classes. The first of said classes shall embrace
all such expenditures as are to be made out of moneys
raised by general tax, and shall be called the general
fund ; the second, such as are to be made out of money
raised by special or local assessment, and shall be called
the special fund ; the third shall consist of accounts of
the sinking fund ; and the fourth shall consist of the revenues of the city from other sources than taxation, to
be called the revenue fund. And no money raised or
received for the use of one of said funds, shall be at any
time used for the purposes of either of the other of said
funds, except as in the next section provided.

§ 37. Section three of said title ten is hereby amended
so as to read as follows :

§ 3. The accounts of the general fund shall always exhibit the receipts and expenditures on account of each
purpose or appropriation for which the general tax shall
be levied in each year, and no receipt or expenditure of
money shall at any time be charged or credited to any
other than its appropriate account. The accounts of the
special fund, in addition to the general account thereof,
shall at all times exhibit the accounts received and paid
under each item composing said fund, with the amounts
received and paid for interest on each. The sinking fund
account shall exhibit the amounts received and paid on
account thereof, specifying from what sources they shall
have been received, together with the amount and description of securities belonging to'said fund. The revenue
fund shall exhibit all the moneys paid into the city treasury for collectors' fees, default and interest for the non-
payment of taxes, costs and fees of the attorney and
counsel, in opening, widening or extending streets, avenues and squares, or other proceedings for taking private
property for public purposes, balance of advertising fees
after paying the actual expenses of advertising, the balance of inspectors' fees, licenses, fees to city after paying the actual expenses of advertising officers or appointees, fees and fines from the police and justices'
courts, penalties for violation of city ordinances, rents
and proceeds of sale of any property of the city, interest
on deposits in bank, and all revenues of the city what-

soever from other sources than taxation, and shall also
exhibit the payments made on account of any judgments
against the city as herein provided. The revenue fund
shall be kept inviolate, except for the payment of such
judgments and the amount thereof standing on the first
day of June in each year shall be deducted from the
amount otherwise necessary to be raised by tax for the
expenses of the city for the next fiscal year, and shall be
transferred and charged to the general fund and applied
accordingly. All bonds and other securities belonging Endorse-
to the sinking fund shall be endorsed as follows: "The bonds.
property of the sinking fund of the city of Brooklyn,
transferable from said fund only by written order of the
mayor, comptroller and treasurer of said city, the commissioners of said fund." Any transfer without such
order of any bond so endorsed shall be null and void.

§ 38. The amount of any judgment recovered against Judgments
and payable by said city and remaining unpaid, with the city.
interest due and to become due thereon, shall be included
by the mayor, in his first statement, after the same shall
become payable, to the joint board of aldermen having
the shorter time to serve, and city supervisors; and
such amount shall be raised in the next levy of taxes
for the expenses of said city. Such judgments shall be
paid out of the first moneys paid into the city treasury
on account of such levy, in the order of their recovery.
Until the moneys so raised shall be paid into the treasury and payments of said judgments refused by the
financial officers of the city, no execution shall issue
against the said city, unless the amount of such judgments shall not have been included in the statement of
the mayor, or in the tax levy, as aforesaid. Provided,
nevertheless, if there be any moneys in the treasury to
the credit of the fund derived from the revenues of the
city other than taxation, sufficient to satisfy said judgments, the common council shall direct the payment
therefrom of said judgments, in the order of their recovery.

§ 39. The city of Brooklyn shall not be liable in City not lia-
damages for any nonfeasance or misfeasance of the feasance or
common council or any officer of the city or appointee nonfeasance
of the common council, of any duty imposed upon them,
or any or either of them, by the provisions of titles four
and five of this act, or of any other duty enjoined upon

them, or any or either of them, as officers of government, by any other provision of this act; but the remedy of the party or parties aggrieved for any such nonfeasance or misfeasance shall be, by mandamus or other proceeding or action, to compel the performance of the duty, or by other action against the members of the common council, officer or appointee, as the rights of such party or parties may by law admit, if at all.

Trustees.

§ 40. The common council of said city and the members thereof are hereby declared to be trustees of the property, funds and effects of the corporation hereby created; and the aldermen of the city of Brooklyn are hereby declared to be trustees of the property, funds and effects of their respective wards, so far as such property, funds and effects, in or derived from their respective wards, are or may be committed to their management or control respectively by the said act of incorporation or the acts amendatory thereof; and every person residing in said city or in any ward, and assessed to pay the taxes therein, who shall pay taxes therein, is hereby declared to be a cestui que trust in respect to the said property, funds and effects respectively; and any co-trustee, or any such cestui que trust, shall be entitled, as against such trustees, and in regard to such property, funds and effects, to all the rights and remedies provided by law of any co-trustee or cestui que trust to prosecute and maintain any action to prevent waste and injury to any property, funds or estate held in trust. Such trustees are hereby made subject to all the duties and responsibilities imposed by law upon trustees, and such duties and responsibilities may be enforced by any co-trustee or cestui que trust aforesaid.

Streets or avenues used five years deemed public streets.

§ 41. All streets and avenues in said city which have been or may be thrown out to public use, and have been or may be used as such for five years continuously, shall be deemed and taken to be public streets and avenues; and the city of Brooklyn and the common council, and the water commissioners thereof, shall have all jurisdiction and power in respect thereto, the same as if such streets and avenues had been or shall be opened by proceedings had for that purpose, under the provisions of this act.

Commissioners of repairs and

§ 42. The office of commissioner of repairs and supplies and all offices dependent upon it, shall cease and be abolished from and after the first day of May, one supplies abolished. thousand eight hundred and sixty-three; and the powers and duties of that office as now established and not modified by this act, shall on and after that day be exercised by the street commisioner, except that the said street commissioner shall have power to appoint with the consent of the common council, only a foreman of repairs and supplies in addition to the appointments now authorized to be made by him.

§ 43. The provisions of the act entitled "An act in In relation to frauds in assessments. relation to frauds in assessments for local improvements in the city of New York," passed April seventeenth, eighteen hundred and fifty-eight, are hereby extended and made applicable to the city of Brooklyn, and to the proceedings relative to any assessment or assessments for local improvements made or to be made therein.

§ 44. The aldermen of each ward shall appoint so Lamp lighters. many lamp lighters as may be designated for his ward.

§ 45. Section five of title two of said act of incorpora- Cleaning streets. tion is hereby repealed; and all contracts for cleaning streets and repairing wells and pumps shall be made by the board of contracts, and the expense thereof shall be as heretofore a charge upon the wards respectively, each for the cleaning of its own streets and repairing its own wells and pumps. Every contract for cleaning streets shall be subject to the powers of the board of health created or to be created in or over said city, and a clause to this effect shall be inserted in the advertisements for proposals, and also in the contract.

§ 46. No member or officer of the common council or No officer to be interested in contracts. board of contracts, or any city or ward officer, whether elected or appointed, or supervisor of said city, shall be directly or indirectly interested in any contract or agreement made by or with the said board of contracts, or in the proceeds or profits of any such contract, nor in furnishing said city for hire or pay, any work, labor, materials or supplies, or any article or service of any kind whatsoever ordered by said board of contracts; nor shall he take or receive any money, article, thing, advantage or promise thereof, as consideration for any vote or act in his official capacity, or for making and consenting in such capacity to any award of any contract, or to any appointment for office or place. Any person offending againt the provisions of this section, shall be deemed guilty of felony, and upon conviction, shall be punished by imprisonment in the state prison for a term not less than three nor more than five years. All contracts made in violation of this section shall be void.

§ 47. Each alderman shall be entitled to receive three dollars for each meeting of the common council or committee of the common council he may attend, provided the aggregate sum which any alderman shall receive for any year shall not exceed five hundred dollars, and provided his attendance in common council be certified by the city clerk, and on committees by the chairmen thereof respectively.

§ 48. All acts and parts of acts inconsistent with this act are hereby repealed.

§ 49. This act shall take effect immediately. Except the forty-seventh section, which shall take effect on the first day of January next.

Chap. 64.

AN ACT to authorize the Port Henry Iron Ore Company of Lake Champlain to borrow money by mortgage on their real estate in Essex county.

Passed March 27, 1862.

The People of the State of New York, represented in Senate and Assembly, do enact as follows :

SECTION 1. The Port Henry Iron Ore Company of Lake Champlain are hereby authorized at any time previous to January first, eighteen hundred and sixty-three, to borrow money to an amount not exceeding thirty-five thousand dollars for the uses of said company, and on such term of time as said company shall choose, not exceeding ten years, and to secure the repayment of the same with annual interest by mortgage upon their real property and franchises in Essex county.

§ 2. This act shall take effect immediately.

Chap. 65.

AN ACT to authorize and direct the Board of Supervisors of the county of Putnam to raise certain moneys by tax to pay certain expenses incurred in laying out and constructing a certain highway in the town of Carmel in said county.

Passed March 27, 1862; three-fifths being present.

The People of the State of New York, represented in Senate and Assembly, do enact as follows:

SECTION 1. The board of supervisors of the county of Putnam are hereby authorized and directed, at their next annual meeting, to levy and assess on the taxable property in the town of Carmel, in said county, a sufficient sum, not exceeding fifteen hundred dollars to pay the following bills for labor with interest from the twenty-third day of November, eighteen hundred and fifty-nine, which bills have been presented to and approved by said board of supervisors in said county, to wit: To Russell White & Company, for labor, six hundred and fifty-six dollars and seventeen cents; to Stephen Voorhis, for labor and team, fifty-seven dollars and seventy-five cents; to Benjamin Brown, for materials, fifteen dollars; to George Avery, for surveys and maps, eighty-nine dollars and seventy-five cents; to James Ganung, for labor, thirty dollars; to Whitlock and Avery, for materials, fifty-one dollars and seventy-four cents; to Edwin Crosby, for cash paid for labor and materials, twenty-four dollars; to Edwin Crosby, for services as commissioner, one hundred dollars; to Cornelius Dean, for services as commissioner, one hundred dollars; to Joel Bunnel, for services as commissioner, fifty-two dollars. Said bills having been incurred in laying out and constructing a public highway from Lake Mahopac, in the town of Carmel, in the county of Putnam to Croton Falls, in the town of North Salem, in the county of Westchester, pursuant to an act passed April sixth, eigh-

[marginal notes: To assess the sum of $1,500. / To whom it shall be paid.]

teen hundred and fifty-nine, and in addition to the amount authorized to be raised by said act.

§ 2. Should the several bills named in section first of this act exceed the said sum of fifteen hundred dollars, then all the bills excepting the bills of Edwin Crosby, for services as commissioner, one hundred dollars, Cornelius Dean, for services as commissioner, one hundred dollars, Joel Bunnel, for services as commissioner, fifty-two dollars, shall first be paid and the balance, if any there be, shall be divided between the said Edwin Crosby, Cornelius Dean and Joel Bunnel, commissioners, in proportion to the several amounts above allowed to each for services.

§ 3. This act shall take effect immediately.

Chap. 66.

AN ACT concerning the Erie Railway Company.

Passed March 28, 1862 ; three-fifths being present.

The People of the State of New York, represented in Senate and Assembly, do enact as follows :

SECTION 1. The Erie railway company, having been duly organized pursuant to the provisions of the act, entitled " An act relative to the foreclosure and sale of the New York and Erie railroad," passed April fourth, eighteen hundred and sixty, and of the act in addition thereto, passed April second, eighteen hundred and sixty-one, and Dudley S. Gregory and J. C. Bancroft Davis, the trustees named in the contract or amicable agreement referred to in said acts, having duly conveyed to the said company all the estate, property, franchises, rights and other things which were purchased by them, pursuant to the provisions of said first named act, and were conveyed to them pursuant to the conditions of sale, and of the several acts and proceedings relative thereto, so as to vest the same in the said Erie railway company, their successors and assigns, and some of the unsecured bonds of the New York and Erie railroad company being still outstanding, it is hereby enacted that any holder of an unsecured bond or bonds of the said New York and Erie railroad company, or of coupons on such bonds which matured before January first, eighteen hundred and sixty-two, or of a judgment debt recovered against said company before the said sale, who shall, before the first day of July next, surrender his said bond or bonds or coupons to the Erie railway company, or discharge said debt, shall be entitled to receive preferred stock therefor in the Erie railway company, upon payment of an assessment of two and one-half per centum on the par value thereof, with interest from the first day of September last, the same as if the surrender had been made pursuant to the provisions of said amicable agreement. And any holder of the stock of the New York and Erie railroad company who shall surrender the certificate of his said stock to the Erie railway company before the said first day of July, and pay a like assessment thereon, shall be entitled to receive the common stock of said Erie railway company, the same as if the surrender had been made pursuant to the provisions of said amicable agreement. *Certain bond holders to receive preferred stock on surrender of their bonds.*

§ 2. The said Erie railway company shall, after the first day of July next, file in the office of the Secretary of State a statement of the whole amount of the stock of said Erie railway company, both common and preferred, outstanding and issued on that day; and certified copies of said statements, and of the articles of association of said Erie railway company, shall be prima facie evidence of the organization of said corporation, and of the facts contained in said articles, and in said statements, in all proceedings to which the said Erie railway company is or may be a party. *File a statement of amount of stock in office of secretary of state.*

§ 3. The aforesaid purchase of the New York and Erie railroad, and other property sold at the sale, having been made by said Dudley S. Gregory and J. C. Bancroft Davis, subject to the rights and interests of the several classes of mortgage bondholders of the New York and Erie railroad company, and of the trustees under the said several mortgages, as the same existed at the time of the sale, in and to the personal property and chattels covered and intended to be covered by said mortgages, the said rights and interest shall continue and be preserved as against all persons and corporations; and it shall not be necessary hereafter to file the said mort- *Not necessary to file mortgages as chattel mortgages.*

27

gages, or any of them, as chattel mortgages, in order to preserve the liens created by them as they existed at the time of said sale.

Consolidation of Buffalo branch. § 4. The Buffalo branch of the Erie railway company, a corporation organized under the provisions of the laws of this state, is authorized to consolidate with the Erie railway company into a single corporation, under the said corporate name of the Erie railway company, provided that the capital stock of the said Erie railway company shall not be increased by such consolidation.

Terms of consolidation. § 5. Such consolidation may be made by an agreement under the respective corporate seals of the two corporations; and upon filing a duplicate or counterpart thereof in the office of the Secretary of State, the said corporation, known as the Buffalo branch of the Erie railway company, shall be merged in the said Erie railway company, and all and singular the rights, franchises and interests of the said Buffalo branch of the Erie railway company, in and to every species of property, real, personal and mixed, and things in action thereunto belonging, shall be deemed to be transferred to and vested in said Erie railway company without any other deed or transfer; and the said Erie railway company shall hold and enjoy the same, together with the rights of way and all other rights of property, franchises and interests, as fully as if the same had been lawfully acquired or constructed by the said Erie railway company; provided, however, that the said Erie railway company shall, when such consolidation takes place, assume all the obligations and liabilities of the said Buffalo branch of the Erie railway company, whether on contract or for misconduct or neglect, and whether to this state or to individuals, and shall be liable to have an action brought against it to enforce the same, and may be made a party to any suit now pending to enforce any such obligation or liability.

Return to secretary of state the amounts to be paid for certain leases. § 6. The Erie railway company shall hereafter, in addition to the returns which it is now required by law to make, return to the Secretary of State, with the other funded debt of the company, the amount of the sums on the thirtieth day of September in each year, required to be paid annually for the leases of the Long Dock property, of the Union railroad, of the Paterson and Ramapo railroad, and the Paterson and Hudson River railroad operated by the Erie railway company, in New Jersey, and of such other railroads as are now or hereafter may be operated by said Erie railway company under a lease, whether in this state or elsewhere: and on failure to make any such return for twelve months, after being required to do so by the Secretary of State, the right to continue such leases or any of them may be determined on information filed in the supreme court by the Attorney General. But no wilful failure to make such return shall operate to relieve such Erie railway company from its obligations to pay any moneys stipulated in and by such lease to be paid by it, And if any corporation duly organized, or to be organized, in the state of New Jersey or Pennsylvania shall undertake to construct a coal road and to connect the same with the road of the Erie railway company, between Oxford Station in Orange county and Deposit in the county of Delaware, for the transportation of coal, said Erie railway company is hereby authorized to lease the said coal road and to contract for the leasing and operation of the same, and for the transportation of coal over said coal road and upon any road that may be owned or operated by said Erie railway company. Provided, however, that this section shall not be deemed to authorize the leasing of but one such road. *Penalty for not filing.*

§ 7. Chapter one hundred and sixty of the laws of eighteen hundred and sixty, and chapter one hundred and nineteen of the laws of eighteen hundred and sixty-one, relating to the re-organization of the New York and Erie railroad company, and conferring on the Erie railway company the franchises, rights and authorities theretofore belonging to the New York and Erie railroad company, are hereby declared to confer upon the Erie railway company, in regard to any railroad, it may now operate including the continuation of their line from Attica to Buffalo and from Corning to Buffalo, all the authority conferred on certain railroad companies by chapter three hundred and two of the act of eighteen hundred and fifty-five.

§ 8. This act shall take effect immediately.

Chap. 67.

AN ACT to amend the charter of the Ætna Fire Insurance Company of New York.

Passed March 28, 1862.

The People of the State of New York, represented in Senate and Assembly, do enact as follows :

SECTION 1. The Ætna Fire Insurance Company of New York, in addition to the powers already vested in them, are hereby authorized and empowered to make insurance against all risks of inland navigation and transportation whatsoever.

§ 2. This act shall take effect immediately.

Chap. 68.

AN ACT to authorize the Bank of Troy to reduce its capital stock.

Passed March 28, 1862.

The People of the State of New York, represented in Senate and Assembly, do enact as follows :

SECTION 1. The Bank of Troy is hereby authorized to reduce its capital stock to an amount not less than two hundred and twenty thousand dollars,

§ 2. Nothing in this act contained shall in any way change or lessen the liability of the stockholders of the said bank to the bill holders or other creditors thereof, or any indebtedness or engagement now existing against said bank, or that may so exist either absolutely or contingently at the time when such reduction shall take place.

§ 3. This act shall take effect immediately.

Chap. 69.

AN ACT to amend an act entitled an "Act to incorporate the Cayuga Asylum for Destitute Children," passed April 10th, 1852.

Passed March 28, 1862; three-fifths being present.

The People of the State of New York, represented in Senate and Assembly, do enact as follows:

SECTION 1. Section thirteen, of chapter two hundred and seven, of the laws of eighteen hundred and fifty-two, entitled "An act to incorporate the Cayuga Asylum for Destitute Children," is hereby amended so as to read as follows:

The board of supervisors of the county of Cayuga are hereby authorized to instruct the superintendents of the poor of said county, to annually contract with the managers of said asylum, to board and clothe all children thrown on said county for support, who are of a proper age to receive its benefits, at a price not exceeding eighty cents each per week for their support. And the said board of supervisors are hereby authorized to levy and collect annually, in advance, in the same manner as other county charges are levied and collected, such sums of money for the above said purpose as the said board of supervisors may deem necessary and expedient; the same to be paid quarterly, by the treasurer of said county, to the treasurer of the Cayuga Asylum, on the presentation to him of bills properly verified, according to contract with the superintendents of the poor; and the said society shall, upon complying with the terms mentioned in the second section of chapter three hundred and sixty-eight, of the laws of one thousand eight hundred and forty-nine, be entitled to a distributive share of the moneys appropriated out of the treasury, and distributed as therein directed, or as shall hereafter be provided by law in relation to the orphan asylums in this state.

Chap. 70.

AN ACT to amend an act entitled "An act to
amend an act entitled 'An act for the benefit of
married women in insuring the lives of their
husbands,' passed April fourteen, eighteen hundred and fifty-eight."

Passed March 28, 1862.

*The People of the State of New York, represented in
Senate and Assembly do enact as follows:*

SECTION 1. Section two of the act entitled "An act to
amend an act entitled 'An act for the benefit of married
women in insuring the lives of their husbands,' passed
April fourteen eighteen hundred and fifty-eight," is
hereby amended so as to read as follows :

The amount of the insurance may be made payable, in
case of the death of the wife before the decease of her
husband, to his or to her children for their use, as shall
be provided in the policy of insurance and to their
guardian, if under age.

§ 2. This act shall take effect immediately.

Chap. 71.

AN ACT authorizing the village of Dunkirk in
the county of Chautauqua, to purchase, take
and hold land within or without the bounds of
said village for a cemetery.

Passed March 28, 1862; three-fifths being present.

*The People of the State of New York, represented in
Senate and Assembly do enact as follows :*

SECTION 1. The trustees of the corporation of the village of Dunkirk in the county of Chautauqua, may purchase, take and hold a lot or tract of land, not exceeding five acres, either within or without the corporate

bounds of said village, but within the town of Dunkirk
in the county of Chautauqua, and enclose with a substantial fence and otherwise suitably prepare the same
as a burial ground, which land when purchased, enclosed
and prepared, shall be exclusively used as a public cemetery, and shall forever be devoted, free of expense, for
the benefit of strangers and other persons who may die
in said village with no other place of interment provided
for them.

§ 2. The said trustees shall have power and are hereby *To remove bodies form- erly inter- red.*
authorized to remove to said cemetery the remains of
the dead heretofore interred in said village upon lands
granted in the year one thousand eight hundred and
thirty-nine as a donation or endowment to the trustees
of the Dunkirk Academy.

§ 3. A general tax may be imposed, levied and col- *Village may lay tax for expenses.*
lected on the taxable property, in the said village of
Dunkirk to defray the expense of purchasing, fencing
and preparing said land to be used as a cemetery and of
removing thereto the dead from the lands of the trustees of the Dunkirk Academy; such tax to be imposed
in the manner prescribed by law for imposing such
general taxes in said village as are now authorized by
law to be imposed thereon for village purposes.

§ 4. The said cemetery shall be and hereby is declared *Cemetery to be exempt from taxa- tion.*
exempted from all public taxes, rates or assessments,
and shall not be liable to be sold on execution or be applied in payment of debts due from said village so long
as the same shall be dedicated to the purpose of a cemetery.

§ 5. This act shall take effect immediately.

Chap. 72.

AN ACT to incorporate the Bay Ridge Fire Company in the town of New Utrecht.

Passed March 28, 1862; three-fifths being present.

*The People of the State of New York, represented in
Senate, and Assembly do enact as follows:*

SECTION 1. It shall and may be lawful for Winant E.
Bennett, Simon G. Wardell, Jaques B. Wardell, Daniel

Van Brunt, Richard Rowland and their associates at
Bay Ridge, in the town of New Utrecht in the county
of Kings, for the purpose of procuring a fire engine or
hooks and ladders and other implements for extinguishing fires, to meet together at any time after the passage
of this act, and choose not less than three nor more
than five of their number to be trustees to be called the
Bay Ridge Fire Company, who shall be a body corporate and shall have perpetual succession, and by that
name be capable of taking, holding and conveying property, real and personal, not exceeding five thousand
dollars in amount, necessary for the purpose of extinguishing fires and the preservation of their engine,
hooks and ladders, and implements of the said company.

§ 2. The said trustees and their successors or a
majority of them shall have full power and authority to
make, establish and ordain such rules and regulations
for the nomination, appointment and government of a
sufficient number of firemen residing at Bay Ridge
within the present boundaries of school district number
two in said town, not exceeding thirty-five to their engine or hooks and ladders belonging to said company to
have the care, management, working and using said fire
engine or hooks and ladders, with the necessary implements belonging thereto, and who shall be ready at all
times to assist in extinguishing fires, and to impose on
them such reasonable fines and penalties, not exceeding
five dollars for any offence, upon such firemen or any of
them in not performing the duties hereby to be enjoined
and required from them.

§ 3. All fines incurred by this act shall and may be
recovered by the trustees aforesaid, in their name, before any justice of the peace in the said county of Kings
with costs of suit. All fines and penalties recovered as
aforesaid, shall be appropriated by the trustees for the
purpose of procuring and keeping in repair the fire engine or hooks and ladders and other implements for extinguishing fires.

§ 4. Each of the said persons so to be nominated and
appointed firemen as aforesaid, shall be exempt from all
jury duty whatsoever, while acting as such firemen.

§ 5. It shall and may be lawful for the members of
the said company, from time to time, to appoint a secretary, who shall enter in a book to be kept for that pur-

pose, the names of the said trustees from time to time chosen, and the names of the firemen from time to time appointed or removed, together with such rules and regulations as shall be made for the government of the company hereby incorporated, or of the persons so to be appointed firemen, and other rules and regulation from time to time made, which entries may be given in evidence in any trial for the recovery of any penalty which may be incurred by virtue of this act.

§ 6. The said trustees shall be chosen by the persons associated under this act or their successors for the time being, pursuant to such rules and regulations as may be prescribed in manner aforesaid, and shall hold their office for one year, or until others shall be chosen in their stead. Term of office.

§ 7. A certificate under the hand of the secretary of the said company shall be deemed and taken in all places as presumptive evidence that the person to whom it is given is a member of said company, and entitled to all the privileges and exemptions in and by this act granted to the members of the said company, but such certificate shall not preclude any court from examining the person presenting it under oath, touching his right to such privilege and exemption. Certificate of company.

§ 8. This act shall be void unless a fire company shall be formed in conformity to its provisions and at least a good and substantial engine or truck and hooks and ladders with their necessary implements and buildings sheltering the same be procured within six months from the passage of this act. Must procure hook and ladders within six months.

§ 9. This act shall take effect immediately.

Chap. 73.

AN ACT supplementary to an act entitled " An act to provide for the continuation of Flatbush Avenue from the city line of Brooklyn into the town of Flatbush," passed April seventeenth, eighteen hundred and fifty-four.

Passed March 28, 1862 ; three-fifths being present.

The People of the State of New York, represented in Senate and Assembly do enact as follows:

SECTION 1. The commissioners of assessment heretofore appointed by the county court of Kings county, under the provisions of the act entitled "An act to provide for the continuation of Flatbush Avenue from the city line of Brooklyn into the town of Flatbush," passed April seventeenth, eighteen hundred and fifty-four or so many of them as are now or may be acting therein, are hereby authorized to receive payment of the unpaid assessments returned by them to the clerk of the county of Kings on the twenty-second day of February, eighteen hundred and fifty-nine, and for that purpose shall, within thirty days after this act takes Meetings of commis-sioners. effect as a law, attend at some public place in the town of Flatbush once a week for four weeks successively, from ten to twelve o'clock on each day, giving six days written notice thereof by posting the same in at least four public places in said town. Upon such payments they shall give duplicate receipts therefor, and the filing of one of said receipts in the office of the clerk of the said county of Kings shall be a sufficient discharge of the assessment liens upon the particular pieces of property to which such payments relate.

To sell lands for unpaid tax-es. § 2. If the said assessments or any of them shall remain unpaid at the expiration of the said thirty days from the first posting of the said notice, the supervisor of the said town of Flatbush is hereby authorized and required to sell each of the several parcels of land upon which the said assessments shall then remain unpaid, at public auction for the lowest term of years for which any person will take the same and pay to the said commissioners the amount remaining unpaid with ten per cent interest from the expiration of said thirty days' notice to pay the same ; the said supervisor first giving thirty days' written notice of said sale by affixing the same in four public places in the said town of Flatbush.

§ 3. Upon such sale being made, the said supervisor shall give certificates of sale to such purchasers as shall become entitled thereto, and shall execute and deliver conveyances of the lands so purchased, unless the same shall be redeemed within two years from the time of sale by the payment to the purchaser or to said commissioners, or either of them, for his use, of the sum paid by the purchaser, with interest at the rate of twelve per cent per annum. *To give conveyances.*

§ 4. So much and such parts of the said act to which this act is supplementary as are inconsistent with the provisions of this act are hereby repealed.

§5 . This act shall take effect immediately.

Chap. 74.

AN ACT to provide for the construction of a bridge across the Oneida river at Caughdenoy.

Passed March 28, 1862 ; three-fifths being present.

The People of the State of New York, represented in Senate and Assembly, do enact as follows :

SECTION 1. The highway commissioners of the towns of Hastings, Oswego county, and Clay, Onondaga county, are hereby appointed commissioners to contract for and superintend the erection of a bridge across the Oneida river at Caughdenoy, Oswego county, or so much thereof as it may be deemed necessary to rebuild, exclusive of that portion which crosses the canal known as the Oneida river improvement.

§ 2. The board of supervisors of the county of Oswego are hereby authorized and required to levy, in the year eighteen hundred and sixty-two, and raise by tax upon the taxable property of said county, in the same manner as other contingent charges of said county are levied *To levy tax of $3,000.*

and raised, the sum of five hundred dollars; and also upon the taxable property of the town of Hastings in said county, the additional sum of five hundred dollars. And the supervisors of the county of Onondaga are hereby authorized and required to levy in like manner, upon the taxable property of the said county of Onondaga, the sum of five hundred dollars, and the additional sum of five hundred dollars upon the taxable property of the town of Clay in said county.

Money to be paid to commissioners. § 3. The moneys raised by virtue of this act shall be paid into the county treasuries of the respective counties aforesaid, (the moneys raised in each county into the treasury thereof,) and by the respective treasurers paid to the order of said commissioners, or a majority of them, provided that before said commissioners shall be entitled to receive said moneys or any part thereof, they shall execute to the board of supervisors of each of said counties of Onondaga and Oswego, a bond in the penal sum of two thousand dollars, with sureties, conditioned for the faithful application of the moneys received by them to the purposes contemplated by this act, which bonds shall be approved by the county judge of Onondaga county and filed in the clerk's office of the county in which the board of supervisors to which they shall be respectively given, resides.

Board of auditors. § 4. The supervisors of the towns of Hastings, Clay and Schroeppel are hereby constituted a board of auditors to examine and audit the accounts of said commissioners, with the same powers as are conferred upon town auditors, and when said bridge is completed are required to meet at some convenient place, of which notice shall be given at some day at least one week preceding the meetings of the boards of supervisors in either of the counties, Oswego or Onondaga, and shall allow the said commissioners to retain, of the moneys appropriated by this act, one dollar and twenty-five cents per day for every day necessarily employed in superintending the building of said bridge ; and said board of auditors shall make a full copy of the accounts presented to them by said commissioners, with the amount audited by them, and the entire cost of said bridge, and file a copy thereof with the clerks of the board of supervisors of said counties, on or before the first day of their next annual session.

§ 5. **The resident** engineer in charge of the Oneida river improvement shall designate what width or length of the bridge structure now erected across said canal or side-cut of the river, is necessary to the use of said Oneida river improvement, and the section thus designated shall be taken care of in the same manner, and be under the same control as other similar structures over the canals of this state. But nothing in this act contained shall make the State of New York subject to any expense, or in any manner liable where it is not now subject or liable. *Duties of resident engineer.*

§ 6. The supervisors designated in the fourth section of this act are hereby constituted a board of commissioners to divide that part of said bridge, exclusive of the portion over the canal, being the part which is northerly from the northerly line of the canal known as the Oneida river improvement, as equally as may be, and assign the northern half to the town of Hastings, and the southern half to the town of Clay, and shall give notice in writing to the town clerk of said towns respectively, of the portions of said bridge assigned to each town. Whereupon it shall be the duty of the highway commissioners of the said towns respectively, to take charge of and keep in repair that portion of said bridge so assigned to the town of which they shall have the charge of the highways. *Supervisors to be a board to divide the portions of bridge to keep in repair.*

§ 7. The said commissioners shall, within fifteen days after the completion of said bridge, file a certificate of the expenses of the same in the town clerk's office in the towns of Hastings and Clay. *File a certificate.*

§ 8. If the expense of said bridge should not amount to the sum of two thousand dollars, the respective boards of supervisors herein specified shall not be required to levy any larger sum than the actual expense of 'constructing said bridge, such sum to be apportioned in the same ratio on the towns and counties, as specified in section two of this act. *Expense of bridge.*

§ 9. This act shall take effect immediately.

Chap. 75.

AN ACT in relation to School District No. Six in the town of Yonkers.

Passed March 28, 1862; three-fifths being present.

The People of the State of New York, represented in Senate and Assembly, do enact as follows :

SECTION 1. George B. Upham, Isaac H. Knox, Ethan Flagg, Justus Lawrence, Peter F. Peck, and John M. Mason, are hereby appointed and declared to be trustees of school district No. Six, in the town of Yonkers, and to constitute the board of education of said school district. The said board shall, at its first stated meeting after the passage of this act, divide the said trustees by lot into three classes, each class to consist of two trustees, and to be denominated, respectively, class No. one, No. two, and No. three. The term of office of the trustees forming such classes shall expire respectively in the order of the number of such classes, on the third Tuesday of October, in each of the years eighteen hundred and sixty-two, eighteen hundred and sixty-three, and eighteen hundred and sixty-four, or as soon thereafter as their successors are elected.

Official term.

§ 2. At the annual meeting of the taxable inhabitants and legal voters of said school district No. six, there shall be elected two trustees of such district, who shall be members of said board of education, and who shall enter upon the duties of their office on the Tuesday succeeding their election, and shall hold their respective offices until the third Tuesday of October, in the third year after their election, or until their successors are elected. In case any vacancy shall occur in said board by reason of death, resignation, removal, refusal to serve, or from any other cause, the remaining members of said board shall be authorized to fill such vacancy, and the person so elected to fill such vacancy, shall hold his office until the next annual meeting of such district, at which meeting there shall be elected a trustee or trustees, for the unexpired term or terms to which the party or parties whose office or offices had become vacant would have been entitled.

Two trustees to be chosen annually.

Fill vacancies.

§ 3. The board of education in said district shall call **Board to call special meetings.** special meetings of said district whenever they may deem it necessary, or whenever petitioned therefor by twenty-five taxable inhabitants of said district, by a petition in writing, stating the object of such meeting. Notice of such special meetings, stating the time and place and object thereof, shall be given by posting such notice in at least five public places in said district, two weeks before the time appointed therefor, and by publishing the same once in each week, for two weeks successively, prior to the time fixed therefor, in all the public newspapers published in said district.

§ 4. The annual meeting of the taxable inhabitants and **Time of holding annual meeting.** legal voters of said district, shall be held on the second Tuesday of October, in each year and unless the time and place of such meeting shall have been fixed by vote of a previous meeting, the same shall be held at eight o'clock, in the evening, at some public place in the district, to be designated by the board of education.

§ 5. The said board of education may make all neces- **Duties of board of education.** sary by-laws for their own government. They shall hold their annual meeting on the third Tuesday of October, in each year; they shall appoint their own officers, and, also, a collector and treasurer for the said district; they shall hold stated meetings for the transaction of business at least once in each month, and at such meetings appoint a committee of not less than two of their own number, to visit the schools of the district, and such committee shall visit all such schools at least once in each month, and report at the next stated meeting of the board, on the condition and prospects thereof. No member of said board shall receive any pay or compensation for his services as such member, nor shall he become a contractor for making any improvements or repairs in or about school property of the district, or furnishing any supplies therefor, nor shall he be directly or indirectly interested in any such contract. All contracts made in violation of this provision shall be absolutely void.

§ 6. The fourth section of the act entitled "An act to **Act of 17th April, 1861, amended.** divide school district No. two, of the town of Yonkers, into separate districts, and to constitute and define the powers of the board of education in the new district,"

passed April seventeenth, eighteen hundred and sixty-
one, is hereby amended so as to read as follows :

§ 4. Whenever, in the opinion of the board of education of school district No. six, it may be advisable to sell
or exchange any of the school houses, lots, or sites, now
or hereafter belonging to or vested in said board, they
shall report a proposition therefor to an annual or special meeting of the district. The said board shall have
power, with the consent of a majority of the taxable
inhabitants present at such meeting, to sell, convey, or
exchange any of the said school houses, lots, or sites,
in the manner that such meeting may approve ; but no
such sale shall be made without the concurrence of a
majority of the taxable inhabitants present and voting
at such meeting, and a majority of all the members of

Moneys
arising from
sale of
school
houses and
lots.

the said board of education. All moneys derived from
any such sale or exchange shall be appropriated by the
said board to the purchase of another site or sites, or
the building or improvement of school houses, or the
payment of any debt or debts, incurred for the purchase, building, or improvement of sites, or school house,
existing at the time of such sale or sales.

Purposes
for which
money may
be raised.

§ 7. The taxable inhabitants of said district, at any
annual, special, or adjourned meeting may vote to authorize such act or acts, and raise such sum or sums of
money as they may deem expedient for the purpose of
purchasing a site or sites, and building a school house
or houses, and purchasing and leasing any suitable lot
or lots, and building or buildings for school purposes,
and of making alterations and improvements with reference to site or structure, and for buying apparatus,
furniture, fixtures, school books and stationery, and for
contingent expenses of the said schools, and for such
other purpose as they may, by a vote of the majority of
the taxable inhabitants present at such meeting, approve, and to direct the trustees to cause the sums voted
to be levied and raised by instalments, or directly by
tax ; and such trustees shall make out a tax list, in the
manner prescribed by law, in case of school district
taxes, and direct such taxes and such instalments to be
levied and raised as directed by such meeting. And the
taxable inhabitants of such district shall have no power
to rescind the vote to raise such money, or to reduce
the amount at any subsequent meeting, unless the same

be done within thirty days after the same shall have
been first voted.

§ 8. In case the taxable inhabitants of the said dis- Relating to moneys for teachers' wages.
trict shall not at their annual meeting, vote to raise a
sum of money for the payment of teachers' wages, and
for procuring the necessary books and stationery, apparatus, fuel, and furniture for the schools then in the district, and carrying on the same until the second Tuesday
of October then next ensuing, and for the payment and
interest on loans to become due prior to such time,
which shall, in the judgment of the said board of education, be sufficient for such purposes, the said board
are hereby authorized and required to levy and raise by
tax such sums as may be necessary for such purposes or
any of them, during the then current school year, in the
same manner as if such sum or sums had been authorized
by the said taxable inhabitants, to be raised according
to the then existing provisions of law.

§ 9. The title to the sites, buildings, furniture, appa- Title of property to be in board of education.
ratus, and all other district school property in the said
district, is hereby vested in the said board of education,
and the same, while used for and appropriated to school
purposes, shall be exempt from all taxes and assessments of every nature and kind whatsoever, and shall
not be liable to be levied upon or sold by virtue of any
warrant or execution.

§ 10. The said board of education are hereby authorized May borrow $4,000.
and empowered to borrow the sum of four thousand dol-
lars, for the purpose of anticipating the collection of the
tax of four thousand dollars, authorized by the last annual
meeting of said district, to be raised for the completion of
the school building now in process of erection therein, and
of grading, fencing, flagging, and improving the school
site, and paying off the mortgage now existing thereon,
and to give their corporate bond for the payment of the
said sum, and the interest thereon, at the time and times
authorized by such meeting, and to mortgage the whole
or any part of the school property of the district to
secure the payment of the said bond; such mortgage to
be executed under the corporate seal of the said board,
and to be signed by their president and clerk, and such
moneys so borrowed shall be appropriated in the manner directed by the said last annual meeting of the said
school district.

§ 11. All the provisions of law now applicable to the said school district and the officers thereof, shall remain as at present existing, except as the same are changed, repealed, or modified by this act.

§ 12. This act shall take effect immediately.

Chap. 76.

AN ACT to authorize the town of Little Falls to raise moneys to reimburse expenditures for families of volunteers in the service of the United States.

Passed March 28, 1862; three-fifths being present.

The People of the State of New York, represented in Senate and Assembly, do enact as follows :

Supervisor to execute bonds to the amount of $5,000.

SECTION 1. The supervisor of the town of Little Falls shall, on or before the first day of April, eighteen hundred and sixty-two, make and execute ten several bonds of the said town, each conditioned for the payment of the sum of five hundred dollars, together with annual interest at a rate not to exceed seven per cent per annum, payable one in each successive year, at the office of the county treasurer of Herkimer county, and negotiate the same for money at not less than par value, and \shall with and out of the moneys which he shall so realize, and borrow upon said several bonds upon the credit and faith of said town, pay over to Henry P. Alexder, Nelson Rust, Zenas C. Priest, Acors Rathbone, Horace M. Burch and William I. Skinner, the relief committee, the said sum of five thousand dollars to reimburse said committee for moneys expended by them as such committee, and to be expended for the relief of families of volunteers who have heretofore enlisted, and are in the service of the United States, and for no other purpose.

Supervisors shall levy tax for principal and interest annually.

§ 2. The supervisor of said town shall, at the annual meeting of the board of supervisors of the county of Herkimer, report the principal and interest to become due on the first day of March following said annual meeting, and the said board of supervisors shall insert the amount of principal and annual interest to become due in the list of taxes for said town, and the said amount shall be chargeable to said town and shall be raised and collected, in each and every year, until said bonds and the interest to accrue thereon as aforesaid shall be collected, and the said amount shall be raised and collected as other town charges and taxes for said town are collected, and said moneys shall be paid over to the treasurer of said county, to the credit of said town, to be applied in payment of said bonds of the town to be issued as aforesaid and to no other purpose.

§ 3. The said county treasurer shall pay the annual interest on said bonds, to the owner or owners thereof, and endorse the same upon the said several bonds, and shall pay the principal due upon said bonds at the time the same shall become due, and payable respectively, and cancel each of the said bonds when fully paid as aforesaid. *County treasurer to pay interest annually.*

§ 4. The several bonds issued in pursuance of this act shall be a charge upon the said town until paid.

§ 5. This act shall take effect immediately.

Chap. 77.

AN ACT to constitute the village of Lowville, in the county of Lewis, a separate road district.

Passed March 28, 1862; three-fifths being present.

The People of the State of New York, represented in Senate and Assembly, do enact as follows:

SECTION 1. The village of Lowville, in the county of Lewis, and the three roads leading therefrom and beyond the corporation limits, viz: from the Stone Church in said village to the east road, so called; from the Bank Building in said village to the east road, so called; and from the Mill Creek bridge in said village, southerly, to the town line between Lowville and Martinsburgh, are hereby declared to be a separate road district, exempt from the superintendence of the commissioners of high-

Trustees to be commissioners of highways. ways of the town of Lowville. The trustees of said village shall be the exclusive commissioners of highways therein, and they alone shall possess and exercise all the powers of commissioners of highways of towns, in repairing, altering describing and discontinuing, and laying out streets and highways, and making assessments of labor and money therefor, within the limits of said village and said three roads, and in laying out such labor and money raised for highways, streets and sidewalks therein.

Powers and duties of trustees. § 2. The trustees of said village shall proceed in the same manner and with the same power, and under the same restrictions as commissioners of highways of towns, in repairing, altering, discontinuing and laying out streets and highways in said village, and assessing damages therefor; and they shall have power and are hereby authorized to assess upon each male inhabitant of said village of the age of twenty-one years and upwards, one day's labor and service upon the highways, streets and alleys of said village, over and above the assessment upon the real and personal property, to be performed under the direction of such trustees, and to have the power to commute for such service and labor for the sum of sixty-two cents for each day so assessed for each and every person; and every person so assessed and having received twenty-four hours previous notice from the street commissioners of said village to appear and perform such labor and service as aforesaid, and who shall not commute, and who shall neglect or refuse to perform such service and labor in person, or by an able-bodied substitute, shall forfeit the sum of one dollar, besides costs, for each day so assessed, to be collected by said street commissioner in accordance with the provisions of article three, title one, chapter sixteen, part one of the Revised Statutes, as near as practicable.

Street commissioner to be elected. § 3. The legal voters of said village shall, at their annual meetings, elect a street commissioner for said village and roads, who shall possess all the powers and discharge all the duties that are given to and enjoined on the overseers of highways in towns, and such as shall be prescribed to him from time to time by the said trustees, being accountable to the said trustees in the same manner as overseers of highways are by law to commissioners of highways.

§ 4. Whenever the office of street commissioner shall Trustees to fill vacancy. become vacant by the death, removal, resignation, or neglect or refusal to serve, of the person elected, the trustees of said village shall have power to appoint a street commissioner, who shall hold the office until his successor shall be elected.

§ 5. This act shall take effect immediately.

Chap. 78.

AN ACT to amend an act entitled "An act to amend and consolidate the several acts in relation to the village of Kingston," passed April eighth, eighteen hundred and sixty-one.

Passed March 28, 1862; three-fifths being present.

The People of the State of New York, represented in Senate and Assembly, do enact as follows:

SECTION 1. Section one of said act is hereby amended Amendment of act of 1861. by inserting after the word "bridge," in the fourth line of said section, the words, "across the Esopus creek."

§ 2. Section four of said act is hereby amended by striking out the words "one police justice," and inserting in lieu thereof, "three inspectors of election."

§ 3. Section five of said act is hereby amended by inserting after the word "assessors," in the first line, the words "inspectors of election," and by striking out the following words, "the police justice shall be elected as hereinafter provided."

§ 4. Section ten of said act is hereby amended so as Inspectors of election to preside at all elections. to read as follows: "The inspectors of election of said village shall preside at all meetings for the election of officers of said village, except in cases otherwise provided for in this act. All laws of this state relating to powers and duties of inspectors of election, and to the election of town officers, and notifying them of their election, shall apply to all elections of officers in said village, so far as the same can be so applied, and are consistent with this act."

§ 5. Section forty-nine of said act is hereby amended by inserting after the word "village," in the tenth line of said section, as follows: "And also by serving the same personally upon such owner or owners, or by leaving the same at their place of residence, with some person of suitable age, if such owner or owners shall reside in said village, at least ten days prior to the time specified in said notice for making the application therein mentioned; or in case such owner do not reside in said village, then such service may in like manner be made on any agent of such owner, residing in said village; but if neither the owner nor any known agent of such owner reside in said village, then such notice shall be posted on the outer door of the court house in said village, and be affixed in some conspicuous manner upon the property, at least ten days before the time of such application, and shall likewise be served by mail upon such owner, if his place of residence be known."

§ 6. Sections sixty-two, sixty-three and sixty-five of said act are hereby repealed.

§ 7. Section sixty-four of said act is hereby amended so as to read as follows:

Jurisdiction
of justices
of the peace
over crimi-
nal and civil
matters.
"The several justices of the peace of the town of Kingston, or any town adjoining the same, in said county of Ulster, shall have jurisdiction in all criminal and civil matters arising under and by virtue of the charter of said village, or any ordinance or by-law thereof, and shall possess the same power to hear, determine, render judgment and issue process and execution in any such matter as in civil actions."

§ 8. Section sixty-six of said act is hereby amended so as to read as follows:

"Every person arrested under or by virtue of the charter of said village, or any ordinance or by-law thereof, shall be taken without unnecessary delay, before any justice of the peace of said town of Kingston, or in case the justices of said town be absent or unable to act for any reason, then before any justice of the peace of any adjoining town in said county, to be dealt with according to law."

§ 9. Section sixty-seven of said act is hereby amended by striking out the words "police justice," wherever and whenever they occur in said section, and inserting in lieu thereof the words "justice of the peace."

§ 10 Section seventy is hereby amended by striking Amend-
ments. out the word "police," in the first line thereof.

§ 11 Section seventy-one of said act is hereby amended by striking out the words "the police justice," in the first line of said section, and inserting in lieu thereof the words "any justice of the peace of the town of Kingston," and by striking out the word "police," in the tenth line of said section.

§ 12. Section seventy-two of said act is hereby amended by striking out all after the word "execute," in line eighteen of said section, to and including the word "justice," in line nineteen of the same, and inserting in lieu thereof the words "such criminal and civil process as shall be issued by any of the justices of the peace of the town of Kingston and delivered to him for service." In regard to process is- sued by jus- tices of the peace.

§ 13. Section seventy-three of said act is hereby amended so as to read as follows:

"The directors may allow the police constable such fees for any services performed by him as are allowed by law for similar services, to town constables, or they may, in their discretion, allow and pay him such compensation, in lieu of such fees, as they may fix and determine, in which case such fees shall be paid into the treasury of the village and credited to the general fund." Fees of po- lice consta- ble.

§ 14. Section seventy-four of said act is hereby repealed. Repeal of 74th section.

§ 15. Section eighty-two of said act is hereby amended by striking out the words "assistant engineer," in the fifth line of said section, and by inserting in lieu thereof the words "a first assistant engineer, a second assistant engineer." In regard to assistant en- gineers.

§ 16. Section eighty-six of said act is hereby amended so as to read as follows:

"The assistant engineers shall aid the chief engineer at all fires; and in case of the absence of the chief engineer his powers and duties shall devolve upon and be discharged by the first assistant engineer; and in case of the absence of both the chief and first assistant engineers, such powers and duties shall devolve upon and be discharged by the second assistant engineer; and in case of the absence of the chief and both such assistant engineers, such powers and duties shall devolve upon Duties of.

and be discharged by such persons as the directors may appoint or designate in the ordinances and by-laws."

Amendment § 17. Section ninety-two of said act is hereby amended by striking out the last word thereof, and inserting in its place the word "board."

98th section repealed. § 18. Section ninety-eight of said act is hereby repealed.

Amendment § 19. Section ninety-nine of said act is hereby amended by striking out the words "the police justice," in the second line thereof.

§ 20. This act shall take effect immediately.

Chap. 79.

AN ACT to amend an act entitled "An act to incorporate the Hermitage Association in the city of New York," passed April seventeenth, eighteen hundred and sixty.

Passed March 28, 1862.

The People of the State of New York, represented in Senate and Assembly, do enact as follows:

SECTION 1. The Hermitage Association in the city of New York shall hereafter be known and designated as the Hermitage National Association.

§ 2. This act shall take effect immediately.

Chap. 80.

AN ACT to provide for the promotion of the public health by draining certain swamp lands in the town of Northfield, in the county of Richmond.

Passed March 29, 1862; three-fifths being present.

The People of the State of New York, represented in Senate and Assembly, do enact as follows:

SECTION 1. Henry Vroom, Hiram J. Corson, and David L. Gardiner, of the town of Northfield, in the county of

Richmond, are hereby appointed commissioners for the purposes and with the powers hereafter mentioned. The said commissioners shall, before entering upon their duties under this act, take an oath or affirmation, well and faithfully to discharge the duties of their trust; the said commissioners are authorized to designate the location of a ditch, with so many lateral ditches or drains as may be necessary for properly draining the swamp, on the east side of the road (known as the plank road) leading from Port Richmond to Springville, in the town of Northfield, in the county of Richmond; and, also, to assess, levy, and collect, by warrant, to be issued to any constable of the said county of Richmond, from the proprietors of the lands subject to such drainage, all sums necessary to defray the expenses thereof, in proportion to their respective interests in said lands and the benefits derived from such improvements, and to pay the said sums to the directors hereinafter mentioned; and, also, inspect said ditch or ditches when completed, and certify the completion thereof, according to the provisions hereinafter contained. *Duties of the commissioners.*

§ 2. The proprietors aforesaid are authorized to meet, two weeks notice of such meeting being given them by the said commissioners, and choose three of their number to be directors, whose duty it shall be to cause the outlets of said swamp to be sufficiently excavated, to drain off the water from the said swamp; the extent and manner of such excavation to be directed by the commissioners aforesaid; and the directors shall cause notice to be given to the several proprietors, through whose lands the said ditch or ditches are to be cleared out and excavated, to clear out and excavate the same, so that the said ditch or ditches shall be of sufficient depth and width to drain off the water from the said swamp, each of said proprietors shall cause such work to be done through his own land, within six weeks after notice given as aforesaid; the work to be done between the first day of April and the first day of November. *Proprietors to choose three directors.*

§ 3. In case any of the said proprietors shall neglect or refuse to cause such clearing and excavations to be done as aforesaid, the said directors shall cause such work to be done, and certify and report the expense thereof to the said commissioners, who shall issue their warrant, in manner aforesaid, to collect from the re- *Duty of directors.*

30

spective proprietors the several sums expended by the directors in clearing and excavating said ditch or ditches through the lands owned by them.

Proprietors to make rules, by-laws, &c.

§ 4. A majority of the said proprietors, at their first or any subsequent meeting, may make proper and suitable rules and by-laws for the holding of annual meetings and choosing directors annually, and for keeping said ditch or ditches cleaned out and free from obstructions, and for defraying and apportioning the expense thereof, by an equitable assessment and tax upon the said proprietors according to their respective interests, to be collected by warrant, to be issued by said directors, and directed to any constable of the said county of Richmond.

Chap. 81.

AN ACT for the relief of Edward S. Dixon heretofore elected a Justice of the peace of the town of Seneca, in the county of Ontario.

Passed March 29, 1862; three-fifths being present.

The People of the State of New York, represented in Senate and Assembly, do enact as follows :

SECTION 1. Edward S. Dixon, heretofore elected a justice of the peace in the town of Seneca, in the county of Ontario, may, at any time after the passage of this act, and before the first Tuesday of April, eighteen hundred and sixty-two take the constitutional oath of office, according to law and file the same with the clerk of Ontario county, and he shall thereupon be confirmed in his said office.

Ratifying his official acts.

§ 2. All official acts of the said Edward S. Dixon done and performed by him as such justice of the peace, are hereby ratified and confirmed. Provided however that nothing herein contained shall effect any suit now pending or any right vested or acquired in opposition to such acts.

§ 3. This act shall take effect immediately.

Chap. 82.

AN ACT authorizing the village of Peekskill to borrow money and to levy taxes for the payment of the same.

Passed March 29, 1862; three-fifths being present.

The People of the State of New York, represented in Senate and Assembly, do enact as follows:

SECTION 1. The board of trustees of the village of Peekskill are hereby authorized, on the faith and credit of said village, to borrow a sum not to exceed three thousand dollars, and to execute either bonds or promissory notes therefor, under the corporate seal of said village and the signatures of the president and clerk thereof; the bonds or promissory notes to be in such form, and the principal and interest made payable at such times and places as may be agreed upon with the lender or lenders, and so that not more than one thousand dollars of the principal shall be payable in each year. *To borrow $3,000.*

§ 2 The said sum hereby authorized to be borrowed, shall be specifically and solely applied and appriated to the erection and repairing of fire engine houses, hook and ladder and hose houses in said village, at the discretion of the trustees. *For engine houses, hook and ladder and hose houses.*

§ 3. The said sum or any part thereof, may be borrowed by the board of trustees of said village, from any person or persons or banking institution, on the best terms that can be obtained, at an interest not exceeding seven per cent per annum payable half yearly; and it shall be and hereby is made the duty of the said board of trustees, and they are hereby authorized to raise by tax upon the real and personal property of said village, in the same manner and at the same time that the general taxes of said village are levied and collected, not to exceed the sum of one thousand dollars annually until the above mentioned loan shall be paid, and also the annual interest on the unpaid portion thereof, and to pay over the same in discharge of said loan or portions thereof, and the interest thereon. *How paid.*

§ 4. The board of trustees shall have power to borrow said sum on the credit of the corporation, to raise the

Trustees to
have power
to borrow.

same and the interest thereon by tax, and to pay the same over in discharge of said loan and the interest thereon, without being thereto specially authorized by a vote, at any time, of the taxable inhabitants of said village.

§ 5. This act shall take effect immediately.

Chap. 83.

AN ACT for the relief of the Ulster and Delaware Plankroad Company.

Passed March 29, 1862 ; three-fifths being present.

The People of the State of New York, represented in Senate and Assembly, do enact as follows :

Charge per weight.

Relating to tolls.

SECTION 1. It shall be lawful for the Ulster and Delaware Plankroad Company, in addition to the tolls now authorized to be collected by law, to charge the sum of one cent for every one hundred pounds or parts thereof, exceeding seven thousand five hundred pounds which any wheeled vehicle and its load may weigh, as and for the toll of any such vehicle and its load which may travel over and pass through the gates of said company or either of them.

Former law applied.

§ 2. All the present provisions of law affecting said company in regard to tolls, shall be applicable to such company whenever the weight of any wheeled vehicle and its load shall be seven thousand five hundred pounds or less ; it being the object of this act to authorize the said company to charge such increased toll for each and every one hundred pounds or part thereof in weight, by which any wheeled vehicle and its load may exceed in weight seven thousand five hundred pounds.

To keep platform scales.

§ 3. It shall be the duty of the said company to keep at each and every toll-gate on their road at which the said increased tolls are proposed to be charged, a good and sufficient platform scales, conveniently located, upon which every wheeled vehicle and load shall be driven when required by the toll gate keeper, in order that the amount of toll to be paid for such vehicle and load may be determined, which toll shall be paid before it shall be lawful for said vehicle and load to pass through said gate.

§ 4. This act shall take effect immediately.

Chap. 84.

AN ACT to authorize the Poormasters of the town of Gorham, in the county of Ontario, to convey certain lands for cemetery purposes.

Passed March 29, 1862; three-fifths being present.

The People of the State of New York, represented in Senate and Assembly, do enact as follows:

SECTION 1. The Poormasters of the town of Gorham, in the county of Ontario, are hereby authorized and required to convey all the lands heretofore vested in them for cemetery purposes in said town, to the president of the Dwelle Cemetery Association, and his successor in office; to be held, used and disposed of by him, as president of such association, only for cemetery purposes in said town, in accordance with the act of incorporation, and the rules and by-laws of said association.

§ 2. Nothing in this act contained shall be construed to give other or greater title to the grantees of said lands, than shall be vested in said Poormasters of said town of Gorham, in and by the conveyance or conveyances made to them.

§ 3. This act shall take effect immediately.

Chap. 85.

AN ACT to authorize the sale and coveyance of the interest of the infant heirs of William C. McVickar, deceased, in the lands of which he died seized, and to provide for the disposition of the proceeds thereof.

Passed March 29, 1862.

The People of the State of New York, represented in Senate and Assembly, do enact as follows :

SECTION 1. The administratrix of the estate of William C. McVickar, late of Malone, in the county of Franklin, with the guardians of the infant children and heirs at law of the said William C. McVickar, are hereby authorized and empowered to sell and convey, in fee simple, all the right, title, interest and estate of the said infant children and heirs at law of the said William C. McVickar, in and to any lands of which said William C. McVickar died seized, and also to convey in fee simple or otherwise, all the right, title, estate and interest of the said infant heirs in any lands which had been contracted to be sold by said William C. McVickar in his lifetime. But no such sale or conveyance shall be valid unless approved by the county court of the county of Franklin, and said court shall have power to require the said administratrix and guardians to give such security and in such form and to renew the same from time to time, as the said court may deem necessary and proper fully to secure and protect the rights and interests of said infant heirs in the premises, and disposition or investment of the moneys that shall come to their hands.

Sale must be approved by county court.

§ 2. The said administratrix and guardians shall report annually to the said court the number of acres and situation of the lands conveyed or sold by them under this act, and the moneys by them received for or as the consideration thereof, and the contracts or securities relating thereto ; and the said moneys shall be applied, paid, secured or invested as the said court shall from time to time order and direct.

Administratrix and guardian to report annually.

§ 3. This act shall take effect immediately.

Chap. 86.

AN ACT relative to the printing of the calendars of causes in the several courts of record in this State.

Passed March 29, 1862 ; three-fifths being present.

The People of the State of New York, represented in Senate and Assembly, do enact as follows :

SECTION 1. The several courts of record in this state, excepting the city and county of New York, at any general term thereafter to be held, may from time to time make orders to be entered in its minutes by which the clerk of such court shall be authorized to cause the necessary number of calendars of causes prepared to be used, either at the general, special or trial terms of such courts or at circuits, to be printed for the use of the court, bar and officers required to attend upon such courts. *Courts to order calendar printed.*

§ 2. The expenses of such printing shall be a charge upon the county in which said printing is done and used, and shall be audited, allowed and paid by the board of supervisors thereof as other contingent county charges are paid. *Expense to be a charge on county.*

§ 3. This act shall take effect immediately.

Chap, 87.

AN ACT releasing to Paul Bresson the interest of the State of New York to certain real estate in the city of Brooklyn.

Passed March 29, 1862.

The People of the State of New York, represented in Senate and Assembly, do enact as follows :

SECTION 1. The right, title and interest of the people of this state, in and to the real estate situate in the city of Brooklyn, in the county of Kings, of which Leopold

Anable Edmond Bresson died seized, and which was devised to Paul Bresson is hereby released to said Paul Bresson his heirs and assigns.

§ 2. Nothing herein contained shall be construed to impair, release or discharge, any right, claim or interest, of any creditor, or of any heir at law capable of taking by descent of or from the said Leopold Anable Edmond Bresson.

§ 3. This act shall take effect immediately.

Chap. 88.

AN ACT to authorize and empower the Shaler and Hall Quarry Company, of Portland, in the State of Connecticut, to convey their real estate lying in the State of New York.

Passed March 29, 1862.

The People of the State of New York, represented in Senate and Assembly, do enact as follows:

SECTION 1. The Shaler and Hall Quarry Company of Portland, in the State of Connecticut, are hereby authorized and empowered to hold, lease, mortgage, sell and convey any or all of their real estate heretofore conveyed to them and situated within the State of New York.

§ 2. This act shall take effect immediately.

Chap. 89

AN ACT for the relief of Horace Allen.

Passed March 29, 1862; three-fifths being present.

The People of the State of New York, represented in Senate and Assembly, do enact as follows:

SECTION 1. The treasurer shall pay, on the warrant of the comptroller, out of any moneys in the treasury not otherwise appropriated, the sum of six hundred dollars to Horace Allen, being the amount awarded to him by the canal appraisers and affirmed by the canal board, for damages caused by the state improvement of Racket river.

§ 2. This act shall take effect immediately.

Chap. 90.

AN ACT to facilitate the construction of the Adirondac Railroad.

Passed March 29, 1862.

The People of the State of New York, represented in Senate and Assembly, do enact as follows:

SECTION 1. The time for the Adirondac Estate and Railroad Company to complete and operate its railroad from Saratoga Springs or Ballston to the Saccandaga river as now limited by law, is hereby extended to the eleventh day of November, A. D., eighteen hundred and sixty-three, and the time to complete and operate the same to the south line of Essex county, is hereby extended to the eleventh day of November, A. D., eighteen hundred and sixty-six, without prejudice to any of the rights, privileges, franchises or exemptions of said company ; provided that the said company shall expend by or before the first day of November next, the sum of thirty thousand dollars upon the construction of that part of its road lying southerly of Stony creek, and the further sum of one hundred thousand dollars on the purchase of materials and in work upon the same part of its road, by or before the first day of July, A. D., eighteen hundred and sixty-three, otherwise this section shall become void. *[Time extended to construct road.]* *[Proviso as to expenditure.]*

§ 2. The evidence of the expenditure of the several sums of money mentioned in the foregoing first section, shall be the affidavit of the president and of the engineer, or of the vice-president and of the engineer of said company, specifying in detail the amount and items of such expenditure, which shall be filed in the comptroller's office within ten days after each of the several days above limited for the making of such expenditure. *[Evidence of the expenditure to be filed in the comptroller's office.]*

§ 3. This act shall take effect immediately.

Chap. 91.

AN ACT providing for the settlement of the claim
of Squire Whipple for the use of his patent iron
truss bridges on the canals of this State.

Passed March 29, 1862; three-fifths being present.

*The People of the State of New York, represented in
Senate and Assembly, do enact as follows :*

SECTION 1. The Canal Board of this state is authorized
and required to hear and examine the subject of the
claim of Squire Whipple, for compensation for the use
of his patent iron truss bridges under his proposition,
dated April twenty-fifth, eighteen hundred and fifty-
four, upon canals of this state, and to make such
award therein as the state would be liable to pay, if it
were an individual or a municipal corporation, and
prosecuted in an action at law for said claim. But no
compensation or damages shall be awarded on account
of bridges specified in or built under a certain agreement in writing, entered into between said Whipple
and John Hutchinson, on the seventh day of February,
eighteen hundred and fifty-six.

§ 2. The sum, if any, so awarded to the said Whipple,
by the said Canal Board, as provided in the first section
Treasurer to of this act, shall be paid to the said Whipple, by the
pay on war-
rant of audi- Treasurer, on the warrant of the Auditor of the Canal De-
tor. partment, out of any money in the treasury at any times
applicable to repairs of the state canals, as far as said
award shall have been made on account of bridges constructed under the head of repairs of the state canals,
and as far as said award shall have been on account of
bridges constructed under the head of enlargement of the
canals, the amount to be paid out of any funds of the
state, not otherwise specially appropriated, and at any
time applicable to the enlargement of the canals upon
which the bridges are respectively located.

§ 3. This act shall take effect immediately.

Chap. 92.

AN ACT to provide for the payment of work done and materials furnished on superintendent's section number twelve of the Erie canal.

Passed March 29, 1862; three-fifths being present.

The People of the State of New York, represented in Senate and Assembly, do enact as follows :

SECTION 1. The Canal Board are hereby authorized to examine the claims of Lewis M. Loss for work done and materials furnished under repair contract, on repair section number twelve on the Erie canal, and if on examination they find that work was done and materials were furnished which were necessary to keep the canal in repair and which were done and furnished under the direction of the Canal Commissioner, superintendent in charge and Resident Engineer, not provided for in his contract, they are to award to him such sum, if any, as may be justly and legally his due. _{Lewis M. Loss.}

§ 2. The Treasurer shall pay, on the warrant of the Auditor, such sum as shall be awarded to said claimant, out of any moneys appropriated to canal repairs.

§ 3. This act shall take effect immediately.

Chap. 93.

AN ACT for the relief of the Sable Iron Company.

Passed March 29, 1862; three-fifths being present.

The People of the State of New York, represented in Senate and Assembly, do enact as follows :

SECTION 1. The stockholders of the Sable Iron Company, incorporated in the year eighteen hundred and thirty-four, and doing business at Ausable Forks, in the town of Jay, county of Essex, may proceed, upon notice given to the stockholders, to elect three trustees for said company, who, and their successors thereafter elected, shall manage and control the affairs of .said company as now provided by law, and the said incorporation is revived and continued with all its original powers.

Chap. 94.

AN ACT to amend an act in relation to highway labor in the county of Livingston, passed April eighteenth, eighteen hundred and thirty-eight.

Passed March 31, 1862 ; three-fifths being present.

The People of the State of New York, represented in Senate and Assembly, do enact as follows:

SECTION 1. Section first of the act entitled An act in relation to highway labor in the county of Livingston, passed April eighteenth, eighteen hundred and thirty-eight, shall be amended by inserting after the word "towns" in the fifth line "said vote shall be taken by ballot upon which shall be written or printed, the words, for money highway tax, or, against money highway tax, which ballot shall be deposited in a separate box to be provided by the inspectors of said town meeting."

§ 2. Section fourth of said act shall be amended by inserting in the fourth line in lieu of "or" the word "and."

§ 3. Section fifth of said act shall be amended by inserting after the word "overseer" in second line "under the direction of the commissioner or commissioners."

§ 4. Section sixth of said act shall be amended by inserting after the word "such," in first line, the words "commissioners and."

§ 5. The said act passed April eighteen, eighteen hundred and thirty-eight, shall not in any way affect former acts in relation to raising money for bridge purposes.

§ 6. This act shall take effect immediately.

Chap. 95.

AN ACT to amend an act entitled "An act authorizing the supervisors of certain towns of Chautauqua and Cattaraugus counties to subscribe for stock in the Erie and New York City Railroad," passed March thirty-first, eighteen hundred and fifty-five.

Passed March 31, 1862; three-fifths being present.

The People of the State of New York, represented in Senate and Assembly, do enact as follows :

SECTION 1. It shall be lawful for the directors of the Erie and New York city railroad or a majority of them, to compromise with the several towns that have issued bonds under the act of March thirty-first, eighteen hundred and fifty-five, and to surrender and cancel said bonds or any part thereof upon the surrender by the supervisors of such town of the certificate for stock in said railroad that has been issued to said town under said act.

§ 2. This act shall take effect immediately.

Chap. 96.

AN ACT to authorize the county of Westchester to acquire land for the construction of the Harlem bridge, pursuant to an act passed April tenth, eighteen hundred and sixty-one, and the appointment of commissioners therefor.

Passed March 31, 1862; three-fifths being present.

The People of the State of New York, represented in Senate and Assembly, do enact as follows :

SECTION 1. It shall be lawful for the commissioners of the Harlem bridge to apply to the supreme court at a general or special term thereof, to be held in the county of Westchester, by a petition, signed by a majority of said commissioners and verified by the president thereof, praying for the appointment of commissioners of appraisal of the land so required for the construction of said bridge, such petition shall contain a description of the property sought to be acquired, and must state that the same is necessary for the proper construction and completion of said bridge, and that said commissioners have been unable to purchase the same from the owner thereof or obtain the use of said land from such owner. The petition shall also state the name and residence of such owner, and copies thereof shall be personally served upon the clerk of the board of supervisors of the county of Westchester, and the owner, owners, or other parties interested in said property so proposed to be taken, together with a notice of the time and place of such application, at least ten days before making such application.

§ 2. On presenting such petition the same proceedings shall be had as are provided for in section fifteen of an act entitled " An act to authorize the formation of railroad corporations and regulate the same," passed April second, eighteen hundred and fifty, except that the number of such commissioners shall be limited to three.

§ 3. The commissioners shall take and subscribe the oath prescribed by the twelfth article of the constitution ; may issue subpœnas, administer oaths to witnesses, and any two of them may adjourn the proceedings, not however more than three times. Whenever the said commissioners shall meet according to appointment they shall cause reasonable notice of such meetings to the parties who are to be affected thereby. They shall view the premises, described in the petition, and hear the proofs and allegations of the parties, and reduce the testimony, if any is taken by them, to writing, and after the testimony is closed, without any unnecessary delay, a majority of them present and acting shall ascertain and determine the compensation which ought justly to be rendered by the county of Westchester to the party owning or interested in the real estate appraised by them. They shall also ascertain what sum shall be paid to the attorney or counsel who may appear for the board of supervisors of the county of Westchester, and for the party or parties whose land shall be taken upon said ap-

Form of petition.

Powers of commissioners.

plication. The commissioners shall make a report to Report to the supreme court. the supreme court within ten days after the testimony on both sides shall have been closed. Said commissioners shall be entitled to three dollars for their expenses and services for each day they are engaged in the performance of their duties, to be paid by the county.

§ 4. On such report being made by the commissioners, notice shall be given to all the parties interested, according to the rules of the supreme court, for the confirmation of the same at a general or special term, and the court may thereupon confirm said report, and upon confirmation thereof shall make an order reciting the substance of the proceedings of the appraisal, description of the real estate appraised, direct to whom the money is to be paid, and shall, also, direct the board of supervisors at their next annual meeting to provide for the payment of the same. Give notice to parties.

§ 5. The board of supervisors of the county of Westchester are hereby directed and required to levy and assess upon the real and personal estate in said county the amount so awarded, with the expenses thereof. Supervisors to levy tax for expenses.

§ 6. Upon the coming in of the report of said commissioners, and confirmation of the same, the title to said land so acquired shall vest in and belong to the county of Westchester.

Chap. 97.

AN ACT to amend an act entitled "An act to incorporate the Conqueror Hook and Ladder and Bucket Company, at Tarrytown, Westchester county," passed April tenth, eighteen hundred and sixty.

Passed March 31, 1862.

The People of the State of New York, represented in Senate and Assembly, do enact as follows :

SECTION 1. Section three of the act entitled "An act to incorporate the Conqueror Hook and Ladder and Bucket Company, at Tarrytown, Westchester county," passed April tenth, eighteen hundred and sixty, is here-

by amended by striking out the word "forty," in said
section, and inserting in lieu thereof the word "sixty."

§ 2. Section four of said act is hereby amended to
read as follows:

To be ex-
empt from
jury and
militia
duty.

Each and all the persons appointed members of said
company under section one of this act, and their successors, who shall serve as such members for five years, and
any officers and trustees they may elect, who shall serve
as such officers or trustees for five years, shall be, during
the terms of their service exempt from serving as jurors,
and the ordinary military duty in time of peace.

§ 3. This act shall take effect immediately.

Chap. 98.

AN ACT to incorporate Knickerbocker Fire Engine Company Number One, at Rockland Lake,
in the town of Clarkstown, in the county of
Rockland and State of New York.

Passed March 31, 1862.

*The People of the State of New York, represented in
Senate and Assembly, do enact as follows:*

SECTION 1. Wm. Hoffman, James L. Conklin, Thomas
H. Woodcock, Henry Brinkerhoff, Austin T. Fitch,
Theodore Ackerson, George Hoffman, John P. Taylor,
Henry M. Reynolds, John F. Rogers, Thaddeus A. Van
Wart, John Van Orden, George Swartwout, Joshua F.
Hazard, William Gillmore, Walter Ackerson, Josiah W.
Conklyn, Charles W. Frances, Cornelius Hennion,
Abram G. Depew, jr., John F. Fullwood, Charles Felter,
Daniel Wheeler, John Tallman, John Tremper, James
Bogart, John A. Hazzard, William Onderdouk, Peter
Nichols, Jacob V. Smith. Thomas J. Belcher, Richard
Swartwout, David Van Wart, Elijah F. Steele. John Mil-
ler, Ferdinand Kerwin, Jacob H. Remsen, Charles Mul-
ford and George Sutherland are hereby constituted a
body corporate by the name of "The Knickerbocker
Fire Engine Company Number One of Rockland Lake,"

and by that name they and their successors shall be capable in law, of purchasing, holding and conveying any real or personal estate necessary for their use as a fire company, to the amount of five thousand dollars; also by their corporate name aforesaid, they and their successors shall and may have perpetual succession and shall be persons in law capable of suing and being sued, pleading and being impleaded, answering and being answered unto, defending and being defended in all courts and places whatsoever, in all manners of actions, suits, complaints, matters and causes whatsoever. *To hold and convey real estate to the amount of $5,000.* *May sue and be sued.*

§ 2. The said corporation shall have full power to make and establish such by-laws, rules and regulations as they from time to time shall think proper, as to their officers, time, place and manner of electing them, the period of their continuance in office, their removal for good cause, their power and duties, and as to the election of members and their removal, and the government of the persons appointed by them as firemen, and with respect to the purposes for which this corporation is constituted. *To make by-laws.*

§ 3. The said corporation shall have full power and authority to nominate and appoint a sufficient number of firemen, not exceeding fifty, to have the care and management of the fire engine and all implements belonging to said company, and who shall be ready at all times to assist in extinguishing fires and to perform all the duties which may be required of them by the regulations of said company, and in case of removal of any members to appoint others in their places. *To appoint firemen.*

§ 4. Each of the persons so appointed firemen as aforesaid, who shall serve as such fireman for five years, including the time they or either of them may have served as a member of Knickerbocker Fire Engine Company Number One of Rockland Lake, previous to this act of corporation, shall, during such service be exempted from serving as a juror in any of the courts of this state, and be exempted from militia duty, except in cases of insurrection or invasion, and a certificate signed by the foreman and secretary of said company shall be conclusive evidence in all cases that the person named therein is or has been a member of said company for the period therein stated. *Term of service.* *Exempt from jury and militia duty.*

§ 5. This act shall take effect immediately.

32

Chap. 99

AN ACT to confirm the acts of the Methodist Episcopal Church in the village of Port Byron and to authorize the corporation to elect nine trustees.

Passed March 31, 1862.

The People of the State of New York, represented in Senate and Assembly, do enact as follows:

SECTION 1. The corporation known as the Methodist Episcopal Church in the village of Port Byron, is hereby authorized to continue to elect nine trustees of the said corporation in the same manner as if that number of trustees had originally been named in the certificate of incorporation, and such trustees shall be classed or continue to be classed in the manner prescribed by the sixth section of the act entitled "An act to provide for the incorporation of religious societies," passed April fifth, eighteen hundred and thirteen, and that all previous acts and doings of the trustees of the said corporation shall be as valid and effectual as they would if no more than five trustees had been elected as provided in the said certificate of incorporation.

§ 2. This act shall take effect immediately.

Chap. 100.

AN ACT for the relief Leonard Van Derkar.

Passed March 31, 1862; three-fifths being present.

The People of the State of New York, represented in Senate and Assembly, do enact as follows:

SECTION 1. The Canal Board is hereby authorized and required to examine the claim of Leonard Van Derkar, for work done on section one of the Erie Canal, by order of the Resident and Assistant Engineer, in the year one thousand eight hundred and fifty-eight, and award to

him such sum as in their judgment the state is justly
liable to pay, and as may be justly and equitably due
him, not exceeding eight hundred dollars.

§ 2. The Treasurer shall pay, upon the warrant of the
Auditor of the Canal Department, such sum as shall be
awarded to said Van Derkar, under the first section of
this act, out of any money in the treasury appropriated
to the payment of canal repairs.

§ 3. This act shall take effect immediately.

Chap. 101.

AN ACT in relation to the support and custody
of indigent insane persons of the county of
Genesee.

Passed April 1, 1862; three-fifths being present.

*The People of the State of New York, represented in
Senate and Assembly, do enact as follows:*

SECTION 1. The superintendent of the poor of the
county of Genesee is hereby authorized and empowered
to take and receive all indigent insane persons now confined in the State Lunatic Asylum at Utica, who have
been admitted into said asylum by virtue of a certificate
granted by the county judge of said county, and said
superintendent of said county of Genesee shall convey
them to and confine them in the lunatic asylum connected with the county poorhouse of said county, there
to be supported at the expense of said county.

§ 2. Whenever the county judge of said county shall,
after the passage of this act, make a certificate concern- Manner of receiving
ing any insane person in indigent circumstances, not a insane and indigent
pauper, in pursuance of chapter twenty, title third, arti- persons.
cle second, part first of the Revised Statutes, such insane person shall be admitted into the insane asylum
connected with said poorhouse mentioned in the first
section of this act, there to remain at the expense of
said county until he or she shall be restored to sound-
ness of mind, or shall be discharged by the superintendent of the poor of said county.

§ 3. This act shall take effect immediately.

Chap. 102.

AN ACT to authorize the election of three superintendents of the poor in the county of Genesee.

Passed April 1, 1862; three-fifths being present.

The People of the State of New York, represented in Senate and Assembly, do enact as follows:

SECTION 1. At the next annual election to be held in this state, there shall be elected in the county of Genesee three superintendents of the poor for said county; one of said superintendents shall hold his office for one year, one for two years and the other for three years from the first day of January next; and the clerk of said county shall on the first day of January next determine by lot which of said superintendents shall hold his office for one year, which for two, and which for three years; and there shall be elected at each annual election thereafter, one superintendent of the poor to hold his office for three years to supply the place of the superintendent whose term of office will expire on the first day of January succeeding such election.

County' clerk to determine by lot.

§ 2. It shall be the duty of the superintendents of the poor of the county of Genesee to appoint a keeper of the poor house of said county, from time to time, as occasion may require.

Superintendents of poor to appoint a keeper of poor house.

§ 3. All acts or parts of acts inconsistent with the provisions of this act, are hereby repealed.

Chap. 103.

AN ACT to correct an error in the assessment of taxes in the city of Brooklyn.

Passed April 1, 1862; three-fifths being present.

The People of the State of New York, represented in Senate and Assembly, do enact as follows:

SECTION 1. The collector of taxes and assessments of the city of Brooklyn is hereby authorized, on the approval of the mayor and comptroller of said city, to receive from the Brooklyn Central and Jamaica Railroad Company the sum of one thousand four hundred and sixteen dollars and seventy-four cents, in payment and satisfaction of the annual taxes against the property of said corporation of said city, which were assessed in the year eighteen hundred and sixty-one; and upon the payment by said corporation of the sum aforesaid, to the said collector, he is hereby authorized and required, on the approval of said mayor and comptroller, to cancel and discharge all taxes against the property of said corporation, contained in the assessment roll in his office for the year aforesaid.

Collector of Brooklyn to receive from the Brooklyn Central and Jamaica R. R. $1,416.74.

§ 2. The deficiency that may be caused by such cancellation and discharge, in the amount of taxes to be collected for the year eighteen hundred and sixty-one, shall be assessed and collected in the year eighteen hundred and sixty-two, as a deficiency upon the city of Brooklyn at large.

Deficiency of 1861 to be collected in 1862.

§ 3. This act shall take effect immediately.

Chap. 104.

AN ACT to amend an act entitled "An act to amend the Revised Statutes in relation to laying out public roads and the alteration thereof, in the towns of North Castle, Bedford and Lewisboro, in the county of Westchester," passed April twelfth, eighteen hundred and fifty-nine.

Passed April 1, 1862; three-fifths being present.

The People of the State of New York, represented in Senate and Assembly, do enact as follows:

SECTION 1. The act entitled " An act to amend the Revised Statutes in relation to laying out public roads and the alteration thereof, in the towns of North Castle, Bedford and Lewisboro, in the county of Westchester," passed April twelfth, eighteen hundred and fifty-nine, is hereby so amended as to apply to and include in its provisions the town of Mount Pleasant, in said county of Westchester.

§ 2. This act shall take effect immediately.

Chap. 105.

AN ACT in relation to John Lent's cemetery.

Passed April 1, 1862; three-fifths being present.

*The People of the State of New York, represented in
Senate and Assembly, do enact as follows:*

SECTION 1. The supervisor of the town of Le Roy, in
the county of Genesee, is hereby authorized and shall
be deemed to have accepted the conveyance upon the
trust therein expressed, executed by John Lent in his
lifetime, bearing date the twenty-sixth day of August,
A. D. eighteen hundred and fifty-seven, and recorded in
the Genesee county clerk's office, in liber one hundred and
forty-seven of deeds, at page three hundred and fifty-five,
on the eighth day of October, A. D. eighteen hundred and
sixty-one, and the land therein described shall be deemed
vested in the said supervisor and his successors in office
forever, subject to the trust aforesaid, that is to say : to
take, hold and possess the same and every part or parcel
thereof and cause the same to be maintained, set apart
and continued as a cemetery or private family burial
ground and a depository for the remains of the family
relatives and descendants of the said John Lent, the
grantor, and so that the same may in no contingency be
sold or conveyed or be hereafter appropriated to any
other use or purpose whatsoever; provided, however,
that nothing herein contained shall in any wise be construed to impose any expense upon the supervisor of the
town of Le Roy.

§ 2. The land so conveyed and in the said deed described, shall forever hereafter be exempt from levy and
sale on execution or taxation.

§ 3. This act shall take effect immediately.

Margin notes:
Land vested in the supervisor and his successors.

To be maintained as a family burying ground.

Exempt from tax.

Chap. 106.

AN ACT to limit the compensation of the Members of the Boards of Supervisors of the counties of Monroe, and Niagara.

Passed April 1, 1862; three-fifths being present.

The People of the State of New York, represented in Senate and Assembly, do enact as follows:

SECTION 1. No member of the Board of Supervisors of the county of Monroe, or of the county of Niagara, shall hereafter be entitled to demand or receive compensation for attendance at any meeting or meetings, session or sessions of said boards hereafter to be held, any number of days exceeding twenty-five for the county of Monroe, and twenty for the county of Niagara, in the aggregate during any one year.

§ 2. Nothing in this act contained, shall be construed to affect the compensation of the members of said boards for attendance at extraordinary meetings or sessions thereof, hereafter held, pursuant to the provisions of the statutes in such case made and provided.

§ 3. This act shall take effect immediately.

Chap. 107.

AN ACT for the protection of fish in the upper portion of the Niagara river.

Passed April 1, 1862; three-fifths being present.

The People of the State of New York, represented in Senate and Assembly, do enact as follows:

SECTION 1. It shall be unlawful to use or draw, for the taking of fish, any seine or net, minnow nets excepted, the meshes or any mesh of which shall be less than one inch and a half square, in that portion of the Niagara river, or its branches or confluents, which are within this state and above the Falls of Niagara. Any person who shall violate, or aid or abet in the violation of this provision, or incite or procure its violation, shall, for each and every offence, forfeit twenty dollars. Penalty of $20.

No fish to be taken with net between April and November.

§ 2. It shall be unlawful to use or draw any seine or net, minnow nets excepted, for the taking of fish, in the said portion of the Niagara river, or its branches or confluents, at any time after the first day of April and before the first day of November in any year. Any person who shall violate, or aid and abet in the violation of this provision, or incite or procure its violation, shall, for each unlawful use or drawing of any seine or net, forfeit twenty dollars.

$20 fine.

Not to use a spear between first of April and first of November.

§ 3. It shall be unlawful to use a spear, in the taking of fish, in the said portion of the Niagara river, or its branches or confluents, at any time after the first day of May and before the first day of November of any year. Any person who shall violate, or aid or abet in the violation of this provision, or incite or procure its violation, shall, for each and every offence, forfeit twenty dollars.

$1 fine for buying and selling fish caught illegally.

§ 4. Every person who shall knowingly sell or buy any fish caught or taken in violation of this act, shall, for each and every fish so sold or bought, forfeit one dollar.

Fines to be recovered in name of the people of the state.

§ 5. All fines or penalties imposed under the provisions of this act, may be recovered with the costs of suit in the name of " The People of the State of New York," before any justice of the peace of any county bordering on said river in this state, and such fines when collected shall be paid, one-half to the person making the complaint, and the other half to the superintendent of the poor in the county ; and in case of non-payment of such fines on rendition of judgment therefor, the defendant or defendants shall be committed to the county jail for a period not less than twenty days.

§ 6. This act shall take effect immediately.

Chap. 108.

AN ACT for the relief of Stephen Van Alstyne.

Passed April 2, 1862; three-fifths being present.

The People of the State of New York, represented in Senate and Assembly, do enact as follows:

SECTION 1. The Canal Board are hereby authorized to settle with Stephen Van Alstyne, for keeping in repair section thirteen of the Erie Canal, under the contract made by the Contracting Board with Thomas B. Morrow and assigned to said Stephen Van Alstyne, and to allow and pay to him such portion of the contract price for the period he has kept said section in repair, as to them shall appear, upon investigation of the case, to be just and equitable, and to settle all questions arising upon said contract, provided that, upon such settlement, the said Thomas B. Morrow and Stephen Van Alstyne shall each of them execute to the state a release in full of all claims against the state for work done or materials furnished under said contract; and said contract and bond accompanying the same shall thereupon be cancelled.

§ 2. In case any sum shall be awarded to said Van Alstyne under this act, the same shall be paid by the auditor, out of the fund for canal repairs.

§ 3. This act shall take effect immediately.

Chap. 109.

AN ACT to incorporate the Firemen of the city of Schenectady, and for other purposes.

Passed April 2, 1862; three-fifths being present.

The People of the State of New York, represented in Senate and Assembly, do enact as follows:

SECTION 1. All persons who now belong or who shall hereafter belong, to any of the fire companies, hose and hook and ladder companies for the extinguishment of

33

fires in the city of Schenectady, are hereby constituted a body politic and corporate by the name of the "Fire Department of the City of Schenectady," and by that name they and their successors,* for the term of thirty years; and they and their successors may have a common seal and may change and alter the same at their pleasure; and, also, they and their successors, by the name of the "Fire Department of the City of Schenectady," shall be in law capable of purchasing, holding and conveying any estate, real or personal for the use of the said corporation; but the amount of the real and personal estate of the said corporation shall not at any time exceed in value the sum of ten thousand dollars.

§ 2. The firemen belonging to the said fire department shall, on or before the first Monday of January, in every year, choose two representatives from each company of firemen, who shall have and exercise all such powers as are herein committed to them.

§ 3. The said representatives shall choose, on the second Monday of January in every year, by ballot, out of their own body, a president and vice president, and from the exempt firemen, who shall have been members of the fire department of said city, and who shall have served as firemen the time prescribed by law, one trustee, a treasurer, secretary and collector. The first representatives shall be F. W. McCamus, James W. Saunders, Henry Holmes, Francis Pfau, Robert Sutliff and James W. Ketchum; the first president F. W. McCamus, the first vice-president James W. Ketchum, the first trustees, of which there shall be three in number, James W. Mairs, John Hulse and David H. Snell; the first treasurer John C. Ellis; the first secretary and collector John McDermott, Jr., to hold their respective offices and places until others are appointed in their stead, agreeably to the provisions of this act. The said trustees shall class themselves into three classes; number one shall go out of office the first year, number two the second year, and number three the third year. The said trustees shall manage the affairs and dispose of the funds of the corporation, according to the by-laws, rules and regulations of the said corporation, from time to time made and established by the said representatives. The trustees shall choose a president, who shall have a right to convene them when he thinks proper, at least once a year. The

* So in the original.

(Margin notes:) To hold and convey real estate. / Choose two representatives annually. / Representatives to choose annually, by ballot, the officers. / Classification of trustees.

treasurer shall give security to the trustees for the faithful performance of his trust, and shall at every annual meeting of representatives, render them an account of the state of the funds; the representatives shall, at their meetings, have a right to enquire into and control the application of their funds, and to displace any of the trustees and officers if guilty of mal-conduct, and elect others in their stead; a majority of the said representatives and also of the said trustees, shall respectively be a quorum to do business; and in case of a vacancy in the office of representative, such vacancy shall be filled by the company from which he is deputed, for the remainder of the year, by a special election to be held for that purpose; and in case of a vacancy in the office of president, vice-president, treasurer, secretary, collector, or any of the trustees, such vacancies shall be filled by the representatives for the remainder of the year, by a special election to be held for that purpose. *Vacancies how filled.*

§ 4. The said representatives shall have full power at any regular meeting thereof, by a vote of two-thirds thereof present and voting to make and prescribe such by-laws, ordinances and regulations as to them, from time to time, shall appear needful and proper, touching the management and disposition of their funds for the purposes aforesaid, and touching the meetings of the corporation, both special and ordinary, except the second Monday in January, in each year, which is hereby declared to be their annual meeting, and touching the duties and conduct of their officers and trustees, and touching all such other matters as appertain to the business ends and purposes for which the said corporation is by this act instituted, and for no other purposes whatsoever; provided that such by-laws, rules, ordinances and regulations be not repugnant to the constitution or laws of the United States or of the State of New York. *Make by-laws.* *Time of annual meeting.*

§ 5. In case any election shall not be made on any day when, pursuant to this act it ought to have been made, the said corporation shall not, on that account, be deemed to be dissolved; but it shall and may be lawful, on any other day, to hold and make such election, in such manner as shall have been regulated by the by-laws and ordinances of the said corporation.

§ 6. The said corporation may prescribe the amount and in what manner each fireman or each company, as *In regard to dues.*

the said corporation may determine, shall pay as dues to the fire department, and it is hereby provided that no member of any company shall be entitled to vote for a representative, until he shall have paid his dues to said department ; and the funds of said corporation, which shall arise from such objects as may have been heretofore or may be hereafter agreed on by the respective fire companies, shall be appropriated to the relief of such indigent or disabled firemen or their families as may be interested therein, and who may, in the opinion of a majority of the trustees, be worthy of assistance ; but if they shall amount to a greater sum than the trustees may think necessary to apply to the said purposes, then the said representatives shall have power to apply such surplus to the purposes of extinguishing fires, under such limitations and restrictions as they may, with the sanction of the corporation of the city of Schenectady, deem proper.

To be exempt from jury and militia duty. § 7. Every person who now is, or hereafter may become a firemen of the city of Schenectady, and shall serve as such, (five years,) after his appointment, shall during and forever after such service, be exempt from serving as a juror in any of the courts of this state, and from all militia duty, except in cases of insurrection and invasion.

Evidence of service. § 8. Certificates of the time that such persons as aforesaid have served as firemen, signed by the president and secretary of the fire department, and countersigned by the mayor of the city of Schenectady, and the clerk of the common council of said city, shall be sufficient evidence thereof

In regard to injured and maimed members. § 9. If any fireman of the city of Schenectady shall, while in the performance of his duty as such, be so maimed or injured as to render him thereafter unable to perform the duties of a fireman, or who shall be so maimed or injured previous to the passage of this act, he shall be entitled to all the benefits of this act ; provided, however, that he shall not receive the certificate granting him the privileges of this act, until the expiration of the time he would have been compelled to serve if he had not been so maimed or injured.

§ 10. This act shall take effect immediately.

Chap. 110.

AN ACT to authorize Josephine Bargagli to take, hold and convey real estate.

Passed April 2, 1862.

The People of the State of New York, represented in Senate and Assembly, do enact as follows :

SECTION 1. Josephine Bargagli, daughter of Jenny Le Coutleux, the latter being a citizen of the United States and a grand daughter of the late Louis Le Coutleux, who was formerly a sergeant at arms of the Senate of this State, is hereby authorized to take and hold real estate, in fee simple or otherwise, and to lease, mortgage, devise or convey the same, in the same manner, and with the like effect, as if she were a citizen of the United States.

§ 2. This act shall take effect immediately.

Chap. 111.

AN ACT for the relief of Francis M. McFarlin and others.

Passed April 2, 1862 ; by a two-thirds vote.

The People of the State of New York, represented in Senate and Assembly, do enact as follows :

SECTION 1. Francis M. McFarlin, Peter Huddleston and Benjamin McFarlin, all of the city of Rochester, are each and all hereby released from any liability or obligation to the State of New York, in consequence of a bond given by them for the repairs of section number one of the Black River Canal, dated the thirteenth day of February, eighteen hundred and sixty-one.

§ 2. The Treasurer shall pay on the warrant of the Auditor of the Canal Department to Francis McFarlin, the sum of two thousand dollars, out of the Canal fund, it being the amount deposited, at the letting of section number one of the Black River Canal, in February, eighteen hundred and sixty-one.

§ 3. This act shall take effect immediately.

Chap. 112.

AN ACT to regulate the use of public highways.

Passed April 2, 1862; three-fifths being present.

The People of the State of New York, represented in Senate, and Assembly do enact as follows:

In regard to wild animals. SECTION 1. It shall not be lawful for any owner or owners of any wild or rare animal, native or imported, which shall be used for exhibition in any menagerie or show, or owned or possessed for the purpose of so exhibiting the same, to convey or cause to be conveyed, or led or driven, over, through or upon any public highway, road or street, such wild or rare animal, unless such owner or owners shall send before the same, a person of mature age, at least one-half of a mile in advance to notify and warn persons traveling or using said highway, road or street, with horses or other domestic animals liable to be frightened by such wild or rare animal, *Punishment for violation.* of the approach of such animal. Any such owner using any public highway, road or street, in violation of the provisions of this act, shall be deemed guilty of a misdemeanor, and may be punished, on conviction, by fine, not exceeding one hundred dollars, or by imprisonment in a county jail not exceeding ninety days, or by both such fine and imprisonment, in the discretion of the court before which such conviction shall be had.

Agent liable. § 2. Any servant or agent of the owner or owners of such wild or rare animal, and having the same in charge, who shall wilfully neglect to give the notice and warning required by the foregoing section, shall be deemed guilty of a misdemeanor, and liable to punishment therefor as prescribed in said section.

§ 3. This act shall take effect immediately.

Chap. 113.

AN ACT conferring additional powers upon the trustees and taxable inhabitants of the village of Fort Edward.

Passed April 2, 1862; three-fifths being present.

The People of the State of New York, represented in Senate and Assembly do enact as follows:

SECTION 1. At any meeting of the electors of the village of Fort Edward, to elect village officers, or at any other meeting of such electors duly notified by the trustees, in the manner provided by the act entitled "An act to provide for the incorporation of villages," passed December seventh, eighteen hundred and forty-seven, and the several acts amending the same, under which the said village is organized, the persons entitled to vote to raise taxes in said village, may by resolution direct the trustees to cause to be raised by tax as other moneys are authorized to be raised for corporate purposes in said village, such sum as shall be named in such resolution, not exceeding the sum of three hundred dollars for the purpose of paying the leader of "the Fort Edward Cornet Band," for services rendered or to be rendered by such leader, in that capacity. But no more than three hundred dollars shall be raised or paid for that purpose annually.

§ 2. And in case of the passage of such resolution, the trustees shall cause the amount of money specified therein, to be levied and raised as aforesaid, and pay the same when raised to the leader of said band, at such time or times and in such installments as the taxable inhabitants aforesaid shall direct, in such resolution requiring said tax to be raised as aforesaid.

§ 3. This act shall take effect immediately.

Chap. 114.

AN ACT to empower St. Patrick's Lodge Number Four of Free and Accepted Masons, in the village of Johnstown, to take, hold and convey real estate and personal property.

Passed April 2, 1862.

The People of the State of New York, represented in Senate and Assembly do enact as follows:

SECTION 1. John Stewart, McIntyre Fraser and Daniel Cameron, trustees of St. Patrick's Lodge Number Four of Free and Accepted Masons, in the village of Johnstown, and their successors in office are hereby empowered to take, hold and convey real estate for the use and benefit of said lodge, in amount not to exceed ten thousand dollars; and are hereby constituted a corporation, with power to sue and be sued by the corporate name of " The trustees of St. Patrick's Lodge Number Four of Free and Accepted Masons."

Not to hold real estate to exceed $10,000.

§ 2. Such real estate as is now held in possession and claimed by the said lodge and the said trustees thereof, not to exceed in the value the amount in the foregoing section expressed, is hereby confirmed in said trustees, as fully and completely as if the said association had had legal power to take and hold real estate at the time of the execution and delivery of the deed of conveyance thereof.

Three trustees to be elected annually.

§ 3. The affairs of said corporation shall be managed by three trustees, to be elected annually, at the first stated meeting of said lodge next preceding the twenty-seventh day of December in each year, from among the members thereof; and until the first election to be held under this act, John Stewart, McIntyre Fraser and Daniel Cameron, the present trustees of said lodge, shall be the trustees of the corporation hereby created.

§ 4. This act shall take effect immediately.

Chap. 115.

AN ACT to amend an act entitled "An act authorizing the Canal Commissioners to build a bridge over the Chenango canal in the city of Utica."

Passed April 2, 1862; three-fifths being present.

The People of the State of New York, represented in Senate and Assembly, do enact as follows:

SECTION 1. Section one of the act entitled "An act authorizing the Canal Commissioners to build a bridge over the Chenango canal in the city of Utica," passed April sixteenth, eighteen hundred and fifty-two, is hereby amended so as to read as follows:

§ 1. The Canal Commissioners are hereby authorized at their discretion to build a bridge over the Chenango canal on Garden street in the city of Utica, or cause the same to be done at the expense of the state, provided said commissioners, upon a personal examination of the place, where said bridge is proposed to be built, shall be of the opinion that the convenience of the public requires the same to be built, and that the same ought to be done at the expense of the state. The expense of building said bridge shall be paid by the Treasurer on the warrant of the Auditor out of any moneys in the treasury not otherwise appropriated.

§ 2. This act shall take effect immediately.

Chap. 116.

AN ACT to appoint a trustee to receive and hold the bequest of Levi Farr, deceased, for the benefit of school district number four, in the town of Greene, Chenango county.

Passed April 2, 1862; three-fifths being present.

The People of the State of New York, represented in Senate and Assembly do enact as follows :

SECTION 1. Robert P. Barnard, of the town of Greene, in the county of Chenango, is hereby appointed as a trustee, with power to have, demand and receive of and from the legal representatives of the estate of Levi Farr, late of said town, now deceased, the legacy bequeathed in the will of said Levi Farr, to the Superintendent of Common Schools for the town of Greene, for the time being and to his successors in office forever, and for the use and benefit of school district number four of said town, and to invest the same when received in a mortgage or mortgages on unincumbered real estate, worth at least twice the amount loaned (exclusive of buildings or other improvements.) The principal of said mortgage or mortgages to be payable at such time or times as said trustee may determine, but the interest to be made payable annually at seven per centum per annum; said mortgage or mortgages to be accompanied by the bond or bonds of the mortgagors, and to be drawn in the name of " the trustee to receive and hold the bequest of Levi Farr, deceased, for the benefit of school district number four, in the town of Greene, Chenango county," as the mortgagee.

Trustee to execute a bond of $8,000.

§ 2. The trustee in the first section of this act named, and his successors in office, shall before entering upon the duties of the office herein created, make, execute and deliver to " the trustees of school district number four in the town of Greene, Chenango county, in their name of office, a bond in the penalty of eight thousand dollars, said bond to be executed by said trustee first named, and two persons as his sureties, and to be approved by the judge of the county of Chenango, and conditioned for the faithful discharge of the trust created by the will of the said Levi Farr, deceased, and the provisions of this act.

§ 3. From time to time, and as often as may be necessary, the principal moneys of the trust fund herein mentioned, shall be reinvested in the manner in the first section of this act provided, and in all cases, in lieu of and as compensation for the discharge of all duties, expenses, work and labor performed, incurred or done by the trustee of the fund herein mentioned, he shall be authorized to retain five per cent upon the interest moneys only actually received by him and paid over to the trustees of said school district number four, and in no case is the principal moneys of such trust fund in any way to be diminished or lessened by any charge for expenses growing out of its management; and such interest moneys so received by him shall immediately thereafter and as often as the same shall be so received, be paid over to the trustees of said school district, to be by them used and applied in the manner provided in the will of the said Levi Farr, deceased, after deducting therefrom his said per centage and no more. *Compensation of trustees.*

§ 4. The trustee of the school district in this act mentioned, shall at all times have the power and right to demand and receive from the trustee herein created, a full and perfect statement of the condition of the trust fund, and may in their discretion require a renewal of the approval of the bond to be given under the second section of this act, at least once in each year, or that a new bond with like securities and to be approved in like manner, shall be executed and delivered to them. *Powers of trustees of school district.*

§ 5. The office of trustee created by the first section of this act, shall become and be vacant by death, resignation, removal from the school district number four, in the town of Greene, of such trustee or his successor or successors, or by a refusal or neglect to comply with the provisions or requirements of the fourth section of this act on the part of said trustee, his successor or successors, and whenever such vacancy shall occur, the judge of the county of Chenango, shall on application of the trustees of said school district, select and appoint some fit and proper person, resident of such district, to be trustee of such trust, who shall thereupon comply with all the requirements of this act, and execute all the *Vacancy and manner of filling the same.*

powers and perform all the duties of such office as herein enacted; but no person other than the person named in the first section of this act as trustee of such trust shall during the term of his office of trustee created by this act nor 'at the time of his appointment thereto, be a trustee of said school district, nor county judge of the county of Chenango.

§ 6. All legal powers and liabilities consistent with and necessary for the execution of the duties and enforcement of the rights of parties in this act mentioned, are hereby conferred upon and attached to the office of trustee created in this act and the trustees of school district number four in said town of Greene, and county of Chenango.

§ 7. The executors of said will shall be absolved from all liability by reason of said legacy upon filing in the office of the surrogate of Chenango county the release of the said legacy executed by the trustee created by this act or subsequently appointed in pursuance thereof.

§ 8. This act shall take effect immediately.

Chap. 117.

AN ACT for the relief of Louis Gabriel Jeanrenaud, and Sophie Adele Jeanrenaud.

Passed April 2, 1862; by a two-thirds vote.

The People of the State of New York, represented in Senate and Assembly, do enact as follows:

SECTION 1. All the claim, right, title, interest and estate of the people of the State of New York, acquired by reason of the alienage of Louis Gabriel Jeanrenaud and Sophie Adele Jeanrenaud, residents of Motiers, in Switzerland, in and to the real estate situate in the city and State of New York, devised to them by the will of their brother, Auguste Jeanrenaud, late of the city of New York deceased, and at the time of his death a citizen of the United States of America, are hereby released to the said Louis Gabriel Jeanrenaud and Sophie Adele Jeanrenaud. And the said Louis Gabriel Jeanrenaud and Sophie Adele Jeanrenaud are hereby authorized and empowered so far as the right of this State therein is concerned to hold,

convey, devise and demise the same, in the same manner
and with the like effect as if they were citizens of the
United States of America.

§ 2. Nothing herein contained shall be construed to
impair, release or discharge, any right, claim or interest,
of any creditor, or of any heir at law capable of taking
by descent of, or from the said Auguste Jeanrenaud
deceased.

§ 3. This act shall take effect immediately.

Chap. 118.

AN ACT to amend an act entitled "An act to
amend act for the more effectual support and
relief of the poor in the county of Fulton,
passed April eighth, eighteen hundred and fifty-
nine.

Passed April 2, 1862; three-fifths being present.

*The People of the State of New York, represented in
Senate and Assembly, do enact as follows:*

SECTION 1. The third section of an act entitled " An
act to amend an act for the more effectual support and
relief of the poor in the county of Fulton," passed April
eighth, eighteen hundred and fifty-nine, is hereby amended so that said section shall read as follows:

§ 3. No superintendent of the poor shall be elected in
said county. At the annual meeting of the board of
supervisors, in the fall of one thousand eight hundred
and sixty-two and every three years thereafter, one
superintendent shall be appointed by said board, who
shall hold his office for three years from the first day of
April following, and shall reside at the poor house in said
county, and be the keeper thereof; said superintendent
shall be subject to the direction of the board of supervisors. Whenever a vacancy occurs in the office of superintendent, the county judge, treasurer and clerk shall
appoint until the next annual meeting of the board of
supervisors. The present superintendent shall hold his
office until the first of April next.

§ 2. This act shall take effect immediately.

*Term of of-
fice of super-
intendent.*

Chap. 119.

AN ACT to incorporate Friendship Hose Company Number Two of New Brighton, in the county of Richmond.

Passed April 2, 1862; three-fifths being present.

The People of the State of New York, represented in Senate and Assembly, do enact as follows :

SECTION 1. William F. Fetherston, William O'Callaghan, John J. Fetherston, Thomas Tathersoll, Michael J. Roughan, Jeremiah O'Callaghan, Andrew Brady, Michael Bannin, Michael Cotter, Edward Howarth, Thomas McCormick, William Finerty, Andrew Fetherston, Charles Birfield, Cornelius Farley, Pierce Chute, John Holt, John Cahill, Thomas Birmingham and Raymond Slater, are hereby constituted a body corporate by the name of "Friendship Hose Company Number Two of New Brighton," and by that name they and their successors shall be capable in law of purchasing, holding and con-

To hold and convey real estate.

veying any real estate or any personal estate necessary for their use as a hose company, to the amount of six thousand dollars; and also by the corporate name aforesaid they and their successors shall and may have perpetual succession, and shall be persons in law capable of suing and being sued, pleading and being impleaded, answering and being answered unto, defending and being defended, in all courts and places whatsoever, in all manner of actions, suits, complaints, matters and causes whatsoever.

Make rules and regulations.

§ 2. The said corporation shall have full power to make and establish such by-laws, rules and regulations as they from time to time shall think proper as to their officers, the time, place and manner of electing them, the period of their continuance in office, their removal for good cause, their powers and duties, and as to the election of members, and their removal, and the government of the persons appointed by them as firemen, and with respect to the purposes for which this corporation is constituted.

Nominate and appoint firemen.

§ 3. The said corporation shall have full power and authority to nominate and appoint a sufficient number of firemen, not exceeding forty, to have the care and management of all the implements belonging to said company, and who shall be ready at all times to assist in extinguishing fires, and to perform all the duties which may be required of them by the regulations of said company, and in case of removal of any members, to appoint others in their places.

§ 4. Each of the persons so to be appointed firemen as aforesaid, who shall serve as such for five years, shall, during such service be exempted from serving as a juror in any of the courts of this state, and from militia duty, except in cases where the militia are ordered into actual service.

§ 5. This act shall take effect immediately.

Chap. 120.

AN ACT requiring the highway tax of the New York Central Railroad Company through the town of Mentz to be applied to the repairs of certain highways in the said town.

Passed April 2, 1862; three-fifths being present.

The People of the State of New York, represented in Senate and Assembly, do enact as follows:

SECTION 1. The highway tax of the New York Central Railroad Company in the town of Mentz shall be expended and paid out by the commissioners of highways of the said town for repairing the highway leading from the railroad depot to the village of Port Byron, and for repairing the highways leading from the railroad depot to the turnpike road, in such manner as John P. Yawger, Porter P. Wethey and the agent of the New York Central Railroad or a majority of them shall determine.

§ 2. This act shall take effect immediately, and continue in force ten years.

Chap. 121.

AN ACT to enable the electors of the town of Sullivan, Madison county, to vote by districts for town officers.

Passed April 2, 1862; three-fifths being present.

The People of the State of New York, represented in Senate and Assembly, do enact as follows:

SECTION 1. The town of Sullivan shall be divided as hereinafter provided into two election districts, for the election of all town officers required by law to be elected by ballot.

District No. 1.
§ 2. District number one shall comprise the present election districts numbers one and two and five in said town, and shall hold its elections in the village of Chittenango.

District No. 2.
§ 3 District number two shall comprise the present election districts numbers three and four of said town, and shall hold its elections in the village of Bridgeport and Lakeport alternately, but the first election in district number two after the passage of this act shall be held at the village of Lakeport.

Supervisors, assessors and town clerk to form a board.
§ 4. The supervisor, assessors and town clerk of the town of Sullivan shall meet at the town clerk's office in said town, on the first Monday in February in each year hereafter, at ten o'clock in the forenoon and form themselves into a board, and in case a majority of said officers for any cause do not attend on that day it shall be the duty of those who do attend to adjourn to some future day, not exceeding five days, and shall immediately thereupon give notice in writing to those officers who do not attend, of the time of such adjournment. And it shall be the duty of said officers to attend on said adjourned day, and to proceed in the same manner as though a majority had attended on the day appointed by them. They shall designate the house in each of the Designate places of holding elections. villages of Chittenango and Bridgeport at which elections shall be held during the year, and they shall thereupon give notice, written or printed, of the annual town elections in said district, together with a list of all such

town officers as are to be elected at such elections, to be posted in at least four public places in each district, at least six days before the holding of such annual town elections, which election shall be the same day on which the annual town meeting is or shall be hereafter held.

§ 5. The said town officers shall also, at the meeting on the first Monday in February, eighteen hundred and sixty-three, and on the first Monday in February each succeeding year thereafter, assign and designate one or more of their number together with one or more of the justices of the peace of said town to hold the elections in each district as shall be necessary to constitute them inspectors of election for each district, and such inspectors shall be allowed to vote in the district where they shall be respectively assigned and designated for each district, and shall at the same time be signed by the board and filed in the office of the town clerk who shall immediately cause written notice thereof to be given to the officers designated as inspectors of election in said district.

§ 6. The officers thus assigned and designated shall Inspectors of election. be inspectors of annual town elections, held in the several districts in said town for which they have been appointed, for the election of all town officers required by law to be elected by ballot.

§ 7. In case of a vacancy in the board of inspectors Vacancy how filled in any election district in said town, or of the absence or inability of any town officer appointed as aforesaid to act as inspector at any election, the inspectors who may be present are hereby authorized and empowered to fill all such vacancies by appointment from among the electors of such district for the time being, who shall take the oath of office as hereinafter provided.

§ 8. The inspectors assigned and designated or ap- Compensation of inspectors. pointed as herein provided, shall receive the same compensation provided by law for inspectors of election in towns and wards.

§ 9. If a special election shall be called to fill a va- Special election. cancy in any town office, the town clerk shall give the like notice as provided in section four, together with a list of such town officers as are to be elected at such election, and the justices of the peace in said town shall meet at the office of the town clerk on the succeeding day and proceed to complete the canvass and declare

35

the result as hereinafter provided for annual town elections.

§ 10. The inspectors of each election district shall
meet at the time and place where an election shall have
been appointed to be held therein, and shall proceed to
organize themselves as a board for the purpose of presiding at and conducting said election.

§ 11. The inspectors shall appoint one of their number chairman of the board, who shall administer to the
other inspectors the oath of office as prescribed by the
constitution, and the same oath shall then be administered to the chairman by one of the other inspectors.

§ 12. The inspectors, or a majority of them having
taken such oath, the board shall then appoint a clerk to
be called the clerk of the poll, who shall take the constitutional oath of office, which shall be administered to him
by the chairman of the board and shall keep a poll list
and make such other minutes as may be required.

§ 13. Before the electors shall proceed to vote for any
town officer, proclamation shall be made of the opening
of the poll and when the poll will close.

§ 14. The inspectors so presiding shall have the same
authority to preserve order, enforce obedience and commit for disorderly conduct as is possessed by the board
of inspectors at a general election, and shall proceed in
the same manner and be governed by the same rules as
is provided for the election of town officers in title
three, article one of the Revised Statutes.

§ 15. As soon as the poll of an election shall have
been finally closed, the inspectors in the several districts
shall proceed to canvass the votes. Such canvass shall
be public, and shall not be adjourned or postponed until
it shall have been finally completed.

§ 16. When the canvass shall have been completed
and the result ascertained, a statement of all the votes
for each candidate shall be made in writing, certified
and signed by the presiding officer and clerk of such
district with one ballot of each kind found to have been
given for the officers chosen at such election, securely
attached to such statement.

§ 17. The inspectors in each district shall designate
one of their number who shall deliver such statement so
made and certified to the board of the annual town
meeting, which shall be held at the office of the town

clerk on the succeeding day on or before ten o'clock in the forenoon of said day.

§ 18. The board of such annual town meeting shall then proceed to complete the canvass by adding all the statements from the several districts together and declare the result the same as though such votes had been polled at such annual town meeting and the person having the greatest number of votes shall be declared elected to the offices for which they have been designated respectively.

§ 19. All such business as is now usually done at the annual town meetings, other than that provided for specially in and by this act, shall hereafter be done by the said board of the annual town meeting at their meeting on the day succeeding the annual town election, immediately after completing the canvass of the votes as herein provided, such business shall be done in the presence of, and under the direction of the said board of the annual town meeting, it shall be done in public, and every elector of said town who shall be present shall be entitled to vote on all questions there decided.

§ 20. Each election district may elect overseers of highways for their respective districts.

§ 21. Highway districts divided by the line which separates the north from the south district shall be under the direction of overseers of highways to be appointed in such election district as the commissioners of highways shall direct.

§ 22. The clerks of said election districts shall make Duty of a list of said overseers of highways so elected in each clerk. of their said districts and file the same in the town clerk's office during the day following said town election.

§ 23. This act shall take effect immediately.

Chap. 122.

AN ACT for the relief of James Irving, and to release to him the interest of the people of the State of New York in certain real estate and premises in the city of Rochester, acquired by him by deed from Hugh McGowan, an alien.

Passed April 2, 1862; by a two-thirds vote.

The People of the State of New York, represented in Senate and Assembly, do enact as follows:

SECTION 1. The interest of the people of the State of New York in the west half of all that tract or parcel of land situate in the city of Rochester, county of Monroe and State of New York, and bounded as follows: Beginning at a stake in the ground on the south line of the road that leads from Rochester to Oliver Culver's land and to the house in which he formerly kept tavern, and on the east line of a lane that leads to Chester Bixby's lime kiln; on this line southerly, eight rods, in a right angle with the road, to a corner; thence easterly, on a line parallel with the main road, five rods; thence northerly on a parallel line with the lane, eight rods; thence westerly on the public highway, five rods, containing one-fourth of an acre, being the same land intended to be conveyed to James Irving by Hugh McGowan, an alien, by deed dated the fourth day of October, eighteen hundred and fifty-nine, and recorded in the office of the clerk of Monroe county, in liber one hundred and forty-seven of deeds, at page four hundred and six, is hereby released to the said James Irving, his heirs and assigns forever.

§ 2. This act shall take effect immediately.

Chap. 123.

AN ACT to amend the charter of the Knickerbooker Life Insurance Company.

Passed April 2, 1862.

*The People of the State of New York, represented in
Senate and Assembly, do enact as follows :*

SECTION 1. All contracts made by the Knickerbooker *In regard to contract of* Life Insurance Company, located in the city of New *company.* York, for insurance on the lives of individuals, against accidents or casualities, for the granting, purchasing or disposing of annuities or otherwise, authorized by the charter of said company, shall be binding and obligatory upon said company when subscribed by the president and secretary thereof, and it shall not be necessary to seal the same with the seal of the company.

§ 2. The board of directors of said company may elect *In relation to board of* annually such a number of its own members, as shall be *directors.* prescribed by its by-laws, to be an executive committee, with such powers as may be delegated to it by said bylaws, to superintend the whole business of said company; and at all meetings of said board of directors, five members shall constitute a quorum for the transaction of business; but a lesser number may meet and adjourn from to time until a quorum shall attend.

§ 3. The insurance business of said company shall be *Manner in* transacted upon the mutual principle; but any person *which busi-* applying for insurance, so electing, may pay, or agree *pany shall* to pay, a fixed sum of money, as may be agreed upon *ca.* by the company, which shall be in full of said insurance, and without any participation in the profits of the company. A balance shall be struck from time to time on the books of the company as the directors may determine, and the profits or losses ascertained, all of which except the reservation provided for in said charter, shall be equitably apportioned among the persons insured who shall, by their policies, be entitled to a participation in the profits of said company; and each insurer to whom any profits shall be so apportioned, shall be entitled to one vote and no more at each election of directors, for every hundred dollars so apportioned to him out of the profits of the company. And mutual policies may be charged with losses to the extent they have been credited with profits, if the losses by insurance require it.

May invest funds. § 4. The capital of said company, and the funds accumulated by its business, or any part thereof, may be invested, and from time to time reinvested, as occasion may require, upon the securities and in the manner allowed by the provisions of the act under which said company is organized, or any amendment thereof.

§ 5. The board of directors of said company may, from time to time, declare dividends upon its guarantee capital, payable to the proprietors or owners of said capital, in cash or scrip as the board may determine, not to exceed twenty per cent of their net earnings; but **Dividends.** no such dividends shall be declared or paid except out of the actual net earnings of the business of said company, and all dividends so paid shall be charged to the expense account of said company.

§ 6. When the benefit or relief fund of said company, specified in its charter, shall amount to the sum of twenty-five thousand dollars, cash dividends, at a rate not exceeding six per cent per annum, may be paid thereon, to the stockholders or insurers, as the board of directors may determine.

§ 7. So much of the charter of said company which was filed in the office of the Secretary of State, on the twenty-ninth day of March, one thousand eight hundred and fifty-three, as is inconsistent with the provisions of this act, is hereby repealed.

§ 8. This act shall take effect immediately.

Chap. 124.

AN ACT to authorize the towns of Manheim, Danube and Little Falls, in the county of Herkimer, to build a bridge across the Mohawk River at a place called Fink's at the Foot of Fall Hill in the town of Danube.

Passed April 2, 1862; three-fifths being present.

The People of the State of New York, represented in Senate and Assembly, do enact as follows:

SECTION 1. John Markell, of the town of Manheim, John Deifendorf, of the town of Danube and Solomon Petrie, of the town of Little Falls, are hereby appointed commissioners to borrow the sum of nine thousand dollars on the credit of said towns, and to locate, construct and build a bridge across the Mohawk River between the towns of Manheim and Danube aforesaid, at a place called Fink's at the foot of Fall Hill. *Commissioners.*

§ 2. Before commencing said bridge the said commissioners shall borrow the said sum of nine thousand dollars on bonds to be issued by them for five hundred dollars each, said bonds shall not be sold at less than par, and to be paid as follows: One-ninth part of the principal sum with the annual interest thereon in each year, which sum shall be ascertained and expressed by coupons with said bonds, and the board of supervisors of the county of Herkimer shall annually cause one-third of the sum so to become due in each year to be levied and collected by a tax in each of said towns as other town charges, until the whole sum shall be fully paid and satisfied. The collectors of the said towns may receive the coupons of such bonds as shall be due or payable for the year when the tax for the payment of the same shall be levied, in payment of taxes. Each of said bonds before being delivered shall be signed by the said commissioners and countersigned by the supervisors of the said towns, and shall not bear more than seven per cent interest. *May borrow $9,000.*

§ 3. The said commissioners shall cause a careful survey and plan of said bridge with an estimate of the cost thereof, including every expense to bring the same

into full use for the public, to be made and approved by
them, and the supervisors of said towns, or a majority of
them, shall advertise for not less than three weeks in
two newspapers printed in the county of Herkimer, in
the state paper printed in Albany, for sealed proposals
to build and construct said bridge according to the plans
and specifications thereof so adopted and approved ; and
shall on the day and at the time and place specified in
said notice open said proposals in public, and award the
contract or contracts for building said bridge to the
lowest responsible bidder, who shall give good and adequate security to be approved by said commissioners for
performing said work, and the said commissioners shall
follow, as nearly as may be, the practice of the Canal
Commissioners in advertising, letting and making payments on the public works. They shall enter into a
sealed and specific contract with the person or persons
to whom such contract shall be awarded, requiring good
and adequate security for the performance thereof and
fixing a method for an amicable adjustment of any dis-
putes that may arise as to the quality of the work, or the
time and manner of finishing the same ; but the said commissioners nor any person employed by them shall not
modify or alter the contract so made nor change or alter
the plans, and specifications of said bridge without the
written consent and approbation of the supervisors of
the towns of Manheim, Danube and Little Falls, or a
majority of them in office at the time of giving such consent and approbation, nor in any case to increase the cost
of said bridge beyond the sum of nine thousand dollars.

§ 4. In case of the removal from the county, sickness,
resignation, death, or inability of either of said commissioners to act, the first judge of the county of Herkimer may appoint in the place of such commission, a new
commissioner, to be an inhabitant and freeholder of the
town in which such vacancy shall occur.

§ 5. Such bridge may be constructed of stone, iron or
wood or partly from either, but its whole cost including
all charges and expenses of the commissioners shall not
exceed the said sum of nine thousand dollars. Such
commissioners shall receive each one dollar per day for
the time actually and necessarily spent in the duties
aforesaid, of which each shall render a minute account
to the supervisor of his town, but neither of said com-

missioners shall receive in the aggregate beyond the sum of three hundred dollars for the whole of his compensation.

§ 6. Each of said commissioners, before entering upon the duties herein authorized, shall give a bond to the people of the State of New York, with two or more good securities to be approved by the supervisor of the town in which he resides, in the penalty of five thousand dollars, conditioned that he will well and faithfully discharge the duty of the commission aforesaid, and pay over and account for all the money which shall come to his hands as such commissioner, and each of said commissioners shall retain and keep in his hands, as nearly as may be, one-third of said bonds, and one-third of the proceeds thereof until the same shall be paid over and applied to the purposes of this act, and the final surplus if any, shall be paid equally to the supervisors of said towns, and said surplus so repaid to the several supervisors, shall belong to the poor fund of said towns respectively.

§ 7. The several bonds to be taken and given under the sixth section of this act, shall be filed with the clerk of Herkimer county, and said commissioners may in their own names as such commissioners, bring any actions in the courts of this state to enforce said bonds so required to be taken from the contractor or contractors.

§ 8. This act shall take effect immediately.

Chap. 125.

AN ACT in relation to the claim of Squire and John M. Whipple, for compensation for erecting a bridge superstructure over the Seneca river, at the village of Seneca Falls.

Passed April 2, 1862; three-fifths being present.

The People of the State of New York, represented in Senate and Assembly, do enact as follows:

SECTION 1. The Canal Board are hereby authorized and empowered to examine the subject of a claim made by Squire and John M. Whipple, for building a bridge

36

across Seneca river on Bridge street, in the village of Seneca Falls, in the year eighteen hundred and fifty-seven, and to award such sum, if any, as the state may be legally and justly liable for.

§ 2. The State Treasurer shall pay upon the warrant of the Auditor of the Canal Department to S. and J. M. Whipple, or order, such sums as shall be awarded to them in pursuance of the provision of the first section of this act, out of any moneys in the treasury appropriated to the enlargement of the Cayuga and Seneca canal.

Chap. 126.

AN ACT to authorize the city of Brooklyn to fix and determine names and numbers for streets, avenues, &c., in said city.

Passed April 2, 1862; three-fifths being present.

The People of the State of New York, represented in Senate and Assembly, do enact as follows:

SECTION 1. The common council of the city of Brooklyn are hereby authorized and empowered to alter, change and fix and determine the names of all streets, avenues, lanes, squares and places in said city, and to designate numbers for houses and lots therein; provided, however, that all such names shall be fixed by ordinance or ordinances to be passed for that purpose, in the same manner as ordinances for other purposes are now made.

§ 2. Any person who shall make use of, put up, display or designate any name or other designation or title for any street, avenue, lane, square or place in said city of Brooklyn, or who shall put up, display or designate any number on any building or lot or otherwise, other than such as may be fixed and determined by the common council of said city, shall be deemed guilty of misdemeanor and be punishable therefor as the law directs.

What shall be a misdemeanor.

§ 3. This act shall take effect immediately.

Chap. 127.

AN ACT to provide for the election of a police constable in the village of Silver Creek.

Passed April 2, 1862; three-fifths being present.

The People of the State of New York, represented in Senate and Assembly, do enact as follows:

SECTION 1. It shall be lawful for the electors of the corporation of the village of Silver Creek, in the county of Chautauqua, at their annual election in each and every year hereafter to elect a police constable, who shall possess the same jurisdiction, and exercise the powers and duties and be entitled to the same fees as constables of towns in said county.

§ 2. Said constable, when so elected, shall hold his office until the next annual election, or until his successor shall be elected and qualified. *Term of office.*

§ 3. In case of the death, removal or inability to serve or neglect to qualify of said constable so elected, it shall be lawful for the trustees of said corporation to appoint a constable to fill any such vacancy until the next annual election of said corporation, or until a successor shall be elected. *Trustees to appoint in case of vacancy.*

§ 4. The trustees of said village shall have power to appoint a police constable for said village, with the powers and duties conferred by the first section of this act, who shall hold said office until the next village election, after the passage of this act, or until his successor shall be elected and have qualified.

§ 5. This act shall take effect immediately.

Chap. 128.

AN ACT to incorporate Protection Fire Engine
Company Number One, in Huntington, Suffolk
county.

Passed April 2, 1862; three-fifths being present.

*The People of the State of New York, represented in
Senate and Assembly, do enact as follows :*

SECTION 1. Fayette Gould, Isaac Adams, Chas N Fleet,
J. Amherst Woodhull, Isaac Rogers, C Smith Sammis,
Amos P. Conklin, Hewlett I. Long, Reuben R. Scudder,
William A. Conant, Joseph G. Conklin, and their associates are hereby constituted a body corporate, by the
name, "The Protection Fire Engine Company Number
One, of Huntington ;" and by that name they, and their
successors, shall be capable, in law, of purchasing, holding
and conveying any real or personal estate necessary for
their use as a fire company, also by their corporate name
they and their successors shall and may have perpetual
succession ; and shall be persons in law capable of suing
and being sued, pleading and being impleaded, defending and being defended, in all courts and places whatsoever, in all manner of actions, suits, complaints and
causes whatsoever.

To make by-laws and regulations.
§ 2. The said corporation shall have full power to
make and establish such by-laws, rules and regulations,
as they from time to time shall think proper, as to their
officers, time, place and manner of electing them, the
period of their continuance in office, their removal for
good cause, their power and duties, and as to the election of members, their removal and the government of
the persons appointed by them as firemen, and with respect to the purposes for which this corporation is constituted.

To appoint firemen.
§ 3. The said corporation shall have full power and
authority to nominate and appoint a sufficient number
of firemen, not exceeding seventy-five, to have the care
and management of the engine and all implements belonging to said company and who shall be ready at all
times to assist in extinguishing fires, and to perform all

the duties which may be required of them by the regulations of said company, and in case of removal of any members to appoint others in their place.

§ 4. Each of the persons so appointed firemen as aforesaid who shall serve as such firemen for five years, including the time they or either of them may have served as a member of the Protection Hook and Ladder Company Number One, or as a member of the Protection Fire Engine Company Number One, of Huntington, previous to this act of incorporation, shall, during such service, be exempted from serving as a juror in any of the courts of this state, and forever hereafter to be exempted from militia duty, except in cases of insurrection or invasion; and a certificate signed by the foreman and secretary of said company, shall be conclusive evidence in all cases that the person named therein is or has been a member of said company for the period stated.

Exemption from jury and military duty.

Chap. 129.

AN ACT in relation to the compensation of the superintendent of common schools in the city of Utica.

Passed April 2, 1862; three-fifths being present.

The People of the State of New York, represented in Senate and Assembly, do enact as follows:

SECTION 1 The commissioners of common schools in the city of Utica, hereafter, in their annual estimate of the amount of money necessary to be raised by the common council of said city, for the payment of teachers' wages, shall include the amount of the annual compensation of the superintendent of said schools, as the same shall, from time to time, be determined by the said commissioners as now by law provided; and the said common council shall cause the same to be levied and collected in the same manner as the said amount of teachers' wages, and other money for school purposes are levied and collected by said common council in said city; and

How to be raised.

so much of the second section of chapter sixty-six of the laws of eighteen hundred and fifty, as requires such compensation to be "audited and allowed as other town charges are in said city," is hereby repealed.

To be paid to the treasurer.

§ 2. The money thus directed by the preceding section to be levied and collected by the common council, shall be paid to the treasurer of said city, who, together with his official sureties, shall be accountable therefor in the same manner as for other money of said city; and the said treasurer shall pay out the same in the same way that other money for the said schools of said city is paid out, and in no other manner.

§ 3. This act shall take effect immediately.

Chap. 130.

AN ACT to authorize the trustees of the village of Elmira to erect bridges over the Chemung Canal in said village.

Passed April 2, 1862; three-fifths being present.

The People of the State of New York, represented in Senate and Assembly, do enact as follows:

SECTION 1. The trustees of the village of Elmira, in the county of Chemung, are hereby authorized to construct one or more bridges over the Chemung Canal in said village; provided, no part of the expense of said bridge or bridges, either in the cost of their construction or in repairs thereafter, nor any damage resulting therefrom, shall be chargeable to the state.

Consent of Canal Commissioners.

§ 2. Before the erection of any of said bridges, the written consent of the Canal Commissioners in charge of the divisions of the canals to which the Chemung Canal belongs, shall be obtained, together with the written opinion of the division engineer having in charge the said canals, that said bridge or bridges will not interfere with the navigation of said canal; nor shall said bridge or bridges be constructed over the canal, until property holders adjoining the approaches to said bridge or bridges shall in writing, release all claims against the state for damages resulting therefrom.

§ 3. The construction of said bridge or bridges shall be under the direction and supervision of the commissioner and engineer in charge of said canal, and whenever in their judgment, the navigation of said canal shall require an alteration in or the removal of said bridge or bridges, they are hereby empowered to order said alteration or removal, and in the event of said order, the said trustees, at the expense of said village, shall make such alteration or removal without delay.

Bridges to be built under direction of Commissioner and State Engineer.

Chap. 131.

AN ACT in relation to the dividends of the Mutual Life Insurance Company of New York.

'Passed April 2, 1862; three-fifths being present.

The People of the State of New York, represented in Senate and Assembly, do enact as follows :

Section 1. The Mutual Life Insurance Company of New York, may appropriate its dividends either to the purchase of additional insurance payable with the policy or at the option of the insured, in reduction of, or towards the annual payment of premiums on policies, such dividends may be declared every five years or oftener at the option of the said company provided, that said company shall not make such appropriation in reduction of any annual premium without the consent first had and obtained of the superintendent of the insurance department, after each dividend, as to all persons entitled to such dividend.

§ 2. This act shall take effect immediately.

Chap. 132.

AN ACT to amend an act entitled "An act to amend and consolidate the several acts in relation to the charter of the city of Rochester," passed April eighth, eighteen hundred and sixty-one.

Passed April 3, 1862; three-fifths being present.

The People of the State of New York, represented in Senate and Assembly, do enact as follows:

Bounds of city.

SECTION 1. Section two of title one of the act entitled "An act to amend and consolidate the several acts in relation to the charter of the city of Rochester," passed April eighth, eighteen hundred and sixty-one, is hereby amended so as to read as follows:

§ 2. The boundaries of said city shall be as follows: Begining at a point in the middle of the ridge road, eight chains and seventy-five links distant from the top of the east high bank of the Genesee river; thence south fifteen minutes east thirty-two chains and forty links to a point on the north side of a road or street called Norton street, leading to the village of Carthage, and on the east side of land now or lately owned by Elisha B. Strong; thence south thirty-nine degrees and fifteen minutes west, along the line between lands now or lately belonging to the State of New York and Elisha B. Strong and others, twenty-one chains and eighty-four links; thence south twelve degrees and forty-five minutes west, sixteen chains and fifty-six links; thence south one degree and forty-five minutes west, thirty chains and seventy-five links to the line between townships number thirteen and fourteen, in the seventh range of townships of Phelps and Gorhams purchase; thence south eighty-nine degrees east along the north line of lots number seventy-two and seventy-one, and a part of sixty-five in said townships number thirteen, one hundred and nine chains and seventy-seven links to the west line of North avenue; thence along the west line of North avenue to Bay street; thence on the south line of Bay street to Hibbard street; thence along the west line of Hibbard

street to the north line of the Auburn and Rochester
Railroad; thence along the northerly line of the Auburn
and Rochester Railroad to the centre of the Goodman
road; thence south twenty-four degrees and thirty minutes west along the east line of lots number fifty-eight,
fifty-nine and sixty, to the south east corner of said lot
number sixty in township number thirteen aforesaid;
thence north eighty-nine degrees and thirty minutes
west along the south line of lot number sixty and part of
lot number nineteen in said township number thirteen
to the centre of the Henrietta road or Mount Hope
avenue; thence south six degrees east, in the centre of
said street, eleven chains and seventy links; thence south
one chain and fifty-one links; thence south twelve degrees west three chains and thirty-five links; thence
south twenty-six degrees and fifteen minutes west two
chains; thence south twenty-nine degrees and thirty
minutes west, twelve chains and fifty links; thence south
twenty-five degrees and fifteen minutes, west three chains
and thirty-five links to the south east corner of the
Mount Hope cemetery lot; thence north eighty-nine degrees west, twenty-three chains and twenty-seven links
to the west line of lot number twenty-four of the first
division of lots in the said township number thirteen;
thence north twenty-five degrees and thirty minutes east,
along the west line of part of lot number twenty-four
aforesaid, and lot number twenty-two, to a point twelve
chains and twenty-seven links south of the original north
line of the Mount Hope cemetery lot, thence north fifty-
four degrees west to the centre of the Genesee river;
thence south-westerly along the centre of the line of said
lot number thirty-six, to a point on lot thirty-five on said
four thousand acre tract, where the east line of lot number one hundred and sixty-nine in township number
one west of the Genesee river, would, if continued, strike
the same; thence north three degrees east, two hundred
and ninety-four chains and ninety-five links to the north
line of lot number thirty-three in the twenty thousand
acre tract, townships number one, short range, west of
the Genesee river; thence south eighty-seven degrees
east, to the top of the west high bank of the Genesee
river; thence northwardly along the top of said bank
to a point due west from the place of beginning; thence
east across the Genesee river to the place of beginning.
37

§ 2. Section seven of title two of the said act is hereby amended so as to read as follows:

§ 7 An election shall be held in each ward annually, on the Tuesday after the first Monday in March, in each year, at such place as shall be designated by the common council, of which a notice shall be published for at least six days previous to the election, in all the daily newspapers printed in said city, at which there shall be chosen by the electors of the whole city, voting in their respective wards, one mayor, who shall hold his office for one year, and one police justice, when the term of office of the then incumbent will expire before the next annual election, who shall hold his office for four years; one treasurer, when the term of office of the then incumbent will expire before the next annual election, who shall hold his office for two years; and one justice of the peace, who shall hold his office for three years; and, also, by the electors of each ward, for such ward one alderman, who shall hold his office for the period of two years; one constable, who shall hold his office for one year; and one commissioner of common schools, when the term of office of the then incumbent will expire before the next annual election, who shall hold his office for two years; and, also, by the electors of each ward, one supervisor, who shall hold his office for one year, and two inspectors of election, in each election district who shall hold their offices for one year.

§ 3. Section eight is hereby amended so as to read as follows:

§ 8. The common council shall annually, or as often as a vacancy exists in any of the offices in the first part of this section named, appoint, by ballot, one city attorney, one city clerk, one chief engineer, one or more assistant engineers, one fire marshal, one overseer of the poor, one superintendent of streets, one sealer of weights and measures, one city surveyor, not less than three nor more than seven persons, of whom the mayor shall be one, to constitute a board of health, and one physician, to be the physician thereof, and so many fire wardens, and so many pound masters as it may deem necessary, each of which said officers shall hold his office during the pleasure of the common council; also, one commissioner of Mount Hope cemetery, who shall hold his office for two years. The common council shall also once in three years, and at some meeting thereof in the month of June, or as often as a vacancy exists, appoint one comptroller, who shall hold his office for three years from the first day of July thereafter. But if the appointment of such commissioner of Mount Hope cemetery, or of such comptroller, is to take effect during the term for which his predecessor was appointed, he shall hold his office only for the unexpired residue of said term.

§ 4. Section fifteen is hereby amended so as to read as follows:

§ 15. Inspectors of elections, so elected under this act as aforesaid, shall be inspectors of elections held in said wards or election districts respectively, as well for the election of state and county, as of the city and ward officers. And in case of the death, inability, or refusal of any such inspector to act, or of his ceasing to be a resident of the ward or election district for which he was so appointed or elected, the common council must thereafter appoint another in his or their place, and file a certificate of such appointment with the city clerk, and the person or persons thus appointed, shall be inspector or inspectors for the ward or election district for which he or they was or were so appointed. The whole compensation to be paid by said city to said inspectors and their clerk or clerks for their services as such, and for all stationery used by them, except for necessary books and blanks, shall not exceed the sum of forty dollars for each election held in such ward or election district.

§ 5. Section nineteen is hereby amended by inserting the words " or election district" after the word " ward " wherever it occurs.

§ 6. Section sixty-six of title four is hereby amended so as to read as follows:

§ 66. All the fines and penalties imposed by the said police justice, and all moneys that shall be paid to, or received by him as such, shall belong to the city of Rochester, and the said police justice shall report, on oath, to the said common council, at the first regular meeting thereof in each month, during the term for which he shall be elected, the number and names of persons fined by him, and the names of persons against whom judgment shall have been rendered by him, for any penalty or penalties, with the dates and amounts of such fines and penalties respectively, and all moneys collected or received by him as such police justice, for fines, or penalties or other wise, and shall pay to the treasurer of said city on the first Monday in each and every month during the term for which the said police justice shall be elected, all moneys received by him, which are hereinbefore declared to belong to said city ; and any neglect to comply with the provisions of this section shall be good ground for the removal from office of said police justice. The said police justice may be removed from office by the county court of Monroe county, for official misconduct, neglect of, or unfaithful, or insufficient performance of any of his duties, on charges preferred by said common council, or by any one or more electors of the said city of Rochester ; but notice of such charges against him, and an oportunity of being heard in his defence, shall first be given in such manner as said court, or the judge thereof, shall direct.

§ 7. Section eighty-seven of said title is hereby amended by striking out the last paragraph, and inserting instead thereof as follows :

In regard to assessments

The said clerk shall make and certify a correct copy of said assessment book, to be delivered to the supervisors of the several wards or election districts respectively, for the use of the board of supervisors of Monroe county, on or before the first day of October in each year, to be by them presented to the board of supervisors of Monroe county, as the ward rolls of the city. And the said board of supervisors shall pay to said clerk for the copy for their use in the same manner as paid to the supervisors of the several towns for the town rolls.

§ 8. Section one hundred and seventeen of said title is hereby amended by striking out the last paragraph thereof, and substituting therefor the following :

And in case any mistake or error has been, or shall be, committed in any of the proceedings in making any tax or assessment upon any property, real or personal, the

Common council to correct error in assessment.

common council shall have power to correct such tax or assessment, or to remit the same if uncollected, and to refund the same if collected ; and the amount or aggregate of the sums so remitted or refunded shall be added to the gross amount of taxes to be assessed and collected the next succeeding year, and shall be collected with the taxes for the general expenses of the city, and in the same manner.

§ 9. Section one hundred and twenty-seven is hereby amended so as to read as follows:

§ 127. After the board of supervisors of the county of Monroe shall have equalized and corrected the assessment rolls of the city of Rochester, and shall have inserted therein the county taxes levied and assessed by them, they shall annex to each roll or warrant, under the hands and seals of the chairman and clerk of the board of supervisors, commanding the said county treasurer to collect from the several persons named in said rolls the sums mentioned in the last column of each roll, opposite their respective names, and authorizing the said treasurer, in case any person named in the rolls shall refuse or neglect to pay his taxes on or before the fifteenth day of February next ensuing, to levy the same by distress and sale of goods and chattels of such person, and they shall on or before the fifteenth day of December next ensuing deliver the said rolls to the treasurer of Monroe county.

Warrant of supervisors.

§ 10. Section one hundred and twenty-eight is hereby amended so as to read as follows:

§ 128. Immediately after receiving such rolls and warrants the county treasurer shall give public notice, by advertisement in all of the daily newspapers printed in the city of Rochester, that all persons named in said rolls are required to pay their taxes to him at his office, on or before the fifteenth day of February then next, and stating the amount to be added if payment shall be delayed. The said county treasurer shall receive the amount of any tax levied on said assessment rolls, with the following additions as charges for collecting, viz.: if the same shall be paid on or before the fifteenth day of December next succeeding levying of such tax, he shall charge and receive an addition of one per cent.; if paid after the said fifteenth day of December, and on or before the first day of January then next, an addition of two per cent.; if paid after the first day of January then next, or on or before the fifteenth day of January then next, an addition of three per cent.; if paid after the fifteenth day of January and on or before the first day of February then next, an addition of four per cent.; if paid after the first day of February then next, an addition of five per cent.

Duty of county treasurer.

§ 11. Section one hundred and thirty-nine of title six is hereby amended so as to read as follows:

§ 139. The said commissioners may appoint a policeman, who shall hold his office during the pleasure of said board, and whose salary shall be fixed and paid by the common council, from the fund raised for the use of the board of education, and who shall have the same powers as the other policemen of said city, and shall perform such duties as said board of education may impose.

§ 12. Section one hundred and fifty-seven of title seven is hereby amended by adding thereto the following:

But no encroachment upon any street, alley or lane of said city, however long continued, shall constitute an adverse possession to, or confer any rights upon the person claiming thereunder, as against said city.

§ 13. Section one hundred and seventy-two of said title is hereby amended by adding thereto the following:

But said common council may set aside said report, and abandon said improvement, at any time before the final confirmation of the assessment roll hereafter mentioned. The provisions of this section shall apply to any proceedings now or hereafter pending before said common council.

§ 14. Section one hundred and eighty-eight is hereby amended by inserting in the second line thereof, immediately after the word "fixed," as follows:

"And the assessment roll shall have been finally confirmed."

§ 15. Section one hundred and eighty-nine is hereby amended by adding thereto the following:

But the said city shall not become obligated to take any such lands or tenements, nor to pay or deposit such damages therefor, nor shall the owners, occupants, or other persons having any liens thereupon, acquire any right to such damages, nor to be paid therefor, until the final confirmation of said assessment roll, as is hereinbefore provided.

§ 16. Section one hundred and ninety-one is hereby amended by inserting immediately after the word "assessments," in the seventh line from the end thereof, the following:

" But the said treasurer may in his discretion, issue his warrant for the collection of the whole or any part of such assessment."

§ 17. Section two hundred and nine of said title is hereby amended by striking out the first two paragraphs and substituting therefor the following :

§ 209. Every tax or assessment authorized by this act, *Tax to be a lien on property.* which has been or shall be assessed upon any lands, tenements or real estate, or upon the owners or occupants thereof, shall be and is hereby declared to be valid and effectual, notwithstanding any irregularity, omission or error in any of the proceedings relating to the same, and shall be and remain a lien on such lands, tenements or real estate, on which or in respect to which the same have been or shall be made, from the time of the passage of the resolution of the common council levying the same, in the case of the annual city taxes, and from the time of the confirmation by the common council of the roll containing the same, in the case of other taxes and assessments, and until the same shall be paid or satisfied.

§ 18. Section two hundred and twenty of title eight is hereby amended by adding thereto the following:

§ 220. The common council of said city may in like *Common council may issue bonds of city to the amount of $10,000.* manner issue the bonds or obligations of said city, payable to the bearer or holder, not less than five nor more than twenty years after their date, for an amount not exceeding ten thousand dollars, with interest payable semi-annually, at a rate not greater than seven per cent per annum, which bonds or obligations shall be used or negotiated by said common council, for the purpose of purchasing, or raising funds to purchase, two additional steam fire engines, their appurtenances and equipments, and repairing centre market in said city, for an engine house, hose depot, and city offices.

§ 19. Section two hundred and twenty-one of said title is hereby amended so as to read as follows :

§ 221. The common council of said city is hereby authorized to borrow sixty-six thousand dollars to pay the amount of the over drafts on its various funds, which had been made up to and including the first day of March, in the year one thousand eight hundred and sixty-two, and to issue the bonds or obligations of said city *Are authorized to borrow money to pay over drafts.* for the moneys so borrowed, which shall be applied exclusively to the payment of the said over drafts. The said bonds or obligations shall, upon their face, purport to be issued in pursuance of this act; shall be issued under the corporate seal of said city; shall be signed by the mayor and clerk thereof, or by such other officers of said city as the common council shall designate; shall be payable to the bearer or holder, not less than five nor more than twenty years after their date, and shall bear interest payable semi-annually, at a rate not greater than seven per cent per annum. The aforesaid sum of sixty-six thousand dollars, shall include any sum or sums which the said common council may have heretofore borrowed under or by virtue of the said two hundred and twenty-fifth section of the act hereby amended; and no more money shall be borrowed under this act, than the difference between the aggregate of the sums heretofore borrowed as aforesaid, and the said sum of sixty-six thousand dollars; and no bonds shall be issued or executed in pursuance of this act, for any sum or sums for which a bond or bonds of the city may have been already issued or executed, unless such previous bond or bonds shall first be taken up and cancelled. All acts and proceedings of the common council of said city in the year eighteen hundred and sixty-one in appropriating and expending the sum of fourteen thousand two hundred and forty-six dollars and twenty-six cents, in raising, equipping and subsisting volunteers and military companies for the military service of the State of New York and of the United States, in said year are hereby legalized and confirmed, and are hereby declared to be of the same validity in all respects, as if the same had been duly authorized by the charter of said city or as if an act specially authorizing all said acts and proceedings had been theretofore duly enacted.

§ 20. Section two hundred and twenty-two of said title is hereby amended by adding thereto the following: "But any member of the fire department who shall have served as such for the period of three years, and shall be prevented from further service as such by the use of steam fire engines in said city, shall be entitled to all the aforesaid privileges and exemptions."

§ 21. Section two hundred and twenty-five of said title is hereby amended so as to read as follows:

§ 225. The fire marshal shall have such powers and perform such duties as the common council shall from time to time direct, and with such a salary as the common council shall determine, payable from the fire department fund.

Relating to fire department.

§ 22. Section two hundred and thirty-eight of title nine is hereby amended by inserting in the fifth line thereof, immediately after the word "attorney," the words " or such person as may he deputed by him or by the police justice."

§ 23. Section two hundred and forty-eight, title eleven is hereby amended by adding thereto the following :

The number of health inspectors and their salaries, shall be determined by the common council.

§ 24. This act shall take effect immediately.

Chap. 133.

AN ACT enabling the Tompkins County Agricultural and Horticultural Society to draw their proportion of the moneys devoted to agricultural purposes from the State Treasury.

Passed April 3, 1862 ; three-fifths being present.

The People of the State of New York, represented in Senate and Assembly, do enact as follows:

SECTION 1. Out of any moneys to which the county of Tompkins would have been entitled, by virtue of the act passed May fifth, eighteen hundred and forty-one, entitled "An act to promote agriculture," and acts for the promotion of agriculture, passed subsequent thereto, there shall be paid to the Tompkins County Agricultural and Horticultural Society, such moneys as appears to have been appropriated and set apart to the county of Tompkins, and have not hitherto been drawn from the treasury of the state.

§ 2. The Treasurer of the state shall pay, on the warrant of the Comptroller, to the order of the treasurer of the said agricultural and horticultural society, countersigned by the president, the sum of five hundred and seventy dollars, out of the treasury of the state ; provided, however, that an equal amount shall be raised by voluntary subscription or otherwise, which shall appear to the satisfaction of the Comptroller. *Treasurer to pay society $570 on certain conditions.*

§ 3. If the sum of five hundred and seventy dollars is not raised by subscription or otherwise, then the Trea-

38

surer is authorized to pay as above, an equal sum, as may appear to the satisfaction of the Comptroller to have been subscribed and paid.

§ 4. The provision of this act are not to apply to the act or acts making annual appropriations for agricultural purposes, but the above sum is in addition to the sum now appropriated annually, to which the county of Tompkins is now by law entitled.

§ 5. This act shall take effect immediately.

Chap. 134.

AN ACT to extend the time of collecting moneys for town purposes in the towns of Suffolk county.

Passed April 3, 1862; three-fifths being present.

The People of the State of New York, represented in Senate and Assembly, do enact as follows:

SECTION 1. If any collector of taxes in the towns of Huntington, Islip, Smithtown, Brookhaven, Riverhead, Southold, Southampton, Easthampton and Shelter Island, in the county of Suffolk, shall within the time which is now or shall hereafter be provided by law, pay over to the treasurer of said county all of the moneys due to the said treasurer for state, school and county purposes, and shall renew his bond with sureties to the satisfaction of the supervisor of said towns, or in case of his absence or disability, of the town clerk, in a penalty not less than double the amount remaining uncollected by virtue of his warrant; such approval to be indorsed upon said bond, and which bond shall be filed and have the effect of a collector's bond as provided by law, then the time for collecting the taxes and making the returns thereof, may be extended to a period not later than the first Monday in May following.

§ 2. This act shall take effect immediately.

Chap. 135.

AN ACT to empower Holley Lodge Number One
Hundred and Forty of the Independent Order
of Odd Fellows of Northern New York, in the
village of Holley and county of Orleans, to hold
and convey real and personal estate, and constitute the same a corporation.

Passed April 4, 1862.

*The People of the State of New York, represented in
Senate and Assembly, do enact as follows:*

SECTION 1. Ransom P. Orr, Asahel Merreman and Ezra
N. Hill, trustees of Holley Lodge Number One hundred
and Forty of the Independent Order of Odd Fellows, in
the village of Holley and county of Orleans, New York,
and their successors in office, are hereby empowered to
take, hold and convey real estate for the use and benefit
of said lodge, in amount not to exceed in value five
thousand dollars, and personal property for the use and
benefit of said lodge, in amount not to exceed in value
five thousand dollars, and shall be constituted a corporation with power to sue and be sued by the corporate
name of " The Trustees of Holley Lodge Number One
Hundred and Forty of the Independent Order of Odd
Fellows of Northern New York."

§ 2. Such real and personal estate as is now held in
possession and claimed by the trustees of such association, not to exceed in value the amounts in the foregoing
section expressed, is hereby confirmed in said trustees,
as fully and completely as if they had had legal power
to take and hold real and personal estate at the time of
the execution and delivery of the deeds of conveyance
thereof, and the personal property of every kind now
held by them.

§ 3. The affairs of said corporation shall be managed
by three trustees, to be elected annually, according to
the by-laws of said lodge, from among the members
thereof, who shall hold their office for one year or until
their successors are elected, and until the first election
to be held under this act, Ransom P. Orr, Asahel Merre-

man and Ezra N. Hill, present trustees of said lodge,
shall be the trustees of the corporation hereby created.

§ 4. This act shall take effect immediately.

Chap. 136.

AN ACT releasing the interests of the state in
certain surplus moneys to Frederick Krutina, as
administrator with the will annexed of William
Keller, deceased.

Passed April 4, 1862 ; by a two-third vote.

*The People of the State of New York, represented in
Senate and Assembly, do enact as follows:*

SECTION 1. All the right, title and interest which the
people of the State of New York have in and to the surplus moneys now remaining on deposit with the chamberlain of the city of New York, and subject to the order
of the supreme court of the State of New York, which
are part of the surplus moneys paid to him in pursuance
of an order of the supreme court, made in an action entitled "William Lee against George Hartmann and
others," belonging to William Keller, deceased, and
escheated to the State of New York by reason of the
alienage of the heirs and devisees of the said William
Keller, is hereby released unto Frederick Krutina ot the
city of New York, as administrator with the testament
annexed of the estate of said William Keller in trust, to
be applied as provided by said last will and testament
of said William Keller, deceased.

§ 2. The supreme court shall, on application of said
Frederick Krutina, make an order for the payment to
him as such administrator of said surplus moneys.

§ 3. Nothing in this act contained shall affect the right
of any creditor of the said William Keller, deceased.

§ 4. This act shall take effect immediately.

Chap. 137.

AN ACT to re-appropriate certain moneys for the enlargement and completion of the canals.

Passed April 4, 1862; three-fifths being present.

The People of the State of New York, represented in Senate and Assembly, do enact as follows:

SECTION 1. The following sums of money arising from the tax imposed for the enlargement and completion of the canals during the present fiscal year or so much thereof as shall remain unexpended on the ninth day of April, one thousand eight hundred and sixty-two shall be and the same is hereby re-appropriated to the following objects and purposes:

To the enlargement and completion of the Erie canal and to furnish an additional and ample supply of water upon the Rome level to maintain seven feet in depth of water, the sum of one hundred thousand dollars. *Erie canal $100,000.*

To the enlargement and completion of the Oswego canal, the sum of thirty-five thousand dollars. *Oswego canal $35,000.*

To the enlargement and completion of the Cayuga and Seneca canal, the sum of thirty thousand dollars. *Cayuga and Seneca $30,000.*

To the completion of the extension of the Genesee Valley canal, the sum of eight thousand dollars. *Genesee Valley $8,000.*

To the completion of the Black river canal and Black river improvement, and the completion of the reservoirs and bridges, the sum of twenty thousand dollars. *Black River $20,000.*

For the improvement of the Champlain canal and Glens Falls feeder, and to rebuild the locks on said canal and to stop the leaks in the Glens Falls feeder as contemplated by the second section of the act entitled "An act to provide the means for the completion of the canals of this state and to fully supply them with water, and for other purposes," passed April nine, eighteen hundred and sixty, the sum of forty-two thousand dollars. *Champlain and Glens Falls feeder $42,000.*

To the enlargement and completion of the Erie canal, the further sum of forty-seven thousand, two hundred and sixty dollars and forty-four cents, being the unexpended balance, and at present unavailable, of the premium moneys on sundry loans made under the constitu- *Erie enlargement the further sum of $47,260.44.*

tion for the enlargement and completion of the canals of this state, which moneys shall be applied to the objects of this appropriation as fast as the same become available in the treasury.

Canal Commissioners may certify to final estimate.

§ 2. The Canal Commissioner in charge may certify the amount due any contractor on a final estimate made on the completion of a contract or a cancellation thereof for work done and materials furnished since the thirteenth day of April, one thousand eight hundred and fifty-nine.

Chap. 138.

AN ACT in reference to highway labor in the village of Oneonta, Otsego county.

Passed April 4, 1862; three-fifths being present.

The People of the State of New York, represented in Senate and Assembly, do enact as follows :

SECTION 1. The trustees of the village of Oneonta, in the county of Otsego, are hereby authorized and required to appropriate one-third part of the highway labor assessed on the inhabitants of said village, to the road recently laid out in the town of Oneonta, and commencing on the Susquehanna river and near the residence of Peter W. Swart, and running thence in a southerly direction up the hill or mountain to the Delaware county line, and being one mile and one hundred rods in length, and to designate the persons so assessed to perform one-third said highway labor on the said new road, instead of the said village, for and during the years eighteen hundred and sixty-two and eighteen hundred and sixty-three.

Trustees to appoint an overseer.

§ 2. The said trustees shall have authority and it is hereby made their duty to designate and appoint some suitable person to act as overseer of said road and to superintend the same and see that it is judiciously laid out and performed ; and the said person so designated and appointed shall be invested with all the powers, duties and responsibilities, and subject to all the liabilities, so far as the said work is concerned, as overseers of highways of the several towns in this state.

§ 3. Any of the persons so designated to work on said new road, as provided in the first section of this act, may perform, during the year eighteen hundred and sixty-two, double the amount of labor for which he is assessed in said year, or any amount thereof less than double thereof, and the work so performed, over and above what may be assessed to him or them in such year eighteen hundred and sixty-two, shall be credited to him or them in the year eighteen hundred and sixty-three, and shall be deducted from the labor assessed to him or them in the year eighteen hundred and sixty-three.

In relation to the performance of the labor.

Chap. 139.

AN ACT to incorporate the Columbian Fire Engine Company Number One of Spring Valley, Ramapo, Rockland county, State of New York.

Passed April 4, 1862; three-fifths being present.

The People of the State of New York, represented in Senate and Assembly, do enact as follows:

SECTION 1. Andrew Smith, John I Cooper, P. Demarest Johnson, Peter S. Van Orden, Albert Tallman, Jr., James F. Parsons, John Wiley, John H. Merritt, Jacob Stephens, Winslow Dorr, John G. Van Houten, Abram Haines, James Wood, Reuben Hope, Jacob D. Cole, John J. Bilyeu, Albert Goetchius, Nelson Hopkins, John D. Blauvelt, Charles G. Merritt, Abram H. Tyson, and Garret S. Cole, are hereby constituted a body corporate by the name of "The Columbian Fire Engine Company, Number One, of Spring Valley," and by that name they and their successors shall be capable in law of purchasing, holding and conveying any real or personal estate necessary for their use as a fire company, to the amount of five thousand dollars; also, by their corporate name aforesaid, they and their successors shall and may have perpetual succession, and shall be persons in law capable of suing and being sued, pleading and being impleaded, answering and being answered unto, defending and being defended, in all courts and places whatsoever, in all manner of actions, suits, complaints, matters and causes whatsoever.

To hold and convey real and personal estate.

Sue and be sued.

To make rules and regulations. § 2. The said corporation shall have full power to make and establish such by-laws, rules and regulations as they from time to time shall think proper, as to their officers, time, place and manner of electing them; the period of their continuance in office; their removal for good cause, their powers and duties, and as to the election of members and their removal, and the government of the persons appointed by them as firemen, and with respect to the purposes for which this corporation is constituted.

To appoint firemen. § 3. The said corporation shall have full power and authority to nominate and appoint a sufficient number of firemen, not exceeding forty, to have the care and management of the fire engine and all implements belonging to said company, and who shall be ready at all times to assist in extinguishing fires, and to perform all the duties which may be required of them by the regulations of said company, and in case of removal of any members, to appoint others in their places.

Firemen exempt from jury and militia duty § 4. Each of the persons so appointed firemen as aforesaid, who shall serve as such firemen for five years, including the time they or either of them may have served as a member of the Columbian Fire Engine Company Number One of Spring Valley, previous to this act of incorporation, shall, during such service, be exempted from serving as a juror in any of the courts of this state, and be exempted from militia duty, except in cases of insurrection or invasion, and a certificate signed by the foreman and secretary of said company shall be conclusive evidence in all cases that the person named therein is or has been a member of said company for the period therein stated.

Chap. 140.

AN ACT to incorporate the Brooklyn Pharmaceutical Society of the City of Brooklyn.

Passed April 4, 1862.

The People of the State of New York, represented in Senate and Assembly, do enact as follows:

SECTION 1. George Reynolds, Herschel Parker, Alexander Hudnut, William J. Watson, J. D. Rice, C. G. C. Hazard, Thomas Scott, Edwin Rulon, J. T. Hogg, Frederick S. Woodward, James T. Burdick, James Fisher, and all such persons who are now members of an association in the city of Brooklyn known as the Brooklyn Pharmaceutical Society, or shall hereafter become members of the same, are hereby constituted a corporation and body politic in law and in fact, by the name, style and title of the "Brooklyn Pharmaceutical Society of the City of Brooklyn," for the purpose of improving the science and art of pharmacy and its collateral branches of science, by diffusing scientific knowledge and making known the best modes of preparing medicines and their compounds, and giving instructions in the same by public lectures. It may hold real and personal estate necessary for the purposes of the association to an amount not exceeding fifty thousand dollars, and may mortgage and sell its property or any part thereof by its bonds and mortgages and conveyances, to be executed under the common seal of the said corporation, and be acknowledged by its president or secretary. The said society may also hold such buildings and collections of books, and of the productions of nature and art, as it may want for the purpose of instruction.

§ 2. The said society may establish by-laws for its government and regulation, and for the preservation and application of the funds thereof, not repugnant to the constitution and laws of the United States or the State of New York, and shall have power to erect an edifice for the accommodation of its members, and to appoint a faculty or learned body to consist of such a number of professors in pharmacy and the collateral

May hold real and personal estate.

May establish by-laws, erect an edifice and appoint a faculty.

39

sciences as may be judged necessary, and when found expedient, to remove them or any of them, and to appoint others in their stead, and to do everything needful and necessary to advance the interest of the society.

Officers.   § 3. The officers of the society shall be a president, two vice-presidents, a secretary and a treasurer, whose respective duties may be assigned by the by-laws, and who shall be elected at the annual meeting to be held in January of each year, and any vacancy that may occur may be supplied by a special election, by the members of said society. There shall also be elected at the said annual meeting, a board of trustees, consisting of not less than seven members, and the officers of the society shall also be ex-officio members of the board of trustees ; and the said board of trustees, of which a majority shall form a quorum, shall conduct the ordinary affairs of the society, and perform such duties as are or may be from time to time committed to them by the society, subject to the revision of the society at each regular meeting.

Powers of trustees.   § 4. The trustees shall have power to issue certificates of membership, to adopt rules and regulations in the examination of candidates, and to grant diplomas to those who shall have passed a satisfactory examination by the trustees, assisted by the professors of the society. Students who have attended one course of lectures in any other constituted society or college of pharmacy, may be entitled to graduate after attending one course of lectures delivered by the professors of this society, by complying with the other requisitions herein set forth.

Relating to annual election of officers.   § 5. If the annual election for officers of said society and members of the board of trustees shall not be held on the stated day in January, the said corporation shall not thereby be dissolved, but the officers and trustees shall hold over until an election of successors.

Privileges of members.   § 6. Every member of this society honorably holding a certificate of fellowship is empowered to compound and dispense physicians prescriptions, sell all compounds or simples, that may be required as medicinal agents.

Seal of society.   § 7. This society shall have a seal which shall be affixed to all diplomas, certificates and title deeds of the society.

§ 8. The corporation hereby created shall be subject to the powers and provisions specified in the third title of the eighteenth chapter of the first part of the Revised Statutes, and the legislature may at any time modify, alter or repeal this act.

Chap. 141.

AN ACT in relation to the superintendents of the poor in the county of Cayuga.

Passed April 4, 1862; three-fifths being present.

The People of the State of New York, represented in Senate and Assembly, do enact as follows :

SECTION 1. Hereafter there shall be three superintendents of the poor in the county of Cayuga.

§ 2. There shall be elected, at the next annual state election, two surperintendents of the poor in said county. The clerk of said county, on the first day of January thereafter, shall determine by lot which of the persons so chosen shall serve three years and which two years, and they shall serve accordingly. At each annual election thereafter there shall be elected one superintendent of the poor in said county, who shall hold his office for three years from the first day of January next after such election.

Clerk to determine by lot the term of superintendents.

§ 3. All the official acts of Grove Bradley and John B. Strong, as superintendents of the poor of the county of Cayuga, since the first day of January, eighteen hundred and sixty, are hereby declared to be as valid and effectual for all purposes as if the said Grove Bradley and John B. Strong had been duly elected to office.

§ 4. This act shall take effect immediately.

Chap. 142.

AN ACT for the relief of Susan Caldwell.

Passed April 4, 1862 ; by a two-third vote.

The People of the State of New York, represented in Senate and Assembly, do enact as follows :

SECTION 1. All the estate and interest of the people of the State of New York, acquired by escheat, by the death of James Caldwell, in and to all the lands and real estate of which said James Caldwell, late of the village of Phœnix, Oswego county, New York, died seized, situate in the county of Oswego, in said state, and the proceeds thereof, is hereby released to Susan Caldwell, widow of the said James Caldwell, deceased, her heirs and assigns forever.

§ 2. This act shall not in any manner affect the rights or claims of any creditor of the said James Caldwell, either by judgment, mortgage, or otherwise, nor any heirs or legal representatives of the said James Caldwell, or any other person or persons lawfully entitled to the lands devised by the said James Caldwell.

§ 3. This act shall take effect immediately.

Chap. 143.

AN ACT permitting the Buffalo and Allegany Valley railroad company to extend their road, and to extend the time for building the same.

Passed April 5, 1862.

The People of the State of New York, represented in Senate and Assembly, do enact as follows :

SECTION 1. The Buffalo and Allegany Valley railroad company, on procuring the necessary additional subscription to the capital stock of said company as required by the general railroad law of this state, authorizing the formation of railroad companies, passed April second, one thousand eight hundred and fifty, and of the several acts amendatory thereof, may extend their road from its present termination at or near Arcade, in the county of Wyoming, to the line of the State of Pennsylvania, near Olean; and upon compliance with the next section of this act, the said company shall acquire all the rights and privileges, and be subject to the same obligations as though the said extension had been embraced in the original articles of association of the said company.

§ 2. Whenever the necessary additional subscription of the capital stock shall be made, which shall not be less than ten thousand dollars for every mile of road required to be constructed by such extension, and ten per cent paid thereon in good faith, and in cash, to the directors of said company, a certificate thereof containing a statement of the length of said proposed extension of the road, a copy of such subscription with the name, place of residence, and number of shares of stock each subscriber agrees to take in said company, and not embraced in the original articles of association of said company, shall be made and signed by at least three of the directors of said company, who shall endorse thereon their affidavit that the amount of stock required by this section has been in good faith subscribed, and ten per cent paid in cash thereon as aforesaid, and that it is intended in good faith to construct or to maintain and operate the said extension as a part of their road.

When $10,000 is subscribed and ten per cent paid in, company may extend their road.

§ 3. Such certificate and affidavit may be filed in the office of the Secretary of State, who shall endorse thereon the day they are filed, and record the same in the book kept by him for the recording of articles of association of railroad corporations; and a copy of said certificate and affidavit filed and recorded in pursuance with this act or of the record thereof, and certified to be a copy by the Secretary of this State or his deputy, shall be presumptive evidence of the facts therein stated.

Certificate to be filed and recorded in office of Secretary of State.

§ 4. The time for constructing said Buffalo and Allegany Valley railroad is hereby further extended for the term of five years.

Time extended five years.

§ 5. This act shall take effect immediately.

Chap. 144.

AN ACT to incorporate the Nanuet Fire Engine Company, at Nanuet, town of Clarkstown, in the county of Rockland.

Passed April 5, 1862; three-fifths being present.

The People of the State of New York, represented in Senate and Assembly, do enact as follows:

SECTION 1. Cornelius L. Ackerman, James W. Demarest, John W. Hutton, Charles E. Smith. David P. Demarest, Henry O. Hutton, Frank Brower, Samuel Blauvelt, John Cooper, Joseph G. Demarest, John Wood, Henry Ferdon, Nicholas Lansing Blauvelt, George Hinton, Jacob Gross, George Gross, Abraham D. Clark, Cornelius I. Demarest, Lucius D. Isham and Jacob C. Haring, and their successors, are hereby constituted a body corporate by the name and title of "The Nanuet Fire Engine Company of Nanuet, Rockland county, New York," and by that name they and their successors may and shall have perpetual succession, and shall be capable in law of purchasing, holding and conveying any estate, real or personal, necessary for use as a fire company, to the amount of five thousand dollars; they shall also by their corporate name aforesaid be capable in law of suing and being sued, answering and being answered unto, defending and being defended in all courts and places whatsoever, in all manner of actions, complaints, matters and causes whatsoever.

To hold and convey real and personal estate to the amount of $5,000.

§ 2. The said corporation shall have full power and authority to make and establish such by-laws, rules and regulations, as from time to time they shall think proper, as to their officers and members, the time and place, and manner of electing such officers, the period of their continuance in office, their removal from office, their powers and duties, and also as to the election of members and their removal or suspension, and the government of the persons appointed by them as firemen, and in regard to all the purposes for which the said body corporate is constituted.

Make by-laws.

§ 3. The said corporation shall have full power to Appoint firemen. nominate and appoint a sufficient number of firemen, not exceeding fifty, to have the care and management of the fire engine and apparatus belonging to or in charge of said company, and who shall be ready at all times to assist in extinguishing fires and to perform all the duties that may be required of them by the by-laws and regulations of said company. And in case of the removal, death, absence or withdrawal of any of the members, the said corporation shall have power to appoint others in their places.

§ 4. Each and all of the persons so appointed firemen, Exempt from jury and militia duty. and who shall serve as such for five years, shall during such service be exempted from serving as jurors in any of the courts of this state and from militia duty, except in cases of war, insurrection or invasion.

§ 5. This act shall take effect immediately.

Chap. 145.

AN ACT to confirm the acts of the board of town officers of the town of Adams, county of Jefferson and State of New York, appointing Graham G. Grennell, Hiram S. Thompson and Orrin H. Rundell as justices of the peace of said town; and to confirm the said appointees, respectively, in their office as justices of the peace of said town.

Passed April 7, 1862; three-fifths being present.

The People of the State of New York, represented in Senate and Assembly, do enact as follows :

SECTION 1. All the acts and proceedings of Charles A. Benjamin, supervisor. Corrill D. Potter, town clerk, and Isaac S. Main, a justice of the peace, of the town of Adams in Jefferson county, State of New York, and done on the second day of January, eighteen hundred and sixty-two, whereby the said supervisor, town clerk and justice of the peace assumed, under their hands and seals, to appoint Graham G. Grennell, Hiram S. Thompson and Orrin H. Rundell to the offices of justices of the peace of said town and in said county, then vacant by the removal from the said county of John Budlong, and the resignation of said office by Orasmus M. Stanley and Nelson Green, respectively, are hereby confirmed. And such appointments shall have the same force, effect and validity, as if the same had been made at the time in full compliance with the law in relation thereto. And the said Graham G. Grennell, Hiram S. Thompson and Orrin H. Rundell, and each of them, shall be and are hereby endued with all the privileges and powers, and made subject to the performance of all the duties of the office of justice of the peace.

Acts of the justices confirmed. § 2. All the acts of, and proceedings before said Graham G. Grennell, Hiram S. Thompson and Orrin H. Rundell, respectively, as justice of the peace, since their said appointment, are hereby confirmed.

Nor affect adversely. § 3. Nothing herein contained shall affect adversely, any action, suit or proceeding commenced before its passage, nor any right vested or acquired in opposition to the acts of the said Graham G. Grennell, Hiram S. Thompson and Orrin H. Rundell, or either of them, while heretofore exercising the said office of justice of the peace.

§ 4. This act shall take effect immediately.

Chap. 146.

AN ACT to incorporate the Newburgh Home for the Friendless.

Passed April 7, 1862; three fifths being present.

The People of the State of New York, represented in Senate and Assembly, do enact as follows:

SECTION 1. Josephine Youngblood, Catharine M. Van Duzer, Phebe E. Montross, Sarah McCarrell, Caroline E. Monell, Elizabeth Case, Margaret S. A. Cumming, Mary Rogers, Elizabeth H. Gray, Deborah B. Falls, Mary S. Wiltsie, Catharine Warren, Julia Ferguson, Jane Leonard, Cynthia Corwin, Elizabeth Stewart, Margaret Hasbrouck, Ellen Walsh, Margaret M. Carlisle, Nancy

Cunningham, Mary F. Thompson, Emily Little, Jane Armstrong, Jane J. Connelly, Mary F. Lawson, Amanda M. Westcott, Harriet E. Bigler, Ethelinda Royce, Jane D. Shelling, Rubie M. Masters, Sarah F. Hermance and Jane E. Langking, and their associates and successors, shall be and they are hereby constituted a body corporate by the name of the Newburgh Home for the Friendless, and by that name shall have perpetual succession, whose object and business shall be, by the publication and diffusion of books, papers and tracts, and by other moral and religious means, to prevent vice and moral degradation, and maintain houses of industry and home for the relief of friendless, destitute or unprotected females, and for friendless and unprotected children.

§ 2. There shall be a board of female managers of the said society, consisting of twelve, to conduct the business of the society in the manner prescribed by the constitution and by-laws of the aforesaid society as the same now exists, or as the same shall be adopted or altered by the corporate body hereby constituted, but the same shall be in accordance with the laws of this state, and such managers shall be elected annually, or otherwise, as is or may be prescribed by such constitution and by-laws. Board of female managers, powers of.

§ 3 Said corporation shall have power to purchase and hold real estate sufficient for the actual occupation and necessary uses of the society, and receive by gift of devise in the same manner and subject to the same restrictions as provided in the general law for the incorporation of religious and benevolent associations, and to hold and convey such real estate, and shall be deemed to be possessed of the rights and to be subject to the liabilities of corporations according to the provisions of title third, chapter eighteen, part first of the Revised Statutes, so far as the same may be applicable, provided, however, that the annual income of any real estate belonging to said corporation shall not exceed the sum of ten thousand dollars. Corporation to hold real estate.

§ 4. The board of managers shall have power to appoint matrons and such other assistants as they may deem necessary in conducting the domestic and internal concerns of their house or houses of industry and home for the friendless; to make any by-laws and regulations for the government of their own proceedings, and those of Powers of board of managers.

40

the persons so appointed, and of other inmates of their house or houses; to govern the children under their care, and prescribe their course of instruction and management to the same extent, and with the same rights as exist in the case of natural guardians.

§ 5. In all cases where a child shall have been surrendered by its natural or other legal guardians to the care and management of the society by any instrument or declaration in writing, it shall be lawful for the said board of managers at their discretion, to place such child by adoption or at service in some suitable employment, and with some proper person or persons, conformably to the laws of this state in regard to the binding out of indigent children, provided that in all such cases the terms of the indenture shall be approved by the police justice of the village of Newburgh, or by the surrogate, or by the superintendent of the alms house, which approval shall be signified on such indenture by the signature of such justice, surrogate or superintendent; but in every such case the requisite provisions shall be inserted in the indenture or contract of binding, to secure the child so bound such treatment, education or instruction as shall be suitable and useful to its situation and circumstances in life.

In regard to binding out children.

§ 6. The children instructed in the schools connected with the houses aforesaid, shall be entitled to draw an annual apportionment from the common school fund, according to the average number in attendance, in the same manner as do the children of other benevolent asylums, and the common or public schools of the village of Newburgh and state.

Children to draw annual apportionment.

§ 7. In case of the death or legal incapacity of a father, or of his imprisonment for crime, or of his abandoning and neglecting to provide for his family, the mother shall be deemed the legal guardian of her children for the purpose of making such surrender as aforesaid; and if, in any such case, the mother be also dead or legally incapable of acting, or imprisoned for crime, or shall have abandoned or neglected to provide for her child or children, the president of the board of trustees of said village, said police justice or surrogate shall be by virtue of his office the legal guardian for the like purpose, and so in all cases where it cannot by diligent inquiry be ascertained that there is within the state any parent or

In case of death or illegal capacity of father.

other person legally authorized to act in the premises, the said president, justice or surrogate shall be ex-officio such guardians for the same purpose; and such guardianship shall extend as well to children already in the care of said society, as to those who may hereafter be offered for admission, or received therein; and in either case whether such surrender be made by the mother or by the said president, justice or surrogate, and whether before or after admission into the said home, it shall be deemed a legal surrender for the purposes, and within the true intent and meaning of the fifth section of this act; but no surrender by a mother as provided by this section, shall be valid, without the consent of the said justice, president or surrogate.

§ 8. There shall be a board of counsellors, consisting of twelve male members, whose duty it shall be to advise the board of managers of said society from time to time in regard to the business of the society, five counsellors shall be a quorum for the transaction of business; no purchase or sale, lease or mortgage of real estate, shall be taken by said corporation without the approval of a majority of the board of counsellors, duly certified by the secretary of said board. *Board of counsellors.*

§ 9. John Forsyth, Homer Ramsdell, Nathaniel Jones, Eli Hasbrouck, John J. Monell, George Cornwell, Selah R. Vanderzee, Wm. L Findlay, John R. Wiltsie, William L. F. Warren, John C Masters and James T. Lawson shall compose the first board of counsellors, and shall act until the next annual meeting of said association, or corporate body, or society, and until their successors shall be elected; such board of counsellors shall be elected annually at the annual meeting of said society, or in such other manner as shall be prescribed by the association. *Who shall compose it, 1st year.*

§ 10. This act shall take effect immediately.

Chap. 147.

AN ACT to repeal an act entitled An act in relation to conveyances and devises of personal
and real estate for religious purposes, passed
April ninth, eighteen hundred and fifty-five.

Passed April 8, 1862.

*The People of the State of New York, represented in
Senate and Assembly, do enact as follows:*

SECTION 1. The act entitled "An act in relation to conveyances and devises of personal and real estate for
religious purposes," passed April ninth, eighteen hundred and fifty-five, is hereby repealed.

§ 2. This act shall take effect immediately.

Chap. 148.

AN ACT to authorize the Greenwood Cemetery
to sell and dispose of a gore of land owned by
them, contained in the block bounded by the
Fifth and Sixth avenues and Twenty-third and
Twenty-fourth streets.

Passed April 8, 1862.

*The People of the State of New York, represented in
Senate and Assembly, do enact as follows:*

SECTION 1. It shall be lawful for the Greenwood Cemetery to sell and dispose of a gore of land owned by them,
contained in the block bounded by the Fifth and Sixth
avenues and Twenty-third and Twenty-fourth streets,
which land not being within the present boundaries of
the cemetery is not required for cemetery purposes, and
to convey the same free and discharged from all or any
of the restrictions and privileges appertaining thereto
as the property of the said corporation.

§ 2. This act shall take effect immediately.

Chap. 149.

AN ACT to amend an act passed April third, eighteen hundred and sixty-one, entitled "An act supplemental to an act entitled 'An act to consolidate the cities of Brooklyn and Williamsburgh and the town of Bushwick into one municipal government and to incorporate the same,'" passed April seventeen, eighteen hundred and fifty-four.

Passed April 8, 1862; three-fifths being present.

The People of the State of New York, represented in Senate and Assembly, do enact as follows:

SECTION 1. Section one of chapter three hundred and twenty-eight of the laws of eighteen hundred and sixty-one, entitled "An act supplemental to an act entitled 'An act to consolidate the cities of Brooklyn and Williamsburgh and the town of Bushwick into one municipal government and to incorporate the same,'" passed April seventeenth, eighteen hundred and fifty-four, is hereby amended by striking out the following words, to-wit: "To Edward A. Lambert for service rendered as mayor of the city of Brooklyn, in the years eighteen hundred and fifty-three and eighteen hundred and fifty-four, the sum of two thousand dollars, to be charged to the first, twelfth and nineteenth wards of said city," and inserting in lieu thereof the following words, to-wit: "To Edward A. Lambert, for service rendered as mayor of the city of Brooklyn, in the years eighteen hundred and fifty-three and eighteen hundred and fifty-four, the sum of two thousand dollars, to be charged to the first, second, third, fourth, fifth, sixth, seventh, eighth, ninth, tenth, eleventh, twelfth and nineteenth wards of said city.

§ 2. This act shall take effect immediately.

Chap. 150.

AN ACT to enable the corporation of the village
of Bath, Steuben county, to raise money for certain purposes.

Passed April 8, 1862; three-fifths being present.

*The People of the State of New York, represented in
Senate and Assembly, do enact as follows :*

SECTION 1. The trustees of the village of Bath in the
county of Steuben, are hereby authorized and required,
at the next annual levy of taxes in said village, after the
passage of this act, to levy and collect from the taxable
property therein in the manner in which the other taxes
in said village are collected, the sum of eleven hundred
dollars over and above the sums which, by the charter
of said village, the trustees thereof are now authorized
to levy and collect by tax.

To build a
court house.
§ 2. Whenever such sum of eleven hundred dollars
shall be collected as above provided, the said trustees
shall pay or cause the same to be paid over to Robert
Campbell, Reuben Robie and David Rumsey, commissioners for building a court house in said village of Bath,
to be appropriated by said commissioners in payment
for the lot purchased by them for an addition to the
court house lot.

§ 3. This act shall take effect immediately.

Chap. 151.

AN ACT relative to the trial of offences committed against joint stock associations.

Passed April 8, 1862.

*The People of the State of New York, represented in
Senate and Assembly, do enact as follows:*

SECTION 1. It shall not be necessary in an indictment
against any person or persons, for an offence commit-

ted against the rights or property of any joint stock association organized under the statutes of this state, to set forth the names of such associa-
, tion, nor to prove the same on the trial of such indictment, but it shall be sufficient to set forth in such indictment the name assumed and used by such association in its business, and to prove the same on the trial accordingly.

§ 2. This act shall take effect immediately.

Chap. 152.

AN ACT to repeal certain sections of chapter two hundred and thirty of the Laws of eighteen hundred and forty-three.

Passed April 8, 1862; three-fifths being present.

The People of the State of New York, represented in Senate and Assembly, do enact as follows :

SECTION 1. Sections eighteen, nineteen, twenty and twenty-one of article second, chapter two hundred and thirty of the Laws of eighteen hundred and forty-three, are hereby repealed.

§ 2. Nothing herein shall apply to, or affect any proceedings, taken under said sections, previous to the passage of this act.

§ 3. This act shall take effect immediately.

Chap. 153.

AN ACT for the relief of Susan A. Schultz and Ida M. Schultz, infants, in certain lands devised to them by Daniel H. Schultz.

Passed April 8, 1862; three-fifths being present.

Whereas, Daniel H. Schultz, late of the town of Clinton in the county of Dutchess, deceased, devised by his last will and testament to his daughters Susan A. Schultz and Ida M. Schultz, certain lands therein described and devised to his son, Theodore A. Schultz, in and by the same will, certain other lands designated as the homestead, and whereas, the said Theodore A. Schultz, deceased, by his last will and testament devised the said homestead to his two sisters, the said Susan A. and Ida M. Schultz, subject to certain legacies in his said will specified, and the said Susan A. and Ida M. are infants, and desire to retain the said homestead, but cannot pay the said legacies without the sale of the whole or some portion of the lands devised them as aforesaid by the said Daniel H. Schultz, Therefore,

The People of the State of New York, represented in Senate and Assembly, do enact as follows:

SECTION 1. On the petition of Reuben Rikert and Louisa Schultz, the supreme court, at any general or special term thereof, or the county court of Dutchess county, may authorize Reuben Rikert, or any freeholder of said county, upon giving security as the court to which such petition may be presented shall prescribe, to sell and convey so much of the lands devised to Susan A. and Ida M Schultz by the last will and testament of Daniel H. Schultz, as may be necessary to pay off and discharge the valid legacies directed to be paid by the last will and testament of Theodore A. Schultz. The money raised by such sale shall be applied to the payment of such legacies, and the surplus, if any there should be after making such payment, shall be invested by the direction of the court in which the proceedings for the sale aforesaid are had, for the benefit of the said Ida M and Susan A. Schultz, and upon such terms and securities as the said court may direct. If a part only of the land hereby authorized to be sold cannot, in the opinion of the court, be sold without materially affecting the value of the remaining part of the said land, then the said court may authorize so much of said land, as in the opinion of the court, will be for the best interests of the infants aforesaid to be sold, and the surplus to be invested as above provided.

§ 2. This act shall take effect immediately.

Margin note: Supreme court to authorize the sale of land to pay off legacies.

Chap. 154.

AN ACT to release the interest of the people of this state, in certain land whereof John Johnson died seized, to John Johnson and James Johnson.

Passed April 8, 1862; by a two-third vote.

The People of the State of New York, represented in Senate and Assembly, do enact as follows:

SECTION 1. All the right, title and interest of the people of this state in the real estate situate in the county of Cattaraugus, whereof John Johnson, late of Franklinville, in said county, died seized, are hereby released to John Johnson and James Johnson, sons of the said deceased, and to their heirs and assigns forever.

§ 2. Nothing herein contained shall be construed to impair, release or discharge any right, claim or interest of any creditor by mortgage, judgment or otherwise, or of any heir or heirs at law of the said John Johnson, or of any person claiming title under or through the said John Johnson. *Not to impair rights of creditors.*

§ 3. This act shall take effect immediately.

Chap. 155.

AN ACT authorizing a loan to the county of Warren, to be applied for the purposes specified in the act chapter two hundred and seventy-four, Laws of eighteen hundred and sixty-one.

Passed April 8, 1862; three-fifths being present.

The People of the State of New York, represented in Senate and Assembly, do enact as follows:

SECTION 1. The comptroller is authorized to loan to the county of Warren the sum of eight hundred dollars, out of any money in the treasury belonging to the capital of the common school fund,

Comptroller
to draw his
warrant on
Treasurer.

§ 2. The comptroller shall draw his warrant on the treasurer for the said sum of eight hundred dollars in favor of the treasurer of the county of Warren, on receiving from the said treasurer his official bond which he is hereby required to execute, to repay the same in four equal annual instalments, with interest at the rate of seven per cent per annum; the said interest shall be paid annually, and the first instalment of said loan shall be paid on the first day of April, one thousand eight hundred and sixty-three.

How the
money shall
be used.

§ 3. The money so loaned shall be applied by the treasurer of Warren county in the manner and according to the provisions specified and contained in chapter two hundred and seventy-four, laws of eighteen hundred and sixty-one, entitled "An act for the relief of the heirs and legal representatives of Ralph Thurman deceased," the same as if said sum had been assessed, levied, collected and paid pursuant to said act.

Board of
supervisors
to lay an
annual tax.

§ 4 The board of supervisors of the county of Warren are authorized and required to levy a tax upon the taxable property, real and personal, upon the town of Johnsburgh in said county, the sum of two hundred dollars, and the interest on the whole sum herein loaned, or on so much as shall remain unpaid, annually for four successive years, until the said sum of eight hundred dollars, with the annual interest thereon, shall be fully paid. The money so to be raised shall be paid to the treasurer of said county annually, who shall, without delay, upon receiving the said money, pay over the same to the treasurer of this state, who shall endorse the same on said bond.

§ 5. This act shall take effect immediately.

Chap. 156·

AN ACT to amend an act entitled "An act to incorporate the Cayuga and Seneca road and Bridge Company," passed April eighteenth, eighteen hundred and forty-three.

Passed April 8, 1862.

The People of the State of New York, represented in Senate and Assembly, do enact as follows :

SECTION 1. The ninth section of the act entitled "An act to incorporate the Cayuga and Seneca Road and Bridge Company," passed April eighteenth, eighteen hundred and forty-three, is hereby amended to read as follows :

The said corporation, while the said road and bridge is in good repair, may exact and collect the following rates of toll : For every vehicle drawn by four horses, oxen or mules, the sum of thirty-one cents ; for every vehicle drawn by three horses, oxen or mules, twenty-five cents ; for every carriage drawn by two horses, oxen or mules, twenty-cents ; for every sleigh or sled drawn by two horses, oxen or mules, fifteen cents ; for every vehicle drawn by one horse, ox or mule, fifteen cents ; for every horse and rider, ten cents ; for each additional horse led or driven, three cents ; for each head of cattle, two cents, and for every score of sheep or swine, ten cents.

§ 2. The charter of this corporation is hereby extended for a period of thirty years, from the passage of this act, subject to all the provisions of their charter.

§ 3. This act shall take effect immediately.

Chap. 157,

AN ACT for the relief of Benjamin B. Clapp for canal damages.

Passed April 8, 1862; three-fifths being present.

The People of the State of New York, represented in Senate and Assembly, do enact as follows :

SECTION 1. Benjamin B. Clapp of the village of Port Byron, in the county of Cayuga, shall have the same right, for the term of two months from the passage of this act, to make and exhibit to the canal appraisers a statement of his claim for damages suffered by him in the year eighteen hundred and fifty-six, in consequence of the appropriation by this state of a portion of a village site owned by him at that time in said village of Port Byron, to its use in making the enlargement to the Erie Canal at that place, that any person suffering such damage has to make and exhibit such claim by section eighty-four, article three, chapter nine, title nine, part first of the fifth edition of the Revised Statutes of this state.

To make exhibit of claim within two months to Canal Appraisers.

§ 2. Before said canal appraisers shall entertain such application, such claim shall be made and exhibited in the same manner and specifying the same with the same particularity as is required by the section of the Revised Statutes named in the first section of this act.

§ 3. Whenever, within the time mentioned in the first section of this act, such statement shall be made and exhibited to the said canal appraisers in the manner prescribed by the second section thereof, it shall be the duty of said canal appraisers to entertain such application and thereafter to take the proceedings in appraising the damages suffered by said Benjamin B. Clapp by the cause mentioned in the first section of this act as are now provided by law for appraising the damages of persons upon claims made and exhibited in pursuance of the section of the Revised Statutes named in the first section herein, and said damages when so appraised, or the amount thereof finally adjudicated by the canal board, in case of an appeal to such board, which appeal is hereby authorized as in other cases, shall be paid in the same manner as the damages appraised under the section last aforesaid are now provided to be paid by law.

Appraisers to examine claims.

§ 4. This act shall take effect immediately.

Chap. 158.

AN ACT for the relief of Benjamin W. Whitcher.

Passed April 8, 1862; three-fifths being present.

The People of the State of New York, represented in Senate and Assembly, do enact as follows:

SECTION 1. The canal appraisers are hereby authorized and required to hear and determine, subject to appeal to the canal board as in other cases, the injuries alleged to have been sustained to the property on his farm by Benjamin W. Whitcher, of Whitestown, in the county of Oneida, in consequence of the opening of the gates of the Whitestown aqueduct on the Erie Canal, by the superintendent in charge, on or about the seventeenth day of August, one thousand eight hundred and fifty-seven, by which the waters of said canal were allowed to flow into the Saquoit creek, and thence over and upon the farm of the said Benjamin W. Whitcher; and if in the judgment of the said appraisers the state is justly liable therefor, to award him such damages as he shall prove himself entitled to.

§ 2. Such damages when awarded or confirmed by the canal board, if appealed from, shall be paid by the treasurer on the warrant of the Auditor of the canal department, out of any moneys appropriated to the payment of canal damages.

Chap. 159.

AN ACT authorizing the appraisal and payment of canal damages to Patrick Buckley, caused by a break in the Champlain Canal in the town of Fort Edward, Washington county.

Passed April 8, 1862; three-fifths being present.

The People of the State of New York, represented in Senate and Assembly, do enact as follows:

SECTION 1. Jurisdiction is hereby conferred upon the canal appraisers to hear and determine the claim of Patrick Buckley, for damages alleged to have been sustained by him from a break in the Champlain Canal in the town of Fort Edward, Washington county, on or about the ninth day of June, one thousand eight hundred and fifty-eight, and if, upon examination, it shall be ascertained that any damages have been sustained by him for which the state is legally liable, said appraisers shall make an award for the same, subject to appeal to the canal board as in other cases.

§ 2. The treasurer shall pay, on the warrant of the Auditor of the Canal Department, such sum, if any, as shall be awarded under the provisions of this act, out of any moneys appropriated or to be appropriated for canal repairs.

§ 3. This act shall take effect immediately.

Chap. 160.

AN ACT to incorporate the Tompkinsville Fire Police Company, of the village of Tompkinsville, town of Castleton, Richmond county.

Passed April 8, 1862; three-fifths being present.

The People of the State of New York, represented in Senate and Assembly, do enact as follows:

SECTION 1. Walter J. Wandel, Jacob B. Wood, H. Mendell, C. F. Grosheim, Jacob Burbank, William Oliffe, C. H. Stebbins, F. Kanenberg, M. Carroll, Phillip Bardes, and their associates are hereby constituted a body corporate, by the name of "The Tompkinsville Fire Police Company," and by that name they and their successors shall be capable of purchasing, holding and conveying real estate, or any personal estate necessary for their use as a Fire Police Company, to the amount of five thousand dollars; also, by the corporate name aforesaid, they and their successors shall be capable of suing and being sued in all courts. *To hold and convey real estate.*

§ 2. The said corporation shall have power to make and prescribe such by-laws rules and regulations for the government of the said corporation, as they from time to time shall deem proper; provided such by-laws, rules and regulations be in accordance with the provisions of this act and the constitution of the State of New York. *Make by-laws.*

§ 3. The said corporation shall have full power and authority to nominate and appoint a sufficient number of fire policemen, not exceeding sixty, to have the care and management of all the implements belonging to said company, and who shall be ready at all times to save and protect property at fires, have the custody of the same during and until after any fire, and to arrest all depredators upon such property, and take them before a magistrate to be dealt with according to law and to perform all the duties which may be required of them by the regulations of said company, and in case of removal or dismissal of any members, to appoint others in their places. *Appoint fire policemen.*

§ 4. Any person appointed fire policemen under the provisions of this act, and serving as such shall, during such service, be exempt from serving as a juror in any of the courts of this state, and from militia duty, except in cases of invasion or insurrection.

§ 5. This act shall take effect immediately.

Chap. 161.

AN ACT to authorize clerks of boards of Excise to take affidavits and acknowledgments in certain cases.

Passed April 8, 1862.

The People of the State of New York, represented in Senate and Assembly, do enact as follows:

SECTION 1. The clerks of the several boards of Excise in this state, shall have the same power to take affidavits and acknowledgments of any instrument to be used before such boards, as justices of the peace; but they shall receive no fees for the same.

§ 2. This act shall take effect immediately.

Chap. 162.

AN ACT to consolidate the towns of Savona and Bath in the county of Steuben.

Passed April 8, 1862; three-fifths being present.

The People of the State of New York, represented in Senate and Assembly, do enact as follows:

SECTION 1. The town of Bath in the county of Steuben shall hereafter consist of all the territory now embraced within the limits of said town of Bath and the said town of Savona in said county.

§ 2. The powers and duties of the supervisor and other officers, except the justices of the peace of the town of Savona as at present constituted, shall cease from and after the second Tuesday of April, one thou-

sand eight hundred and sixty-two, and the supervisor
and town clerk of the said town are hereby directed to
deposit in the county clerk's office of the county of Steuben the books, papers and records of the said town, on
or before the first day of April next.

§ 3. The justices of the peace of said town of Savona,
elected prior to the passage of this act, shall continue to
hold their respective office for and during the term for
which they severally have been elected.

§ 4. The supervisor of the said town of Savona shall, Supervisor to pay over all moneys.
on or before the first day of April, one thousand eight hun-
dred and sixty-two, pay over to the supervisor of the
town of Bath, all moneys and securities remaining in his
hands and belonging to the said town of Savona. And
the commissioner of highways of the said town of Savona
shall, in like manner pay over to the commissioner of
highways of the town of Bath, all moneys remaining in
his hands and belonging to the said town of Savona.

§ 5. All acts and parts of acts inconsistent with the
provisions of this act, are hereby repealed, so far as they
relate to the said towns of Savona and Bath.

§ 6. This act shall take effect immediately.

Chap. 163

AN ACT to reduce taxation in the city of New
York, by applying to that purpose the surplus
revenues of the sinking fund for the payment
of interest on the city debt.

Passed April 9, 1862 ; three-fifths being present.

*The People of the State of New York, represented in
Senate and Assembly, do enact as follows :*

SECTION 1. It shall and may be lawful for the mayor,
aldermen and commonalty of the city of New York to
transfer the surplus revenues of the sinking fund for
the payment of interest on the city debt, at the end of
the present and every future year, to the fund known as
the general fund of said corporation, to be applied to
the diminution of the taxes of said city, as hereinafter
provided.

42

Duties of the Comptroller.

§ 2. It shall be the duty of the comptroller of said city to prepare and submit to the board of supervisors of the county of New York, at least four weeks before their annual meeting, in each and every year, for the purpose of imposing the annual taxes, a statement setting forth the amounts by law authorized to be raised by tax in that year, on account of the corporation of the city of New York or for city purposes within said city, and also an estimate of the probable amount of receipts into the city treasury during the then current year, from all the sources of revenue of said general fund, including such surplus revenues from the said sinking fund ; and the said board of supervisors are hereby authorized and directed to deduct the total amount of such estimated receipts from the aggregate amount of all the various sums which by law they are required to order and cause to be raised by tax in said year for the purposes aforesaid, and to cause to be raised by tax only the balance of said aggregate amount, after making such deduction.

Mayor, aldermen and commonalty prohibited from altering rates.

§ 3. It shall not be lawful for the said mayor, aldermen and commonalty to make or cause to be made any alteration of rates or charges affecting any item or source of the revenues of either of the sinking funds of said city or of the general fund aforesaid, which may tend to a diminution of the receipts from such sources of revenue, or either of them ; and all the revenues of said corporation not by law otherwise specifically appropriated, shall, when received into the city treasury, be credited to the said general fund, and said revenues are hereby appropriated and shall be applied exclusively to the purpose specified in the second section of this act.

§ 4. All acts and parts of acts heretofore passed, inconsistent with the provisions of this act, are hereby repealed ; such repeal to take effect from and after the passage of an ordinance by the said mayor, aldermen and commonalty, authorizing and directing the transfer of the said surplus revenues of the sinking fund for payment of interest on the city debt to the general fund aforesaid at the end of each year, as provided in the first section of this act.

§ 5. This act shall take effect immediately.

Chap. 164.

AN ACT for the relief of Hiram H. Walbridge, Gilbert Peterson and Charles A. Danolds.

Passed April 9, 1862; three-fifths being present.

The People of the State of New York, represented in Senate and Assembly, do enact as follows:

SECTION 1. The Canal Board are hereby authorized to hear and determine the alleged claim of Charles A. Danolds, for work done on sections three hundred and sixty-one, three hundred and sixty-two, three hundred and sixty-three, three hundred and sixty-five, and three hundred and sixty-six of the Erie canal, under a contract made between the canal contracting board and Henry S. Danolds, Michael Kerr and Nehemiah Osborn, bearing date on the twenty-ninth day of January, one thousand eight hundred and sixty-one; and also the alleged claims of Gilbert Peterson and Hiram H. Walbridge, assignees of a contract made between said board and Myron H. Mills, and bearing date on the first day of September, one thousand eight hundred and fifty-four, for work done under the said contract on section three hundred and sixty-four of said canal, and allow the said Charles A. Danolds, Gilbert Peterson and Hiram H. Walbridge, for work done and to be done under the said contracts, such additional compensation above the compensation specified in the said contracts as shall by the said board be deemed just and equitable.

§ 2. The Treasurer shall pay, on warrant of the Auditor of the Canal Department, such sums as may be allowed and awarded to the said Charles A. Danolds, Gilbert Peterson and Hiram H. Walbridge, under the provisions of the first section of this act, out of any money appropriated or to be appropriated to the Erie canal enlargement.

§ 3. The Canal Commissioners are hereby prohibited to hold out any inducements to contractors on the canals, to continue work on said canals by assurances that the legislature will reimburse them any losses they now suffer by virtue of a fulfilment of their said contracts.

Prohibition to Canal Commissioners.

§ 4. This act shall take effect immediately.

Chap. 165.

AN ACT to authorize the city of Schenectady to purchase a steam fire engine.

Passed April 9, 1862; three-fifths being present.

The People of the State of New York, represented in Senate and Assembly, do enact as follows:

SECTION 1. The city of Schenectady may sell such and so many of its engine houses and lots, fire engines, implements and equipments as it may deem proper, and apply the proceeds thereof towards the purchase of a steam fire engine and its equipments.

Borrow
$3,000.

§ 2. The said city may borrow upon its notes or bonds a sum not exceeding three thousand dollars at not over seven per cent. interest, which sum so borrowed, with the proceeds of the property said city is authorized to sell by this act, shall be applied to the purchase of a steam fire engine and its equipments.

§ 3. This act shall take effect immediately.

Chap. 166.

AN ACT to amend an act entitled "An act to incorporate the Firemen's Benevolent Association of Buffalo," passed March twenty-third, eighteen hundred and thirty-seven.

Passed April 9, 1862.

The People of the State of New York, represented in Senate and Assembly, do enact as follows:

SECTION 1. The first section of the act entitled "An act to incorporate the Firemen's Benevolent Association of Buffalo," passed March twenty-third, eighteen hundred and thirty-seven, is hereby amended so as to read as follows:

§ 1. All such persons as now are or who hereafter shall be engineers of the fire department, or members of any fire engine, hook and ladder or hose company in the city of Buffalo, and all persons residents of said city, who now have or shall hereafter have served the time required by the charter of the city of Buffalo, to entitle them to exemption from service as jurors and militia duty, and who have or shall hereafter receive the certificate required by said charter as evidence of such service and exemption, are hereby constituted a body corporate by the name of "The Firemen's Benevolent Association of Buffalo," for the relief of indigent and disabled firemen and their families, and for that purpose shall have power to purchase, take and hold, transfer and convey real and personal property to an amount not exceeding fifty thousand dollars.

§ 2. The second section of said act is hereby amended so as to read as follows:

§ 2 The control and disposal of the funds, property and estate of the said corporation and the management of its affairs, shall be vested in a board of fifteen trustees, who shall be elected by ballot by those members of said association who are or may be entitled, by the by-laws of said association, to vote. An annual election of trustees of said association shall be held on the second Wednesday of December, in each year, hereafter. At the election of trustees of said association, which shall be held on the second Wednesday of December, in the year one thousand eight hundred and sixty-two, fifteen trustees shall be elected; one of whom shall be chosen from the members of each fire engine, hook and ladder and hose company then existing within the city of Buffalo, and the remainder of said trustees from the members of said association who shall have completed their term of service as firemen, and received as evidence thereof the certificate required by the charter of said city. At the first meeting of said trustees, succeeding said election, there shall be chosen by said trustees, from their own number, one president, one vice-president, one secretary and one treasurer of said board of trustees, who shall hold their respective offices for one year and until their successors are chosen. Said officers shall immediately proceed to divide by lot the whole number of trustees, including themselves, into three equal classes. Those in the first class shall hold their offices as trustees for one year. Those in the second class shall hold their offices for two years, and those in the third class shall hold their offices for three years, and there shall be elected annually thereafter five trustees who shall hold their offices for three years. All officers of said board of trustees shall be elected by the board from among their own number, at the first meeting succeeding each annual election of trustees. All trustees of said association shall hold their offices until their successors shall be appointed, except as hereinafter provided, and whenever the term of office of any trustee who shall have been elected from any fire engine, hook and ladder or hose company shall be about to expire, the person who shall be elected to succeed such trustee, shall be elected from the same company from which said trustee whose term of office is about to expire is chosen, unless said company shall have been disbanded, or shall have otherwise ceased to exist, in which case his successor shall be chosen from the members of said association who shall have completed their term of service as firemen, and received the certificate thereof required by the charter of said city. In case any trustee of said association shall be absent from three regular meetings of the board of trustees of said association in succession, or shall become a member of another company than the one of which he was a member at the time of his election, his office shall be deemed vacant, and the board of trustees shall have power to appoint a trustee to fill such vacancy, and the trustee so appointed shall hold his office until the next election of trustees, or until his successor is appointed.

§ 3. The first and second sections of the act entitled "An act to amend an act entitled 'An act to incorporate the Firemen's Benevolent Association of Buffalo,' passed March twenty-third, eighteen hundred and thirty-seven," passed April tenth, eighteen hundred and sixty, are hereby repealed.

Official term. (margin)

Vacancies. (margin)

Chap. 167.

AN ACT to authorize the board of supervisors of the county of New York to raise money by loan, and to create a public fund or stock to be called "The New York County Court House stock," and to authorize the commissioners of the sinking fund to receive and purchase said stock.

Passed April 9, 1862; three-fifths being present.

The People of the State of New York, represented in Senate and Assembly, do enact as follows :

SECTION 1. It shall be lawful for the board of supervisors of the county of New York to raise by loan, from time to time, a sum of money not exceeding ten hundred thousand dollars by the creation of a public fund or stock, to be called "The New York County Court House Stock," which shall bear an interest not exceeding seven per cent per annum, and shall be redeemable in such annual instalments, commencing in the year eighteen hundred and seventy-five, as the said board shall provide.

§ 2. It shall be lawful for the said board of supervisors, by ordinance to be passed in the usual manner, to determine what shall be the nominal amount or value of each share of said stock, and of what number of shares the same shall consist, and upon such determination being made by the said board, the comptroller of the city of New York is hereby authorized and directed to sell and dispose of said stock either at public auction or private sale, or by subscription for the same on such terms not less than its par value, as the said board of supervisors may deem expedient, and to prepare and deliver to the purchasers thereof the usual certificates for the same, which shall be signed by the said comptroller and countersigned by the mayor of the city of New York, and sealed with the common seal of said board of supervisors, attested by the clerk of said board of supervisors, and the said stock shall be transferable, in the usual manner in the office of said comptroller.

(marginal notes: To borrow $1,000,000. — Supervisors to set value on shares of stock.)

§ 3. 'The moneys to be raised by virtue of this act shall be applied by the said board of supervisors to the payment of the award made and confirmed by the supreme court to the mayor, aldermen and commonalty of the city of New York, for the value of land acquired for a court house in said county, pursuant to the act entitled "An act to enable the supervisors of the county of New York to acquire and take lands for the building of a court house in said county," passed April tenth, eighteen hundred and sixty-one, and to the erection of a court house on said land; and for the payment of the said stock, the said land, and the building which shall be erected thereon shall be irrevocably pledged.

§ 4. The said board of supervisors are hereby authorized and empowered to order and cause to be raised. by 'tax on the estates, real and personal, subject to taxation according to law, within the county of New York, and to be collected, in addition to the ordinary taxes, yearly and every year, a sum of money sufficient to pay the interest annually accruing on said stock, and also in like manner to cause to be raised and collected by tax, commencing with the year eighteen hundred and seventy-five, such amount of money as may be necessary to meet the annual instalments on said stock as hereinbefore provided.

§ 5 It shall be lawful for the commissioners of the sinking funds of the city of New York to receive in settlement of the said award made to the said mayor, aldermen and commonalty of the city of New York for the value of the land taken for said court house, an amount of said stock equal to the amount of said award, and from time to time, if the said commissioners shall deem it expedient, to invest the moneys of the said sinking funds in the purchase of additional amounts of said stock, and to hold and dispose of the stock which may be so received or purchased in the manner provided by law, in relation to other securities received and held for the redemption of certain debts by the corporation of the said city by the said commissioners.

§ 6. Sections seven, eight and nine of the said act entitled "An act to enable the supervisors of the county of New York to acquire and take lands for the building of a court house in said county," passed April tenth, eighteen hundred and sixty-one, are hereby repealed.

§ 7. It shall be the duty of the commissioners appoint- Commissioners to appoint a treasurer. ed pursuant to the act entitled "An act in relation to the city hall in the city of New York," passed April seventeenth, eighteen hundred and fifty-eight, under whose direction said court house is being constructed, and their successors, to appoint one of their number to be known as treasurer in connection with the construction of said court house, under their direction, and to perform such other duties as the board of commissioners shall provide; such treasurer shall be entitled to receive such compensation for his services as shall be prescribed and fixed by the said board of supervisors.

§ 8. This act shall take effect immediately.

Chap. 168.

AN ACT to confer additional powers upon the Metropolitan Police relating to the inspection of steam boilers.

Passed April 9, 1862; three-fifths being present.

The People of the State of New York, represented in Senate and Assembly, do enact as follows:

SECTION 1. Every owner of a steam boiler or boilers in use in the Metropolitan police district shall annually, and at such convenient times, and in such manner and form as may by rules and regulations to be made therefor by the Metropolitan Police Board be provided, report to the said Metropolitan Police Board at its head quarters, the location of such steam boiler or boilers, and thereupon, and as soon thereafter as practicable, the Metropolitan sanitary company or such member or members thereof as may be competent for the duty herein prescribed, and may be detailed for such duty by the Metropolitan Police Board, but no person shall be detailed for such duty except he be a practicable engineer who shall proceed to inspect such steam boiler or boilers, and all apparatus and appliances connected therewith, and the strength and security of each boiler shall be tested by hydrostatic pressure; and they shall limit the

43

pressure of steam to be applied to or upon such boiler, certifying each inspection and such limit of pressure to the owner of the boiler inspected, and also to the engineer in charge of the same; and no greater amount of steam or pressure than that certified in the case of any boiler, shall be applied thereto. In limiting the amount of pressure, wherever the boiler under test will bear the same, the limit desired by the owner of the boiler shall be the one certified.

A record to be kept by police board.

§ 2. The Metropolitan Police Board shall preserve in proper form a correct record of all inspections of steam boilers, and of the amount of steam or pressure allowed in each case, and in cases where any steam boiler or the apparatus or appliances connected therewith, shall be deemed by the board after inspection to be insecure or dangerous, the board shall prescribe such changes and alterations as may render such boilers, apparatus and appliances secure and devoid of danger. And in the mean time and until such changes and alterations are made and such appliances attached, such boiler, apparatus and appliances may be taken under the control of the police board, and all persons prevented from using the same, and in cases deemed necessary the appliances, apparatus or attachments for the limitation of pressure may be taken under the control of the said police board. And no owner or agent of any steam boilers shall employ any person as engineer without their having a certificate as to qualification from practical engineers to be countersigned by the commissioners of police.

Penalty for violation of this act.

§ 3. Any person applying or causing to be applied to any steam boiler a higher pressure of steam than that limited for the same, in accordance with the provisions of this act, and any person violating the provisions of the second section of this act, shall be guilty of a misdemeanor, and wherever any owner of any steam boiler in the Metropolitan district shall fail or omit to have the same reported for inspection as provided for by this act, such boiler may be taken under the control of the Metropolitan Police Board, and all persons prevented from using the same until it can be satisfactorily tested as herein provided for, and the owner shall in such case be charged with the expense of so testing it.

§ 4. This act shall take effect immediately.

Chap. 169.

AN ACT relating to the enlargement and com-
completion of the canals of this State, and to
reduce the number and regulate the employment of engineers thereon.

Passed April 10, 1862; three-fifths being present.

*The People of the State of New York, represented in
Senate and Assembly, do enact as follows :*

SECTION 1. All contracts for the enlargement and com- Contracts to be finished
pletion of the canals of this state, as contemplated by prior to 1st
section three of article seven of the constitution, and September, 1862.
not hereinafter provided for, shall be executed and performed in accordance with the plans, maps and specifications heretofore prescribed and adopted on or before
the first day of September next after the passage of this
act, and the accounts for the said enlargement and completion shall be closed as soon thereafter as may be, and
no more work shall thereafter be done, or materials procured, under pretence of enlarging and completing said
canals, and the same shall be deemed and considered
finished and completed, and from that time all the
powers and authority of the contracting board in relation to the enlargement, completion and construction of
such canal shall cease.

§ 2. After the passage of this act the Canal Board shall Canal Board prohibited
not have power to change the plan of finishing and from chang-
completing the work of enlarging and completing ing plan of completing
said canals as heretofore fixed and determined by canals.
the resolutions of said board; nor shall the said board
have the power to change the plan of construction
of a completed canal, its banks, locks, waste wiers, cul-
verts, bridges, or any other structure or matter or thing
connected therewith, except to allow and certify to such
works of extraordinary repairs and improvements in a
completed canal as is contemplated by the existing statutes of the state.

§ 3. After the first day of September next no more Reduction
than one engineer and one assistant engineer shall be of engineer force.
employed upon each division of the said canals. The

said engineer and assistant engineer shall be appointed
by the Canal Board, and they shall be practical engineers
and have the certificate of the State Engineer as to fitness, capacity and integrity, and the said board shall fix
the compensation of such engineers. The State Engineer and Surveyor shall prescribe and define the duties
of the engineers so appointed, and shall assign each
engineer and assistant engineer to a division of the
canals corresponding with the division of each of the
canal commissioners. The first, second, third and fourth
sections of the act entitled "An act prescribing the
powers and duties of the State Engineer and Surveyor,
and of the engineers employed on the public works,"
passed April tenth, eighteen hundred and fifty, are hereby repealed.

§ 4. In case it may be necessary to employ temporarily
additional assistance to aid the said engineers in the
performance of some specific job of work or duty, the
same may be done by the engineer in charge where the
work is to be performed, with the assent of the State
Engineer and Surveyor and the commissioner in charge
of the division where the work is to be performed, and
the said State Engineer and Surveyor and canal commissioner shall file a statement in the canal department
containing the names of the persons to be employed,
the nature of their duties severally, and the daily compensation to be paid to each, and the periods during
which such employment is to continue. And every
engineer appointed by the Canal Board under this act
shall, before entering upon the duties of his office, file
in the canal department his bond, duly executed to the
people of the state, in such sum and with such surety
for the faithful discharge of his duties as the Auditor
shall approve, and shall take and subscribe the constitutional oath of office, which oath shall be filed in the
office of the Secretary of State No money shall be advanced to any engineer on account of services rendered,
nor shall any account of moneys disbursed by him be
audited until the provisions of this section shall have
been fully complied with.

§ 5. The services and duties performed by the said
engineers shall be such as relate strictly to the repairs
and maintenance of the completed canals of the state,
and the compensations allowed and expenses incurred

under the provisions of this act, shall be paid out of the appropriation for superintendence, collection and ordinary repairs of the canals.

§ 6. The limitation fixed by the first section of this act for closing the construction accounts and contracts for work on the canals of this state, shall not apply to the work now in progress on the Champlain canal and Glens Falls feeder, authorized by the act entitled " An act to provide the means for the completion of the canals of this state, and fully supply them with water, and for other purposes," passed April ninth, eighteen hundred and sixty, nor to any work on the said canal and feeder under the authority of said act.

§ 7. This act shall take effect immediately.

<small>Champlain and Glens Falls feeder exempted from limitation.</small>

Chap. 170.

AN ACT relating to superintendents of the poor and temporary relief in Richmond county.

Passed April 10, 1862; three-fifths being present.

The People of the State of New York, represented in Senate and Assembly, do enact as follows:

SECTION 1. There shall hereafter be five superintendents of the poor in the county of Richmond, instead of the number now provided by law, one of whom shall reside in each of the towns in said county. They shall be divided into five classes, of whom one shall hold his office for one year, one for two, one for three, one for four and one for five years, from the first day of January next; Edward Reilly shall be the superintendent of the first class, and hold his office for one year from the first day of January next, and Edward P. Barton shall be the superintendent of the second class, and hold his office for two years from the first day of January next, and the said Edward Reilly shall, for the purposes of this act, be deemed a resident of the town of Castleton, and the said Edward P. Barton of the town of Southfield, until the expiration of their terms of office. There shall be elected at the next annual election in said

<small>Number and classification of superintendents.</small>

county, three superintendents of the poor, one of whom shall reside in each of the other towns, and the clerk of said county shall, on the fifteenth day of December next, determine by lot which of said three superintendents shall hold his office for three, which for four, and which for five years, and there shall annually thereafter be elected one person to fill the office of the superintendent whose term expires on the first of January next ensuing. and who shall reside in the same town.

Overseer of poor abolished. § 2. The office of overseer of the poor in said county is hereby abolished, and all of the powers, duties and liabilities which now are or hereafter may be conferred or imposed upon the overseers of the respective towns, are hereby vested in and conferred upon the superintendents of the poor residing in said town, and all suits and proceedings authorized to be instituted or prosecuted by such overseers shall be instituted or prosecuted by such superintendent in his name of office.

Duties of overseers and justices conferred on superintendents. § 3. The powers and duties of the overseers and of justices of the peace of the several towns in said county, in relation to temporary relief and the support of the poor, are hereby conferred upon the superintendent of the poor residing in such town, and the powers of justices of the peace to act in such cases are hereby abolished.

Superintendent to keep an entry of all relief granted. § 4. Each of the said superintendents of the poor shall keep a book in which he shall enter the name, age, sex and native country of every person to whom temporary relief shall be granted by him, and the date thereof, and the amount expended for each and every such person, and stating the causes, direct or indirect, which shall have operated to render such person a pauper. Each of the said superintendents shall furnish the board of supervisors, at their annual meeting, with a certified transcript of the entries in such book for the next preceding year.

Supervisors to publish statement. § 5. The board of supervisors of said county shall, in addition to the statements now required from them by law, annually publish a statement of all moneys raised during the year. for the support of the poor of said county, the amount expended in the several towns for temporary relief, and the amount allowed each superintendent for fees and services, and for this purpose the board of superintendents of the poor shall furnish the

supervisors, at their annual meeting, with a true statement of all moneys expended by them.

§ 6. All laws inconsistent with this act are hereby repealed.

§ 7. This act shall take effect immediately.

Chap. 171.

AN ACT to change the name of Jeremiah Truman Brown.

Passed April 12, 1862; without the approval of the
Governor.*

*The People of the State of New York, represented in
Senate and Assembly, do enact as follows:*

SECTION 1. From and after the passage of this act,
Jeremiah Truman Brown, an adopted child of Nelson N.
North, of Brooklyn, shall be known and designated as
Jeremiah Anthony North.

* Pursuant to section nine, article four of the constitution of the State of
New York.

Chap. 172.

AN ACT to amend the act entitled "An act concerning the rights and liabilities of husband and wife," passed March twentieth, eighteen hundred and sixty.

Passed April 10, 1862; three-fifths being present.

*The People of the State of New York, represented in
Senate and Assembly, do enact as follows:*

SECTION 1. The third section of the act entitled "An
act concerning the rights and liabilities of husband and
wife," passed March twentieth, eighteen hundred and
sixty, is hereby amended so as to read as follows:

May bargain, sell and convey real and personal property.

§ 3. Any married woman possessed of real estate as her separate property, may bargain, sell and convey such property and enter into any contract in reference to the same, with the like effect in all respects as if she were unmarried, and she may in like manner enter into such covenant or covenants for title as are usual in conveyances of real estate, which covenants shall be obligatory to bind her separate property, in case the same or any of them be broken.

§ 2. The fourth, fifth, sixth, ninth, tenth and eleventh sections of the said act are hereby repealed.

§ 3 The seventh section of the said act is hereby amended so as to read as follows:

May sue and be sued, also bring actions for injuries to her person or character in her own name.

§ 7. Any married woman may, while married, sue and be sued in all matters having relation to her sole and separate property, or which may hereafter come to her by descent, devise, bequest, purchase, or the gift or grant of any person in the same manner as if she were sole; and any married woman may bring and maintain an action in her own name, for damages, against any person or body corporate, for any injury to her pe son or character, the same as if she were sole; and the money received upon the settlement of any such action or recovered upon a judgment, shall be her sole and separate property. In case it shall be necessary in the prosecution or defence of any action brought by or against a married woman, to enter into any bond or undertaking, such bond or undertaking may be executed by such married woman with the same effect in all respects as if she were sole, and in case the said bond or undertaking shall become broken or forfeited the same may be enforced against her separate estate.

§ 4. The eighth section of the said act is hereby amended so as to read as follows:

Her bargains not to bind husband.

§ 8. No bargain or contract made by any married woman, in respect to her sole and separate property, or any property, which may hereafter come to her by descent, devise, bequest, purchase, or the gift or grant of any person (except her husband,) and no bargain or contract entered into by any married woman in or about the carrying on of any trade or business, under any statute of this state, shall be binding upon her husband, or render him or his property in any way liable therefor.

§ 5. In an action brought or defended by any married _{Husbands} woman in her name, her husband shall not neither shall ^{property} his property be liable for the costs thereof, or the re- ^{for costs.} covery therein. In an action brought by her for an injury to her person, character or property, if judgment shall pass against her for costs, the court in which the action is pending shall have jurisdiction to enforce payment of such judgment out of her separate estate, though the sum recovered be less than one hundred dollars.

§ 6. No man shall bind his child to apprenticeship or ^{Mother to} service or part with the control of such child or create ^{give con-} any testamentary guardian therefor, unless the mother ^{prenticing} if living, shall in writing signify her assent thereto. ^{child.}

§ 7. A married woman may be sued in any of the ^{Judgment} courts in this state, and whenever a judgment shall be ^{to be en-} recovered against a married woman the same may be ^{against her} enforced by execution against her sole and separate ^{tate.} estate in the same manner as if she were sole.

§ 8. This act shall take effect on the first day of July next.

Chap. 173.

AN ACT to make the common schools free in district number five, in the town of Rome in the county of Oneida, and to provide a tax for that purpose.

Passed April 10, 1862; three-fifths being present.

The People of the State of New York, represented in Senate and Assembly, do enact as follows:

SECTION 1. The common schools in school district _{Trustees} number five, in the town of Rome, in the county of _{may raise} Oneida, shall be free to all children between the ages of _{ceed $1,000} five years and twenty-one years, residing in said district; _{in one year.} and rate bills therein are hereby abolished. The trustees of said district shall have the power, and it is hereby made their duty to raise from time to time by tax to be levied equally upon all the real and personal property in said school district, which shall be liable for ordinary

44

school district taxes, such sum or sums of money not exceeding one thousand dollars in any one year, as the trustees of said district may deem necessary for the payment of teachers' wages after applying all other moneys belonging to the said district which may be applicable to the payment of the wages of teachers. But all moneys which shall be due for teachers' wages on the first day of April next shall be provided for, as now prescribed by law.

Annual or special meeting may raise an additional sum of $500.

§ 2. In case the moneys directed to be raised by tax in the first section of this act, shall be insufficient for the payment of the teachers' wages, the said district may, at a regular annual meeting, or at a special meeting called for that purpose, vote a tax for any one year, in addition to the one thousand dollars authorized by the said first section, not exceeding five hundred dollars. A notice of a special meeting called for the purpose of voting a tax under this section, shall be published at least two weeks successively in the newspapers printed in the said town of Rome, in addition to the existing requirements prescribed by law.

§ 3. This act shall take effect immediately.

Chap. 174.

AN ACT to amend an act entitled "An act making appropriations for the support of government for the fiscal year commencing on the first day of October, in the year eighteen hundred and sixty-one," passed April thirteen, eighteen hundred and sixty-one.

Passed April 11, 1862; three-fifths being present.

The People of the State of New York, represented in Senate and Assembly, do enact as follows:

SECTION 1. The act entitled "An act making appropriations for the support of government for the fiscal year commencing on the first day of October, in the year one thousand eight hundred and sixty-one," passed April thirteen, one thousand eight hundred and sixty-one, is

hereby amended by striking out from the clause of said
act making an appropriation for commissary department,
and for the pay of keepers of arsenals, the word " ten "
and insert in lieu thereof the word " twenty," so that the
clause will read as follows :

" For the commissary department and for the pay of
the keepers of arsenals, twenty thousand dollars."

§ 2. This act shall take effect immediately.

Chap. 175.

AN ACT to authorize the board of supervisors of
the county of Kings to borrow money to erect a
court house for said county.

Passed April 11, 1862; three-fifths being present.

*The People of the State of New York, represented in
Senate and Assembly, do enact as follows:*

SECTION 1. The treasurer of the county of Kings is Treasurer
hereby authorized, under the direction of the board of on credit of
supervisors thereof, to borrow on the credit of said county
$100,000.
county a sum not exceeding one hundred thousand dollars, and to issue bonds, in such form as the said board
may prescribe, for the payment of the same, with interest payable annually or semi-annually, as the said board
may direct; the money so borrowed to be expended
under the direction of said board in the erection of a
building or buildings for the accommodation of the
courts and county officers of said county; such bonds
shall be issued in the name of and under the seal of the
county of Kings, and shall be signed by the president of
the board of supervisors of the county and the county
treasurer, and countersigned by the clerk of the board
of supervisors.   The said clerk shall keep a record
showing the date, amount and rate of interest of said
bonds respectively, with the time they may become
due.

§ 2. The said board of supervisors shall cause to be Supervisors
annually to
levied and collected and paid annually, such sums as lay tax for
interest and
may be necessary to pay interest on the money so bor- principal.

rowed, and to pay the principal in annual instalments, as the same becomes due ; the number and times of payment of such instalments shall be determined by the said board of supervisors, when they shall give the first directions to the county treasurer to borrow money under this act, and the treasurer shall immediately apply the money so collected and paid to him towards the payment of the interest and principal of the money so borrowed.

§ 3. This act shall take effect immediately.

Chap. 176.

AN ACT to amend an act entitled "An act to alter the map or plan of the city of New York," passed April seventeenth, eighteen hundred and sixty.

Passed April 11, 1862; three-fifths being present.

The People of the State of New York, represented in Senate and Assembly, do enact as follows :

Section 1. The act entitled " An act to alter the map or plan of the city of New York," passed April seventeenth, eighteen hundred and sixty, chapter four hundred and sixty-six, is hereby amended by striking out the word " five " after the words four hundred and twenty, in said act, so as to read " four hundred and twenty feet distant easterly, from the easterly line of the Fifth avenue."

§ 2. The proceedings heretofore commenced for the opening of Madison avenue, under said act, shall be amended in conformity with this act.

§ 3. This act shall take effect immediately.

Chap. 177.

AN ACT to confirm certain acts of the officers and constituted authorities of the town of New Lotts, county of Kings and State of New York.

Passed April 12, 1862 ; three-fifths being present.

Whereas, a company has been organized by the name of the Union Gas Light Company, under the act entitled "An act to authorize the formation of Gas Light Companies," passed February sixteenth, eighteen hundred and forty-eight, for the purpose of manufacturing and supplying gas for lighting the streets, avenues and highways and public and private buildings in the town of New Lotts, and the officers and constituted authorities of the said town, by a contract bearing date the twenty-sixth day of June, eighteen hundred and sixty-one, consented that the said company might build gas works and lay down all necessary conductors for conducting gas through the streets, avenues and highways in said town of New Lotts, and in and by the said contract do agree to exempt such corporation formed as aforesaid from taxation on their personal property for a period of three years from the date of the organization of said company, and that the said company should enjoy the exclusive privileges of lighting the streets, avenues and highways and public and private buildings in the said town by gas as aforesaid, and of laying gas pipe through the said streets, avenues and highways ; therefore, *In regard to constructing gas works.*

The People of the State of New York, represented in Senate and Assembly, do enact as follows :

SECTION 1. The powers, privileges, exemptions and rights given and granted, or intended to be given and granted as above recited, by the constituted authorities of the town of New Lotts, county of Kings, to the Union Gas Light Company, are hereby granted to and vested in the said the Union Gas Light Company, its successors and assigns, for the period of twenty years. Nothing herein contained shall prevent any person from manufacturing gas, and using the same upon his own premises or property. *Vesting the powers granted by officers of New Lotts.*

§ 2. The legislature may at any time alter, modify or repeal this act.

§ 3. This act shall take effect immediately.

Chap. 178.

AN ACT to regulate the size of apple, pear and potatoe barrels.

Passed April 12, 1862.

The People of the State of New York, represented in Senate and Assembly, do enact as follows:

SECTION 1. A barrel of apples, pears or potatoes shall represent a quantity equal to one hundred quarts of grain or dry measure, and all persons buying or selling those articles in this state, by the barrel, shall be understood as referring to the quantity specified in this act.

§ 2. This act shall take effect by the first day of June, eighteen hundred and sixty-two.

Chap. 179.

AN ACT supplementary to an act passed April sixteenth, eighteen hundred and sixty, and supplementary to an act passed April third, eighteen hundred and sixty-one to provide for rebuilding a bridge in the village of Adams, Jefferson county, and for raising money by tax for that purpose, upon the town of Adams, in said county.

Passed April 12, 1862; three-fifths being present.

The People of the State of New York, represented in Senate and Assembly, do enact as follows:

Supervisors to levy on town of Adams $500.

SECTION 1. The board of supervisors of the county of Jefferson are hereby authorized and directed, at their annual meeting in eighteen hundred and sixty-three, to

cause to be levied and collected on the town of Adams,
in said county, in like manner as other town charges are
by law directed to be levied and collected, the further
sum of five hundred and fifty-five dollars, and to cause
to be levied and collected in like manner the annual interest thereon, in each and every year, interest to commence on the first day of January, eighteen hundred
and sixty-two, to be expended in completing the rebuilding the bridge across Sandy Creek in said village
of Adams, where Main street crosses the same. The
collector of said town of Adams shall pay over the said
money, when collected, to Daniel Griggs, Asa Lyon and
Chauncey Bartlett, of said town, who shall apply the
said moneys to the purpose of rebuilding the bridge
aforesaid, and the expenses incurred by them thereon.

§ 2. It shall be the duty of the said Daniel Griggs, Duties of
Asa Lyon and Chauncey Bartlett, to account to the commis-
town auditors of said town of Adams, at its annual ses- sioners.
sion in the year eighteen hundred and sixty-two, for all
moneys received by them, by virtue of the acts to which
this act is a supplement, or by virtue of this act, stating
each item of expenditure; and the balance, if any, remaining on hand after the completing of such bridge,
shall be applied by said board for repairs made and to
be made on the roads and bridges in said town.

§ 3. The said Daniel Griggs, Asa Lyon and Chauncey
Bartlett are hereby authorized to borrow the said sum
of five hundred and fifty-five dollars to finish rebuilding
the said bridge, and to pay the expenses incurred thereon
by them, in anticipation of the levying and collecting
of such tax, and to apply the moneys authorized by this
act to be levied and collected, to the payment of the
said sum of five hundred and fifty-five dollars borrowed,
with lawful annual interest.

§ 4. This act shall take effect immediately.

Chap. 180.

AN ACT to further amend an act entitled "An act appointing commissioners to lay out a road between the village of Dunkirk and the village of Cherry Creek in the county of Chautauqua," passed April thirteenth, eighteen hundred and fifty-seven.

Passed April 12, 1862; three-fifths being present.

The People of the State of New York, represented in Senate and Assembly, do enact as follows:

SECTION 1. Section first, chapter two hundred and fifty-one of the Laws of eighteen hundred and sixty is hereby amended as follows:

Levi Baldwin, Martin H. Town and John C. Griswold are hereby appointed commissioners to review so much of the laying out of the highway described in said act as lies in the town of Arkwright, with the same powers and under the same regulations as prescribed for the said commissioners appointed for the towns of Cherry Creek and Sheridan, and a majority of such commissioners after reasonable notice of meeting to all, may act with the same force and effect as if all had joined in the determination.

§ 2. This act shall take effect immediately.

Chap. 181.

AN ACT to amend an act entitled "An act to incorporate the Long Island College Hospital of the city of Brooklyn," passed March sixth, eighteen hundred and fifty-eight.

Passed April 12, 1862.

The People of the State of New York, represented in Senate and Assembly, do enact as follows :

SECTION 1. The fourth section of the act entitled "An act to incorporate the Long Island College Hospital of the city of Brooklyn," passed March sixth, eighteen hundred and fifty-eight," is hereby amended so as to read as follows :

§ 4. To carry into effect the objects of the said corporation, the members thereof shall, at an annual meeting to be held at such time and place as the by-laws of the said corporation shall direct and appoint, elect from their own number by ballot, and by a majority of the votes given at such election, five persons as regents of the said corporation; and the persons so elected, together with those whose term of service has not yet expired, shall constitute a board of regents. The regents so elected shall hold their offices until others are elected in their places. In case of any vacancy by resignation or otherwise, in the board, the remainder of the regents shall have power to fill such vacancies.

Chap. 182.

AN ACT for the appraisal of the damages of Nathaniel M. Sargeant, caused by a break in the Black River canal.

Passed April 12, 1862; three-fifths being present.

The People of the State of New York, represented in Senate and Assembly, do enact as follows:

SECTION 1. The canal appraisers are hereby authorized and directed to hear and determine the claim of Nathaniel M. Sargeant, of the town of Boonville, Oneida county, New York, for alleged damages to his lands, mill and chair factory in said town of Boonville, caused by a break in the embankment of the basin of the Black River canal, on summit level, at the waste wier thereof on the twentieth day of June, eighteen hundred and fifty-nine; and if upon such examination they find that said Sargeant has, for the cause above named, suffered any injury to his said property for which the state is legally and justly liable, to award said Sargeant such damages therefor as shall in their opinion be just and equitable, subject to appeal to the Canal Board as in other cases.

§ 2. The Treasurer shall pay on the warrant of the Auditor, such sum as shall be finally awarded in pursuance of the first section of this act, out of any moneys appropriated, or that shall be appropriated for the payment of canal damages.

Chap. 183.

AN ACT to amend the charter of the village of North Watertown, Jefferson county.

Passed April 12, 1862; three-fifths being present.

The People of the State of New York, represented in Senate and Assembly, do enact as follows:

SECTION 1. There shall be in and within the village of North Watertown, in the county of Jefferson, only one street commissioner.

§ 2. The street commissioner in and for the said village shall be appointed by resolution of the trustees of said village; he shall hold his office during the pleasure of said board of trustees, and shall receive such compensation as shall be fixed by the said trustees, not exceeding, however, the sum of one dollar and fifty cents per day while engaged as such commissioner.

§ 3. This act shall take effect immediately.

Chap. 184.

AN ACT to authorize the extending of certain streets in the city of Brooklyn, to the East river and to the permanent Bulk-head line.

Passed April 12, 1862; three-fifths being present.

The People of the State of New York, represented in Senate and Assembly, do enact as follows:

SECTION 1. The common council of the city of Brooklyn are hereby authorized and empowered to open, continue and complete to the East river and to the permanent bulk-head line, any and all of the streets in the late city of Williamsburgh, the westerly terminations of which are now at First street in said late city, or at the East river and also all those certain parts of streets lying between Division avenue or Broadway and the late boundary line between the late cities of Brooklyn and

Williamsburgh, and to grade, pave, curb, gutter, flag, and bridge the same; and all provisions of law relating to the opening, grading, paving, guttering, flagging and bridging of streets of said city of Brooklyn, except such part thereof as requires a petition or consent of the owners of property affected thereby, shall apply thereto.

§ 2. This act shall take effect immediately.

Chap. 185.

AN ACT to provide for the payment of the bonds issued by the city of New York for the defence of the National Union.

Passed April 12, 1862; three-fifths being present.

The People of the State of New York, represented in Senate and Assembly, do enact as follows:

SECTION 1. The board of supervisors of the county of New York are hereby authorized and required, as hereinafter provided, to order and cause to be levied and raised for the corporation of the city of New York, by tax upon the estates by law subject to taxation within said county, the several sums specified in this act.

§ 2. In the year eighteen hundred and sixty-two, said board shall cause to be so raised the sum of five hundred thousand dollars, or so much thereof as shall be necessary to pay the volunteer soldiers' family aid fund bonds of said corporation, payable in eighteen hundred and sixty-two, issued under an ordinance passed July seventeenth, eighteen hundred and sixty-one, and such additional sum as may be required to pay the interest payable in eighteen hundred and sixty-two upon said bonds, and upon the union defence fund bonds, and the union defence fund redemption bonds, hereinafter mentioned.

Supervisors to raise by tax $500,000 in 1862.

§ 3. In the year eighteen hundred and sixty-three, said board shall cause to be so raised the sum of five hundred thousand dollars, or so much thereof as may be necessary to pay the volunteer soldiers' family aid fund bonds number two, of said corporation, payable in eighteen hundred and sixty-three, issued under an ordinance

$500,000 in 1863.

passed December sixteenth, eighteen hundred and sixty-one, and such additional sum as may be required to pay the interest payable in eighteen hundred and sixty-three, upon said bonds, and upon the union defence fund redemption bonds, hereinafter mentioned.

§ 4. It shall be lawful for the mayor, aldermen, and commonalty of the city of New York to borrow, upon the faith and credit of said corporation, such sum or sums of money as may be necessary to pay and redeem the union defence fund bonds, payable May first, eighteen hundred and sixty-two, issued under the ordinance passed April twenty-third, eighteen hundred and sixty-one, and for the moneys so borrowed to issue other bonds of said corporation, which shall be known and designated as the union defence fund redemption bonds, and be payable on the first day of November, eighteen hundred and sixty-four, and bear interest at a rate not exceeding seven per cent per annum, payable semi-annually on the first days of May and November in each year. *[Union defence fund and redemption fund.]*

§ 5. In the year eighteen hundred and sixty-four, the said board of supervisors shall likewise cause to be raised the amount required to pay and redeem the said union defence fund redemption bonds, and the interest thereon, payable in said year. *[To be redeemed in 1864.]*

§ 6 All moneys reimbursed to or received by said corporation, on account of the expenditure made under said three ordinances, shall be applied to the payment and redemption of said bonds, and of the interest thereon as provided in said ordinances respectively, or to the payment and redemption of the union defence fund redemption bonds, authorized by this act. *[Certain funds applied to the redemption of the bonds.]*

§ 7. The several amounts authorized to be raised by tax under this act shall be levied and collected in the same manner as other taxes are by law levied and collected in said county, and shall be applied and expended for the payment of the said several loans and interest thereon as hereinbefore provided, and for no other purpose or purposes whatever.

§ 8. This act shall take effect immediately.

Chap. 186.

AN ACT to authorize the county court or court of sessions of the county of Steuben, to make an order declaring Seymour S. Wood innocent of the crime of which he was convicted on the eleventh day of June, eighteen hundred and forty-two, and to provide that the record of his conviction shall not be used as evidence in the courts.

Passed April 12, 1862; three-fifths being present.

The People of the State of New York, represented in Senate and Assembly, do enact as follows:

SECTION 1. The county court or court of sessions of the county of Steuben, shall have full power and authority, on the application of Seymour S. Wood, and upon being satisfied of the innocence of said Seymour S. Wood of the crime of which he was convicted and sentenced on the eleventh day of June, eighteen hundred forty-two, in the county of Steuben, to make an order declaring him innocent of such crime; which order shall be entered in the minutes of the court and a copy thereof shall be attached to the record of his conviction now filed in said county, and thereafter the said record shall not be evidence or used as such in any court, and shall not be certified except in connection with such order.

§ 2. This act shall take effect immediately.

Chap. 187.

AN ACT to incorporate the Board of Foreign
Missions of the Presbyterian church of the
United States of America.

Passed April 12, 1862.

*The People of the State of New York, represented in
Senate and Assembly, do enact as follows:*

SECTION 1. Walter Lowrie, Gardner Spring, Wm. *To hold and convey real or personal estate.*
W. Phillips, George Potts, Wm Bannard, John D. Wells,
Nathan L. Rice, Robert L. Stuart, Lebbeus B. Ward,
Robert Carter, John O. Lowrie, citizens of the state of
New York, and such others as they may associate
with themselves, are hereby constituted a body corporate and politic forever, by the name of the Board
of Foreign Missions of the Presbyterian church in the
United States of America, for the purpose of establishing and conducting christian missions among the une-
vangelized or pagan nations, and the general diffusion of
christianity ; and by that name they and their successors
and associates shall be capable of taking by purchase,
grant, devise or otherwise, holding, conveying or otherwise disposing of any real or personal estate for the
purposes of said corporation ; but which estate within
this state shall not at any time exceed the annual income
of twenty thousand dollars.

§ 2. The said corporation shall possess the general
powers, rights and privileges, and be subject to the
liabilities and provisions contained in the eighteenth
chapter of the first part of the Revised Statutes, so far
as the same are applicable, and also subject to the provisions of chapter three hundred and sixty of the laws
of eighteen hundred and sixty.

§ 3. This act shall take effect immediately.

Chap. 188.

AN ACT to incorporate the New York State Convention of Universalists.

Passed April 12, 1862.

The People of the State of New York, represented in Senate and Assembly, do enact as follows :

SECTION 1. E. G. Brooks, Ebenezer Fisher, Nathan Crary, F. M. Alvord, Benjamin Austin, E. W. Reynolds, J. M Austin, T. J. Sawyer, C. C. Gordon, Ely T. Marsh, A. Kelsey, G. W. Montgomery, L. C. Brown, E. M. Whitney, J. M. Pullman, Wm. M. De Long, I. George, their associates and successors, are hereby made a corporation by the name of the New York State Convention of Universalists, with all the powers and privileges, and subject to all the provisions and restrictions contained in the third title of the eighteenth chapter of the first part of the Revised Statutes, and chapter three hundred and nineteen of the laws of eighteen hundred and forty-eight, and said corporation may hold real and personal estate to the value of two hundred thousand dollars, to be devoted exclusively to the diffusion of christian knowledge by means of missionaries, publications and other agencies.

Chap. 189.

AN ACT to incorporate the Mutual Aid Society of the East Genesee Annual Conference.

Passed April 12, 1862; three-fifths being present.

The People of the State of New York, represented in Senate and Assembly, do enact as follows :

SECTION 1. Edward O. Hall, Kasimer P. Jervis. Robert Hegaboon, Augustus C. George, Porter McKinstry, Thompson Jolly, Daniel Chase, Sylvester C. Congdon, and such other persons, clergymen of the Methodist

Episcopal church, as may become associated with them, and* other such clergymen, their successors, are hereby constituted a body corporate and politic, by the name and style of "The Mutual Aid Society of the East Genesee Annual Conference."

§ 2. The object of the said corporation is to render pecuniary aid to such of its members as shall become disabled for the performance of labor as such clergymen, and to provide for the destitute widows and heirs-at-law of those of its members who may die. *Object of corporation.*

§ 3. The said corporation may make such rules, regulations and by-laws relative to the admission of the members, the election of officers, the disposition, disbursement and general management of its funds and affairs, as to it shall seem meet from time to time : provided, however, that such rules, regulations and by-laws shall be in conformity with the constitution and laws of the United States, the constitution and laws of the State of New York. *Make by-laws.*

§ 4. The said corporation shall possess the general powers, rights and privileges, and be subject to the restrictions, liabilities and provisions contained in the eighteenth chapter of the first part of the Revised Statutes, so far as the same are applicable.

§ 5. The said corporation shall be capable and authorized to take, receive and hold real estate or other property, by purchase, gift, grant or devise, or otherwise, and to sell, convey or demise* the same, provided, however, that the gross value thereof shall at no time exceed the sum of twenty thousand dollars, and provided, further, that such corporation shall not take, by the last will and testament of any person leaving a husband, wife, child or parent, more than one-half part of his or her estate remaining after his or her debts are paid, nor shall it take anything by any last will and testament which shall be made within two months of the death of the testator. *To take and hold real estate.*

§ 6. This act shall take effect immediately.

*So in the original.

46

Chap. 190.

AN ACT to amend an act entitled "An act to constitute the village of Farmersville, in the county of Seneca, a separate road district, and to regulate the same," passed April fourteenth, eighteen hundred and sixty.

·Passed April 12, 1862; three-fifths being present.

The People of the State of New York, represented in Senate and Assembly, do enact as follows:

SECTION 1. The second section of an act entitled "An act to constitute the village of Farmersville, in the county of Seneca, a separate road district, and to regulate the same," passed April fourteenth, eighteen hundred and sixty, is hereby amended by adding thereto, as follows:

Pay of pathmaster.
Provided, that said pathmaster shall be entitled to one dollar per day for every day he shall be necessarily employed as such pathmaster, over and above his assessment to be retained by him out of any moneys received by him as commutation or fine money.

§ 2. The fourth section of said act is hereby amended by adding thereto, as follows:

Duty of path-master
It shall be the duty of the pathmaster of said district to provide a yard in said district in which to keep such animals so running at large until such penalty, together with the charges of confining and keeping such animals shall be paid. It shall be lawful for any elector of said district to confine any such animal so running at large in said district in such yard, and he shall immediately give notice thereof to said pathmaster. Any animals so confined shall be kept and cared for by said pathmaster, until said penalty and charges are paid, or said animals are sold. On being notified that such animals are so confined he shall immediately give notice thereof to the owner personally, if known and a resident of said village. And within twenty-four hours after receiving said notice, said pathmaster shall give notice of the sale of said animal by posting written notices thereof in three of the most public places in said district, stating

Notice of sale of animals impounded.

the time and place of said sale. Such sale shall not take place in less then ten days from the posting of the notice thereof. If the value of such animals exceed thirty dollars such notice shall also be published once in each week for two successive weeks in a newspaper printed in such district if there be one, and if there be none, then in the newspaper printed nearest to such district; and if the owner of such animal or animals be known and not a resident of said district, the pathmaster shall also give such owner notice of such sale by putting the same into the postoffice and paying postage thereon in said district, properly folded and directed to said owner at least ten days before said sale. Such sale may be postponed from time to time by said pathmaster for want of buyers, but in such case the postponement shall be posted under the three posted notices of sale. The owner or owners of said animals may at any time Terms upon which owners may redeem. redeem the same before the sale thereof by paying the penalty for their running at large, and the charges of confining and keeping said animals and the fees hereinafter named. Such pathmaster shall be entitled to receive for posting said notices twenty-five cents; for sale in pursuance thereof, twenty-five cents; for notifying said owner personally or by mail, twelve cents; and for publishing said notice, the same fees as are now allowed by law for publishing legal advertisements, and twelve cents per mile for going to have such notice published in said newspaper; for keeping each horse, per day, twelve cents; for each head of cattle, per day, seven Fees. cents; for each sheep or swine, per day, four cents. If said penalty, charges and fees are not paid before the time advertised for the sale thereof, said pathmaster shall proceed to sell said animals at public auction, and shall apply the proceeds of such sale to the payment of such penalties, charges and fees, and the residue he shall pay to the owner of such animals on demand if demanded within one year after such sale. If not so demanded it shall be paid to the commissioners of highways of said town for the benefit of the highways therein.

§ 3. The fifth section of said act is hereby repealed.

§ 4. This act shall take effect immediately.

Chap. 191.

AN ACT to repeal an act entitled "An act to incoporate the Metropolitan Medical College of the city of New York," passed March twenty-eight, eighteen hundred and fifty-seven.

Passed April 12, 1862.

The People of the State of New York, represented in Senate and Assembly, do enact as follows :

SECTION 1. The act entitled "An act to incorporate the Metropolitan Medical College of the city of New York," passed March twenty-eighth, eighteen hundred and fifty-seven, is hereby repealed.

§ 2. This act shall take effect immediately.

Chap. 192.

AN ACT making an appropriation for the payment to the United States of the direct tax assumed by the State of New York, and also appropriating the proceeds of the tax levied in pursuance of chapter two hundred and seventy-seven of the Laws of eighteen hundred and sixty-one.

Passed April 12, 1862; three-fifths being present.

The People of the State of New York, represented in Senate and Assembly, do enact as follows:

$2,603,918.- 67 appropriated to pay direct tax to U. S.

SECTION 1. The sum of two million six hundred and three thousand nine hundred and eighteen dollars and sixty-seven cents, or so much thereof as may be necessary, is hereby appropriated out of any moneys in the treasury not otherwise appropriated, to pay to the United States so much of the direct tax levied by the act of Congress, approved the fifth day of August, eighteen hundred and sixty-one, as was by the said act apportioned to this state and which has been assumed by this Legislature ; and the Comptroller is hereby authorized to apply towards the payment of the said tax the indebtedness of the United States to this state, when the amount thereof shall have been ascertained as provided in said act.

§ 2. The sum of one million two hundred and fifty thousand dollars is hereby appropriated for the redemption of Comptroller's bonds, issued for loans to the treasury in anticipation of the state tax to provide for the public defence, imposed by chapter two hundred and seventy-seven, Laws of eighteen hundred and sixty-one, reimbursable, viz.: one hundred thousand on the first day of June, and one million one hundred and fifty thousand on the first day of July, eighteen hundred and sixty-two ; and the further sum of ninety-one thousand three hundred and twenty dollars and eighty-four cents for the payment of the accruing interest on said bonds.

$1,250,000 appropriated to pay Comptroller's bonds.

§ 3. This act shall take effect immediately.

Chap. 193.

AN ACT to repeal an act entitled "An act for the better regulation of a road in Bethlehem, Albany county," passed April third, eighteen hundred and sixty-one.

Passed April 12, 1862; three-fifths being present.

The People of the State of New York, represented in Senate and Assembly, do enact as follows :

SECTION 1. Chapter one hundred and twenty-nine of the Laws of New York, passed April third, eighteen hundred and sixty-one, is hereby repealed.

§ 2. This act shall take effect immediately.

Chap. 194.

AN ACT in relation to warrants issued by county treasurers against defaulting collectors.

Passed April 12, 1862; three-fifths being present.

The People of the State of New York, represented in Senate and Assembly, do enact as follows :

SECTION 1. In all cases where any county treasurer shall issue his warrant against a defaulting collector, the said warrant shall direct the sheriff to collect of the said collector, in addition to the amount in which the said collector shall be in default, all costs and fees for collecting.

§ 2. The said sheriff shall receive the same fees as on executions issued out of the supreme court.

Chap. 195.

AN ACT in relation to the election of county superintendents of the poor in the county of Columbia.

Passed April 12, 1862; three-fifths being present.

The People of the State of New York, represented in Senate and Assembly, do enact as follows:

SECTION 1. There shall be elected in and for the county of Columbia, at the next general election, and annually thereafter, one county superintendent of the poor, who shall hold his office for three years.

§ 2. This act shall take effect immediately.

Chap. 196.

AN ACT to amend an act entitled " An act to consolidate and amend the several acts relating to the village of Warsaw, and to enlarge the powers of the corporation of said village," passed March seventeenth, eighteen hundred and sixty.

Passed April 12, 1862 ; three-fifths being present.

The People of the State of New York, represented in Senate and Assembly, do enact as follows:

SECTION 1. Title six of the act entitled " An act to consolidate and amend the several acts relating to the village of Warsaw, and to enlarge the powers of the corporation of said village," passed March seventeenth, eighteen hundred and sixty, is hereby amended so as to read as follows:

§ 1. The said village shall constitute one highway dis- *Trustees to* trict, and the powers and duties of commissioners of *act as commissioners* highways are hereby devolved upon and shall be exer- *of highways* cised by the board of trustees of said village, except in the erection and repairs of bridges over the streams in said village, subject to the provisions hereinafter contained ; and the jurisdiction of the commissioners and overseers of highways of the town of Warsaw within the limits of said village, and over the taxable inhabitants, corporations and banking associations and property therein, and the taxes levied or to be levied on the same, or any of them, or any part thereof, is hereby entirely abrogated ; but this act shall not exonerate the taxable *Inhabitants* property in said village from contributing its proportion *to contri-* of any moneys which shall be raised in the town of *bute for repairs of* Warsaw for the repairs of roads and bridges, pursuant *roads and* to the fourth section of title first of chapter sixteen of *bridges.* the first part of the Revised Statutes, or chapter two hundred and seventy-four of the laws of eighteen hundred and thirty-two, or from contributing its proportion for the payment of any debt which has heretofore been incurred for building and repairing bridges in said town.

§ 2. This act shall take effect immediately.

Chap. 197

AN ACT to repeal chapter four hundred and ten, passed April fourteenth, eighteen hundred and sixty, and chapter three hundred and three, passed April seventeenth, eighteen hundred and sixty-one, and to divide the crime of murder into two degrees, and to prescribe the punishment of arson.

Passed April 12, 1862; three-fifths being present.

The People of the State of New York, represented in Senate and Assembly, do enact as follows :

Act of April 14, 1860, and act of May 4, 1861, repealed. SECTION 1. The act entitled "An act in relation to capital punishment, and to provide for the more certain punishment of the crime of murder," passed April fourteenth, eighteen hundred and sixty, and the act entitled "An act in relation to cases of murder, and of arson in the first degree, occurring previously to the fourth day of May, in the year one thousand eight hundred and sixty," passed April seventeenth, eighteen hundred and sixty-one, are hereby repealed.

Effect on offences previously committed. § 2. No offence committed previous to the time when this statute shall take effect, shall be affected by this act, except that when any punishment shall be mitigated by the provisions of this act, such provision shall control any judgment to be pronounced after the said act shall take effect for any offences committed before that time.

No prosecution of offences pending to be affected. § 3. No prosecution for any offence pending at the time the aforesaid statutory provisions shall be repealed, shall be affected by such repeal; but the same shall proceed in all respects as if such provision had not been repealed

Sec. 1st of title one chap. one of the fourth part of Revised Statutes altered. § 4. Section first of title one, chapter one, of the fourth part of the Revised Statutes, shall be so altered as to read as follows :

Division of crime of murder. § 1. Every person who shall hereafter be convicted— First. Of treason against the people of this State ; or, Second. Of murder in the first degree ; as those crimes are respectively declared in this title, shall suffer death for the same.

§ 5. Section four of the said title shall be so altered as to read as follows: Section 4, of same title amended.

§ 4. The killing of a human being, without the authority of law, by poison, shooting, stabbing, or any other means, or in any other manner, is either murder in the first degree, murder in the second degree, manslaughter or excusable or justifiable homicide, according to the facts and circumstances of each case. Defining murder.

§ 6. Section five of the said title shall be so altered as to read as follows: Section 5 of same title amended.

§ 5. Such killing, unless it be manslaughter or excusable or justifiable homicide, as hereafter provided, shall be murder in the first degree, in the following cases : First. When perpetrated from a premeditated design to effect the death of the person killed, or of any human being ; Second. When perpetrated by any act imminently dangerous to others, and evincing a depraved mind regardless of human life, although without any premeditated design to effect the death of any particular individual ; Third. When perpetrated in committing the crime of arson in the first degree. Such killing, unless it be murder in the first degree, or manslaughter, or excusable or justifiable homicide, as hereinafter provided, or when perpetrated without any design to effect death by a person engaged in the commission of any felony, shall be murder in the second degree. Murder in the first degree. Second degree.

§ 7. Add to the said title another section, in these words :

Every person who shall be convicted of murder in the second degree, or of arson in the first degree, as herein defined, shall be punished by imprisonment in a state prison for any term not less than ten years. Punishment of second degree.

§ 8. In title three, chapter one, part four of the Revised Statutes, alter section nine so as to read as follows :

§ 9 Every person who shall be convicted of any degree of arson herein specified, shall be punished by imprisonment in a state prison, as follows ; First. Of arson in the second degree, for a term not more than ten years, nor less than seven years ; Second. Of arson in the third degree, for any term not more than seven years, nor less than four years ; Third. Of arson in the fourth degree, for any term not more than four years, and not less than one year ; or by imprisonment in a county jail not exceeding a year. Punishment of arson.

Arson in
the third
degree.

§ 10. Every person who shall willfully set fire to or burn in the night time any store or warehouse not adjoining to or within the curtilage of any inhabited dwelling house, so that such house shall not be endangered by such firing, shall, upon conviction, be adjudged guilty of arson in the third degree.

Chap. 198.

AN ACT to amend an act entitled "An act to supply Sing Sing prison with Croton water, and for the sale of certain lands of the State," passed April seventeenth, eighteen hundred and sixty-one.

Passed April 12, 1862; three-fifths being present.

The People of the State of New York, represented in Senate and Assembly, do enact as follows:

SECTION 1. The second section of the act entitled "An act to supply Sing Sing prison with Croton water, and for the sale of certain lands of the State," passed April seventeenth, eighteen hundred and sixty-one, is hereby amended to read as follows:

To lease
certain land
to the city
of New
York.

§ 2. The commissioners of the land office, upon the execution of the contract authorized by the first section of this act, are directed and required to execute to the "mayor, aldermen and commonalty of the city of New York," letters patent, or a lease for a term of years, of a strip of land in the village of Sing Sing, in the county of Westchester, being thirty-three feet in width on each side from the centre of the Croton aqueduct, as the same now runs through and across the lands owned by this state in said village of Sing Sing, and

The land to
revert to
the state on
termination
of supply of
water.

known as the State Farm. The said letters patent or lease to contain the condition that upon the termination of the supply of water by the Croton Aqueduct Board, the lands conveyed by such letters patent shall revert to the people of the State of New York, and the letters patent or lease then and thereupon to become void, and also to contain such other conditions and provisions as the said the commissioners of the land office shall deem necessary for the preservation of the interests of the people of this state.

§ 3. This act shall take effect immediately.

Chap. 199.

AN ACT to amend an act entitled "An act to authorize the laying of a double railroad track in the city of Brooklyn and the town of Newtown, in the county of Queens," passed April sixteenth, eighteen hundred and sixty.

Passed April 12, 1862; three-fifths being present.

The People of the State of New York, represented in Senate and Assembly, do enact as follows:

SECTION 1. It shall be lawful for the Grand Street and Newtown railroad company, under their present charter, to construct a double railroad track through and upon Graham avenue, in the city of Brooklyn, from their present track on Grand street to Meeker avenue, and thence through and upon Meeker avenue, or some other street or avenue adjacent thereto, and not over one thousand feet therefrom, to Newtown creek at the Penny bridge.

§ 2. The said company may use single horse cars on their road and charge for the transportation of passengers a sum on the extension not exceeding three cents; and the board of directors shall consist of not less than five nor more than thirteen directors. *May use single horse cars.*

§ 3. All acts and parts of acts inconsistent herewith, are hereby repealed.

§ 4. This act shall take effect immediately.

Chap. 200.

AN ACT for the relief of families of volunteers in the service of the United States from the town of Salisbury, in the county of Herkimer.

Passed April 12, 1862 ; three-fifths being present.

The People of the State of New York, represented in Senate and Assembly, do enact as follows :

May raise $1,100.

Section 1. The board of supervisors of the county of Herkimer, at their regular annual meeting to be held for the year eighteen hundred and sixty-two, are hereby authorized and required to raise by tax to be levied upon the taxable property of the town of Salisbury, in said county in the same manner as other town charges are levied and raised, eleven hundred dollars, for the purpose of refunding moneys and interest expended, and to provide a fund for the support of families of volunteers in the service of the United States. But no moneys to be raised by virtue of the provisions of this act shall be paid out to any person hereafter volunteering or enlisting ; nor to any relative of his ; nor to any member of his family ; nor to any person for any money voluntarily paid or subscribed, or article voluntarily furnished to any volunteer, or relative, or family of such volunteer.

Money to be paid to relief committee.

§ 2. The money raised by virtue of this act, when collected, shall be paid over to Lorenzo Carryl, John C. Pitt, James H. Ives, John Ives, John D. Lamberson, George K. Rogers, James J. Cooke, the volunteer relief committee of the town of Salisbury, by the treasurer of Herkimer county, and said committee shall apply so much thereof as may be needed therefor to reimburse said committee for moneys expended by them as such committee, and to be expended for the relief of families of volunteers who have heretofore enlisted and are in the service of the United States, and for no other purposes.

§ 3. This act shall take effect immediately.

Chap. 201.

AN ACT to authorize the town of Manheim to raise moneys to reimburse expenditures for volunteers in the service of the United States.

Passed April 12, 1862; three-fifths being present.

The People of the State of New York, represented in Senate and Assembly, do enact as follows:

SECTION 1. The supervisor of the town of Manheim shall, at the next annual meeting of the board of supervisors of the county of Herkimer, report the amount of moneys which has been expended by the relief committee of said town in assisting volunteers and their families, together with the interest which may have or may hereafter become due, and any other expenditures which may have been necessarily incurred by said committee; and the whole sum shall be chargeable to the said town, and shall be raised and collected with the tax for the present year, in the same manner as other town charges and taxes for said town are levied and collected; but the amount hereby authorized to be raised shall not exceed five hundred dollars. *May raise by tax $500.*

§ 2. The sum levied, raised and collected, as authorized by this act, shall on or before the first day of March, one thousand eight hundred and sixty-three, be paid over by the supervisor of the said town to John Feeter, Hiram Broat, William Feeter, Daniel Snell and James Brown, the relief committee aforesaid, to reimburse them for moneys expended by them for the purposes mentioned in section one. *Money to be paid to relief committee.*

§ 3. This act shall take effect immediately.

Chap. 202.

AN ACT to authorize the West Winfield Bank to reduce its capital stock.

Passed April 12, 1862.

The People of the State of New York, represented in Senate and Assembly, do enact as follows:

SECTION 1. The directors of the West Winfield Bank are hereby authorized to reduce the capital stock of said bank to the sum of one hundred thousand dollars.

§ 2. Whenever said directors shall by resolution have determined to reduce said capital stock, they shall within six months thereafter pay over to the stockholders of said bank the amount of the stock so reduced, in sums proportioned to the amount of stock held by said stock-holders respectively, and upon such payment each of said stockholders shall surrender to said bank the certificate of stock heretofore held by him, and shall be entitled to receive of and from said bank new certificates for the balance of said capital stock. Nothing in this act shall impair any of the obligations or contracts entered into by or with said bank, nor change or lessen the liability of the stockholders thereof.

§ 3. This act shall take effect immediately.

Chap. 203.

AN ACT to authorize the town of Herkimer to raise moneys to reimburse expenditures for families of volunteers in the service of the United States.

Passed April 12, 1862; three-fifths being present.

The People of the State of New York, represented in Senate and Assembly, do enact as follows :

County
Treasurer
to execute

SECTION 1. The county treasurer of the county of Herkimer shall, on or before the first day of May, eighteen hundred and sixty-two, make and execute four several bonds in the name of and for and in behalf of the town of Herkimer, in said county, each conditioned for the payment of the sum of five hundred dollars, together with annual interest at a rate not to exceed seven per cent per annum, payable one in each successive year, at the office of the county treasurer of Herkimer county, and negotiate the same for money at not less than their par value, and shall with and out of the moneys which he shall so realize, for and borrow upon said several bonds upon the credit and faith of said town, pay over to Dean Burgess, Henry O. Crouch and Ezra Graves, the relief committee of said town, the sum of two thousand dollars, to reimburse said committee for moneys expended by them as such committee, and to be expended for the relief of families of volunteers who have heretofore enlisted, and are in the service of the United States, and for no other purpose.

§ 2. The said county treasurer shall, at the annual meeting of the board of supervisors of the county of Herkimer, report the principal and interest to become due on the first day of March following said annual meeting, and the said board of supervisors shall insert the amount of principal and annual interest to become due in the list of taxes for said town, and the said amount shall be chargeable to said town and shall be raised and collected, in each and every year, until said bonds and the interest to accrue thereon as aforesaid, shall be collected, and the said amount shall be raised and collected as other town charges and taxes for said town are collected, and said moneys shall be paid over to the treasurer of said county, to the credit of said town, to be applied in payment of said bonds of the town to be issued as aforesaid and to no other purpose.

§ 3. The said county treasurer shall pay the annual interest on said bonds, to the owner or owners thereof, and endorse the same upon the said several bonds, and shall pay the principal due upon said bonds at the time the same shall become due and payable, respectively, and cancel each of the said bonds when fully paid as aforesaid.

§ 4. The several bonds issued in pursuance of this act shall be a charge upon the said town until paid.

§ 5. This act shall take effect immediately.

Chap. 204.

AN ACT for the relief of the families of the New York State volunteers, in the town of Morristown.

Passed April 12, 1862; three-fifths being present.

The People of the State of New York, represented in Senate and Assembly, do enact as follows:

Elect volunteer aid commissioners.

SECTION 1. The electors of the town of Morristown, in the county of St. Lawrence, at any annual or special town meeting may appoint by resolution, not less than three nor more than five persons, who shall hold their office for one year, and shall be residents and tax payers of said town, to act as volunteer aid commissioners, whose duty it shall be to provide for the indigent families of New York State volunteers of said town, from any tax raised for that purpose.

Duties of commissioners.

§ 2. The said commissioners shall meet as soon as practicable after their appointment and decide what families and to what extent they shall receive aid under this act; make out a statement thereof in writing, sign and file the same in the town clerk's office of the said town, to be by them revised as often as the same shall become necessary; but no money shall be paid or article furnished to the family or relative of any volunteer or soldier hereafter enlisted or mustered into service, nor shall any money be paid to reimburse any subscription voluntarily made, or money voluntarily paid for the purpose contemplated in this act.

Shall render an account.

§ 3. The said commissioners shall render a just and true account, duly attested, of their proceedings and expenditures under this act, (stating particularly the articles, the price thereof, and to whom furnished,) to the board of town auditors of said town, which accounts of expenditures shall be audited and as audited allowed by the said board, and levied and collected in the same manner as other town charges.

§ 4. The electors of said town, in town meeting assembled, may by vote limit the amount to be expended under this act.

§ 5. This act shall take effect immediately.

Chap. 205.

AN ACT to amend the act entitled "An act for the incorporation of companies formed to navigate the lakes and rivers," passed April fifteenth, eighteen hundred and fifty-four.

Passed April 12, 1862; three-fifths being present.

The People of the State of New York, represented in Senate and Assembly, do enact as follows:

SECTION 1. The act entitled "An act for the incorporation of companies formed to navigate the lakes and rivers," passed April fifteenth, eighteen hundred and fifty-four, is hereby amended by adding to the first section of said act the following sentences and paragraphs: The number of directors specified in the certificate of any company organized under the provisions of this act may be increased or diminished in the following manner: Whenever any such company shall desire to call a meeting of the stockholders, for the purpose of increasing or diminishing the number of directors, it shall be the duty of the directors to publish a notice, subscribed by at least a majority of them, at least thirty successive days, as is prescribed in section three, previous to the day fixed upon for holding such meeting, specifying the object of such meeting, the time and place when and where such meeting shall be held, and the number to which it shall be proposed to increase or diminish such directors. A vote of at least two-thirds of all the shares of stock shall be necessary to an increase or diminution of the number of directors, and if at least two-thirds of the stockholders, in person, shall vote in favor of such increase or reduction, the number of directors shall be increased or diminished accordingly; and thereupon the number of directors to which the same shall have been increased or diminished, shall be elected as directors, in the manner provided for in this act. *Manner of increasing and diminishing directors.*

§ 2. The proceedings of such meeting, so far as the same may relate to the increase or reduction of the number of directors, shall be signed and certified to under oath by the chairman or president of such meeting and *Proceedings to be signed and certified to under oath.*

48

by the secretary thereof and filed as provided for in the
first section of the act hereby amended and shall be recorded by the secretary of the company in the books of
the company which contain the record of the proceedings.   And the copy of such certificate so filed and certified by the county clerk in whose office the same shall be
filed, in the manner provided for in the ninth section of
the act hereby amended, shall be received in all courts
and places as legal evidence of the matter therein stated.
§ 3. This act shall take effect immediately.

Chap. 206.

AN ACT to enable Cuyler Copeland and others to
file claims with the canal appraisers for canal
damages, and to provide for the payment thereof.

Passed April 12, 1862; three-fifths being present.

*The People of the State of New York, represented in
Senate and Assembly, do enact as follows :*

SECTION 1. Cuyler Copeland, Abiel West, Warren
Ashley, Thomas Campbell, James T. Sargent, Elisha
Smith, and George Tucker shall have the same right, for
two months from the passage of this act, to file with the
canal appraisers their several claims for damages done
them in consequence of the appropriation by this state
of their real estate and buildings in the village of Fort
Ann, in the town of Fort Ann, Washington county, New
York, in building a piece of new canal, and in the construction of locks on the Champlain canal, at that place,
in the year eighteen hundred and fifty-four, which they
had by law for one year from the time such appropriation was made; and whenever, within the said two
months, said claims or any of them shall be presented to
said appraisers in the manner and with the particularity
required by section eighty-four of chapter nine of title
nine of article three of the third part of the Revised
Statutes, it shall be their duty to appraise and determine
the amount of such damages, and make their award or
awards thereon as if the same had been filed within the

time required by law, from which determination and
award or awards an appeal may be taken to the canal
board as in other cases.

§ 2. The treasurer shall pay, upon the warrant of the Treasurer
Auditor of the canal department, such sum or sums as award.
shall be finally awarded by the said appraisers or the
canal board, upon the claim or claims mentioned in the
first section of this act, out of any moneys in his hands
applicable to the repairs or enlargement of the canals of
this state, not otherwise appropriated.

§ 3. This act shall take effect immediately.

Chap. 207.

AN ACT to amend an act entitled "An act for
the incorporation of the village of Oxford and
for other purposes," passed April sixth, one
thousand eight hundred and eight, and the
acts amending the same.

Passed April 12, 1862; three-fifths being present.

*The People of the State of New York, represented in
Senate and Assembly, do enact as follows :*

SECTION 1. On the first Tuesday of May, eighteen Classifica-
hundred and sixty-two, there shall be elected in the tion of trus-
manner now required by law, at the annual election in tees.
said village of Oxford six trustees of said village, who
shall possess all the rights and powers now or hereafter
conferred upon the trustees of said village. The trustees so elected on the first Tuesday of May next, shall
be classified by lot to be publicly drawn by the presiding officer at such election, immediately after the
completion of the canvass of such election. The classes
shall be divided into three and numbered one, two and
three, according to the term of service of each ; the
class having the shortest term to serve being number
one, and the term of office of the two persons drawn in
class number one shall expire on the first Tuesday of
May, eighteen hundred and sixty-three ; those in class
number two on the first Tuesday of May, eighteen hun-

dred and sixty-four; those in class number three on the
first Tuesday of May, eighteen hundred and sixty-five.
The said trustees shall hold their office until others are
elected or appointed in their place and qualify.

Two trus-
tees to be
elected an-
nually

§ 2. At the annual elections held in said village after
the first Tuesday in May, eighteen hundred and sixty-
two, there shall be elected in said village, in the manner
now required by law, two trustees of said village who
shall hold their office for the term of three years, and
until others are elected or appointed in their place and
qualify.

Trustees to
fill vacancy.

§ 3. In case of any vacancy now or hereafter existing
in the office of trustee of said village, arising from any
cause, the trustees in office may appoint any elector
of such village, being a freeholder, to fill such vacancy
until the next annual election in such village and until
others shall be elected to fill such vacancy and qualify.

Vacancies.

§ 4. If at any annual election any vacancy in the office
of trustee is to be filled, the electors shall designate on
their ballot the person or persons to fill such vacancy or
vacancies, and who shall serve for the full term; and in
case no person shall be elected to fill such vacancy, then
the trustees in office shall appoint some elector in such
village, being a freeholder, to fill the same until the
next annual election and until others shall be elected in
their place and qualify.

Animals
running at
large.

§ 5. Any person may take up any animals running at
large in said village, and put them in the public pound
now or hereafter established in said village, and shall
immediately give notice thereof to the pound keeper
who shall receive and detain them in the pound until
discharged by law. Within twenty-four hours after
receiving notice of the impounding as aforesaid, said
pound master shall give notice of the sale of said animal or animals by posting written notices thereof in
three of the most public places in said village, stating
the time and place of said sale, and describing said
animals. Such sale shall not take place in less than ten
days from the posting of the notices thereof in any
case, and if the value of such animals exceed twenty-
five dollars, such notice shall also be published once in
each week for four successive weeks, before the sale
thereof, in a newspaper printed in such village, if there
be one, and if none, then in the newspaper printed near-

est to such village; and if the owner or owners of such animal or animals is known to the pound master, he shall give said owner or owners notice of the sale thereof; if a resident of said village he shall give notice personally, if not a resident, by depositing, postage pre-paid, a notice of said sale in the postoffice, properly folded and directed to said owner at his place of residence, at least six days before said sale; said sale may be postponed for want of bidders, in which case said pound master shall give notice of postponement as required herein for notice of ——.* The owner or owners of such animals may at any time redeem the same before the sale thereof by paying the fees, penalty and expenses of keeping the same; if not paid, the said pound master shall, at the time and place named, proceed to sell the same, and shall be entitled to charge and receive for publishing notice of sale the same fees as are now allowed by law for publishing legal advertisements. In case of sale, the pound keeper shall pay the surplus money arising from said sale, after deducting his fees and charges, to the treasurer of said village, who shall retain thereof the penalty of the by-laws under which such animal was impounded, and hold the balance thereof for the benefit of the owner of such animal, if claimed within one year from the day of such sale, if not so claimed, then said balance shall belong to said village.

Owners may redeem

§ 6. The trustees of said village shall fix the compensation and fees of the pound keeper or keepers in said village. The trustees of said village shall have power to pass any and all by-laws regulating the pound or pounds now or hereafter established in said village, and the keeping of the same and fixing the penalties for breaking of the same, and for the rescuing of any animal therefrom or while being driven thereto; and to fix suitable penalties for the violation of any such by-law to be sued for and collected in the corporate name of said village.

Trustees to fix fees of pound keeper.

§ 7. This act shall take effect immediately.

* So in the original.

Chap. 208.

AN ACT to authorize the construction and maintenance of a bridge over the Genesee Valley Canal, at Atkinson street, in the city of Rochester, upon certain conditions.

Passed April 12, 1862; three-fifths being present.

The People of the State of New York, represented in Senate and Assembly, do enact as follows:

SECTION 1. The canal commissioners are hereby authorized to construct or cause to be constructed and maintained, at the expense of the state over the Genesee Valley canal, in the city of Rochester, at the point where Atkinson street intersects the Genesee Valley canal, a common single track bridge with sidewalks, to be paid for out of any moneys appropriated for repairs of the Genesee Valley canal, and to be undertaken whenever it shall be proved to the satisfaction of the said commissioners that said street was opened and used before the construction of the said canal, and continues to be a public street of said city on both sides of said canal.

§ 2. This act shall take effect immediately.

Chap. 209.

AN ACT to authorize the board of town auditors of the town of Southeast, in the county of Putnam, to provide for the relief of families of volunteers.

Passed April 12, 1862; three-fifths being present.

The People of the State of New York, represented in Senate and Assembly, do enact as follows:

SECTION 1. The board of town auditors of the town of Southeast, in the county of Putnam, are hereby authorized and directed to act as a committee to furnish relief to the families of volunteers from said town in the military service of the United States or the State of New York, with power to borrow money for that purpose to an amount not exceeding six hundred dollars, until the same can be raised by tax. The money so borrowed, or such portion thereof as shall be necessary for that purpose, shall be appropriated for relief of volunteer families as aforesaid, from the first day of October, eighteen hundred and sixty-one to the first day of October, eighteen hundred and sixty-two and for no other purpose whatever.

§ 2. The board of supervisors of the county of Putnam shall, at their next annual meeting, cause to be levied and collected, on the town of Southeast in said county, the sum of six hundred dollars to pay the money authorized to be borrowed by section one of this act.

Supervisors to levy on Southeast $600

Chap. 210.

AN ACT to amend an act entitled "An act to amend an act entitled 'An act to vest certain powers in the freeholders and inhabitants of the village of Jamacia*, in the county of Queens,' passed April twenty-fifth, eighteen hundred and fourteen, and to enlarge the powers of the corporation of said village," passed April, tenth, eighteen hundred and fifty-five.

Passed April 12, 1862; three fifths being present.

The People of the State of New York, represented in Senate and Assembly, do enact as follows:

SECTION 1. Section sixteen of title five of " An act to amend an act entitled ' An act to vest certain powers in the freeholders and inhabitants of the village of Jamacia,* in the county of Queens,' passed April twenty-

*So in the original.

fifth, eighteen hundred and fourteen, and to enlarge the powers of the corporation of said village," passed April tenth, eighteen hundred and fifty-five, is hereby amended so as to read as follows :

Duties of assessors. Assessments imposed and sums directed to be raised by the trustees for the costs and expenses of laying down, making, repairing, building, improving and opening drains, sewers and cisterns, shall be laid or assessed and distributed or proportioned by the assessors. Those which the trustees shall judge or determine to be of general utility or for the general benefit of the village, shall be assessed by the assessors in the same manner as other taxes and assessments assessed by them for general purposes. Those which the trustees shall adjudge and declare to be local, shall be assessed by the said assessors upon the lots, buildings and real estate upon or in front of which such drains, sewers and cisterns shall be laid down, made, repaired, built, improved or opened, and upon such other lots, buildings and real estate in said village, which they shall deem benefited thereby, in proportion, as near as may be, to the benefits and advantages which each shall acquire from such drain, sewer or cistern.

§ 2. This act shall take effect immediately.

Chap. 211.

AN ACT to amend an act entitled " An act to establish the grade of Flatbush avenue in the city of Brooklyn, and to conform the adjacent and intersecting streets thereto," passed April nineteenth, eighteen hundred and sixty.

Passed April 12, 1862; three-fifths being present.

The People of the State of New York, represented in Senate and Assembly, do enact as follows :

SECTION 1. The second section of the act entitled "An act to establish the grade of Flatbush avenue in the city of Brooklyn, and to conform the adjacent and intersecting streets thereto," passed April nineteenth, eighteen hundred and sixty, hereby amended, shall read as follows:

§ 2. The common council shall cause application to be made to the supreme court at a special term to be held in the county of Kings, or to the county court of Kings county, for the appointment of three persons as commissioners, who shall estimate and assess the expense of such regrading and repaving, and the amount of damages and benefits to be sustained and derived therefrom by the owners of such lands and such buildings as may be affected thereby. The said common council shall fix and determine the district of assessment upon which shall be levied the said expense and damages. For the purpose of paying the balance of the awards for damages allowed by said commissioners, the Comptroller of said city shall issue under the city seal, assessment certificates payable out of the first moneys received on the assessment levied for said expense and damages; such certificate shall bear interest at the rate of seven per cent. per annum, and shall be countersigned by the clerk of said city, and shall be paid to the several parties entitled thereto. *Three commissioners to be appointed.* *Certificates to bear interest.*

§ 2. Nothing in this act contained shall be construed to require the appointment of commissioners of estimate and assessment in place of those heretofore appointed, and the commissioners so appointed are hereby authorized to perform the duties required by the act as hereby amended.

§ 3. This act shall take effect immediately.

Chap. 212.

AN ACT to facilitate the ingress of salmon into Cayuga Lake, and for the protection of the same.

Passed April 12, 1862; three-fifths being present.

The People of the State of New York, represented in Senate and Assembly, do enact as follows:

SECTION 1. The owner or owners of each and every dam, whether such owner be an individual, several in- *Alter the dams on or before the*

49 · . . . .

dividuals, or the state, made across the Oswego or other rivers leading from the Cayuga lake into Lake Ontario, so as to prevent the usual course of the salmon from going up the said rivers into Cayuga lake, shall, on or before the first day of October next, so alter such dam, by making a slope apron in the channel of said river, at least five feet wide, smoothly planked, descending from the top of the dam on an angle of not more than thirty degrees and extending to the bottom of the river below, with a side plank of at least one foot in width attached to each side of said apron, in such a manner as to confine the water to the channel-way of said apron in its passage over the dam. Each such dam shall be made at least one foot lower at the place where such apron is joined thereto to create a sufficient draught and depth of water on said apron for the free passage of salmon up said river and over said dams to the waters in Cayuga lake.

Penalty for neglect.

§ 2 The owner or owners of every such dam, who shall refuse or neglect to build and keep in repair an apron, according to the provisions contained in the foregoing section, shall forfeit the sum of one hundred dollars and costs of suit, for every month he or they may so neglect or refuse, and any person feeling himself aggrieved may prosecute therefor in his own name, by action of debt, in any court having cognizance thereof. The one-half of said penalty when so recovered, shall be paid to the person prosecuting therefor, and the other half to the commissioners of highways of the town where such recovery shall be had, to be applied in repairing the roads and bridges in such town.

For preservation of fish.

§ 3. It shall not be lawful for any person to spear, or in any manner catch or destroy any salmon or other fish, while passing up said apron or aprons, or within the distance of ten rods thereof, whereby they may be prevented or disturbed from pursuing their usual course up said river. Every person offending against the provisions of this section shall, for every such offence, forfeit the sum of twenty-five dollars and costs of suit, to be recovered in the same manner and applied in the same way as provided in the last preceding section.

§ 4 All acts and parts of acts heretofore passed, in relation to dams or obstructions in the rivers above recited in the first section of this act, conflicting with this act, or regulating the fishery in the same, are hereby repealed,

§ 5. This act shall take effect immediately.

Chap. 213.

AN ACT to provide for keeping in repair the highway leading from the Sacandaga river to Mount Pleasant.

Passed April 12, 1862; three-fifths being present.

The People of the State of New York, represented in Senate and Assembly, do enact as follows:

SECTION 1. Sherman Batcheller is hereby appointed a commissioner to superintend and keep in repair, and in proper condition for the public travel at all seasons of the year, that portion of the highway leading from Sacandaga river to Mount Pleasant, in the county of Saratoga, lying between the points in said highway known as the hill, or Fox school house, on the westerly side of the woods, or forest through which said road passes, and the steam mill on the easterly side of said forest near Mount Pleasant. Commis. sioner.

§ 2. For the purpose of defraying the expense of keeping said highway in repair as aforesaid, the assessors of the town or towns through which the said highway passes between the points mentioned in the first section shall assess, for five consecutive years, two cents per acre on the following lots of land, to wit: Lot number fifty, forty-nine, forty-eight, sixty-two, sixty-one, sixty, fifty-nine, fifty-eight, sixty-three, eighty-two, eighty-one, eighty, one hundred nine, one hundred eight, one hundred twelve, one hundred one, one hundred two, sixty-four, sixty-five, and subdivision lots number one, two, three, four, five, six, seven, eight, nine, ten, in great lots number eighty-five, eighty-six, eighty-seven, eighty-eight, all in the patent of land known as the patent of John Glen and forty-four others, one cent per acre on the following lots in the same patent, to wit: seventy-six, seventy-seven, seventy-eight, seventy-nine, thirty-nine, forty-five, forty-six, forty-seven, one hundred thirty-four, one hundred thirty-five, one hundred thirty-six, one hundred fifteen, one hundred sixteen, one hundred seventeen, ninety-nine, one hundred eighty-nine, which shall be levied and collected in the same Expense to be assessed on certain lots.

manner as other taxes, and when so collected shall be paid over to the treasurer of the county of Saratoga, and by him to be paid over to said commissioner in such sums as are from time to time required by him for the purposes aforesaid.

Commissioner to execute and deliver his bonds to treasurer. § 3. Before said commissioner shall receive any money under this act he shall execute and deliver to said county treasurer a bond, with one or more sureties to be approved by him, in double the sum to be raised annually by this act, conditioned for the faithful application of the moneys so to be appropriated under this act. In case of the death, removal, resignation, or other disability of said commissioner to serve under this act, the office of commissioner may be filled by appointment by the county judge of Saratoga county.

Commissioner to report to supervisors of Saratoga. § 4. Said commissioner is hereby required to report in writing to the board of supervisors of Saratoga county on the first day of their regular annual meeting in each year, the condition of said highway between the points named in the first section, the amount of moneys received by him under this act, and the manner in which he has expended or disposed of the same and his vouchers therefor.

Pay of commissioner. § 5. Said commissioner shall receive from the moneys hereby appropriated for his services in performing the duties imposed by this act, two dollars per day for each day's actual service ; but he shall not receive for such services any sum to exceed in the aggregate thirty dollars per year.

Treasurer to invest surplus. § 6. In case moneys raised by virtue of this act shall at any time exceed the sum necessary to keep said highway in repair as aforesaid, such excess shall be invested by said county treasurer upon securities in such manner as said board of supervisors shall approve, and said moneys so invested shall be and remain a fund to be applied in keeping said road in repair as aforesaid, and the whole sum shall be so expended by said commissioner until the same is exhausted.

§ 7. This act shall take effect immediately.

Chap. 214.

AN ACT to erect the village of Preston Hollow, in the county of Albany, into a separate road district.

Passed April 12, 1862; three-fifths being present.

The People of the State of New York, represented in Senate and Assembly, do enact as follows :

SECTION 1. That part of the village of Preston Hollow, Bounds. in the town of Rensselaerville, in the county of Albany, consisting of the lands on each side of the centre of the turnpike, between the Methodist church on the south, and the north line of the lands of Kenyon and Devereux on the north, running back from said turnpike for the distance of one hundred rods on each side thereof, is hereby declared to be, and hereby is constituted a separate road district ; and all the highway labor assessed upon the inhabitants of said village, residing within said district, shall be applied in said district in grading the streets and constructing stone or plank sidewalks in said village ; and the said inhabitants, so residing as aforesaid, shall be exempt from working in any other road district in said town.

§ 2. The commissioners of highways of the town of Power of Rensselaerville, and their successors in office, shall have commis-sioners. the same powers, and be charged with the same duties over said district as is now possessed by them over other road districts in said town, except that they shall not have power to change the limits of said district, or to assign the inhabitants of said road district hereby created to any other district in said town. James A. Kenyon, of the village of Preston Hollow, is hereby appointed the overseer of highways of said district, for the ensuing year, and shall have the same powers and be charged with the same liabilities as other overseers.

§ 3. Any inhabitant of said district, with the consent Inhabitants and under the direction of the overseer of said district, may grade their own may grade and construct the sidewalk in front of his pre- sidewalks. mises, and the expense thereof shall be ascertained and fixed by said overseer ; and in case the amount thereof shall exceed his highway labor for the year, at the rate of sixty-two and a half cents per day, such excess shall be credited to him at the said rate on any future assessment.

§ 4. This act shall take effect immediately.

Chap. 215.

AN ACT to prevent abuses in town and county charges in criminal cases in the county of Herkimer.

Passed April 12, 1862; three-fifths being present

The People of the State of New York, represented in Senate and Assembly, do enact as follows:

SECTION 1. The fees of justices of the peace and constables and sheriffs in the county of Herkimer, in cases of complaint and prosecution, for obtaining money or property, or other valuable thing, by means of false pretences, shall not be chargeable to the town or county until after conviction, and a record thereof duly filed. The party complaining shall be liable to the justice and constable or sheriff for their fees in such cases, and no justice of the peace shall be required to issue process in such cases, nor any officer be required to serve such process without payment of his fees in advance. After conviction, the amount of fees so paid shall be a valid charge against the county.

Supervisors may limit the amount of fees.

§ 2. The board of supervisors of the county of Herkimer may, by resolution, prescribe such reasonable limits as they may deem sufficient and reasonable for the aggregate amounts of fees to be allowed to all the justices and to all constables of the respective towns in said county, for services in criminal cases chargeable to said towns, and also to said county in each town severally. But such limitations of constables' fees shall not apply to those cases of felony in which extraordinary services shall be rendered by the written direction of the district attorney given in advance of the services, and specifying as nearly as may be the particular service required.

§ 3. The several justices of the peace and constables Justices of the several towns in which the amount of fees shall and con- be so limited, shall keep an account of the services by stables to keep an ac- them rendered in criminal cases, distinguishing between count of ser- vices. those chargeable to the town and county, respectively; and the auditing boards of the respective towns, and the board of supervisors of the county, shall respectively audit and allow such accounts at amounts not exceeding in the aggregate the amount so prescribed, and where the legal fees at the rates established by law of the justices and constables in any town, shall exceed the prescribed limit, they shall be reduced to such limit and apportioned rateably among the several officers rendering the services.

§ 4. This act shall take effect immediately.

Chap. 216.

AN ACT to amend an act entitled "An act relating to the support of the poor of Rensselaer county," passed April thirteenth, eighteen hundred and sixty.

Passed April 12, 1862; three-fifths being present.

The People of the State of New York, represented in Senate and Assembly, do enact as follows:

SECTION 1. Section ten of an act entitled "An act relating to the poor of Rensselaer county," passed April thirteenth, eighteen hundred and sixty, is hereby amended so as to read as follows:

§ 10. The board of superintendents of the said county Board of su- shall appoint the keeper of the house of industry, who perinten- dents to ap- shall be the manager of the county farm, subject to the point keep- general directions of the acting superintendent, which er of house of industry directions the acting superintendent shall communicate and a phy- in writing whenever requested so to do by the said keeper, sician. and said board shall also appoint a physician of the said house of industry, and said keeper and physician respectively shall hold their offices during the pleasure of the said board. The annual salaries of the said acting superintendent, keeper and physician shall be fixed by the board of supervisors, and shall be neither increased nor diminished during their term of office.

§ 2. Section eleven of the aforesaid act is hereby amended so as to read as follows:

No money to be paid until delivery of articles. § 11. No money shall be paid nor draft delivered to any contractor or to any other person for articles furnished under the contract before mentioned or for any other property furnished by any person until the said articles shall have been actually delivered at the house of industry, and the same shall have been examined, their weight or measure ascertained by the keeper; which delivery, weight and measure shall be verified by the affidavit of the keeper, which shall state that at date thereof he has personally received, inspected and weighed or measured such articles, and that the quantity and quality is correct as charged.

Relating to temporary relief and duties of superintendent. § 3. It shall be the duty of the said acting superintendent to grant the necessary temporary relief to poor persons residing in the city of Troy, whose relief would be by law a county expense, in the same manner as town overseers of the poor are now required to grant relief to poor persons residing in their respective towns, and under the same restrictions of law, so far as the same shall be applicable, as said town overseers now are, excepting the compensation for such services, which shall be fixed by the board of supervisors of the county; and also excepting that said acting superintendent shall not be required to apply to any officer for authority. The expenses incurred for temporary relief under this section shall, in no case, exceed the cost of maintaining the person relieved at the house of industry, for the same length of time as that for which relief is granted, except when the removal of such person to said house of industry shall be clearly impracticable; and the said acting superintendent shall keep a book of record in his office, in which shall be entered in full the name and residence of each person receiving any relief or assistance, together with the date and amount of the same, and also the manner or means by which such relief or assistance has been rendered; such book to be free and open for the inspection of any tax-payer of the county, from nine o'clock in the forenoon until twelve o'clock at noon, and from two o'clock until four o'clock in the afternoon of each and every day in the year, Sundays and legal holidays excepted.

§4. This act shall take effect immediately.

Chap. 217.

AN ACT to authorize persons convicted of vagrancy in the county of Ontario, in certain cases, to be sentenced to the work house in the county of Monroe.

Passed April 12, 1862; three-fifths being present.

The People of the State of New York, represented in Senate and Assembly, do enact as follows:

SECTION 1. Whenever any justice of the peace in the county of Ontario shall, in accordance with section three, title two, chapter twenty, part one of the Revised Statutes, be satisfied that any person brought before him, under the provisions of the said title, is a vagrant within said title, and is an improper person to be sent to the poor house of the said county, he shall sentence and commit such person to the work house in the county of Monroe, for a term of not less than sixty days nor more than ninety days.

§ 2 It shall be lawful for the board of supervisors of Ontario county, and it is hereby required to enter into an agreement with the board of supervisors of the county of Monroe, (or with any person in their behalf and by them appointed,) to receive and keep in said work house any person or persons who may be sentenced in pursuance of the first section of this act. *Supervisors of Ontario county make agreement with supervisors of Monroe county.*

§ 3 Any officer of the said county of Ontario, to whom any person shall be delivered by a justice of the peace thereof, with a commitment to the said work house, in pursuance of any sentence under the first section of this act, is hereby authorized to take and deliver such person to the superintendent of said work house, who shall receive such person and safely keep him for the term for which he may be sentenced, and keep him at work according to the rules and discipline of said *Officers who shall take vagrants to work house*

50

work house; and the officer taking such person to said work house shall be paid by the county of Ontario such fees for such taking as the board of supervisors of said county shall audit and direct.

§ 4. This act shall take effect immediately.

Chap. 218.

AN ACT to regulate the taking of tolls upon the Geneva and Rushville Plank Road.

Passed April 12, 1862; three-fifths being present.

The People of the State of New York, represented in Senate and Assembly, do enact as follows:

Supervisor and commissioners of highways of Seneca to examine track of road.

SECTION 1. On or before the last Tuesday in April, eighteen hundred and sixty-two, the supervisor and the commissioners of highways of the town of Seneca, in the county of Ontario, shall meet together in said town and shall proceed to view the track or roadway of the Geneva and Rushville Plank Road Company, for the whole length thereof. And if, in their opinion or in the opinion of a majority, the said tract or roadway is in such a state of repair as not to justify the taking of tolls thereon, they shall, or the said majority shall draw up a notice in writing to that effect, and shall therein order and direct the said Geneva and Rushville Plank Road Company to throw open and leave open its toll gate or gates and to collect no tolls thereon. Said notice shall be signed by them, or a majority of them, and shall be filed in the office of the town clerk of the town of Seneca. Any person interested may procure from said town clerk a copy of such notice certified by him, and may serve the same upon any officer or director of the plank road company. And after the lapse

Gates to be thrown open.

of twenty-four hours from the time of service it shall not be lawful for the said plank road company to ask or receive any tolls at any gate upon the said road, until the said supervisor and the said highway commissioners shall have again met and proceeded over said track or roadway, and shall have again viewed the same in its whole length, and shall have made and signed a certificate in writing to the effect that the said track or roadway is in a good and fitting state of repair, and that the said plank road company ought to have the right again to ask and receive tolls upon the said road. Said certificate shall be filed in the office of the town clerk of the said town of Seneca. And the said plank road company, after the lapse of twenty-four hours from the time of said filing, may proceed to ask and receive at any gate, toll at the rate now prescribed by law from any person, to whom shall be exhibited, on request by him, a copy of said certificate by the town clerk of the town of Seneca. And if, after the granting of said certificate, the said supervisor and commissioners of highways shall be thereunto required at any time, by any freeholder of the town of Seneca, they shall, upon payment or tender of said freeholder of their and each of their per diem allowance as now fixed by the law, again proceed over and view the said track or roadway, and shall reduce to writing the opinion of them, or a majority of them, as to the state of repairs of the said road, and whether the same is in such a condition as to justify the said plank road company in asking and receiving tolls for travel thereon; which writing by them, or a majority of them, they shall file in the office of the town clerk in the town of Seneca. And if, by said writing it shall appear that in their opinion, or in the opinion of a majority of them, the said company ought not to ask and receive toll, then, after twenty-four hours from the time of service by any one upon any officer or director of the said company of a copy of said writing, certified by said clerk, it shall not be lawful for the said company to ask or receive any toll for travel on the said road, until the said decision shall have been changed or reversed as heretofore provided.

§ 2. The said plank road company, or any freeholder of the town of Seneca, shall have the right to appeal from the decision of the said supervisor and commissioners of highways, to the county court of Ontario county, which appeal shall be made by serving upon the said supervisor and commissioner of highways, within twenty days after the time of filing of a decision in the office of the town clerk of the town of Seneca a notice in writing of intention to appeal; such appeal shall be

Right of appeal.

How appeal shall be made. brought to a hearing in said county court, according to the rules and practice of said county court, and the provisions of law; and shall be heard upon affidavits or upon the oral examination of witnesses, as such county court shall direct to be served or produced according to its rules or practices, and according to the provisions of law. And the said county court, on hearing such appeal, need not hold its courts at the court house, in Canandaigua, but may, by order to be entered upon its minutes, designate any place in the town of Seneca for the hearing of said appeal; and may on the decision of said appeal in its discretion award costs against either party, to be enforced by order.

Per diem allowance to supervisor and commissioners. § 3. The per diem allowance of the said supervisor and commissioners of highways for their first meeting and view of the said track or roadway as hereinbefore provided shall be a town charge upon the town of Seneca, and shall be audited and paid in the same manner as other town charges or accounts. The per diem allowance of said supervisor and commissioner of highways for any services rendered at the request of the said plank road company shall be paid by said company, and before the service is rendered, if demanded, and the per diem allowance herein mention shall be the same as now allowed by law to such officer.

§ 4. This act shall take effect immediately.

Chap. 219.

AN ACT to authorize the board of supervisors of Monroe county to correct erroneous assessments for county or state taxes.

Passed April 12, 1862; three-fifths being present.

The People of the State of New York, represented in Senate and Assembly, do enact as follows:

SECTION 1. The board of supervisors of Monroe county are hereby authorized and empowered to correct erroneous assessments for personal property, upon individuals or corporations in the city of Rochester, for either county or state taxes, and to refund to any indi-

vidual or corporation so erroneously assessed, the
amount of any tax which may at any time heretofore
have been levied by said board and collected upon such
erroneous assessment, and that such sum or sums be
levied upon the city of Rochester.

§ 2. This act shall take effect immediately.

Chap. 220.

AN ACT to re-organize the State Asylum for
Idiots, and to provide for the government and
management thereof.

Passed April 12, 1862; three-fifths being present.

*The People of the State of New York, represented in
Senate and Assembly, do enact as follows:*

SECTION 1. The management of the asylum for idiots
shall be vested in a board of trustees, consisting of the
Governor, Lieutenant-Governor, Secretary of State,
Comptroller, Superintendent of Public Instruction, and
eight other persons.

§ 2. Henry N. Pohlman, James H. Titus, Hamilton Trustees.
White, Allen Munroe, Hiram Putnam, Franklin Townsend, Lyman Clary and George H. Middleton, present
trustees of the asylum for idiots, shall continue to be
such trustees, and shall hold their office as follows: the
said Franklin Townsend and George H. Middleton for
two years, the said Allen Munroe and Hamilton White
for four years, the said Henry N. Pohlman and Lyman
Clary for six years, and the said James H. Titus and
Hiram Putnam for eight years, from the thirty-first day
of December, one thousand eight hundred and sixty-one
and until others are appointed in their places, subject,
however, to being removed at any time by the Senate,
upon the recommendation of the Governor. Their suc- How ap-
cessors shall be appointed by the Senate upon the nomi- pointed
nation of the Governor, and shall hold their offices for hereafter.
eight years, and subject to be removed in the manner
aforesaid. The Senate may, in like manner, appoint a
trustee for the unexpired term of office of any incum-

bent who shall die, resign, be removed from office, or cease to be an inhabitant of the state during his term, and such trustee shall be subject to removal in the manner above provided. Five members of the said board shall constitute a quorum for the transaction of business.

Powers and duties of board of trustees.

§ 3. Said board shall have the general direction and control of all the property and concerns of the said asylum not otherwise provided by law, and shall take charge of its general interests, and see that its general design be carried into effect, and everything done faithfully according to the requirements of the legislature, and the by-laws, rules and regulations of the asylum

§ 4. The board shall appoint a superintendent, who shall be a well educated physician, and a treasurer, who shall reside in the city of Syracuse, and give bonds to the people of the state, for the faithful performance of his trust, in such sum and with such sureties as the Comptroller of the state may approve. The superintendent shall appoint a steward and a matron, who, together with the superintendent, shall constantly reside in the asylum, and shall 'be denominated the resident officers thereof.

Determine amount of salaries of officers.

§ 5. The board shall, from time to time, determine the annual salaries and allowances of the resident officers of the asylum. But no determination as to said salaries, or either of them, nor any alteration of them, or either of them, shall be made unless there shall be present at a meeting of the board of trustees, the Governor, Lieutenant-Governor, Secretary of State, Comptroller, Superintendent of Public Instruction, or a majority of those officers, of whom the Comptroller shall be one.

§ 6. The salaries and allowances of the resident officers of the asylum shall be paid quarterly on the first days of October, January, April and July in each year, by the treasurer of the asylum, on presentation of the bills therefor, audited, allowed and certified, as prescribed in the by-laws.

May hold in trust donations.

§ 7. The trustees may take and hold in trust for the state any grant or devise of land, or any donation or bequest of money or other personal property, to be applied to the maintenance and education of idiots, and the general use of the asylum.

Establish by-laws.

§ 8. The trustees are hereby directed and empowered to establish such by-laws as they may deem necessary

and expedient for regulating the appointment and duties
of officers, teachers, attendants and assistants, for fixing
the conditions of admission, support and discharge of
pupils, and for conducting in a proper manner the business of the asylum ; also, to ordain and enforce a suitable system of rules and regulations for the internal government, discipline and management of the asylum.

§ 9. The superintendent shall be the chief executive Duties of
officer of the asylum. He shall have the general super- superinten-
intendence of the buildings, grounds and farm, together dent.
with their furniture, fixtures and stock, and the direction and control of all persons employed in and about
the same, subject to the laws and regulations established
by the trustees. He shall have the appointment of his
co-resident officers, with power to assign them their
respective duties, subject to the by-laws. He shall employ, subject to the supervision of the board of trustees,
such teachers, attendants and assistants as he may think
proper and necessary for the economical and efficient
carrying into effect of the design of the institution, prescribe their several duties and places, and fix their compensation, and may discharge any of them. He shall,
also, from time to time, give such orders and instructions
as he may judge best calculated to induce good conduct,
fidelity and economy in any department of labor and expense, and he is authorized and enjoined to maintain
salutary discipline among all who are employed by the
institution, and to enforce strict compliance with such
instructions and uniform obedience to all the rules and
regulations of the asylum. He shall further cause full
and fair accounts and records of all his doings, and of
the entire business and operations of the institution, together with the condition and prospects of the pupils, to
be kept regularly, from day to day, in books provided
for that purpose ; and he shall see that all such accounts
and records shall be fully made up to the first days of
April and October in each year, and that the principal
facts and results, with his report thereon, be presented
to the board at its semi-annual meetings. The exercise
of the foregoing powers shall be subject to the approval
of the trustees, except as herein otherwise provided.
He shall conduct the official correspondence of the institution, and keep a record of the applications received,
and the pupils admitted, and he shall be accountable for

the careful keeping and economical use of all furniture, stores and other articles provided for the asylum, and prepare and present to the board at its semi-annual meetings a true and perfect inventory of all the personal property and effects belonging to the asylum.

Officers exempt from jury, highway and militia duties.

§ 10 The resident officers of the asylum and all the teachers, attendants and assistants actually employed therein, during the time of such employment shall be exempt from serving on juries, from all assessments for labor on the highways, and in time of peace from all service in the militia; and the certificate of the superintendent shall be conclusive evidence of such employment.

Board to keep a record.

§ 11. The board shall keep in a bound book, to be provided for that purpose, a fair and full record of all its doings, which shall be open at all times to the inspection of any of its members, and of all persons whom the Governor or either house of the legislature may appoint to examine the same.

Times of meeting of board of trustees.

§ 12. The board of trustees shall maintain an effective inspection of the affairs and management of the institution; for which purpose the board shall meet at the asylum twice in each year, at such time as the by-laws shall provide; and a committee of three trustees to be appointed by the board, at the annual meeting thereof, shall visit it once in every month,; such committee shall also perform such other duties, and exercise such other powers as shall be prescribed by the by-laws, or as the board may, from time to time, ordain.

Trustees shall have access to accounts and building.

§ 13. It shall be the duty of the resident officers to admit any of the trustees into every part of the asylum, and to exhibit to him or them, on demand, all the books, papers, accounts and writings belonging to the institution, or pertaining to its business, management, discipline or government; also, to furnish copies, abstracts and reports whenever required by the trustees.

Duties of treasurer.

§ 14. The treasurer shall have the custody of all moneys, bonds, notes, mortgages and other securities and obligations belonging to the asylum. He shall keep full and accurate accounts of receipts and payments, in the manner directed in the by-laws, and such other accounts as the trustees shall prescribe. He shall balance all the accounts on his books annually, on the first day of October, and make a statement of the balances thereon, and an abstract of all the receipts and payments of the past year; which he shall, within three days thereafter, deliver to the auditing committee of the trustees, who shall compare the same with his books and vouchers, and verify the same by a further comparison with the books of the superintendent, and certify the correctness thereof to the trustees at their annual meeting. He shall further render a quarterly statement of his receipts and payments to said auditing committee, who shall compare and verify the same as aforesaid, and report the result, duly certified, to the trustees at the annual meeting thereof, who shall cause the same to be recorded in one of the books of the asylum. He shall further render an account of the state of his books, and of the funds and other property in his custody, whenever required so to do by the trustees.

§ 15. Said treasurer is also authorized to receive for the use of the asylum, any and all sums of money which *Authority of treasurer.* may be due upon any note or bond in his hands belonging to the asylum; also any and all sums which may be charged and due according to the by-laws of the asylum, for the support of any pupil therein, or for actual disbursements made in his behalf for necessary clothing and traveling expenses, in an action in the supreme court, to be brought in said treasurer's name, as treasurer of the asylum of idiots; and which shall not abate by his death, removal or resignation, against the individual or county liable therefor, and having neglected to pay the same when demanded by the treasurer; in which action judgment shall be rendered for such sum as shall be found due, together with costs, and interest from the time of the demand made as aforesaid. Every such action may be brought in the county of Onondaga. Said treasurer may, also, upon the receipt of the money due upon such judgment, or upon any mortgage in his hands belonging to the asylum, execute a release, and acknowledge full satisfaction thereof, so that the same may be discharged of record.

§ 16. The superintendent shall, at the time of the admission of any pupil into the asylum, enter in a book to be printed and kept for that purpose, a minute, with *Name and residence of pupil to be kept.* date, of the name and residence of the pupil, and of the person or persons upon whose application he is received; together with a copy of the application, statement,

51

certificate and all other papers accompanying such idiot; the originals of which he shall file and carefully preserve.

§ 17. The supervisors of any county in the state, from which state pupils may be selected and received into the asylum, are hereby authorized and required while such pupils remain at the asylum, to raise the sum of twenty dollars annually, for the purpose of furnishing suitable clothing for each pupil from said county; and on or before the first day of April in each year, pay over the same to the treasurer of the asylum. The superintendent shall immediately, on receiving any pupil, give notice thereof to the clerk of the board of supervisors of the county from which such pupil shall have been sent to said asylum.

§ 18. There shall be received and supported gratuitously in the asylum one hundred and twenty pupils, to be selected in equal numbers, as near as may be, from each judicial district, from those whose parents or guardians are unable to provide for their support therein, to be designated as state pupils; and such additional number of idiots as can be conveniently accommodated, may be received into the asylum by the trustees, on such terms as may be just. But no idiot shall be received into the asylum, without there shall have been first lodged with the superintendent thereof, a request to that effect, under the hand of the person by whose direction he is sent, stating the age, and place of nativity, if known, of the idiot, his christian and surname, the town, or city, and county in which they severally reside, the ability or otherwise of the idiot, his parents or guardians, to provide for his support in whole or in part, and if in part only, then what part; and the degree of relationship, or other circumstance of connection between him and the person requesting his admission; which statement shall be verified in writing, by the oath of two disinterested persons, residents of the same county with the idiot, acquainted with the facts and circumstances so stated, and certified to be credible by the county judge of the same county. And no idiot shall be received into said asylum unless the county judge, of the county liable for his support, shall certify that such idiot is an elligible and proper candidate for admission to said asylum as aforesaid.

§ 19. Whenever the trustees shall direct a state pupil to be discharged from the asylum, the superintendent thereof is authorized to return such pupil to the county from which he was sent to the asylum, and deliver him to the keeper of the poor house of such county; and the superintendents of the poor of said county shall audit and pay the actual and reasonable expenses of such removal, as part of the contingent expenses of said poor house. But if any town, county or person be legally liable for the support of such pupil, the amount of such expenses may be recovered for the use of the county, by such superintendents of the poor. If such superintendents of the poor neglect, or refuse to pay such expenses, on demand, the treasurer of the asylum may pay the same and charge the amount to the said county; and the treasurer of the said county shall pay the same, with interest, after thirty days, out of any fund in his hands not otherwise appropriated; and the supervisors of the said county shall levy and raise the amount as other county charges.

Relating to discharge of pupil and payment of expenses.

§ 20. The superintendent is authorized to agree with the parent, guardian or committee of any idiot, or with any other person or persons, for the support, maintenance and clothing of any idiot, at the asylum, upon such terms and conditions as may be prescribed by the by-laws or approved by the trustees. But every parent, guardian, committee or other person applying for the admission into the asylum of any idiot who, or whose parents or guardians, are of sufficient ability to provide for his maintenance therein, shall, at the time of his admission, deliver to the superintendent a bond, with one or more sureties, to be approved by the trustees in such a manner as they shall prescribe, in the penal sum of at least three hundred dollars, conditioned to pay to the treasurer, for the time being, of the asylum, by his name of office, all such sum or sums of money, at such time or times as shall be agreed upon as aforesaid; and to remove such idiot from the asylum, free of expense to the trustees, within twenty days after the service of the notice hereinafter provided. And if such idiot, or his parents or guardians, are of sufficient ability to pay only some portion less than the whole of the expenses of supporting and clothing him at the asylum, said bond shall be conditioned only for his removal as aforesaid;

Relating to support of pupils.

and the superintendent may take security by note or other written contract or agreement, with or without sureties, as he may deem proper, for such portion of the said expenses as the idiot, his parents or guardians, are able to pay, subject, however, to the approval of the trustees, in the manner that shall be prescribed in the by-laws. Notice to remove any idiot from the asylum, shall be in writing, signed by the superintendent; it shall be directed to the parents, guardians, committee or other person or persons, upon whose request he was received, at the place or places of residence mentioned in such request, and may be served by depositing the same in the postoffice at the city of Syracuse, and with the postage prepaid. If the idiot shall not be removed from the asylum, according to the conditions of said bond, within twenty days after the service of such notice in manner aforesaid, he may be removed and disposed of by the superintendent, as directed in the last preceding section in relation to state pupils, and all the provisions of that section respecting the payment and recovery of the expenses of the removal and disposition of a state pupil, shall be equally applicable to similar expenses arising under this section.

§ 21. The provisions of section nineteen of this act shall be applicable to all state pupils now in the asylum. And any bond, bill, note, agreement, undertaking or other security for the maintenance or support of any pupil at the asylum, heretofore made by any person in his behalf, and now belonging to the asylum, shall be valid and effectual in law, and may be prosecuted as provided in section fifteen of this act.

§ 22. All laws and parts of laws inconsistent with the provisions of this act, are hereby repealed.

§ 23. This act shall take effect immediately.

Chap. 221.

AN ACT to amend an act entitled "An act to promote the public health in the town of New Utrecht," passed April thirteenth, eighteen hundred and fifty-nine.

Passed April 12, 1862; three-fifths being present.

The People of the State of New York, represented in Senate and Assembly, do enact as follows:

SECTION 1. In case the total estimate of expense of the improvement contemplated by the act entitled "An act to promote the public health in the town of New Utrecht," passed April thirteenth, eighteen hundred and fifty-nine, shall exceed the sum of twenty thousand dollars, the said improvement shall not be made; and the said commissioners shall not make any assessment therefor. They shall, in such case, file their estimate of the expense, together with the map which shall have been made as required by the said act, in the office of the clerk of the town of New Utrecht, for the use of the assessors thereof, and for any public purpose for which it may be applied by the said town. The compensation for the services of the commissioners, surveyors and assistants, incurred in pursuance of the provisions of the act hereby amended, shall also in such case be a charge against the district described in the second section of that act, and shall be audited by the board of town auditors of the town of New Utrecht, and by them certified to the board of supervisors of the county of Kings, and included by them in and form a part of the annual taxes imposed or levied upon the said district by the said board of supervisors next after the filing of the estimate of expense aforesaid, which compensation shall be paid by the county treasurer of said county to the parties respectively in whose favor the same shall be audited whenever said taxes shall be collected.

Improvement not to be made if it exceed $20,000.

In that case shall file statement and map with town clerk.

In regard to compensation of commissioners.

Supervisors to include the same in annual tax.

§ 2. For the purpose of enabling the said board of supervisors to levy the amounts audited as aforesaid, it shall be the duty of the assessors of said town, in mak-

Duty of assessors.

ing out the next assessment roll, after the filing of such estimate, as aforesaid, to designate the property in said town within the bounds of the district hereinbefore mentioned.

§ 3. No person shall be disqualified from acting as commissioner for the purpose of carrying out the provisions of the said act by reason of being a freeholder in said district and liable to be assessed for the expenses of the improvements contemplated by the said act.

§ 4. The commissioners appointed under said act shall have power to appoint an attorney to conduct the proceedings under said act, whose compensation shall not exceed one hundred and fifty dollars, to be audited as aforesaid.

§ 5. The operation of the said act is hereby suspended for one year.

§ 6. Such of the provisions of the act hereby amended as are inconsistent with this act are hereby repealed.

Marginal notes:
Being a freeholder of district no disqualification from acting as commissioners.

Commissioners to appoint an attorney.

Suspended for one year

Chap. 222.

AN ACT for the relief of Adden Bardin, George Hahn, Nathaniel P. Osborn and John Fabrig for canal damages.

Passed April 12, 1862; three-fifths being present.

The People of the State of New York, represented in Senate and Assembly, do enact as follows:

SECTION 1. Jurisdiction is hereby conferred upon the canal appraisers to hear and determine the several claims, to-wit: The claim of Adden Bardin, the claim of George Hahn, the claim of Nathaniel P. Osborn, and also of John Fabrig, for damages claimed to have been heretofore sustained by each of said persons severally, in consequence of the raising of an embankment for a bridge across the enlarged Erie canal at the junction of St. Pauls and Griffith streets in the city of Rochester, and by the change of location of said canal, and for property, sidewalks and fences destroyed by reason of said embankment, belonging to said persons, severally, and to make such award thereon, if any, as the state shall be legally and justly liable for.

§ 2. The Treasurer shall pay, on the warrant of the Auditor of the Canal Department, such sum, if any, as shall be awarded and finally adjudicated as provided for by the preceding section of this act, out of any moneys in the treasury appropriated or to be appropriated to the canal enlargement *Treasurer to pay the award.*

§ 3. This act shall take effect immediately.

Chap. 223.

AN ACT to provide for the examination of the accounts of the Treasurer and other State officers.

Passed April 14, 1862; three-fifths being present.

The People of the State of New York, represented in Senate and Assembly, do enact as follows:

SECTION 1. There shall be nominated by the Governor and appointed by him, with the advice and consent of the Senate, three officers by the name of commissioners of public accounts, who shall hold their offices for three years, and until their successors shall be duly qualified. *Commissioners of public accounts appointed by Governor and senate.*

§ 2. The three commissioners to be appointed next after the passage of this act shall hold office as follows, namely: one for the term of one year, one for the term of two years, and one for the term of three years, which terms shall be respectively designated by the Governor at the time of appointment. *Term of office.*

§ 3. The commissioners so appointed shall, within ten days after receiving notice of their appointment, give notice of their acceptance, which, with the oath of office duly signed and certified by an officer authorized to administer oaths, shall be placed on file in the office of the Secretary of State. *Shall notify within ten days their acceptance, which with oath shall be filed in Secretary of State's office.*

§ 4 The commissioners shall meet at twelve o'clock on the first Tuesday of October in each year, at the office of the Treasurer in the city of Albany, and shall proceed at once to inspect the accounts of the treasury, *Time of meeting of commissioners.*

and shall examine the accounts and vouchers relating to all moneys received and paid from the treasury during the year ending on the thirtieth day of the preceding September.

Duties of commissioners relative to Treasurer, Comptroller and Auditor § 5. The commissioners shall compare the warrants drawn on the treasury by the Comptroller and by the Auditor of the canal department for the preceding fiscal year, with the several laws under which such warrants are claimed to have been drawn, and shall certify and report whether such warrants were duly authorized by law. In case that any warrant shall be discovered which in their judgment was not duly authorized by law, the commissioners shall state that fact in their report, with their reasons for such judgment.

Accounts to be examined—canal fund, canal commissioners, superintendent of repairs, collectors. § 6. The commissioners shall also inspect the accounts of the commissioners of the canal fund, the accounts of the canal commissioners, the accounts of the superintendents of repairs, and of the collectors of tolls, and all other accounts kept in the canal department. They shall also inspect the accounts of the Inspectors of State Prisons, and of the several wardens and agents employed at the state prisons. *State prison inspectors.* They shall also inspect the condition, securities, and all the books and papers of *Banking and insurance departments.* the banking and insurance departments, and ascertain whether the same are kept in compliance with law. They shall also ascertain whether the moneys have been duly paid into the treasury as directed by law, from the several banking corporations for the maintenance of the banking department and the compensation of the superintendent and other persons connected with that department; from the several insurance companies for the maintenance of the insurance department and the compensation of the superintendent and other persons employed in that department; from the several gas light companies for the compensation of the inspectors of gas metres, and other expenditures made a charge upon such companies; and from the several railroad companies for expenses charged upon them for reports and services *State Engineer.* rendered in the department of the State Engineer and Surveyor.

Report annually to Governor. § 7. The commissioners shall deliver to the Governor, during the month of January in each year, a report duly signed and certified, which it shall be his duty to transmit immediately to the legislature. The report

shall contain a full statement of all the proceedings of ^{What to}
the commissioners, and a certificate of the amount of ^{contain.}
money received into the treasury during the preceding
fiscal year; the amount paid from the treasury during
the same period, by virtue of warrants from the Comptroller; what amounts have been paid from the treasury
upon warrants which they did not consider to be duly
authorized by law; the amount of money received by
the Treasurer when he entered upon the duties of his
office, and the remainder in the treasury at the close of
the last fiscal year. Such report shall also contain a
full statement of the condition of all accounts kept in
the canal department; the receipts and disbursements on
account of each and every canal and canal improvement,
and whether every such receipt and disbursement was
duly authorized by law; also, a full statement of the condition of all accounts kept at the several state prisons,
the receipts and disbursements on account of each and
every prison, and whether every such receipt and
disbursement was duly authorized by law; also, a full
statement of the condition of the banking department,
and whether the business of that department has been
managed and transacted in strict compliance with statute; and also, a like statement of the condition and
business of the insurance department. It shall also
state the amounts assessed to the several banking corporations for the maintenance of the banking department; to the several insurance companies for the maintenance of the insurance department, and to the several
gas light companies for the compensation of the inspectors of gas metres, and other expenses made a charge
on said companies, and shall specify the amount paid in
each year by every such company or corporation, and
the purposes to which the moneys so paid were applied,
and from the several railroad companies for expenses
charged on them for compensation of persons preparing
reports in the office of the State Engineer and Surveyor.

§ 8. Whenever any Treasurer, Auditor of the canal ^{On death of}
department, or Superintendent of the banking depart- ^{Treasurer, Auditor,}
ment, or Superintendent of the insurance department, ^{Superin- tendent of}
shall die or vacate his office during the term for which ^{banking or insurance}
he was chosen or appointed, or shall be succeeded at ^{depart-}
the close of his term by another person duly elected or ^{ment, Gov- ernor may}

require commissioners to examine accounts. appointed, the Governor may require, if he shall consider it to be necessary for the public interest, that these commissioners of public accounts shall make an examination of the accounts of such Treasurer, Auditor or Superintendent.

Majority of commissioners may act.

What considered a vacancy. § 9. The majority of the commissioners may perform all the duties required by this act. But any commissioner who shall omit or neglect, without sufficient reason, to perform the duties imposed by this act, shall be held to have' vacated his office, and the Governor shall proceed to appoint his successor.

Compensation of commissioners. § 10. The commissioners appointed under this act shall receive a compensation of five dollars for each day actually employed in the discharge of their duties, and the same allowance for mileage which is made to members of the legislature ; but such compensation shall not exceed five hundred dollars to each commissioner for Chapter 597 of laws of 1857 repealed. any one year. Chapter five hundred and ninety-seven of the laws of eighteen hundred and fifty-seven, is hereby repealed.

§ 11. This act shall take effect immediately.

Chap. 224.

AN ACT to release the interest which the State of New York may have acquired to the real estate of which Joseph Laville died seized to his widow, Catharine Laville.

Passed April 14, 1862 ; by a two-third vote.

The People of the State of New York, represented in Senate and Assembly, do enact as follows :

Description of premises. SECTION 1. All the right, title and interest of the people of the State of New York in and to the following described premises, to wit : " All that certain lot of land, with the buildings thereon, situated in the Fifth ward of the city of New York, and known and distinguished as number seventy-five, formerly eighty-three Leonard street, in said city of .New York;" and also sixteen certain lots of land, with the buildings thereon, situated

in the town of Newtown, near the village of Astoria,
Queens county and State of New York, and known on a
map of valuable building lots in the village of Astoria
and town of Newtown, in Queens county, Long Island,
" surveyed May one thousand eight hundred and fifty by
E. A. Smith, surveyor, filed or intended to be filed in
Queens county clerk's office as lots numbers from six
hundred and eighty-eight to six hundred and ninety-five,
both inclusive, and as lots numbers from seven hundred
and twelve to seven hundred and nineteen, both inclusive," of all which premises Joseph Laville, late of the
city of New York, died seized, is hereby released to
Catharine Laville, the widow of the said Joseph Laville,
to have and to hold to her the said Catharine Laville,
her heirs and assigns forever.

§ 2. Nothing herein contained shall be construed to No rights of
impair, release or discharge any right, claim or interest creditors to be released
of any creditor by mortgage, judgment or otherwise, or by this act.
of any heir or heirs at law of the said Joseph Laville,
or of any person claiming title under or through the said
Joseph Laville.

§ 3. This act shall take effect immediately.

Chap. 225.

AN ACT to authorize and require the Comptroller
of the State of New York to settle with the
treasurers of Essex and Warren counties in relation to rejected non-resident taxes.

Passed April 14, 1862; three-fifths being present.

*The People of the State of New York, represented in
Senate and Assembly, do enact as follows* :

SECTION 1. The Comptroller of the State of New York Sacketts
is hereby authorized and directed in his statement and Harbor and Saratoga R.
settlement of the accounts of non-resident taxes returned R. Com-
from the counties of Essex and Warren as non-resident, pany's lands in Es-
and of the state tax apportioned on and charged to said sex and Warren
county, to credit the treasurers of said counties of Essex counties.
and Warren with the amount of all taxes heretofore re-

jected by the Comptroller from the non-resident taxes returned as unpaid for the years eighteen hundred and fifty-seven, eighteen hundred and fifty-eight, eighteen hundred and fifty-nine and eighteen hundred and sixty, which were so rejected on the ground that the same were exempt from taxation by the provisions of an act entitled " An act exempting the land of the Sackett's Harbor and Saratoga Railroad Company from taxation, until the sale of the same or the maturity of their bonds," passed March thirteenth, eighteen hundred and fifty-seven, or of an act entitled " An act to facilitate the completion of the Lake Ontario and Hudson River Railroad," passed February eighteenth, eighteen hundred and sixty, or of both of said acts, and to cause any amount that may be found due to said treasurers of said counties of Essex, and Warren, after such credit, and after stating the account of said counties of Essex and Warren, as in other respects provided by law, to be paid to the treasurer of said counties of Essex and Warren, out of the treasury of this state.

§ 2. The Comptroller shall hereafter in his annual statements or settlements of the account of non-resident taxes returned from the counties of Essex and Warren as unpaid, not reject or disallow any part of said taxes so returned on the ground that the lands on which the same are assessed are exempt from taxation, under the acts above named in the first section of this act, or either of them ; but if said taxes are in other respects legally assessed and returned as unpaid, he shall admit and allow the same to the credit of said treasurers of said counties of Essex and Warren.

§ 3. This act shall take effect immediately.

Comptroller to return accounts of unpaid taxes in said counties.

Chap. 226.

AN ACT for the relief of Henry W. Best, a justice of the peace of the town of Cherry Valley, county of Otsego.

Passed April 14, 1862; three-fifths being present.

The People of the State of New York, represented in Senate and Assembly, do enact as follows:

SECTION 1. All the official acts of Henry W. Best, a justice of the peace of the town of Cherry Valley, in the county of Otsego, shall be deemed valid and effectual for all purposes, the same as though his oath of office had been filed in the office of the county clerk of Otsego county, previous to the first day of January, eighteen hundred and sixty-one.

§ 2. The said Henry W. Best shall have full power and authority to make and file his oath of office in the clerk's office of Otsego county, at any time within twenty days after this act shall become a law, and said oath so filed to have the same force and effect as though the same had been filed on or before the first day of January, eighteen hundred and sixty-one.

§ 3. This act shall not affect or inpair any suit or legal proceeding that may have been had or commenced by or before the said Henry W. Best as a justice of the peace.

§ 4. This act shall take effect immediately.

Chap. 227.

AN ACT granting and releasing all the right, title, and interest of the people of the State of New York in and to a messuage lot of land in the nineteenth ward of the city New York to Augusta Theresa Arnold and Mary Ulrich.

Passed April 14, 1862 ; by a two-third vote.

The People of the State of New York, represented in Senate and Assembly, do enact as follows :

Description of premises SECTION 1. All right, title, and interest of the people of the State of New York, in and to a lot of land in the nineteenth ward of the city of New York, containing as follows : Beginning at a point on the southerly side of Fifty-sixth street, distant one hundred feet easterly from the easterly side of Lexington avenue, running thence southerly and parallel with Lexington avenue one hundred feet ; thence easterly and parallel with Fifty-sixth street twenty-five feet ; thence northerly and parallel with Lexington avenue one hundred feet ; thence westerly along the southerly side of Fifty-sixth street twenty-five feet to the place of beginning, is hereby granted and released to Augusta Theresa Arnold, her heirs and assigns as heir at law of Wilhelm Ulrich, subject to the right of dower of Mary Ulrich, wife of Wilhelm Ulrich, deceased, therein ; and they are hereby authorized to take, hold, convey, and dispose of the same as aforesaid, in the same manner, and with the same force and effect as if they had been citizens of the United States at the time of the death of said Wilhelm Ulrich.

Not to affect creditors. § 2. This act shall not apply to or in any way affect the right of any judgment creditor, mortgagee, or any other person who may have any legal or equitable claim upon said lands, excepting as aforesaid.

§ 3. This act shall take effect immediately.

Chap. 228.

AN ACT in relation to non-resident highway taxes upon certain lands in the county of Hamilton, and to provide for laying out and constructing a public highway in said county.

Passed April 14, 1862; three-fifths being present.

The People of the State of New York, represented in Senate and Assembly, do enact as follows :

SECTION 1. William Burnham and Elijah Cole, of the town of Wells, in the county of Hamilton, are hereby appointed commissioners to lay out a public highway, commencing on the west side of Sacandaga river at the northeast line of township number one and lot number six, and running up said river to the Lake Pleasant branch, and thence up the Lake Pleasant branch to the foot of Lake Pleasant, a distance of about ten miles. Commis- sioners to lay out road

§ 2. The highway tax on all the following non-resident lands, shall be applied to the construction and repair of said highway, viz: all the non-resident lands in township number one in Totten and Crossfield's purchase, except the southwest corner; all of the non-resident lands in township number nine, Totten and Crossfield's purchase, and all of the non-resident lands in townships numbers ten and twenty-nine, in Totten and Crossfield's purchase, all of said lands being in the said county of Hamilton, not otherwise appropriated by chapter three hundred and thirteen of the Laws of eighteen hundred and sixty. Lands to be taxed.

§ 3. The county treasurer of Hamilton county shall pay over to the Comptroller of the state, when he makes his annual return of the arrears of the taxes, the amount of any highway taxes assessed upon any of said tracts or townships, which may have been paid over to the said treasurer, and the Comptroller shall pay over annually, all such moneys so received by him, to the said commissioners. Treasurer of Hamilton county to pay to Comptrol- ler highway tax on said lands.

§ 4. If the officers, or any of them, whose duty it shall be to assess the highway tax on said tracts of land mentioned in the second section of this act, shall omit Commis- sioners to assess the tax in cer- tain cases.

to make any assessment of the same, the commissioners appointed by this act shall make such assessment, and the tax so assessed by said commissioners shall be as valid in all respects, and shall be collected in the same manner as other highway taxes on non-resident lands are collected.

Commis-
sioners may
expend tax
on road.
§ 5. The said commissioners shall have power to expend the highway tax assessed on the several tracts and townships of land mentioned in the second section of this act, in laying out, constructing and keeping in repair said public highway.

Shall give a
bond.
§ 6. The said commissioners shall give a bond, with satisfactory sureties, to the treasurer of the county of Hamilton, in the sum of one thousand dollars, for the faithful performance of their duties, before entering upon the discharge thereof.

Exhibit an-
nually ac-
count of
their ex-
penditures.
§ 7. The said commissioners shall render, on oath, to the treasurer of the county of Hamilton, annually, before the first day of December in each year, an exhibit of their expenditures, with the necessary vouchers for the same.

Treasurer
of Hamilton
county to
fill vacancy
in commis-
sioners.
§ 8. The treasurer of the county of Hamilton shall have power to fill all vacancies that may occur in the office of said commissioners for any cause.

Per diem of
commis-
sioners.
§ 9. The said commissioners shall be paid and receive for their services one dollar and fifty cents for each day actually employed in the performance of their duties.

§ 10. This act shall take effect immediately, and continue in force six years.

Chap. 229.

AN ACT to amend an act entitled "An act to amend an act concerning the proof of wills,. executors and administrators, guardians and wards, and surrogate courts, passed May sixteenth, eighteen hundred and thirty-seven.

Passed April 14, 1862; three-fifths being present.

The People of the State of New York, represented in Senate and Assembly, do enact as follows:

SECTION 1. Section twenty-five of "An act to amend an act concerning the proof of wills, executors and administrators, guardians and wards, and surrogate courts, passed May sixteenth, eighteen hundred and thirty-seven," is hereby amended so as to read as follows : *(margin: Section 25 of act of May 16th, 1837, amended.)*

§ 25. Whenever any person interested in the estate of the deceased shall discover that the sureties of any executor or administrator are becoming insolvent, that they have removed or are about to remove from this state, or that for any other causes they are insufficient, such person may make application to the surrogate who granted the letters testamentary or of administration for relief. *(margin: When sureties are becoming insolvent, or are about to remove, &c.)*

§ 2. Section twenty-six of said act is hereby amended so as to read as follows : *(margin: Section 26 of said act amended.)*

§ 26. If the surrogate shall receive satisfactory evidence that the matter requires investigation, he shall issue a citation to such executor or administrator requiring him to appear before such surrogate, at a time and place to be therein specified, to show cause why he should not give further sureties or be superseded in the administration ; which citation shall be served personally on the executor or administrator at least six days before the return day thereof ; or if he shall have absconded or cannot be found, it may be served by leaving a copy at his last place of residence. *(margin: Executor or administrator to be cited to show cause in regard to sureties.)*

§ 3. Section twenty-seven of said act is hereby amended so as to read as follows : *(margin: Section 27 amended.)*

§ 27. On the return of the citation, or at such other time as the surrogate shall appoint, he shall pro- *(margin: If sureties insufficient, further)* sureties may be required.

ceed to hear the proofs and allegations of the parties, and if it shall satisfactorily appear that the sureties are for any cause insufficient, the surrogate may make an order requiring such executor or administrator to give further sureties in the usual form within a reasonable time, not exceeding five days.

Section 28 amended.

§ 4. Section twenty-eight of said act is hereby amended so as to read as follows:

When surrogate to revoke letters testamentary or administration.

§ 28. If such executor or administrator neglect to give further sureties to the satisfaction of the surrogate within the time prescribed, the surrogate shall by order revoke the letters testamentary or of administration issued to such executor or administrator whose authority and rights as an executor or administrator shall thereupon cease.

Section 29 amended.

§ 5. Section twenty-nine of said act is hereby amended so as to read as follows:

Sureties may make application to surrogate for relief.

§ 29. When either or all of the sureties of any executor or administrator shall desire to be released from responsibility on account of the future acts or defaults of such executor or administrator, they may make application to the surrogate who granted letters testamentary or of administration for relief.

Section 30 amended.

§ 6. Section thirty of said act is hereby amended so as to read as follows:

Executor and administrator to give new sureties.

§ 30. The surrogate shall thereupon issue a citation to such executor or administrator requiring him to appear before such surrogate at a time and place to be therein specified, and give new sureties in the usual form for the faithful discharge of his duties, which citation shall be served in the manner prescribed by the second section of this act.

Section 31 amended.

§ 7. Section thirty-one of said act is hereby amended so as to read as follows:

Release of old sureties.

§ 31. If such executor or administrator shall give new sureties to the satisfaction of the surrogate, the surrogate may thereupon make an order that the surety or sureties who applied for relief in the premises, shall not be liable on their bond for any subsequent act, default or misconduct of such executor or administrator.

Section 32 amended.

§ 8. Section thirty-two of said act is hereby amended so as to read as follows:

If new sureties not given letters.

§ 32. If such executor or administrator neglect to give new sureties to the satisfaction of the surrogate, on the return of the citation, or within such reasonable ters to be revoked. time as the surrogate shall allow, not exceeding five days, the surrogate shall by order revoke the letters testamentary or of administration issued to such executor or administrator whose authority and rights as an executor or administrator shall thereupon cease.

§ 9. Section thirty-three of said act is hereby amended Section 33 amended. so as to read as follows:

§ 33 In all cases in which letters testamentary or administration shall have been granted to more than one person, and the surrogate granting the same shall have revoked the same in pursuance of the previous provisions of this act, as to part only of such executors or administrators, the person or persons whose letters have not been revoked, shall have the further administration of the respective estates, subsequent to such revocation; When letters are revoked, as to part only, of several executors or administrators, the others continue to serve. any suit brought previous to such revocation may be continued the same as if no such revocation had taken place. In all other cases of revocation as aforesaid the surrogate shall grant administration of the goods, chattels and credits, not administered, in the manner prescribed by law. Not to affect pending suits.

§ 10. Section thirty-six of said act is hereby amended Section 36 amended. so as to read as follows:

§ 36. The surrogate shall have the same jurisdiction in requiring any executor or administrator, whose letters have been revoked, as hereinbefore provided, to render an account of his proceedings, as is conferred by the third article of title three, chapter six of the second part of the Revised Statutes. The new executor or administrator shall, within a reasonable time, or in case of his neglect, the other person mentioned in such article, may make application for such account, and such application may be made at any time after the revocation of the letters as aforesaid. Jurisdiction of surrogate to require accounting. New executor, administrator or other person, &c., may require accounting.

Chap. 230.

AN ACT for the release of certain lands and real estate of which Thomas Britton died seized to Eleanor Britton, his widow.

Passed April 14, 1862; by a two-third vote.

The People of the State of New York, represented in Senate and Assembly, do enact as follows:

SECTION 1. All the estate, right, title and interest of the people of the State of New York, of, in and to all the lands and real estate situate in the town of Albion in the county of Oswego, whereof the said Thomas Britton died siezed, or possessed, and devised by him to the said Eleanor Britton of said town, is hereby released to the said Eleanor Britton, his widow, her heirs and assigns forever.

§ 2. Nothing hereinbefore contained shall be construed to impair, release or discharge any right, claim or interest of any creditor by mortgage, judgment or otherwise.

§ 3. This act shall take effect immediately.

Chap. 231.

AN ACT to authorize Hanson A. Risley, as late clerk of Chautauqua county, to sign the records made during his term of office as such clerk.

Passed April 14, 1862.

The People of the State of New York, represented in Senate and Assembly, do enact as follows:

SECTION 1. Hanson A. Risley, the late clerk of Chautauqua county, is hereby authorized by the first day of July next to sign his name as such clerk to any records made in the books of records belonging to the clerk's office of said county during his term of office, which he omitted to sign before the expiration of his term of

office, and that such signing have the same force and
effect as if it had been made by him before the expiration of his said term of office; provided, however, that
no suit, action or proceeding now pending, nor any right
already acquired shall be affected hereby.

§ 2. This act shall take effect immediately.

Chap. 232

AN ACT to amend an act entitled "An act for
the better regulation of firemen in the city of
Brooklyn," passed February seventeenth, eighteen hundred and fifty-seven.

Passed April 14, 1862; three-fifths being present.

*The People of the State of New York, represented in
Senate and Assembly, do enact as follows:*

SECTION 1. The present commissioners of the fire department of the western district of the city of Brooklyn, and their successors in office, shall have the sole
charge, control, arrangement and government of the
organization now known as the fire department of the
western district of the city of Brooklyn, and shall have
full power to make and establish rules and regulations
for the government of all officers, members and companies thereof, and to punish any violation of such rules
and regulations, by reprimand, suspension, expulsion or
disbandment of the members or companies thereof.

§ 2. Said commissioners shall also have power to organize the said fire department, to increase or decrease
the number of companies or the members of such companies, and from time to time to make such changes therein
as they may deem necessary and proper, and generally
to exercise full and complete control and jurisdiction
over the said fire department, and no fire companies
shall be organized or located unless approved by the
said commissioners.

§ 3. It shall be the duty of the chief engineer of the
said fire department to present to the said commissioners the names of all persons applying to be appointed

Marginal notes:
Present fire commissioners to have full powers.
To organize fire department.
Duties of chief engineer.

firemen, and of all persons expelled or resigned from the
department, and on the same being duly investigated
and determined, the decisions of the said commissioners
thereon shall be final, unless an appeal shall be taken, as
hereinafter provided.

Board of appeals. § 4. There shall be appointed by the board of representatives a board of appeals, consisting of five exempt
firemen, who shall have ceased to be active members of
the department at least five years previous to their election; neither shall they be attached to any company
during their term of office, under the penalty of forfeiting their right to office.

Election for said board. § 5. The first election for the board of appeals under
this act, shall be held on the second Thursday in May,
eighteen hundred and sixty-two, and within ten days
after the said election, the persons so elected shall, in
the presence of the president of the fire department of
the city of Brooklyn, draw for the respective terms of
Their official term. office, to wit: one for the term of five years, one for the
term of four years, one for the term of three years, one
for the term of two years, one for the term of one year;
and annually thereafter there shall be elected one member of the board of appeals, to hold his office for the
term of five years; but each and every member of the
board of appeals shall hold his office until his successor
has been elected and duly qualified, and in case of a
vacancy occurring in the office of either or all of the
said members of the said board of appeals, either by
Vacancy how filled. death, removal or resignation, the vacancy shall be filled
at the next meeting of the board of representatives.

Members may appeal. § 6. Should any of the members or companies of the
fire department of the city of Brooklyn, against whom
sentence shall have been pronounced by the fire commissioners, think themselves aggrieved by such action,
they may, within ten days after the decision of the said
board of fire commissioners, bring their case before the
board of appeals, which board shall meet within twenty
days after notice of such appeal, and review the case.
Fire commissioners to review decisions. Should any disagreement arise between the board of appeals and the fire commissioners in regard to any decision of the latter, the same shall be referred back to
the fire commissioners for reconsideration, within thirty
days after the same shall have been first presented to
the board of appeals; and should the fire commission-

ers refuse to recede therefrom or reconsider the same, then their action shall be final, unless the board of appeals shall overrule such decision within ten days after it has been returned to them by the fire commissioners.

§ 7. All parties charged with a violation of any of the laws or ordinances relative to the fire department, shall be served with a notice, either personally or by leaving the same at their last place of residence, containing a copy of the said charges and the time and place of trial. *Violation of ordinances.*

§ 8. This act shall take effect immediately.

Chap. 233.

AN ACT to authorize the Watervliet Turnpike Company to construct and maintain a Railroad on their present road and to extend the same into and through the villages of West Troy and Cohoes and the town of Watervliet and the city of Albany, to increase the capital stock and to alter their corporate name.

Passed April 15, 1862; three-fifths being present.

The People of the State of New York, represented in Senate and Assembly, do enact as follows:

SECTION 1. The Watervliet Turnpike Company, in addition to their present rights, powers, franchises and privileges are also hereby authorized and permitted to construct and maintain one or more railroad tracks and ways, with all the necessary turnouts, branches and switches, upon the bed, or* one or both sides of their present turnpike road. And are also authorized, with the consent of the board of trustees of the village of West Troy, to extend, construct and maintain said railroad track or ways, from the northerly termination of said turnpike road, or any other more convenient point on said turnpike, on and through Broad street or any of the other streets in said village to some convenient point at or near the bridge across the west sprout of the Mohawk river, and to construct and maintain a branch railroad southerly through Broad street and any other street in *May construct one or more railroad tracks.* *To extend said track.*

* So in the original.

said village; and also to construct and maintain the same, and diverging branch or branches thereof by any eligible and convenient route to the village of Cohoes, and also to construct and maintain such railroad or ways with necessary branches, switches and turnouts in and through any of the streets or highways or alleys in the village of Cohoes, on first obtaining the consent of the trustees of said village of Cohoes to the construction thereof, within the corporate limits of said village; and are also empowered and authorized to extend their present turnpike road to the northerly line of the city of Albany, and to construct and maintain thereon one or more railroad tracks or ways; and are also hereby autho-

rized, with the consent and with such restrictions as may be deemed proper by the common council of the city of Albany, to extend and maintain such railroad track or tracks and ways from the southerly termination of said turnpike road, in and through Broadway, in said city to South Ferry street, by a single or double track where the carriage-way of said Broadway is of the width of forty-five feet and over, and by a single track where said carriage-way is less than forty-five feet; and the

said company are hereby required in winter to remove the snow from the surface of said carriage-way down to within one foot of the pavement where the width thereof will admit of it, where a double track is laid for a space of twenty feet in width on each side of said track from the outside rail, and where a single track is laid and the carriage-way is less than thirty-five feet wide, for the space of fifteen feet in width on each side of said

track from the rail; provided always that if said company construct said railroad through Broadway, in the city of Albany, they shall extend and maintain a branch track therefrom, through North Ferry street, to and through the Lumber District to the north bounds thereof, for a distance not exceeding in all one mile from their main road, and they are hereby authorized so to

do: also to use any existing bridge or bridges across the Erie and Champlain canal for the purpose of construct-ing, maintaining and operating thereon such railroad

tracks or ways, and to erect and maintain new and ad-ditional bridges for such purposes: provided however that the consent of the canal board shall be obtained thereto, and subject to such conditions and restrictions as the canal board shall from time to time impose: provided, always, that such new bridges shall not interfere with the use or navigation of the Erie or Champlain canals, and shall be constructed in a manner to be approved by the canal board.

§ 2. The track or tracks of said railroad or way, and all the branches, turnouts and switches thereof, shall be constructed with the most approved rail, and that part thereof which shall be constructed in, through or upon any of the public and paved street or streets in the city of Albany or the village of West Troy, or the village of Cohoes, shall be constructed and maintained flush with the surface of such street or streets, as they now are or may be from time to time established or altered, and the said company shall keep the surface of every such street inside the rail and for two feet outside thereof, at all times in good and proper condition and repair; and said railroad tracks or ways shall be so constructed and used as to leave on each side thereof a portion of the carriage way sufficient for the safe and convenient passage of carriages going in one direction and so as not to occupy more than half of the width of the present turnpike road or of the carriage way of any of the streets in the city of Albany or the villages of West Troy and Cohoes, through which the same may be constructed, and so as not unnecessarily to impair the public use of the remaining portion of the turnpike road and such street or streets by causing or permitting snow or dirt, taken from the said tracks or ways, to be placed thereon, or in any other manner, and in case said company neglect to keep the surface of the portion of any part of said Broadway, in the city of Albany, used by them, in good condition or repair, as hereinbefore provided, or cause or permit snow or dirt from the same to be placed on the remaining portion of said street, as above referred to, or otherwise obstruct said remaining portion, or neglect to remove therefrom surplus snow above one foot in depth, in the cases above herein provided, they shall be liable to the owner or occupant of the property on the line of said street opposite which any of the above grievances exist or have been done or permitted, in the penalty of fifteen dollars, to be recovered by an action at law, before any Justice of the Peace, on one day's notice being given to said company, and said suit may

Manner of constructing and maintaining said road.

Liable in penalty of $15 in certain cases.

May be sued before a justice

on notice being given be commenced by the service of a summons, on notice as aforesaid, being given, on any director of said company.

§ 3. It shall be lawful for said company, in constructing and operating such railroad track or ways, to construct, operate and run the same over and across the track of any existing highway or turnpike road, or the track and rails of any existing railroad company, but said company shall construct, maintain, and keep every such crossing in a proper, safe, and sufficient condition and repair, so as to allow at all times the ready, safe, and free passage of cars, and other vehicles, on and across the same, without hindrance or delay, nor shall such company cross or run over the track of the New York Central Railroad Company, unless on terms to be agreed upon between the two companies, and in case of disagreement between them, such terms shall be settled and determined on due notice to both parties, by the Supreme Court of the Third District at special term.

§ 4. The said turnpike company are hereby authorized to take, transport and carry property and persons upon the said railroad track or tracks, for compensation, by the power of horses, animals, or any mechanical or other power, or the combination of them, which the said company may choose to employ, except the force of steam, and may charge and collect from each and every person so carried, a fare not to exceed for any distance, not exceeding two miles, five cents, and for any excess over two miles at the rate of two cents per mile for such excess; and the board of directors of said company may regulate the time and manner in which property and passengers shall be transported and carried thereon; and may also, from time to time, fix, regulate, and establish the rates of charges and compensation to be paid and collected for the transportation of property and merchandize on its railroad, and may alter or modify the same at pleasure. But said company shall not, on Sunday, run their cars more than once an hour, to six o'clock P. M., and half hourly after six o'clock P. M., from each end of their road, for the transportation of passengers and their ordinary baggage, or for any other purpose, and nothing in this act shall authorize said company to run the freight cars of any other railroad upon their track through the city of Albany; nor shall said company carry on said track freight to or from any other railroad on which steam is used as a propelling power.

Marginal notes:

May run their track across highways, turnpikes or railroads.

Proviso as to Central railroad.

Not to use steam.

Rate of fare.

Powers of board of directors.

Sunday regulations.

Not to run freight cars of other companies. Nor any freight between certain railroads.

§ 5. For the purpose of defraying the costs and ex- May increase capital stock. penses of constructing and equipping and putting in full and complete operation the aforesaid railroad track and ways, with the branches, turnouts, switches and other necessary fixtures and appurtenances as above authorized, the said company may and they are hereby authorized to increase their capital stock, not exceeding one hundred and fifty thousand dollars. The amount of such increase of capital stock shall be determined by a resolution of board of directors of said company, within ninety days after the final passage of this act; such increase of the capital stock shall be divided into shares of one hundred dollars each, and shall be considered personal property, and shall be assignable and Stock transferable. transferable on the books of the company, in the same manner and as now authorized in relation to the present capital stock.

§ 6. Gilbert C. Davidson, Henry A. Brigham, Archi- Commissioners, to open books for subscription. bald A. Dunlop, James D. Wasson, Charles Van Benthuysen, James Roy, Charles B. Lansing, Joseph Badgley and Cornelius W. Armstrong, are hereby appointed commissioners, who shall, on or before the first day of January, eighteen hundred and sixty-three, meet at some suitable place in the village of West Troy, and also in the city of Albany, which they or a majority of them shall designate, to open books, and receive subscriptions to such increase of capital stock of said company. Public notice of the time and place of every Public notice to be given thereof. such meeting for such purpose, shall be given for at least six days previous to the same, in at least one newspaper printed in the village of West Troy, and one other newspaper printed in the city of Albany; the books when opened by the commissioners, shall remain Relating to subscribing for stock. open from nine o'clock in the forenoon until five o'clock in the afternoon of the day, for not exceeding three successive days, so that all persons may have a fair opportunity of becoming subscribers, and the sum of ten dollars on each share subscribed for, shall be paid by every subscriber, in current money, to the commissioners in attendance at the time of making such subscription, and no subscription shall be complete or valid without such payment at the time when the subscription is made. If more than the amount of the increase of the capital stock, as fixed, shall have been subscribed, then the commissioners shall proceed to distribute and apportion the same among the subscribers thereof, in such a manner as they shall deem most advantageous to the company.

§ 7. The said commissioners, after closing the books of subscriptions, provided at least eighty thousand dollars of such additional stock shall have been subscribed for, and ten per cent shall have been paid thereon as required in the previous section, shall then give six days' public notice in at least one newspaper printed in the city of Albany, and also in one of the newspapers printed in the village of West Troy, for a meeting of the owners of the present capital stock, and also of the subscribers to the additional stock, to choose nine directors and three inspectors of election. The said commissioners, or such of them as shall attend, shall preside at such election, receive and canvass the votes, and declare and certify the result. Every stockholder and subscriber for the additional stock, who may attend in person or by proxy, shall be entitled to one vote in each share held or subscribed for by him at the time of giving notice of such election. The directors and inspectors shall be chosen by ballot, and shall hold their office until the next annual election, as provided for by the present charter of the company; and the term of office of the directors and inspectors of said company who shall be in office at the time of such election, shall expire on the day of such election. If any vacancy in the office of directors or inspectors chosen at such election shall happen by death or resignation, such vacancy may be filled by the remaining directors until the next annual election.

§ 8. The said commissioners shall also, before opening the books for subscription to such additional stock, ascertain and appraise the fair value per share of the present capital stock of the said company on the amount actually paid in, and shall certify such valuation to the board of directors elected as prescribed in the last section, and shall also, without delay, deliver over to the said board of directors the subscription books and moneys received by them from the subscribers to the additional stock of the company; and the said board of directors and their successors in office may from time to time receive additional subscriptions for any part of

Side notes:

When commissioners shall call a meeting of stockholders.

Commissioners to preside.

Qualification of voters.

Manner of choosing officers and official term

Manner of filling vacancies of director or inspector.

Duties of commissioners.

such additional stock remaining unsubscribed for, or
which may have been forfeited by reason of non-payment of the same as required by the board of directors,
and without giving any new notice, and upon such terms
and conditions, not inconsistent with the provisions of
this act, which the board of directors may direct.

§ 9. The said commissioners, before performing any To be
of the duties imposed on them by this act, shall be sev- sworn.
erally sworn and qualified before some officer authorized
to administer oaths, that they will faithfully and impar-
tially execute and discharge all the duties imposed on
and required of them under this act.

§ 10. The directors of said company may demand and Powers of
require from the several subscribers to the additional directors.
stock of the company, payment of the stock by them
subscribed for, at such time and place and in such proportions as they may deem proper, under the penalty of
forfeiture of their respective shares, and all previous
payments thereon, and may also sue for and recover the
balance due on such subscriptions, but no subscriber for Amount re-
or owner of such additional stock shall be required to quired of
pay, in the aggregate, a greater sum on each share of to stock.
stock subscribed for or owned by him, than the appraised
valuation per share of the present stock, on the amount
paid in, as the same shall be appraised and certified by
the commissioners in the manner aforesaid.

§ 11. The said company, in addition to the powers, Company
authority and privileges granted and conferred by this have certain
act, shall have the power and authority mentioned and granted by
defined in and by the first, second, third, fifth, sixth, 2, 1850.
eigth, ninth and tenth subdivisions of the twenty-eighth
section, and in the thirty-fifth, forty-second and forty-
fifth sections of the act entitled "An act to authorize
the formation of railroad corporations, and to regulate
the same," passed April second, eighteen hundred and
fifty; but nothing in this section contained shall authorize the said company to use steam as a propelling power
on said road.

§ 12. Unless the said company shall construct and put Must build
in operation at least six continuous miles of said railroad a certain
track, with the necessary turnouts, branches and switch- within
es, within three years after the passage of this act, this three years.
act shall cease and be of no effect.

Corporate
name.
§ 13. The corporate name of the said company shall hereafter be the Watervliet Turnpike and Railroad company.

§ 14. This act shall take effect immediately.

Chap. 234.

AN ACT to provide for the payment of certain moneys expended in equipping the twentieth regiment of New York State militia.

Passed April 15, 1862; three-fifths being present.

The People of the State of New York, represented in Senate and Assembly, do enact as follows:

Treasurer
to pay not
to exceed
$12,000.
SECTION 1. The treasurer is hereby authorized and required to pay out of moneys in the treasury raised in pursuance of chapter two hundred and seventy-seven, of the laws of eighteen hundred and sixty-one, on the warrant of the Comptroller, a sum not exceeding twelve thousand dollars for moneys loaned and advanced in April, eighteen hundred and sixty-one, by the banks located in the town of Kingston, for the purpose of equipping the then twentieth regiment of New York State militia now in the service of the United States; the moneys hereby appropriated, to be paid only on the presentation of proper vouchers showing the loan and advance of said moneys, and the proper application thereof to the purposes above stated

Auditing
Board.
§ 2 The Inspector General, Judge Advocate General and Quartermaster General are hereby constituted /an auditing board to audit such claims as may be presented under the provisions of this act.

Governor to
present ac-
counts to U.
S. Govern-
ment.
§ 3. It shall be the duty of the Governor of this State to cause to be presented to the proper officers of the United States, accounts setting forth all payments made under the provisions of this act, with the proper vouchers thereof, and to effect the reimbursement of the same, and to pay into the treasury of this State all sums received in settlement for the same.

Chap. 235.

AN ACT to enable the people of this State to acquire certain lands situate in the town of Ossining, in the county of Westchester, for the use of the Sing Sing prison.

Passed April 15, 1862 ; three-fifths being present.

The People of the State of New York, represented in Senate and Assembly, do enact as follows :

SECTION 1. The Governor of this State is hereby autho- rized to take possession for the use of the people of this state, for the convenience of the Sing Sing prison, of the whole or of a part of a piece of land lying and being in the town of Ossining, in Westchester county, adjoining the Sing Sing prison ground on the south and bounded as follows : On the west by the Hudson river, on the north by the prison grounds, on the east by state land, and on the south by lands belonging to John Ryder and to others. Such piece of land so to be taken, not to exceed in quantity four acres of ground, and to be as much less as the Governor, with the advice of the inspectors of state prisons, shall deem necessary for the use and pur- poses of said Sing Sing prison. *(marginal note: Bounds of land taken. Quantity.)*

§ 2. The Governor is hereby authorized to cause a survey and map of so much of said land as he shall so decide to be necessary to be taken for said purposes, to be made and filed in the office of the State Engineer and Surveyor, and in case the Governor shall be unable to agree with the owner or owners of such lands and tena- ments for the purchase thereof, he shall proceed to cause the damages of such owner or owners to be assessed and paid in the manner pointed out in article four, title two of chapter nine, of part three of the Revised Statutes. The provisions of which article are hereby declared to be, and are made to apply to the land so to be acquired in all respects so far as the same shall be applicable thereto. *(marginal note: Map and survey to be made and filed in the office of State Engi- neer. Damages to be assessed in case of disagree- ment.)*

§ 3. This act shall take effect immediately.

Chap. 236.

AN ACT to release the interest of the State in certain lands of which John Turnbull died seized to Margaret Turnbull.

Passed April 15, 1862; by a two-third vote.

The People of the State of New York, represented in Senate and Assembly, do enact as follows:

SECTION 1. All the right, title, interest and estate of the people of this state in and to any real estate, lands and premises situate in the town of Bovina and county of Delaware and state aforesaid, of which John Turnbull died seized, acquired by the escheat of the same on the death of the said John Turnbull, is hereby released to Margaret Turnbull, her heirs and assigns forever.

This act not to impair any right or claim. § 2. Nothing herein contained shall be construed to impair, release or discharge any right, claim or interest of any creditor by mortgage, judgment or otherwise, or of any heir or heirs at law, now capable of taking the same by descent, or of any person lawfully claiming title under or through the said John Turnbull.

§ 3. This act shall take effect immediately.

Chap. 237.

AN ACT for the relief of Eliza Harrison, an alien.

Passed April 15, 1862; by a two-third vote.

The People of the State of New York, represented in Senate and Assembly, do enact as follows:

SECTION 1. The conveyance of a certain lot or parcel of land situate in the village of Niagara Falls, in the county of Niagara and State of New York, made by Samuel Goulding to Eliza Harrison, bearing date the twentieth day of February, in the year one thousand eight hundred and sixty-one, and recorded in the office of the clerk of Niagara county, in said state, in book number eighty-three of deeds, on page four hundred and fifty-three, and so forth, shall be of the same force, effect and validity, and confer the same title as if the said Eliza Harrison and George Harrison had always been citizens of the United States; and the said Eliza Harrison is hereby authorized to hold, devise and convey the said lot or parcel of land, and all the claim, right, title and interest of the people of this state to the said lot or parcel of land, by reason of the alienage of the said Eliza Harrison and George Harrison, are hereby released to the said Eliza Harrison.

§ 2. Nothing herein contained shall be so construed to impair, release, or discharge any right, claim or interest of any creditor, by mortgage, judgment or otherwise. *This act not to impair any right or claim.*

§ 3. This act shall take effect immediately.

Chap. 238.

AN ACT to amend an act entitled "An act to authorize the improving and keeping in repair a certain highway in the county of Putnam, and to assess certain non-resident lands along the line of said road to pay the expense of keeping the same in repair," passed March twenty-fourth, eighteen hundred and fifty-seven.

Passed April 15, 1862; three-fifths being present.

The People of the State of New York, represented in Senate and Assembly, do enact as follows:

SECTION 1. The county judge of Putnam county is hereby empowered and directed, between the first and fifteenth days of April next, to appoint three commissioners in the place of the three named in section one of said act, whose terms of office expire on the first day of May next. One of the commissioners so appointed shall be appointed for one year, one for two years, and one for three years, and the said county judge shall between the first and fifteenth days of April in each year hereafter, appoint one commissioner for three years to fill the

Appointment of commissioners.

Their official term.

55

vacancy that will occur by the expiration of the term of office of one of said commissioners on the first day of May in each year.

Parts of section 2 and 3 of act of March 24, 1857, repealed. § 2. The portions of sections second and third of said act, which limits the powers and duties of the commissioners to five years, are hereby repealed, and all the powers vested in and duties imposed upon the said commissioners named in section first of said act, by sections second and third of said act for five years, and all other powers vested in and duties imposed upon said commissioners by said act or by any amendments thereafter, are hereby vested in and imposed upon the commissioners hereafter appointed by the county judge as provided in section one of this act.

Road regulations. § 3. No person or persons shall at any time pass, ride, drive or carry on or over the said road or any part or portion thereof, more than forty hundred pounds at one load, on any vehicle on wheels, the rims or tires of which are less than five inches in width, nor shall any person drive over any part of said road with a wheel chained or in any other manner so fastened as to prevent it from turning on its axle except by the use of a shoe not less than six inches wide. **Penalty.** Whoever shall offend against any of the above provisions shall forfeit and pay to the commissioners the sum of ten dollars for each and every such offence, to be recovered with costs by said commissioners in their name in a civil action before any justice of the peace in Putnam county. All money so collected and recovered by said commissioners under and by virtue of this provision, shall be expended by them the same year in improving and keeping said road in repair.

Commissioners to make an annual exhibit. § 4. Said commissioners shall at the annual meeting of the supervisors of said county, submit to them on affidavit a true account of all money received by them and the amount expended with the proper voucher therefor.

§ 5. This act shall take effect immediately.

Chap. 239.

AN ACT to legalize the acts and proceedings of Samuel P. Marsh, as justice of the peace of the town of Verona, Oneida county.

Passed April 15, 1862; three fifths being present.

The People of the State of New York, represented in Senate and Assembly, do enact as follows :

SECTION 1. All proceedings by and before Samuel P. Marsh, acting as a justice of the peace in and for the town of Verona in Oneida county, prior to the first day of January, eighteen hundred and sixty-two, are hereby confirmed and shall be held to be of full force and validity.

§ 2. Nothing in this act shall be construed to affect any cause of action or suit or proceeding in cases where any suit has been commenced before the passage of this act, except as provided in the foregoing section.

§ 3. This act shall take effect immediately.

Chap. 240.

AN ACT to incorporate the fire department of the village of Corning.

Passed April 15, 1862; three-fifths being present.

The People of the State of New York, represented in Senate and Assembly, do enact as follows:

SECTION 1. All such persons as now are or shall here- *Name of* after be members of each and every fire company organ- *organiza-* ized by the trustees of the village of Corning, in the *tion.* county of Steuben, under the charter of said village, shall be and continue a body corporate by the name of "The Fire Department of the village of Corning," and they and their successors, by the said name, are autho- *May hold and convey* rized to purchase, receive by gift, or otherwise hold and *real and personal* convey any real and personal property for the use of *estate.*

said corporation, not exceeding in value the sum of ten thousand dollars

Board of trustees.

§ 2. There shall be a board of trustees, who shall have the management and control of the affairs and property of the said corporation, and such other powers, and subject to such obligations as hereinafter provided. The first trustees shall be Alexander Olcott, Alfred Jones, Charles H. Thomson, John N. Hungerford, Thaddeus E. Hunt, Hiram Pritchard, George W. Pratt, H. Alonzo Gorton, Cyrus D. Sill and William F. Ingle, of whom the following shall be the first officers, viz: Alexander Olcott, president; Alfred Jones, vice-president; George W. Pratt, secretary; who shall hold their respective offices until others are chosen in their stead.

President, vice-president and secretary.

Annual meeting.

§ 3. The said several fire companies shall, on the first Monday in January next, and on said day in each year thereafter, hold an election and thereat elect three persons from the members of said companies respectively, and the persons thus elected shall thereafter form the said board of trustees; and said board shall, on the first Wednesday after the first Monday in January next, and on said day in each year thereafter, choose, out of their own body, by ballot, a president, vice-president and secretary; the said secretary to be secretary of the department. The said companies shall also, on the third Tuesday in April next, and on said day in each year thereafter, hold an election and thereat elect a chief engineer, first assistant engineer, second assistant engineer and treasurer. The said elections shall be held by each company separately, and at their respective engine houses (unless it shall be necessary to hold the same at different places, in which case the same shall be held at such places as the said board shall direct.) The said board shall appoint from its members three inspectors of the first election of each of said companies, under this act, who shall act as such inspectors; and thereafter the three persons elected by said companies respectively, as their respective trustees, shall be the inspectors of all elections by their respective companies. The inspectors shall bring the returns of each election before the board of trustees aforesaid, at their first meeting after such election, and the said board shall meet within three days after each election, and examine into and decide the result thereof. And the said board shall, by

Election for engineers and treasurer.

Board appoint inspectors of election.

Duties of.

their president, or otherwise, as the board shall direct, make known to the trustees of the village aforesaid the result of each election for the offices of chief and assistant engineers, within three days after the same shall have been decided by them ; and said trustees of the village shall thereupon approve or disapprove of the engineers so elected ; and if said trustees of the village shall disapprove thereof, or of either thereof, or shall neglect to approve or disapprove thereof, or of either thereof, for two weeks after being thus notified of such election, then the board of trustees, by its secretary, shall call a special election of said companies, at their respective houses, at which shall be elected persons to fill said offices, or such of them as are not filled by such prior election and approved by said trustees of the village. All of the officers aforesaid shall hold their respective offices until the next election and until their successors shall be chosen as aforesaid.

Board to report result of election.

Trustees to approve or disapprove

Official term.

§ 4. The said trustees shall have power to make such by-laws, rules and regulations, from time to time, as they may deem expedient and proper, not inconsistent with the charter and by-laws of said village, and the laws of this State, and may be convened by the president, or as may be provided by said laws, rules and regulations. The treasurer shall give security to said board of trustees for the faithful performance of his duties ; and at every annual meeting, or oftener if required by the trustees, shall render to them a true account of the property of the department and of his action as treasurer. The said trustees shall have power to remove any of the officers of the board of trustees after three days previous notice in writing of the charges preferred, and elect others in their stead. A majority of the trustees shall constitute a quorum for the transaction of business. The board of trustees shall fill, from its members, all vacancies which may occur in the offices of said board until the next election after the occurrence of such vacancies ; and may by its president, or otherwise, as said board shall direct, call special elections to fill vacancies in any of the offices in this act mentioned. Notice of the time of all elections under this act shall be given by the secretary, at least five days before the time thereof, in at least one of the newspapers of the village.

Powers of board.

Treasurer.

Trustees may remove from office.

Fill vacancies.

Call special elections.

§ 5. The board of trustees shall apply the funds of said corporation which shall arise from chimney fines, certificates of membership, money paid by insurance companies in pursurance of law, fire warden's fines, penalties recovered for. violation of village fire ordinances, and donations, or such parts of said funds or of the income thereof, as they shall deem proper, to the relief of indigent and disabled firemen or their families ; and also defray such contingent expenses as may be necessary in the transaction of the business of said board of trustees.

§ 6. The fire companies aforesaid shall consist of at least thirty persons each, and the members of any of said companies which shall not contain that number, shall not be members of this corporation, except that if any company shall be reduced below said number the same shall not be disbanded nor forfeit any of its rights or privileges under this act, provided its said full number shall be filled within thirty days after said company shall be required so to do by the said board of trustees.

§ 7. Each of said fire companies shall have the right to pass by-laws for its own government, not inconsistent with the by-laws, rules and regulations established by the said board of trustees, or the charter and by-laws of the said village, and the laws of this state.

§ 8. The said fire department shall possess the general powers of a corporation, as defined and limited in title three of the eighteenth chapter of part first of the Revised Statutes of this state, and shall be subject to the provisions of such chapter so far as they may be applicable to said department and the organization thereof, and so far as the same are not inconsistent with this act.

§ 9. The said board of trustees shall have power to impose reasonable fines and penalties for violation by the members of said corporation of the by-laws, rules and regulations of said board, and to sue in the corporate name for the recovery of such penalties.

§ 10. All moneys which by law now are or hereafter may be directed to be paid into the treasury of said village, for the purposes of said fire department, and which now are or may hereafter by law be directed to be paid by any insurance companies or other companies or persons, or applied or recovered for the purposes of the fire department of said village, shall be payable to the treasurer of the said corporation.

§ 11. This act shall take effect immediately.

Chap. 241.

AN ACT to confirm certain acts of the officers and constituted authorities of the town of Newtown, county of Queens.

Passed April 15, 1862; three-fifths being present.

Whereas, the officers and constituted authorities of the town of Newtown, in the county of Queens, by a contract dated the twenty-sixth day of March, eighteen hundred and sixty-one, have consented that Stephen Scammon and Aaron Smith might build gas works, and lay down all necessary conductors for conducting gas through the streets, avenues and highways in said town of Newtown, and in and by the said contract have agreed to exempt the personal property employed for the purpose aforesaid from taxation, for a period of three years from the date of said contract, and that the said Stephen Scammon and Aaron Smith, and their assigns, should enjoy the exclusive privilege of lighting the streets, avenues and highways and public and private buildings in the said town by gas as aforesaid, and of laying gas pipe through the said avenues, streets and highways therefor, *(Contract made with S. Scammon and A. Smith.)*

The People of the State of New York, represented in Senate and Assembly, do enact as follows:

SECTION 1. The powers, privileges, exemptions and rights given and granted, or intended to be given and granted as above recited, by the constituted authorities of the town of Newtown, in the county of Queens, to the said Stephen Scammon and Aaron Smith as aforesaid, are hereby granted to and vested in the said Stephen Scammon and Aaron Smith, and their assigns, for the period of twenty years. But nothing herein contained shall prevent any person from manufacturing gas and using the same upon his own premises or property. *(Contract hereby confirmed.)*

§ 2. The legislature may at any time alter, modify or repeal this act.

§ 3. This act shall take effect immediately.

Chap. 242.

AN ACT to amend an act entitled "An act for the better support of the poor in the town of Newburgh, in the county of Orange," passed March twenty-third, eighteen hundred and fifty-three.

Passed April 15, 1862 ; three-fifths being present.

The People of the State of New York, represented in Senate and Assembly, do enact as follows :

SECTION 1. The fourth section of the act entitled "An act for the better support of the poor in the town of Newburgh, in the county of Orange," is hereby amended by striking out " all reasonable hours," and inserting instead thereof, such hours as said commissioners may designate.

§ 2. This act shall take effect immediately.

Chap. 243.

AN ACT making further provisions relative to encroachments upon highways.

Passed April 15, 1862 ; three-fifths being present.

The People of the State of New York, represented in Senate and Assembly, do enact as follows :

Proceedings upon hearing before jury.

SECTION 1. Upon the hearing before a jury, as provided in section one hundred and six of article fifth, title first, chapter sixteenth and part first of the Revised Statutes, the justice who has issued the precept to such party shall preside at the trial, in the same manner as upon the trial of an issue joined in a civil action com-

menced before him; six of the jurors summoned shall
be drawn and impanneled in the same manner as upon
trial by jury in civil action before him, and he shall
have the power and it shall be his duty to decide as to the
competency of jurors, the competency and admissibility
of evidence, and all other questions which may arise
before him, in the same manner and with the like effect
as upon a jury trial in civil actions before him; and
such justice shall adjust and determine the costs of such
inquiry, and in case the jury shall find an encroachment, Judgment
he shall render and docket a judgment to that effect, and dered.
for such costs against the person or persons who shall
have denied such encroachment; in case the jury find
no encroachment, he shall render and docket a judgment
to that effect against the commissioner or commissioners prosecuting the proceedings, and also for such costs,
together with the damages, if any, which may have been
fixed by the jury, and payment thereof shall be enforced
by such justice, as in other cases of judgments rendered
by him.

§ 2. The person or party against whom such judg- Right of ap-
ment shall be rendered, may, within sixty days after peal.
filing the certificate of the jury, appeal from the finding
and judgment to the county court of the same county;
such appeal shall be made by the service, within twenty
days after the docketing of said judgment, of notice of
appeal upon the justice and upon the successful party
or parties, or one of them, stating the grounds of such
appeal. It shall be the duty of such justice, in his return to such appeal, to embrace copies of all the papers
made and served in the proceeding prior to issuing the
precept for such jury, and all the evidence and proceedings before him, together with the finding of the jury
and judgment entered thereon. All the provisions Provisions
of title eleven, chapters third and fifth of the Code of chapters 3
Procedure are hereby extended to such appeals, so far and 5 of
as the same are applicable thereto.   plied.

§ 3. In case the decision of the jury finding an en- Proceed-
croachment shall be affirmed by the appellate court, such peal.
court, in addition to the costs now allowed by law, may
in its discretion order judgment against the appellant
for the penalties provided by section one hundred and
four of article one, title one, chapter sixteen, part first
of the Revised Statutes aforesaid, for such period as

56

shall intervene between the time fixed for the removal
of fences, as provided by section one hundred and seven
of the said article, title and chapter, and the decision of
such appeal; and in case of the continued neglect or
refusal of the occupant, after judgment, to make such
removal, the court rendering judgment may, by order
from time to time, enforce the additional penalties incurred, or may provide for the removal of such fences
at the expense of the occupant, payment of such expense to be enforced by order. Such applications to be
made according to the usual practice of the court.

§ 4. This act shall apply to all proceedings now pending in relation to encroachments upon highways, where
a hearing has not already taken place, and all acts or
parts of acts inconsistent with this act are hereby repealed, so far as proceedings had or continued under
this act are concerned.

§ 5. This act shall take effect immediately.

Chap. 244.

AN ACT to provide for taxing dogs and for the
collection of such tax, and to create a fund to
pay for injuries upon sheep occasioned by dogs.

Passed April 15, 1862; three-fifths being present.

*The People of the State of New York, represented in
Senate and Assembly, do enact as follows:*

SECTION 1. Section first, title seventeen, chapter twenty, part first of the Revised Statutes is hereby amended
so as to read as follows:

In all the counties of the state except the city and
county of New York, there shall be annually levied and
collected the following tax upon dogs: Upon every
bitch owned or harbored by any one or more persons, or
by any family, three dollars; upon every additional
bitch owned or harbored by the same person or persons
or family, five dollars; upon every dog other than a
bitch owned or harbored by one or more persons or by
any family, fifty cents, and upon every additional dog,

Marginalia:
Penalties incurred after judgment, how enforced.

Applied to pending proceedings—certain acts repealed.

Section 1, title 17, chapter 20, first part of Revised Statutes repealed.

Tax.

other than a bitch, owned or harbored by the same person or persons or families, two dollars.

§ 2. Section four of said title, chapter and part, is hereby amended so as to read as follows:

The assessors of every town or city or ward of a city, _{Duty of as-} except the city of New York, shall annex to the assess- _{sessors.} ment roll of real and personal estate therein, made by them annually, the name of each and every person or persons liable to the tax imposed hereby, together with the number of bitches and dogs for which such person or persons is or are assessed, and return the same to the supervisor of their respective towns, cities, or wards of cities, to be laid by said supervisor before the board of supervisors, to be by them collected in the same manner as other state and county and town taxes are collected. And if any person duly assessed shall refuse _{When dog} or neglect to pay the tax so assessed within five days of _{to be killed.} the demand thereof, it shall be lawful for any person, and it shall be the duty of the collector to kill the dog so taxed.

§ 3. Section five of said title, chapter and part, is _{Section 5 of} hereby amended by striking out the words " sixty days _{said chap-} from the time of such delivery," and inserting the _{ter amend-} words, " the time now required by law for the collection _{ed-} of taxes laid by said supervisors."

§ 4. Section seven of said title, chapter and part, is _{Section 7 of} hereby amended so as to read as follows: _{said chapter amended.}

Each collector shall be allowed to retain a commission of ten dollars on every hundred dollars collected, and at that rate upon all sums collected by him pursuant to the direction of the supervisors; and said collectors shall also, on filing his affidavit of the fact with the county treasurer, be entitled to retain as a further compensation, from the moneys collected by him, the sum of one dollar for every dog or bitch killed by him under the provisions of the second section of this act.

§ 5. Section ten of the said chapter, title and part, is _{Section 10} hereby amended by inserting after the words " fence _{of said chapter} viewers of the town" therein, the further words, " or _{amended.} assessors of the city or of the ward of the city."

§ 6. Section eleven of the said title, chapter and part, is _{Section 11} hereby amended by striking out the words "due notice" _{of said chapter} and inserting in the place thereof the words " notice in _{amended.} writing of the time and place of such view, shall have been served, at least twenty-four hours before, on the said owner or possessor, either personally or by leaving at his dwelling house with a person who usually dwells therein and who shall have arrived at the age of sixteen years," and by striking out the words "to the fence viewers" in the last line thereof.

Sections 12 and 13 of said chapter amended. § 7. Section twelve of the said title, chapter and part, is hereby amended by striking out the words "of the fence viewers," and inserting the words "mentioned in the tenth section," and section thirteen thereof is hereby amended by striking out the words "constituted by the eighth section of this title," and inserting the words "to be raised by said tax."

Power of collectors. § 8. The several collectors to whom any warrant for the collection of the tax herein mentioned shall be delivered, shall have all the powers, for the collection thereof, which such collectors now have, and they and their sureties shall be subject to all the liabilities there for which such collectors and their sureties are now subject to.

When payment of tax to be proved § 9. In any action brought for the killing of any dog, it shall be incumbent on the plaintiff in said action to prove that the tax imposed upon such dog by the provisions of this act has been paid.

Certain acts repealed. § 10. Section two of said title, chapter and part, and all acts or parts of acts, whether general or local, inconsistent with the act hereby amended or repugnant thereto, are hereby repealed.

§ 11. This act shall take effect immediately, except section nine, which shall take effect on the first of November next.

Chap. 245.

AN ACT to amend an act entitled "An act in relation to the auditing accounts by the boards of supervisors of Onondaga and other counties and the duties of certain officers in said counties," passed March twenty-sixth, eighteen hundred and sixty-one.

Passed April 15, 1862 ; three-fifths being present.

The People of the State of New York, represented in Senate and Assembly, do enact as follows :

SECTION 1. Section first of the act entitled "An act in relation to the auditing of accounts by the boards of supervisors of Onondaga, Tioga, Oneida, Fulton, Monroe, Broome, Delaware, Cayuga, Orange. Jefferson, Richmond, Livingston, Chenango, Suffolk, Ulster, Dutchess, Steuben and Niagara, and the duties of certain officers in said counties in connection therewith," passed March twenty-sixth, eighteen hundred and sixty-one, is hereby amended so as to read as follows : *Act of March 26, 1861, amended.*

§ 1. The supervisors of the counties of Onondaga, Tioga, Oneida, Fulton, Monroe, Broome, Delaware, Cayuga, Orange, Jefferson, Richmond, Livingston, Chenango, Chemung, Ulster, Dutchess, Steuben, Niagara, Columbia and Herkimer, by their clerks, shall provide boxes with suitable inscriptions thereon and with openings in the top, to be kept in the offices of the clerks of said counties and in their charge, under lock and key, in which shall be deposited by said clerks, all accounts and claims against said counties, duly verified according to law ; and whenever said boards shall severally for themselves order, the clerks of said boards shall take from said boxes all bills and accounts against said counties, which they shall then file and number, and it shall not be lawful for the said boards of supervisors, in any one year, to audit as against said counties any other bill or account than such as shall have been deposited in said boxes, or otherwise in their possession, upon the morning of the fourth day of the annual meeting of said boards ; except bills for the services of supervisors, *Clerks of boards of supervisors to provide boxes for accounts and claims.* *Accounts to be audited must be in their possession on fourth day of meeting except in certain cases.*

their clerks and janitors, and except bills for services or disbursements rendered or made during the session of the board.

Further amended. § 2. Said act is hereby further amended by adding thereto a new section as follows:

This law may be made applicable to any other county. Whenever the board of supervisors of any county of this state shall by resolution declare that the provisions of this act shall be extended and made applicable to such county, the provisions of this act shall thereafter be applicable to such county.

§ 3. This act shall take effect immediately.

Chap. 246.

AN ACT to amend the provisions of the Revised Statutes in relation to jurisdiction over divorces.

Passed April 15, 1862; three-fifths being present.

The People of the State of New York, represented in Senate and Assembly, do enact as follows:

SECTION 1. The second subdivision of the thirty-eighth section of article third, title first, part second, chapter eighth of the Revised Statutes, is hereby amended so as to read as follows:

When marriage dissolved for adultery. Where the marriage has been solemnized or has taken place within this state, or where the injured party at the time of the commission of the offence and at the time of exhibiting the bill of complaint shall be an actual inhabitant of this state.

§ 2. Section thirty-one of article second of title one of chapter eight of the scond part of the Revised Statutes, is hereby amended so as to read as follows, to wit:

When marriage not to be annulled No marriage shall be annulled on the ground of force or duress, if it shall appear that at any time before the commencement of the suit, there was a voluntary cohabitation of the parties as husband and wife, nor on the ground of fraud, where there was such voluntary cohabitation with full knowledge of the facts constituting the fraud.

§ 3. This act shall take effect immediately.

Chap. 247.

AN ACT to authorize the city of Brooklyn to issue bonds in payment of moneys borrowed for the equipment of volunteers and militia for the present war, and the support of their families.

Passed April 16, 1862; three-fifths being present.

The People of the State of New York, represented in Senate and Assembly, do enact as follows:

SECTION 1. The temporary bonds heretofore issued by the common council of the city of Brooklyn to banks in said city and to other persons, for moneys advanced for the equipment of volunteers and militia and the support of their families, and amounting in the aggregate to the sum of one hundred and fifteen thousand five hundred and eighty-eight dollars and fifty-six cents, are hereby legalized and declared to be valid claims against the said city of Brooklyn. *The temporary bonds legalised.*

§ 2. For the purpose of paying said temporary bonds, the mayor, comptroller and clerk of said city are hereby authorized and directed to issue the corporate bonds of said city for said sum of one hundred and fifteen thousand five hundred and eighty-eight dollars and fifty-six cents, bearing seven per cent semi-annual interest for a term not exceeding three years from their date. The joint board of aldermen and supervisors of the city of Brooklyn are hereby directed to make provision for the payment of said interest and of the principal of said bonds from time to time, as the same may become due and payable. *Corporate bonds to be issued.*

§ 3. Nothing in this act contained shall be construed to impair the claim of the said city to be refunded by the state or general government such portion of said moneys as were advanced for the equipment of militia and volunteers for the present war. *Claim of city in state and general government not to be impaired.*

§ 4. This act shall take effect immediately.

Chap. 248.

AN ACT in relation to plank roads and turnpike roads.

Passed April 16, 1862; three-fifths being present.

The People of the State of New York, represented in Senate and Assembly, do enact as follows:

Certain plank roads and turnpike companies deemed duly incorporated.

SECTION 1. No plank road or turnpike road company, corporation or association heretofore formed or organized under the act entitled "An act for the incorporation of companies to construct plank roads and companies to construct turnpike roads," passed May seventh, eighteen hundred and forty-seven, and the several acts amending the same, shall be deemed invalid, or to have forfeited any of its powers, rights or franchises by reason of any failure on the part of such company or the persons organizing the same, to have complied with the requirements of such acts in the formation or organization of such company, as to the number of stockholders or persons who signed the articles of association of such company or association, or in the publication of notices in the organization thereof, or by reason of any informality or defect in the signing such articles of association or in the publication of the notices aforesaid; and the stockholders, officers and creditors of every such company are hereby declared to have the same rights and the stockholders to be subject to the same obligations and liabilities as if such company had strictly complied with all the requirements of the law aforesaid, to create and perfect a complete body corporate; provided

Proviso.

that this act shall only apply to such companies as shall have attempted an organization, and shall have actually constructed a road wholly or in part according to their articles of association.

Pending suits or proceedings not affected

§ 2. Nothing in this act contained shall affect any suit or proceeding now pending in any court of this state.

Chap. 249.

AN ACT to alter the map of the late village of Williamsburgh, now part of the city of Brooklyn.

Passed April 17, 1862 ; three-fifths being present.

The People of the State of New York, represented in Senate and Assembly, do enact as follows:

SECTION 1. The map of the late village of Williamsburgh, made under and by virtue of the nineteenth section of the act entitled "An act to incorporate and vest certain powers in the freeholders and inhabitants of the village of Williamsburgh, in the county of Kings," passed April fourteenth, eighteen hundred and twenty-seven, is hereby altered and amended as follows :

All that part of a certain street laid down on the said map west of and parallel with First street, commonly known as River street, which lies north of Grand street in the fourteenth ward of the city of Brooklyn, is hereby discontinued and closed.

§ 2. This act shall take effect immediately.

Chap. 250.

AN ACT to amend an act entitled "An act to incorporate the Citizens' Savings Bank of the city of New York," passed April fifth, eighteen hundred and sixty.

Passed April 17, 1862.

The People of the State of New York, represented in Senate and Assembly, do enact as follows :

SECTION 1. Section first of the act entitled "An act to incorporate the Citizens' Savings Bank of the city of New York," passed April fifth, eighteen hundred and sixty, is hereby amended by inserting after the words "seventeenth ward," the words "or sixth ward."

§ 2. This act shall take effect immediately.

Chap. 251.

AN ACT relative to documentary evidence.

Passed April 17, 1862; three-fifths being present.

The People of the State of New York, represented in Senate and Assembly, do enact as follows:

SECTION 1. The record of any bill of sale, mortgage, hypothecation or conveyance of any vessel of the United States, duly recorded in the office of the collector of customs where such vessel is registered or enrolled, or a transcript or copy thereof duly certified by said collector, may be read in evidence in any of the courts of this state, and in any judicial proceedings in this state, with the like force and effect as the original bill of sale, mortgage, hypothecation or conveyance.

§ 2. This act shall take effect immediately.

Chap. 252.

AN ACT to amend an act to increase the number of firemen in the village of Rhinebeck, passed February sixth, eighteen hundred and forty.

Passed April 17, 1862; three-fifths being present.

The People of the State of New York, represented in Senate and Assembly, do enact as follows:

SECTION 1. In addition to the powers already granted to the trustees of the village of Rhinebeck, they shall have power and they are hereby authorized at their discretion to form a hose company to be composed of twenty-five members, in accordance with section twelve of the act passed April twenty-third, eighteen hundred and thirty-four, entitled "An act to incorporate the village of Rhinebeck," and the amendment thereto, passed February sixth, eighteen hundred and forty, entitled "An act to increase the number of firemen in the village of Rhinebeck."

§ 2. This act shall take effect immediately.

Chap. 253.

AN ACT to cede the jurisdiction of this State to the United States over lands in the city of Buffalo.

Passed April 17, 1862; three-fifths being present.

The People of the State of New York, represented in Senate and Assembly, do enact as follows:

SECTION 1. Consent is hereby given to the Government of the United States of America to purchase such lands in the city of Buffalo for the erection of forts, magazines, arsenals, dock-yards and other needful buildings as it shall deem necessary for the protection and defence of said city, and on acquiring title thereto the jurisdiction over the same shall vest in the said United States; but the jurisdiction hereby granted shall not impede or prevent the execution of any legal process, civil or criminal, under the authority of this state, except such as may affect the real or personal property of said United States.

§ 2. The jurisdiction hereby granted shall cease whenever the said United States shall cease to occupy said lands for the purposes aforesaid, but during such occupancy, and no longer, said lands shall be exempt from all taxes, assessments or other charges under the authority of this State.

§ 3. This act shall take effect immediately.

Chap. 254.

AN ACT for the relief of John Lloyd.

Passed April 17, 1862; three-fifths being present.

The People of the State of New York, represented in Senate and Assembly, do enact as follows:

SECTION 1. The sum of five hundred dollars awarded to John Lloyd by the canal appraisers, on the twenty-second day of December, eighteen hundred and fifty-nine, by virtue of the power conferred upon them by chapter two hundred and forty-four of the laws of eighteen hundred and fifty-seven, shall be paid by the treasurer on the warrant of the Auditor, to the said John Lloyd, out of any moneys in the treasury hereafter appropriated to pay canal damages, notwithstanding that two years have elapsed since the passage of the act chapter two hundred and forty-four of the laws of eighteen hundred and fifty-seven.

§ 2. This act shall take effect immediately.

Chap. 255.

AN ACT for the relief of the estate of David S. Colvin, deceased.

Passed April 17, 1862; three-fifths being present.

The People of the State of New York, represented in Senate and Assembly, do enact as follows:

SECTION 1. The executrix of the estate of David S. Colvin, deceased, is hereby authorized to file with the appraiser a claim for damages to the property of said Colvin, by the Erie Canal enlargement, with the same effect as though said claim had been filed within one y   after the appropriation of the land of said Colvin by the state.

§ 2. This act shall take effect immediately.

Chap. 256.

AN ACT to authorize the appraisal and payment of canal damages to Conley M. Morgan and Carter H. Morgan.

Passed April 17, 1862; three-fifths being present.

The People of the State of New York, represented in Senate and Assembly, do enact as follows :

SECTION 1. The canal appraisers are hereby authorized and required to hear and determine the claim of Conley M. Morgan and Carter H. Morgan for alleged damages sustained by them by reason of a portion of their land situated in the town of Cuba, in the county of Allegany, being taken by the state for the construction of Oil Creek reservoir, and other damages sustained by them by reason of such construction ; and if upon such examination they find that said Morgans have from the cause above named suffered any injury to their said property, for which the state is legally and justly liable, they shall award said Morgans such damages therefor as shall in their opinion be just and equitable, subject to appeal to the canal board as in other cases. *Right to appeal given.*

§ 2. Nothing in this act contained shall be construed to authorize the canal appraisers to award any damages for land taken or injuries sustained from the cause above named for which an award has already been made.

§ 3. The treasurer shall pay on the warrant of the auditor, such sums as may be finally awarded in pursuance of the first section of this act, out of any moneys appropriated or to be appropriated for the payment of canal damages.

§ 4. This act shall take effect immediately.

Chap. 257.

AN ACT to authorize the appraisal and payment of canal damages to Walter O. Talcott.

Passed April 17, 1862; three-fifths being present.

The People of the State of New York, represented in Senate and Assembly, do enact as follows:

SECTION 1. The canal appraisers are hereby authorized and required to hear and examine the alleged claim of Walter O. Tallcott, for permanent and temporary injury done to his farm, situated about one mile from the village of Cuba, in the county of Allegany, and injuries done to the crops thereon, by surplus water from the Oil Creek reservoir overflowing a portion of the said premises, since the first day of April, one thousand eight hundred and fifty-eight; and if, upon such examination, they find that said Talcott has sustained damages from the aforesaid cause, for which the state is justly liable, they shall appraise such damage, and make such awards therefor as they deem just and reasonable, subject to an appeal to the canal board, as in other cases.

Right to appeal given.

§ 2. The state treasurer shall pay, on the warrant of the auditor of the canal department, the sum finally awarded to said claimant, in pursuance of the first section of this act, out of any money in the treasury appropriated or to be appropriated to the payment of canal damages.

§ 3. This act shall take effect immediately.

Chap. 258.

AN ACT to enable the schools of the childrens' aid society to participate in the distribution of the common school fund.

Passed April 17, 1862; three-fifths being present.

The People of the State of New York, represented in Senate and Assembly, do enact as follows:

SECTION 1. The industrial schools established and maintained under the charge of the childrens' aid society in the city of New York, shall participate in the distribution of the common school fund, in the same manner and degree as the common schools of the city and county of New York, and shall be subject to the same regulations and restrictions as are now by law imposed on the common schools of the city and county of New York.

§ 2. This act shall take effect immediately.

Chap. 259.

AN ACT for the relief of Levi Bennett.

Passed April 17, 1862; three-fifths being present

The People of the State of New York, represented in Senate and Assembly, do enact as follows:

SECTION 1. The canal appraisers are hereby authorized and directed to examine the claim of Levi Bennett for damages alleged to have been sustained by him on account of the damming up and diversion of the waters of the Cowassalon creek, in the year eighteen hundred and fifty-seven, caused by the obstruction of a culvert under the Erie canal, at the town of Lenox, in Madison county, in that year; and if they find that he has, for that cause, suffered any damages for which the state is legally and justly liable, they shall appraise the same and make such award therefor as shall be just

Right to appeal given. and equitable, subject to an appeal to the canal board as in other cases.

§ 2. The treasurer shall pay, on the warrant of the auditor of the canal department, such sum, if any, as shall be awarded under the first section of this act, to the said Levi Bennett, out of any money in the treasury appropriated or to be appropriated to the payment of canal damages.

§ 3. This act shall take effect immediately.

Chap. 260.

AN ACT for the relief of Otis Smith.

Passed April 17, 1862; three-fifths being present.

The People of the State of New York, represented in Senate and Assembly, do enact as follows:

SECTION 1. The canal appraisers are hereby authorized and required to examine the claim of Otis Smith, of Pittsford, in the county of Monroe, for damages alleged to have been sustained by him since the passage of chapter six hundred and seventy of the laws of eighteen hundred and fifty-seven, on account of the discharge of the waters from the Erie canal through the waste-wier at or near Cartersville on said canal, and which from the same cause he will sustain hereafter; and if the said Otis Smith has sustained and is likely hereafter to sustain damages from the cause aforesaid, for which the state ought justly to remunerate him, the said canal appraisers are hereby authorized to appraise the same, and to make such award to him therefor as shall to them seem just Right to appeal given. and equitable, subject to appeal to the canal board as in other cases; such award when made to be in full for all damages, past and future, that may be or have been sustained by the said Otis Smith for the cause aforesaid, his heirs and assigns.

§ 2. The Treasurer shall pay, on the warrant of the Auditor of the canal department, such sum, if any, as may be awarded in pursuance of the first section of this act, to the said Otis Smith, out of any money in the treasury appropriated or to be appropriated to the payment of canal damages.

§ 3. This act shall take effect immediately.

Chap. 261.

AN ACT for the relief of Allen T. Goldsmith for canal damages.

Passed April 17, 1862; three-fifths being present.

The People of the State of New York, represented in Senate and Assembly, do enact as follows:

SECTION 1. Allen T. Goldsmith, of the town of Palmyra, in the county of Wayne, shall have the same right for the term of two months from the passage of this act, to make and exhibit to the canal appraisers a statement of his claim for damages suffered by him in consequence of the appropriation by the state of a portion of a farm owned by him, at the time of the enlargement of the Erie canal at Palmyra, to its use in making such enlargement, that any person suffering such damage has to make and exhibit such claim, by section eighty-four, article three, chapter nine, title nine, part first of the fifth edition of the Revised Statutes of this state.

§ 2. Before such canal appraisers shall entertain such application, such claim shall be made and exhibited in the same manner, and specifying the same with the same particularity as is required by the section of the Revised Statutes named in the first section of this act.

§ 3. Whenever, within the time mentioned in the first section of this act, such statement shall be made and exhibited to the said canal appraisers in the manner prescribed by the second section thereof it shall be the duty of the canal appraisers to entertain such application, and thereafter to take the same proceedings in appraising the damages suffered by the said Allen T. Goldsmith, by the cause mentioned in the first section of this act, as are now provided by law for appraising the damages of persons upon claims made and exhibited in pursuance of the section of the Revised Statutes named in the first section herein; and said damages, when so appraised, or

58

the amount thereof finally adjudicated by the canal board in case of an appeal to such board, which appeal is hereby authorized, as in other cases, shall be paid in the same manner as the damages appraised under the section last aforesaid are now provided to be paid by law.

§ 4. This act shall take effect immediately.

Chap. 262.

AN ACT for the relief of James O'Brien.

Passed April 17, 1862; three-fifths being present.

The People of the State of New York, represented in Senate and Assembly, do enact as follows:

SECTION 1. The canal appraisers are hereby authorized and directed to examine the claim of James O'Brien, for damages alleged to have been sustained by him in consequence of the inundation of certain lands owned by him in the town of Fort Edward in Washington county, alleged to have been caused by the overflow of the banks of the Champlain canal on or about the ninth day of June, eighteen hundred and fifty-eight; and, in case they shall find that he has thereby suffered damages for which the state is justly liable, to make such award therefor as shall be just and equitable, subject to an appeal to the canal board as in other cases.

Right to appeal given.

§ 2. The Treasurer shall pay, upon the warrant of the Auditor of the canal department, such sum as shall be awarded under the provisions of this act, out of any moneys in the treasury appropriated to the payment of repairs upon the Champlain canal.

§ 3. This act shall take effect immediately.

Chap. 263.

AN ACT to authorize the appraisal and payment of canal damages to Samuel Morgan.

Passed April 17, 1862; three-fifths being present.

The People of the State of New York, represented in Senate and Assembly, do enact as follows:

SECTION 1. The canal appraisers are hereby authorized and required to hear and determine the claim of Samuel Morgan, for alleged damages sustained by him by reason of a portion of his land situated in the town of Cuba, in the county of Allegany, being taken by the state for the construction of Oil creek reservoir, and injuries done to his land and buildings thereon by reason of such construction; and if upon such examination they find that said Morgan has, from the cause above named, suffered any injury to his said property, for which the state is legally and justly liable, they shall award said Morgan such damages therefor as shall in their opinion be just and equitable, subject to appeal to the canal board as in other cases.

§ 2. Nothing in this act contained shall be construed to authorize the canal appraisers to award any damages for land taken or injuries sustained from the cause above named for which an award has already been made. *Saving clause.*

§ 3. The Treasurer shall pay, on the warrant of the Auditor, such sum as may be finally awarded in pursuance of the first section of this act, out of any moneys appropriated for the payment of canal damages.

§ 4. This act shall take effect immediately.

Chap. 264.

AN ACT to increase the Auditing Board of the town of Dunkirk, and to authorize the erection of a Jail in said town.

Passed April 17, 1862 ; three-fifths being present.

The People of the State of New York, represented in Senate and Assembly, do enact as follows:

Members of board.

SECTION 1. The board of town auditors of the town of Dunkirk shall consist of the supervisor, justices of the peace, and clerk of said town and the president and treasurer of the village of Dunkirk, to have the exclusive power, and it shall be their duty at their annual meeting to audit the accounts of the justices of the peace and constables of said town and all other town accounts as is now provided by law.

Duties of trustees, relating to jail.

§ 2. It shall be the duty of the trustees of said village of Dunkirk to furnish a suitable jail or prison at the expense of the corporation of the said village, for the safe keeping and confinement of prisoners. Said jail to be under the control of the sheriff of Chautuaqua county, who shall maintain and feed all prisoners committed thereto, and all expenses incurred in maintaining said prisoners, and all expenses incident to said jail shall be

Expenses to be audited.

audited and allowed by the board of supervisors of said county in the same manner as expenses connected with the county jail are allowed and paid. And it shall be

Duties of justices.

the duty of all justices of the peace in said town of Dunkirk, to commit to said jail in said village of Dunkirk all culprits and criminal offenders whose term of imprisonment shall not exceed ninety days.

Bonds to raise monies.

§ 3. Said board of trustees are hereby authorized to issue bonds in the name of the corporation of said village to raise money to an amount not exceeding two thousand dollars payable within five years from the fourth day of July, eighteen hundred and sixty-two, for the purpose of building said jail ; said bonds to draw seven per cent interest payable semi-annually at the

How paid.

office of the treasurer of said village ; said bonds to be paid from the general fund of said village and the trustees of said village are hereby authorized to pay said bonds and the interest thereon as the principal thereof and the said interest shall from time to time become due and payable from any moneys in the treasury of the said village, and if there are no moneys in the said treasury for that purpose they are hereby authorized to raise moneys for that purpose by tax upon the property of said village in manner provided by law.

Chap. 265.

AN ACT to provide for the licensing of ballast lighters in the port of New York.

Passed April 17, 1862; three-fifths being present.

The People of the State of New York, represented in Senate and Assembly, do enact as follows :

SECTION 1. No boat, lighter or vessel shall be employed in the business of carrying ballast in the port of New York, unless licensed for that purpose under the provisions of this act; and any person using or employing any boat, lighter or vessel for the purpose of carrying ballast in the port of New York, not duly licensed as in and by this act provided, or of which the license shall have expired, shall pay a fine of twenty-five dollars for each and every day on which such boat, lighter or vessel is so used or employed, to be recovered by the captain of the port of New York, and the amount of such fine shall be a lien on the boat, lighter or vessel so used or employed. *License required.* *Penalty.*

§ 2. The captain of the port of New York shall have power to license such boats, lighters or vessels as he shall, after inspection by him or under his direction, deem suitable for the purpose of carrying and discharging ballast, such licenses to be issued to the owner thereof, and to continue in force for one year from the date thereof, and shall be renewable from year to year. *Who may grant license.*

§ 3. The sum of ten dollars shall be paid to the said captain of the port of New York for every license issued under this act, and the sum of five dollars for every renewal thereof; all license fees, fines and penalties col- *Fees.*

lected under this act shall be paid over and accounted for by the captain of the port of New York, in like manner as is now required by law in respect to fees, fines and penalties collected or recovered by him.

§ 4. This act shall take effect immediately.

Chap. 266.

AN ACT to amend an act entitled " An act to amend and modify the several acts relating to the village of Newburgh, and to combine the same into one act," passed May twenty-fifth, eighteen hundred and thirty-six.

Passed April 17, 1862; three-fifths being present.

The People of the State of New York, represented in Senate and Assembly, do enact as follows:

SECTION 1. The trustees of the village of Newburgh are hereby authorized to raise annually in said village for the purposes mentioned in the thirty-third section of the act entitled " An act to amend and modify the several acts relating to the village of Newburgh, and combine the same into one act," passed May twenty-fifth, eighteen hundred and thirty-six, a sum not exceeding nine thousand dollars, which shall be raised and applied according to the said thirty-third section of said act.

§ 2. All acts and parts of acts heretofore passed, inconsistent with the provisions of this act, are hereby repealed.

§ 3. This act shall take effect immediately.

Chap. 267.

AN ACT to change the name of the town of Newark in the county of Tioga to Newark Valley.

Passed April 17, 1862.

The People of the State of New York, represented in Senate and Assembly, do enact as follows :

SECTION 1. The name of the town of Newark in the county of Tioga is hereby changed to that of Newark Valley.

§ 2. This act shall take effect immediately.

Chap. 268.

AN ACT to incorporate the Homœopathic Medical society of the State of New York.

Passed April 17, 1862.

The People of the State of New York, represented in Senate and Assembly, do enact as follows:

SECTION 1. It shall be lawful for each of the county homœopathic medical societies incorporated under the session laws of eighteen hundred and fifty-seven, chapter three hundred and eighty-four, to elect by ballot, at their annual meeting, or at a special meeting to be held for that purpose, on five days notice, from their members respectively, as many delegates to a state homœopathic medical society to be organized under this act, as there are members of assembly from such county.

§ 2. Said delegates shall meet together for their first meeting at the city of Albany, on the first Tuesday of May, eighteen hundred and sixty-two, and being met, not less than nine in number may elect by ballot a president, three vice presidents, a secretary and treasurer, who shall hold their office for one year, and until others shall be chosen in their places. If the said delegates should not meet and organize themselves at such

time and place as aforesaid, it shall be lawful for them
to meet at such other time and place as a majority of
them shall think proper, and their proceedings shall be
as valid as if such meeting had been held at the time
and place before specified.

§ 3. Such delegates when met together as aforesaid,
and such persons as shall be elected in like manner,
from time to time, by said county medical societies in
accordance with this act, shall constitute a body politic
and corporate, to be known as the Homœopathic Medical
Society of the state of New York. Such society shall
be subject to all the liabilities, and entitled to all the
powers and privileges of the medical society of the
state of New York, incorporated under the act entitled
"An act to incorporate medical societies for the purpose of regulating the practice of physic and surgery
in this state," passed April ten, eighteen hundred and
thirteen, and the acts amendatory of the same, not inconsistent with this act, and shall also possess the
powers and be subject to the provisions and liabilities
of the eighteenth chapter of the first part of the Revised
Statutes.

§ 4. This act shall take effect immediately.

Chap. 269.

AN ACT to amend the charter of "The Excelsior
Fire Insurance Company" in the city of New
York.

Passed April 17, 1862 ; three-fifths being present.

*The People of the State of New York, represented in
Senate and Assembly, do enact as follows :*

SECTION 1. The Excelsior Fire Insurance Company is
hereby authorized to reduce the number of its Directors
to twenty-one, instead of forty as provided for by its
charter.

§ 2. All the provisions of said charter in relation to
the election* Directors, and their powers and duties shall
apply to those authorized by this act.

§ 3. This act shall take effect immediately.

*So in original.

Chap. 270.

AN ACT in relation to certain school moneys and property of the fourteenth and fifteenth townships in the county of Chenango.

Passed April 17, 1862; three-fifths being present.

The People of the State of New York, represented in Senate and Assembly, do enact as follows:

SECTION 1. The office of School Land Agent of the fifteenth township, one of the "twenty townships," in the county of Chenango, is hereby abolished, and all its powers, rights and duties are hereby transferred to and devolved on the supervisors of the towns of Norwich and New Berlin.

§ 2. The supervisors of the towns of Norwich, New Berlin and Preston shall meet at the office of the town clerk of the town of Norwich on the first day of May, eighteen hundred and sixty-two, where shall be produced the moneys, securities and all other school property belonging to the fourteenth and fifteenth townships of the "twenty townships;" and the supervisors of the towns of Preston and Norwich shall proceed to make a just and equitable division of the school moneys and property belonging to the fourteenth township, between the said towns of Preston and Norwich. The supervisors of the towns of Norwich and New Berlin shall also at the same time proceed to make a just and equitable division of school moneys and property belonging to the fifteenth township, between the said towns of Norwich and New Berlin.

§ 3. In case the supervisors of the towns of Preston and Norwich cannot agree upon a division of the said moneys and property of the fourteenth township, the supervisor of New Berlin shall be associated with them, and the division shall be made by a majority of their votes. In case of disagreement in the division of the moneys and property of the fifteenth township between the towns of Norwich and New Berlin, the supervisor of Preston shall be associated with the supervisors of those

Office of school land agent abolished.

Duties of certain supervisors.

towns, and the division shall be made by a majority of their votes.

Division of school moneys. § 4. The divisions of such school moneys and property above directed to be made, shall be in writing and signed by the supervisors agreeing to the same. They shall set forth fully the moneys, property and securities divided and the specific shares and interests allotted to each town, and such writings shall be recorded in the offices of the town clerks of the towns affected thereby.

Interest of school moneys, &c., of Norwich. § 5. The interest of all school moneys or other school property belonging to the town of Norwich, shall be applied to the support of common schools in said town, in such manner as the inhabitants of said town shall in annual town meeting direct.

County judge. § 6. In case the supervisors of the said towns fail to agree upon the division of said fund, they are hereby authorized to call upon the county judge of Chenango county whose decision shall be final.

§ 7. This act shall take effect immediately.

Chap. 271.

AN ACT to amend chapter five hundred and five of the laws of eighteen hundred and sixty.

Passed April 17, 1862; three-fifths being present.

The People of the State of New York, represented in Senate and Assembly, do enact as follows:

SECTION 1. Section three of chapter five hundred and five of the laws of the year eighteen hundred and sixty, entitled "An act to provide for a police court in the city of New York," is hereby amended so as to read as follows:

So much of the premises as may be set apart as a place for the detention of prisoners as aforesaid, shall be maintained and controlled by the commissioners of public charities and correction. The board of police justices shall designate and regulate the portions of said buildings which shall be set apart for the use of the police justices.

§ 2. Section four of the said act is hereby amended so as to read as follows:

A sum equal to the amount actually paid for the ground upon which the said building is located, to wit: twelve thousand dollars is hereby authorized to be applied for the completion of said building in the manner provided for in the second section of the act hereby amended, which amount the board of supervisors of the county of New York are hereby directed to levy and raise by tax in the manner provided by law for levying taxes, in the year eighteen hundred and sixty-two, upon the estates, real and personal, within said city, subject by law to taxation.

§ 3. This act shall take effect immediately.

Chap. 272

AN ACT for the release of certain lands and real estate of which Thomas Walmsley died seized to Alexander Walmsley.

Passed April 17, 1862; by a two-third vote.

The People of the State of New York, represented in Senate and Assembly, do enact as follows:

SECTION 1. All the estate, right, title and interest of the people of the State of New York, of, in and to all the lands and real estate situate in the town of Rotterdam, in the county of Schenectady, whereof Thomas Walmsley died seized or possessed, and devised by him to Alexander Walmsley, of the province of Lower Canada, is hereby released to the said Alexander Walmsley, his heirs and assigns forever.

§ 2. Nothing herein contained shall be construed to impair, release or discharge any right, claim or interest of any creditor by mortgage, judgment or otherwise. Saving clause.

§ 3. This act shall take effect immediately.

Chap. 273.

AN ACT to amend an act entitled "An act to regulate the sale of poisons," passed April sixteenth, eighteen hundred and sixty.

Passed April 17, 1862; three-fifths being present.

The People of the State of New York, represented in Senate and Assembly, do enact as follows:

Amendment.

SECTION 1. The first section of the act entitled "An act to regulate the sale of poisons," passed April sixteenth, eighteen hundred and sixty, is hereby amended so as to read as follows:

Book to be kept.

No person shall sell or give any poison or poisonous substance without recording in a book, to be kept for that purpose, the name of the person receiving said poison, and his or her residence, excepting upon the written order or prescription of some regularly authorized practicing physician, whose name must be attached to such order. Such book shall be kept open for inspection.

Repeal.

§ 2. The third section of said act is hereby repealed.

§ 3. This act shall take effect immediately.

Chap. 274.

AN ACT for the relief of Ebenezer Murdock.

Passed April 17, 1862; three-fifths being present.

The People of the State of New York, represented in Senate and Assembly, do enact as follows:

SECTION 1. The canal appraisers are authorized and required to hear, investigate and decide upon the claims of Ebenezer Murdock, for alleged damages on account of the removal or destruction of his buildings by the enlargement of the Erie canal, opposite the lower lock in the village of Lockport; and if, upon due proof, it shall appear that said buildings were the property of said Murdock at the date of said removal or destruction, they may make such award therefor as may be just, not exceeding the sum of six hundred dollars ; such appraisement and award, if any be made, shall be subject to appeal to the canal board as in other cases.

§ 2. The sum which shall be finally awarded under the provisions of this act the Treasurer shall pay, on the warrant of the Auditor, to the said Ebenezer Murdock. out of any money in the treasury hereafter to be appropriated for the payment of canal damages.

§ 3. This act shall take effect immediately.

Chap. 275.

AN ACT to amend an act in relation to the Glébe lands in the village of Newburgh, Orange county, passed April tenth, eighteen hundred and fifty-five.

Passed April 17, 1862; three-fifths being present.

The People of the State of New York, represented in Senate and Assembly, do enact as follows :

SECTION 1. The third section of chapter two hundred and thirty-six of the laws of eighteen hundred and fifty-five, is hereby amended so as to require and make it the duty of the treasurer of the village of Newburgh, as soon as practicable after he shall receive the commutation moneys mentioned in the second section of the said act, or any part of the said moneys amounting to the sum of one hundred dollars or upwards, to invest the same and to keep the same invested in bonds or other written securities of the village of Newburgh, or on bond and mortgage on unincumbered real estate in the county of Orange, worth at least double the amount of the investment, and at an interest not less than six per cent per annum, payable annually. The said treasurer is also authorized and required, when unable to obtain securities of the nature above specified, to keep the said moneys deposited upon interest in any savings bank incorporated under the law of this state. The interest and income to be derived from the said moneys, shall be paid over by said treasurer from time to time to the board of education of the village of Newburgh, to be by them applied as required by the said act.

§ 2. This act shall take effect immediately.

Chap. 276.

AN ACT to alter the commissioners' map of the city of Brooklyn.

Passed April 17, 1862; three-fifths being present.

The People of the State of New York, represented in Senate and Assembly, do enact as follows :

SECTION 1. All that part of Twenty-fourth street, as laid down upon the map made by the commissioners appointed to lay out streets, avenues and squares in the city of Brooklyn, lying east of the Sixth avenue, is hereby discontinued and closed.

§ 2. All that part of Twenty-fifth street, as the same is laid down upon said commissioners' map, lying east of the Fifth avenue, is hereby discontinued and closed.

§ 3. All that part of Twenty-sixth street, as the same is laid down upon said commissioners' map, lying east of the Fifth avenue, is hereby discontinued and closed.

§ 4. All that part of Sixth avenue, as laid down upon said commissioners' map, which lies between the southerly side of Twenty-fourth street and the southerly side of Twenty-fifth street, is hereby discontinued and closed.

§ 5. This act shall take effect immediately.

Chap. 277.

AN ACT for the relief of Russel Martin and Theodore H. Luckey, assignees of a contract to William McArthur for the repairs of section number three, Genesee Valley canal.

Passed April 17, 1862; three-fifths being present.

The People of the State of New York, represented in Senate and Assembly, do enact as follows:

SECTION 1. If the canal board upon investigation shall find that Russel Martin and Theodore H. Luckey have furnished materials and performed labor on repair section three, Genesee Valley canal, not contemplated by the terms of the contract of William McArthur, then the canal board are hereby authorized to award said Martin and Luckey for the labor so done and materials furnished, such sum or sums as shall be just and equitable; but nothing in this act shall be construed to alter or change the terms and conditions of their said contract.

§ 2. Such sum or sums of money as the canal board may award under this act, shall be paid by the treasurer, on the warrant of the Auditor of the canal department, out of any money appropriated for canal repairs.

§ 3. This act shall take effect immediately.

Chap. 278.

AN ACT for the relief of John N. Elmore.

Passed April 17, 1862; three-fifths being present.

The People of the State of New York, represented in Senate and Assembly, do enact as follows:

SECTION 1. The Lieutenant Governor, Attorney General and Comptroller shall be and they are hereby constituted and appointed commissioners to adjust and settle a certain judgment in the supreme court in favor of the people of this state against John N. Elmore, late county treasurer of the county of Chemung, upon such terms and conditions as they shall deem just and equitable or proper; and upon such settlement being made by said commissioners, said judgment shall be deemed cancelled, and said Elmore discharged from his imprisonment thereon.

§ 2. This act shall take effect immediately.

Chap. 279.

AN ACT for the better improvement of highways at Rockland Lake and vicinity.

Passed April 17, 1862; three-fifths being present.

The People of the State of New York, represented in Senate and Assembly, do enact as follows:

Certain highways united in one district.

SECTION 1. That all the highways in the town of Clarkstown, in the county of Rockland and State of New York, included in districts numbers one, two, nineteen, forty-one, twenty-nine, seventeen, thirteen and eight be and they are hereby united into one district, known as the Rockland Lake highway district.

Three superintendents to be chosen.

§ 2. All the highways in said district shall hereafter be worked under the direction of three superintendents, to be chosen after the first year by the electors in said district, in the manner of electing members of the legislature of this state and at the annual town meeting.

Powers.

§ 3 The superintendents are hereby authorized to collect the taxes of all the persons in said district in money, at the rate of sixty-two and a half cents a day for all the days assessed by the commissioner or commissioners of highways of said town, for the improvement of the highways in said district, and in case of default or refusal of any person to pay said taxes, the superintendents are hereby authorized to distrain for the same, as in cases of execution for debt.

Notice for payment of taxes to be given.

§ 4. One week's notice shall be given in the usual way for payment of said taxes, and one per cent only shall be allowed for the collection of the same, if paid on or before the day appointed, but in case of default to pay on said day, then five per cent shall be allowed for the collection of the same.

§ 5. It shall be the duty of said superintendents to hire such men and teams and to provide all suitable tools and materials necessary for the proper improvement of all the highways in said district, either by contract or otherwise, as in their judgment shall be for the best interest of the tax payers. *Duties of superintendents.*

§ 6. It shall be unlawful for the said superintendents to perform any work on said highways for pay, nor shall they be interested, directly or indirectly, in any contract made for improvements upon such highways, nor shall they receive any compensation for their services as such superintendents. *Certain things forbidden.*

§ 7. The superintendents shall be divided into three classes, known as the first, second and third class. Each class shall be determined by lot, and shall hold their offices respectively for one, two and three years, as determined by the class in which they draw; and all persons who shall be elected to fill the place of the superintendent whose term of office shall have expired under this act shall be elected for the full term of three years. *Term of office.*

§ 8. It shall be the duty of the superintendents to expend at least two-thirds of the whole amount of moneys received for said highway taxes, on or before the first day of July in each and every year, for the repairs of said highways, and such repairs shall be so made as to be just and equal to all the tax payers in said district, and when in their judgment it shall be advisable so to do they may construct sidewalks in the village of Rockland Lake. *Moneys how appropriated.*

§ 9. The superintendents shall subscribe to an oath faithfully to perform all duties devolving upon them under this act, and shall render an account of all receipts and expenditures to the people at the next annual meeting to elect superintendents. *Oath of office.*

§ 10. Jacob V. Smith, Moses G. Leonard and Ludlow Smith are hereby appointed superintendents according to the provisions of this act.

§ 11. All the provisions of this act shall be applicable to any highway district or districts in any of the towns composing the county of Rockland, who shall hereafter, by petition signed by a majority of persons liable to be assessed for highway labor in such district, apply to the *Application of this act.*

commissioner or commissioners of highways at least two weeks before the annual town meeting, and said commissioner or commissioners shall hereby be empowered to apply the provisions of this act to any district or consolidated districts, who may so apply for the same.

§ 12. This act shall take effect immediately.

Chap. 280.

AN ACT to provide for the better assessment of real estate for highway labor and for the better working of the same, and for the better keeping highways in repair in the town of Seneca in the county of Ontario.

Passed April 17, 1862; three-fifths being present.

The People of the State of New York, represented in Senate and Assembly, do enact as follows:

SECTION 1. The commissioners of highways of the town of Seneca in the county of Ontario, shall have the power and are hereby required in making and laying any assessment for highway labor upon the real estate in the said town, in cases where the owner or owners of such real estate shall reside in the same town with the said commissioners, and in a road district different from that in which said real estate shall lie, to specify and direct in the lists which they shall issue to the respective overseers of highways for such districts, whether the highway labor assessed upon such real estate shall be worked in the road district where such land shall lie or in the road district where the owner thereof resides. And the highway labor thus assessed shall be worked out according to the provisions of law, as shall be directed in the said lists.

§ 2. All the soil lying within the outer lines of any highway in said town, and the exclusive use thereof, shall be and belong to the owner of the fee of the land within said lines subject to the public right of travel over the same, and subject to the right of the commissioners and owners of highways and their agents, to take and use the said soil to any depth and extent not injurious to the lands adjoining said highway, for the purpose of making and repairing any highway or highways in the same town.

§ 3. This act shall take effect immediately.

Chap. 281.

AN ACT to regulate places of public amusement in the cities and incorporated villages of this State.

Passed April 17, 1862; three-fifths being present.

The People of the State of New York, represented in Senate and Assembly, do enact as follows:

SECTION 1. It shall not be lawful to exhibit to the public in any building, garden or grounds, concert room, or other place or room within the city of New York, any interlude, tragedy, comedy, opera, ballet, play, farce, negro minstrelsy, negro or other dancing, or any other entertainment of the stage, or any part or parts therein, or any equestrian, circus or dramatic performance, or any performance of jugglers, or rope dancing, acrobats until a license for such exhibition shall have been first had and obtained pursuant to and at the same rate provided for theatrical performances in an act entitled "An act to amend an act entitled 'An act to create a fund in aid of the society for the reformation of juvenile delinquents in the city of New York, and for other purposes,' passed February first, eighteen hundred and thirty-nine;" and every manager or proprietor of any such exhibition or performance, who shall neglect to take out such license, or consent to, cause, or allow any such exhibition or performance, or any single one of them without such license, and every person aiding in such exhibition, and every owner or lessee of any building, part of a building, garden, grounds, concert room or other room or place, who shall lease or let the same for the purpose of any such exhibition or performance, or assent that the same be used for any such purpose, ex-

Certain amusements forbidden until licensed.

Penalty.

cept as permitted by such license, and without such
license having been previously obtained and then in
force, if the same shall be used for such purpose, shall
incur the penalties and be subjected to the proceedings
for an injunction provided for by the other provisions
contained in the said act, which penalty the society for
the reformation of juvenile delinquents in said city are
hereby authorized to prosecute, sue for and recover for
the use of the said society, in the name of the people of
the State of New York.

§ 2. It shall not be lawful to sell or furnish any wine,
beer or strong or spirituous liquors to any person in the
auditorium or lobbies of such place of exhibition or
performance mentioned in the first section of this act, or
in any apartment connected therewith by any door, window or other aperture; nor shall it be lawful to employ
or furnish or permit or assent to the employment or attendance of any female to wait on or attend in any manner or furnish refreshments to the audience or specta-
tors or any of them, at any of the exhibitions or performances mentioned in the first section of this act, or at
any other place of public amusement in the city of New
York.

§ 3. No license shall be granted for any exhibition or
performance given in violation of the second section of
this act, and any and every exhibition or performance
at which any of the provisions of the second section of
this act shall be violated, shall of itself vacate and annul and render void and of no effect any license which
shall have been previously obtained by any manager,
proprietor, owner or lessee consenting to, causing or
allowing or letting any part of a building for the purpose of such exhibition and performance; and any
license provided for by the first section of this act, may
be revoked and annulled by the officer or officers granting the same, upon proof of a violation of any of the
provisions of this act; such proof shall be taken before
such officer upon notice of not less than two days, to
show cause why such license should not be revoked.;
said officer shall hear the proofs and allegations in the
case, and determine the same summarily, and no appeal
shall be taken or review be had from such determination, and any person whose license shall have been revoked or annulled, shall not thereafter be entitled to a

(margin notes)
Selling liquor pro-hibited.

And female waiters.

In certain cases no li-cense given.

In certain cases an-nulled.

In certain cases re-voked.

license under the provisions of this act. On any examination before an officer pursuant to a notice to show cause as aforesaid, the accused party may be a witness in his own behalf.

§ 4. Any person violating any of the provisions of this act or employing or assenting to the employment or attendance of any person contrary to the provisions of this act, shall be deemed guilty of a misdemeanor, and upon conviction, shall be punished by imprisonment in the penitentiary for a term not less than three months nor more than one year, or by a fine not less than one hundred dollars nor more than five hundred dollars, or by both such fine and imprisonment.

§ 5. It shall be the duty of every chief of police, sheriff, deputy sheriff, constable, captain of police, policeman, and every other police officer, to enter at any time said places of amusement, and to arrest and convey any person or persons violating any provision of this act, forthwith, before any police justice or recorder or magistrate having jurisdiction in said city, there to be dealt with according to law.

§ 6. The provisions of this act shall apply to all the cities and incorporated villages of this State, but the license to be obtained in every city or incorporated village, other than the city of New York, shall be issued under such terms and under such regulations as the municipal authorities of the said cities or villages may respectively prescribe; and the fines and penalties for any violation of any of the provisions of this act in such other cities or incorporated villages respectively, other than as mentioned in section four of this act, shall be sued for and recovered in the name of the overseer of the poor of such city or incorporated village, or the town in which such incorporated village is situate, or such other officer as the municipal or village authorities thereof may direct, for the benefit of the poor thereof.

§ 7. This act shall take effect immediately.

Violation of act misdemeanor.

Penalty.

Duty of chief of police and other officers.

Applied to all cities and incorporated villages.

Overseers of the poor and other officers may sue for penalties.

Chap. 282.

AN ACT to amend an act entitled "An act to incorporate the Williamsburgh Savings Bank," passed April ninth, eighteen hundred and fifty-one.

Passed April 17, 1862.

The People of the State of New York, represented in Senate and Assembly, do enact as follows :

SECTION 1. It shall be lawful for the trustees of the Williamsburgh Savings Bank to loan the funds of the said institution upon unencumbered productive real estate, worth double the amount to be secured thereby; provided that no single loan shall exceed the sum of twenty thousand dollars.

§ 2. This act shall take effect immediately.

Chap. 283.

AN ACT to alter and amend an act entitled "An act to authorize the appointment of commissioners to take the proof and acknowledgment of deeds and other instruments and to administer oaths in Great Britain and France and other foreign countries."

Passed April 17, 1862.

The People of the State of New York, represented in Senate and Assembly, do enact as follows :

SECTION 1. The first section of the act entitled "An act to authorize the appointment of commissioners to take the proof and acknowledgment of deeds and other instruments and to administer oaths in Great Britain and France," passed April seventeenth, eighteen hundred and fifty-eight, is hereby amended so as to read as follows :

§ 1. The Governor of this state is hereby authorized to appoint and commission one or more, and not exceeding three commissioners in each of the following cities: London, Liverpool and Glasgow, in Great Britain ; in Dublin, Belfast, Cork and Galway, in Ireland ; and Paris and Marseilles, in France ; who shall continue in office for four years, and until a successor shall be appointed and shall have authority to take the acknowledgment or proof of the execution of any deed or written instrument to be recorded or read in evidence in this state, except bills of exchange, promissory notes, and last wills and testaments ; and also to administer an oath or affirmation to any person or persons who may desire to take the same, and to certify the taking of such oath or affirmation, and also to certify the existence of any patent, record, or other document remaining of record in any public office or official custody in Great Britain or Ireland or France, and the correctness of a copy of any such patent, record, or other document. The certificate of any one of such commissioners, under his official seal and subscribed by him, in regard to the acknowledgment or proof of the execution of any such deed or written instrument, or the taking of such oath or affirmation, or the existence or correctness of a copy of such patent, record, or document, when authenticated by the Secretary of State, as hereinafter mentioned, shall have the same effect to authorize the recording or reading in evidence of such deed or written instrument, oath or affidavit, patent, record, or document, as is given by law to like certificates made by justices of the supreme court of this state, or to any certificate or exemplification by any officer of this state, of any patent, record, or other document. The Governor may, in his discretion, at any time hereafter, appoint a commissioner for any other foreign state or country, who shall have the like powers as the commissioners above named. *Additional commissioners may be appointed.*

Other commissioners may be appointed.

§ 2. The seventh section of said act is hereby amended so as to read as follows :

§ 7. The fees of such commissioner, for services under this act, shall be as follows : In Great Britain and Ireland, for administering each oath and certifying the same, and for making each certificate attached to a patent, record, or other document, one shilling sterling ; in France, one franc and twenty-five centimes. In *Fees.*

Great Britain and Ireland, for taking each acknowledgment or proof of any deed or other written instrument to be recorded or read in evidence, four shillings sterling ; in France, five francs; and in all other countries the same compensation as is allowed the commissioners in France.

Chap. 284.

AN ACT in relation to Agricultural and Horticultural Associations.

Passed April 17, 1862 ; three-fifths being present.

The People of the State of New York, represented in Senate and Assembly, do enact as follows:

SECTION 1. In addition to the powers now vested by statute in the board of managers of any agricultural or horticultural association, the officers of such association shall have power to regulate and prevent all kinds of theatrical, circus or mountebank exhibitions and shows, as well as all huckstering or traffic in fruits, goods, wares and merchandise of whatever description, for gain, on the fair days, and within a distance of two hundred yards of the fair grounds of said association, if in the opinion of said officers, the same shall obstruct or in any way interfere with the free and uninterrupted use of the highway around and approaching such fair grounds; and the police employed by any such association shall possess the same power for a space of two hundred yards from said grounds, as is now vested in them by law within said grounds and be under the same control of the officers of the association within that space ; and the same fines and penalties shall be incurred for any violation of the rules and regulations of said officers of any such association within two hundred yards of the fair grounds, as is now by law incurred for any violation of the rules and regulations within the grounds of any such association.

Chap. 285.

AN ACT to amend chapter four hundred and twenty-seven of the Laws of eighteen hundred and fifty-five.

Passed April 17, 1862; three fifths being present.

The People of the State of New York, represented in Senate and Assembly, do enact as follows:

SECTION 1. The eighty-second section of the act entitled "An act in relation to the collection of taxes on lands of non-residents, and to provide for the sale of such lands for unpaid taxes," passed April thirteenth, eighteen hundred and fifty-five, is hereby repealed. Repeal.

§ 2. It shall be unlawful for the Comptroller of this State, and for any person employed in the office of such Comptroller, to be interested directly or indirectly in any tax sale made by such Comptroller, or in the title acquired by such sale, or in any money paid or to be paid for the redemption of any lands sold for taxes or on the cancellation of any tax sale; and it shall be unlawful for any person to pay to the Comptroller or to any employee in his office, and for the said Comptroller or any employee in his office to receive, directly or indirectly any compensation, reward or promise thereof, from any person or persons who are interested in any purchase or purchases of lands sold for taxes, for any service or services performed or to be performed in regard to such sale, redemption, cancellation or such tax title. If any person offend against any provision of this section, he shall be deemed guilty of a misdemeanor; and the sale by the Comptroller of any lands in which such person shall be interested contrary to the provision of this section, is hereby declared to be void. Comptroller &c. not to be interested in tax sales. Misdemeanor.

61

Chap. 286.

AN ACT to enable the president, directors and company of the Albany and Greene turnpike road to abandon a part of their road.

Passed April 17, 1862; three-fifths being present.

The People of the State of New York, represented in Senate and Assembly, do enact as follows:

SECTION 1. The president, directors and company of the Albany and Greene turnpike road may abandon all that part of their said road being in the town of Coxsackie, in the county of Greene, lying northerly of the dwelling house now owned and occupied by Benjamin Tryon, and situate on said road, whenever said president and directors shall execute or cause to be executed a release of that part of said road so to be abandoned, signed by said president under the corporate seal of said company, and cause the same to be recorded in the clerk's office of said county of Greene.

§ 2. Upon the execution and recording of said release, the said corporation shall thereafter be exonerated from all further charges or liabilities on account of that part of said road so released and abandoned; and the same shall be declared a public highway; but nothing in this Proviso. act contained shall be so construed as to affect or impair the right of said turnpike company from demanding and collecting the same rates of tolls at their gates on the remaining part of their said road that they are now entitled by law to demand and collect.

§ 3. This act shall take effect immediately.

Chap. 287.

AN ACT to amend the act entitled "An act to provide for the incorporation of villages," passed December seventh, eighteen hundred and forty-seven, and of the several acts amendatory thereof, so far as relates to the village of Middletown, in the county of Orange.

Passed April 17, 1862; three-fifths being present.

The People of the State of New York, represented in Senate and Assembly, do enact as follows:

SECTION 1. The members of the different companies composing the fire department of the village of Middletown, shall biennially, and at such time or times and in such manner as the trustees shall designate, vote for a chief engineer and for two assistant engineers, and each person who shall receive the highest number of votes for such offices shall be appointed thereto by said trustees, unless in their judgment for good cause such appointment shall not be made. In case either of such nominations shall not be ratified by the trustees, they shall order a new election, and at such new election the person thus rejected shall be ineligible, and all votes given for him at such new election shall be void.

§ 2. Such chief engineer shall, under the direction of the trustees, have the general superintendence and custody of all the property and conveniences for the prevention and extinguishment of fires in said village. It shall be his duty to be present at such fires of buildings, and take the command of the several fire companies, and direct and control the movements for the extinguishment of such fires. On the first day of January of each year, and as much oftener as the trustees shall require, he shall make detailed written reports to them of the condition of the department, the fire apparatus, and of all the village property held for the extinguishment of fires, and he shall perform such specific duties as shall be prescribed by such trustees.

§ 3. The assistant engineer or engineers shall aid the chief engineer at all fires, and in the absence of the chief engineer or from incapacity to serve, the duties and powers of the office shall be exercised and performed by such assistant or assistants. In case of the death, removal, resignation or other incapacity to serve of either of such engineers, the trustees shall appoint some suitable person to supply such vacancy for the balance of the term.

Chap. 288.

AN ACT in relation to the Union Turnpike company.

Passed April 17, 1862.

The People of the State of New York, represented in Senate and Assembly, do enact as follows :

SECTION 1. Whenever the "Union turnpike company," an incorporation in the county of Albany, formed under the act passed May seventh, eighteen hundred and forty-seven, entitled "An act to provide for the incorporation of companies to construct plank roads and for companies to construct turnpike roads," and the amendments thereto, shall have finished their road for the distance specified in the articles of association of said company, and had the same inspected, it shall be lawful for said company to erect a toll gate thereon and exact tolls thereat, at the rates provided in the before mentioned act.

§ 2. This act shall take effect immediately.

Chap. 289.

AN ACT to change the name of "The Rose Hill Savings Bank," in the city of New York.

Passed April 17, 1862.

The People of the State of New York, represented in Senate and Assembly, do enact as follows:

SECTION 1. The name of the "Rose Hill Savings Bank," in the city of New York, is hereby changed, and said corporation shall be hereafter called and known by the name of "The New York Savings Bank," and by that name shall have the same rights and powers that it would have if such change had not been made.

§ 2. Nothing in this act contained shall in any way Proviso. change or lessen any liability of said corporation that may exist, either absolutely or contingently, at the time such change of name may take place.

Chap. 290.

AN ACT to prescribe the fire limits in the village of Newburgh.

Passed April 17, 1862; three-fifths being present.

The People of the State of New York, represented in Senate and Assembly, do enact as follows:

SECTION 1. The board of trustees of the village of Newburgh are hereby authorized and empowered to prohibit the erection, moving or placing of any wooden building without the permission in writing of said board of trustees, within any part of said village which is bounded on the north by Nicoll street, on the west by Liberty street, on the south by South William street, and east by the west side of Front street; and to direct that all or any buildings hereinafter erected or put up within the above described limits shall be made or constructed

of stone or brick, with partition walls and roof of stone
or metal, under such penalties as may be prescribed by
the said board of trustees

§ 2. All acts or parts of acts heretofore passed, inconsistent with this act, are hereby repealed.

§ 3. This act shall take effect immediately.

Chap. 291.

AN ACT to amend the charter of the village of Geneseo.

Passed April 17, 1862; three-fifths being present.

*The People of the State of New York, represented in
Senate and Assembly, do enact as follows:*

Power of
electors.
SECTION 1. It shall be lawful for, and the electors of
the village of Geneseo are hereby authorized at any
annual meeting of the electors of said village, or at any
special meeting called by the trustees of said village as
herein prescribed for that purpose, to vote to raise by
tax upon the taxable property of said village, such sum
or sums of money as shall be necessary for constructing
proper and suitable water works, and laying down and
permanently locating iron or other pipes and fixtures, and
erecting hydrants for the purpose of carrying water into
all or any parts of said village, for the use of said village
and the inhabitants thereof; and also to raise by like tax
such sum or sums of money as may be necessary and
suitable to erect proper lamp posts and fixtures, to be
connected with the works of the Geneseo gas light company, for the purpose of lighting all or any of the streets
or public places or buildings of said village with gas.

Ib.
§ 2. In case the electors of said village shall by vote
at said meeting or meetings direct that such sum or sums
of money be raised by tax in installments, they may by
vote also authorize the trustees of said village to borrow
upon the credit of said village such sum or sums of
money as to such meeting may seem proper, to be repaid
by the moneys thereafter to be raised by tax in said in-
Exception. stallments, but said trustees shall not be authorized to

borrow any sums of money over and above the amounts voted to be raised by tax by the electors at any such meeting.

§ 3. Said trustees are hereby authorized to levy and raise by tax upon the taxable property of said village, such sum or sums of money as may be voted at such meeting, in the times and manner by the vote of said meeting designated; said tax to be levied and collected in the manner now prescribed by law for raising and collecting the taxes for said village.

§ 4. Said trustees are also hereby authorized to borrow upon the credit of said village, such sum or sums of money as they may be authorized by the vote of said meeting to borrow, and to issue the bonds or obligations of said village for the payment thereof, such bonds or obligations to be executed by the order of said trustees in such form as they shall prescribe by resolution of said trustees, passed at any regular meeting thereof, which resolution shall be recorded in the book of records of said village.

§ 5. The said trustees are hereby authorized to expend the sums of money so raised or borrowed in pursuance of said vote of said meeting of electors, for the purposes authorized by said vote, consistent with this act, and in pursuance thereof, to construct such buildings, erections and water works, and lay down such pipe as shall be necessary or suitable for the purpose of supplying the said village and its inhabitants with water; and also to erect the proper lamp posts and fixtures for the purpose of lighting said streets with gas; and they are hereby authorized to expend such sums of money from time to time as shall be necessary to keep said water works and gas fixtures in repair, and to pay for gas furnished for lighting the streets and public places and buildings of such village with gas.

§ 6. The said trustees shall have power from time to time to fix the rates at which the inhabitants of said village may use the water from said water works, and to enforce the collection of such rates by warrant therefor issued to the collector of said village, who by virtue of said warrant, shall be empowered and shall have authority to collect the same with fees in addition to be fixed by said trustees of the person or persons against whom the same are issued, in the same manner as other taxes of said village are collected. Said trustees, in case the rates imposed by them are not paid, shall have full power to prevent the person or persons not paying from using said water. Said trustees shall have power to impose penalties for any violation of ordinances enacted by them in relation to regulating said water works and the use of the water from the same.

Notice of meeting of electors. § 7. The trustees shall give eight days public notice of the time and place of the meeting of said electors, for the purpose of voting such tax as is herein authorized, by posting copies of such notices in eight public places in said village, and said notices shall contain a statement of the object of such meeting and of the amount intended to be raised by tax at such meeting, and the purposes for which it is intended to be raised.

§ 8. This act shall take effect immediately.

Chap. 292.

AN ACT to change the name of the town of Bucktooth in the county of Cattaraugus to Salamanca.

Passed April 17, 1862.

The People of the State of New York, represented in Senate and Assembly, do enact as follows:

SECTION 1. The name of the town of Bucktooth in the county of Cattaraugus is hereby changed to that of Salamanca.

§ 2. This act shall take effect immediately.

Chap. 293.

AN ACT to provide for the collection of agricultural statistics in the several counties of this State.

Passed April 17, 1862; three-fifths being present.

The People of the State of New York, represented in Senate and Assembly, do enact as follows:

SECTION 1. It shall be the duty of all county agricultural or horticultural societies, or, in the absence of such county societies, town societies, that receive an annual appropriation of money and books, or either, from the state treasury, to procure the collection of the statistics of agricultural and horticultural products and improvements each year in their respective counties, by procuring proper answers to such questions as shall be contained in blanks to be provided for that purpose. *Duties of agricultural and horticultural societies.*

§ 2. It shall be the duty of the board of managers, or other proper officers of such county agricultural or horticultural societies, or, in the absence of such county societies, the presidents of the several town societies which receive money from the state, to select and appoint some suitable person in each school district and each joint district in said county, whose duty it shall be to procure the proper answers from all persons residing in the said school district or joint district to the questions contained in the blanks to be furnished for that purpose, and the said board of managers or president shall furnish the person so appointed with the proper blanks on or before the first of January of each and every year, with such instructions as may be necessary to his correct understanding of the duties to be performed. *Duties of board of managers.*

§ 3. The persons thus appointed in the several school districts and joint districts shall proceed at once to procure the proper answers to the several question contained in said blanks, by calling on the persons of whom the information is to be obtained, or in such other manner as in the judgment of said officers may best secure the correct answers; which answers he shall enter upon said blanks, under their appropriate heads, and opposite the *Answers to be obtained* name of the respective persons from whom they are obtained. When the answers shall have been obtained

from all the residents of said districts, and properly entered upon said blanks, the said blanks shall be returned to the president of said agricultural or horticultural society, who shall cause the same to be added up, and the aggregate result for each school district or joint district entered in a column on similar blanks, opposite the number of the respective district, in such manner as to show the result in each town by school districts, which

blanks containing such aggregate results shall be forwarded to the Secretary of the New York State agricultural society, on or before the first of February in each year.

§ 4 The several officers appointed in school districts, as provided in section two of this act, and who shall perform the duties of said office, shall be entitled to receive and shall be furnished by the president of the agricultural or horticultural society of his respective county one copy of the transactions of the New York State agricultural society, and one copy of the transactions of the American institute, published for the year that the statistics thus collected represents. The county agricul-

tural or horticultural society, or, in the absence of such county societies, the town societies, whose officers shall faithfully perform the duties specified in the several sections of this act, shall be entitled to receive from the Comptroller of this State such amounts of money annually as they have heretofore been authorized to receive under the provisions contained in the act entitled "An act for the encouragement of agriculture," passed May fifth, one thousand eight hundred and forty-one, an act to amend an act entitled "An act to promote agriculture," passed May fifth, one thousand eight hundred and forty-one, and the acts amendatory thereof, passed April sixteenth, one thousand eight hundred and sixty-one, without procuring a like sum to be raised by subscription or otherwise, as provided by said act.

§ 5. It shall be the duty of the Comptroller to provide blanks by the first day of December in each year, of such form and containing such questions as shall be approved by the executive committee of the New York State agricultural society, and furnish the same to the presidents of said county or town agricultural or horti-

cultural societies, with such instructions as shall enable
said officers to discharge the duties required of them as
contemplated by this act.

§ 6. If there should be any counties in this state in *Duty of executive committee of state society.* which there is no such agricultural or horticultural society, or town societies, receiving appropriations from the
state treasury, then it shall be the duty of the executive
committee of the New York State agricultural society to
appoint a suitable person in each of said counties, whose
duty it shall be to appoint suitable persons in the re- *Appointments.* spective school districts of his county, as provided in section two of this act; and the persons so appointed shall
proceed in all respects as if they had been appointed by
the board of managers or other officers of a county agricultural or horticultural society, as provided by section
two of this act.

§ 7. Such persons as shall be appointed by the execu- *Pay of persons appointed.* tive committee of the New York State agricultural
society, shall be entitled to receive a suitable compensation, to be paid out of any moneys that would properly
belong to a county agricultural or horticultural society,
if such society existed in said county, and the Treasurer
of the State shall pay such sum, on the warrant of the
Comptroller, to be given on the certificate of the Secretary of the State agricultural society, that such service
has been duly and faithfully performed, but such compensation shall not in any case exceed in amount the
sum that such county agricultural or horticultural society would be entitled to receive.

§ 8. This act shall take effect immediately.

Chap. 294.

AN ACT to amend an act entitled "An act to amend and condense the several acts in relation to the village of Hamilton," passed May eleventh, eighteen hundred and forty, and to amend subdivision three of section three of chapter two hundred and ninety-seven of the Laws of eighteen hundred and fifty-nine.

Passed April 17, 1862; three-fifths being present.

The People of the State of New York, represented in Senate and Assembly, do enact as follows :

Time of holding town meeting. SECTION 1. Section two of chapter two hundred and sixty-six of the laws of eighteen hundred and forty, is hereby amended so as to read as follows : The inhabitants qualified by law to vote at town meetings, and residing within the aforesaid limits, shall meet on the last Tuesday of February in each year, except the year eighteen hundred and sixty-two, at the hour and place to be designated by said inhabitants at their last preceding annual meeting, and if none be designated then at such hour and place as the trustees may appoint.

Overseer of highways to be appointed. § 2. Subdivision three of section three of chapter two hundred and ninety-seven, of the laws of eighteen hundred and fifty-nine, is hereby amended so as to read as follows : To appoint an overseer of highways for said village, who shall hold his office during the pleasure of the trustees, which said overseer shall possess all the powers and perform all the duties which overseers of highways now possess and perform, shall be subject to the direction and control of the trustees, and to removal *Certain corporations to furnish highway labor.* by them for cause. Any moneyed or stock corporation located and doing business in said village, shall be notified to furnish the amount of highway labor, assessed to such corporation, in the same manner as individuals residing in said village by the said overseer of highways, giving written notice to the president, cashier, or any clerk or other officer thereof, at the principal office or place of transacting the business or concerns of the said corporation, which labor shall be performed within the corporate or territorial limits of the said village as the said overseer of highways shall direct, any number of days work not exceeding ten, may be required to be performed by any such corporation in any one day. Every such corporation may commute for the highway *May commute.* labor assessed upon it, at the same rate as is allowed by law to individuals by paying such commutation money to the said overseer of highways, and the commutation money so paid shall be expended by the said overseer of highways in the improvement of the roads, streets, and bridges in said village. The president of said vil- *Power of president of village.* lage shall possess the same powers to enforce the performance of highway labor from such corporation and to enforce the penalties for the non-performance thereof as is possessed by the commissioners of highways by statute. The board of trustees of said village of Hamil- *And of trustees.* ton are hereby authorized to reduce the amount of commutation fees for highway labor as now established by law, but shall not reduce said fees below fifty cents per day for each day's highway labor due.

Chap. 295.

AN ACT for the relief of E. Norman Leslie, and to authorize the trustees of the village of Skaneateles to raise one hundred and eighty-eight dollars by tax.

Passed April 17, 1862 ; three-fifths being present.

The People of the State of New York, represented in Senate and Assembly, do enact as follows:

SECTION 1. The trustees of the village of Skaneateles shall assess, apportion and raise by tax, in said village, the sum of one hundred and eighty-eight dollars, in addition to any and all sums they otherwise might raise, or have authority to raise by law, and it shall be lawful for said trustees to assess and cause the said tax to be collected and enforced, in the same manner as other taxes are assessed, collected and enforced in said village, and when the treasurer shall have collected the taxes under the tax roll and warrant to be delivered to him, it shall be the duty of the said treasurer to pay to E. Norman Leslie, the said sum of one hundred and eighty-eight dollars, on account of a certain judgment (together with the interest and expenses accrued thereon,) recovered against him by Thaddeus Edwards for an alleged trespass arising out of the collection of the expenses of making a sidewalk in said village, which sidewalk was made under the direction of the board of trustees of said village, of which the said E. Norman Leslie was a member.

§ 2. This act shall take effect immediately.

Chap. 296.

AN ACT to legalize the election held in the village of Avon on the fourth day of March, eighteen hundred and sixty-two.

Passed April 17, 1862; three-fifths being present.

The People of the State of New York, represented in Senate and Assembly, do enact as follows:

SECTION 1. The election held in the village of Avon, in the county of Livingston, on the fourth day of March, eighteen hundred and sixty-two, is hereby legalized, and the said officers elected at said election, shall have the same powers in all respects as they would have had if the required three weeks notice had been given, and all business transacted at said election is hereby made as legal as though the said notice had been given.

§ 2. This act shall take effect immediately.

Chap. 297.

AN ACT to incorporate the fire department of the village of Owego.

Passed April 17, 1862 ; three-fifths being present.

The People of the State of New York, represented in Senate and Assembly, do enact as follows :

SECTION 1. All persons who now are or hereafter shall become members of any fire engine, hook and ladder or hose company now organized, or which hereafter be organized by the trustees of the village of Owego, in the county of Tioga, in conformity with the charter of said village, shall be and are hereby ordained and constituted a body politic and corporate in fact and in name, by the name of "The Fire Department of the village of Owego," and by that name they and their successors shall have perpetual succession, and shall have a common seal, and may sue and be sued in any of the courts of the state, by or in the name of the president of the said fire department ; and also they and their successors, by their corporate name, may purchase, receive by gift or otherwise, and hold and convey any real estate or personal property for the use and benefit of said corporation, provided the amount of real and personal estate so held shall not exceed the sum of ten thousand dollars. *Fire department.* *Powers.*

§ 2. There shall be a board of trustees, who shall have the management and control of the affairs and property of said corporation, and be vested with such other power, and subject to such restrictions as are hereinafter provided. The first trustees shall be Charles Ogden, Jonathan S. Houck, William H. S. Bean, John W. Kennedy, Edward Forman, Edward L. Legg, Hamlin Jones and George A. Madill, of whom the following shall be the first officers, viz., George A. Madill, president; Charles Ogden, vice-president ; William H. S. Bean, secretary ; and Edward Forman, treasurer, to hold their respective offices until the first annual meeting, to be held agreeably to the provisions of this act. *Trustees.*

§ 3. The said several fire companies composing the said corporation shall, on the last Wednesday of January, one thousand eight hundred and sixty-three, and on *Election of trustees.*

said day in each year thereafter, hold an election at
their respective rooms (unless it shall be necessary to
hold the same at a different place, when the same shall
be held at such places as the said board of trustees shall
direct,) and choose by ballot two persons from the members of each of said companies, and the persons thus
chosen shall thereafter constitute the board of trustees
President, of said corporation. And the said board of trustees
&c., to be shall, on the first Wednesday of February, one thousand
chosen. eight hundred and sixty-three, and on said day in each
year thereafter, choose out of their own number, by
ballot, a president, vice-president and secretary, the said
secretary to be the secretary of the corporation. And
Firemen to the firemen of the several fire companies constituting the
choose en- said corporation shall also hold a meeting on the last
gineer, &c. Wednesday of January, one thousand eight hundred and
sixty-three, and on said day in each year thereafter, at
the place designated by said board of trustees for that purpose, at which meeting they shall elect from among their
own number, by ballot, a chief engineer, first assistant
Treasurer. engineer, second assistant engineer and treasurer. The
said board of trustees shall appoint from its members
two inspectors, who shall act as inspectors of the election last aforesaid. The said inspectors shall bring the
returns of the said election before the board of trustees
at its first meeting after such election, and the said board
of trustees shall meet within three days after such election and examine into and decide the result thereof.
And the said board of trustees shall, by its president or
otherwise, as it shall direct, make known to the trustees
of the said village the result of said election last aforesaid, at the first meeting of the trustees of said village
after such result shall be ascertained as aforesaid. And
Power of if the trustees of said village shall, by notice in writing
trustees. to the secretary of said department, disapprove of said
engineers, or either of them, so elected as aforesaid,
within two weeks from the time they are notified of the
result of said election as above provided, then the board
of trustees of said corporation shall, within three days
after the service of the said notice on its secretary as
Special elec- aforesaid, call a special election of the firemen of the
tion. several companies, to be held within five days from the
date of said call, at the place therein designated, at which
shall be elected persons from among their own number,

other than those disapproved of as aforesaid, to fill the said offices, or such of them as are made vacant by said disapproval. All officers of said corporation whose election is provided for by this act, shall hold their respective offices until their successors are chosen as above provided. *Term of office.*

§ 4. A majority of the board of trustees shall constitute a quorum for the transaction of business; and the acts of said board herein authorized may be done by such majority. *Majority may act.* The trustees shall have full power, and it shall be their duty to make and prescribe such laws and regulations, not inconsistent with the charter of said village and the laws of this state, as they shall deem necessary for the proper management of the affairs and disposition of the funds of said corporation, and may be convened by the president or as may be provided by said laws and regulations. *Duties.* Said board of trustees shall have power to appoint such meetings of said fire department (other than the annual meeting) as they shall deem advisable; and it shall be the duty of said board to appoint at least one day in each year for a general review of said fire department; and said board may affix such penalties for neglect to attend such general review, or *Penalties.* other omisions and violations of duty as firemen, and to sue in the corporate name of said department for the recovery of the same. Said board shall fill from its members all vacancies which may occur by resignation, or otherwise, in the offices of said board; and in case of any vacancy in said board the same shall be filled by the company in which such vacancy occurs. In case of *Vacancies in office of engineer, &c., how filled.* vacancy in the office of chief engineer, or assistant engineer or treasurer, it shall be filled at an annual or special meeting. If at a special meeting it shall be called by the secretary of the board, and under its direction. Notice of the time of all elections under this act shall be given by the secretary of the department at least five days before the time thereof, in at least one of the newspapers of the village. The treasurer shall give security *Treasurer to give security.* to said board of trustees for the faithful performance of his duties; and at every annual meeting, or oftener if required by the trustees, shall render to them a full and true account of the property of the said corporation, and of his action as treasurer. The said board of trustees *Power of removal from office.* shall have power to remove any of the officers of the

63

board of trustees after three days previous notice of the charges preferred.

§ 5. The board of trustees may apply the funds of the said corporation, or such parts of said funds, or of the income thereof, as they shall deem proper, to the relief of indigent and disabled firemen, or their families; and also to defray such contingent expenses as may be necessary in the transaction of the business of said board of trustees.

§ 6. The fire companies composing said corporation shall consist of at least thirty persons each, except hose companies, which shall consist of at least twenty persons. And the members of any of said companies which shall not contain said number shall not be members of this corporation, except that, if any company shall be reduced below said number the same shall not be disbanded, or forfeit any of its rights or privileges under this act, provided its said full number shall be filled within thirty days after said company shall be required so to do by the said board of trustees, by notice in writing served upon the acting foreman of said company.

§ 7. Each of said fire companies shall have the right to pass by-laws for its own government not inconsistent with this act, or the laws and regulations established by the said board of trustees or the charter and by-laws of the said village.

§ 8. The said fire department shall possess the general power of a corporation as defined and limited in title three of the eighteenth chapter of part first of the Revised Statutes of this state; and shall be subject to the provisions of such chapter so far as they may be applicable to said department, and so far as the same are not inconsistent with this act

§ 9. All moneys and evidences of indebtedness, now in the hands of, or belonging to the treasurer of the fire department of said village, as the same before the passage of this act has been and is organized, shall be paid to the treasurer of the said corporation upon his demand thereof, reserving the rights therein of such companies as may not become members of the corporation hereby created in consequence of provisions of section six. And all moneys which by law now are or may hereafter be directed to be paid into the treasury of said village or otherwise, for the purposes of said department and which now are or may hereafter by law be directed to be paid by any insurance company, or other companies or persons, shall be paid to the treasurer of the said corporation.

§ 10. Certificates signed by the president of the said corporation, and the foreman of any company to which any member of this department belongs, and bearing the seal of said corporation, declaring the term the said member has served as fireman in the said corporation, or that the term of service required by the laws of this state has been fully completed by said member, shall be sufficient evidence to entitle him to all the privileges and exemptions secured to firemen by the laws of this state.

§ 11. This act shall take effect immediately.

Chap. 298.

AN ACT in relation to superintendents of the poor.

Passed April 17, 1862; three-fifths being present.

The People of the State of New York, represented in Senate and Assembly, do enact as follows:

SECTION 1. Section one of chapter four hundred and ninety-eight of the laws of eighteen hundred and forty-seven, passed December sixteen, eighteen hundred and forty-seven, is hereby amended by adding thereto the following: And after the board of supervisors of any county shall have, by resolution, directed that only one superintendent of the poor shall be elected in and for such county, the said board may, at any annual meeting thereof, revoke such resolution, and may, by resolution, direct that thereafter three superintendents of the poor shall be elected in and for such county. The superintendent of the poor who shall be in office at the time of the adoption of the resolution hereby authorized, shall hold his office (subject to all provisions of law) until the expiration of the term of office for which he was elected. If the term of office of such superintendent will expire on the thirty-first day of December of the same year of the adoption of said resolution, then three superinten-

Election of superintendents. dents of the poor for said county shall be elected at the next general election, whose term of office respectively shall be determined in accordance with the provisions of section three of said chapter four hundred and ninety-eight. If the term of office of the superintendent of the poor in office at the time of the adoption of said resolution will not expire during the year of the adoption of said resolution, then, at the general election to be held next thereafter, there shall be elected two superintendents of the poor for said county, and their term **Term of office.** of office shall be determined in accordance with the provisions of section three of chapter four hundred and ninety-eight of the laws of eighteen hundred and forty-seven, but for such term that the terms of the three superintendents of the poor shall so expire that one of them shall be to be filled at each annual election thereafter. In any county where such resolution has been already adopted, there shall be elected annually thereafter, at the general election in each year, one county superintendent of the poor, who shall hold his office for three years; and, in each of the counties of this state having a county poor house, the superintendent of the **To appoint keeper.** poor of such counties, or superintendents, if there be more than one, shall appoint a keeper or keepers of such county poor house, and shall have full power, at any time, to remove any keeper and appoint another in his stead. And if the keeper of any such poor house shall **Power to remove keeper.** neglect or refuse to leave the same, or surrender to the superintendent or superintendents the possession of the same, when such possession is demanded, the said superintendent or superintendents shall have power and are hereby authorized to proceed against said keeper in his or their name of office, and to remove said keeper from such poor house by summary proceedings, in the same manner as is provided by article second of chapter eight of part third of the Revised Statutes, entitled " Summary proceedings to recover possession of land in other cases," so far as the same are applicable, except that it shall only be necessary for the superintendent to **Warrant of removal.** set forth in his affidavit, or prove upon the hearing the following facts, to entitle him to the warrant of removal.

1. That the party commencing the proceedings is the superintendent or superintendents of the poor of the county.

2. That the county has a county poor house; and that the keeper is in possession of such poor house, or living therein, and that he refuses to surrender up the possession of such poor house, or remove from the same after the possession shall have been demanded by such superintendent of the poor.

But nothing in this act shall affect the tenure of office of any present incumbent. *Saving clause.*

§ 2. This act shall take effect immediately.

Chap. 299.

AN ACT to authorize the construction of a bridge over the Allegany river on the Indian Reservation, in the town of Carrolton, in the county of Cattaraugus.

Passed April 17, 1862 ; three-fifths being present.

The People of the State of New York, represented in Senate and Assembly, do enact as follows :

SECTION 1. George Van Campen, of the town of Allegany, county of Cattaraugus, a special road commissioner appointed by the board of supervisors of said county, at their annual session in the month of November, eighteen hundred and sixty-one, is hereby authorized to construct a bridge over the Allegany river, at or near the east bounds of the town of Carrolton, on the Indian Reservation, in said county, and to lay out such roads as may be necessary in connection therewith.

§ 2. The said bridge shall be erected as, and shall be, a joint bridge between the towns of Allegany and Carrolton.

§ 3. The commissioner or commissioners of highways of said towns, respectively, are hereby authorized, in their discretion, to contribute, from any moneys applicable to roads and bridges in said towns, towards the construction of such bridge, four hundred dollars on the part of Allegany, and two hundred dollars on the part of Carrolton; one-half of such amounts as they shall contribute to be paid from any moneys applicable to the year eighteen hundred and sixty-two, and the other half from any moneys applicable to the year eighteen hundred and sixty-three.

Chap. 300.

AN ACT to amend an act entitled "An act to provide for the incorporation of life and health insurance companies, and in relation to agencies of such companies," passed June twenty-fourth, eighteen hundred and fifty-three, and to amend several acts amending the same.

Passed April 17, 1862.

The People of the State of New York, represented in Senate and Assembly, do enact as follows:

SECTION 1. Section second of the act entitled "An act to provide for the incorporation of life and health insurance companies, and in relation to agencies of such companies," passed June twenty-fourth, eighteen hundred and fifty-three, is hereby amended by adding thereto at the end thereof the following provisions:

Companies to make insurance on life only, and the granting, &c., of annuities. No company, partnership, or association, organized or incorporated by or under the laws of this or any other state of the United States or any foreign government, transacting the business of life insurance in this state, shall be permitted or allowed to take any other kind of risks except those connected with or appertaining to making insurance on life, and the granting, purchasing and disposing of annuities; nor shall the business of life insurance in this state be in any wise conducted or transacted by any company, partnership or association, which in this, or any other state or country, makes insurance on marine or fire risks, excepting by such *Exception.* foreign companies and associations as shall have already made the deposit in the insurance department required for the transaction of life insurance business in this state.

§ 2. The first section of the act entitled "An act to amend an act entitled 'An act to provide for the incorporation of life and health insurance companies, and in relation to agencies of such companies,' passed June twenty-fourth, eighteen hundred and fifty-three, and the amendment thereto passed July eighteenth, eighteen hundred and fifty-three," passed April twelfth, eighteen hundred and sixty, is hereby so amended as to read as follows:

§ 1. Section one of the act entitled "An act to amend an act entitled 'An act to provide for the incorporation of life and health insurance companies, and in relation *agencies of such companies,' passed June twenty-fourth, eighteen hundred and fifty-three," passed July eighteenth, eighteen hundred and fifty-three, is hereby amended, so as to read as follows:

No company shall be organized under this act for the purposes mentioned in the first department, with a less capital than one hundred thousand dollars, and no company shall be organized, for the purposes mentioned in the second department, with a less capital than twenty-five thousand dollars. The whole capital of such company shall, before proceeding to business, be paid in and invested in stocks or in treasury notes of the United States or of the State of New York, or in bonds and mortgages on improved and unincumbered real estate within the State of New York, worth seventy-five per cent more than the amount loaned thereon, (exclusive of farm buildings thereon,) or in such stocks or securities as now are or may hereafter be receivable by the bank department. And it shall be lawful for any company organized under this act to change and reinvest its capital, or any part thereof, at any time they may desire, in the stocks or bonds and mortgages or securities aforesaid. No company organized for the purposes mentioned in the first department shall commence business until they have deposited with the Superintendent of the Insurance Department of this state the sum of one hundred thousand thousand dollars in United States or New York State stocks, in all cases to be. or to be made to be, equal to stock producing six per cent per annum, and not to be received at a rate above their par value, or above their current market value, or in bonds and mortgages of the description and character above indicated ; and no company organized for the purposes named in the second department shall commence business until they have

Marginal notes: Capital $100,000 in first department and $25,000 in second department. To be paid in before proceeding to business. Deposit in insurance department

*So in the original.

deposited with the Superintendent of the Insurance Department of this state the sum of twenty-five thousand dollars, invested as hereinbefore provided for the investment of the capital of such company. The Superintendent of the Insurance Department shall hold such securities as security for policy holders in said companies, but so long as any company so depositing shall continue solvent, may permit such company to collect the interest or dividends on its securities so deposited, and from time to time to withdraw any of such securities on depositing with the said Superintendent such other securities of like value as those withdrawn, and of the same character and to be received as those above mentioned.

§ 3. The second section of the act entitled ' An act to amend an act entitled 'An act to provide for the incorporation of life and health insurance companies, and in relation to agencies of such companies,' passed June twenty-fourth, eighteen hundred and fifty-three, and the amendment thereto passed July eighteenth, eighteen hundred and fifty-three," passed April twelfth, eighteen hundred and sixty, is hereby so amended as to read as follows :

§ 2. Section eight of the act entitled "An act to provide for the incorporation of life and health insurance companies, and in relation to the agencies of such companies," passed June twenty-fourth, eighteen hundred and fifty-three, is hereby amended so as to read as follows :

§ 8. It shall be lawful for any company organized *May invest its funds in bonds and mortgages or stocks.* under this act to invest its funds or accumulations in bonds and mortgages on unincumbered real estate within the State of New York, worth fifty per cent more than the sum so loaned thereon, exclusive of buildings, unless such buildings be insured in a good and solvent insurance company or companies and the policy or policies of insurance be assigned as collateral security for the monies loaned, or in stocks or treasury notes of the United States, stocks of this state, or stocks of any incorporated city of this state, and to lend the same or any part thereof on the security of such bonds and mortgages, and upon the pledge of such stocks, or treasury *Proviso.* notes ; provided that the current market value of such stocks or treasury notes shall be at least ten per cent more than the sum so loaned thereon.

§ 4. Section second of the act entitled "An act to amend an act entitled 'An act to provide for the incorporation of life and health insurance companies, and in relation to agencies of such companies, passed June twenty-fourth, eighteen hundred and fifty-three,' passed July eighteenth, eighteen hundred and fifty-three," is hereby so amended as to read as follows:

§ 2. Section fourteen of said act is hereby amended so as to read as follows:

It shall not be lawful for any person to act within this state, as agent or otherwise, in receiving or procuring applications for insurance, or in any manner to aid in transacting the business of insurance referred to in the first section of this act, for any company or association incorporated by, or organized under, the laws of any other state government, unless such company is possessed of the amount of actual capital required by the sixth section of this act, for companies in this state, and the same is invested in stocks or treasury notes of the United States, or of the State of New York, or of the state in which said company is located, or in bonds and mortgages on improved, unincumbered real estate within the state where such company is located, or in such stocks or securities as now are, or may hereafter be, receivable by the bank department; but all mortgages deposited by any company under this section shall be upon improved, unincumbered real estate worth seventy-five per cent more than the amount loaned thereon, which stocks and securities shall be deposited with the Auditor, Comptroller, or chief financial officer of the state, by whose laws said company is incorporated; and the Superintendent of the Insurance Department of this State furnished with the certificate of such Auditor, Comptroller or chief financial officer aforesaid under his hand and official seal, that he, as such Auditor, Comptroller, or chief financial officer of such state, holds in trust and on deposit, for the benefit of all the policy holders of such company, the security before mentioned, which certificate shall embrace the items of the security so held, that he is satisfied that such securities are worth one hundred thousand dollars, if the company proposes to transact the business referred to in the first department, or that they are worth twenty-five thousand dollars if the company proposes to transact

[margin note: Agents within this state not to act for foreign companies unless capital is invested in certain stocks, &c., or in bonds and mortgages.]

[margin note: Certificate to be furnished as to security.]

64

Saving
clause. the business referred to in the second department. But
nothing herein contained shall be construed to invalidate the agency of any company incorporated by another
state by reason of such company having from time to
time exchanged the securities so deposited with the Auditor, Comptroller, or chief financial officer of the state
in which such company is located, for other stock or
securities, authorized by this act, or by reason of such
company having drawn its interest and dividends, from

Attorney to
be appointed on whom
process may
be served.
Charter to
be filed. time to time, for such stocks and securities. Such company shall also appoint an attorney in this state, on
whom process of law can be served; and such attorney
shall file with the Superintendent of the Insurance Department a certified copy of the charter of said company, and also a certified copy of the vote or resolution
of the trustees or directors of the said company appointing such attorney, which appointment shall continue
until another attorney be substituted. And in case any
such insurance corporation shall cease to transact business in this state according to the laws thereof, the
agents last designated or acting as such for such corporation, shall be deemed to continue agents for such corporation for the purpose of serving process for commencing actions upon any policy or liability issued or
contracted while such corporation transacted business in

Service of
process. this state, and service of such process for the causes
aforesaid upon any such agent, shall be deemed a valid
personal service upon such corporation Such company

Statement
to be filed
in insurance department. shall also file a statement of its condition and affairs in
the office of the Superintendent of the Insurance Department, in the same form and manner required for the
annual statements of similar companies organized under

Certificate
of superintendent to
be procured
before
agent can
act. the laws of this state. It shall not be lawful for any
agent to act for any company referred to in this section,
directly or indirectly, in taking risks, collecting premiums, or in any manner transacting the business of life
insurance in this state, without procuring from the said
Superintendent a certificate of authority, stating that the
foregoing requirements have been complied with, and
setting forth the name of the attorney for such company; a certified copy of which certificate shall be filed
in the county clerk's office of the county where the
agency is to be established, and shall be the authority of
such company and agent to commence business in this

state; and such company or its attorney shall annually, in the month of January, file with the superintendent of the Insurance Department of this state a statement of its affairs for the preceding year, in the same manner and form provided in the twelfth section of this act for similar companies in this state; and if the said annual statement shall be satisfactory evidence to the Superintendent of the Insurance Department of the solvency and ability of the said company to meet all its engagements at maturity, and that the said deposit is maintained as above required and provided, he shall issue renewal certificates of authority to the agents of said company, certified copies of which shall be filed in the county clerk's office of the county where the agency is located, during the month of January in each year; and which renewal certificates shall be the authority of such agents to issue new policies in this state for the ensuing year. To be filed in county clerk's office.

§ 5. Section fifteen of the act entitled "An act to provide for the incorporation of life and health insurance companies, and in relation to the agencies of such companies," passed June twenty-fourth, eighteen hundred and fifty-three, is hereby amended so as to read as follows:

§ 15. It shall not be lawful for any person to act in this state as agent or otherwise, in receiving or procuring applications for life or health insurance, or in any manner to aid in transacting the business of any life or health insurance company, partnership or association, incorporated by or organized under the laws of any foreign government, until such company, partnership or association shall have deposited with the Superintendent of the Insurance Department, for the benefit of the policy holders of said company, partnership or association, citizens or residents of the United States, securities to the amount of one hundred thousand dollars, of the kind required or which may hereafter be required for similar companies of this state, and shall have appointed an attorney in this state on whom process of law can be served; and the said company, partnership or association shall have filed with the Superintendent of the Insurance Department a duly certified copy of the charter or deed of settlement of the said company, partnership or association, and also a duplicate original copy of the letter or power of attorney of such company or associa- Agent not to act until company deposit in the insurance department securities to the amount of $100,000. An attorney to be appointed on whom process may be served. Charter and power of attorney to be filed.

tion appointing the attorney thereof, which appointment shall continue until another attorney be substituted. And in case any such insurance corporation shall cease to transact business in this state according to the laws thereof, the agents last designated or acting as such for such corporation, shall be deemed to continue agents for such corporation for the purpose of serving process for commencing actions upon any policy or liability issued or contracted while such corporation transacted business **Service of process.** in this state, and service of such process for the causes aforesaid upon any such agent, shall be deemed a valid **Statement to be filed.** personal service upon such corporation. Such company, partnership or association shall also file a statement of its condition and affairs in the office of the Superintendent of the Insurance Department, in the same form and manner required for the annual statements of similar companies organized under the laws of this state. **Agents not to act without certificate of superintendent.** It shall not be lawful for any agent or agents to act for any company, partnership or association referred to in this section, directly or indirectly, in taking risks, collecting premiums, or in any manner transacting the business of life insurance in this state, without procuring from the said Superintendent a certificate of authority (which shall be renewable annually) stating that the foregoing requirements have been complied with, and setting forth the name of the attorney for such **Certificate to be filed.** company, a certified copy of which certificate shall be filed in the county clerk's office of the county where the agency is to be established, and which shall be the authority of such company and agent to commence **Annual statement to be filed.** business in this state; and such company, partnership or association shall annually, on the first day of January, or within thirty days thereafter, file with the Superintendent of the Insurance Department a statement of all its affairs in the same manner and form provided in the twelfth section of this act for similar companies in this state; which statement shall be made up for the year ending on the preceding thirtieth day of June, accompanied also by a supplementary annual statement, duly verified by the attorney or general agent of the com- **What to contain.** pany or association in this state, giving a detailed description of the policies issued and those which have ceased to be in force during the year, the amount of premiums received and claims and taxes paid in this state and the United States for the year ending on the preceding thirty-first day of December; said supplementary statement shall also contain a description of the investments of such company or association in this country, and such other information as may be required by said Superintendent; and if the said annual statement shall be satisfactory evidence to the said Superintendent of the solvency and ability of the said company to meet all its engagements at maturity, he shall issue renewal certificates of authority to the agents of said company, partnership or association, certified copies of which shall be filed by such agents in the county clerk's office of the county where the agency is located, within sixty days after the first day of January in each year, and which renewal certificates shall be the authority of such agents to issue new policies in this state for the ensuing year. All such foreign insurance companies, partnerships and associations engaged in the transaction of the business of life or health insurance in this state, shall annually, on or before the first day of March in each year, pay to the Superintendent of the Insurance Department a tax of two per cent on all premiums received in cash or otherwise by their attorneys or agents in this state, during the year ending on the preceding thirty-first day of December, upon which a tax on premiums has not been paid to any other state. The avails of said tax shall be paid into the state treasury, and shall be applicable, as far as necessary, towards defraying the expenses of the insurance department. In case of neglect or refusal by any such company to pay said tax, the Superintendent is hereby authorized to collect the same out of the interest on the stocks and securities deposited by such company in the insurance department.

[marginal notes:] When superintendent to issue renewal certificates to agents. — Foreign companies to pay tax. — Avails of tax to be paid into state treasury.

Chap. 301.

AN ACT for the relief of Frederick D. Van
          Wagenen.

Passed April 17, 1862; three-fifths being present.

*The People of the State of New York, represented in
Senate and Assembly, do enact as follows:*

SECTION 1. The canal board is hereby authorized and
required to investigate the claim of Frederick D. Van
Wagenen, in which he alleges that he sustained loss and
damage, while constructing the stone dam number four
on the Oswego river, in consequence of the state failing
to maintain its coffer dam erected for the protection of
said Van Wagenen, while executing said work, and the
amount, if any awarded to him by said board, shall be
paid by the commissioner in charge of the middle division
of the canals of the state, out of the moneys of the canals
devoted to or set apart for repairs.

§ 2. This act shall take effect immediately.

Chap. 302.

AN ACT to amend an act entitled "An act for the
    incorporation of benevolent, charitable, scientific
    and missionary societies," passed April twelfth,
    eighteen hundred and forty-eight.

Passed April 17, 1862.

*The People of the State of New York, represented in
Senate and Assembly, do enact as follows:*

SECTION 1. Section first of the act entitled "An act for
the incorporation of benevolent, charitable, scientific
and missionary societies," passed April twelfth, eighteen
hundred and forty-eight, is hereby amended by adding
to said section after the word "scientific," in the fourth
line thereof, the words "historical, literary," so that said
act shall authorize the incorporation of historical and

literary societies in the same manner as in case of the organization of societies "for benevolent, charitable, scientific or missionary purposes."

Chap. 303.

AN ACT for the relief of Patrick Colwell.

Passed April 17, 1862; three-fifths being present.

The People of the State of New York, represented in Senate and Assembly, do enact as follows:

SECTION 1. The Lieutenant-Governor, Comptroller and Attorney General, shall examine or cause to be examined, the claim of Patrick Colwell, of New York city, for damages alleged to have been sustained by him by the falling of the new state arsenal on the nineteenth day of November, eighteen hundred and fifty-eight, destroying his property in a stable adjoining said arsenal, and on said examination to award the said Patrick Colwell such sum as he may be legally and equitably entitled thereto, if any.

§ 2. The treasurer shall pay, on the warrant of the Comptroller, out of any moneys not otherwise appropriated, such sum as shall have been awarded to the said Patrick Colwell.

§ 3. This act shall take effect immediately.

Chap. 304.

AN ACT to declare the village of Belleville a separate road district.

Passed April 17, 1862; three-fifths being present.

The People of the State of New York, represented in Senate and Assembly, do enact as follows:

SECTION 1. The village of Belleville shall constitute a separate road district in the town of Ellisburgh, exempt from the superintendence of the commissioners of highways of said town, with the exception of the bridges across Big Sandy creek, which shall remain under the superintendence of the commissioners of highways of said town. And the trustees of said village shall be commissioners of highways for said village, and shall have the same powers and be subject to the same duties as commissioners of highways of towns in like cases, and may in their discretion appoint a street commissioner, whose special duty it shall be to superintend, subject to the control of said trustees, the construction and repairs of all roads, side walks and cross walks in said village, and who shall receive for his services such an amount as a majority of the board of trustees may deem proper, not exceeding the compensation allowed to overseers of highways.

§ 2. This act shall take effect immediately.

Chap. 305.

AN ACT in relation to the First Congregational church and society of Moravia.

Passed April 17, 1862.

The People of the State of New York, represented in Senate and Assembly, do enact as follows:

SECTION 1. The trustees of the First Congregational church and society of Moravia, are hereby authorized and empowered to convey by deed to the trustees of the village of Moravia, and their successors in office, to be held by said trustees and their successors as a public cemetery, as the same is now held by the trustees of the said First Congregational church and society of Moravia, all that certain piece or lot of land in the village of Moravia, in the county of Cayuga, owned and held by the said church and society as a cemetery.

§ 2. This act shall take effect immediately.

Chap. 306.

AN ACT to prevent and punish fraud in the use of false stamps, brands, labels, or trade marks.

Passed April 17, 1862; three-fifths being present.

The People of the State of New York, represented in Senate and Assembly, do enact as follows:

SECTION 1. Any person or persons who shall knowingly and wilfully forge or counterfeit, or cause or procure to be forged or counterfeited, any representation, likeness, similitude, copy, or imitation of the private stamp, brand, wrapper, label or trade mark, usually affixed by any mechanic, manufacturer, druggist, merchant, or tradesman, to and upon the goods, wares, merchandize, or preparation of such mechanic, manufacturer, druggist, merchant or tradesman, with intent to pass off any work, goods, manufacture, compound or preparation to which such forged or counterfeited representation, likeness, similitude, copy or imitation to be affixed or intended to be affixed, as the work, goods, manufacture, compound or preparation of such mechanic, manufacturer, druggist or tradesman, shall, upon conviction thereof, be deemed guilty of a misdemeanor, and shall be punished by imprisonment in the county jail for a period of not less than six months, nor more than twelve months, or fined not more than five thousand dollars.

§ 2. Any person or persons who shall, with intent to defraud any person or persons, body corporate or politic have in his or their possession, any die or dies, plate or plates, brand or brands, engraving or engravings, or printed labels, stamps, imprints, wrapper, or trade marks, or any representation, likeness, similitude, copy, or imitation of the private stamp, imprint, brand, wrapper, label, or trade mark usually affixed by any mechanic, manufacturer, druggist, merchant, or tradesman, to or upon articles made, manufactured, prepared, or compounded by him or them, for the purpose of making impressions, or selling the same when made, or using the same upon any other article made, manufactured, prepared, or compounded, and passing the same off upon

65

the year eighteen hundred and sixty-two, and the other half from any moneys applicable to the year eighteen hundred and sixty-three.

Chap. 300.

AN ACT to amend an act entitled "An act to provide for the incorporation of life and health insurance companies, and in relation to agencies of such companies," passed June twenty-fourth, eighteen hundred and fifty-three, and to amend several acts amending the same.

Passed April 17, 1862.

The People of the State of New York, represented in Senate and Assembly, do enact as follows:

SECTION 1. Section second of the act entitled " An act to provide for the incorporation of life and health insurance companies, and in relation to agencies of such companies," passed June twenty-fourth, eighteen hundred and fifty-three, is hereby amended by adding thereto at the end thereof the following provisions:

Companies to make insurance on life only, and the granting, &c., of annuities.

No company, partnership, or association, organized or incorporated by or under the laws of this or any other state of the United States or any foreign government, transacting the business of life insurance in this state, shall be permitted or allowed to take any other kind of risks except those connected with or appertaining to making insurance on life, and the granting, purchasing and disposing of annuities ; nor shall the business of life insurance in this state be in any wise conducted or transacted by any company, partnership or association, which in this, or any other state or country, makes insurance on marine or fire risks, excepting by such foreign companies and associations as shall have already made the deposit in the insurance department required for the transaction of life insurance business in this state.

Exception.

§ 2. The first section of the act entitled "An act to amend an act entitled 'An act to provide for the in-

corporation of life and health insurance companies, and
in relation to agencies of such companies,' passed June
twenty-fourth, eighteen hundred and fifty-three, and the
amendment thereto passed July eighteenth, eighteen
hundred and fifty-three," passed April twelfth, eighteen
hundred and sixty, is hereby so amended as to read as
follows:

§ 1. Section one of the act entitled "An act to amend
an act entitled 'An act to provide for the incorporation
of life and health insurance companies, and in relation
*agencies of such companies,' passed June twenty-
fourth, eighteen hundred and fifty-three," passed July
eighteenth, eighteen hundred and fifty-three, is hereby
amended, so as to read as follows:

No company shall be organized under this act for the
purposes mentioned in the first department, with a less
capital than one hundred thousand dollars, and no company shall be organized, for the purposes mentioned in
the second department, with a less capital than twenty-
five thousand dollars. The whole capital of such company shall, before proceeding to business, be paid in and
invested in stocks or in treasury notes of the United
States or of the State of New York, or in bonds and
mortgages on improved and unincumbered real estate
within the State of New York, worth seventy-five per
cent more than the amount loaned thereon, (exclusive
of farm buildings thereon,) or in such stocks or securities
as now are or may hereafter be receivable by the bank
department. And it shall be lawful for any company
organized under this act to change and reinvest its capital, or any part thereof, at any time they may desire, in
the stocks or bonds and mortgages or securities aforesaid. No company organized for the purposes mentioned
in the first department shall commence business until
they have deposited with the Superintendent of the Insurance Department of this state the sum of one hundred thousand thousand dollars in United States or New York State
stocks, in all cases to be, or to be made to be, equal to
stock producing six per cent per annum, and not to be
received at a rate above their par value, or above their
current market value, or in bonds and mortgages of the
description and character above indicated; and no company organized for the purposes named in the second
department shall commence business until they have

*So in the original.

deposited with the Superintendent of the Insurance Department of this state the sum of twenty-five thousand dollars, invested as hereinbefore provided for the investment of the capital of such company. The Superintendent of the Insurance Department shall hold such securities as security for policy holders in said companies, but so long as any company so depositing shall continue solvent, may permit such company to collect the interest or dividends on its securities so deposited, and from time to time to withdraw any of such securities on depositing with the said Superintendent such other securities of like value as those withdrawn, and of the same character and to be received as those above mentioned.

§ 3. The second section of the act entitled ' An act to amend an act entitled 'An act to provide for the incorporation of life and health insurance companies, and in relation to agencies of such companies,' passed June twenty-fourth, eighteen hundred and fifty-three, and the amendment thereto passed July eighteenth, eighteen hundred and fifty-three," passed April twelfth, eighteen hundred and sixty, is hereby so amended as to read as follows:

§ 2. Section eight of the act entitled "An act to provide for the incorporation of life and health insurance companies, and in relation to the agencies of such companies," passed June twenty-fourth, eighteen hundred and fifty-three, is hereby amended so as to read as follows:

May invest its funds in bonds and mortgages or stocks. § 8. It shall be lawful for any company organized under this act to invest its funds or accumulations in bonds and mortgages on unincumbered real estate within the State of New York, worth fifty per cent more than the sum so loaned thereon, exclusive of buildings, unless such buildings be insured in a good and solvent insurance company or companies and the policy or policies of insurance be assigned as collateral security for the monies loaned, or in stocks or treasury notes of the United States, stocks of this state, or stocks of any incorporated city of this state, and to lend the same or any part thereof on the security of such bonds and mortgages, and upon the pledge of such stocks, or treasury **Proviso.** notes; provided that the current market value of such stocks or treasury notes shall be at least ten per cent more than the sum so loaned thereon.

§ 4. Section second of the act entitled "An act to amend an act entitled 'An act to provide for the incorporation of life and health insurance companies, and in relation to agencies of such companies, passed June twenty-fourth, eighteen hundred and fifty-three,' passed July eighteenth, eighteen hundred and fifty-three," is hereby so amended as to read as follows:

§ 2. Section fourteen of said act is hereby amended so as to read as follows:

It shall not be lawful for any person to act within this state, as agent or otherwise, in receiving or procuring applications for insurance, or in any manner to aid in transacting the business of insurance referred to in the first section of this act, for any company or association incorporated by, or organized under, the laws of any other state government, unless such company is possessed of the amount of actual capital required by the sixth section of this act, for companies in this state, and the same is invested in stocks or treasury notes of the United States, or of the State of New York, or of the state in which said company is located, or in bonds and mortgages on improved, unincumbered real estate within the state where such company is located, or in such stocks or securities as now are, or may hereafter be, receivable by the bank department; but all mortgages deposited by any company under this section shall be upon improved, unincumbered real estate worth seventy-five per cent more than the amount loaned thereon, which stocks and securities shall be deposited with the Auditor, Comptroller, or chief financial officer of the state, by whose laws said company is incorporated; and the Superintendent of the Insurance Department of this State furnished with the certificate of such Auditor, Comptroller or chief financial officer aforesaid under his hand and official seal, that he, as such Auditor, Comptroller, or chief financial officer of such state, holds in trust and on deposit, for the benefit of all the policy holders of such company, the security before mentioned, which certificate shall embrace the items of the security so held, that he is satisfied that such securities are worth one hundred thousand dollars, if the company proposes to transact the business referred to in the first department, or that they are worth twenty-five thousand dollars if the company proposes to transact

Agents within this state not to act for foreign companies unless capital is invested in certain stocks, &c., or in bonds and mortgages.

Certificate to be furnished as to security.

64

the business referred to in the second department. But nothing herein contained shall be construed to invalidate the agency of any company incorporated by another state by reason of such company having from time to time exchanged the securities so deposited with the Auditor, Comptroller, or chief financial officer of the state in which such company is located, for other stock or securities, authorized by this act, or by reason of such company having drawn its interest and dividends, from time to time, for such stocks and securities. Such com-

pany shall also appoint an attorney in this state, on whom process of law can be served; and such attorney shall file with the Superintendent of the Insurance Department a certified copy of the charter of said company, and also a certified copy of the vote or resolution of the trustees or directors of the said company appointing such attorney, which appointment shall continue until another attorney be substituted. And in case any such insurance corporation shall cease to transact business in this state according to the laws thereof, the agents last designated or acting as such for such corporation, shall be deemed to continue agents for such corporation for the purpose of serving process for commencing actions upon any policy or liability issued or contracted while such corporation transacted business in

this state, and service of such process for the causes aforesaid upon any such agent, shall be deemed a valid personal service upon such corporation Such company

shall also file a statement of its condition and affairs in the office of the Superintendent of the Insurance Department, in the same form and manner required for the annual statements of similar companies organized under

the laws of this state. It shall not be lawful for any agent to act for any company referred to in this section, directly or indirectly, in taking risks, collecting premiums, or in any manner transacting the business of life insurance in this state, without procuring from the said Superintendent a certificate of authority, stating that the foregoing requirements have been complied with, and setting forth the name of the attorney for such company ; a certified copy of which certificate shall be filed in the county clerk's office of the county where the agency is to be established, and shall be the authority of such company and agent to commence business in this state; and such company or its attorney shall annually, in the month of January, file with the superintendent of the Insurance Department of this state a statement of its affairs for the preceding year, in the same manner and form provided in the twelfth section of this act for similar companies in this state; and if the said annual statement shall be satisfactory evidence to the Superintendent of the Insurance Department of the solvency and ability of the said company to meet all its engagements at maturity, and that the said deposit is maintained as above required and provided, he shall issue renewal certificates of authority to the agents of said company, certified copies of which shall be filed in the county **To be filed in county clerk's office.** clerk's office of the county where the agency is located, during the month of January in each year; and which renewal certificates shall be the authority of such agents to issue new policies in this state for the ensuing year.

§ 5. Section fifteen of the act entitled " An act to provide for the incorporation of life and health insurance companies, and in relation to the agencies of such companies," passed June twenty-fourth, eighteen hundred and fifty-three, is hereby amended so as to read as follows:

§ 15. It shall not be lawful for any person to act in **Agent not to act until company deposit in the insurance department securities to the amount of $100,000.** this state as agent or otherwise, in receiving or procuring applications for life or health insurance, or in any manner to aid in transacting the business of any life or health insurance company, partnership or association, incorporated by or organized under the laws of any foreign government, until such company, partnership or association shall have deposited with the Superintendent of the Insurance Department, for the benefit of the policy holders of said company, partnership or association, citizens or residents of the United States, securities to the amount of one hundred thousand dollars, of the kind required or which may hereafter be required for similar **An attorney to be appointed on whom process may be served.** companies of this state, and shall have appointed an attorney in this state on whom process of law can be served; and the said company, partnership or association shall have filed with the Superintendent of the Insurance Department a duly certified copy of the charter **Charter and power of attorney to be filed.** or deed of settlement of the said company, partnership or association, and also a duplicate original copy of the letter or power of attorney of such company or associa-

tion appointing the attorney thereof, which appointment
shall continue until another attorney be substituted.
And in case any such insurance corporation shall cease
to transact business in this state according to the laws
thereof, the agents last designated or acting as such for
such corporation, shall be deemed to continue agents for
such corporation for the purpose of serving process for
commencing actions upon any policy or liability issued
or contracted while such corporation transacted business
Service of process. in this state, and service of such process for the causes
aforesaid upon any such agent, shall be deemed a valid
Statement to be filed. personal service upon such corporation. Such company,
partnership or association shall also file a statement of
its condition and affairs in the office of the Superinten-
tendent of the Insurance Department, in the same form
and manner required for the annual statements of similar companies organized under the laws of this state.
Agents not to act without certificate of superintendent. It shall not be lawful for any agent or agents to act for
any company, partnership or association referred to in
this section, directly or indirectly, in taking risks, collecting premiums, or in any manner transacting the
business of life insurance in this state, without procuring from the said Superintendent a certificate of authority (which shall be renewable annually) stating that
the foregoing requirements have been complied with,
and setting forth the name of the attorney for such
Certificate to be filed. company, a certified copy of which certificate shall be
filed in the county clerk's office of the county where
the agency is to be established, and which shall be the
authority of such company and agent to commence
Annual statement to be filed. business in this state; and such company, partnership or
association shall annually, on the first day of January,
or within thirty days thereafter, file with the Superintendent of the Insurance Department a statement of all
its affairs in the same manner and form provided in the
twelfth section of this act for similar companies in this
state; which statement shall be made up for the year
ending on the preceding thirtieth day of June, accompanied also by a supplementary annual statement, duly
verified by the attorney or general agent of the com-
What to contain. pany or association in this state, giving a detailed description of the policies issued and those which have
ceased to be in force during the year, the amount of premiums received and claims and taxes paid in this state

and the United States for the year ending on the preceding thirty-first day of December ; said supplementary statement shall also contain a description of the investments of such company or association in this country, and such other information as may be required by said Superintendent; and if the said annual statement shall be satisfactory evidence to the said Superintendent of the solvency and ability of the said company to meet all its engagements at maturity, he shall issue renewal certificates of said company, partnership or association, copies of which shall be filed by such agents in the county clerk's office of the county where the agency is located, within sixty days after the first day of January in each year, and which renewal certificates shall be the authority of such agents to issue new policies in this state for the ensuing year. All such foreign insurance companies, partnerships and associations engaged in the transaction of the business of life or health insurance in this state, shall annually, on or before the first day of March in each year, pay to the Superintendent of the Insurance Department a tax of two per cent on all premiums received in cash or otherwise by their attorneys or agents in this state, during the year ending on the preceding thirty-first day of December, upon which a tax on premiums has not been paid to any other state. The avails of said tax shall be paid into the state treasury, and shall be applicable, as far as necessary, towards defraying the expenses of the insurance department. In case of neglect or refusal by any such company to pay said tax, the Superintendent is hereby authorized to collect the same out of the interest on the stocks and securities deposited by such company in the insurance department.

When superintendent to issue renewal certificates to agents.

Foreign companies to pay tax.

Avails of tax to be paid into state treasury.

Chap. 301.

AN ACT for the relief of Frederick D. Van Wagenen.

Passed April 17, 1862; three-fifths being present.

The People of the State of New York, represented in Senate and Assembly, do enact as follows:

SECTION 1. The canal board is hereby authorized and required to investigate the claim of Frederick D. Van Wagenen, in which he alleges that he sustained loss and damage, while constructing the stone dam number four on the Oswego river, in consequence of the state failing to maintain its coffer dam erected for the protection of said Van Wagenen, while executing said work, and the amount, if any awarded to him by said board, shall be paid by the commissioner in charge of the middle division of the canals of the state, out of the moneys of the canals devoted to or set apart for repairs.

§ 2. This act shall take effect immediately.

Chap. 302.

AN ACT to amend an act entitled "An act for the incorporation of benevolent, charitable, scientific and missionary societies," passed April twelfth, eighteen hundred and forty-eight.

Passed April 17, 1862.

The People of the State of New York, represented in Senate and Assembly, do enact as follows:

SECTION 1. Section first of the act entitled "An act for the incorporation of benevolent, charitable, scientific and missionary societies," passed April twelfth, eighteen hundred and forty-eight, is hereby amended by adding to said section after the word "scientific," in the fourth line thereof, the words " historical, literary," so that said act shall authorize the incorporation of historical and literary societies in the same manner as in case of the organization of societies "for benevolent, charitable, scientific or missionary purposes."

Chap. 303.

AN ACT for the relief of Patrick Colwell.

Passed April 17, 1862; three-fifths being present.

The People of the State of New York, represented in Senate and Assembly, do enact as follows:

SECTION 1. The Lieutenant-Governor, Comptroller and Attorney General, shall examine or cause to be examined, the claim of Patrick Colwell, of New York city, for damages alleged to have been sustained by him by the falling of the new state arsenal on the nineteenth day of November, eighteen hundred and fifty-eight, destroying his property in a stable adjoining said arsenal, and on said examination to award the said Patrick Colwell such sum as he may be legally and equitably entitled thereto, if any.

§ 2. The treasurer shall pay, on the warrant of the Comptroller, out of any moneys not otherwise appropriated, such sum as shall have been awarded to the said Patrick Colwell.

§ 3. This act shall take effect immediately.

Chap. 304.

AN ACT to declare the village of Belleville a separate road district.

Passed April 17, 1862; three-fifths being present.

The People of the State of New York, represented in Senate and Assembly, do enact as follows:

SECTION 1. The village of Belleville shall constitute a separate road district in the town of Ellisburgh, exempt from the superintendence of the commissioners of high-

Chap. 316.

AN ACT to amend the charter of the Atlantic
Fire Insurance Company of Brooklyn.

Passed April 17, 1862.

*The People of the State of New York, represented in
Senate and Assembly, do enact as follows:*

SECTION 1. The fourth article of the certificate of incorporation of the Atlantic Fire Insurance company of
Brooklyn, is hereby amended so as to read as follows:

John D. Cocks, Czar Dunning, G. A. Jarvis, J. S. T.
Stranahan, Walter S. Griffith, J. A. Davenport, Ezra
Lewis, Robert H. Berdell, S. L. Husted, Nehemiah
Knight, J. J. Van Nostrand, Nathaniel Putnam,
Edward Bridge, C. C. Roumage, Levi H. Brigham, Cur-
tis Noble, Joseph W. Green, Seymour Burrell, Charles
Stanton, William W. Wicks, Samuel Osborne, S. W.
Moore, William L. Cogswell, Joseph R. Skidmore, James
W. Martens, William H. Slocum, Matthew Vassar, Jr.,
C. S. Knight, Percy R. Pyne, William M. Wilson, John
O. Hoyt, David R. Baylis, John Schenck, John Alstyne,
Cornelius J. Sprague, William Evans, John Woolsey,
Walter M. Franklin, Albert G. Lee and E. W. Dunham
shall constitute the board of directors of said company
for the present year, and shall continue in office until
the first Wednesday of February, in the year one thousand eight hundred and sixty-three, on which day, and
annually thereafter, not less than twenty nor more
than forty directors shall be elected by the shareholders
by ballot, at the office of the company in the city of
Brooklyn. Each shareholder shall be entitled to one
vote for every share of stock which he shall have held
in his own name for at least thirty days prior to such
election. Notice of every such election shall be published at least two weeks immediately previous thereto, three times in each week, in two newspapers printed
in the city of Brooklyn.

§ 2. The fifth article of the said certificate of incorporation shall be amended so as to read as follows:

The first board of directors, immediately after the corporation shall be authorized to commence business, and

the directors thereafter to be chosen as soon as may be
after each annual election, shall, by the vote of at least ten
members, convened at a meeting of the board, choose
one of their number to be president, who shall hold his
office until his successor shall have been elected. In case
of the death, resignation or other disability of the president or of any director, the vacancy shall in like manner
be filled by the board for the remainder of the term or
for the time being, as the case may require. The first
board of directors shall also appoint three inspectors to
conduct the first election for directors, and at each annual election thereafter three inspectors shall be elected
by the shareholders for the like purpose.

§ 3. The sixth article of the said certificate of incorporation shall be amended by adding to the end of the
said section the following words :

" And eight members of the said board shall constitute a quorum for the transaction of business."

Chap. 317.

AN ACT to amend an act entitled " An act to incorporate a fire company in Union Village, Washington county," passed March twenty-second,
eighteen hundred and thirty-seven.

Passed April 17, 1862; three-fifths being present.

*The People of the State of New York, represented in
Senate and Assembly, do enact as follows :*

SECTION 1. Section one of the act entitled " An act to
incorporate a fire company in Union Village, Washington county," passed March twenty-second, eighteen hundred and thirty-seven, is hereby amended so as to allow
fifty as the number of members of said company, in
place of twenty-four as now authorized.

§ 2. This act shall take effect immediately.

Chap. 318.

AN ACT to provide the means to pay the indebtedness of the State incurred for the enlargement and completion of the canals, and to increase the revenue of the sinking fund, under section three of article seven of the Constitution.

Passed April 18, 1862; three-fifths being present.

The People of the State of New York, represented in Senate and Assembly, do enact as follows :

Additional tax to be levied. SECTION 1. In addition to any other tax now authorized to be levied and collected, there shall be imposed for the fiscal year commencing on the first day of October, one thousand eight hundred and sixty-two, a tax of six-eighths of one mill on each dollar of valuation of real and personal property taxable in this state, or a tax at such rate or proportion as may be necessary to raise the sum of one million three hundred and fifty thousand dollars, to be assessed raised and collected upon and by the annual assessments and collections of taxes for the said fiscal year, in the manner prescribed by law, to be paid by the county treasurers respectively, into the treasury of this state, to be there received, held and paid to and for the uses and purposes in this act prescribed.

Where paid. § 2. The whole of the taxes levied and collected under this act shall be paid into the treasury of this state to the credit of the canal fund, and shall be held, applied, and is hereby appropriated as follows :

How taxes applied. 1st. To increase the revenues of the sinking fund under sections three of article seven of the constitution of this state, so as to make the said fund sufficient to preserve the public faith in the payment of the interest on the debt contracted under said section three of article seven, for the enlargement and completion of the canals, the sum of two hundred and fifty-two thousand dollars.

Ib. 2d. To pay the fifteen per cent reserved on contracts entered into pursuant to laws enacted in accordance with said section three of article seven, for the enlargement and completion of the canals, which may be due to contractors and not provided for by other appropriations, the sum three hundred thousand dollars.

3d. For the payment of awards made by the canal appraisers and the canal board since April thirteenth, eighteen hundred and fifty-nine, and interest thereon at the rate of six per cent per annum, from and after ninety days from the date of such awards to the time when the Auditor of the canal department shall give notice in the state paper that funds have been provided for that purpose ; also for the payment of interest in accordance with the provisions of chapter four hundred and ninety of the laws of eighteen hundred and sixty, together with the payment of such portion of principal as may be due and unpaid, on which the payment of interest is provided for by said act, the sum of eight hundred thousand dollars.

§ 3. To meet the appropriation made under the last clause of the second section of this act, of the moneys to be collected upon said tax, with as little delay as practicable, the commissioners of the canal fund may, from time to time, invest in said tax any surplus moneys of the canal debt sinking fund under section one of article seven of the constitution, not exceeding in all the sum of six hundred thousand dollars, and the moneys thus invested shall be applied to pay the appropriations made for the payment of awards by the canal appraisers, and interest thereon as provided in this act, and of any increase to such awards as may have been made by the canal board ; and so much of the moneys arising from such tax as may be necessary, shall be, when paid into the treasury, and hereby is pledged and shall be applied in the first instance to reimburse the said sinking fund for the amount invested in said tax, and for the interest on the same, at a rate not exceeding five per cent per annum from the time of investment to the day of payment.

§ 4. In case the net proceeds of said tax shall not, when paid into the treasury, be sufficient to pay the appropriation in full, made by this act, then such net proceeds shall be apportioned to the several appropriations herein made in proportion to the several sums appropriated.

§ 5. This act shall take effect immediately.

Chap. 319.

AN ACT to amend the charter of the Schoharie Kill bridge company, and laws relating thereto.

Passed April 18, 1862; three-fifths being present.

The People of the State of New York, represented in Senate and Assembly, do enact as follows:

Liability to pay toll.

SECTION 1. The inhabitants of the towns of Windham, Ashland and Prattsville, except such of said inhabitants as are exempt from paying tolls by part one, chapter eighteen, title one, article three, section thirty-six, of the Revised Statutes, shall hereafter be liable to pay the usual full rates of toll for passing the middle gate on the turnpike road of the Schoharie Kill bridge company, situated on said turnpike road between Windham Center

Exception.

and the village of Ashland, unless each inhabitant claiming the right to pass said gate by virtue of chapter eighty of the laws of eighteen hundred and seventeen shall produce and show to the gate keeper of said gate a certificate, signed by the treasurer of said company, that the highway labor and assessments required to be worked by such inhabitants as reside on said turnpike has been worked out upon said turnpike road. or commuted for the same as required by section three of the act passed April seventeenth, eighteen hundred and fifty-one, by the first day of July in each and every year as required by said act, or commuted for in each and every

Duty of certain inhabitants.

year by the fifteenth day of June; and said inhabitants liable to work their assessments on said turnpike shall in each year work out such assessments or commute therefor by said fifteenth day of June, or any day thereafter, in writing,* or otherwise on which day it shall be the duty of said treasurer, on demand at his office, to grant such certificate as aforesaid; which certificate shall entitle the holder thereof, who has the right to pass said gate by virtue of said act, to pass free of toll one year from said fifteenth day of June.

§ 2. This act shall take effect immediately.

*So in the original.

Chap. 320.

AN ACT making an appropriation for the benefit
of the Stockbridge Indians.

Passed April 18, 1862; by a two-third vote.

*The People of the State of New York, represented in
Senate and Assembly, do enact as follows :*

SECTION 1. The Treasurer shall pay, on the warrant of
the Comptroller, out of any money in the treasury not
otherwise appropriated, to the sachem and councillors of
the Stockbridge Indians, or their duly authorized agent
or . attorney, the sum of ten thousand dollars, to be expended, or so much thereof as may be necessary, in the
erection of a meeting house, school house, and for such
other improvements and purposes as they may deem best
calculated to promote the best interest and happiness of
their people, and the remainder, if any, shall be divided
among the members of said tribe according to the customs and usages thereof.

§ 2. The Governor of this state shall appoint a suitable and proper person to act as agent for said Indians,
whose duty it shall be to take charge of the money
hereby appropriated, and to see that the same is properly
and economically expended for the purposes intended by
this act, whose compensation shall be paid out of said
money; but in no case shall such agent be entitled to
receive more than five hundred dollars for his services.
It shall be the duty of such agent to render an account
in writing and under oath to the Governor of this state,
on or before the first day of April, eighteen hundred and
sixty-three, showing the condition of said money, and
specifying in what manner the same has been expended.
Before such agent shall receive any money under this
act, he shall execute to the people of this state, a bond
with a penalty of double the amount to be received with
such surety as the Governor shall approve, conditioned
for the faithful application of said money, according to
the true intent and meaning of this act.

§ 3. This act shall take effect immediately.

67

Chap. 321.

AN ACT for the relief James Oswold and Daniel A. Van Valkenburgh.

Passed April 18, 1862; three-fifths being present.

The People of the State of New York, represented in Senate and Assembly, do enact as follows :

SECTION 1. The canal board are hereby authorized to settle with and allow to James Oswold and Daniel A. Van Valkenburgh such amount as the said board shall deem just and equitable for labor peformed or materials furnished by them as the assignees of William H. Douglass, under a certain contract for the enlargement of the Erie canal, made the fourteenth day of February, eighteen hundred and sixty, by the said William H. Douglass with the people of the State of New York, for work to be done on sections three hundred and sixty-one, three hundred and sixty-two, three hundred and sixty-three, three hundred and sixty-five and three hundred and sixty-six, provided that before any payment shall be made to the said Oswold and Van Valkenburgh, they, together with the said William H. Douglass shall release to the state all claim for damages for the abandonment or which might arise under the said contract.

§ 2. Any sum which may be found due said Oswold and Van Valkenburgh shall be paid out of any money appropriated to the Erie canal enlargement by the Treasurer on the warrant of the Auditor of the canal department.

Chap. 322.

AN ACT to authorize a loan to the town of Westfield.

Passed April 18, 1862; three-fifths being present.

*The People of the State of New York, represented in
Senate and Assembly, do enact as follows:*

SECTION 1. The Comptroller is hereby authorized to
loan to the town of Westfield from the school fund such
sum, not exceeding three thousand dollars, as may be
necessary to rebuild the bridge across Chautauqua creek,
in the village of Westfield.

§ 2. The money so to be loaned shall be expended
under the direction of the commissioner of highways of
said town, who is hereby authorized to draw for the
same at such times and in such sums as may be necessary
to pay for the materials and work on said bridge.

§ 3. The board of supervisors of the county of
Chautauqua is hereby required to raise by tax on the
town of Westfield, the sum of five hundred dollars
annually for six years, or until the whole principal sum
shall be paid, and such further sum as may be necessary
to pay the annual interest on the amount loaned to said
town, or on so much thereof as may remain unpaid from
year to year until the whole principal sum shall be paid.

Chap. 323.

AN ACT for the relief of Samuel Burns for canal
damages.

Passed April 18, 1862; three-fifths being present.

*The People of the State of New York, represented in
Senate and Assembly, do enact as follows:*

SECTION 1. Samuel Burns of the town of Brutus, in the
county of Cayuga, shall have the same right, for the
term of two months from the passage of this act, to
make and exhibit to the canal appraisers a statement of

his claim for damages suffered by him in the year eighteen hundred and fifty-six, in consequence of the appropriation by this state of a portion of his land, owned by him at that time in said town of Brutus, to its use in making the enlargement to the Erie canal at that place, that any person suffering such damage has to make and exhibit such claim by section eighty-four, article three, chapter nine, title nine, part first of the fifth edition of the Revised Statutes of this state.

Proviso.

§ 2. Before said canal appraisers shall entertain such application, such claim shall be made and exhibited in the same manner and specifying the same with the same particularity as is required by the section of the Revised Statutes named in the first section of this act.

Duty of canal appraisers.

§ 3. Whenever, within the time mentioned in the first section of this act, such statement shall be made and exhibited to the said canal appraisers in the manner prescribed by the second section thereof, it shall be the duty of said canal appraisers to entertain such application and thereafter to take the same proceedings in appraising the damages suffered by said Samuel Burns by the cause mentioned in the first section of this act as are now provided by law for appraising the damages of persons upon claims made and exhibited in pursuance of the section of the Revised Statutes named in the first section herein, and said damages when so appraised, or the amount thereof, finally adjudicated by the canal

Appeal.

board, in case of an appeal to such board, which appeal is hereby authorized as in other cases, shall be paid in the same manner as the damages appraised under the section last aforesaid are now provided to be paid by law.

§ 4. This act shall take effect immediately.

Chap. 324.

AN ACT to provide for the opening and laying out of a highway in the towns of Wayne and Bradford, in the county of Steuben.

Passed April 18, 1862; three-fifths being present.

The People of the State of New York, represented in Senate and Assembly, do enact as follows:

SECTION 1. John Birdseye, of the town of Wayne, Jonathan C. Wolcott, of the town of Bradford, and William H. Bull, of the town of Bath, in the county of Steuben, or a majority of them, shall have power, and they are hereby required to lay out and construct a public highway in said towns, to commence at the Bath and Penn Yan road, in the town of Wayne, in said county, near the residence of Charles Crookston, and running thence, on the most direct and feasible route, and as they shall deem best for the traveling public, in a southerly direction through the so called Birdseye Hollow; and thence through the town of Bradford, near the residence of Jonathan Walcott, until it meets the Bradford Hollow and Sonora road, near the residence of widow Bartholomew.

§ 2. The expense of laying out and obtaining the right of way for the said highway shall be levied upon and paid by the said towns of Wayne and Bradford in equal proportions, as taxes are usually levied and collected in said county ; and there shall be levied and collected in the same manner, upon said county of Steuben, for constructing said highway, an amount not exceeding five hundred dollars, and after said amount of five hundred dollars shall have been expended upon said highway, and it shall not then be completed, so much of the highway labor assessed upon said towns, as can be spared from the highways of said towns, shall be applied to the highway to be laid out under this act, each town applying its labor upon the portion thereof which shall lay within its limits.

§ 3. This act shall take effect immediately.

Chap. 325.

AN ACT for the relief of John C. Adams for canal damages.

Passed April 18, 1862 ; three-fifths being present.

The People of the State of New York, represented in Senate and Assembly, do enact as follows :

SECTION 1. Jurisdiction is hereby conferred upon the Canal Appraisers to hear and determine the claim of John C. Adams, for damages claimed to have been heretofore sustained by him in consequence of a portion of his farm, situate in the town of Cuba, in the county of Allegany, being taken and appropriated by the state for the construction of the Genesee Valley canal, and hear and determine all the legal and equitable claims of said Adams, arising from such construction. The said appraisers shall make such award thereon as shall be just and reasonable, subject to appeal to the canal board as in other cases.

§ 2. The said John C. Adams may file his claim for damages with the Canal Appraisers, within one year from the passage of this act.

§ 3. The Treasurer shall pay, on the warrant of the Auditor of the canal department, such sum, if any, as shall be awarded and finally adjudicated, as provided for by the first section of this act, out of any moneys in the treasury appropriated or to be appropriated to the payment of canal damages.

§ 4. This act shall take effect immediately.

Chap. 326.

AN ACT for the relief of Peter Smith.

Passed April 18, 1862; three-fifths being present.

The People of the State of New York, represented in Senate and Assembly, do enact as follows:

SECTION 1. The Comptroller is hereby authorized and directed to draw his warrant on the Treasurer in favor of Peter Smith, for such sum as the Comptroller, Attorney-General and Lieutenant-Governor shall certify to be legally or justly due to him for the difference in the cost of iron used in the construction of the shelves, roofing, &c., of the state library at the time the contract for furnishing the same was made, and the time to which the execution of said contract was delayed by the committee of Regents of the University having charge of said buildings, in consequence of improvements in the plan thereof.

§ 2. The Treasurer shall pay the said warrant out of any moneys in the treasury appropriated to the general fund of the state.

§ 3. This act shall take effect immediately.

Chap. 327.

AN ACT for the relief of Richard Calrow, junior.

Passed April 18, 1862; three-fifths being present.

The People of the State of New York, represented in Senate and Assembly, do enact as follows:

SECTION 1. The Lieutenant-Governor, Comptroller and Secretary of State of this State, are hereby appointed referees to hear and determine the alleged claim of Richard Calrow, junior, against the state, growing out of the construction and erection of the arsenal in the city of New York.

§ 2. The said referees shall have full power and authority to compel the attendance of witnesses, and to swear and examine the same, and shall by their report, find and certify what sum, if any, is equitably due to the said Richard Calrow, junior, for work done and materials furnished in the construction and erection of the said arsenal, whether the same was done and furnished under the contract thereof or otherwise, provided the referees are satisfied that said work was performed by authority from either of the commissioners, or any one of them, or their architects, and the state is legally and equitably liable therefor.

§ 3. In case such referees shall certify and report any sum to be due to the said Richard Calrow, junior, under the provisions of this act, the amount so reported due, not exceeding the sum of thirty-five hundred dollars, which shall be paid by the Treasurer, on the warrant of the Comptroller, out of the fund heretofore appropriated by chapter two hundred and seventy-three of the laws of eighteen hundred and fifty-nine.

§ 4. The provisions of said chapter two hundred and seventy-three, of the laws of eighteen hundred and fifty-nine, shall apply to this act so far as the same is consistent herewith.

§ 5. This act shall take effect immediately.

Chap. 328.

AN ACT for the relief of C. Amelia Vernam and McNeil Seymour, administrators of the goods, chattels and credits of Abraham Vernam, deceased.

Passed April 18, 1862; three-fifths being present.

The People of the State of New York, represented in Senate and Assembly, do enact as follows :

SECTION 1. The canal board are hereby authorized and empowered to examine the claim of C. Amelia Vernam and McNeil Seymour, administrators of the goods, chattels and credits of Abraham Vernam, deceased, repair contractor on repair section number one of the Erie canal, for compensation for extra labor performed and

materials furnished on said section by him or his administrators, by direction of the Canal Commissioner in
charge of said section, and not embraced in said contract; and if it shall be established by competent proof
to the satisfaction of said board, that such labor has
been performed or such materials furnished by said
Vernam or his administrators, under the direction of
the Canal Commissioner, for which the state has not
paid the said Vernam or his administrators, to award to
said administrators such sum therefor as shall be just
and equitable and legal.

§ 2. Such sum, if any, as shall on such examination be
found due said administrators, shall be paid to them by
the Treasurer, on the warrant of the Auditor, out of
any moneys appropriated for canal repairs.

§ 3. This act shall take effect immediately.

Chap. 329.

AN ACT for the appraisal and payment of canal damages to Richard Claxton.

Passed April 18, 1862; three-fifths being present.

*The People of the State of New York, represented in
Senate and Assembly, do enact as follows :*

SECTION 1. The canal appraisers are hereby authorized and required to hear and investigate and decide
upon the claims of Richard Claxton, for alleged damages
to his boat yard and lot, occasioned by the enlargement
of the Oswego canal, at the village of Liverpool, in the
county of Onondaga, and make such award if any therefor as shall be just, and as in their judgment the state is
liable to pay, not exceeding in the aggregate four hundred dollars; such appraisement and award, if any be
made, shall be subject to appeal to the canal board, as
in other cases.

§ 2. The sum, if any, which may be awarded under
the provisions of the first section of this act, or the sum
determined by the canal board, in case of an appeal from
the award of the canal appraisers, shall be paid by the

Treasurer, on the warrant of the Auditor, to Richard Claxton or his legal representatives, out of any money in the treasury appropriated or to be appropriated for the enlargement of the Oswego canal.

§ 3. This act shall take effect immediately.

Chap. 330.

AN ACT for the relief William Monteath.

Passed April 18, 1862; three-fifths being present.

The People of the State of New York, represented in Senate and Assembly, do enact as follows:

Section 1. The canal board are hereby authorized and required to examine the claim of William Monteath, for damages alleged to have been sustained to his canal boat Chatham of Buffalo, by the sinking of the same at a place called Oberry's Bridge, about seven miles east of the city of Buffalo, on the twelfth day of May, eighteen hundred and sixty-one, and award to him such sum, if any, as the state shall be legally and equitably liable for ; but nothing in this act contained shall be construed to authorize the said canal board to award damages for any injuries sustained by the cargo of said boat.

§ 2. In case any sum shall be awarded to said William Monteath under this act, the same shall be paid by the Treasurer, on the warrant of the Auditor of the canal department, out of money appropriated for the enlargement of the Erie canal.

Chap. 331.

AN ACT to authorize the payment of interest on certain canal drafts protested for non-payment.

Passed April 18, 1862; three-fifths being present.

The People of the State of New York, represented in Senate and Assembly, do enact as follows :

SECTION 1. The Treasurer shall pay, on the warrant of the Auditor, the sum of eight hundred and forty-five dollars and seventeen cents, to Horace Hunt and Andrew Kingsley, for the payment of interest accruing, at the rate of six per cent per annum, on certain canal drafts issued by Frederick Follet, Canal Commissioner, in the years eighteen hundred and fifty-two and eighteen hundred and fifty-three, to Hunt and Kingsley, on contract to construct locks numbers seventy-eight, seventy-nine and eighty, on the Genesee Valley canal; to Bradley Sherman on contract for construction of locks numbers ninety, ninety-one and ninety-two on said canal; and to John T. Wright, on contract to construct locks numbers seventy-two, seventy-three, seventy-four, seventy-five, seventy-six and seventy-seven, and section number seventy-eight on said canal. The last two mentioned contracts having been duly assigned to said Horace Hunt and Andrew Kingsley; payment to be made out of any moneys appropriated, or to be appropriated to the Erie canal enlargement.

§ 2. This act shall take effect immediately.

Chap. 332.

AN ACT to amend an act entitled "An act to amend an act incorporating the village of Geneva, in the county of Ontario, passed May sixth, eighteen hundred and thirty-seven," passed April fourteenth, eighteen hundred and fifty-five.

Passed April 18, 1862; three-fifths being present.

The People of the State of New York, represented in Senate and Assembly, do enact as follows:

SECTION 1. Section seventeen of the act entitled "An act to amend an act incorporating the village of Geneva in the county of Ontario, passed May sixth, eighteen hundred and thirty-seven, passed April fourteenth, eighteen hundred and fifty-five," is hereby amended by adding thereto the following:

Sales at auction.

And the said trustees shall have power to forbid or regulate sales at auction, within the corporate bounds of the village of Geneva: And the said trustees may pass and enact such by-laws and ordinances in relation to sales by auction, as shall not contravene the provisions of the said section seventeen as to the penalties to be named therein, but all such by-laws shall be published before they shall take effect.

Street commissioners appointed by trustees.

§ 2. The street commissioner named in section second of the said act, shall no longer be elected by the people, as in said section prescribed, but shall be appointed by the board of trustees on the Wednesday after the first Monday of March in each year, or as often as a vacancy shall occur in the said office, and he shall hold his office until the Wednesday after the first Monday of March, next succeeding his appointment, or until a successor shall be appointed; and it shall require a vote of the majority of the trustees elected, to appoint any one to the said office of street commissioner or to remove any one therefrom.

§ 3. Section thirty-one of the said act is hereby amended by striking out the word "six" in the last line

but one of the said section, and inserting the word " four"
in the place thereof.

§ 4. The acts of the board of trustees of the said village of Geneva, in expending certain moneys from the treasury of the said village for the purpose of raising and equipping volunteers for the military service of the United States government, in the year eighteen hundred and sixty-one, and the year eighteen hundred and sixty-two, are hereby legalized and confirmed, notwithstanding anything to the contrary in the said act contained. *Certain acts confirmed.*

§ 5. This act shall take effect immediately.

Chap. 333.

AN ACT authorizing the appraisal and payment of damages to Amos Kelsey, caused by a break in the Erie canal in the town of Gaines, Orleans county.

Passed April 18, 1862; three-fifths being present.

The People of the State of New York, represented in Senate and Assembly, do enact as follows:

SECTION 1. Jurisdiction is hereby conferred upon the canal appraisers to hear and determine the claim of Amos Kelsey, for damages alleged to have been sustained by him from a break in the Erie canal, in the town of Gaines, Orleans county, on or about the twenty-first day of July, eighteen hundred and fifty-seven; and from another break in said Erie canal on the fifth day of July, eighteen hundred and sixty-one, and if, upon examination, it shall be ascertained that any damages have been sustained by him, in consequence of such break for which the state is legally liable, and that such break was caused by the defective construction of the culvert under such canal; said appraisers shall make an award for the same, subject to appeal to the canal board, as in other cases.

§ 2. The Treasurer shall pay, on the warrant of the Auditor, such sum, if any, as shall be awarded under the provisions of this act, out of any moneys appropriated or to be appropriated for the payment of canal awards.

§ 3. This act shall take effect immediately.

Chap. 334.

AN ACT to authorize the trustees of the village
of Dunkirk to pay certain military expenses,
and to issue bonds for the same.

Passed April 18, 1862; three-fifths being present.

*The People of the State of New York, represented in
Senate and Assembly, do enact as follows:*

Trustees may issue bonds. SECTION 1. The board of trustees of the village of
Dunkirk are hereby authorized and directed to issue
bonds in the name of said village to the amount of four
thousand three hundred and seventy-five dollars, payable one-third in one year, one-third in two years, and
one-third in three years, from the first day of January,
eighteen hundred and sixty-two, and bearing interest at
seven per cent per annum, and payable at the office of
the treasurer of said village.

Proceeds on sale of bonds. § 2. The said board of trustees are also authorized and
required to appropriate said bonds and to negotiate the
sale thereof at a rate not less than par, and apply the
proceeds thereof to the payment of certain liabilities incurred and expenses paid by citizens of said village, for
clothing and uniforming companies D and E of the volunteers from said village. The president and treasurer
Board of auditors of certain accounts. of said village, and the supervisor of the town of Dunkirk, shall constitute a board of auditors for the purpose
of auditing and liquidating the actual amount of money
expended or liabilities incurred by any citizen of said
village under resolutions for the purpose of providing
such clothing and uniforms; and said auditors are hereby directed not to audit or allow to any citizen of said
village any amount for money paid or liabilities incurred
Exception. except where the same shall have been paid or incurred
in furnishing clothing and equipping the members of
companies " D and E," under the said resolutions; that
no bonds shall be issued by said president and trustees
for money paid or liabilities incurred, unless the same
shall have been previously audited and allowed by said
board of auditors.

Interest on bonds. § 3. The said board of trustees are also authorized
and required, out of any moneys in the treasury of said

village not otherwise especially appropriated, and out of the taxes hereafter to be levied and collected in said village, to pay the interest on said bonds from time to time as the same shall fall due, and the principal sum secured by said bonds as it shall grow due.

§ 4. This act shall take effect immediately.

Chap. 335.

AN ACT to amend existing laws which prohibit fishing with nets in the Crooked lake, in the counties of Steuben and Yates, and to increase penalties for taking trout therefrom.

Passed April 18, 1862; three-fifths being present.

The People of the State of New York, represented in Senate and Assembly, do enact as follows:

SECTION 1. All acts and parts of acts heretofore passed prohibiting fishing with nets in the Crooked lake, so called, situate in the counties of Steuben and Yates, are hereby repealed, except as provided in section two of this act.

§ 2. It shall not be lawful to take the fish called trout from the said Crooked lake in the months of November, December, January and February, nor to take fish from said lake with gill, trap or fike nets at any time. Any person who shall offend against this act shall be deemed guilty of a misdemeanor, and on due conviction thereof shall be subject to a fine of twenty-five dollars, or imprisonment in the county jail wherein the conviction shall take place, and for a second offence by both fine and imprisonment as above, in the discretion of the court. Any person, a citizen of this state, may in his or her own name prosecute for the above named penalty of twenty-five dollars, before any justice of the peace of said counties, and shall, if judgment be obtained, be entitled to one-half of said penalty, the other half to go to the support of the poor of the county in which suit is brought.

§ 3. This act shall take effect immediately.

Chap. 336.

AN ACT authorizing the commissioners of highways of the town of Westfield, Richmond
county, to lay out and open a road in said
town.

Passed April 18, 1862; three-fifths being present.

*The People of the State of New York, represented in
Senate and Assembly, do enact as follows:*

Laying out road.   SECTION 1. The commissioners of highways of the
town of Westfield, in the county of Richmond, are hereby authorized and empowered to lay out and open a
public road in said town, as follows: Commencing on
the southerly side of the Woodrow road and the easterly
side of a private road belonging to Felix or Hugh Mc-
Keon and Dominick McGuire, and from thence running
southerly along the easterly side of said private road to
and through the lands of Jane Sprague and of Rachael Depew: and also through the land of Joseph Bedell to the
Qurantine road near the Willow-swamp bridge; thence
running westerly forty-nine and a half feet; thence
northerly parallel with the easterly side of said road as
it shall be laid out, and said private road to the said
Woodrow road; the said road to be forty-nine and a
half feet in width, and the easterly side of said private
road to be the easterly boundary thereof, so far as the
same extends, and for that purpose they hereby have
power to lay said highway through any orchards or
gardens that may interfere with the opening thereof.

Appraisal of damages.   § 2. The county judge of Richmond county shall appoint three disinterested persons not residents of said
town of Westfield, who shall appraise and assess the
damages that may be sustained by the occupants of any
lands for the purposes of the opening of said road.
Said commissioners shall file their report with the town
clerk of said town, and the supervisors of said county
shall at their next annual meeting after the filing of
said report, cause to be levied and collected the amount
stated in said report upon the taxable property in said
town of Westfield, in the same manner as other town

and county taxes; and the county treasurer is directed to pay, on the certificate and certified copy of report of said commissioners, the amount or amounts awarded the person or persons whose lands have been taken.

§ 3. This act shall take effect immediately.

Chap. 337.

AN ACT in relation to the justices' courts and police courts in the city of Brooklyn.

Passed April 18, 1862; three-fifths being present.

The People of the State of New York, represented in Senate and Assembly, do enact as follows:

SECTION 1. The police justice and the justices of the peace in the city of Brooklyn, shall each nominate, and with the consent of the common council of the city of Brooklyn, appoint, one clerk for each of said courts, who shall hold his office during the pleasure of the justice so appointing him. Appointment of clerks.

§ 2. Each of said clerks shall execute, before entering upon the discharge of the duties of the office, a bond to the said city of Brooklyn, in the sum of two thousand five hundred dollars, with two sufficient sureties, to be approved by a justice of the supreme court, conditioned for the faithful performance of the duties of the office as such clerk, and for the accounting and paying over, as directed by law, all moneys which shall be received by them as such clerks. Bond.

§ 3. This act shall take effect immediately.

Chap. 338.

AN ACT relating to awnings in the city of Brooklyn.

Passed April 18, 1862; three-fifths being present.

The People of the State of New York, represented in Senate and Assembly, do enact as follows:

SECTION 1. The common council of the city of Brooklyn shall have power to make and enforce an ordinance or ordinances, regulating the erection, construction and maintenance of awnings and awning posts in said city, or for the removal of the same.

§ 2. The said common council shall have power to make, declare and enforce penalties for the violation of any such ordinance; and the owner of any awning or awning posts shall be liable for any violation thereof, and the penalty therefor may be enforced against such owner.

§ 3. This act shall take effect immediately.

Chap. 339.

AN ACT to amend the act entitled "An act to incorporate the village of Cleveland, Oswego county," passed April fifteenth, eighteen hundred and fifty-seven; and its several amendments to enlarge its powers.

Passed April 18, 1862; three-fifths being present.

The People of the State of New York, represented in Senate and Assembly, do enact as follows:

Special election of police justice.

SECTION 1. The village of Cleveland shall have power, and is hereby authorized at a special charter election, to be called within twenty days after the passage of this act, by the Trustees, as provided in their charter for calling special elections, to elect a police justice for said village, and who shall hold his office four years from the

Tuesday succeeding the last annual election, and a police justice shall in like manner be elected every fourth year thereafter at the annual election of village officers, and in case of a vacancy happening in the said office of police justice, the trustees of said village are hereby au- *Authority* thorized to call a special election of the electors to fill *of trustees.* such vacancy, and the person so elected shall fill the office during the unexpired term of the person whose office has become vacant : or such vacancy may be filled by the said electors at the next annual election of village officers, if no special election shall be ordered by said trustees for that purpose

§ 2. The police justice shall, before entering upon *Official oath* the duties of his office, and within five days after being notified of his election, take and file his official oath in the county clerk's office of Oswego county. The said police justice shall be a resident and a legal voter in said village, and keep an office therein.

§ 3. The police justice shall possess the same powers in *Jurisdic-* all criminal cases or proceedings as justices of the peace *tion.* of towns And he shall have the exclusive power and jurisdiction, except as hereinafter provided, in all civil actions for forfeitures and penalties imposed for the violation of any of the laws, by-laws or ordinances of said village, and for the collection of all unpaid taxes or assessments provided for in said act, to incorporate the village of Cleveland, and be subject to the same duties and liabilities, and in the same manner collect and receive the same fees as justice of the peace of towns. The said police justice shall also have the same powers as commissioners of deeds in the several cities in this state.

§ 4. In any action brought before said police justice *Provision* to recover a penalty imposed for a violation of the laws, *as to ac-* by-laws or ordinances of said village, it shall only be *tions.* necessary to state in the complaint the title and sections of said law, by-law or ordinance alleged to have been violated, and the amount of the penalty claimed, and other facts may be given in evidence without being stat- *Evidence.* ed in the complaint, and every by-law, ordinance, resolution or proceeding of the trustees may be read in evidence in all courts in this state, either first from a copy of such by-law, resolution, ordinance or proceeding, signed by the president or clerk of said village, or from any printed volume containing such by-law, ordinance, resolution or proceeding, and accompanied by a certificate signed by the clerk, that such volume was printed by authority of the trustees of said village.

§ 5. The said police justice shall have power in cases of persons brought before him charged with having committed any offence in violation of any ordinance of the village, to proceed summarily without a jury, unless the person thus charged shall demand a trial by jury, to try such person and determine the alleged offences and charges, and in case any person shall be found guilty of having violated any ordinance of the village, for which a penalty is by the ordinance imposed, said justice shall require such penalty with costs and fees to be paid to him within twenty-four hours, and during that time the defendant shall remain in the custody of the constable, and if the penalty and costs and fees be not paid within that time, may order the defendant to be confined in the lock-up or county jail for a time not exceeding sixty days, unless the penalty and costs and fees be paid sooner.

§ 6. In case of and during any vacancy in the office of such police justice, and during the sickness or absence or other inability, or refusal of such officer to act, then in that case any justice of the peace of the town of Constantia, shall have full power, and it shall be his duty to perform all the duties referred to in the foregoing sections, the same as if this act had not been passed.

§ 7. This act shall take effect immediately.

Chap. 340.

AN ACT to incorporate the Presbyterian Committee of Home Missions of the General Assembly of the Presbyterian church in the United States of America.

Passed April 18, 1862.

The People of the State of New York, represented in Senate and Assembly, do enact as follows:

SECTION 1. Edwin F. Hatfield, Albert Barnes, Benjamin J. Wallace, George L. Prentis, Thomas S. Hastings, Charles S. Robinson, Joseph Allison, Jonathan F. Stearns, Henry Darling, Edward A. Lambert, Joseph F. Joy, Matthew W. Baldwin, James B Pinneo, J. Milton Smith and Alfred O. Post (designated for the purpose by the general assembly of the Presbyterian church which met in Syracuse, New York, in May eighteen hundred and sixty-one), and their successors in office, are hereby constituted a body corporate and politic by the name of the "Presbyterian Committee of Home Missions," the object of which shall be to assist in sustaining the preaching of the Gospel in feeble churches and congregations, in connection with the Presbyterian church in the United States, and generally to superintend the whole course of home missions in behalf of the said church, as its general assembly may from time to time direct ; also to receive, take charge of, and disburse any property or funds which at any time, and from time to time, may be intrusted to said church or said committee for home missionary purposes. *Corporate name.*

§ 2. The said corporation shall possess the general powers and be subject to the provisions contained in title three of chapter eighteen of the first part of the Revised Statutes, so far as the same are applicable and have not been repealed or modified. *Powers.*

§ 3. The management and disposition of the affairs and funds of said corporation shall be vested in the individuals named in the first section of this act and their successors in office, who shall remain in office for such period and be displaced and succeeded by others, to be elected at such time and in such manner as the said church, represented in general assembly, shall direct and appoint. *Ib.*

§ 4. The said corporation shall be in law, capable of taking, receiving and holding any real or personal estate, which has been, or may hereafter be given, devised or bequeathed to it, or to the said church for the purposes aforesaid, or which may accrue from the use of the same ; but the said corporation shall not take and hold real and personal estate above the value of two hundred thousand dollars. *May take property not exceeding $200,000*

§ 5. No inhabitant of this state who shall die leaving a wife, child or parent shall devise or bequeath to the corporation hereby created more than one-half of his or her estate, after the payment of his or her debts ; but a *Limitation as to devises and bequest.*

devise or bequest by such inhabitant shall be valid to
the extent of such one-half; in no case however shall
any devise or bequest to such corporation be valid in
any will made by any inhabitant of this state, which
shall not have been made and executed at least two
months before the death of the testator or testatrix.

§ 6. This act shall take effect immediately.

Chap. 341.

AN ACT relating to the jail and penitentiary in
the county of Kings.

Passed April 18, 1862; three-fifths being present.

*The People of the State of New York, represented in
Senate and Assembly, do enact as follows :*

Jail under
control of
keeper.

SECTION 1. From and after the first day of January,
eighteen hundred and sixty-four, the jail of the county
of Kings shall be under the control and management of
a keeper, (instead of the sheriff of said county,) subject
to the restrictions hereinafter contained. Keepers of the
jail of said county shall hold their office for three years
unless sooner removed by the appointing power for in-
competency or improper conduct, specified in writing.

Term of
office.

Appointed
by super-
visors.

§ 2. The first keeper shall be appointed by the board
of supervisors of said county, by a vote of a majority of
all the members elected to said board, at a meeting to
be held on the first Tuesday of October, eighteen hundred and sixty-three. On the first Tuesday of October,
every third year after said first Tuesday of October,
eighteen hundred and sixty-three, said board of supervisors shall in like manner appoint a keeper, whose term
of office shall commence on the first day of January
succeeding his appointment. Vacancies in said office
may in like manner be filled at any regular meeting of
said board, and persons appointed to fill the same shall
hold during the remainder of the term of the individual
in whose place they are appointed.

Deputy
keeper.

§ 3. Said keeper may appoint a deputy to assist him
in the discharge of his duties, who shall hold his office
during the pleasure of said keeper, which deputy shall

possess all the powers of the keeper in case of his absence or inability to act, and be subject to like liabilities ; and the said keeper shall also appoint so many subordinates and assistants as said board of supervisors may direct, who shall hold their offices during the pleasure of said keeper and of said board of supervisors.

§ 4. All keepers and deputy keepers appointed in pursuance of the provisions of this act, shall, before entering upon the duties of their office, take the constitutional oath and file the same in the office of the clerk of said county, and give such security for the faithful performance of their trusts as said board of supervisors may direct. *Oath of office.*

§ 5. The keeper of said jail, and during his absence or inability, his deputy, shall possess all the powers which are conferred by law upon sheriffs in relation to the confinement and detention of prisoners, and shall be subject to the same liabilities in case of escape, and shall pay over all moneys received in his official capacity to the persons legally entitled to receive the same. *Power of deputy.*

§ 6. All supplies necessary for the maintenance of the inmates of said jail shall be furnished by said board of supervisors by contract or otherwise, as they may deem expedient, and all fixtures and furniture furnished and necessary repairs made, under their orders and directions. *Supplies, &c., to be furnished by supervisors.*

§ 7. Nothing in this act shall be construed to interfere with the powers of the sheriff, constables and policemen of said county of Kings at all times taking the prisoners confined in said county jail to and from said jail when required or authorized so to do by any law, or confining in said jail such prisoners as said sheriff may legally hold by virtue of civil process and for the purpose of confining prisoners held on civil process, the sheriff of said county shall have the exclusive custody of a suitable portion of the jail of said county, to be assigned by the board of supervisors for that purpose anything in this act contained to the contrary notwithstanding. *Saving clause as to power of sheriff.*

§ 8 The compensation to be allowed said keeper, his deputy and his subordinates, shall be fixed by the board of supervisors of said county ; shall be paid quarterly unless otherwise directed by said board, and shall not be increased or diminished during the continuance in office of said keeper, deputy and subordinates. *Compensation of keeper, &c., fixed by supervisors*

When prisoners to be sent to penitentiary.

§ 9. From and after the first day of May, one thousand eight hundred and sixty-four, it sha'l be the duty of all magistrates and courts in said county to sentence all prisoners who on conviction are liable (except in capital cases) to imprisonment in the county jail, for more than ten days, to imprisonment in the penitentiary instead of said jail; and the keeper of said penitentiary shall receive such persons and safely keep for the term for which they are sentenced, and employ them according to the discipline and rules established for the government of said penitentiary.

Chap. 342.

AN ACT to incorporate the Canandaigua Walton Club.

Passed April 18, 1862.

The People of the State of New York, represented in Senate and Assembly, do enact as follows:

SECTION 1. James C. Smith, Henry O. Chesebro, Elbridge G. Lapham, William Jeffrey, J. Albert Granger, Charles W. Gulick, Gideon Granger, George Gorham, John C. Draper, John H. Morse, George B. Bates, Leander M. Drury, John Rankin, junior, H. Fay Bennett, and Walter S. Hubbell, who now are members of the Canandaigua Walton Club, and such other persons as shall hereafter be associated with them or with their successors, are hereby constituted and created a body corporate by the name of "The Canandaigua Walton Club," whose object is hereby declared to be the providing, establishing and maintaining suitable boats, apparatus, boat houses and lodge on the shore of Canandaigua lake, at a point known as "Walton Point," for fishing, hunting, sporting and promoting the physical development of its members and others, which corporation shall continue for ninety-nine years.

Corporate name.

Directors.

§ 2. The direction, management and control of the affairs and property of the said corporation shall be vested in the persons named in the first section of this act, and their successors, subject to such by-laws and regulations as they may, from time to time, adopt.

By-laws.

§ 3. The officers of such club shall consist of a presi- *Officers.* dent, vice-president, secretary, treasurer and commissary, who shall be elected annually to their respected offices by such of the members of the corporation as are or may be entitled by its rules to vote at such elections. Said annual elections shall take place on the first Tuesday of September in each year, at the lodge of said club now built on said Walton Point, and until the next annual election, the officers of said club. at the *Elections.* time of the passage of this act, shall continue to hold their respective offices, and the officers elected at any annual election shall hold their offices for one year, and until their successors shall be elected.

§ 4 The said corporation shall have power to take, *Power to hold property not exceeding $5000.* hold and convey real and personal property to the amount of not exceeding five thousand dollars, and also all apparatus and furniture necessary to the object of said corporation.

§ 5. All personal property, apparatus, furniture, tools, *Property of club is vested in corporation* implements and machinery, and other property, and all structures and buildings, and any contract, or contracts or agreement for the purchase of any real estate, now held by the officers of said "club," or any or either of them, or any other person or persons in trust for the said club, or for the use and benefit of the same, shall, by virtue of this act, vest in and become the property of the corporation hereby created. And the said corporation shall assume and be liable for all contracts, agreements and responsibilities, which have been en- *Liability.* tered into or incurred previous to the passage of this act, by the officers of the said club, or any of them, lawfully acting in behalf said club.

§ 6 In case the aforesaid corporation shall, at any *Forfeiture.* time, appropriate their funds or any part thereof, to any purpose or purposes other than those contemplated by this act, and shall thereof be convicted by due course of law, the said corporation shall thenceforth cease and determine, and the estate, real and personal, whereof it may be seized and possessed, shall vest in the people of this state.

§ 7. The provisions contained in title three of chapter *Certain provisions of revised statutes applied.* eighteen of the first part of the Revised Statutes shall be deemed and taken as part of this act. Except where they are herein altered, modified or changed.

§ 8. This act shall take effect immediately.

70

Chap. 343.

•AN ACT to continue the incorporation of the Brooklyn Institute, to amend the charter thereof, and to consolidate the acts relating thereto.

Passed April 18, 1862.

The People of the State of New York, represented in Senate and Assembly, do enact as follows:

SECTION 1. The incorporation of the Brooklyn Institute is hereby continued until the same shall be repealed by the Legislature.

Purpose of corporation

§ 2. The purposes of the said incorporation shall be the continuing of the library, collecting and forming a repository of books, maps, pictures, drawing apparatus, models of machinery, tools and implements generally, for enlarging the knowledge in literature, science and art, and thereby improving the condition of mechanics, manufacturers, artizans and others.

Powers.

§ 3. The said incorporation for the purposes thereof shall be capable of taking and holding by purchase, devise and otherwise and of selling leasing, mortgaging, or otherwise disposing of, in whole or in part, any real or personal estate, the annual income of which shall not exceed ten thousand dollars.

Corporate powers in directors.

§ 4. The corporate powers of the said institute shall be vested in a board of directors of fifteen persons, who shall be elected on the second Monday in January of each year, in such manner and form, and at such place as the by-laws of said corporation may direct, who shall, at the time of such election, be members of the said Institute, and shall enter on the duties of their offices on the first day of May next ensuing their election.

Election thereof.

The board of directors which shall be elected on the second Monday in January, eighteen hundred and sixty-three, shall be divided by the board into three classes, to be drawn by lot: the first class drawn shall hold their offices for one year; the second class for two

Term of office.

years, and the third class for three years. On the second Monday in January, eighteen hundred and sixty-four, and on the second Monday in January, in each year thereafter, there shall be elected five directors who shall hold their offices for three years, and until others shall be elected in their places.

§ 5. The officers of the corporation shall be a presi- *Officers.* dent, vice-president, treasurer and secretary, who shall be chosen by the directors from their board on the first Saturday in the month of May in each year, and shall hold their offices for one year, and until others shall be chosen in their places. Any vacancies which may occur *Vacancies.* in the board of directors, or in the offices, shall be filled in such manner as the by-laws shall provide; and the officers elected at the election on the second Monday of January last, shall hold their offices until the first day of May, eighteen hundred and sixty-three, and until others are chosen in their places.

§ 6. The trust funds of the corporation shall be con- *Trustees.* trolled and managed by seven trustees, who shall be known as "The trustees of the Brooklyn Institute," of whom, for the time being, the president of the Brooklyn Savings Bank shall be one, the president of the said institute shall be one, and the treasurer of the said institute shall be one. The said trustees shall have power to keep the trust funds of the corporation securely invested, and pay over the income arising therefrom to the treasurer of the said Institute, to be applied by the board of directors to the purposes of the trusts committed to the said corporation. Isaac H. Frothingham, James Howe, Crawford C. Smith and S. Warren Sneden, and the president of the Brooklyn Savings Bank, and the president and treasurer of the said institute, for the time being, shall be the first trustees for the purposes of this act. Any vacancies in the said trustees, (except *Vacancies.* the president of the Brooklyn Savings Bank and the president and treasurer of the said Institute,) by resignation or death, or otherwise, shall be filled by the trustees remaining in office at the time of such vacancy, provided that every person chosen to fill such vacancy shall, at the time of his selection, be a member of the said institute.

§ 7. There shall be a joint meeting of the board of *Meeting of* directors and trustees on the first Monday of February, *directors and trustees* in each year, at the directors' rooms in the Institute, or such other place as may be agreed upon, at which time the trustees shall report to the board of directors the state of the funds entrusted to them, and the accounts relative thereto during the year next previous; and the treasurer of the said Institute shall at the same time report to said trustees the total amount of income of the institute, from what sources received and for what purpose expended; and between the first day of January and the first day of February of each year, the said trustees shall make a report to the Legislature of this state, of the state of the funds entrusted to them, and the uses to which they have been applied during the year next previous.

By-laws.   § 8. The said corporation shall have power to make and prescribe such by-laws, rules and regulations as may be proper and necessary for the purposes of said incorporation, and are not inconsistent with the constitution and laws of this state.

Powers.   § 9. This corporation shall possess the general powers and be subject to the general restrictions and liabilities prescribed in the third title of the eighteenth chapter of the first part of the Revised Statutes.

Repeal.   § 10. The act entitled "An act to incorporate the Brooklyn Appentices Library Association," passed November twentieth, eighteen hundred and twenty-four, and the act entitled "An act to extend the charter of the Brooklyn Apprentices Library Association, and for other purposes," passed April thirteenth, eighteen hundred and forty-three, are hereby repealed, without prejudice to any rights accrued under the same.

Saving clause.   § 11. The Legislature may at any time alter, amend or repeal this act.

Chap. 344.

AN ACT to incorporate the Starr Institute.

Passed April 18, 1862; three-fifths being present.

The People of the State of New York, represented in Senate and Assembly, do enact as follows:

Corporate name.   SECTION 1. Mary R. Miller, Joshua S. Bowne, William Kelly, Freeborn Garrettson, senior, Lewis Livingston, A. W. H. Judson, Theophilus Gillender, Homer Gray,

William R. Schell, Ambrose Wager, Henry M. Taylor, James A. A. Cowles, William B. Platt, Theophilus Nelson, M. D., John N. Cramer and Andrew J. Heermance, and their successors, are hereby constituted a body corporate by the name of "The Starr Institute," to be located in the village of Rhinebeck, in the county of Dutchess.

§ 2. The object and purpose of said corporation are hereby declared to be to furnish facilities for the intellectual and moral improvement of the inhabitants of the town of Rhinebeck. Object.

§ 3. The above named persons shall constitute a board of trustees of said corporation, with power, from time to time to adopt such by-laws as they may deem expedient for the management and transaction of the business and affairs of the said corporation, and any vacancy which may occur in the office of trustee may be filled by the board and their successors, from time to time. By-laws.

§ 4 The said corporation may receive from the said Mary R. Miller a conveyance of the lot and premises on the westerly side of Montgomery street, in the village of Rhinebeck, whereon the building known as the Starr Institute now stands, together with the library, furniture, and all the appurtenances thereof, and hold the same for the purposes of the corporation; and may also purchase, take and hold such other real and personal estate as may be given, granted, devised or bequeathed to it for the purposes of the corporation, provided the net annual income thereof do not, when so acquired, exceed the sum of two thousand five hundred dollars. May hold real estate. Proviso.

§ 5. The said corporation shall possess the general powers and be subject to the general restrictions and liabilities contained in the third title of chapter eighteen of part first of the Revised Statutes. Powers.

§ 6. This act shall take effect immediately.

Chap. 345.

AN ACT authorizing the appraisal and payment of canal damages to Andrew J. Rowley, caused by a break in the Erie canal, in the town of Gaines, Orleans county.

Passed April 18' 1862; three-fifths being present.

The People of the State of New York, represented in Senate and Assembly, do enact as follows :

SECTION 1. Jurisdiction is hereby conferred upon the Canal Appraisers to hear and determine the claim of Andrew J. Rowley, for damages alleged to have been sustained by him from a break in the Erie Canal, in the town of Gaines, Orleans county, on the fifth day of July, eighteen hundred and sixty-one; and if, upon examination it shall be ascertained that any such damages have been sustained by him, for which the State is legally liable, and that such breach was caused by the defective construction of a culvert under said canal, said Appraisers shall make an award for the same, subject to appeal to the Canal Board as in other cases.

§ 2. The Treasurer shall pay, on the warrant of the Auditor, such sum, if any, as shall be awarded under the provisions of this act, out of any moneys appropriated, or to be appropriated for the payment of canal awards.

§ 3. This act shall take effect immediately.

Chap. 346.

AN ACT to amend an act entitled " An act to incorporate the New York College of Veterinary Surgeons," passed April sixth, eighteen hundred and fifty-seven.

Passed April 19, 1862.

The People of the State of New York, represented in Senate and Assembly, do enact as follows :

SECTION 1. In addition to the trustees named in section one of the act entitled " An act to incorporate the

New York College of Veterinary Surgeons," passed April sixth, eighteen hundred and fifty-seven, there shall be added the following residents of New York or adjacency : E. G. Rawson, Charles S. Roe, Charles H. Birney, Isaac Ootheal, Thomas Wall, Richard Kelly, S. P. Nichols, James Crawford, Thomas Palmer, Daniel W. Clark, Forbes Holland, George Murray, E. Van Ranst, Barry Cornell.

§ 2. The board of examiners or censors of said college shall be elected by its faculty, from the faculties, respectively, of the medical colleges of the city of New York, or other medical or veterinary medical practitioners.

§ 3. Five of the trustees shall form a quorum for the transaction of business. Any trustee refusing or neglecting to attend six regular meetings, the board may declare his place vacant.

Chap. 347.

AN ACT to repeal chapter seven hundred and thirty-nine of the Laws of eighteen hundred and fifty-seven, and chapter two hundred and eighty-five of the Laws of eighteen hundred and fifty-eight, in relation to town insurance companies.

Passed April 19, 1862.

The People of the State of New York, represented in Senate and Assembly, do enact as follows :

SECTION 1. Chapter seven hundred and thirty-nine of the laws of eighteen hundred and fifty-seven, and chapter two hundred and eighty-five of the laws of eighteen hundred and fifty-eight, relating to town insurance companies, are hereby repealed; but nothing in this act contained shall affect any company or companies heretofore formed or organized under said chapters or either of them, or any rights acquired by such company or companies by virtue of such organization or organizations.

Chap. 348.

AN ACT in relation to the publication of notices by the contracting board.

Passed April 19, 1862; three-fifths being present.

The People of the State of New York, represented in Senate and Assembly, do enact as follows :

Publication of notices.

SECTION 1. The public notice required to be published by the first section of the act entitled "An act to enlarge the powers and define the duties of the contracting board," passed March four, eighteen hundred and fifty-seven, shall be published at least thirty days in the state paper and shall also be published at least three weeks, in not more than three newspapers published in the division districts in which the work or portion of the canal intended to be let is located, and not otherwise; and all the provisions of the said first section of the said act, inconsistent with the provisions of this act, are hereby repealed; but this repeal shall not affect or invalidate any notice given by the said contracting board in accordance with the provisions of the act hereby amended, and which may be pending at the date of the passage of this act.

Saving clause.

§ 2. This act shall take effect immediately.

Chap. 349.

AN ACT to repeal the charter of the Westfield and Chautauqua Lake Plankroad Company.

Passed April 19, 1862; three-fifths being present.

The People of the State of New York, represented in Senate and Assembly, do enact as follows :

SECTION 1. The charter of the Westfield and Chautauqua Lake Plankroad Company is hereby repealed; and the said road where the same was a public highway, previous to the construction of said plank road, is here-

by declared to be a public highway, and the commissioners of highways of the several towns shall have authority to take possession of the same; and the said road
shall be worked and used as other highways are worked
and used in said towns.

§ 2. It shall be the duty of the commissioners of highways in the several towns through which the said road
passes, immediately after the passage of this act, to divide the said road into districts and appoint overseers
for the several districts to serve until the first annual
town meetings after such appointment.

§ 3. This act shall take effect immediately.

Chap. 350.

AN ACT authorizing the Supervisor of the town
of Hempstead, to call a special town meeting to
determine, by ballot, whether the public lands
of said town (called the Hempstead Plains) shall
be sold or not.

Passed April 19, 1862; three-fifths being present.

*The People of the State of New York, represented in
Senate and Assembly, do enact as follows:*

SECTION 1. The supervisor of the town of Hempstead, *Supervisor
in the county of Queens, shall, whenever two hundred when to call
freeholders and inhabitants of said town present him town meet-
with a petition to that effect, direct the town clerk of ing.*
said town to call a special town meeting of the inhabitants thereof without delay, for the purpose of voting,
by ballot, whether the public lands of said town (called
the Hempstead Plains) shall be sold or not. But no such
town meeting shall be held oftener than once in twelve
months.

§ 2. The town clerk of said town, shall give notice of *Town clerk
the time and place of said meeting by publication in to give
two newspapers in the town, for two successive weeks, notice.*
and by posting a notice of such meeting in five public
places in the town at least ten days before such meeting,
and shall provide a suitable box for depositing all the *Provide box
and tickets.*

votes so given, and also a sufficient number of tickets, one-half of which shall contain "in favor of selling the plain lands," the other half shall contain "against selling the plain lands." The justices of the peace and the town clerk shall preside at such meeting, and the polls shall be held open from nine o'clock A. M. to six o'clock P. M.

§ 3. If, at any such meeting, the vote so given shall be in favor of selling said plain lands, the supervisor and the justices of the peace, shall, without delay, cause said lands to be surveyed and mapped, and shall direct the commissioners of highways of said town to lay out, on actual survey, such and so many highways on said plain lands as, in their judgment, the public good may require, and enter the same of record as now required by law.

§ 4. After said lands shall have been surveyed and said highways entered of record as aforesaid, the supervisor of said town shall direct the said town clerk to call a special town meeting of the inhabitants thereof, and every three years thereafter of which meetings notice shall be given as is provided in the second section of this act, who, when assembled, shall elect, by ballot, three commissioners for the sale of said plain lands, also a town treasurer; the said commissioners and town treasurer shall hold their offices for three years and until others are elected and duly qualified, in the same manner as herein provided.

§ 5. The said commissioners shall have power to sell at public auction from time to time, of which auctions notice shall be given as is provided in the second section of this act, said plain lands in parcels of not less than twenty-five nor more than one hundred and sixty acres and execute good and valid conveyances therefor. The moneys arising from such sale or sales shall be paid to said town treasurer, who shall execute a bond with ample security to the supervisor of said town, to be approved by the board of town auditors, and who shall receive and retain for his services as town treasurer, the same fees as now allowed by law to county treasurers; said commissioners shall receive for their services a reasonable compensation, to be allowed and audited by the board of town auditors; all contingent expenses incurred in the sale of said plain lands, surveying, and

Marginal notes:
Justices and town clerk preside.
When lands to be surveyed and highways laid out.
When commissioners and treasurer to be chosen.
Term of office.
Power of commissioners to sell lands.
Compensation of commissioners and treasurer.

all other charges, shall be audited by said board of town
auditors, and paid by said town treasurer.

§ 6. All the monies arising from the sale of said plain Appropria-
lands shall be paid into the hands of said town treasurer monies.
and shall be by him securely and safely invested on bond
and mortgage or in stocks of this state, and two-thirds
of the interest arising therefrom shall be apportioned
by him and paid to the several school districts, and
drawn by the trustees thereof, in the same manner that
other public moneys are now apportioned and drawn till
otherwise directed by law, and one-third of the interest thereof shall be paid by said town treasurer for
the support of the poor of the town, under the order of
the overseer of the poor.

§ 7. The said commissioners for the sale of said lands Commis-
shall make a full report of all their proceedings at each treasurer to
and every annual town meeting, and the said town treasu- report.
rer shall also make, at the same time, a full and complete
report of all the moneys received and disbursed by him,
and a particular statement of the amount loaned and the
securities held by him.

§ 8. This act shall take effect immediately.

Chap. 351.

AN ACT to amend an act entitled "An act to extend the benefits of instruction to the blind, and
for other purposes," passed April eighteenth,
eighteen hundred and thirty-nine.

Passed April 19, 1862; three-fifths being present.

*The People of the State of New York, represented in
Senate and Assembly, do enact as follows :*

SECTION 1. Section five of the act entitled "An act to
extend the benefits of instruction to the blind," passed
April eighteenth, eighteen hundred and thirty-nine, is
hereby amended so as to read as follows :

The supervisors of any county in this state from which Supervisors
state pupils shall be sent to and received in the said in- may raise
stitution, whose parents or guardians shall, in the money for
opinion of the superintendent of public instruction, be

unable to furnish them with suitable clothing are hereby authorized and directed, in every year while such pupils are in said institution, to raise and appropriate thirty dollars for each of said pupils, and to pay the sum so raised to the said institution, to be by it applied to furnishing such pupils with suitable clothing while in said institution. And if in any case all or any of said moneys are not expended before the expiration of the periods of appointment of such pupils, then the unexpended residue shall go into the general clothing fund of the said institution, to be by it devoted to furnishing

Clothing. state pupils with suitable clothing. If said sums shall not be paid to the said institution within six months after the annual meeting of the supervisors of any of said counties, the sums so unpaid shall bear interest at the rate of seven per centum per annum, from the expiration of said six months until the same be paid. The

When monies to be paid to Comptroller supervisors of any county in this state from whose pauper institutions pupils shall be sent to the said institution for the blind, shall raise, appropriate and pay to the order of the Comptroller of the state, towards the expense of educating and clothing such pupils, a sum equal to that which the county would have to pay to support the pupils as paupers at home.

§ 2. Section six of the same act is also hereby amended so as to read as follows :

Superintendent of public instruction may visit institution for the blind and report to legislature. The superintendent of public instruction is hereby authorized to visit and inspect the New York institution for the blind, in all its departments, to report to the legislature such matters and things as he may deem necessary, and in the selection and appointment of pupils he may, in those cases where in his opinion absolute indigence is not established, require and impose conditions whereby some proportionate share of the expense of educating and clothing such pupils shall be paid by their parents or guardians, in such way, manner and time as he may designate.

Chap. 352.

AN ACT to authorize the commissioners for loaning certain moneys from the United States, of the county of Ontario, to release certain land from the lien of a mortgage.

Passed April 19, 1862; three-fifths being present.

The People of the State of New York, represented in Senate and Assembly, do enact as follows:

SECTION 1. The commissioners for loaning certain moneys from the United States, of the county of Ontario, are hereby authorized to execute, acknowledge and to deliver to the trustees of school district number twelve, in the town of Farmington, a release from the lien from and operation of a mortgage, held by said commissioners in their official capacity, of the following described premises, to wit: All that certain piece or parcel of land lying in the town of Farmington, in the county of Ontario, begining at a point in the centre of the highway running past the dwelling of A. R. Bullis, M. D., at a point seven chains and forty-five links north, thirty-one and three-fourth degrees west, from the intersection of the centre of said highway with the centre of the highway leading past the dwelling of Israel F. Chilson; thence north fifty-eight degrees and a quarter east, along the line of B. B. Ketchum's land four chains and fifty links; thence north thirty-one degrees and three-quarters west, parallel with first mentioned highway and along the line of said Ketchum's land two chains and fifty links; thence south fifty-eight and a quarter degrees west, four chains and fifty links to the centre of the highway; thence south thirty-one degrees and three-quarters east, two chains and fifty-links to the place of beginning, containing one acre and twenty rods of land.

§ 2. This act shall take effect immediately.

Chap. 353.

AN ACT to incorporate The Ten Broeck Free
Academy.

Passed April 19, 1862.

The People of the State of New York, represented in
Senate and Assembly, do enact as follows:

Corporate name.

SECTION 1. Jonas K. Button of Franklinville; John
T. Cummings of Farmersville and Herman G. Button of
Machias, in the county of Cattaraugus, and their successors in office to be appointed as hereinafter provided
for, shall be, and are hereby created a body corporate
by the the name of "The Trustees of the Ten Broeck
Free Academy" and by that name shall have perpetual
succession for the purpose of organizing, conducting
and maintaining a free academy for the instruction of
youth in the village of Franklinville in the said county
of Cattaraugus, to be known as the "Ten Broeck Free
Academy."

Trustees may hold real and personal property.

§ 2. The said trustees may receive by gift, grant or
devise, and hold real and personal property, the yearly
income or revenue of which shall not exceed the sum of
ten thousand dollars in addition to the real estate
whereon their academy may be erected.

Free in-struction.

§ 3. The instruction in said academy shall forever be
free so far as the revenue from the endowment thereof
will permit, the preference always to be given to pupils
who may reside in the said towns of Farmersville, Machias and Franklinville, under such regulations as the
said trustees may adopt.

Trustees to execute bond.

§ 4. Every trustee under this act, shall, before entering upon his duties execute a bond to the treasurer of
said county of Cattaraugus in his name of office to be
approved by the county judge of Cattaraugus county, in
a penal sum equal to the amount of the assets and property of the said corporation, excepting the value of the
academy lot, building, library and apparatus with at
least two sureties satisfactory to the said county judge,
conditioned for the faithful discharge of his duties, and
that he will well and truly account for all the moneys

which he may receive as such trustee. And if at any
time any such bond shall be deemed insufficient by the
said county judge, a new bond shall be given as aforesaid to the satisfaction of the said judge within twenty
days after notice that the same shall have been so required, and upon default thereof the office of such
trustee so neglecting to renew his bond, shall become
vacant. The said trustees shall annually account to the
county treasurer of the said county for all their receipts
and expenditures as such trustees, and it shall be the
duty of the county treasurer to make a full report of
the same to the board of supervisors at each annual
session of the said board with such particulars as he
may deem proper, and the said county treasurer is
hereby authorized and it shall be his duty with the
approval of the county judge to prosecute the official
bond of any trustee for any breach of duty of which
he may have been guilty, and the moneys collected in
any such action shall be paid over to the said trustees.

§ 5. The county judge and surrogate of Cataraugus *Appointing board.*
county together with the supervisors of the said towns
of Farmersville, Franklinville and Machias shall constitute an appointing board, who shall have power to fill
any vacancies that may occur in the office of trustee
under this act. The concurrence of a majority of said
board, shall be necessary to fill any such vacancy and
the appointment shall be made in writing and filed in
the county clerks office of said county. One of the
said trustees shall always be a resident of the said town
of Farmersville, one of Machias and of Franklinville,
and the vacancies shall be filled accordingly. And unless any person so appointed shall give the security
required as aforesaid, within thirty days after proper
notice of such appointment, he shall be considered as
having declined the appointment of the office of trustee
aforesaid. Whenever a vacancy shall occur in the office
of trustee under this act the remaining trustee or trustees
or either of them shall notify the members of the said
appointing board of the existence of such vacancy, to
the end that the same may be filled without delay.

§ 6. The said trustees shall receive as a compensation *Compensation of trustees.*
for the duties imposed upon them the same percentage
on net income only as administrators receive for their
services not exceeding twenty-five dollars in all in any

one year. The said appointing board shall receive the same compensation paid to supervisors for attending meetings of their board, not exceeding in all in any one year the sum of twenty dollars.

Moneys to be loaned on bond and mortgage. § 7. The principal moneys which the trustees may receive from time to time, shall be loaned by them without delay on bond and mortgage on productive unincumbered real estate in this state, worth at least twice and one half times the amount loaned thereon exclusive of buildings, and after the erection of the academy building and purchasing suitable furniture therefor, and a suita-**Prohibition.** ble library and apparatus the trustees shall in no event use or expend any part of the principal of the funds in their hands or in any way belonging to the said institution but only the interest thereon, for the purpose of maintaining instruction in said academy and keeping the building, premises, furniture and library in good and proper condition and repair. Upon the receipt of ten thousand dollars the trustees may without delay commence the erection of the requisite academy buildings.

Authority to Peter Ten Broeck. § 8. Peter Ten Broeck of the said town of Farmersville is hereby authorized and empowered to give, grant, devise and bequeath to the aforesaid corporation by his last will and testament whenever the same may be made any portion of his estate real and personal within the limits allowed by law, any existing act or statute to the contrary notwithstanding.

Visitation. § 9. The said Ten Broeck Free Academy shall be subject to the visitation of the Regents of the University in like manner as other Academies, but shall not be entitled to participate in the distribution of the Literature Fund.

Trustees may be removed. § 10. Any trustee under this act may be removed by the county judge of said county upon hearing, on notice and good cause shown, and if any trustee shall remove from the town from which he was appointed, his office shall thereupon become and be vacant.

§ 11. This act shall take effect immediately.

Chap. 354.

AN ACT for the protection of bridges belonging to the State, or under its control.

Passed April 19, 1862; three-fifths being present.

The People of the State of New York, represented in Senate and Assembly, do enact as follows:

SECTION 1. It shall not be lawful for any person to lead, ride or drive any horse or horses, mule or mules, faster than on a walk over any bridge belonging to or under the control of this state, which is now or may hereafter be erected over any canal, canal feeder, stream or river thereof. No driving over bridges of the state faster than a walk.

§ 2. No person shall hereafter drive any cattle across any bridge or bridges referred to in the first section of this act, at a faster rate than upon a walk, and shall not, in so driving them over, permit more than twenty-five cattle to be upon any such bridge at one time. Cattle.

§ 3. Any person violating either of the provisions of this act shall be liable to a penalty, for each offence, fifteen dollars, to be sued for and recovered in any court having cognizance thereof, by the contractor, in the name of the people of this state, whenever such bridge or bridges, where the offence shall be committed, shall be embraced within his repair contract, and in all other cases by the superintendent of canal repairs. Such penalty when recovered shall be credited to the state in the first settlement thereafter of the accounts of such contractor or superintendent with the state. Penalty.

§ 4. This act shall take effect first day of June, one thousand eight hundred and sixty-two. Time of taking effect.

Chap. 355.

AN ACT to incorporate "The Exchange Company of New York."   .

Passed April 19, 1862; three-fifths being present

The People of the State of New York, represented in Senate and Assembly, do enact as follows :

SECTION 1. Abraham B. Bayliss, Stewart Brown, William Butler Duncan, Frederick C. Gebbard, James W. Gerard, Charles Gould, Moses H. Grinnell, D Henry Haight, Carroll Livingston, A. A. Low, Charles H. Marshall, E. E. Morgan, U. A. Murdock, Royal Phelps, Charles H. Russell, Paul Spofford, H. G. Stebbins, James Stewart, Thomas Tileston, Henry F. Vail, William R. Vermilyea, J. E. Williams, with their associates and all other persons who may hereafter be holders of the stock hereinafter mentioned, are hereby constituted a body

Corporate name. corporate by the name of "The Exchange Company of New York." The said corporation shall have perpetual succession, with power to sue and be sued, to make and use a common seal, and alter the same at pleasure.

Powers. § 2 The said corporation shall have power, in and by their corporate name, to purchase, lease, hold and convey real or leasehold estate in the city of New York, and to erect thereon a building suitable for the purpose of an exchange, and such other purposes as may, in the opinion of the trustees of said corporation, tend to carry out the design of such institution, and promote the convenient transaction of business in the city of New York; and when said building shall have been erected, they shall have power to lease the same and receive the rents and profits thereof, and divide the same among the stockholders.

Capital not less than $50,000. § 3. The capital stock of said corporation shall consist of not less than fifty thousand dollars, with liberty to increase the same when a majority of the trustees shall so determine, to any amount not exceeding one million of dollars. The said capital stock shall be divided into shares of one hundred dollars each, and the same shall be deemed personal property, and the same shall be transferable in such manner as the by-laws of such corporation shall direct. The said corporation may commence business and shall be deemed fully organized when fifty thousand dollars shall have been fully subscribed, and ten per cent on each share subscribed for paid in.

§ 4. All the affairs, concerns and business of such corporation shall be managed and conducted by and under the direction of thirteen trustees, who shall be stockholders and citizens of this state, and who shall be elected by the stockholders annually, on the first Monday of March in each year, by ballot, by plurality of the votes of the stockholders present and represented, by proxy, each share having one vote; and if for any cause such election shall* be then so held, the said corporation shall not be deemed dissolved, but such election shall be held within six months thereafter. Notice of the time and place of every such election shall be published for three weeks immediately preceding the day appointed therefor, in two of the daily newspapers printed and published in the city of New York. *(Trustees to be chosen. Notice of election.)*

§ 5. The first trustees shall be Abraham B. Baylis, William Butler Duncan, Frederick O. Gebhard, James W. Gerard, A. A. Low, E. E. Morgan, U. A. Murdock, Royal Phelps, Charles H. Russell, Paul Spoffard, Thomas Tileston, Henry F. Vail, William R. Vermilyea, who shall continue in office until others shall be chosen in their places, and so from time to time the trustees who may be duly elected shall continue in office and hold over until others shall be duly elected in their stead. *(Term of office.)*

§ 6. The trustees aforesaid or the survivors of them, and those who may from time to time be duly elected, shall by a majority vote, as soon as may be after their election, appoint from among their number a president, vice-president and treasurer, and the same re-appoint and remove at pleasure. And said trustees shall have power to fill vacancies in their board, occasioned by death, resignation, removal from the state, or otherwise, and to make all such by laws not inconsistent with the laws of this state or of the United States, as they may deem proper for the management of the affairs of such corporation, the holding of elections, the transfer of stock, and calling in of subscriptions thereto; and they shall have power to alter or amend the said by-laws from time to time. *(Officers.)*

*So in the original.

§ 7. A majority of the trustees for the time being,
shall constitute a quorum for the transaction of business;
and all committees, officers, clerks or servants, authorized
or created by this act, or by the by-laws of this corporation, shall be appointed by the trustees aforesaid ; and
said trustees may from time to time, re-construct, repair
or alter, or remodel any edifice or edifices, standing or
to be erected, on any real or leasehold estate that may
be acquired or held by said corporation, pursuant to the
provisions hereinbefore contained.

§ 8. The persons hereinbefore named as trustees are
hereby authorized, by themselves or by a committee to
be appointed from among their number, to receive
subscriptions to the capital stock of said corporation, at
such times and places in the said city of New York, as
they may appoint, by giving at least one week's public
notice thereof, in two daily newspapers published in said
city.

§ 9. It shall be lawful for the trustees of the corporation hereby created, to call in and demand from the
stockholders or subscribers, respectively, all such sums
of money as shall be payable on the shares subscribed
for by them, at such times and in such payments and
installments as the said trustees shall deem proper ; and
in case of default in such payment, may enforce the same
by action against any defaulting subscriber or stockholder, his representatives or assigns, or at their option
may declare forfeited said stock, and all previous payments made thereon.

§ 10. Each and every stockholder shall be individually
liable to the creditors of such corporation, for all debts
that may be due and owing by said corporation to their
laborers and servants for services performed, and for all
other debts and liabilities of said corporation to an
amount equal to the amount of stock held by him until
he shall* paid, in full, the amount of such stock so held
but no stockholder shall be personally liable for the
payment of any debt contracted by such corporation,
unless a suit for the collection of such debt shall be
brought against the said corporation within six years
after the debt shall become due ; and no suit shall be
brought against any stockholder in said corporation
until an execution against the corporation shall have
been returned unsatisfied in whole or in part.   No person

Majority of trustees may act.

Subscrip-tions.

Payment of same.

Liability of] stockhold-ers.

* So in the original.

holding stock in such corporation as executor, administrator, guardian or trustee, and no person holding such stock as collateral security, shall be personally subject to any liability as a stockholder of said company ; but the person pledging such stock shall be considered as holding the same, and shall be liable as a stockholder accordingly ; and the estate and funds in the hands of such executor, administrator, guardian, or trustee, shall be liable in like manner, and to the same extent, as the testator or intestate, or the ward or person interested in such fund, would have been if he had been living or competent to act and hold the stock in his own name. Every such executor, administrator, guardian or trustee shall represent the shares of stock owned by him, as such, at all meetings, and may vote as a stockholder; and every person pledging his stock as aforesaid may, in like manner represent the same and vote accordingly.

§ 11. This act shall be treated and considered as a public act, and nothing herein contained shall be construed or held as intending to confer any banking or insurance privileges. Public act.

§ 12. This act, and the corporation created thereby, and all the powers and privileges, conferred on, or granted to said corporation shall cease and be void if the said corporation be not organized within two years after the passage of this act. When to cease.

§ 13. The said corporation is hereby authorized from time to time to borrow such sums of money as may be necessary, not exceeding the sum of five hundred thousand dollars for the purpose of purchasing said land or building, or for the purpose of discharging any indebtedness incurred by such corporation in completing such purchase, or for the purpose of reconstructing, altering, repairing, or re-modeling the edifice standing on the premises aforesaid, or any part thereof, and for any such purpose from time to time to issue the bonds of said company for any amount so borrowed, and from time to time mortgage such land, building, and other corporation property, or any part or parts thereof, to secure the payment of such bonds, or any of them. The mortgage or mortgages herein authorized, may be made directly to the holder or holders of said bonds, or to some person or persons in trust for them, in such manner, and with such clauses and conditions as the trustees of said com- May borrow money.

pany shall see fit, and none of said bonds shall be for a less amount than five hundred dollars.

§ 14. This act shall take effect immediately.

Chap. 356.

AN ACT to provide for the regulation and inspection of buildings, the more effectual prevention of fires, and the better preservation of life and property in the city of New York.

Passed April 19, 1862; three-fifths being present.

The People of the State of New York, represented in Senate and Assembly, do enact as follows:

Building limits.

SECTION 1. All that portion of the city of New York, lying south of a line drawn east and west, from the East to the Hudson river, one hundred feet north of the northerly line of Fifty-second street, in the city of New York, shall constitute the building limits designated under this act, in which no building shall hereafter be built, except in conformity to the provisions of this act; and the several provisions of this act shall apply to all stone, brick, or iron buildings north of said building limits, and within the city of New York, except as hereinafter provided.

Buildings.

§ 2. All buildings hereafter erected within the building limits of the city of New York shall have all outside or party walls constructed of stone, brick, or iron, and all such walls shall be built to a line, and be carried up plumb and straight, with close joints; and the several component parts of all such buildings shall be built and constructed in such manner as herein provided.

Construction regulated.

Ibid.

§ 3. All foundation walls shall be built of stone or brick, and shall be laid not less than four feet below the surface of the earth, on a good solid bottom, and in case the nature of the earth should require it, a bottom of driven piles, or laid timbers, of sufficient size and thickness shall be laid, to prevent the walls from settling, the top of such pile or timber bottom to be driven or laid below the water line; and all piers, columns, posts or pillars resting on the earth shall have a footing course, and shall be set upon a bottom in the same manner as the foundation walls.

§ 4. The footing, or base course, under all foundation Ibid. walls, shall be of stone or concrete, and shall be at least twelve inches wider than the bottom width of the foundation walls. And if the walls be built of isolated piers, then there must be inverted arches, at least twelve inches thick turned under and between the piers, or two footing courses of large stone, at least ten inches thick in each course. All foundation walls, other than those of dwellings, shall be at least four inches thicker than the wall next above them, to a depth sixteen feet below the curb level, and shall be increased four inches in thickness for every additional five feet in depth below the said sixteen feet. Foundation walls in dwelling-houses shall be; below the basement-floor beams, four inches thicker than the walls next above them. All foundation walls shall be understood to mean that portion of the wall below the level of the street curb, and depth shall be computed from the curb level downward.

§ 5. In all dwelling-houses not above thirty feet in Ibid. height, and not more than twenty-five feet in width, the party and outside walls shall not be less than eight inches thick. In all dwelling-houses from thirty to thirty-eight feet in height, and not more than twenty-eight feet in width, the outside walls shall not be less than eight inches thick, and the party walls shall not be less than twelve inches thick. In all dwelling-houses thirty-eight to fifty-five feet in height, and not more than thirty feet in width, the outside and party walls shall not be less than twelve inches thick; and if above fifty-five feet the walls shall not be less than sixteen inches thick, to the top of the second-story beams, provided the same is twenty feet above the curb level, and if not, then to the under side of the third-story beams; and also provided that portion of the wall twelve inches thick shall not exceed fifty-five feet in height from the said sixteen inch wall.

§ 6. In all buildings other than dwelling-houses, not Ibid. above thirty-five feet in height, and not more than twenty-seven feet in width, the outside walls shall not be less than eight inches thick, and the party walls not less than twelve inches thick; if above thirty-five feet

and under fifty feet in height, the walls shall not be less
than twelve inches thick; if above fifty feet and under
sixty-five feet in height, the walls shall not be less than
sixteen inches thick, to the height of twenty feet, and not
less than twelve inches thick from thence to the top;
and if above sixty-five feet, and under eighty feet in
height, the walls shall not be less than sixteen inches
thick to the height of thirty feet, and not less than
twelve inches thick from thence to the top. In all buildings over twenty-seven feet in width, and not having
either brick partition walls or girders, supported by columns running from front to rear, the walls shall be increased an additional four inches in thickness, to the
same relative thickness in height as required under this
section, for every additional ten feet in width of said
building, or any portion thereof. It is understood that
the amount of materials specified may be used either in
piers or buttresses, provided the walls between the same
shall in no case be less than eight inches in thickness, to
the height of forty feet, and if over that height, then
twelve inches thick.

§ 7. In all buildings in which there are stone or brick
partition walls, the said partition walls shall be subject
to the clauses and provisions above set forth, with regard to foundations, thickness, and heights; and if there
should be substituted iron or wooden girders, supported
upon iron or wooden columns, in place of the partition
walls, they shall be made of sufficient strength to bear
safely the weight of two hundred and fifty pounds for
every square foot of the floor or floors that rest upon
them, exclusive of the weight of material employed in
their construction, and shall have footing courses and
foundation wall equal to that of the party wall, with inverted arches under and between the columns, or two
footing courses of large, well shaped stone, laid cross-
wise, edge to edge, and at least ten inches thick, in each
course, the lower footing course to be equal in area to
that under a party wall; and under every column as
above set forth, a cap of cut granite, at least twelve inches thick, and of a diameter twelve inches greater than
that of the column, must be laid.

Ibid.   § 8. No wall of any building now erected, or hereafter
to be built or erected in the said city, shall be cut off or
altered below, to be supported in any manner, in whole

or in part, by wood, but shall be wholly supported by stone, brick or iron ; and no wood or timber shall be used between such wall and such supporters. Every temporary support placed under any wall, girder, or beam, during the erection, finishing, alteration, or repairing of any building, shall be equal in strength to the permanent support required for such wall, girder, or beam. And the walls of every building shall be strongly braced from the beams of each story until the next tier of beams are on and leveled up.

§ 9. All stone walls less than twenty-four inches thick, Stone walls. shall have at least one header, extending through the walls, in every six square feet ; and if over twenty-four inches in thickness, shall have one header for every six superficial feet on both sides of the wall, and running into the wall at least two feet. In every brick wall every Brick wall. fifth course of bricks shall be a heading course, except where walls are faced with brick, in which case every fifth course shall be bonded into the backing by cutting the courses of the faced brick, and putting in diagonal headers behind the same, or by splitting face brick in half, and backing the same by a continuous row of headers. In all walls which are faced with thin ashlar, All walls. anchored to the backing, or in which the ashlar has not either alternate headers and stretchers in each course, or alternate heading and stretching courses, the backing of brick shall not be less than eight inches thick, and all eight-inch backing shall be laid up in cement mortar, and shall not be built to greater height than prescribed for eight-inch walls. All heading courses shall be good, hard perfect brick.

§ 10. In all buildings where the walls are built hollow, Walls. the same amount of stone or brick shall be used in their construction as if they were solid, as above set forth ; and no hollow walls shall be built unless the two walls forming the same shall be connected by continuous vertical ties of the same materials as the walls, and not over twenty-four inches apart. The heights of all walls shall be computed from the curb level. No swelled or refuse brick shall be allowed in any wall or pier.

§ 11. The mortar used in the construction of any build- Mortar. ing shall be composed of lime or cement, mixed with sand, in proper proportions. No inferior lime or cement shall be used ; and all sand shall be clean, sharp grit,

73

free from loam, and all joints in all walls must be filled with mortar.

Partition walls. § 12. Any building except a private dwelling, over thirty feet in width, if built (or used) for the purpose of a hotel or boarding house, shall have one or more brick, stone, or fire-proof partition walls running from front to rear. These walls shall be so located that the space between any two of the bearing walls of the building shall not be over twenty-five feet.

Bond stone. § 13. Every isolated pier less than six superficial feet at the base, and all piers supporting a wall built of rubble stone or brick, or under any iron beam or arch girder, or arch on which a wall rests, or lintel supporting a wall, shall, at intervals of not more than thirty inches in height, have built into it a bond-stone not less than four inches thick, of a diameter each way equal to the diameter of the pier, except that in front piers above the curb, the bond-stone may be four inches less than the pier in diameter; and all piers shall be built of good hard burnt brick and cement, and all the brick in such piers shall be of the hardest quality, and be well wet before laid; and the walls and piers under all compound girders, iron or other columns, shall have a bond-stone every thirty inches in height from the bottom, whether said piers are in the walls or not, and a cap-stone at least twelve inches in thickness by the whole size of the bearing.

Anchors. § 14. All walls shall be securely anchored with iron anchors, to each tier of beams. The front, rear, side, end, and party walls shall, if not carried up together, be anchored to each other, every six feet in their height, by tie anchors, made of one and a quarter inch by three-eights of an inch wrought iron. The said anchors shall be built into the front and rear walls, at least one half the thickness of the front and rear walls, so as to secure the front and rear walls to the side, end, or party walls; and all stone used for the facing of any building except where built with alternate headers and stretchers, as hereinbefore set forth, shall be strongly anchored with iron anchors; and all such anchors shall be let into the stone at least one inch. The side, end, or party walls, shall be anchored to each tier of beams, at intervals of not more than eight feet apart, with good, strong wrought iron anchors, three-eights of an inch by one inch, well built into the side walls and well fastened to the side of the beams; and where the beams are supported by girders, the ends of the beams resting on the girders shall be strapped by wrought iron straps of the same size, and at the same distance apart, and in the same beam as the wall anchors; all wall anchors used in any building except dwellings, shall be three-eights by one inch wrought iron, and shall hook over a three-quarter round bolt of wrought iron running through the beam.

§ 15. All side or party, and front or rear walls, not corniced, and where no gutter is required on any building over fifteen feet high, shall be built up and extended at least twelve inches above the roof, and shall be coped with stone or iron; provided, that where partition walls are carried up, and where Mansard or French roofs are built over a hotel or block of houses, the partition and division walls may be carried up above the roofing and coped with some fire-proof material, or shall be carried up to the under side of the roof-planking; and the roof-planking must, in all such cases, have a space of at least four inches left, extending the entire length of the wall between the ends or sides of said planking, filled up to the top of the planking with good mortar, and the slating or other roof material may then be carried over the same. *Side walls, &c.* *Partition walls.* *Roof planking.*

§ 16. Compound beams with cast-iron arches and wrought-iron ties, used to span openings not more than ten feet in width, shall have a bearing of at least twelve inches by the thickness of the wall to be supported, and for every additional foot of span over and above the said ten feet, the bearing shall be increased one inch; provided the same are supported at the ends on walls or piers of brick or stone, and on the front of any building where the supports are of iron or solid cut stone, they shall be at least twelve inches on the face, and the width of the thickness of the wall to be supported, and in all cases shall be of sufficient strength to bear the weight to be imposed upon them, and shall rest upon a cut granite base block at least twelve inches thick by the full size of the bearing, and all compound beams or girders used in any building, shall be, throughout, of a thickness not less than the thickness of the wall to be supported, and shall be made in the best manner. All compound beams shall have a cast-iron shoe on the *Compound beams, &c*

upper side, to answer for the skew back of a brick or
cut stone arch, which said arch shall always be turned
over the same, and the arch shall, in no case, be less
than eight inches in height by the width of the wall to
be supported, and the shoe shall be made strong enough
to resist the pressure of the arch in all cases. Cut stone
or hard brick arches, with two wrought-iron tie-rods, of
sufficient strength, may be turned over any openings
less than forty feet, provided they have skew backs of
cut stone or cast or wrought-iron into which the bars or
tension rods shall be properly secured by heavy wrought-
iron washers, necks, and heads of wrought-iron, properly secured to the skew backs. The above clause is
intended to meet cases where the arch has not abutments of sufficient size to resist its thrust.

Openings
for doors
and win-
dows.

§ 17. All openings for doors and windows in all buildings, except as otherwise provided, shall have a good
and sufficient arch of stone or brick, well built and
keyed, and with good and sufficient abutments, or a lintel of stone or iron, as follows: For an opening not
more than four feet, the lintel shall not be less than
eight inches in height; and for an opening not more
than five feet in breadth, the lintel shall be twelve inches in height; and for an opening exceeding five feet
in breadth, the lintel shall increase in height over and
above the twelve inches before provided, one inch for
every additional foot in breadth of the opening; and
every such opening less than five feet in breadth, in all
walls over eight inches in thickness, shall have a lintel
of stone or iron not less than seven inches in breadth,
and one-third the thickness of the walls on which it
rests; and in all openings, as aforesaid, in any eight-
inch wall, the lintel shall be one-half the thickness of
the wall; and on the inside of all openings in which the
lintels shall be less than the width of the wall, there shall
be a good timber lintel on the inside of the other lintels,
which shall rest, at each end, not more than four inches
on any wall. column, post or pillar, and shall be cham-
fered at each end, and shall have a double rolock arch
over the said lintel; or the said arch may be turned on
a centre, which may be struck after the arch is turned,
provided the piers or abutments are of a sufficient

Arches, &c. strength to bear the thrust of the arch; and all arches
over openings or fire-places shall be built of good hard

brick, and well keyed; all lintels over openings returned
on a corner building shall be of iron or stone, of the
breadth before provided for, and of the full thickness of
the wall to be supported; and where the second-story
window sills rest upon the said lintel course, the lintel
shall be of iron or stone, and shall be the full size of the
wall to be supported. Where hollow cast-iron lintels
are placed over openings, they shall have a brick arch
of sufficient thickness, with skew backs and tie-rods of
sufficient strength to support the superincumbent weight,
independent of the cast-iron lintel.

§ 18. All stores or storehouses, or other buildings Stores and
which are more than two stories, or above twenty-five houses.
feet in height above the curb level, except dwelling-
houses, school-houses or churches, shall have doors,
blinds or shutters made of fire-proof metal, on every
window and entrance above the first story, where the
same do not open upon a street. Where, in any such
building, the shutters, blinds or doors cannot be put on
the outside of such door or window, they shall be put
on the inside; and every such door, blind or shutter
shall be closed on the completion of the business of each
day; and if fire-proof shutters or blinds are put upon
the front or sides of any building on the street fronts,
they must be so constructed that they can be opened
from the outside, above the first story.

§ 19. All chimneys, and all flues in stone or brick Chimneys.
walls, in any buildings, without reference to the purpose
for which they may be used, shall be properly pargetted
on the inside with good parging mortar, or the joints
shall be struck smooth on the inside. And no tin or other
metal flue or flues, pipe or pipes of a single thickness of
metal, to convey heated air in any building hereafter to
be built, altered or erected, in any part of the said city,
shall be allowed, unless the same be so constructed as to
have a thickness of not less than one inch of plaster of
paris between the said metal pipe, flue or flues, and any
of the timber or wood work adjoining the same. Unless the plaster of paris is put on as above set forth, the
pipes in all cases must be double, that is, two pipes, one
inside the other, at least one inch apart, and filled with
plaster of paris. Fire brick pipes, for conveying hot
air, may also be put in wooden partitions, provided they
have a spigot and faucet joint filled with plaster. No.

steam pipe shall be placed within two inches of any timber or wood work as aforesaid ; where the said space of two inches around the steam pipe is objectionable, it shall be protected by a soapstone or an earthen ring or tube. No base or flooring, or roofing, or any other wood work shall be placed against any brick or other flue, until the same shall be well plastered with plaster of paris behind such wood work. All flues in any build- ing shall be properly cleaned, and all rubbish removed, and the flues left smooth on the inside, upon the com- pletion of all such buildings, as aforesaid. No chimney shall be started or built upon any floor or beam, and in no case where the breast of a chimney shall project more than four inches in any eight-inch wall, or eight inches in a twelve-inch wall, shall it be commenced in any wall, but shall be started and built on the same line from the foundation ; and if supported by piers, the said piers shall start from the foundation and on the same line with the chimney breast, and shall not be less than sixteen inches on the face ; and all such piers shall be well built into the wall. All hearths shall be supported by arches of stone or brick, and no chimneys projecting over the distance above specified shall be cut off below, in whole or in part, and supported by wood, but shall be wholly supported by stone, brick or iron, and all chimneys in any building or buildings as aforesaid, already erected, or hereafter to be erected or built, or any other chimney or chimneys in any part of the said city, which shall be dangerous in any manner whatsoever, shall be repaired or taken down. In all chimneys which are corbelled out from the walls as above described, they shall be sup- ported by five courses of brick.

§ 20 No smoke pipe in any building with wooden or combustible floors and ceilings, shall enter any flue, unless the said pipe shall be at least eighteen inches from either the floors or ceilings ; and in all cases where smoke pipes pass through stud or wooden partitions of any kind, whether the same be plastered or not, they shall be guarded by either a double collar of metal, with at least four inches air space, and holes for ventilation ; or by a soapstone ring, not less than three inches in thickness, and extending through the partition, or by a solid coating of plaster of paris, three inches thick, or by an earthenware ring, three inches from the pipe. In

Smoke-
pipes.

all cases where hot water, steam, hot air, or other furnaces are used, the furnace smoke pipe must be kept at least two feet below the beams or ceiling above the same, unless said beams or ceiling shall be properly protected by a shield of tin plate suspended above said smoke pipe, with sufficient space for the free circulation of air above and below said shield; and the smoke pipe shall, in all cases, be kept at least eight inches from the beams or ceilings, as aforesaid; and the top of all furnaces set in brick must be covered with brick, slate, or tin plate, supported by iron bars, and so constructed as to be perfectly tight; said covering to be in addition to and not less than six inches from the ordinary covering to the hot-air chamber. If, however, there is not height enough to build the furnace top at least four inches below the floor beams or ceiling, then the floor beams must be trimmed around the furnace, and said covering and the trimmers and headers must be at least four inches from the same. The top of portable furnace or furnaces, not set in brick, shall be kept at least one foot below the beams or ceiling, with a shield of tin plate, made tight, and suspended below the said beams or ceiling, and extend one foot beyond the top of the furnace on all sides. All hot-air registers, hereafter placed in Registers. the floor of any building, shall be set in soapstone borders, not less than two inches in width. All soapstone borders to be firmly set in plaster of paris or gauged mortar; all floor register boxes to be made of tin plate, with a flange on the top to fit the groove in the soapstone, the register to rest upon the same. There shall also be an open space of two inches on all sides of the register box, extending from the under side of the ceiling below the register, to the soapstone in the floor; the outside of said space to be covered with a casing of tin plate, made tight on all sides, to extend from the under side of the aforesaid ceiling up to and turn under the said soapstone. Registers twelve by nineteen inches, or less than fifteen by twenty-five inches, shall have a space of three inches between the register box and casing; registers of fifteen by twenty-five, and more, shall have a space of three and a half inches.

§ 21. In no building, whether the same be a frame Beams. building or otherwise, shall any wooden beams or timbers be placed within eight inches of any flue, whether the same be a smoke, air, or any other flue. All wooden beams and other timbers in the party wall of every building hereafter to be erected or built of stone, brick or iron, shall be separated from the beam or timber entering into the opposite side of the wall by at least four inches of solid mason work. No floor beam shall be supported wholly upon any wooden partition, but every beam, except headers and tail beams, shall rest, at each end, not less than four inches in the wall, or upon girder, as authorized by this act. And every trimmer or header more than four feet long, used in any building except a dwelling, shall be hung in stirrup irons of suitable thickness for the size of the timbers. No timber shall be used in any wall of any building where stone, brick or iron is commonly used, except bond timbers and lintels, as hereinbefore provided for, and no bond timber in any wall shall in width and thickness exceed that of a course of brick. No bond timber shall be more than three feet in length, and such bond timber shall be laid eighteen inches apart, parallel to each other, and there shall be eight inches of brick or mason work between the ends of the same. In all buildings where the floor beams are of wood, the end of the beams resting on the wall shall be cut to the bevel of three inches. In every building already erected or hereafter to be

Floors.   built, the floors shall be of sufficient strength to bear the weight to be imposed upon them, exclusive of the weight of the material used in their construction. And all timbers or beams used in any building, whether the same be a frame building or otherwise, shall be of good sound material, free from rot, sap, shakes or rotten knots, and of such size and dimensions as the purpose for which the building is intended requires.

Cornices.   § 22. Wooden cornices may be placed on buildings not over forty feet in height, or on three story and basement dwelling houses, provided that the said cornices, whether used for a gutter or not, shall have the brackets well built into the walls, and well fastened to wall strips built into the wall for that purpose; and in all cases, the walls shall be carried up to the planking of the roof, and when the cornice projects above the roof, the walls shall be carried up to the top of the cornices, and no wooden cornice shall extend across two or more buildings, but the same shall return against the building on which it is placed, and the party walls shall in all cases extend up above the planking of the cornice and be coped; and all exterior cornices and gutters of all other buildings, hereafter to be erected or built, shall be of some fire-proof material; and in every case the greatest weight of stone, iron or other material of which the cornice shall be constructed shall be on the inside of the outer line of the wall on which the cornice shall rest, in the proportion of three of wall to two of cornice in weight, allowance being made for the excess of leverage produced by the projection of the cornice beyond the face of the wall; and all fire-proof cornices shall be well secured to the walls with iron anchors, independent of any wood work, and all exterior wooden cornices or gutters that may be unsafe or rotten, shall be made safe or be taken down.

§ 23. The planking and sheathing of the roof of every Roof. building erected or built as aforesaid, shall in no case be extended across the front, rear, side, end or party wall thereof; and every such building, and the top and sides of every dormer window thereon, shall be covered and roofed with slate, tin, zinc, copper or iron, or such other equally fire-proof roofing as a majority of the insurance companies of the city of New York, which are incorporated under the laws of this state, will insure at the same rate of premium as other articles in this section mentioned, or which shall be approved by the board of inspection appointed under this act. And no wooden building hereafter erected or built, or already erected in any part of the said city more than two stories or above thirty feet in height above the curb level, to the highest part thereof, which shall require roofing, shall be roofed with any other roofing or covering except as aforesaid. Nothing in this section shall be construed to prohibit the repairing of any shingle roof, provided the building is not altered in height. All buildings in the city of New York, whether already erected or hereafter to be built, shall have scuttle frames and doors, or bulkheads leading to the roof, made of or covered with some fire-proof material, and shall have ladders or stairways leading to the same, and all such scuttles and stairways, or ladders leading to the roof shall be kept so as to be ready for use at all times, and all scuttles shall not be less in size than two by three feet.

§ 24. All gas, water, steam or other pipes which may
be introduced into any building other than a dwelling
house, shall not be let into the beams unless the same be
placed within thirty-six-inches of the end of the beams;
and in no case shall be let into the beams more than two
inches in depth.

Floors.

§ 25. In all buildings, every floor shall be of sufficient
strength, in all its parts, to bear safely upon every
superficial foot of its surface, seventy-five pounds; and
if used as a place of public assembly, one hundred and
twenty pounds; and if used as a store, factory, warehouse, or for any other manufacturing or commercial
purpose, from one hundred and fifty to five hundred
pounds and upwards; the weight in each class of these
buildings being determined by the department for the
survey and inspection of buildings, created by this act,
who shall form a schedule of the weights required to be
supported safely on the floors of each class, and furnish
a printed copy of this schedule to any person applying
for it. Every floor shall be of sufficient strength to bear
safely the weights aforesaid, in addition to the weight of
the materials of which the floor is composed; and every
column post, or other vertical support, shall be of sufficient strength to bear safely the weight of the portion
of each and every floor depending upon it for support,
in addition to the weight required, as above, to be supported safely upon said portions of said floors. In all
calculations for the strength of materials to be used in
every building, the proportion between the safe weight
and the breaking weight shall be as one to three, for all
beams, girders, and other pieces subjected to a cross
strain; and shall be as one to six for all posts, columns,
and other vertical supports, and for all tie rods, tie
beams, and other pieces subjected to a tensile strain.
And the requisite dimensions of each piece of material
is to be ascertained by computation, by applicable rules
given by Tredgold, Hodgkinson, Barlow, and other re-
liable writers on the strength of materials, using for
constants in the rules only such numbers as have been
deduced from experiments on materials of like kind
with that proposed to be used.

§ 26. In all fire-proof buildings, either brick walls
with wrought iron beams, or cast or wrought iron
columns with wrought iron beams, must be used in the
interior; and the following rules shall be observed:

1st. All metal columns shall be planed true and smooth Columns. at both ends, and shall rest on cast iron bed plates and have cast iron caps, which shall also be planed true. If brick arches are used between the beams, the arches shall have a rise of at least an inch and a quarter to each foot of span between the beams.

2d. And all arches shall be at least four inches thick. Arches. Arches over four feet span shall be increased in thickness toward the haunches by additions of four inches in thickness of brick; the first additional thickness shall commence at two and a half feet from the centre of the span; the second addition, at six and a half feet from the centre of the span; and the thickness shall be increased thence four inches for every additional four feet of span toward the haunches.

3d. The said brick arches shall be laid to a line on the Ibid. centres with a close joint, and the bricks shall be hard burnt, and shall be well wet and the joints well filled with cement mortar, in proportions of not more than two of sand to one of cement, by measure. The arches shall be well grouted, and pinned with slate, and keyed.

4th. All iron beams in stores or storehouses shall have Ties. wrought iron ties, which shall be at least one inch in diameter, placed not more than six feet from the centres, and the said ties shall be well secured to the lower half of each beam, and into a beam or continuous piece of angle iron at both walls against which the arches abut.

5th. Under the ends of all the iron beams, where they rest on the walls, a stone template must be built into the walls; said templates to be eight inches wide in twelve- Templates. inch walls, and in all walls of greater thickness, to be in width not less than four inches less than the width of said walls, and not to be, in any case, less than four inches in thickness and eighteen inches long.

§ 27. All dwelling houses, in any part of the city of Stairway. New York, already erected, or that may hereafter be built, that now are, or may be more than forty feet high, that shall be occupied by or built to contain six or more families above the first story, and all dwelling houses that shall be occupied by or built to contain eight or more families above the first story, shall have a stairway connected with a proper scuttle or other opening, leading to the roof, and all the rooms on each floor shall connect by doors from front to rear, and every such dwelling house shall have placed thereon a practical fire-proof fire escape that shall be approved of by the department for the survey and inspection of buildings, in the city of New York, and all front and rear tenement houses on

the same lot shall be connected by an iron bridge; provided, that where any such building shall be built fire-proof throughout, or where there are two or more dwelling houses adjoining, and of equal height and with flat roofs, the same may be exempt from the requirements of this section; and no dwelling houses, such as are mentioned in this section, now built, or which may hereafter be built, shall have any hay, straw, hemp, flax, wood, shavings, burning fluid, turpentine, camphene, or any other combustible material, stored therein, or kept on sale, except in such quantities as shall be provided for by ordinances of the common council of said city.

§ 28. It shall not be lawful for the owner or owners of any brick front or wooden building already erected in said city, that has a peak roof, to raise the same for the purpose of making a flat roof thereon, unless the same be raised with the same kind of material as the building, and except that such new roof be covered with any of

the articles of roofing mentioned in the twenty-third section of this act; and, unless all such buildings, when so raised, shall not exceed forty feet in height to the highest part thereof, and all such brick dwelling houses that have eight inch walls, the said walls shall not exceed forty feet in height; and, also, provided that all such dwelling houses exceed twenty-five feet in height to the peak, before the said alteration. If any such building shall have been built before the street upon which it is located is graded, or, if the grade is altered, all such buildings may be raised or lowered, to meet the requirements of said grade. And no brick front or wooden building whatsoever, in said city, southward of said line, shall be enlarged or built upon, unless the exterior walls of such addition or enlargement be of fire-proof materials; provided, however, that such brick front, or wooden building only, may be raised, lowered or altered, under the circumstances, and in the same manner especially provided for in this section; and no wooden building shall be removed from one lot to another, southward of said line.

§ 29. No wooden shed shall be erected southward _{Wooden} of said line, unless one whole side of the same shall be _{sheds.} left entirely and constantly open. And also, provided the same does not exceed twelve feet in height to the peak or highest part thereof, from the level on which it is placed, and shall not contain any straw, hay, hemp, flax, or any combustible materials (fuel excepted). Nothing in this section shall be construed to prohibit _{Proviso.} the erection of any wooden building, provided the same does not exceed twelve feet in height to the peak or highest part thereof, above the level of the earth on which it is placed; and also, provided the same be wholly covered on the outside with any fire-proof material. No outside wooden stairs shall be erected south- _{Wooden} ward of said line, which shall extend above the second _{stairs.} story floor of any such building to which the same shall be attached; and if any such stairway shall be enclosed, the same shall be wholly covered with some fire-proof material.

§ 30. Any piazza, platform or balcony that does not _{Piazza or} exceed ten feet in width, and that does not extend more _{balcony.} than three feet above the second story floor of any building to which the same may be attached, or the roof of which does not exceed the same height may be built of wood, provided the same is open on the side; and such piazza, platform or balcony may be built higher, or may be inclosed, provided the same shall have end or party walls of stone or brick not less than eight inches thick, which shall be started and built from the foundation and carried up above the roof, and coped with stone or iron; and the roofs of all piazzas shall be covered with some fire-proof material. Any bay or oriel window that does not extend more than three feet above the third story floor of any dwelling house to which the same shall be attached, may be built of wood.

§ 31. All privies not exceeding ten feet square and _{Privies, fer-} ten feet high, and all ferry houses which shall be erect- _{ry houses, &c.} ed with the express permission of the corporation of the city of New York, may be built and covered with wood, boards or shingles.   All ash holes or ash houses within the said city shall be built of stone, brick or iron without the use of wood in any part thereof.

§ 32. Every wooden building or frame building with _{Repairing} a brick front, or any other front, situated in the said _{wooden buildings.}

city, south of the said line, which may hereafter be
damaged by fire or otherwise to any amount not greater
than one-half the value thereof. at the time of such
damage may be repaired or rebuilt; but if such damage
shall amount to more than one-half of such value thereof, exclusive of the value of the foundation, then such
building shall not be repaired or rebuilt but shall be taken
down.

Damage by fire. § 33. The amount and extent of such damage by fire,
or otherwise, shall be determined by the deputy superintendent created under this act and one surveyor
appointed by the fire insurance company or companies,
if such building or buildings are insured, and one surveyor appointed by the owner or owners. But if such
building or buildings be not insured, then the damage
shall be determined by the deputy superintendent and a
surveyor appointed by the owner or owners; and in
case these two do not agree they shall appoint a third
party, and a decision of a majority of them, reduced to
writing, and sworn to, shall be conclusive in the premises; and such building shall in no manner be repaired
or rebuilt, until after such decision shall have been
rendered.

Prohibition concerning building. § 34. No building already erected or hereafter to be
built in said city, shall be enlarged, raised, altered, or
built upon in such manner that were such building
wholly built or constructed after the passage of this act,
it would be in violations of any of the provisions of
this act, except as herein provided. And all buildings
built of stone, brick or iron, and all wooden buildings, with or without brick fronts, in any part of
said city, before the same shall be enlarged, raised or
built upon, shall be first examined by said department, to ascertain if the building or buildings, or
either of them, are in a good and safe condition
to be enlarged, raised, or built upon. And no such
buildings as aforesaid shall be enlarged, raised or built
upon, until after such examination and decision; and
the decision of said department, under such examination, shall be final and conclusive in the premises, and
shall be made without delay.

Plans and specifica- tions to be made. § 35. All plans and specifications for the erection,
construction, alteration or repair of any building or
part of a building in the city of New York, may, at the
option of the owner, before execution thereof, be sub-

mitted for examination and approval to the department
for the survey and inspection of buildings in the city of
New York ; and it shall be the duty of the superintendent of buildings, under said department, to examine the
same without delay, and when found or made to conform to the requirements of the several provisions of
this act, to certify the approval of said department to
the same, and where such approved plans and specifications shall be strictly followed in the construction,
alteration or repair of any such building or part of
a building, then the owner of such building and all persons executing the work under such approved plans and
specifications, shall be exonorated from all liability
under the several provisions of this act.

§ 36. The department created under this act shall have Power of
full power, in passing upon any question relative to the department.
mode, manner of construction or materials to be used in
the erection, alteration or repair of any building in the
city of New York, where the same is not specially provided for herein, to make the same conform to the true
intent, meaning and spirit of the several provisions
hereof ; and shall also have discretionary power, upon
application therefor, to modify or vary any of the several provisions of this act to meet the requirements of
special cases, where the same do not conflict with public
safety and the public good, so that substantial justice
may be done ; but no such deviation shall be permitted
except a record of the same shall be kept by said department, and a certificate be first issued to the party
applying for the same. Such certificate shall be issued
only upon an order first being obtained therefor, upon a
sworn petition setting forth the facts upon application to
a special term of the supreme court in the city of New
York, said supreme court hereby being authorized to
grant such order in its discretion.

§ 37. The owner or owners of any dwelling house, Punishment
store, storehouse, or other building, or of any frame tion of this
building, with or without a brick front, or any wooden act.
building, or of any ash house, ash hole, or wooden shed
upon which any violation of this act may be placed or
shall exist, whether he or they be the owner or owners
of the land in fee, or not, or be the lessee or lessees
thereof, or has or have a qualified or contingent interest
therein, by virtue of some agreement or contract in

writing, or in any other manner, and any master architect or architects who may be employed or assist therein, or any and all other persons who shall violate any provision of this act, or fail to comply therewith, shall, for each and every such violation or non-compliance, respectively forfeit and pay the sum of fifty dollars, and any master builder or builders, master carpenter or carpenters, master mason or masons, master roofer or roofers, furnace maker or makers, or other persons who shall violate any provision of this act, or who may be employed or assist therein, shall, for every such violation, not removed within ten days after notice of the violation shall be given to him or them, respectively forfeit and pay the additional sum of fifty dollars: provided, however, in all cases of violation that shall be in existence at the time this act takes effect, that no penalty shall attach until after a notice of ten days shall be given requiring the removal of such violation or violations.

Jurisdiction of courts, in relation to this act. § 38 All courts of civil jurisdiction in the city of New York shall have cognizance and jurisdiction over all suits or proceedings herein authorized to be brought for the recovery of any penalty, and the enforcement of any of the several provisions of this act; and any court of record in said city shall have power at any time after the service of notice of violation, to enjoin and restrain by injunction order the further progress of any violation named in this act; and all courts in which such suits of proceedings are instituted, upon the rendition of a verdict for any penalty or penalties, shall give judgment for the amount of such penalty or penalties and costs, and for the removal of such violation or violations, and may enforce the removal of all such violations and the collection of such penalties by first issuing a precept, before the entry of said judgment, to the superintendent and inspectors of building, commanding the removal of said violations; said violations to be removed and a return of said precept, with the expense of such removal endorsed thereon, to be made in the same manner as provided for the removal of unsafe buildings, under section forty-three of this act; such expenses thus returned to be adjusted and inserted in the entry of judgment, and said judgment collected upon execution; but nothing in this section contained shall confer equity powers upon any but courts of equity jurisdiction.

§ 39. The notice of violation named under this act Notices of violations of this act to be given. shall be signed by the superintendent of buildings or his deputy, and may be served by any of the inspectors or messenger, by leaving a copy of the same with any person or persons violating, or who may be liable under any of the several provisions of this act, and shall contain a description of the building, premises or property upon which such violation shall have been put or may exist, a duplicate copy of which, together with a notice of commencement of suit for the recovery of any or all of the penalties herein prescribed, may be at any time thereafter, filed in the county clerk's office in the city of New York, in the same manner as now by law provided for the filing of lis pendens, and thereupon shall have the like effect; and any judgment recovered upon the suit named in the notice so filed, shall be a lien upon said property therein described from the time of such filing, and may be enforced against said property in every respect, notwithstanding the same may be transferred subsequent to the filing of said notice.

§ 40. Any and all persons who, after having been per- Punishment sonally served with the notice of violation, as hereinbefore prescribed, shall fail to comply therewith, and shall continue to violate any of the several provisions of this act, or who shall be accessory thereto, shall be guilty of a misdemeanor, punishable by fine or imprisonment; and upon complaint made before any police justice, or any court of criminal jurisdiction within the city of New York, shall be arrested and held to bail by said justice or said court; and, upon conviction of such offence, shall pay all costs of such arrest, and shall be fined in a sum not to exceed two hundred and fifty dollars, or may be imprisoned for a term not to exceed six months; said fine and imprisonment to be imposed in the discretion of the court by whom said person so arrested and held to bail shall be tried; and said criminal courts, and the judges thereof, respectively, are hereby authorized to act and do as aforesaid.

§ 41. Any building or buildings, part or parts of a building, wall, walls, parts of walls, or party walls, shed, chimney, staging or other structure, in the city of New Buildings, walls, &c., becoming dangerous. York, that from fire, excavation, improper erection or construction, or from any other cause, shall at any time become dangerous or unsafe, and endanger life or limb, may be taken down and removed or made secure, in manner following : Immediately upon such unsafe or dangerous building or buildings, part or parts of building, wall, walls, parts of walls or party walls, shed, chimney, staging or structure, being so reported to any of the officers of said department, the same shall be immediately entered upon the docket of unsafe buildings, and the owner, or any one of the owners, agents, lessees, or other parties having a vested or contingent interest

Notice to
be given. in the same, shall be served with a notice in writing, containing a description of the premises deemed unsafe or dangerous, requiring the same to be made safe and secure, or removed, as the same may be necessary, which said notice shall require the person thus served to immediately certify to the office of said department his or their assent or refusal to secure or remove the same ; and that in case of refusal or neglect so to do, or his or their refusal or neglect to secure or remove the same, a survey thereof will be made, at a time and place therein named, and that in case the same shall again be reported unsafe or dangerous, after such survey, that said report will be placed before a court therein named, and a jury trial upon the allegations and statements contained in said report will be had before said court at a time and place therein named, to determine whether said unsafe or dangerous building or premises shall be repaired and secured, or taken down and removed.

Duty of
persons re-
ceiving no-
tice. § 42 If the person so served with notice shall certify his or their assent to the securing or removal of said unsafe or dangerous premises, he or they shall be allowed until twelve o'clock, M., of the day following the service of such notice, in which to commence the securing or removal of the same ; and he or they shall employ sufficient labor to secure or remove the same as expeditiously as the same can be done ; but upon his or their refusal

In case of
neglect. or neglect to comply with any of the requirements of said notice so served, then a survey of the premises named in said notice shall be had at the time and place therein named, by three competent persons, either practical builders or architects, to be composed of the superintendent or deputy superintendent of buildings, one person who shall be appointed by the American Institute of Architects of the city of New York, and one person to be appointed by the owner, agent, lessee, or other

interested person thus notified, upon whose refusal to
appoint such surveyor, however, the said other two
surveyors may make such survey; and in case of a disagreement, shall appoint a third person to take part in
such survey, whose decision shall be final; and a report
of such survey, reduced to writing, shall constitute the
issue to be placed before the court for trial.

§ 43. Whenever the report of any such survey, had as
aforesaid, shall cite that the buildings or premises, thus
surveyed, are unsafe and dangerous, or in a condition
endangering life and limb; the attorney of the fire department of the city of New York shall immediately
file a note of issue with the clerk of any court of equity
jurisdiction in the city of New York, and said clerk
shall thereupon place said issue before said court, or, if
in case said court is not in session, then before a judge
or justice thereof, and said court or said judge or justice
shall, at the time designated in said notice, proceed to
the trial of said issue before a jury, whose verdict shall
be conclusive and final, and shall try said issue without
delay, giving precedence to the trial of such issue over
all others; and said court, judge or justice shall have
power to empanel a jury for that purpose, and upon the
rendition of a verdict against said party so served with
notice and before entry of judgment, the judge or justice
trying said cause shall issue a precept out of said court,
directed to the superintendent of buildings and inspectors appointed under this act, citing said verdict, and
commanding them to forthwith repair and secure, or
cause to be repaired and secured, or take down and
remove, or cause to be taken down and removed, as the
same may be, in accordance with said verdict, said
unsafe or dangerous building, buildings, part or parts of
a building, wall, walls, parts of walls, party walls, shed,
chimney, staging, or structure, or other premises that
shall have been named in said notice; and shall immediately, thereupon, proceed to execute and enforce the
commands of said precept, and may employ such labor,
and furnish such materials, as may be necessary for that
purpose, the expense of which, together with the costs
of such survey, and an allowance of twenty dollars costs
of said trial added thereto, to be endorsed upon said
precept, shall be a charge against the owner or owners
of said premises, and a lien against the same, and shall

Report of surveyor, and pro-ceedings thereon.

be collected as hereinafter provided; and after having so done, said officers shall make return of said precept, with an endorsement of their action thereunder, and the costs and expenses thereby incurred, to said court; and thereupon said court, or a judge or justice thereof shall tax and adjust the amount endorsed upon said precept, and insert the same in the judgment roll in said action or proceeding, and the amount of said judgment shall be a lien upon said property, and shall be collected upon execution, by the sheriff of the city and county of New York.

Proviso.   § 44. Provided, nevertheless, that immediately upon the issuing of said precept, the owner or owners of said building or premises, or any party interested therein, upon application to said superintendent of buildings, shall be allowed to execute and enforce the commands of said precept, at his or their own proper costs and expenses, provided the same shall be done immediately, and in accordance with the requirements of said precept, upon the payment of all costs incurred up to that time. And it is further provided, that in case no person having an interest in said unsafe or dangerous buildings, walls, or premises can be found, after diligent search, within twenty-four hours after said premises shall have been entered upon the docket of unsafe buildings, upon whom to serve said notice, then said notice may be served by posting the same in some conspicuous place upon the said premises, which shall be deemed a personal notice, to all parties having any interest therein.

§ 45. There is hereby created in the city of New York, under and subject to the charter of said city, an executive department, to be known and designated as the Department for survey, &c., created "Department for the survey and inspection of buildings in the city of New York," which shall have charge of enforcing the several provisions of this act, and this department shall also perform all the duties and possess all the powers heretofore performed and possessed by the fire wardens of the city of New York. And said department shall be provided with office room and all the necessary supplies for the proper transaction of its business, in the same manner as now provided for other executive departments in said city.

Superintendent of buildings.   § 46. The chief officer of said department shall be called the "superintendent of buildings," who shall be qualified for such position as hereinafter provided, and who shall be appointed by the mayor of said city, by and with the advice and consent of the board of supervisors in said city, on or before the first day of May, eighteen hundred and sixty-two, and he shall hold office for the term of four years, or until his successor shall take office, but may be sooner removed, for malfeasance, incapacity, or neglect of duty, by the mayor, with the concurrence of said board of supervisors. He shall be ex-officio a member of the board of trustees of the New York fire department, but shall hold no other office in said board of trustees. And the superintendent of buildings shall appoint, as subordinate officers under said department, a deputy superintendent of buildings, eight inspectors of buildings, a clerk, and a messenger, all of whom shall hold office for the term of four years, but may be sooner removed by said superintendent, for malfeasance, incapacity, or neglect of duty; and any position held under this act, upon becoming vacant from any cause, shall be filled in the same manner as herein provided.

§ 47. All the officers under said department, except the clerk and messenger, shall be either practical architects, house carpenters or masons, and before their appointment shall each pass an examination before a committee on examination appointed by the American institute of architects in said city, and shall furnish a certificate of such examination, signed by said committee, certifying to their knowledge and competency to perform all the duties of such office, and in addition to such qualifications, the superintendent, deputy superintendent, and one half in number of the inspectors shall be exempt firemen of the fire department of the city of New York. And the superintendent, in addition to such qualifications, shall also have been engaged in conducting or carrying on business as an architect, house carpenter or mason, at least seven years, of which he shall make oath to beforesaid mayor. *Qualification of officers.*

§ 48. It shall be the duty of the superintendent of buildings to sign all "certificates" and "notices," required to be issued under this act; to make return of violations to the attorney of the New York fire department for prosecution; to have kept in proper books for that purpose, a register of all transactions in said department; *Duty of superintendent.*

to submit to the mayor and common council, once in every six months, a detailed statement of said transactions; to return quarter yearly, to the board of trustees of the New York fire department a statement under oath of all the transactions of said department in detail, and perform such other duties as are herein required of him, and he shall have a general supervision and direction over the officers of said department.

Duty of deputy superintendent. § 49. It shall be the duty of the deputy superintendent of buildings to examine all buildings whereon violations are reported, and all buildings reported dangerous or damaged by fire, and make a written report of such examinations to the superintendent, with his opinion relative thereto; to examine all buildings under application to raise, enlarge, alter or build upon, and report to the superintendent the condition of the same, with his opinion relative thereto, and in the absence of the superintendent he shall be empowered to act with all the powers enjoyed and possessed by said superintendent.

Inspector of buildings. § 50. The inspectors of buildings shall be under the direction of the superintendent and deputy, and shall attend all fires occurring in their respective districts, and report to the chief engineer or assistant engineers present, all information they may have relative to the construction and condition of the buildings or premises on fire, and the adjoining buildings, whether the same be dangerous or otherwise, and report, in writing, to said department all such buildings damaged by fire or otherwise, with a statement of the nature and amount of such damages, as near as they can ascertain, together with the street and number of such building, the name of the owners, lessees and occupants, and for what purpose occupied; and said inspectors shall examine all buildings in course of erection, alteration and repair, throughout their respective districts, at least once every day (Sundays and holidays excepted), and shall report, in writing, forthwith to the deputy superintendent, all violations of any of the several provisions of this act, together with the street and number of the building or premises upon which violations are found, and the names of the owners, agents, lessees, occupants, builders, masons, carpenters, roofers, furnace builders, and architects, and all other matters relative thereto, and shall report in the same manner all new buildings in their respective districts, and the clerk and messenger shall each perform such duties as may be assigned them by the superintendent or deputy. All the officers appointed under this act shall, so far as may be necessary for the performance of their respective duties, have the right to enter any building or premises in said city.

§ 51. The officers under said department shall receive Salary. an annual salary, payable in equal monthly parts, as follows : the superintendent of buildings in the sum of two thousand five hundred dollars ; the deputy superintendent of buildings in the sum of two thousand dollars ; the inspectors of buildings in the sum of one thousand dollars each ; the clerk in the sum of nine hundred dollars ; the messenger in the sum of eight hundred dollars ; and shall each (except the clerk and messenger), before entering upon the discharge of their respective duties, execute to the corporation a bond conditioned for the faithful performance of their respective duties, in a penal sum in amount twice that of their respective salaries, with such sureties as shall be approved of by the comptroller of said city.

§ 52. All suits or proceedings instituted for the en- Proceedings forcement of any of the several provisions of this act, or for in suits regulated. the recovery of any penalty thereunder, shall be brought in the name of the fire department of the city of New York by the said attorney, under the direction of the board of trustees of said fire department, and it shall be the duty of said attorney to take charge of the prosecution of all such suits or proceedings, in the same manner as now provided for the prosecution of violations of corporation ordinances, and for that purpose shall have the same power as the corporation attorney, collect and receive all moneys upon judgment, suit or proceedings, so instituted, pay all necessary costs and disbursements thereon, and upon payment of judgment and removal of violations thereunder, execute satisfaction thereof ; he shall keep a correct and accurate register of all such suits and proceedings, and an account of all moneys received and paid out thereon, and shall quarter-yearly render an account of such suits, proceedings and moneys to the board of trustees of the fire department of said city, and shall thereupon pay over the amount of all such penalties, when collected, to the treasurer of the fire department of the city of New York for the use and benefit of said fire department.

Ibid.

§ 53. No suit or proceeding commenced or penalty incurred for any violation under this act, or fine or penalty recovered upon judgment, shall be discontinued, compromised or remitted, except by an order of the court, or judge or justice thereof, having jurisdiction over the same; and said court, judge or justice, shall have discretionary power so to do in whole or in part, upon the joint application of the party aggrieved, said attorney and the trustees of said fire department, upon a sworn petition of the party aggrieved, setting forth the grounds of such application.

Tax to pay salaries.

§ 54. The board of supervisors in the county of New York shall, for the year eighteen hundred and sixty-two, and annually thereafter, raise and collect by tax upon the real and personal property taxable within the city of New York, such sum of money as shall be requisite and necessary to pay salaries provided for under this act; such sum of money, when collected, shall be paid into the treasury of the city of New York, and shall be disbursed to the several officers under this act as they shall be entitled thereto.

Repeal.

§ 55 Chapter four hundred and seventy of the Laws of the State of New York, for the year eighteen hundred and sixty, entitled "An act to provide against unsafe buildings in the city of New York," and all other acts or parts of acts inconsistent with the several provisions of this act, are hereby repealed; but such repeal shall

Saving clause.

not effect any suit, prosecution or proceeding commenced, or penalty or forfeiture incurred or offence committed previous to the time when this act shall take effect; but every such suit, prosecution or proceeding may lawfully proceed, and every such offence be prosecuted and punished as if the said laws and parts of laws hereby repealed had remained in full force.

§ 56. This act shall take effect on the first day of May next, and the common council of the city of New York shall publish this act once a week in every paper employed by said common council, from the time of its passage until said first day of May.

Chap. 357

AN ACT to extend the time for the completion of the Erie and New York city railroad.

Passed April 19, 1862.

The People of the State of New York, represented in Senate and Assembly, do enact as follows :

SECTION 1. The time for the completion of the Erie and New York city railroad, is hereby extended for the period of ten years from the time now fixed by law for the completion of the same, and all the rights, privileges, franchises, actions and rights of action in behalf of said corporation shall exist in the same manner and to the same extent as though this act had been passed and taken effect on the first day of March, eighteen hundred and sixty-two.

§ 2. This act shall take effect immediately.

Chap. 358.

AN ACT to incorporate the American Missionary Association.

Passed April 19, 1862.

The People of the State of New York, represented in Senate and Assembly, do enact as follows ;

SECTION 1. William E. Whiting, Thomas Ritter, Henry Belden, James O. Bennett, Anthony Lane, Thomas C. Fanning, Samuel Wilde, O. B. Wilder, John Lowrey, Josiah Brewer, William B. Brown, Alonzo S. Ball, Lewis Tappan, S. S. Jocelyn and George Whipple, and others now acting as officers and members of the American Missionary Association, located in the city of New York, together with such others as may be hereafter associated with or succeed them, shall be and are hereby constituted a body corporate, by the name of " The American Missionary Association," for the purpose of conducting

76

missionary and educational operations, and diffusing a knowledge of the Holy Scriptures in the United States and in other countries.

§ 2. The said corporation shall possess the general powers, and be subject to the provisions contained in the third title of chapter eighteen of the first part of the Revised Statutes, so far as the same are applicable and have not been repealed or modified

§ 3 The management of the affairs and concerns of the said corporation shall be conducted by an executive committee, to be from time to time appointed or elected by the said association, and to consist of not less than twelve members, any five of whom shall constitute a quorum for the transaction of its business; and all persons now holding office in said association shall be like officers in said corporation; and with like function, until the next annual meeting of the association.

§ 4. The said corporation shall have power to receive and disburse funds, and to purchase or take by donation, deed, devise or bequest any real or personal estate, given, granted, devised or bequeathed to it for the purpose stated in section first, but it shall at no time hold property beyond the value of three hundred thousand dollars and shall always have full power to grant, bargain, lease or otherwise dispose of the same; provided that the proceeds from such grant, bargain, lease or disposal shall never be in any manner directed to any other purpose than that for which the property was originally donated.

§ 5. No inhabitant of this state who shall die leaving a wife, child or parent, shall devise or bequeath to the aforesaid corporation created, more than one-fourth of his or her estate, after the payment of his or her debts, but a devise or bequest by such inhabitant shall be valid to the extent of such one-fourth; in no case, however, shall any devise or bequest to such corporation be valid in any will made by any inhabitant of this state which shall not have been made at least two months before the death of the testator or testatrix.

§ 6. This act shall take effect immediately.

Chap. 359.

AN ACT to incorporate the New York Commercial Association.

Passed April 19, 1862; three-fifths being present.

The People of the State of New York, represented in Senate and Assembly, do enact as follows:

SECTION 1. The members of the association known as Corporate the New York Commercial Association, and all other name. persons who may hereafter become associated with them under the provisions of this act, are hereby created a body corporate by the name of the New York Commercial Association, with perpetual succession and power to use a common seal and alter the same at pleasure, to sue and be sued, to take and hold by grant, purchase and devise, real and personal property to an amount not exceeding three hundred thousand dollars, for the purposes of such association, and to sell, convey, lease and mortgage the same or any part thereof.

§ 2. The property, affairs, business and concerns of the Officers. corporation hereby created shall be managed by a president, vice president, treasurer and twelve managers, who, together, shall constitute a board of managers, to be elected annually at such time and place as may be provided by the by-laws; and the present officers and managers of the said association as now constituted shall be the officers and managers of the said corporation until their present term of office shall expire, and until others under the provisions of this act shall be elected in their place. All vacancies which may occur Vacancies. in the said board by death, resignation or otherwise shall be filled by the said board. A majority of the members of such board shall constitute a quorum for the trans- Quorum. action of business.

§ 3. The purposes of said corporation shall be to pro- Purposes of corporation vide and regulate a suitable room or rooms for a produce exchange in the city of New York, to inculcate just and equitable principles in trade, to establish and maintain uniformity in commercial usages, to acquire, preserve and disseminate valuable business information, and to adjust controversies and misunderstandings between persons engaged in business. The said corporation shall have power to make all proper and needful by-laws, not contrary to the constitution and laws of the state of New York or of the United States.

Members. § 4. The said corporation shall have power to admit new members and expel any member in such manner as may be provided by the by-laws.

Arbitration committee. § 5. The board of managers shall annually elect by ballot five members of the association, who shall not be members of the board, as a committee to be known and styled the arbitration committee of the New York Commercial Association. The board of managers may at any time fill any vacancy or vacancies that may occur in said committee for the remainder of the term in **Duty.** which the same shall happen. It shall be the duty of said arbitration committee to hear and decide any controversy which may arise between the members of the said association or any persons claiming by, through or under them, and as may be voluntarily submitted to said committee for arbitration, and such members and persons may by an instrument in writing signed by them and attested by a subscribing witness agree to submit to the decision of such committee any such controversy, which might be the subject of an action at law or in equity, except claims of title to real estate or to any interest therein, and that a judgment of the supreme court shall be rendered upon the award made pursuant to such submission

Proceedings regulated. § 6. Such arbitration committee or a majority of them shall have power to appoint a time and place of hearing of any such controversy and adjourn the same from time to time as may be necessary, not beyond the day fixed in the submission for rendering their award, except by consent of parties; to issue subpoenas for the attendance of witnesses residing or being in the metropolitan police district. All the provisions contained in title fourteen, part third, chapter eight of the Revised Statutes and all acts amendatory or in substitution thereof relating to issuing attachments to compel the attendanc of witnesses shall apply to proceedings had before the said arbitration committee. Witnesses so subpoenaed as aforesaid shall be entitled to the fees prescribed by law for witnesses in the courts of justices of the peace.

§ 7. Any number not less than a majority of all the *Majority may act.* members of the arbitration committee shall be competent to meet together and hear the proofs and allegations of the parties, and an award by a majority of those who shall have been present at the hearing of the proofs and allegations shall be deemed the award of the arbitration committee, and shall be valid and binding on the parties thereto. Such award shall be made in writing, *Award.* subscribed by the members of the committee concurring therein and attested by a subscribing witness. Upon filing the submmission and award in the office of the clerk of the supreme court of the city and county of New York, both duly acknowledged or proved in the same manner as deeds are required to be acknowledged or proved in order to be recorded, a judgment may be *Judgment thereon.* entered therein according to the award, and shall be docketed, transcripts filed and execution issued thereon, the same as authorized by law in regard to judgments in the supreme court. Judgments entered in conformity with such award shall not be subject to be removed, reversed, modified or in any manner appealed from by the parties thereto, except for frauds, collusion or corruption of said arbitration committee, or some member thereof.

§ 8. This act shall take effect immediately.

Chap. 360.

AN ACT to renew the charter of the New York Institution for the instruction of the Deaf and Dumb.

Passed April 19, 1862; three-fifths being present.

The People of the State of New York, represented in Senate and Assembly, do enact as follows:

SECTION 1. The act entitled "An act to incorporate the members of the New York institution for the instruction of the Deaf and Dumb," passed on the fifteenth day of April, one thousand eight hundred and seventeen, shall be and the same is hereby re-enacted, renewed and extended for the term of twenty-five years, from and after the first day of April, one thousand eight hundred and sixty two.

§ 2. This act shall take effect immediately.

Chap. 361.

AN ACT to correct abuses in the city of New York, in the relaying of pavement by property owners and others whenever a portion of the pavement is temporarily removed.

Passed April 19, 1862; three-fifths being present.

The People of the State of New York, represented in Senate and Assembly, do enact as follows:

Croton aqueduct department to control the relaying of certain pavements. SECTION 1. The Croton Aqueduct department of the city of New York shall have cognizance, control and general direction in the relaying of all pavement removed for the purposes of constructing vaults or lateral drains, digging cellars, laying foundations of buildings or other structures, making sewer connections or repairing sewers, and in the laying down of gas and water pipes or introducing the same into buildings, or for any other purpose, and no removal of pavement for such purposes shall be made until a permit is first had of the said Croton Aqueduct department.

Proceedings relating thereto. § 2. Whenever any portion of the pavement in any street or avenue in said city shall have been removed for any of the purposes mentioned in the preceding section, and such pavement shall not be relaid in a manner satisfactory to the Croton Aqueduct board, the president of said board may cause a notice in writing to be served upon the person or corporation by whom the same was removed, or if such removal was for the purpose of making connection between any house or lot and any sewer or pipes in the street, or for constructing vaults, or otherwise improving any house or lot, upon the owner or occupant of such house or lot, requiring such person or corporation, or the owner or occupant of such house or lot, to have such pavement properly relaid within five days after service of such notice. Such notice may be served upon the owner or occupant of a house or lot by leaving the same with any person of adult age upon said premises. In case such pavement or portion thereof shall not be relaid to the satisfaction of said Croton Aqueduct board within the time specified in such notice, it shall be lawful, and authority is hereby given to said board to have such pavement or the portion thereof which shall have been so unsatisfactorily laid, put in proper order and repair, in such manner as the said board may deem best, on account of the person or corporation by whom such pavement was removed, or of the owner of the premises for whose benefit such removal was made. Upon the cost of such work being certified to the comptroller of the city of New York by said Croton Aqueduct board, with a description of the lot or premises to improve which such removal was made, said comptroller shall pay the same, and the amount so paid shall become a lien and charge upon the premises so described, and on being certified by the comptroller to the clerk of arrears may be collected in the same manner that arrears of Croton water rents are collected under the direction of the clerk of arrears. But if such removal was made by any person or corporation and not for a connection between any house and sewer or pipes, or to otherwise benefit any house or lot, upon the said Croton Aqueduct board certifying in writing such facts to the said comptroller with the cost of repair, and the name of the person or corporation by whom or by whose direction the pavement so repaired was removed, said comptroller shall pay such cost, and shall transmit a copy of the said certificate to the counsel to the corporation who shall proceed to collect the same by suit against the person or corporation by whom the pavement was removed, and such person or corporation are hereby made liable to pay the same. Upon the trial of any such suit the said certificate of the Croton Aqueduct board shall be conclusive evidence of the cost of such repair.

§ 3. This act shall take effect immediately.

Chap. 362.

AN ACT to authorize the Supervisors of Orleans county to raise money for the support of volunteers.

Passed April 19, 1862; three-fifths being present.

The People of the State of New York, represented in Senate and Assembly, do enact as follows:

Tax may be raised, not exceeding $10,000 for volunteers. SECTION 1. The supervisors of the county of Orleans are hereby authorized to raise by tax, in the same manner in which ordinary county taxes are raised and collected, a sum not exceeding ten thousand dollars, to be called "The Volunteer Relief Fund," and to be used for the relief of families of volunteers who have heretofore enlisted and are now in the army or service of the United States. The said sum may be raised at the same time or at different times, in the discretion of the supervisors

Committee to disburse fund. § 2. The chairman of the board of supervisors of said county, the county judge, and the county treasurer, shall be a committee for disbursing the aforesaid fund; and the money raised shall be paid from time to time to such families of volunteers, as, in the judgment of said committee, shall need assistance, and under such regulations and restrictions as the committee shall adopt. The committee shall keep an account of all moneys received **Report.** and paid under this act, and shall report the same to the board of supervisors at their annual meeting. But no **Saving clause.** moneys shall be paid out under the provisions of this act, save to the families of volunteers heretofore enlisted, and save to the families of such volunteers as enlisted heretofore under the promise that their families should receive relief.

May borrow money. § 3. It shall be lawful for the supervisors of said county to anticipate the whole or any part of the aforesaid sum, by borrowing the same upon the credit of the county and issuing bonds therefor and paying interest therefor not exceeding the rate of seven per cent per annum.

§ 4. This act shall take effect immediately.

Chap. 363.

AN ACT to amend an act entitled "An act in relation to certain streets, avenues and roads in the city of Brooklyn," passed April seventeenth, eighteen hundred and sixty.

Passed April 19, 1862; three-fifths being present.

The People of the State of New York, represented in Senate and Assembly, do enact as follows:

SECTION 1. The first section of an act entitled "An act in relation to certain streets, avenues and roads in the city of Brooklyn," passed April seventeenth, eighteen hundred and sixty, is hereby repealed.

§ 2. Section two of said act is hereby amended so as to read as follows:

§ 2. All that part of the old Flatbush road, which is embraced between Hanson Place and Atlantic avenue, Canton street and Flatbush avenue, is hereby closed and discontinued.

§ 3. This act shall take effect immediately.

Chap. 364.

AN ACT to close part of Partition street in the twelfth ward of the city of Brooklyn.

Passed April 19, 1862; three-fifths being present.

The People of the State of New York, represented in Senate and Assembly, do enact as follows:

SECTION 1. So much and such part of Partition street in the twelfth ward of the city of Brooklyn as lies between a line parallel with and distant four hundred and seventy-five feet northwesterly of Ferris street, and the exterior water line is hereby declared to be closed and discontinued, and the owner or owners of the lands adjoining and fronting upon such part of said street, and their heirs, successors and assigns may hold, convey,

77

improve and use the lands forming such part of said
street in the same manner and with like effect as if the
same had never been laid out as a public street.

§ 2. This act shall take effect immediately.

Chap. 365.

AN ACT to authorize the discharge of mortgages of record in certain cases.

Passed April 19, 1862; three-fifths being present.

*The People of the State of New York, represented in
Senate and Assembly, do enact as follows :*

When mortgage may be discharged on petition of mortgagee.
SECTION 1. The mortgagor named in, or the owner of
any lands described in any mortgage of real estate in
this state, which is recorded in this state, and which
from the lapse of time is presumed to be paid, may
present his petition to the courts mentioned in this act,
asking that such mortgage may be discharged of record.
Such petition shall be verified ; it shall describe the
mortgage and when and where recorded, and shall allege
that such mortgage is paid ; that the mortgagee has, or
if there be more than one mortgagee, that all of them
have been dead for more than five years, specifying the
time and place of his or their death and place of residence at the time of the death ; that no letters testamentary, or of administration, have been taken out in
this state ; the names and places of residence so far
forth as the same can be ascertained of the heirs of such
mortgagee or mortgagees, and that such mortgage has
not been assigned or transferred, and if such mortgage
has been assigned state to whom, and the facts in regard
to the same.

Where presented.
§ 2. Such petition may be presented to the supreme
court in the county where the mortgaged premises are
situate, or when situate in the city of New York to the
superior court thereof, or when situate in the city of
Buffalo to the superior court thereof.

Order to show cause.
§ 3. The court upon the presentation of such petition,
shall make an order requiring all persons interested to
show cause at a certain time and place, why such mort-

gage should not be discharged of record. The names of
the mortgagor, mortgagee and assignee, if any, the date
of the mortgage and where recorded and the town or
city in which the mortgaged premises are situate shall
be specified in the order. The order shall be published
in such newspaper or newspapers, and for such time as
the court shall direct. The court may also direct the
order to be personally served upon such persons as it
shall designate.

§ 4. The court may issue commissions to take the
testimony of witnesses, and may refer it to a referee to
take and report proofs of the facts stated in the petition.
The certificate of the proper surrogate or surrogates that
no letters testamentary or of administration, have been
issued shall be evidence of the fact; and the certificate
of the clerk of the county or counties in which the
mortgaged premises have been situate since the date of
said mortgage, that no assignment thereof has been
recorded, and no notice of the pendency of an action
thereon has been filed, shall be evidence that the mortgage has not been assigned or transferred. Upon being
satisfied that all the matters alleged in the petition are
true, the court may make an order that the mortgage be
discharged of record.

§ 5. The county clerk upon being furnished with a
certified copy of such order and paid the fees allowed
by law for discharging mortgages, shall record said
order and discharge the mortgage of record.

Chap. 366.

AN ACT to amend the provisions of chapters
twenty-eight and thirty-eight, Session Laws of
eighteen hundred and fifty-seven, in relation to
the addition of cash capital to existing funds of
the Orient Mutual Insurance Company.

Passed April 19, 1862.

*The People of the State of New York, represented in
Senate and Assembly, do enact as follows:*

SECTION 1. The Orient Mutual Insurance Company
having united a cash capital to its other corporate funds

in accordance with the provisions of chapters twenty-eight and thirty-eight of the Session Laws of eighteen hundred and fifty-seven, shall be and is hereby authorized to return to the purely mutual system, by paying off and returning such cash capital at its par value to the holders thereof, provided however, that such company after the repayment of such cash capital shall have capital and invested assets amounting to five hundred thousand dollars, or more, over and above all debts, claims and liabilities, due and to become due, including a reinsurance fund adequate to safely reinsure all outstanding risks, and provided also, that the written consent to such change of three-fourths of the stockholders and of the same number of the trustees of the company shall be previously obtained.

§ 2. The holders of the cash capital shall each be individually liable to the amount of the sum or sums so received by them, for all the losses under contracts or policies of insurance pending at the time of such repayment which the other assets of the company shall be insufficient to discharge, unless the holders of such contracts or policies of insurance shall have released them from such liability by assenting to the change.

§ 3. This act shall take effect immediately.

Chap. 367.

AN ACT to amend an act entitled "An act to provide for the incorporation of fire insurance companies," passed June twenty-fifth, eighteen hundred and fifty-three.

Passed April 19, 1862 ; three-fifths being present.

The People of the State of New York, represented in Senate and Assembly, do enact as follows :

SECTION 1. The sixth section of the act entitled "An act to provide for the incorporation of fire insurance companies," passed June twenty-fifth, eighteen hundred and fifty-three, is hereby amended so as to read as follows :

§ 6. No joint-stock company shall be incorporated under this act in the city and county of New York, nor in the county of Kings. nor shall any company incorporated under this act establish any agency for the transaction of business in either of said counties, with a smaller capital than two hundred thousand dollars, nor in any other county in this state with a smaller capital than fifty thousand dollars ; nor shall any company formed for the purpose of doing the business of fire or inland navigation insurance, on the plan of mutual insurance, commence business, if located in the city of New York or in the county of Kings, nor establish any agency for the transaction of business in either of said counties, until agreements have been entered into for insurance with at least four hundred applicants, the premiums on which shall amount to not less than two hundred thousand dollars, of which forty thousand dollars at least shall have been paid in cash, and notes of solvent parties, founded on actual and bona fide applications for insurance, shall have been received for the remainder ; nor shall any mutual insurance company in any other county of the state commence business until agreements have been entered into for insurance with at least two hundred applicants, the premiums on which shall amount to not less than one hundred thousand dollars, of which twenty thousand dollars at least shall have been paid in cash, and notes of solvent parties, founded on actual and bona fide applications for insurance, shall have been received for the remainder. No one of the notes received as aforesaid shall amount to more than five hundred dollars ; and no two shall be given for the same risk, or be made by the same person or firm, except where the whole amount of such notes shall not exceed five hundred dollars ; nor shall any such note be represented as capital stock unless a policy be issued upon the same within thirty days after the organization of the company, upon a risk which shall be for no shorter period than twelve months. Each of said notes shall be payable, in part or in whole, at any time when the directors shall deem the same requisite for the payment of losses by fire or inland navigation, and such incidental expenses as may be necessary for transacting the business of said company. And no note shall be accepted as part of such capital stock unless the same shall be accompanied by a certificate of a justice of the peace or supervisor of the town or city where the person making such note shall reside, that the person making the same is, in his opinion, pecuniarily good and responsible for the same, and no such note shall be surrendered during the life of the policy for which it was given. No fire insurance company organized under this act or transacting business in this state, shall expose itself to any loss on any one fire or inland navigation risk, or hazard, to an amount exceeding ten per cent of its paid up capital.

§ 2. The eighth section of said act is hereby amended so as to read as follows:

Capital how invested.

§ 8. It shall be lawful for any fire insurance company organized under this act, or incorporated under any law of this state, to invest its capital, or the funds accumulated in the course of its business, or any part thereof, in bonds and mortgages on unincumbered real estate within the state of New York worth fifty per cent more than the sum loaned thereon, exclusive of buildings, unless such buildings are ensured and the policy transferred to said company, and also in the stocks of this state, or stocks or treasury notes of the United States, and to lend the same or any part thereof, on the security of such stocks or bonds or upon bonds and mortgages, as aforesaid, and to change and re-invest the same as occasion may from time to time require; but any surplus money, over and above the capital stock of any such fire and inland navigation insurance companies or of any fire insurance company incorporated under any law of this state, may be invested in or loaned upon the pledge of the stock, bonds, or other evidences of indebtedness of any institution incorporated under the laws of this state, except their own stock; provided, always, that the current market value of such stocks, bonds, or other evidences of indebtedness shall be at least ten per cent more than the sum so loaned thereon.

§ 3. The twelfth section of said act is hereby amended by adding thereto at the end thereof the following provisions:

Funds and dividends.

No fire insurance company, chartered by this state, shall hereafter divide to its stockholders, in any one year, an amount greater than one-tenth of its capital, unless such company shall have accumulated and be in possession of a surplus fund, in addition to the amount of its capital and of such dividend, equal to the whole amount received by such company for premiums on policies which shall be in force at the time of declaring such dividend; and such accumulated fund is hereby declared to be the unearned premiums of such company. This section shall not apply to any companies chartered by this state which are authorized to issue certificates of profits, and to redeem the same, from future earnings. _Exception._

§ 4. The eighteenth section of said act is hereby so amended as to read as follows:

§ 18. Any existing joint-stock fire insurance company heretofore incorporated under the laws of this state, and any company organized under this act, having a capital of at least one hundred and fifty thousand dollars, may, without increasing its capital, at any time, within two years previous to the termination of its charter, after giving notice, at least once a week for six weeks successively in a newspaper published in the county where such company is located, of such intention, and with a declaration, under its corporate seal, signed by the president and two-thirds of its directors, of their desire for such extension, extend the term of its original charter to the time specified in the twenty-sixth section of this act, by altering and amending the same so as to accord with the provisions of this act, and filing a copy of such amended charter, with the declaration aforesaid, in the office of the Superintendent of the Insurance Department, whereupon the same proceedings shall be had as are required in the tenth section of this act; and any mutual insurance company heretofore incorporated or organized under any of the laws this state, having surplus assets aside from premium and stock notes, sufficient to reinsure all its outstanding risks, after having given notice once a week for six weeks, of their intention, and of the meeeting hereinafter provided for, in the state paper, and in a newspaper published in the county where such company is located, may, with the consent of two-thirds of the corporators or members present at any regular annual meeting, or at any special meeting duly called for the purpose, or with the consent in writing of two-thirds of the corporators or members of such company, and the consent also of three-fourths _Existing companies._

of the trustees or directors, (unless otherwise provided
in the charter,) become a joint-stock company, by conforming its charter to and otherwise proceeding in accordance with this act; and every member of such
company, on the day of said annual or special meeting,
or the date of said written consent, shall be entitled to
priority in subscribing to the capital stock of said company, for one month after the opening of the books of
subscription to such capital stock, in proportion to the
amount of cash premiums paid in by such members, on
unexpired risks in force on the day of said annual or
special meeting or the date of said written consent;
and every company so extended or changed, shall come
under the provisions of this act, in the same manner as
if it had been incorporated originally under this act.
Every mutual insurance company heretofore incorporated under the laws of this state, and doing business with
a capital, in premium notes, of at least fifty thousand
dollars, may, at any time, within two years previous to
the termination of its charter, without increasing its
capital, after giving notice, at least once a week for six
weeks successively, in a newspaper published in the
county where such company is located, of such intention,
and with a declaration, under its corporate seal. signed
by its president and two-thirds of its directors, of their
desire for such extension, extend the term of its original charter to the time specified in the twenty-sixth
section of this act, by altering and amending the same
so as to accord with the provisions of this act, and
filing a copy of such amended charter, with the declaration aforesaid, in the office of the Superintendent of the
Insurance Department, whereupon the same proceedings
shall be had as are required in the tenth section of this
act, except as to its capital, which shall be certified to
be in accordance with the provisions of this section, applicable to the reorganization of mutual insurance companies. Every mutual insurance company so extended
shall, except as to the amount of its capital, come under
the provisions of this act, in the same manner as if it
had been incorporated originally under this act.

§ 5. The twenty-third section of said act is hereby so
amended as to read as follows :

Foreign cor
porations
act to take

§ 23. It shall not be lawful for any fire insurance company, association or partnership, incorporated by or

organized under the laws of any other state of the United States or any foreign government, directly or indirectly to take risks or transact any business of insurance in this state, unless possessed of the amount of actual capital required of similar companies formed under the provisions of this act ; and any such company desiring to transact any such business, as aforesaid, by an agent or agents in this state, shall first appoint an attorney in this state on whom process of law can be served, and file in the office of the Superintendent of the Insurance Department a certified copy of the vote or resolution of the directors appointing such attorney, which appointment shall continue until another attorney be substituted ; in case any such insurance company shall cease to transact business in this state, according to the laws thereof, the agents last designated or acting as such for such corporation, shall be deemed to continue agents for such corporation for the purpose of serving process for commencing actions upon any policy or liability issued or contracted while such corporation transacted business in this state ; and service of such process for the causes aforesaid upon any such agent shall be deemed a valid personal service upon such corporation ; and also a certified copy of their charter or deed of settlement together with a statement, under the oath of the president or vice-president, and other chief officer, and secretary of the company for which he or they may act, stating the name of the company and place where located ; the amount of its capital, with a detailed statement of its assets, showing the amount of cash on hand, in bank, or in the hands of agents ; the amount of real estate, and how much the same is encumbered by mortgage ; the number of shares of stock of every kind owned by the company, the par and market value of the same ; amount loaned on bond and mortgage ; the amount loaned on other security, stating the kind, and the amount loaned on each, and the estimated value of the whole amount of such securities ; any other assets or property of the company ; also stating the indebtedness of the company, the amount of losses adjusted and unpaid, the amount incurred and in process of adjustment ; the amount resisted by the company as illegal and fraudulent ; and any other claims existing against the company ; also a copy of the last annual report, if any, made under any law of the state by which such company was incorporated; and no agent shall be allowed to transact business for any company, whose capital is impaired to the extent of twenty per cent thereof, while such deficiency shall continue; and any company incorporated by or organized under any foreign government shall, in addition to the foregoing, deposit with the Superintendent of the Insurance Department for the benefit and security of policy holders residing in the United States, a sum not less than two hundred thousand dollars, in stocks of the United States or of the state of New York in all cases to be, or to be made to be equal to a stock producing six per cent per annum, said stocks not to be received by said Superintendent at a rate above their par value or above their current market value; or in bonds and mortgages on improved unincumbered real estate in the state of New York, worth fifty per cent more than the amount loaned thereon; or in such stocks and securities as now are or which may hereafter be receivable by the Bank Department as security for circulating notes; the stocks and securities so deposited may be exchanged from time to time for other securities receivable as aforesaid, and so long as the company so depositing shall continue solvent and comply with the laws of this state, may be permitted by the said Superintendent to collect the interest or dividends on said deposit; the said deposit shall be in lieu of the investments in the name of trustees as heretofore required, and upon its being duly made either by the transfer of the trust funds or otherwise the trustees shall thereby be discharged from all liability; and where a deposit is made of bonds and mortgages accompanied by full abstracts of title and searches the fees for an examination of title by counsel to be paid by the party making the deposit shall not exceed twenty dollars for each mortgage; and the fees for an appraisal of property shall be five dollars to each appraiser, not exceeding two, besides expenses for each mortgage; nor shall it be lawful for any agent or agents to act for any company or companies referred to in this section, directly or indirectly, in taking risks or transacting the business of fire or inland navigation insurance in this state, without procuring from the Superintendent of the Insurance Department a certificate of authority stating that such company has complied with all the requisitions of this act which apply to such companies, and the name of the attorney appointed to act for the company ; a certified copy of such certificate of authority, with statement, must be filed by the agent in the office of the clerk of every county where such company has agents, and shall be published in the paper in which the state notices are required to be inserted, four successive times after the filing of such statement as aforesaid ; and within thirty days thereafter proof of such publication, by the affidavit of the publisher of such newspaper, his foreman or clerk, shall be filed in the office of the said superintendent. The statements and evidences of investments required by this section shall be renewed from year to year in such manner and form as may be required by said Superintendent, with an additional statement of the amount of premiums received and losses incured in this state during the preceding year, so long as such agency continues ; and the said Superintendent, on being satisfied that the capital, securities and investments remain secure, as hereinbefore provided, shall furnish a renewal of his certificate, as aforesaid, and the agent or agents obtaining such certificate, shall file a certified copy of the same in the office of the clerk of the county in which such agency shall be established, within the month of January; the fees for each certificate of authority and certified copy thereof shall be five dollars. But any company organized under or incorporated by any foreign government may furnish and file such annual statements and evidences in the month of January in each year, made out for the year ending on the preceding thirtieth day of June if accompanied also by an annual supplementary statement, duly verified by the attorney or general agent of the company in this state showing the amount of risks written, premiums received, losses sustained, and taxes paid in this state for the year ending on the preceding thirty-first day of December, said supplementary statement shall also contain a description of the investments of such company in this country ; and such other information as may be required by the said Superintendent. Any violation of any of the provisions of this section shall subject the party violating to a penalty of five hundred dollars for each violation, and of the additional sum of one hundred dollars for each month during which any such agent shall neglect to make such publication or to file such affidavits and statements as are herein required. Every agent of any fire insurance company shall, in all advertisements of such agency, publish the location of the company, giving the name of the city, town or village in which the company is located, and the state or government under the laws of which it is organized. The term agent or agents, used in this section, shall include an acknowledged agent or surveyor, or any other person or persons, who shall, in any manner, aid in transacting the insurance business of any insurance company not incorporated by the laws of this state. The provisions of this section shall apply to all foreign companies, partnerships, associations and individuals, whether incorporated or not.

Lien.

§ 6. Any fire or fire and marine insurance company, chartered by this state, may have a lien, by passing a by-law to that effect upon the stock or certificate of profits owned by any member for any debt hereafter to become due the said company for premiums, by stating that the said stock is subject to any such lien upon the certificates of stock or profits, and such lien may be waived in writing by the consent of the president of said company upon the transfer of any such stock.

§ 7. The twenty-fifth section of said act is hereby amended by adding thereto at the end thereof the following words:

Penalties.

Such penalties may also be sued for and recovered in the name of the people, by the Attorney General, and when sued for and collected by him, shall be paid into the state treasury.

Chap. 368.

AN ACT to amend section thirty-six, of article two, title ten, chapter eight, of the third part of the Revised Statutes.

Passed April 19, 1862; three-fifths being present.

The People of the State of New York, represented in Senate and Assembly, do enact as follows:

SECTION 1. Section thirty-six of article two, title ten, chapter eight, of the third part of the Revised Statutes is hereby amended so that the same shall read as follows:

Six of the persons so summoned shall be drawn in like manner as jurors in justices' courts, and shall be sworn by such magistrate, well and truly to hear, try and determine the matters in difference between the parties. Whenever a sufficient number of jurors, duly drawn and summoned, do not appear, or cannot be obtained to form a jury, the magistrate may order any sheriff, constable or marshal to summon from the bystanders or from the county at large, so many persons qualified to serve as jurors as shall be sufficient, and return their names to the magistrate. Every person so summoned or summoned under the provisions of this article as hereby amended, shall attend forthwith and serve as a juror, unless excused by the magistrate, and for every neglect or refusal so to attend shall be subject to fine by said magistrate in the same manner as is now provided by law in the case of jurors in courts of record.

(margin note: Summoning jury in summary proceedings to recover possession of land.)

Chap. 369.

AN ACT for the relief of William Rumble and others.

Passed April 19, 1862; three-fifths being present.

The People of the State of New York, represented in Senate and Assembly, do enact as follows:

SECTION 1. On payment to the Attorney-General of the costs of the action now pending, wherein the People of the State of New York are plaintiffs, and William Rumble and others are defendants, all claims in behalf of the people, upon the bond on which said action is brought, is released, provided the Canal Commissioner in charge of the Genesee Valley canal and Attorney-General shall, in writing, approve of such release.

§ 2. This act shall take effect immediately.

Chap. 370.

AN ACT to amend the charter of the Guardian Life Insurance Company of New York.

Passed April 19, 1862.

The People of the State of New York, represented in Senate and Assembly, do enact as follows:

SECTION 1. The charter of "The Guardian Life Insurance Company of New York" is hereby amended by striking out and removing from said charter sections seventeen and eighteen, and is hereby further amended so that sections fifteen and sixteen thereof shall respectively read as follows:

§ 15. Within sixty days after the expiration of five years from the first day of January, eighteen hundred and sixty, and within the sixty days next succeeding every term of five years thereafter, the board of directors shall cause a general statement of the affairs of the company to be made, which shall fully and truly exhibit its property and liabilities, and also its profits remaining after deducting a sum sufficient to reinsure and cover all outstanding risks and other contingencies.

§ 16. The company shall, within sixty days after the expiration of each of said terms of five years, pay in cash to the holders of its capital stock, in proportion to the amount of stock respectively owned by them, twenty per cent of the profits to be thus ascertained at each succeeding period of five years, and shall equitably divide the remaining eighty per cent thereof in cash, among the holders of policies then existing for the whole term of life, holders of endowment policies then existing, and the holders of such other policies as the board of directors may deem advisable, excepting such holders of policies as may, at the time of the issuing of their policies have expressly waived all interest in the profits of the company; provided, however, that the company may in lieu of paying such cash dividends to policy holders, apply the amount of the said eighty per cent of the net profits due any policy holder to the payment of any note or notes, whether due or otherwise, which the company may hold against the said policy holder, paying the balance, if said amount be in excess of the amount of the said note or notes with accrued interest, to the said policy holder in cash. In case of the death of any party prior to the declaration of the policy dividend then next ensuing, who was insured at the making of the policy dividend then last declared, and was then entitled as a policy holder under the provisions of the charter, to an interest in the aforesaid division of net profits, he shall be entitled to his ratable proportion of the said eighty per cent of the net profits which may have accrued prior to his death and since the declaration of the policy dividend then last declared, to be paid or applied at the declaration of the policy dividend then next ensuing, in the same manner as in this section is heretofore provided for holders of policies then existing for the whole term of life.

§ 2. This act shall take effect immediately.

Chap. 371.

AN ACT to amend "An act to incorporate the village of Panama," passed March twenty-first, eighteen hundred and sixty-one.

Passed April 19, 1862; three-fifths being present.

The People of the State of New York, represented in Senate and Assembly, do enact as follows:

SECTION 1. Section four of "An act to incorporate the village of Panama," passed March twenty-first, eighteen hundred and sixty-one, is hereby amended so it shall read as follows:

Mode of conducting elections.

§ 4. One or more of the trustees shall preside at elections, and in case no trustee shall be present at the hour appointed for opening the polls, the electors assembled may appoint a president to preside. The presiding officer or officers at such elections are authorized and required to preserve order, judge of the qualifications of electors, canvass the ballots, and declare the persons elected by the greatest number of votes; and all the powers possessed by inspectors of elections by the election laws of this state, are hereby conferred upon them for the purposes of such charter election; and the persons elected shall hold their offices respectively one year, and until others shall be elected; except as hereinafter provided. All officers of said corporation shall hold their respective offices one year, and until others are elected or appointed to fill their places. All elections under this section shall be by ballot and determined by a plurality of votes.

§ 2. Section twenty-five of said act is amended by adding to said section the following:

Corporation to receive certain moneys.

And said corporation shall be entitled to and shall receive from said commissioners of highways of the town of Harmony, such proportion of the road and bridge money thus raised for said town as the taxable property within said corporation bears to the taxable property of said town of Harmony.

§ 3. Section twenty-seven of said act is amended by adding to said section the following:

And the trustees of said corporation shall have *Power of trustees.* authority to build all necessary sidewalks in said corporation, and to levy and collect a tax on the real and personal estate in said corporation to defray the expenses of the same.

Chap. 372.

AN ACT to regulate the fees of associate justices of the peace in criminal causes and in cases of bastardy.

Passed April 19, 1862; three-fifths being present.

The People of the State of New York, represented in Senate and Assembly, do enact as follows:

SECTION 1. Whenever any justice of the peace shall be associated with any other justice of the peace in the trial or examination of any criminal cause, or in cases of bastardy, the compensation of such justice of the peace so associated, shall be two dollars for each day actually and necessarily devoted to such service.

§ 2. This act shall take effect immediately.

Chap. 373.

AN ACT to amend title one, part two, chapter five, article eight, of the Revised Statutes.

Passed April 19, 1862; three-fifths being present.

The People of the State of New York, represented in Senate and Assembly, do enact as follows:

SECTION 1. Section nineteen of article eight, title one, chapter five, part two, of the Revised Statutes, is hereby amended to read as follows:

§ 19. If any controversy shall arise between the trustees and any other person in the settlement of any demands against such debtor, or of debts due his estate, *Reference of controversies.*

79

the same may be referred to one or more indifferent persons, who may be agreed upon by the trustees and the party with whom such controversy shall exist, by a writing to that effect signed by them.

§ 2 Section twenty of said article is hereby amended to read as follows:

§ 20. If such referee or referees be not selected by agreement, then the trustees or the other party to the controversy, may serve a notice of their intention to apply to the officer who appointed said trustees, or to any judge of the supreme court at chambers, residing in the same district with said trustees, for the appointment of one or more referees, specifying the time and place when such application will be made, which notice shall be served at least ten days before the time so therein specified.

§ 3. Section twenty-one of said article is hereby amended to read as follows:

§ 21. On the day so specified, upon due proof of the service of such notice, the officer before whom the application is made shall proceed to select one or more referees, the same in all respects as they are now selected according to the rules and practice of the supreme court.

§ 4 Section twenty-two of said article is hereby repealed, and the following substituted in lieu thereof:

§ 22. When any witness to such controversy shall reside out of the county where the said trustees resided at the time of their appointment, the referee or referees appointed to hear said controversy shall have power to issue a commission or commissions in like manner as justices of the peace are now authorized to issue the same, and the testimony so taken shall be returned to said referee or referees in the same manner, and be read before them on a hearing, in like manner as testimony taken on commission before justices of the peace.

Chap. 374.

AN ACT to prevent attempts to commit burglaries and other crimes.

Passed April 19, 1862 ; three-fifths being present.

The People of the State of New York, represented in Senate and Assembly, do enact as follows :

SECTION 1. If any person in this state who shall be found by night armed with any dangerous or offensive weapon or instrument whatsoever, with intent to break or enter into any dwelling house, building, room in a building, cabin, state room, railway car or other covered enclosure where personal property shall be and to commit any larceny or felony therein, or with the intent to commit any larceny or felony, or if any person shall be found by night having in his possession any picklock, crow, key, bit, jack, jimmey, nippers, pick, bettey or other implements of burglary with the intent aforesaid, or if any person shall be found in any dwelling house, building or place where personal property shall be, with intent to commit any larceny or felony therein, under such circumstances as shall not amount to an attempt to commit felony, every such offender shall be deemed guilty of a misdemeanor. If any person shall commit any such offence after a previous conviction, either for felony or petit larceny, or such misdemeanor as aforesaid, he shall be deemed guilty of a felony and may be punished by imprisonment in a state prison not to exceed five years.

§ 2. Whenever any larceny shall be committed by stealing, taking and carrying away from the person of another, the offender may be punished as for grand larceny although the value of the property taken shall be less than twenty-five dollars. Attempts under similar circumstances may be punished as for attempts to commit grand larceny.

§ 3. Every person who shall lay hand upon the person of another or upon the clothing upon the person of another, with intent to steal under such circumstances as shall not amount to an attempt to rob or an attempt to commit larceny, shall be deemed guilty of an assault

[margin notes: Arming at night with dangerous weapons, with felonious intent. Misdemeanor. Felony. When grand larceny, though less than $25 in value be stolen. Laying hands upon another, with intent to steal or rob.]

with intent to steal, and shall be punished as now provided by law for the punishment of misdemeanors. It *As to proof.* shall not be necessary to allege or prove in any prosecution for an offence under this section any article intended to be stolen, or the value thereof, or the name of the person so assaulted.

§ 4. This act shall take effect immediately.

Chap. 375.

AN ACT to amend the Revised Statutes in relation to taking the testimony of witnesses out of the State.

Passed April 19, 1862.

The People of the State of New York, represented in Senate and Assembly, do enact as follows:

SECTION 1. Whenever a default shall have been taken for want of any appearance or answer or other pleading in any action, and in any proceeding pending in any court of record, and whenever any issue of fact shall have been joined in any such action or proceeding, and it shall appear on the application of either party that any witness not residing in this state is material in the prosecution or defence of such action or proceeding, the court may, upon such terms as it shall think proper, award a commission to one or more competent persons, authorizing them or any one of them to examine such witness on oath upon the interrogatories annexed to such commission, to take and certify the deposition of such witness, and return the same according to the directions given with such commission; but in all cases of default for want of appearance, no notice of such application shall be required to be served on the adverse party.

§ 2. This act shall take effect immediately.

Chap. 376.

AN ACT to provide·for a Night Police in the village of Canandaigua.

Passed April 19, 1862; three-fifths being present.

The People of the State of New York, represented in Senate and Assembly, do enact as follows:

SECTION 1. The trustees of the village of Canandaigua, in the county of Ontairo, in this state, are hereby authorized to give notice in the manner now provided by law, prior to any election hereafter to be held in and for said village, of a tax to be raised to employ a night police force for said village, the number proposed for such police force to be designated in the notice aforesaid: and the number of said night policemen, and the sum required to employ the same, may be voted by the taxable inhabitants and electors of said village at any election hereafter to be held in and for said village; and when voted, the same shall be assessed and collected in the same manner as other taxes of said village, as now provided by law.

§ 2. The trustees of the village aforesaid, are hereby authorized. to appoint such number of night policemen as may be authorized by the vote taken in pursuance of the provisions of the first section of this act; and such trustees shall also have power to prescribe the duties of, and regulations for, such night police

§ 3. This act shall take effect immediately.

Tax for night police

Power of trustees.

Chap. 377.

AN ACT to authorize the appraisal and payment of canal damages to James Hyde.

Passed April 19, 1862; three-fifths being present.

The People of the State of New York, represented in Senate and Assembly, do enact as follows:

SECTION 1. The Canal Appraisers are hereby authorized and required to hear and examine the alleged claim of

James Hyde for permanent and temporary injuries done to his farm and buildings thereon situate on the Genesee Valley canal. near Black Creek Corners, in the town of New Hudson, in the county of Allegany, and injuries done to crops thereon since the first day of January, eighteen hundred and fifty-seven, by reason of waters from the waste weirs of the said canal, or water from the said canal overflowing the lands of the said Hyde; and if, upon such examination, they find that said Hyde has sustained damages from the aforesaid causes, they shall appraise such damages and make such award therefor as they shall deem just and reasonable, subject to an appeal to the canal board as in other cases.

§ 2. The Treasurer shall pay on the warrant to the Auditor of the Canal Department, the sum finally awarded to said claimant in pursuance of the first section of this act, out of any money appropriated or to be appropriated to the payment of canal damages.

§ 3. This act shall take effect immediately.

Chap. 378.

AN ACT to amend an act entitled "An act in relation to jurors and to the appointment and the duties of a commissioner of jurors in the county of Kings," passed April seventeenth, eighteen hundred and fifty-eight.

Passed April 21, 1862; three-fifths being present

The People of the State of New York, represented in Senate and Assembly, do enact as follows:

Appointing board.

SECTION 1. The appointment of the commissioner of jurors for the county of Kings shall hereafter be vested in a board, consisting of the county clerk, the district attorney and the surrogate of said county.

Term of office.

§ 2. The term of the present commissioner of jurors for said county of Kings shall expire on the second Monday of May, eighteen hundred and sixty-two, and the said board shall appoint his successor on the first Monday of May, eighteen hundred and sixty-two at such hour and place as shall be designated by said county clerk; and the term of said office shall be four years, to commence at the expiration of the present incumbent's term of office as herein provided, and upon complying with the provisions of section five of the act of which this act is amendatory.

§ 3. Said commissioner of jurors may be removed at any time by the Governor for cause, in the same manner in which sheriffs may now be removed by law, and the said board shall fill any vacancy that may occur in said office, and the concurrence of two members of said board shall make a valid appointment of said commissioner. *Removal.*

§ 4. If the said commissioner of jurors or any other person shall corruptly and without sufficient cause omit the name of any person from the list of persons to be summoned as jurors, or from the box provided for in section fourteen of the act hereby amended, or shall directly or indirectly receive from any person liable to do jury duty, any money, fee, reward, compensation or advantage in consideration of omitting the name of such person from such list or box, he shall, on conviction, be deemed guilty of a felony, and shall be punished by imprisonment in the state prison for a term not less than two nor more than five years. *Punishment for omitting name.*

§ 5. All acts and parts of acts inconsistent with this act, are hereby repealed. *Repeal.*

§ 6. This act shall take effect immediately.

---

*Chap. 379.

AN ACT to exempt all that part of the city of Albany lying west of Allen street from certain taxes and assessments, and for auditing the accounts of the commissioner and overseers of highways in that district.

Passed April 21, 1862; three-fifths being present.

The People of the State of New York, represented in Senate and Assembly, do enact as follows:

SECTION 1. All the estates, real and personal, situate within the city of Albany, west of Allen street, shall be and hereby are declared exempted from taxation and assessment for the purpose of raising money to pay the expenses of maintaining and supporting a fire department in the city of Albany ; for the support of the police department in said city ; for the making, repairing and cleansing of drains and sewers ; for all damages, costs and other expenses arising from the stoppage or overflow of drains and sewers ; for the cleaning of streets and the removal of street dirt, garbage and other nuisances ; for the expenses of building and repairing of wells and pumps and cleaning the same ; for the expense of furnishing gas or oil for the street lamps and for furnishing lamps and putting up the same ; and for repairing, cleaning. superintending and lighting the lamps which now are or hereafter may be erected within that part of the city of Albany which is situated east of Allen street aforesaid ; for the grading, excavating and filling and repairs of pavements, or making or repairing crosswalks in any streets of said city east of Allen street ; also for the salaries of the city superintendents and their clerk, and for all the incidental expenses of the offices of city superintendents.

§ 2. The accounts of the commissioner and overseers of highways in the separate road districts west of Allen street in the city of Albany, shall be annually submitted to the inhabitants in town meeting, the day before the annual election in said district, and when audited and approved by the supervisors of the ninth and tenth wards, and the city surveyor of the city of Albany, shall be filed in the chamberlain's office for the inspection of the inhabitants and tax payers of the said district.

§ 3. This act shall take effect immediately.

Chap. 380.

AN ACT to amend an act entitled "An act to incorporate the village of Mount Morris," passed May second, eighteen hundred and thirty-five, and the several subsequents acts amending the same.

Passed April 21, 1862; three-fifths being present.

The People of the State of New York, represented in Senate and Assembly, do enact as follows:

SECTION 1. The electors of the village of Mount Morris, at the next annual meeting for the election of officers in said village, and every two years thereafter, shall, in addition to the officers now required by law to be chosen and elected in said village, elect one police justice, to be designated "police justice of the village of Mount Morris," who shall be a resident and elector of the village of Mount Morris, and who shall hold his office during the period of two years, and until his successor be elected and qualified; and two police constables, who shall also be residents and electors of said village, and who shall hold their office for the period of one year respectively, and until others are elected in their places and qualified. *Police justice.*

§ 2. The police justice so elected shall, within five days after his election, file with the clerk of the county of Livingston his acceptance of said office, with the same oath and surety as justices of the peace of towns are by law required to file with the clerk of their respective counties, and shall enter upon the duties of his office as soon as such acceptance, oath and sureties are so filed. *Oath and surety.*

§ 3. The said police justice shall have criminal jurisdiction of all crimes, misdemeanors and offences committed in said village of Mount Morris, of which justices of the peace of towns have jurisdiction in their respective towns. And shall have civil jurisdiction in all actions wherein the trustees of said village are parties, in actions to recover penalties for the violation of *Jurisdiction.*

80

any of the ordinances of said village, and in no other cases, and in reference to those matters of which he has jurisdiction he shall possess the like powers, rights and authority, and be subject to the like obligations and duties as appertain and belong to justices of the peace in relation to criminal matters, and to actions for the recovery of penalties for the violation of any ordinances of said village in the several towns in this state ; and all criminal proceedings before said police justice shall be conducted by him before trial, and (if a trial is demanded by the accused,) shall be tried by h m as a court of special sessions, in the same manner as such proceedings are now by law required to be conducted before justices of the peace, or tried before a court of special sessions. And the trial of all actions before him for the recovery of a penalty for the violation of village ordinances shall be conducted in the like manner as trials of the same actions before a justice of the peace of towns.

Compensation. § 4. The said police justice shall receive, as a compensation for services rendered by him as such police justice in criminal matters, the same fees and he shall be entitled to charge for such services the same fees as justices of the peace of towns are entitled to receive **Fees paid to treasurer.** and charge for like services All fees and perquisites receivable by him shall be by him received, and shall, with all fines and penalties for the violation of village ordinances collected or received by him, be by him paid into the treasury of said village quarterly, at the end of each quarter. And each payment shall be accompanied by a statement in writing, signed by the said police justice, **Account.** containing a particular account of all fees and perquisites received and earned by him during the preceding quarter, and of all fines and penalties received by him during the same time, for violation of village ordinances, which said statement shall be verified as to its fullness and accuracy, by his affidavit attached thereto. And the money thus paid by said police justice into the treasury shall form a separate fund in the hands of said treasurer for the payment of said police justice of his compensation for criminal services performed by him as such police justice as herein provided, and in case the same is more than sufficient to pay said justice the balance shall be applied by the trustees of said village to other incidental expenses of the same, as they may direct.

§ 5. The said police justice shall, at the end of each quarter. make out and deliver to the trustees of said village a statement, in items, as justices of the peace are now required to state their accounts. or his fees for services as such police justice during the preceding quarter, verified as to its correctness by his oath, which the said trustees shall audit if correct, and the amount so audited shall, on the draft of the president of the board of trustees, countersigned by the clerk of said village, under the seal of said village, be paid by the treasurer to said police justice, out of the fund herein provided for that purpose, providing such fund is sufficient for that purpose ; if not then sufficient the amount on hand applicable thereto shall be paid and endorsed on said draft. *Statement of items, to be made quarterly.*

§ 6. In case the fund herein provided for the payment of the fees of said justice. in criminal proceedings, shall prove insufficient for that purpose, then and in that case the deficiency shall be levied, assessed and collected by the board of supervisors of the county of Livingston, in the same manner as other fees for criminal proceedings in the different towns in said county are levied and collected, and for that purpose the said police justice shall make out and deliver. at the proper time, and to the proper auditing bodies, a statement of his account for such deficiency for services rendered, in items showing the proceeding in which such services were rendered, which statement shall be made and verified in the same manner as justices of the peace are now by law required to make statements for similar services *Deficiency in fund.*

§ 7. The said police justice shall not be required to perform any services in civil proceedings, until his legal fees therefor are paid, and in civil actions he may charge for services rendered the same fees as justices of towns charge for similar services, and issue executions upon judgments for penalties in the same manner as justices of the peace in actions for penalties. *Fees to be paid.*

§ 8. An appeal may be taken from any judgment rendered by said police justice in a civil action to the county court of Livingston county in the same manner as from a judgment rendered by a justice of the peace of towns. *Appeal.*

Constables. § 9. The police constables herein provided for shall have power and authority to serve all process, whether civil or criminal, issued by the said police justice, and all civil process when the trustees of said village are parties, and criminal process in the county of Livingston. They shall respectively take the same oath of

Oath and security. office, give the same security and receive the same compensation, and be paid in the same manner as constables of towns.

Repeal. § 10 Section four of an act amending the charter of the village of Mount Morris, passed April eighteenth, eighteen hundred and thirty-eight, is hereby repealed.

Additional power of trustees. § 11. In addition to the powers and authority already conferred on the trustees of said village, by the act of incorporation and its amendments, they shall have power and authority to hire for a term of years, or for such time as they may deem expedient, some suitable building, room or rooms in the village of Mount Morris at such rent as they in their judgment may see fit to pay, and cause the same to be fitted up in a proper and secure manner, for the purpose of a lock-up, and to keep the same so fitted up and in repair and provided with necessary accommodations of fuel and other necessaries, and it shall be lawful for the constables of the town of Mount Morris or the police constables of the village of Mount Morris to detain in such look-up all persons lawfully arrested by them or either of them, in the night or day time, either upon view or information of felony or crime; if in the day time, until such person or persons can be brought before the proper officer for trial or examination, and if in the night time, until the following morning, when they shall be taken by the constable making the arrest before some justice of the peace of the town of Mount Morris or the police justice of the village of Mount Morris, to be dealt with according to

Power of constables. law. It shall also be lawful for such constables to detain in such lock-up, when necessary to secure their attendance on the trial or examination of persons charged with offences, persons who may be necessary witnesses on such trial or examination, and who cannot otherwise safely be kept, on the requirement or authority of any justice of the peace of said town of Mount Morris or the police justice of said village of Mount Morris, until such trial or examination can be had and their testimony therein be taken, and for such services in detaining such persons and for necessary supplies furnished them during such detention, such constables shall receive such compensation as constables of towns are now entitled to by law, for like services and supplies; and such further compensation as the trustees of said village may direct. *Fees.*

§ 12. The necessary expenses of renting, fitting up, supplying and keeping in proper condition and repair the said lock-up and all other necessary expenses connected therewith shall be a corporation charge on the village of Mount Morris, and shall be estimated and reported by the trustees in their annual report, as they are now required to report corporation expenses; and the inhabitants of said village qualified to vote for the raising of money by tax in said village may, at any annual meeting of said inhabitants, or at a special meeting, duly called for that purpose, vote to raise such sum as will cover such expenses, by tax upon the taxable property of said village, and thereupon the same may be levied and collected in the same manner as other taxes are collected in said village. *Expenses a charge on village.*

§ 13. The said lock-up shall be in charge and custody of the police constables of said village, who shall receive such compensation for their services in taking care of the same as the trustees shall from time to time designate, to be paid out of the fund for that purpose provided. *Lock-up.*

§ 14. This act shall take effect immediately.

Chap. 381.

AN ACT to legalize the tax levied by the board of trustees of the village of Olean for the year eighteen hundred and sixty-one, and to provide for the collection of the amount of such tax as the same has been heretofore levied and assessed by said trustees.

Passed April 21, 1862; three-fifths being present.

The People of the State of New York, represented in Senate and Assembly, do enact as follows:

SECTION 1. The tax heretofore levied and assessed by the board of trustees of the village of Olean for the year eighteen hundred and sixty-one, against the taxable property of said village for the purpose of paying and discharging the indebtedness of said village, incurred in the purchase of a fire engine and apparatus and other indebtedness and expenditures of said village, the tax roll for the collection of which is now in the hands of the collector of the said village, is hereby ratified, legalized and confirmed, and shall be deemed a legal and valid tax.

§ 2 The collector of said village of Olean is hereby authorized to collect said tax from the persons and out of the property against which the same has been so as aforesaid assessed.

§ 3. This act shall take effect immediately.

Chap. 382.

AN ACT entitled an act in regard to tolls on the Jordan and Skaneateles plankroad.

Passed April 21, 1862; three-fifths being present.

The People of the State of New York, represented in Senate and Assembly, do enact as follows:

SECTION 1. For every team of three animals drawing loads on the Jordan and Skaneateles plankroad, the directors thereof may charge and receive the same amount of tolls now allowed by law for teams of four animals, and for every additional ton or part of a ton of weight over four thousand pounds, excluding the carriage, the amount of tolls now allowed by law for teams of two animals, in addition to the present rates.'

§ 2. All teams drawing wagons with tire six inches wide may pass over said road free of tolls.

Chap. 383.

AN ACT to re-incorporate the Rockbottom Bridge Company of the village of Binghamton.

Passed April 21, 1862.

The People of the State of New York, represented in Senate and Assembly, do enact as follows:

SECTION 1. Whereas, the Rockbottom Bridge Company of the village of Binghamton, which was incorporated by an act of the legislature of the State of New York, passed April first, eighteen hundred and fifty-three, having become dissolved by insolvency, and by operation of section forty-six, title four, chapter eight of article two, part three of the Revised Statutes, therefore, Joseph B. Abbot, Horatio Evans, Eli Pratt, Allen Perkins and B. N. Loomis, and all persons who shall become stockholders pursuant to this act, shall be and they are hereby constituted a body corporate by the name of " The Rockbottom Bridge Company of the village of Binghamton. *Corporate name.*

§ 2. The capital stock of said corporation shall be ten thousand dollars, or two hundred shares of fifty dollars each, which shall be issued in the first instance under the direction of the directors of said company to the stockholders or proprietors, according to their respective interests or advances in or on account of the bridge here nafter mentioned, which shares shall be deemed personal estate and shall be thereafter assignable and transferable on the books of said corporation according to the by-laws thereof. *Capital.*

Paying for bridge and repairs. § 3. The directors of said company may demand from the stockholders all such sums of money proportionable to the amount of stock owned by each, for the purpose of paying for said bridge property and keeping the same in repair, at such times and in such proportions as they think proper, under the penalty of forfeiting their respective shares and all previous payments thereon.

Owners of stock to meet and choose directors. § 4. On the passage of this act, the owners of the stock of said bridge company hereby incorporated, shall meet on due notice to each personally, at a time and place designated by two of their number and choose from the stock owners five of their number to be directors, who shall hold their offices respectively until January, eighteen hundred and sixty-three, and until others are chosen in their places; but after that day the number of directors and the day and manner of choosing them, and the duration of their offices shall be regulated **Term of office.** by the by-laws of said company.

Elections. § 5 In all future elections for directors, each stockholder shall be entitled to one vote for every share of stock owned by him standing in his name upon the books of the company, and the persons having the greater number of votes shall be the directors.

Officers of company. § 6. The directors chosen at any election, shall as soon thereafter as conveniently may be, choose from their number one person to be president, one person to be secretary and one person to be treasurer of said company.

Rights and privileges. § 7. The said corporation may purchase and hold the bridge and the lands, and all the property owned by the former Rockbottom Bridge Company of the village of Binghamton, and have and enjoy all the rights and privileges formerly held and enjoyed by the said coporation.

Toll. § 8. The corporation hereby created may demand and receive the same rates of toll as the Susquehanna Bridge Company of the village of Binghamton are now authorized by law to demand and receive.

Penalty for non-payment of toll. § 9. If any person shall wilfully cross said bridge and pass the toll gate without paying toll and with the intent to evade the payment thereof, said toll being demanded by the toll gatherer, the person so offending shall forfeit and pay to said company the sum of five dollars for every such offence, to be recovered with costs of suit in the name of the corporation.

§ 10. If any toll gatherer shall unreasonably delay or *Toll gatherer.* hinder any passenger at the gate, or shall demand or receive more than the legal toll, he shall for every such offence forfeit the sum of five dollars, to be recovered with costs to the use of the person so unreasonably delayed, hindered or defrauded.

§ 11. It shall be the duty of said corporation, in the sea- *Snow.* son of sleighing, to keep said bridge covered with snow. during such time as the sleighing on the adjacent river roads shall be reasonably suitable for loaded sleighs, so as to allow the convenient passage of said sleighs over said bridge without delay or embarrassment.

§ 12. All parts or provisions of an act authorizing the building of a toll bridge across the Susquehanna river at the village of Binghamton, passed April twenty-first, eighteen hundred and twenty-five, and of the act entitled "An act incorporating the Susquehanna Bridge Company of the village of Binghamton," passed January thirty-first, eighteen hundred and twenty-nine, which are *Repeal and* prohibitory or restrictive of any of the rights, powers or *its effect.* privileges given or granted by this act, are so far hereby repealed as to give full force and effect to this act in all its provisions.

§ 13. The legislature may at any time alter, modify or repeal this act.

Chap. 384.

AN ACT to amend the Statutes concerning Teachers' Institutes, and otherwise in relation to Public Instruction.

Passed April 21, 1862; three-fifths being present.

The People of the State of New York, represented in Senate and Assembly, do enact as follows:

SECTION 1. The Treasurer shall pay, on the warrant *Pay to* of the Comptroller, to the order of any one or more of *school com-* the school commissioners, such sum or sums as the Su- *missioners.* perintendent of Public Instruction shall certify to be due for expenses incurred by any one or more of them, in holding teachers' institutes in their respective counties or assembly districts, as required by section eight, chapter one hundred and seventy-nine, Laws of eighteen hundred and fifty-six.

Duty of Superintendent of Public Instruction. § 2. It shall be the duty of the Superintendent of Public Instruction to advise and co-operate with the school commissioners in regard to the time and place of holding teachers' institutes, and the employment of teachers and lecturers to conduct the exercises of the same; and he shall visit or cause to be visited, by any person or persons employed in the Department of Public Instruction, such and so many institutes as he may find it practicable to reach, for the purpose of examining into the course and method of instruction pursued, and of rendering such assistance as he may find expedient; and he shall establish the basis upon which the yearly appropriation for the support of teachers' institutes shall be distributed to the several counties, having reference in such distribution to the number of teachers in the county and in attendance at the institute, to the facilities for securing their attendance at the institute, and the assistance of those competent to conduct the exercises, and also to the length of time during which the institute shall be held.

Certificates. § 3. The Superintendent of Public Instruction may establish such regulations in regard to the forms of certificates issued by school commissioners, as shall in his judgment best serve as an incentive and an encouragement to teachers to attend upon the sessions of **Teachers may attend institutes.** the institute; and the closing of school by any teacher, for a term not exceeding two weeks, for the purpose of attending the institute held in the county where such teacher shall be employed, shall not work a forfeiture of the contract under which he may be teaching, and he shall be allowed to make up the time spent at the institute, not exceeding two weeks, immediately after the close of his original term of engagement.

Authority of trustees. § 4. The trustees of any school district are hereby authorized, in their discretion, to give to the teacher or teachers employed by them, the time, either wholly or in part, spent by such teacher or teachers at any regular session of the institute in the county where they are employed, without deducting from the wages of such teacher or teachers any portion thereof on account of such absence; and

whenever any district shall be reported as having supported a school but five and one-half months during the year,
and it shall be shown to the satisfaction of the Super- _{Authority}
intendent of Public Instruction that the failure to sup- _{of superintendent.}
port a school six months was owing to the absence of
the teacher while attending a teachers' institute in the
county in which such district shall wholly or partly lie,
the Superintendent of Public Instruction may direct
that such district be included in the apportionment of
school moneys, provided that in all other respects such
district shall appear legally entitled to such apportionment.

§ 5. Section number fourteen of chapter one hundred
and fifty-one of the Laws of eighteen hundred and fifty-
eight is hereby amended so as to read as follows:

Nothing contained in this act shall be so construed as <sub>Saving
clause.</sub>
to affect or interfere with any special school act now
in force in any city or incorporated village, or with any
district organized under the provisions of the union
free school law, passed June eighteenth, eighteen hundred and fifty-three, except so far as relates to the time of
making the annual report and of holding the annual
school meeting.

§ 6. Whenever it shall be satisfactorily shown to the <sub>Neglect of
school com-</sub>
Superintendent of Public Instruction that any school _{missioner.}
commissioner has persistently neglected the duties prescribed by law for him to perform, he may withhold his
order for the payment of the whole or any part of the
salary of said commissioner as the same shall become
due, and the sum so withheld shall be forfeited by such
commissioner as a penalty for such neglect; but the
Superintendent of Public Instruction shall have power
to remit such penalty, if the commissioner shall subsequently disprove or satisfactorily justify such neglect.

§ 7. All laws or parts of laws, so far as they are inconsistent with the provisions of this act, are hereby
repealed.

§ 8. This act shall take effect immediately.

Chap. 385.

AN ACT to amend and consolidate the several acts relative to the city of Schenectady.

Passed April 21, 1862; three-fifths being present.

The People of the State of New York, represented in Senate and Assembly, do enact as follows:

TITLE I.

BOUNDARIES AND CIVIL DIVISIONS.

Corporate name.

SECTION 1. The inhabitants of that portion of the territory of this state heretofore known as the city of Schenectady, shall continue to be a body politic and corporate, by the name of "the city of Schenectady," with the powers, privileges and liabilities of corporations as provided by chapter eighteen, part one, title three of the Revised Statutes, as well as those conferred by this act, which shall be known as the charter of said city, and the wards and boundaries thereof shall remain as they now are.

They sue and be sued.

§ 2. The inhabitants of said city shall be a corporation by the name of "the city of Schenectady," and may sue and be sued, complain and defend in any court, or before any tribunal, and may appear and act in all matters and proceedings whatsoever, relative to the affairs and business of the said city and corporation.

Seal.

They may have and use the present public seal of the said city as their common seal, and may alter the same at pleasure.

May hold property.

They shall continue in law capable of holding, enjoying and conveying all the estate, real and personal, and of collecting, recovering and disposing of all the property, rents, income, funds and effects whatsoever, now held and owned by or belonging to the said city, or which they now are or may become possessed of or entitled to in as full and ample a manner as the same are now held and possessed by the mayor, recorder, aldermen and commonalty of the city of Schenectady; and they may receive by gift, grant, devise, bequest or purchase, any real or personal property or estate whatsoever, and may hold and convey such real and personal estate as the purposes of the corporation may require.

TITLE II.

OFFICERS, THEIR ELECTION AND APPOINTMENT.

§ 1. The officers of said city shall be one mayor, one recorder, one treasurer, one police justice, one high constable, three assessors, four justices of the peace, and one superintendent of streets, and for each ward one supervisor, three aldermen, two commissioners of common schools, three inspectors of election and one constable, all to be chosen by ballot by the electors of said city, who are qualified, as hereinafter provided, to vote therefor. And the following officers to be appointed by the common council, namely : One clerk, one marshal, one attorney, one physician, one printer, one chief engineer, two assistant engineers, one surveyor, one overseer of the poor, one sealer of weights and measures, one board of magistrates, to consist of the police justice and two aldermen, one board of health, to consist of the mayor, city physician and one alderman from each ward ; commissioners of deeds not exceeding twenty, and so many pound masters, fence viewers, lamplighters, fire wardens and firemen, keepers of hospitals, policemen for special occasions, laborers and servants, as the common council shall, from time to time deem necessary, direct, which officers, except commissioners of deeds, shall be appointed by the common council on the first Tuesday of May, by majority of votes, and such appointments shall be made by ballot, unless the common council shall otherwise order ; commissioners of deeds shall be appointed at the time, in the mode and for the term now provided by law.

§ 2. The term of office of superintendent of streets, supervisor, constable, inspectors of election, clerk, marshal, attorney, physician, printer, chief engineer and assistant, surveyor, overseer of the poor, sealer of weights and measures, board of magistrates, board of health, pound masters, fence viewers and lamplighters, shall be one year : of the mayor, treasurer, high constable and commissioners of common schools, two years ; of the aldermen and assessors, three years ; and of the recorder, justices of the peace and police justice, four years. The term of office of the mayor, recorder and aldermen, shall commence with the second Tuesday of April, and of the other officers named, with the second

Tuesday of May. All other officers appointed by the common council, and whose term of office is not fixed above, shall hold their offices during the pleasure of the common council.

§ 3. No person shall be eligible to either of the offices in the last preceding section specified, unless he shall be a resident of said city; and if any such officer, after his election, shall cease to be a resident of said city, his office shall thereby become vacant.

§ 4. An election for the officers who are to be chosen by the electors of said city, shall be held on the first Tuesday of April in each year, at such place in each ward as the common council shall designate, at least eight days prior to said election; and if the common council shall fail to designate such places within the time prescribed, then such election shall be held at the place in each ward at which the last general election for state officers was held; and it shall be the duty of the clerk of the common council to publish notice of such election for at least six days previous thereto, in all of the newspapers printed in said city, which notice shall state the time when and place where the election is to be held, the hour of the opening and closing of the polls, and the officers to be elected thereat.

§ 5. There shall be chosen on the first Tuesday of April, after this act shall take effect, by the electors of the whole city, voting in their respective wards, on general ticket, one mayor, one treasurer, one superintendent of streets, three assessors, one justice of the peace and one high constable; and there shall be chosen at the same time, by the electors of each ward, one supervisor, one alderman, one constable and three inspectors of election; and there shall be chosen in like manner, at each annual election thereafter, all such city and ward officers whose term of office will expire prior to the next annual election, and whose election by the people is provided for by this act.

§ 6. The common council shall at the same meeting, when they determine as to the election of such assessors, proceed to determine by lot which of said assessors shall hold his office for one year, which for two years, and which for three years, and shall enter such determination in their minutes, and the said assessors shall hold their respective offices according to such determination.

§ 7. If at any annual election, to be held in said city, *Vacancies.* there shall be any vacancy to be supplied in any office, and any person is at the same time to be chosen for the full term of such office, or if two or more persons are to be elected to the same office for different terms, the term which each person is voted for shall be designated upon the ballot, and every ballot that does not contain such designation shall be rejected by the canvassers, so far as it relates to such office.

§ 8. The polls of any election held under this act, *Polls of election.* shall be opened in each ward, at the several places where they are to be held, at ten o'clock in the morning, and shall be kept open without intermission or adjournment until five o'clock in the afternoon, when they shall be finally closed.

§ 9. Two inspectors of elections for each ward or elec- *Inspectors.* tion district in said city shall be elected, and one shall be appointed at each charter election, in the manner provided by section twenty-one of article three, title three, of the act entitled "An act respecting elections other than for militia and town officers," passed April fifth, eighteen hundred and forty-two, and the provisions of said act are hereby declared to be applicable to the city of Schenectady and to the elections to be held therein under this act, except so far as they may be inconsistent with the provisions of this act.

§ 10. The common council shall provide two ballot *Ballot boxes and tickets.* boxes for each ward or election district, with locks and keys, in which the ballots shall be deposited ; one box shall be the city box, the other the ward box. The officers to be elected by general ticket for the whole city shall be upon one ballot, which shall be endorsed upon the outside thereof " city ticket," and the officers to be elected for the several wards shall be upon one ballot, which shall be endorsed upon the outside thereof "ward ticket ;" and such ballots when received by the inspectors shall be deposited in the box indicated by the endorsement thereon.

§ 11. Every person entitled to vote for member of *Qualification of voters.* assembly, who shall have been for thirty days preceding the charter election a resident of said city, and for the last ten days an actual resident of the ward in which he offers his vote, and who is at the time an actual resident of such ward, shall be entitled to vote in the ward in

which he resides, and not elsewhere, for all or any of
the officers to be chosen at such election, providing such
person shall have complied with the provisions of chapter three hundred and eighty of the laws of eighteen
hundred and fifty-nine.

Canvass of
inspectors.

§ 12. Immediately after the closing of the polls, the
inspectors of election shall forthwith, and without adjournment, canvass the votes received by them and declare the result; they shall on the same or the next day
make a statement and certificate in writing of the number of votes given for each person for each office on the
city ticket, and file the same on the day of election or
the next day with the city clerk, and shall at the same
time certify and declare in writing the several persons
who shall have been elected to the several ward offices
at such election, and shall file such certificate and declaration with said clerk within the same time above directed.

Determina-
tion by
common
council.

§ 13. The common council shall convene on Thursday
next succeeding such election, at seven o'clock in the
evening, at their usual place of meeting, and the clerk
shall thereupon deliver to the common council the statements and certificates of the votes given for city officers,
filed with him by the inspectors of elections as aforesaid; and the said common council shall forthwith estimate, determine and declare what persons were duly
elected at such election to the several city offices voted
for respectively; the persons having the greatest number of votes for each office shall be declared to be duly
elected; and the said common council shall thereupon
make and sign in duplicate a certificate of their determination and declaration, which shall be signed by the
members present, or a majority of them, one of which
shall be filed with their clerk, and the other with the
clerk of Schenectady county.

§ 14. If at any election authorized by this act, any officer
shall not have been chosen by reason of two or more candidates having received an equal number of votes,
whether it be a city or ward office, the common council
shall at the same meeting when they determine and declare the election of city officers, by a majority vote and
by ballot, elect such officer from the two candidates
having the greatest number of votes; or they may in
their discretion by a like vote, order a special election

to be held within two weeks thereafter, for the election
of such officer; which special election shall be held and
conducted and the votes canvassed and result declared
in the same manner herein prescribed for the holding of
the annual charter election.

§ 15. If a vacancy shall occur in any city or ward office *Vacancies how filled.* from any other cause than that provided for in the last
preceding section, the common council shall, within one
month thereafter, by a majority vote and by ballot, fill
such vacancy by the appointment of some suitable person; or they shall within the same time and by a like
vote, order a special election to be held to fill such
vacancy; and any person elected to fill a vacancy, shall
hold his office if it be that of mayor, recorder or alderman, until the second Tuesday of April after his election;
and if it be that of any other city or ward office, until
the second Tuesday of May after his election; but if the
vacancy thus filled be one of a class and the unexpired
term shall extend beyond the time above limited, then a
successor shall be chosen at the first annual charter
election after such vacancy, to serve out such unexpired
term, which special election shall be held and conducted
and the votes canvassed and declared in the same manner herein prescribed for the holding of the annual
charter election.

§ 16. It shall be the duty of the city clerk to give *Clerk to give notice to persons elected.* notice in writing to every person elected or appointed
to any office under this act, within three days after the
election or appointment of such person shall have been
officially declared, of his election or appointment, which
notice shall be served personally, or by leaving it at the
residence of such person.

§ 17. The officers of said city who are by this act *Oath of office.* made elective by the people, and the city clerk, police
justice and high constable, shall, within ten days after
they shall be notified of their election and before they
enter upon the duties of their offices, severally take
and subscribe the constitutional oath of office and file
the same with the city clerk. Such oath shall be taken
before the city clerk, by all of said officers except said
clerk, who shall take such oath before the mayor. In
case of the inability of the clerk to act from any cause,
such oath may be taken before the mayor or recorder,

and shall in such case be filed within three days thereafter with the said clerk.

Notice of acceptance.

§ 18. Every person chosen or appointed by the common council to any office except those enumerated in the last section, shall, within ten days after he shall be notified of his appointment and before he enters upon the duties of his office, file with the city clerk a notice in writing signifying his acceptance of such office.

Refusal to serve.

§ 19. If any person elected or appointed to any office specified in the last two sections, shall not take and subscribe the oath of office and file the same, or shall not file the notice of acceptance as therein directed, or shall fail to execute in due form and file any official bond required of him and within the time required, such neglect shall be deemed a refusal to serve.

Clerk to keep book.

§ 20. The city clerk shall keep a book ruled in columns in which he shall enter the name of every person elected or appointed to any office in said city by the electors or the common council thereof, the name of the office, when elected or appointed, the commencement of the term, the expiration thereof, time of filing oath of office or notice of acceptance, and time of filing official bond; and every person so elected or appointed to any such office shall, upon filing his oath of office or notice of acceptance, subscribe his name opposite the office to which he was elected or appointed, which book shall be open at all times to the inspection of any elector of said city.

Resignation.

§ 21. The resignation of office of any person elected or appointed under this act shall be made to the common council of the city, and shall be subject to its acceptance.

Inability to serve, from sickness &c

§ 22. In case any officer elected or appointed under this act, except justice of the peace, shall, from sickness, absence, or from any other cause, be unable, in the judgment of the common council, to discharge the duties of his office, the common council may appoint some suitable person to discharge such duties during such disability; and the person so appointed by the common council to fill such vacancy or discharge such duties, shall have and exercise all the powers, and discharge all the duties, and be subject to all the provisions of law applicable to the officer whose place they shall supply, or to the office to which they may respectively be appointed, or the duties of which they may be authorized to discharge.

§ 23. Any officer who may be elected or appointed **Removal from office.** under this act, except the mayor, recorder, aldermen, police justice and justices of the peace, may be removed from office by the common council by a vote of two-thirds of all the members thereof, to be taken by yeas and nays and recorded, for any refusal or neglect to discharge the duties of his office, or for the unfaithful or insufficient discharge of such duties, or for mal-conduct in office; but notice of the charges against him, and an opportunity of being heard in his defence, shall be first given to such officer.

The police justice and justices of the peace may be **Expense of** removed for cause, in the mode provided by law for the **election.** removal from office of justices of the peace in the several towns of this state.

§ 24. The expenses of any election to be held under this act, shall be a city charge, and be paid in the same manner as other contingent expenses of the city.

TITLE III.

OF THE COMMON COUNCIL.

§ 1. The mayor, recorder and aldermen of the said **Meetings.** city, for the time being, shall be the common council thereof. The meetings of the common council shall be held at the city hall or in such other place in said city as it shall appoint. The annual meeting shall be held on the first Tuesday of May in each year, and it shall meet monthly thereafter, and oftener in its discretion. Special meetings may also be called by the mayor, or in his absence, by the recorder; and special meetings may also be called by the direction, in writing, to the marshall of a majority of the aldermen. Notice, in writing, of all meetings shall be given by the marshal to each member of the common council by delivering it to him personally, or by leaving it at his residence. The presence of two-thirds of the members of the common council shall be required to make a quorum to transact business.

§ 2. The mayor shall preside at the meetings of the **Presiding** common council; in his absence the recorder shall preside, and in his absence the common council may appoint one of its number to preside.

§ 3. In the proceedings of the common council each member shall have a vote.

Minutes to be kept. § 4. The meetings of the common council shall be open to the public, except when the public interests shall, in its judgment, require secrecy. The minutes of the proceedings shall be kept by the clerk, and the same shall be open at all times to the inspection of any elector of said city. The common council shall prescribe, from time to time, such rules to govern its proceedings as it shall deem advisable, not inconsistent with the provisions of this act.

Mode of voting. § 5. Whenever required by two members, the vote by yea and nay of all the members of the common council present shall be taken upon any act, proceeding, resolution or proposition had at any meeting, except appointments directed herein to be made by ballot, and such votes shall be entered at large on the minutes.

When two-third vote required. § 6. No sale, lease, gift or other disposition whatever of the lands, quit rents, assets or other property of the said city shall be made, nor shall any tax or assessment be ordered, or any ordinance, contract or resolution for taxing or assessing the citizens of said city, or involving the expenditure or appropriation of the public money, be entered into or adopted, except upon the concurrent vote of two-thirds of all the members composing the common council, to be taken by yea and nay, and recorded in the minutes at length.

Execution not to be stayed. § 7. The common council shall not, nor shall any of its officers, or any officer of said city have power to stay the execution of, or the execution issued upon, any judgment or sentence imposed in pursuance of any of its ordinances, nor to release, remit or discharge, in whole or in part, any such judgment, fine or sentence, nor in any other manner whatever, to control or interfere with the same.

Contracts &c., limited to three years. § 8. The common council shall not make or enter into, or renew or extend any contract or agreement, to continue in force for a longer period than three years from the time the same shall be made, or entered into, or renewed, or extended by it; and said common council shall not renew, or extend, or covenant to renew or extend any contract or agreement when more than one year of its term is unexpired.

§ 9. No member of the common council shall, during the period for which he was elected, be appointed to or be competent to hold any office of which the emoluments are paid from the city treasurer, or paid by fees directed to be paid by any resolution or ordinance of the common council, or be directly or indirectly interested in any contract as principal, surety or otherwise, the expense or consideration whereof are to be paid under any ordinance of the common council. *Members of common council, not to hold certain other offices.*

§ 10. The common council shall have the management and control of the fiscal and prudential affairs of the city and of all property, real and personal, belonging to said city, and may make such orders and adopt such ordinances, and take such action in relation to the same as they shall deem proper and necessary. And the said common council shall also have the power to adopt, make, continue, modify and repeal such ordinances and regulations as they shall deem proper and necessary for the following purposes: *Jurisdiction of common council*

To preserve the public peace and good order, and to protect and preserve the property of said city and the property of the inhabitants thereof.

To prevent, restrain and suppress vice, immorality, gaming, drunkenness, fighting, any riot, rout, noise, disturbance, and all riotous and disorderly conduct and assemblages in any tavern, grocery, street or place within said city.

To suppress disorderly, gaming and bawdy houses, instruments and devices used for gaming, billiard tables and bowling alleys, and to restrain disorderly persons and vagrants.

To restrain and prevent the vending or other disposition of liquors and intoxicating drinks to be drank in any canal boat, store, or other place not duly licensed, and to forbid the selling or giving to be drank any intoxicating liquors to any minor without the consent of his or her parent, guardian or master.

To prohibit, restrain and regulate all shows, sports, exhibition of natural and artificial curiosities, caravans of animals, circuses, theatrical exhibitions, or other public performances and exhibitions, or to grant licenses therefor, under such restrictions as they may deem proper, and may receive for any such license a sum not exceeding twenty dollars for any one license.

To direct and regulate the location of all slaughter houses, abate or remove nuisances of every kind, and to compel the owner or occupant of any grocery, tallow chandlery shop, slaughter house, butcher's stall, soap factory, tannery, stable, privy, hog-pen, sewer, or other offensive and unwholesome house or place, to cleanse, remove or abate the same whenever the common council shall deem it necessary for the health and comfort of the inhabitants of said city and the enjoyment of their property by them.

To direct the location of all buildings for storing gunpowder or other combustible substances, and to regulate the sale and use of gunpowder, fire crackers, fireworks, or other combustible materials, the exhibition of fireworks, the discharge of firearms, the use of candles and lights in barns, stables and other buildings, and to restrain the making of bonfires in streets and yards.

To prevent the cumbering of the sidewalks, streets, avenues, walks, public squares, lanes, alleys, bridges and basins in said city, and the storing or piling thereon of casks, boxes, or other articles, and to regulate and prescribe as to the erection of awnings, signs and outside steps.

To prevent and punish horse racing and immoderate driving or riding in any street or avenue, and to authorize the stopping and detaining of any person who shall be guilty of immoderate driving or riding in any street or avenue in said city.

To restrain and regulate the rate of speed of locomotive engines and cars upon the railroads within said city, and to prevent the blowing of steam whistles, and the unnecessary interruption of the passage in the streets of said city, and to prescribe rules for and the warning to persons of the approach of locomotives in said city, and to prevent persons not employees or passengers on any engine or cars, from jumping on or off such engine or cars.

To fix and establish the lamp district within which the lamp tax shall be assessed and levied in said city.

To regulate and prohibit bathing in any public water.

To restrain drunkards, vagrants, disorderly persons, mendicants, street beggars and persons soliciting alms or subscriptions for any purpose whatever.

To establish and regulate pounds, and to regulate and restrain the running at large of horses, cattle, swine and other animals, geese and other poultry, and to authorize the impounding and sale of the same for the penalty incurred and the charges and fees for the keeping and impounding of the same, and to fix and determine such penalty, charges and fees.

To regulate and prevent the running at large of dogs, and to prevent dog fighting in said city.

To prohibit any person from bringing or depositing within the limits of said city, any dead carcass or other unwholesome or offensive substance, and to require the removal or destruction thereof, and of any putrid meats, fish, hides or skins of any kind, by any person who shall have the same upon his premises; and on his default, to authorize the removal or destruction thereof by some officer of the city.

To compel all persons to keep sidewalks in front of premises owned or occupied by them, clear from snow, ice, dirt, wood and obstructions.

To regulate the ringing of bells, and the crying of goods and other commodities for sale at auction or private sale, and to prohibit and prevent the blowing of horns, beating of pans, and other disturbing noises in said city.

To require the removal from the populous parts of the city of all persons having infectious or pestilential diseases.

To regulate the burial of the dead.

To establish order and regulate markets; to regulate the vending of wood, charcoal, hay, meats, vegetables, fruit, fish, and provisions of all kinds, and to prescribe the mode, time and place of selling the same, and the fees to be paid by butchers for license; but nothing herein contained shall authorize the common council to prevent the sale of wholesome meats by the quarter.

To establish and regulate the assize and quality of bread.

To establish, construct, regulate and preserve public cisterns, reservoirs, wells and pumps, and to prevent the waste of water.

To establish and regulate public scales, appoint weighers, and prescribe their fees.

To require and compel the destruction of Canada thistles and other noxious weeds.

To regulate sextons and undertakers for burying the dead, cartmen and their carts, hackney carriages and their drivers, scavengers, porters, and chimney sweeps, and their fees and compensation, and to prescribe the sum to be paid by them into the city treasury for license.

To prevent runners, stage drivers, hackmen or others, from soliciting persons to travel or ride in any stage, omnibus, carriage, boat, or upon any railroad, or to go to any hotel or other place of entertainment.

To provide for and regulate the lighting of streets and alleys, and the protection and safety of public lamps, and the lamps of citizens or of corporations.

To regulate and restrain hawking and peddling in the streets, and to regulate pawn-brokers, and to regulate and restrain auction sales and street sales by transient persons, and to grant licenses therefor under such regulations as the common council may prescribe, and may receive for any such license a sum not exceeding five dollars a day during the continuance thereof.

To protect and preserve shade trees in the streets, parks, squares, avenues, and alleys of said city.

To require every merchant or trader, or dealer in merchandise or property of any description, which is sold by measure or weight, to cause his weights or measures to be sealed by the city sealer and to be subject to his inspection.

To require, prescribe and regulate the building and maintaining of partition and street fences, and the fencing of vacant and other lots, and the erection and maintaining of balustrades on buildings in said city.

To prescribe the duties of all of the elective officers of said city, in addition to those herein prescribed, and to prescribe the duties, in addition to those herein prescribed, of all officers who receive their appointment from the common council.

To fix the compensation of all such officers, and mode of payment thereof, and the penalty for failing to perform their duties.

To require bonds for the faithful discharge of such duties; and to prescribe as to the penalty, condition, sureties and mode of execution of all official bonds to be given to said city, and the time for executing the same in cases not otherwise provided for in this act or by law.

To require the punctual attendance of the members of the common council and of its officers at the meetings thereof.

And, generally, to adopt such ordinances for the good government, order and safety of said city and the trade and manufactures therein, as the common council may deem necessary, not repugnant to the constitution or laws of this state, and not inconsistent with this act.

§ 11. Where, by the provisions of this act, the common council have authority to pass ordinances on any subject, it may punish any violation thereof by fine not exceeding one hundred dollars and the costs, the offender to stand committed until such fine and costs be paid, but such commitment shall in no case exceed six months; or, by imprisonment in the county jail, at hard labor or not, in the discretion of the police justice, for a period not exceeding six months, or by both such fine and imprisonment. And the police justice is hereby invested with power and authority to impose such fine and commitment, and sentence to such imprisonment, under any such ordinance, and to carry such judgment of commitment and imprisonment into effect by a warrant of conviction under his hand, to be issued to the keeper of the county jail. Or the said common council, instead imposing such fine and imprisonment for the violation of any such ordinance, may prescribe any penalty not exceeding one hundred dollars for a violation thereof, and may provide that the offender on failing to pay the penalty recovered, shall be imprisoned in the common jail of Schenectady county for any term not exceeding thirty days; which penalties may be sued for and recovered with costs in the name of said city.

§ 12. No ordinance of the common council imposing Ordinance. a penalty shall take effect until the expiration of at least three days after the first publication thereof in a newspaper of said city. A record or entry of the first publication thereof made by the city clerk, or a copy of such record or entry duly certified by him, shall be *prima facie* evidence of such first publication. And all ordinances and regulations of the common council may be read in evidence in all courts of

83

justice, and in all proceedings before any officer, body or board in which it shall be necessary to refer thereto, either from a copy thereof certified by the city clerk with the common seal of said city affixed, or from the volume of ordinances printed by authority of the common council.

Lock-up. § 13. The common council may establish a "lock-up" for the temporary detention of vagrants, intoxicated or disorderly persons, petty offenders, or persons held for examinations or trial before the police justice, and may appoint during pleasure a person to take charge thereof, and fix his compensation, and may pass ordinances regulating said "lock-up" and prescribing the duties of the person in charge thereof; but no person shall be detained in said "lock-up" for more than twenty-four hours.

Salaries. § 14. The common council shall, in the month of March in each year, after the passage of this act, fix the salaries or compensation of all officers to be elected at the then succeeding charter election or to be appointed by the succeeding common council, which salaries or compensation shall not be increased or diminished during the term of office of any such officer; and if, from any cause, the common council shall fail to fix such salaries or compensation as herein directed, then they shall continue as previously fixed until they shall be changed by the common council pursuant to this section; any person appointed or elected to fill any vacancy shall receive the salary or compensation pro rata of the officer whose place he supplies.

Constables. § 15. The common council shall have the power, when, in its judgment the public safety or preservation of good order require it, to appoint special constables, not exceeding ten in number, whose time of service shall be limited in the resolution appointing them, and shall not exceed forty-eight hours in any case. A certificate of such appointment, signed by the city clerk, shall be authority for any person so appointed to act as such special constable and the special constables so appointed shall possess all the powers of any constable of the county of Schenectady, except the service of process in civil actions.

TITLE IV.

POWERS AND DUTIES OF CITY OFFICERS.

§ 1. It shall be the duty of the mayor to take care that Mayor. the laws of the state and the ordinances of the common council be faithfully executed; to exercise a constant supervision and control over the conduct of all subordinate officers, and to receive and examine into all complaints against them relative to the discharge of their duties; to attend the meetings of and to recommend to the common council such measures as he shall deem expedient, and, in general, to maintain the peace and good order of the city. He shall have the power, when, in his judgment, the public safety or preservation of good order shall require it, to appoint special constables, not exceeding five in number, whose time of service shall be limited in the order appointing them, and shall not exceed twenty-four hours in any case; such appointment shall be in writing, dated and subscribed by the mayor, and shall be filed by him with the city clerk. A copy thereof shall be delivered to the person appointed, and shall be his authority for acting. In case of the absence or inability to act of the mayor, this power of appointment may be exercised by the person acting as mayor for the time being. Such special constables so appointed shall possess all the powers of any constable of the county of Schenectady, except the service of process in civil actions.

§ 2. It shall be the duty of the recorder to attend the Recorder. meetings of the common council, and in the absence or inability to act of the mayor, he shall discharge the duties of that office, and he is, in such case, hereby invested with power so to do.

§ 3. It shall be the duty of every alderman in said Alderman city to attend all the meetings of the common council; to act upon committees when thereupon duly appointed; and he may arrest or order the arrest of all persons violating the laws of the state or the ordinances, or police regulations of the city; to report to the mayor all subordinate officers who are guilty of any official misconduct or neglect of duty; and to aid in maintaining peace and good order.

§ 4. The mayor, recorder and aldermen of said city, by virtue of their office, shall have and exercise all the

power and authority of justice of the peace, in the towns
of this state, in criminal cases, and in enforcing the
laws of this state relating to the police thereof.

Treasurer.   § 5. The treasurer shall collect and receive all moneys
belonging to the city ; he shall be receiver of all taxes
assessed or collected in said city, and shall deposit and
keep all moneys that shall be received by him, and shall
keep accounts of all his receipts and disbursements in
such manner as the common council shall direct, and at
the expiration of his office he shall render a just and
true account of all moneys received and disbursed by
him as treasurer, and shall pay over to his successor in
office all moneys remaining in his hands, received by him
as such treasurer, and shall deliver to such successor all
the books, deeds, securities and other papers and property in his possession belonging to said city, or which
said city shall have placed in his hands for safe keeping ;
he shall also, on or before the first Tuesday of May in
each year, execute to the city of Schenectady, and deliver the same to the common council at their annual
meeting a bond, with two or more sureties, in such
penalty as the common council shall direct, not less than
ten thousand dollars, conditioned that he will faithfully
perform all the duties of the office of treasurer of the
city of Schenectady, and will account for and pay over
all moneys in his hands whenever required to do so by
the common council or by law ; he shall have the custody of the common seal of said city ; and he shall keep
the maps, deeds, leases and all other evidences of title
or of debt, and other valuable papers belonging to said
city ; he shall pay no money from the city treasury
except in pursuance of the order or resolution of the
common council, to be certified and signed by the clerk
thereof ; the books and accounts of the treasurer shall,
at all reasonable hours, be open to the examination of
any member of the common council of said city ; and
he shall, between the first and fifteenth day of March in
each year, transmit to the mayor, to be presented to the
common council, and shall publish in a newspaper, a
detailed statement of the funds and property of said
city, and of its debt and time of maturity thereof, with
a full account, under appropriate heads, of all his receipts and disbursements for the last preceding year,
which statement shall be signed and verified by him to

the effect that the same is correct and true, and that there are no errors or omissions therein, so far as he knows or believes.

§ 6. It shall be the duty of the superintendent of streets to superintend, under the direction of the common council, or their committee on roads and bridges, all work to be done, performed or ordered, or required to be done or performed upon or in relation to any of the public streets, walks, bridges, sewers, reservoirs, wells or public pumps of said city.

§ 7. The clerk shall attend the meetings of the common council, and keep a book in which he shall record the minutes in full of all its proceedings, and in which he shall also record at length all ordinances adopted by the common council; and all official bonds given by any officer to said city, and which shall be approved and accepted by the common council, or which shall be required by this act to be recorded by him, and shall keep all papers that by any provision of law, or by direction of the common council, shall be required to be filed with or kept by him; and copies of all papers filed in his office, and transcripts from his book of minutes, including bonds and other instruments in writing, required by this act to be recorded therein, when certified by him under the common seal of said city, shall be evidence in all places of the matters therein contained.

§ 8. The assessors, justices of the peace, supervisors, overseers of the poor, inspectors of election, commissioners of deeds, and constables provided to be elected or appointed under this act, shall severally have and exercise all the powers, and perform all the duties, and be subject to all the provisions of law now applicable to those officers respectively in the several towns of this state, except as limited by this act or as shall be inconsistent therewith. Commissioners of deeds shall have and exercise the powers heretofore exercised by those officers in cities, but they may discharge their duties at any place within the county of Schenectady, and the justices of the peace of said city shall not act as commissioners of deeds.

§ 9. The supervisors to be elected under this act shall be members of the board of supervisors of the county of Schenectady, and shall be entitled to the same compensation, to be paid in the same manner.

Jurors.

§ 10. The supervisors of the said city, with the assessors, shall make out and return to the county clerk of Schenectady county a list of persons to serve as petit jurors and as grand jurors in the several courts held in said county, at the same time and in the same manner prescribed by law for supervisors, assessors and town clerks of the several towns of this state, and for that purpose they shall assemble at such place as a majority of said supervisors shall appoint.

Term of office.

§ 11. All officers provided to be elected or appointed under this act, shall hold their offices for the terms herein respectively limited, and until their successors shall be elected and duly qualified to serve.

Official bonds.

§ 12. The official bonds of all persons elected or appointed to any office in said city under this act, who are required by the laws of this state, or by this act, to give bonds, shall be executed to the city of Schenectady, and shall be acknowledged or proved in the manner provided by law for the acknowledgment or proof of conveyances of real estate, and except where otherwise directed by this act, shall be approved and accepted by the common council. After being so approved and accepted, such bonds shall be recorded at length in the minutes of the common council as hereinbefore directed, and be deposited with the mayor of the city for safe keeping, and it shall be his duty to deliver the same to his successor in office.

Ibid.

§ 13. Every person elected or appointed to the office of constable in said city, shall execute with two or more sureties a joint and several bond in such penalty as the common council shall direct, conditioned that such constable will faithfully discharge all the duties of the office of constable, and that he will pay to each and every person who may be entitled thereto all such sums of money as he may become liable to pay, on account of any execution that may be delivered to him for collection. And upon any default of said constable in collecting any execution when collectable, or in returning any execution when returnable, or in paying over any money collected by virtue of any execution, or to discharge any other of the duties of said office, the person aggrieved, may, in his own name, prosecute upon said bond, and recover of said constable and his sureties, or any or either of them, the sum, with interest, to which he may be entitled on account of any such execution delivered to said constable, or he may recover the damages which such person may have sustained by reason of the default of said constable in performing any of the other duties of said office; but no such action shall be brought after the expiration of two years from the commencement of the term of office of such constable.

TITLE V.

TAXES AND FINANCES.

§ 1. The assessors to be elected under this act, shall Assessors. be a board of assessors, and shall meet in said city on the first Monday of May in each year, and elect one of their number chairman; and between that day and the first day of July in each year, they shall assess, in the manner provided by law, all property, real and personal, in said city, not exempt by law from taxation; and in making such assessments they shall provide and use a separate book for each ward.

§ 2. The assessors, after completing their assessment Notice. rolls, instead of posting notice thereof, shall give such notice by publishing the same for three weeks in two newspapers published in said city.

§ 3. The said assessors shall each be paid for his ser- Pay of assessors. vices under this act, a sum not exceeding one hundred dollars in any one year, which compensation shall be fixed by the common council as hereinbefore provided.

§ 4. The common council shall examine, settle and Accounts. allow all accounts chargeable against the city as well of other persons as of its officers; and shall have authority to direct the raising of such sums as shall be necessary to defray the same, and the contingent expenses of the said city, and such other sums as they are by this act required to raise, subject to the limitations and restriction herein contained.

§ 5. The common council of the city of Schenectady Tax may raise annually by tax, for the purpose of constructing and repairing highways and bridges, and the necessary public buildings and constructions of said city, for providing necessary apparatus and means for the prevention and extinguishment of fires, for lighting the streets of said city, for defraying the expenses of the poor of said city, for defraying the expenses of the police of said city, for salaries of officers of said city, and for necessary contingent expenses of said city, a sum not exceeding in the aggregate seventeen thousand dollars, the amount required to be raised under each head to be specified separately.

Ibid. § 6. The said common council shall make up on the first Tuesday of November in each year, an account of the city expenditures from and including the first day of March preceding to that date for the several purposes named in the last preceding section, and shall at the same time estimate the expenditures to be incurred for the same purpose, to and including the last day of February thereafter; and it shall be the duty of the said common council to be caused to be raised by tax, in the mode now provided by law, the entire amount, after deducting the moneys received by the common council, which are applicable thereto, of such ascertained and estimated expenditures, not exceeding the aforesaid sum of seventeen thousand dollars; and shall also cause to be raised, by tax, such sum as the board of education shall, in the manner hereinafter provided, certify to be necessary for school purposes, and such further sum as shall be necessary to pay the city debt, and interest thereon, and which shall become due prior to the first of March of the next ensuing fiscal year; and the moneys so to be raised shall be applied to the purposes for which they were raised; and the said common council shall pay such city debt as it shall become due; and the said common council shall not incur any expenditure or liability for any purpose whatever, except those named in the last preceding section, nor beyond the aforesaid sum of seventeen thousand dollars, except for school purposes as hereinafter provided.

To be levied § 7. The board of supervisors of the county of Schenectady, on being served with copies of the resolution of said common council, requiring the several sums of money to be raised as aforesaid, shall cause the same to be assessed, levied and collected, with the other taxes to be collected in said city, according to law, and paid to the treasurer of the said city in the manner directed in and by this act, which several amounts shall be expended and applied under the direction of the common council, for the purposes for which the same were raised, assessed and collected; and the treasurer of the said city is hereby required to keep separate accounts of the same; and it shall be the duty of the said city treasurer to pay over to the county treasurer the state and county taxes to be collected in said city, at the time and in the manner the town collectors are required to do.

§ 8. The supervisor of each ward shall, on or before the fifteenth day of December in each year, deliver to the said treasurer the tax list for his ward, with the warrant of the board of supervisors for the collection thereof. All taxes assessed in said city may be paid to said treasurer, without any charge for collecting, for thirty days after said treasurer shall have given public notice of receiving said tax lists in the city newspapers, which notice it shall be his duty to give immediately after receiving said tax lists. *Warrant to collector.*

§ 9. The constable elected in each ward of said city shall also be collector of taxes in his ward. He shall within five days after being notified by the treasurer that the tax list is ready for him, give bond for the faithful discharge of his duty as such collector, in such form, penalty and security as shall be approved of by the mayor and treasurer of said city; and shall collect and pay to the city treasurer all moneys assessed and to be collected in his tax list within the time required by law. But in case any such collector shall refuse or neglect to enter into the said bond, or if from any cause he shall be incapable of serving, then, and in such case, the mayor of said city shall appoint some suitable person to act in his stead, who shall give the like security, and have the same powers and perform the duties required of said collector. The bonds required to be taken under this section, shall be reported and delivered by the mayor to the common council at its next meeting, and shall be recorded by the clerk as hereinbefore provided, and be deposited with the mayor for safe keeping. *Constable to be collector.*

§ 10. After the expiration of said thirty days and upon the giving of the bond by the collector as above required, the said tax lists, with a warrant to collect the same, shall be delivered over by the treasurer to the collector of each ward, who shall collect and pay over the same to the city treasurer within the time required by law, and may charge and collect for his fees, in addition to the tax on each inhabitant, five per cent. on the amount of such tax collected by him. *Tax list and warrant.*

84

§ 11. The proceeds of the property of the city of Schenectady shall, when sold, be applied to the payment of the debts of said city.

Deposits.

§ 12. The board of managers of the Schenectady Savings Bank are hereby authorized to invest in any stock or bonds issued or to be issued by the city of Schenectady, pursuant to law, in addition to the stocks in which they are now authorized to invest by their charter, so much of their deposits as they shall deem advisable.

Exemption.

§ 13. All the estate, real and personal, situate within the city of Schenectady, lying outside of the boundaries as said city existed under and by virtue of chapter two hundered and fifteen of the Laws of eighteen hundred and fifty-three, shall be and is hereby declared exempt from assessment and taxation for the purposes of raising money to pay the expense of the lamp department, the expense of the fire department.

TITLE VI.

PUBLIC SCHOOLS AND EDUCATION.

Commissioner.

§ 1. There shall be elected in said city, at a special election to be held on the first Tuesday of May in each year, in the same manner and under the same regulations as other ward officers are elected, one commisioner of common schools for each ward, to supply the places of those whose terms are about to expire; they shall hold their offices for two years, and until others are elected and have taken the oath of office. The term of office of all the commissioners elected pursuant to this title shall commence on the Tuesday next after the election.

Vacancies.

§ 2 The common council of said city may make appointments of commissioners of common schools to fill vacancies which may occur from any other cause than the expiration of the term of office of those elected. The commissioners so appointed, shall hold their office until the Tuesday next succeeding the next annual election; and at each annual election there shall be chosen a commissioner to supply the place of any person so appointed, and the person thus elected shall serve out the unexpired term.

Removal

§ 3. Any commissioner of common schools in said city may be removed from office for official misconduct, by the common council of said city, by a vote of two-thirds of the members thereof; but a written copy of the charges preferred against said commissioner shall be served upon him, and he shall be allowed an opportunity of refuting any such charges of misconduct before removal.

§ 4. The commissioners of common schools in said city shall constitute a board to be styled "The Board of Education of the City of Schenectady," which shall be a corporate body in relation to all the powers and duties conferred upon them by virtue of this title. A majority of the board shall constitute a quorum. The annual meeting of said board shall be held on the Wednesday succeeding the second Tuesday of May in each year. At such annual meeting they shall elect one of their number president of the board, and whenever he shall be absent, a president pro tempore may be appointed. The said commissioners shall receive no compensation for their services, nor shall they be interested, directly or indirectly, in any contract for building or for making any improvement or repairs provided for by this title. *Board of education.*

§ 5. The said commissioners shall meet for the transaction of business as often as once in each month, and may adjourn for any shorter time. Special meetings may be called by the president, or in his absence or inability to act, by any member of the board, as often as necessary, by giving personal notice to each member of the board, or by causing a written or printed notice to be left at his last place of residence at least twenty-four hours before the hour for such special meeting. *Meetings.*

§ 6. The said commissioners shall appoint a secretary and librarian, who shall hold his office during the pleasure of the board, and whose compensation shall be fixed by the board. The said secretary shall keep a record of the proceedings of the board, have charge of the library, and perform such other duties as the board may prescribe. The said record or transcript thereof certified by the secretary, shall be received in all courts as prima facie evidence of the matters therein set forth; and such record, and all the books, accounts, vouchers and papers of said board, shall at all times be subject to the inspection of the common council or any committee thereof. *Secretary and librarian.*

§ 7. The common council of said city shall have power, and it shall be its duty, to raise from time to time by tax, to be levied upon all the real and personal estate in said city which shall be liable to taxation for city and county charges, in like manner as other city taxes are raised, such sums as may be determined and certified by the said board of education to be necessary and proper for any and all of the following purposes:

1. To purchase, lease or improve sites for school houses, or sites with buildings thereon for the same purpose.

2. To build, purchase, lease, enlarge, alter, improve and repair school houses, and their outhouses and appurtenances.

3. To purchase, exchange, improve and repair school apparatus, books, furniture and appendages; but the power herein granted shall not be deemed to authorize the furnishing with class or text books any scholar whose parents or guardian shall be able to furnish the same.

4. To procure fuel and defray the contingent expenses of the common schools, including the academical department therein and the expenses of the school library of said city, and the necessary contingent expenses of said board, including the salary of the secretary of the board, and the compensation allowed to the assistant librarians.

5. To pay teachers' wages after the application of public moneys which may by law be appropriated and provided for that purpose.

6. The amount raised for teachers' wages and contingent expenses shall not exceed the sum of ten thousand dollars in any one year, nor shall there be raised in any one year for buying sites, or sites with buildings thereon, erecting and repairing school houses and the appurtenances, a sum exceeding two thousand dollars, except as herein otherwise provided for. And the common council is authorized and directed to borrow, upon the promissory note of the city in anticipation of the amount to be raised by tax as aforesaid, such sums as the board of education shall from time to time certify is required by it.

§ 8. All moneys to be raised pursuant to the provisions of this title, and all school moneys by law appropriated

Purposes thereof.

Not to exceed $10,000 in any one year.

Monies paid to Treasurer.

to or provided for said city, whether from the school or literature funds, or under the act to establish free schools throughout the state, or otherwise, shall be paid to the treasurer of said city, who, together with the sureties on his official bond, shall be accountable therefor, in the same manner as for other moneys of said city. The said treasurer shall be liable to the same penalties *Penalties.* for official misconduct in relation to the said money as for any similar misconduct in relation to other moneys of said city.

§ 9. All moneys required to be raised by virtue of this *Deposits where made* title, or received by said city for the use of the common schools therein, or of the academical department hereinafter mentioned, shall be deposited for the safe keeping thereof with the treasurer of said city, to the credit of said board of education, until drawn from said treasurer as hereinafter provided for; and the said treasurer shall keep the fund authorized by this title to be received by him, separate and distinct from any other funds which he is or may by law be authorized to receive.

§ 10. The treasurer shall pay out the moneys autho- *Drafts.* rized by this title to be received by him, upon drafts drawn by the president and countersigned by the secretary of said board of education, which drafts shall not be drawn except in pursuance of a resolution or resolutions of said board, and shall be made payable to the person or persons entitled to receive said money.

§ 11. The said board shall have power and it shall be *Powers of board.* its duty:

1. To organize and establish such and so many schools in said city as it shall deem requisite and expedient, and to alter and discontinue the same.

2. To purchase and hire school houses and rooms, lots, or sites for school houses, or sites with buildings thereon to be used as school houses, and to fence and improve such sites, as it may deem proper.

3. Upon such lots and upon such sites, owned by said city, to build, enlarge, alter, improve and repair school houses, out houses and appurtenances, as it may deem advisable.

4. To have the custody and safe keeping of the school houses, out houses, books, furniture and appurtenances, and to see that the ordinances of the common council in relation thereto be observed.

5. To contract with, license and employ all teachers in said schools and the academical department therein, and at its pleasure to remove them.

6 To pay the wages of the teachers in said schools out of the moneys appropriated and provided by law for the support of common schools in said city, and the wages of the teachers of the academical department out of the moneys appropriated to said department from the income of the literature and United States deposite funds, so far as the same shall be sufficient, and the residue of the wages of the teachers in said schools and academical department from the money authorized to be raised for that purpose, by section seven of this title, by tax upon said city.

7. To defray the contingent expenses of the said common schools and academical department, and the expenses of the school library of said city, and the necessary and contingent expenses of the board, including the annual salary of the secretary of the board, and the compensation allowed to the assistant librarians, provided the account of such expenses shall first be audited and allowed by the common council.

8. To have in all respects the superintendence, supervison and management of the common schools of said city, and, from time to time, to adopt, alter, modify and repeal, as they may deem expedient, rules and regulations for their organization, government and instruction, or the reception of pupils and their transfer from one school to another, and generally for their good order, prosperity and utility; and to have power to establish in said schools an academical department, to receive into said schools or academical department pupils residing out of said city, and to regulate and establish the tuition fees of such non-resident pupils in the several departments of said schools and in such academical department, and to collect such fees in the name of the said city ; to regulate the transfer of scholars from the primary to the academical departments; to direct what text books shall be used in said schools and academical department ; to provide and keep in repair school apparatus, books for indigent pupils, furniture and appendages, fuel and other necessaries for the schools and academical department; and to appoint assistant libra-

rians as they may, from time to time, deem necessary, and to regulate their compensation.

9. Whenever, in the opinion of the board of education, it may be advisable to sell any of the school houses, lots, or sites, or any of the school property now or hereafter belonging to the city, to report the same to the common council.

10. To prepare and report to the common council such ordinances and regulations as may be necessary and proper for the protection, safe keeping, care and preservation of school houses, lots and sites, and appurtenances, and all the property belonging to the city connected with or appertaining to the schools; and annually; on or before the first day of June, in each year, to determine and certify to the said common council the sums, in their opinion, necessary or proper to be raised under the seventh section of this title for the year commencing on the first day of July thereafter, specifying the amount required for each of the purposes therein mentioned, and the reason therefor.

11. Between the first day of July and the first day of August, in each year, to make and transmit to the county clerk, or such other officer as may be designated by law, a report, in writing, bearing date the first day of July, in the year of its transmission, and stating:

1. The number of school houses in said city, and an account and description of all common schools kept in said city during the preceding year, and the time they have severally been taught.

2. The number of children taught in said schools respectively, and the number of children over the age of four years, and under the age of twenty-one years, residing in said city, on the first day of January in each year.

3. The whole amount of school moneys received by the treasurer of said city during the preceding year, distinguishing the amount received by him from the city tax and from any other source.

4 The manner in which such moneys have been expended, and whether any and what part remains unexpended, and for what cause.

5. The amount of moneys received for tuition fees from foreign pupils during the year, and the amount paid for teachers' wages in addition to the public moneys,

5. To contract with, license and employ all teachers in said schools and the academical department therein, and at its pleasure to remove them.

6 To pay the wages of the teachers in said schools out of the moneys appropriated and provided by law for the support of common schools in said city, and the wages of the teachers of the academical department out of the moneys appropriated to said department from the income of the literature and United States deposite funds, so far as the same shall be sufficient, and the residue of the wages of the teachers in said schools and academical department from the money authorized to be raised for that purpose, by section seven of this title, by tax upon said city.

7. To defray the contingent expenses of the said common schools and academical department, and the expenses of the school library of said city, and the necessary and contingent expenses of the board, including the annual salary of the secretary of the board, and the compensation allowed to the assistant librarians, provided the account of such expenses shall first be audited and allowed by the common council.

8. To have in all respects the superintendence, supervison and management of the common schools of said city, and, from time to time, to adopt, alter, modify and repeal, as they may deem expedient, rules and regulations for their organization, government and instruction, or the reception of pupils and their transfer from one school to another, and generally for their good order, prosperity and utility; and to have power to establish in said schools an academical department, to receive into said schools or academical department pupils residing out of said city, and to regulate and establish the tuition fees of such non-resident pupils in the several departments of said schools and in such academical department, and to collect such fees in the name of the said city ; to regulate the transfer of scholars from the primary to the academical departments; to direct what text books shall be used in said schools and academical department ; to provide and keep in repair school apparatus, books for indigent pupils, furniture and appendages, fuel and other necessaries for the schools and academical department; and to appoint assistant libra-

rians as they may, from time to time, deem necessary, and to regulate their compensation.

9. Whenever, in the opinion of the board of education, it may be advisable to sell any of the school houses, lots, or sites, or any of the school property now or hereafter belonging to the city, to report the same to the common council.

10. To prepare and report to the common council such ordinances and regulations as may be necessary and proper for the protection, safe keeping, care and preservation of school houses, lots and sites, and appurtenances, and all the property belonging to the city connected with or appertaining to the schools; and annually, on or before the first day of June, in each year, to determine and certify to the said common council the sums, in their opinion, necessary or proper to be raised under the seventh section of this title for the year commencing on the first day of July thereafter, specifying the amount required for each of the purposes therein mentioned, and the reason therefor.

11. Between the first day of July and the first day of August, in each year, to make and transmit to the county clerk, or such other officer as may be designated by law, a report, in writing, bearing date the first day of July, in the year of its transmission, and stating:

1. The number of school houses in said city, and an account and description of all common schools kept in said city during the preceding year, and the time they have severally been taught.

2. The number of children taught in said schools respectively, and the number of children over the age of four years, and under the age of twenty-one years, residing in said city, on the first day of January in each year.

3. The whole amount of school moneys received by the treasurer of said city during the preceding year, distinguishing the amount received by him from the city tax and from any other source.

4 The manner in which such moneys have been expended, and whether any and what part remains unexpended, and for what cause.

5. The amount of moneys received for tuition fees from foreign pupils during the year, and the amount paid for teachers' wages in addition to the public moneys,

5. To contract with, license and employ all teachers in said schools and the academical department therein, and at its pleasure to remove them.

6 To pay the wages of the teachers in said schools out of the moneys appropriated and provided by law for the support of common schools in said city, and the wages of the teachers of the academical department out of the moneys appropriated to said department from the income of the literature and United States deposite funds, so far as the same shall be sufficient, and the residue of the wages of the teachers in said schools and academical department from the money authorized to be raised for that purpose, by section seven of this title, by tax upon said city.

7. To defray the contingent expenses of the said common schools and academical department, and the expenses of the school library of said city, and the necessary and contingent expenses of the board, including the annual salary of the secretary of the board, and the compensation allowed to the assistant librarians, provided the account of such expenses shall first be audited and allowed by the common council.

8. To have in all respects the superintendence, supervison and management of the common schools of said city, and, from time to time, to adopt, alter, modify and repeal, as they may deem expedient, rules and regulations for their organization, government and instruction, or the reception of pupils and their transfer from one school to another, and generally for their good order, prosperity and utility; and to have power to establish in said schools an academical department, to receive into said schools or academical department pupils residing out of said city, and to regulate and establish the tuition fees of such non-resident pupils in the several departments of said schools and in such academical department, and to collect such fees in the name of the said city ; to regulate the transfer of scholars from the primary to the academical departments; to direct what text books shall be used in said schools and academical department ; to provide and keep in repair school apparatus, books for indigent pupils, furniture and appendages, fuel and other necessaries for the schools and academical department; and to appoint assistant libra-

rians as they may, from time to time, deem necessary, and to regulate their compensation.

9. Whenever, in the opinion of the board of education, it may be advisable to sell any of the school houses, lots, or sites, or any of the school property now or hereafter belonging to the city, to report the same to the common council.

10. To prepare and report to the common council such ordinances and regulations as may be necessary and proper for the protection, safe keeping, care and preservation of school houses, lots and sites, and appurtenances, and all the property belonging to the city connected with or appertaining to the schools; and annually; on or before the first day of June, in each year, to determine and certify to the said common council the sums, in their opinion, necessary or proper to be raised under the seventh section of this title for the year commencing on the first day of July thereafter, specifying the amount required for each of the purposes therein mentioned, and the reason therefor.

11. Between the first day of July and the first day of August, in each year, to make and transmit to the county clerk, or such other officer as may be designated by law, a report, in writing, bearing date the first day of July, in the year of its transmission, and stating:

1. The number of school houses in said city, and an account and description of all common schools kept in said city during the preceding year, and the time they have severally been taught.

2. The number of children taught in said schools respectively, and the number of children over the age of four years, and under the age of twenty-one years, residing in said city, on the first day of January in each year.

3. The whole amount of school moneys received by the treasurer of said city during the preceding year, distinguishing the amount received by him from the city tax and from any other source.

4 The manner in which such moneys have been expended, and whether any and what part remains unexpended, and for what cause.

5. The amount of moneys received for tuition fees from foreign pupils during the year, and the amount paid for teachers' wages in addition to the public moneys,

with such other information relating to the common schools of said city as may, from time to time, be required by the State Superintendent of Common Schools.

School commissioner. § 12. Each school commissioner shall visit all the schools in said city, at least twice in each year of his official term ; and said board of education shall provide, that each of said schools shall be visited by a committee of three or more of its number at least once in each term.

Duty of board. § 13. It shall be the duty of said board, in all its expenditures and contracts, to have reference to the amount of moneys which shall be subject to its order during the then current year, for the particular expenditures in question, and not to exceed that amount.

Trustees of school library. § 14. The said board of commissioners shall be trustees of the school libraries in said city, and all the provisions of law which now are or hereafter may be passed relative to school district libraries, shall apply to said commissioners in the same manner as if they were trustees of a school district comprehending said city ; they shall, also, be vested with the same discretion as to the disposition of the moneys appropriated by the laws of this state for the purchase of libraries, which is therein conferred on the inhabitants of school districts ; it shall be their duty to provide room or rooms for such libraries, and the necessary furniture therefor ; the librarian shall report to the board the condition of the library or the libraries under his charge; and the said board or secretary thereof, under the direction and by the resolution of said board, may make all purchases of books for said library or libraries, and may direct the mode of their distribution, and may cause to be repaired damaged books belonging thereto, and may sell any book in said library or libraries that may be deemed useless, and apply the proceeds to the purchase of other books for said library or libraries.

Title of property. § 15. The title of the school houses, sites, lots, furniture, books, apparatus and appurtenances, and all other school property in this title mentioned, shall be vested in the city of Schenectady, and the same while used or appropriated for school purposes, shall not be levied upon or sold by virtue of any warrant or execution, nor be subject to taxation for any purpose whatever ; and the said city, in its corporate capacity, shall be able to take and hold any personal or real estate transferred to it by grants, gifts, devise or bequest, in trust for the benefit of the common schools of said city, or of the academical department therein, whether the same be transferred in terms to said city, by its corporate name, or by any other designation, or to any person or persons, or bodies for the benefit of said schools or academical department.

§ 16. The common council of said city shall, upon the recommendation of said board of education, sell any of the school houses, sites, lots, or any of the school property now or hereafter belonging to said city, upon such terms as the common council shall deem reasonable ; the proceeds of all such sales shall be paid to the treasurer of said city, and shall be, by said board, expended in the purchase, repairs or other improvement of school houses, lots, or school furniture, apparatus or appurtenances. *Sales of property.*

§ 17. It shall be the duty of said board, at least fifteen days before the annual election for commissioners, in each year, to prepare and report to the common council true and correct statements of the receipts and disbursements of moneys under and in pursuance of the provisions of this title, during the preceding year, in which account shall be stated under appropriate heads : *Report of commissioners.*

1. The moneys raised by the common council, under the seventh section of this title. *What to contain.*

2. The school moneys received by the treasurer of the city from the county treasurer.

3. The money received by the treasurer of the city, under the seventh section of this title.

4. All other moneys received by the treasurer of said city, subject to the order of the board, specifying the sources from which they shall have been derived.

5. The manner in which sums of money shall have been expended, specifying the amount under each head of expenditure ; and the common council shall, at least ten days before such election, cause the same to be published in all newspaper* of said city.

§ 18. The common council shall have power, and it shall be its duty to pass such ordinances and regulations as the said board may report as necessary for the protection, preservation, safe keeping and care of the school houses, lots, sites, appurtenances and appendages, libraries and all necessary property belonging to or connected *Ordinances relating to school houses &c.*

* So in the original.

with the schools of said city, and to impose such penalties for the violation thereof as the common council are authorized to impose by this act, and when collected to be paid to the treasurer of the city, to the credit of the said board of education, and shall be subject to its order in the same manner as other moneys raised, pursuant to the provisions of this title.

Notice of election to commissioner. § 19. It shall be the duty of the clerk of said city, immediately after the election of any person as commissioner of common schools, personally or in writing to notify him of his election, and if any such person shall not, within ten days after receiving such notice of his election, take and subscribe the constitutional oath, and file the same with the clerk of said city, the common council may consider it as a refusal to serve, and proceed to supply the vacancy occasioned by such refusal, and the person so refusing shall forfeit and pay to the city treasurer, for the benefit of the schools of said city, a penalty of ten dollars.

Regents. § 20. Every academical department, to be established as aforesaid, shall be under the visitation of the Regents of the University, and shall be subject, in its course of education and matters pertaining thereto, (but not in reference to the buildings or erections in which the same is conducted, unless in case the buildings or erections aforesaid are separate from those of the common school department) to all the regulations made in regard to academies by the said Regents, and in such department the qualifications for the entrance of any pupil shall be the same as those established by the said Regents for admission into any academy of the state under their supervision; and such academical department shall share in the distribution of the income of the Literature Fund, and of the income of the United States Deposit Fund, with academies in the state subject to the visitation of the Regents.

Board may purchase certain property. § 21. The said board of education shall have power to purchase, in the corporate name of the city of Schenectady, from the trustees of Union College, and the said trustees of Union College shall have power to sell and convey to said city, the building called the west college, and the buildings connected therewith, and the site on which they stand, situate on Union street, in said city, and lying between College street and the Erie canal, and the New York Central Railroad, for the use of the said common schools and academical department, and upon such trusts and upon such terms, and subject to such conditions, as shall be agreed upon by and between the said board of education and the said trustees of Union College; and said buildings and premises, after the same shall be conveyed to the city of Schenectady, in pursuance of such agreement, shall be held by said city for such uses and purpose, and upon such trusts, and subject to such conditions, as shall so be agreed upon, and as shall be specified in the deed of conveyance. The preceding provisions of this title in relation to the purchase of school houses, sites and lots, and other real property, and to the taking, holding, disposition and sale of the same, so far as the same are inconsistent with this section, shall not be applicable to the purchase, sale, and conveyance authorized in this section.

§ 22. The said board of education and the said trustees of Union College shall have power, from time to time, to enter into such contracts as they may deem expedient in relation to the organization, superintendence and management of the said academical department, the prescribing the course of studies and system of discipline, and the appointment and payment of the professors and teachers in such academical department; and also in relation to the terms upon which the pupils in said academical department may receive books from the libraries of Union College or attend the lectures of the professors in said college, or be admitted, when prepared, as members in full standing of its several classes; such contract, when entered into, shall be binding on said board of education and the said trustees of Union College, and shall be faithfully executed. The preceding provisions of this title, in relation to the powers and duties of said board of education, in reference to the academical department, shall be deemed modified by this section, and such powers and duties shall be exercised only in conformity to the contracts which may be entered into under this section.

§ 23. This title shall extend over and be applicable to all the territory lying within the corporate limits of said city; and the office of town superintendent of common schools, so far as it is applicable to the said city of Schenectady, is hereby abolished.

TITLE VII.

STREETS AND PUBLIC IMPROVEMENTS.

Commis-
sioners of
highways. § 1. The common council shall be commissioners of highways in said city; and it may invest any three of its members with power to lay out, alter or discontinue any street, highway or lane, in the mode now provided by law for laying out, altering or discontinuing highways in towns, subject however to the approval of the common council; and the same appeal shall lie from the decision of the common council, and the same proceedings shall be had on such appeal, and other appeals may be taken by either party as are now provided by law as aforesaid; or the said common council may open, widen or improve any street, highway, lane, walk, square or park, at the expense of the owners of houses or lots intended to* benefited thereby, in the mode hereinafter provided.

Care of
streets. § 2. The common council shall have the care and superintendence of the streets, highways, lanes, alleys, bridges, parks and public squares in said city, and of the sewers, vaults, drains, wells, pumps and reservoirs therein; and shall have the power to cause sewers, vaults, drains, wells, reservoirs, bridges, arches and pumps, to be constructed or repaired either at the expense of the city or at the expense of the owners of houses or lots intended to be benefited thereby, in the mode hereinafter provided.

§ 3. The common council shall have power:

Powers of
common
council. 1. To direct and require the repairing and preservation of the streets, bridges, lanes, alleys, parks and public squares, and cause them to be repaired, cleansed, improved and secured from time to time as may be necessary.

2. To regulate the roads, streets, lanes, parks, and alleys already laid out, or which shall hereafter be laid out, and to alter such of them as it shall deem inconvenient, subject to the restrictions hereinafter contained.

3. To cause such of the streets and alleys in said city as shall have been used for ten years and are not sufficiently described, or have not been duly recorded, to be ascertained, described and entered of record, in the city clerk's office; and the record of such streets, lanes, alleys or public squares so ascertained and described, or which

*So in the original.

shall hereafter be laid out by the said common council, in books kept by the clerk of the said city, by order of the said common council, shall be evidence of the existence of such streets, alleys, lanes and squares, as therein described.

§ 4. In every case where a street in said city has been, or shall be encroached upon by any fence, building or otherwise, the common council of said city may cause the same to be surveyed and the extent of such encroachment ascertained, and may, by resolution, specifying the nature of such encroachment and the extent thereof, require the owner or owners, if known, and if unknown, the occupant or occupants of the premises so encroaching or adjoining such encroachment, to remove the same within such time as shall be specified in such resolution, which time shall not be less than ten days from the passage thereof. A copy of such resolution shall, within two days after the passage thereof, be served by or under the direction of the superintendent of streets, or such other person as the common council shall direct, upon the owner if he resides in the county of Schenectady, and if not then upon the occupant of the premises aforesaid. If such removal shall not be made within the time specified in such resolution, the owner or occupant of the premises upon whom a copy of such resolution shall have been served, as hereinbefore required, personally, or by leaving it at his place of residence with some person of suitable age, shall forfeit to the said city the sum of five dollars for each and every day after the time mentioned in said notice that such encroachment shall continue unremoved; and the said common council, or the superintendent of streets, may remove or cause to be removed, such encroachments, and may collect of such owner or occupant all reasonable charges therefor, with costs, in any court having jurisdiction of civil actions, and upon a judgment rendered in such action, execution may issue against the person of the defendant in such action.

§ 5. If any person upon whom a copy of such resolution shall have been served, shall, within five days after such service, file with the clerk of said city a notice that he or they deny such encroachment, the mayor or attorney of said city, may apply to the county judge of Schenectady county, for a precept directed to the sheriff of said county, commanding him to summon twenty-four freeholders of said city, to be named in said precept, to meet at a certain day and place specified therein, not less than two days after the issuing thereof, to inquire into the premises. The said mayor or attorney, shall give the person or persons denying such encroachment, at least twenty-four hours' notice of the time and place at which such freeholders are to meet. On the day and at the place specified in such precept, a jury of twelve persons shall be drawn by said judge, from those so summoned, and who shall appear, which jury shall be sworn by said judge well and truly to inquire whether any such encroachment has been made, to what extent, and by whom. Said county judge shall preside at such investigation, and shall decide all questions of law that may arise upon the evidence offered by either party thereto, and may give instructions to the jury as to the law of the case as in civil actions. The jury shall hear the proofs and allegations that may be submitted by either party. If they shall find that any encroachment has been made, they shall make and subscribe a certificate in writing, stating the particulars of such encroachment, and by whom made, which shall be filed by said judge, with a brief record of the proceedings made and subscribed by him, in the office of the clerk of said city The person or persons denying such encroachment within ten days after the finding of such jury, that there is an encroachment, shall, under the penalty provided in the next preceding section, remove the same, or in case of neglect so to do, the common council of said city, or the superintendent of streets, may proceed to remove the same and collect charges therefor in the manner provided in the next preceding section. If the jury find that no encroachment has been made, they shall so certify.

Fees of jurors and witnesses. § 6. The persons summoned as jurors, and persons summoned and attending as witnesses, shall be entitled to the same fees as jurors and witnesses summoned to attend courts of record of this state. The party prevailing in such proceeding shall recover costs as against the other, which costs shall be ascertained and certified by the said judge, and collected by a warrant issued by him to the sheriff of the county of Schenectady, commading him to collect the same of the goods and chattels of the party against whom such warrant shall issue. Such costs shall consist of the sheriff's, jurors', and witnesses' fees, and such an amount as the judge shall allow for attorney's fees, not exceeding twenty dollars.

§ 7. Any determination in a proceeding instituted by virtue of the foregoing sections may be removed to the supreme court by the party aggrieved thereby, by certiorari, to be allowed by any judge of the supreme court, within thirty days from such determination, but certiorari in favor of any owner or occupant, shall not be allowed in favor of any owner or occupant, unless the party suing out the same shall execute, with two sureties, to be approved by the judge allowing such certiorari, an undertaking conditioned to pay all costs and damages against him on such certiorari, which undertaking shall be filed with the Schenectady county clerk. The allowance of such certiorari, and the giving and filing of such undertaking shall stay all proceedings under and by virtue of such determination from and after notice thereof to the mayor of said city. The return to such certiorari shall be made by said county judge, and the same shall be entitled to a preference over other causes on the calendar at any general term in the third or fourth judicial districts. The court, upon the hearing of the same, may review any determination made by the said judge during such proceding, and the correctness of the finding of such jury and shall give such judgment thereon as said court shall deem proper. Costs may be allowed as in other cases of certiorari. *Certiorari.* *Costs.*

§ 8. The common council shall have power, from time to time, to adopt ordinances, directing and requiring any of the streets, highways, lanes, alleys, walks or squares in said city or any part of either of them, to be graded, paved, flagged, macadamized, planked or covered with broken stone or gravel, at the expense of the owners or occupants of the lots and buildings lying upon the street, highway, lane, or alley where such work shall be required to be done; and may, in like manner, direct and require the altering and repairing of the same; and said common council shall prescribe the time and manner in which such work shall be done, and which work shall be done under the superintendence and direction of the superintendent of streets. *Ordinances concerning streets &c.*

§ 9. The common council shall, within eight days after the adoption of any ordinance provided for in the last *Publication of ordinance.*

preceding section, cause the same to be published in a newspaper-printed in said city, and shall continue the publication thereof once a week for three successive weeks.

Service thereof.

§ 10. Immediately after the adoption of any such ordinance, and at least thirty days prior to the expiration of the time therein limited for the doing of such work, the superintendent of streets shall serve or cause to be served a written or printed copy of such ordinance on each of the owners or occupants of the lots and buildings affected thereby, either personally or by leaving the same directed to such owner or occupant, or both of them, with some person of suitable age and discretion, upon such lot or lots.

§ 11. In case any of the said buildings or lots shall be vacant or unoccupied, or no person of suitable age and discretion shall be found thereon, and the owner or owners thereof shall not reside in said city, or shall be unkown, or an infant or infants, in addition to publishing such ordinance as above directed, it shall be sufficient service of notice thereof to affix a copy of the same, on some conspicuous part of said vacant or unoccupied premises, directed to the owner generally if not known, or by name if known.

Ibid.

Proof of service,

§ 12. The said superintendent shall immediately, after serving the said ordinance, file an affidavit with the city clerk of the time and manner of serving the same, annexing thereto a copy of such ordinance so served; and the printer or publisher of the newspaper which published such ordinance shall, upon the completion of such publication, file with the said clerk an affidavit of such publication, and such affidavits shall be presumptive evidence in all courts and places of the matters therein contained.

If owner or occupant fails to comply with requirements of ordinance superintendent may act.

§ 13. If the owner or occupant of any lot or building affected by any such ordinance shall fail to comply with the requirements thereof, the common council shall cause the same to be done, by or under the direction of the said superintendent, for and at the cost and expense of such owner or occupant. The said superintendent shall keep an account of such cost and expense, which shall include the cost of survey, and shall certify to the correctness of the same, and return it to the common council within thirty days after the completion of the work. The common council shall audit and allow such account at such sum as it shall deem proper, and which shall be final and conclusive, and upon the payment thereof by the said city, it shall be lawful for said city to sue for and recover from such owner or occupant, or his legal representative, the sum so allowed and paid, with interest and cost, in an action for money paid and expended for such owner or occupant by the said city; and the said account, with the certificate of the city clerk thereon of the amount allowed thereon, with proof of the payment of such amount, shall be sufficient presumptive evidence to entitle the plaintiff to recover in any such action.

§ 14. Instead of suing the owner or occupant of any such lot for such cost and expense, as provided in the last preceding section, or in case of inability to collect the same of the goods and chattels of such owner or occupant, the said city may publish a notice in a newspaper printed in said city, and also in the state paper, once a week for eight weeks successively, requiring the owner of any such lot to pay to the treasurer of said city the aforesaid cost and expense, with interest from the time it was so paid by said city, at the rate of ten per cent, together with his pro rata share of the cost and expense of publishing such notice, within three months from the time of the first publication thereof; and that, if default shall be made in such payment, such lots will be sold at public auction, by or under the direction of the city treasurer, at a day and place therein to be specified, for the lowest term of years at which any person shall offer to take* same, in consideration of advancing the sum so chargeable to said lot; and, if the owner or owners shall refuse or neglect to pay the same, with the interest and costs, and charges of the advertisement as aforesaid, then it shall be lawful for the said city to cause the said lots to be sold at public auction as aforesaid, for a term of years, for the purposes and in the manner expressed in the said advertisement, and to give a declaration of such sale to the purchaser thereof, under the common seal of the said city; and such purchaser, his executors, administrators and assigns shall, by virtue thereof and of this act, lawfully hold and enjoy the same for his and their own proper use, against

*So in the original.

the owner or owners thereof, and all claiming under him or them, until his term therein shall be fully complete and ended, being at liberty to remove all the buildings and materials which he or they shall erect or place thereon, but leaving the ground in sufficient fence, and with the street or streets fronting the same, in the order required by any such ordinance; and, further, the amount of the costs and expenses incurred and paid by the said city for conforming the streets, highways, lanes or alleys in front of any such lots, shall remain a lien thereon, and be entitled to a preference over any other lien thereon, until paid or otherwise satisfied.

§ 15. If the cost and expenses that may be incurred and paid by the said city as aforesaid, shall be paid by any person, when by agreement or by law, the same ought to have been borne or paid by some other person, then it shall be lawful for the person paying the same to sue for and recover the same, with interest and costs of suit, in any court having cognizance thereof, as so much money paid for the use of the person who ought to have paid the same; and the account of such expenses, certified as aforesaid by the city superintendent, and proof of payment, shall be conclusive evidence in such suit; and, in all cases where there is no agreement to the contrary, the owner or landlord, and not the occupant or tenant, shall be deemed the person who in law ought to bear and pay such expenses.

§ 16. Whenever any application shall come before the common council to open, widen or improve any street, highway, lane, walk, square or park in said city, the expense thereof to be paid by local assessment, the common council shall proceed as follows:

It shall enter a brief description in its minutes of the proposed improvement and its extent, and shall refer the subject to a committee of its body, with instructions to cause a survey and map to be made of the proposed improvement, showing the locality thereof, and the particular lots, tracts and parcels of land and buildings required therefor, and the owners thereof; such committee shall cause a survey and map as aforesaid to be made, and shall make an estimate of the probable cost and expense of such improvement, and shall thereupon give at least five days notice in a newspaper published in said city, of the time and place when they will hear the parties interested. The said committee shall meet

Ibid.

Proceedings to open or improve streets, &c.

at the time and place specified, and, after hearing such parties, shall make their report, in writing, to the common council, with their opinion as to the propriety of making such improvement, designating particularly that portion of the city that should be assessed for such improvement, and shall submit such survey, map and estimate with their report. The common council shall, thereupon, take such action thereon as it shall deem proper. But no such improvement shall be ordered except by the concurrent vote in the affirmative of two-thirds of all the members composing the common council.

§ 17. Whenever the common council shall determine in the manner aforesaid, that it is proper to make such improvement, it may, by ordinance, require and direct that the same be done, the expense thereof to be defrayed by local assessment; which ordinance shall contain a description of the land required for such improvement, and that portion of said city which will be assessed therefor, and the common council may thereupon purchase the land so required for said improvement and take a conveyance therefor to said city. *Ordinance relating thereto.*

§ 18. In case no agreement can be made by the common council for the purchase of the land required for such improvement, it may, upon notice, apply to the Schenectady county court, or to the supreme court of the third or fourth judicial districts, at any special term thereof, for the appointment of three commissioners to inquire into and appraise the damages and compensation to be made for the property to be taken for such improvement, and who shall also apportion and assess such damages and compensation, together with the costs of such proceedings upon the owners of the property to be benefitted thereby, and within the limit designated as aforesaid. *Application to county court.*

§ 19. Notice of such application shall be given by publishing the same in a newspaper published in said city, at least eight days prior to the time named therein for such application, and by serving a copy thereof within the same time upon the owner or his agent, of every lot or building, any part of which is to be taken for such improvement, if such owner or agent be a resident of the county of Schenectady; if there be no such owner or agent resident within said county, then upon the occupant of such lot or building, which notice shall *Notice thereof.*

be served personally or by leaving the same at the residence of said owner, agent or occupant.

Appointment of commissioners. § 20. At the term of the court in such notice specified, the said court, upon proof by affidavit being filed of the publication and service of such notice, as is in the last section specified, or upon sufficient reason being shown for the omission to serve such notice, and upon hearing the city by its attorney, and also the parties interested, if desired, shall appoint three commissioners who shall be freeholders of said city, not interested in any of the land described in such notice, nor of kin to any owner or occupant thereof, or any other party in interest.

Oath and proceedings of commissioners. § 21. The said commissioners so appointed shall be sworn faithfully to discharge their duties according to the provisions of this act, without favor or partiality. They shall give five days public notice in a newspaper published in said city of the time and place they will meet to enter upon their duties; and if the said city shall not have fixed the value, by agreement or purchase, with the owner, as hereinbefore provided, said commissioners shall, at the time appointed, proceed to view the land and buildings proposed to be taken, and then, or at any other time to which they may adjourn, shall appraise the damage which the owners of such land or buildings, and if there be any occupants who are not owners, which such occupants of the lands or buildings to be taken for such public improvement, will severally sustain by being deprived thereof, and the compensation which they shall severally receive therefor, and shall thereupon proceed to apportion and assess the whole amount of such value as agreed upon as aforesaid, or such damages as appraised by them, and all the costs and expenses of the common council in the proceedings, upon the property to be benefitted thereby within the territory designated in said ordinance, as near as may be in proportion to the benefit which each shall be deemed to acquire thereby.

Costs, &c. § 22. The costs and expenses of said proceedings, which shall include the expenses of making survey and map, printers' fees, commissioners' fees for the appraisal and apportionment, and all other disbursements made or to be made by said common council in such proceedings, and also the costs of the city attorney, which shall not in any case exceed fifty dollars, shall be adjusted and allowed by the county judge at such sum as he shall deem just; of the time and place of which adjustment the city attorney shall give five days public notice in a newspaper published in said city.

§ 23. When such damages and compensation shall Assessment have been thus fixed by agreement or appraised, the therefor. commissioners shall add thereto the amount of the aforesaid costs and expenses, as allowed by the county judge, and shall thereupon apportion and assess the whole amount of such damages and costs upon the owners of the land, and if there be any owners of buildings who are not the owners of the land upon which such buildings stand, then upon the owners of such buildings embraced within the territory designated in the ordinance directing such improvement, and to be benefitted thereby, as near as may be in proportion to the benefit which each shall be deemed to acquire thereby.

§ 24. The said commissioners shall, as soon as may be, Report. make their report to the common council upon the matters referred to them, and shall at the same time submit a roll in which they shall describe, with all practicable certainty, the several parcels of land, and the buildings where they are owned, separate from the land, to be taken for such improvement, and the names and residences of the owners thereof, and the particular right and interest of such owners, so far as can be ascertained, and the amount of compensation which should be paid to each of said owners and to the occupants, in the cases in which such occupants shall be entitled to compensation as above provided; and which roll shall also contain their apportionment and assessment of such damages and costs, and the names, if known, of all persons upon whom any part of such damages and costs are apportioned or assessed, the description of the land or building in respect to which they are assessed, the amount assessed to each, the amount of compensation, if any, to which such persons are respectively entitled by the appraisal of said commissioners, and the amount of the excess, if any, to be collected of any such person.

§ 25. Upon the filing of such report and roll, the said Confirmation. common council shall assign a time for the confirmation tion. thereof, and at the time assigned shall hear the allegations of all persons interested, and may take proof in relation thereto, and shall confirm the same without any alteration, or with such alterations therein as they deem proper, or may set the same aside, and refer the matter to the same or to new commissioners to be appointed by the court as before, who shall thereupon proceed as hereinbefore provided.

When possession may be taken. § 26. Upon the confirmation by the common council of such report and roll, the same shall be final and conclusive, and the common council may take and enter upon the lands and buildings specified therein and which had been determined by the common council to be necessary for such public improvement, on paying the amount of compensation awarded to the owners or occupants thereof in such roll, or depositing the same in the Schenectady Savings Bank, to the credit of the person to whom the same was awarded.

When title to land vests in city § 27. When any damages shall be awarded and any assessment for benefits of the improvements in respect to which such damages are awarded, shall be made upon the same person or persons, or in respect to the ownership of any entire parcel of land, a part of which shall be taken for such improvement, in that case the said city of Schenectady shall become vested with the title of such land, (free from all incumbrances) upon paying or depositing according to law, the amount of the difference between the sums of money so awarded or assessed.

When damages to be paid. § 28. Whenever the amount of any damages for taking any lands as aforesaid shall be finally ascertained and fixed, the common council shall, within four months thereafter, pay the amount of such damages to the owners and occupants of lands and tenements, or to persons having any liens thereon, to whom the same shall have been allowed, or deposit the same as hereinbefore provided ; and in case such owners be unknown, non-residents of the said city, married women, infants, idiots or lunatics, or the right and interests of persons claiming the same, shall, in the opinion of the common council, be doubtful, it shall be lawful for the said common council in any such case, to direct the amount of such damages to remain with the treasurer of said city, and it shall be the duty of such treasurer to credit the same to the parcel of land so taken for the benefit of whomsoever may be entitled to the same.

§ 29. Until such damages shall be paid or said direc- _{Lands not to be enter-} tion made, it shall not be lawful 'for the said common _{ed upon un-} council, or any of its officers or agents, to take or enter _{til damages are paid.} upon any lands or tenements for the taking of which any such damages shall have been allowed.

§ 30. Upon the confirmation of the aforesaid appraise- _{Treasurer to give no-} ment and assessment report and roll, the same as con- _{tice of as-} firmed, shall be entered at length by the city clerk in his _{sessment roll, &c.} book of minutes, and shall thereupon be delivered to the city treasurer, who shall give public notice to all persons interested by publishing the same in a newspaper published in said city, once a week for. four successive weeks, that such appraisement and assessment roll has been delivered to him, and requiring all persons upon whom any assessment is made therein, to pay the same within four weeks from the first publication of said notice.

§ 31. In case any person against whom any assess- _{When as-} ment is so charged, shall fail to pay the same within _{sessment is not paid the} such time, it shall be lawful for said city to sue for and _{city may sue therefor.} recover from any such person the sum so assessed against him with interest and cost, in an action for money paid and expended for such person by said city; and in such action, the aforesaid roll or a copy thereof from the book of minutes of the city clerk, duly certified by him, shall be sufficient presumptive evidence to entitle the plaintiff to recover in any such action.

§ 32. Instead of suing the person so charged upon such _{When lands may be sold} roll for the sum assessed upon him, as provided in the last preceding section, or in case of inability to collect the same by suit of the goods and chattels of such person, the said city may enforce the payment thereof by advertising and selling the lands or buildings in respect to which such person shall have been so assessed ; notice of which sale shall be given, and the same shall be conducted and made and have the same effect in all respects as is herein above provided for the sale of any lot charged with the cost and expense of grading or paving any street.

§ 33. Every assessment made as aforesaid upon the _{Lien.} owners or occupants of any lands or buildings, shall be and remain a lien and charge on such lands or buildings on which or in respect to which such assessment shall have been made, from the time of the confirmation by the common council of the aforesaid appraisement and assessment roll until the same shall be paid.

Who to pay assessment. § 34. In all cases where there is no agreement to the contrary, the owner or landlord, and not the occupant or tenant, shall be deemed in law the person who ought to bear and pay every such assessment made for the expense of any public improvement in the said city.

Ibid. § 35. Where any such assessment shall be made upon or paid by any person, when, by agreement or by law, the same ought to be borne or paid by any other person, it shall be lawful for the one so paying to sue for and recover of the person bound to pay the same, the amount so paid, with interest.

Saving clause. § 36. Nothing herein contained shall impair, or in any way affect, any agreement between any landlord and tenant, or other person, respecting the payment of any such assessments.

When greater assessment is made than is necessary § 37. If upon completion of any such improvement, for which such assessment shall have been made, it shall appear that a greater amount has been assessed and collected than is necessary to defray the expenses thereof, the common council shall apportion such excess among the persons and property assessed, in proportion to the amount collected of them, and shall pay the same to such persons, and the owners of such property entitled thereto, on demand.

Removal of buildings. § 38. It shall be lawful for the said common council to order and direct the removal of any building standing on any lots or other real estate which shall have been required and appraised as aforesaid, for any of the purposes aforesaid, on giving thirty days' previous notice to make such removal; and in case of neglect or refusal on the part of such owner or owners to remove such building, it shall be lawful for the said common council to direct the city superintendent to take down and remove the same at the expense of such owner or owners to be paid out of the proceeds of the sale of the materials of such building, which the said common council are, in such cases, authorized to cause to be sold at public vendue, on giving eight days' previous notice of the time and place of such sale, in one of the newspapers printed in the city of Schenectady.

When lease or agreement to cease. § 39. In all cases where the whole of any lot, or other real estate within the bounds of the said city, which is subject to a lease or other agreement, shall be required and taken by the said common council for any of the purposes. aforesaid, all the covenants and stipulations contained in such lease or agreement, shall, upon the confirmation of such assessment roll as aforesaid, cease, determine, and be absolutely discharged; and in all cases where a part only of such lot or other real estate shall be required and taken as aforesaid, the covenants, contracts and stipulations shall cease, determine, and be absolutely discharged, so far only as relates to such part; and it shall be lawful for the said county court of Schenectady county, upon the application in writing of either the landlord or tenant, or other party interested in the part of such lots or real estate, to appoint three disinterested freeholders, inhabitants of the said city, to determine the rents to be thereafter payable by virtue of such lease or agreement, for the residue of such lot or real estate which shall be required and taken as aforesaid; and the determination in writing. under the hands of the persons so appointed, or any two of them, on being confirmed by the said court shall be conclusive and binding on all the parties who may be interested in the part of such lot, or other real estate, required and taken as aforesaid.

§ 40 Whenever any application shall come before the common council to direct the building, repairing or cleansing of any common sewer, vault or drain, or the building or repairing of any bridge or arch, or to order the digging or building of any well, reservoir or pump in said city, to be paid for by local assessment, the common council shall proceed as follows : Proceedings relating to sewers, &c.

It shall enter a brief description in its minutes of the proposed improvement and its extent, and shall refer the subject to a committee of its body, with instructions to cause a survey and map to be made thereof, showing its locality, and the particular lots and buildings to be affected thereby, and the owners thereof; such committee shall cause a survey and map as aforesaid to be made, and also an estimate of the probable cost and expense of such improvement, and shall, thereupon, give at least five days' notice in a newspaper published in said city of the time and place when they will hear the parties interested. The said committee shall meet at the time and place specified, and, after hearing such parties, shall make their report, in writing, to the common council, with their opinion as to the propriety of making such improvement, designating particularly that portion of the city that should be assessed therefor, and shall submit such survey, map and estimate with their report. The common council shall, thereupon, take such action thereon as it shall deem proper. But no such improvement shall be ordered except by the concurrent vote in the affirmative of two-thirds of all the members composing the common council.

§ 41. Whenever the common council shall determine in the manner aforesaid that it is proper to make such improvement, it may, by ordinance, require and direct that the same be done, by or under the direction of the superintendent of streets, the expense thereof to be defrayed by local assessment, which ordinance shall prescribe the time and manner in which said improvement shall be done, and the portion of the city which will be assessed therefor.

§ 42. The said superintendent shall proceed to do such work according to such ordinance, and shall keep a particular account of the cost and expense thereof, including the expense of survey map, and shall certify to the correctness of the same, and return it to the common council within thirty days after the completion of the work. The common council shall audit and allow such account at such sum as it shall deem proper, and which shall be final and conclusive, and shall, thereupon, appoint three disinterested persons, and who are not of kin to any of the parties interested, to apportion and assess the cost and expense of such improvement upon the owners of the lots to be benefited by such improvement, within the portion of the city designated in said ordinance.

§ 43. The said commissioners so appointed shall be sworn faithfully to discharge their duties according to the provisions of this act, without favor or partiality. They shall give five days public notice in a newspaper published in said city of the time and place they will meet to enter upon their duties; and, at the time appointed, shall proceed to view the location of said improvement, and the lands and buildings upon which the cost and expense thereof is to be apportioned and assessed, and then or at any other time to which they may adjourn, they shall apportion and assess the whole

amount of such cost and expense upon the property
aforesaid, or the owners thereof, as near as may be in
proportion to the benefit which each shall be deemed to
acquire thereby.

§ 44. The said commissioners shall, as soon as may be, Report.
make their report, in writing, to the common council,
upon the matters referred to them ; and they shall, at
the same time, submit a roll which shall contain their
apportionment and assessment of such cost and expense,
and the names, if known, of all persons upon whom any
part thereof is apportioned or assessed, the description
of the lands or buildings assessed, or in respect to which
such owners are assessed, and the amount assessed upon
or to each.

§ 45. Upon the filing of such report and roll, the said Confirma-
common council shall assign a time for the confirmation tion.
thereof ; and, at the time assigned, shall hear the allegations of all persons interested, and may take proof in
relation thereto, and shall confirm such roll without any
alteration or with such alterations therein as they shall
deem proper, or may set the same aside and refer the
matter to the same or to new commissioners, to be
appointed by the common council, and who shall proceed
thereupon as above provided.

§ 46. Upon the confirmation by the common council Entry by
of such roll, the same shall be final and conclusive, and clerk.
shall be entered at length by the city clerk in his book
of minutes, and shall thereupon be delivered to the city
treasurer, who shall thereupon proceed to give the notice Proceed-
and receive and collect such assessments, and the city ings.
may sue for and recover the same, or advertise and sell
the lands and buildings assessed, or in respect to which
the owners thereof are assessed, in the same manner,
within the same time and with the same effect in all respects, and every such assessment shall be a lien in the
same manner as is hereinbefore prescribed in relation to
local assessments for opening streets.

§ 47. The provisions contained in sections thirty-four, Certain sec-
thirty-five, thirty-six and thirty-seven of this title, as to tions of this
the liability of the owner, the right to collect by one to assess-
who has paid, of the person who is liable to pay, that ments for
the agreement between landlord and tenant as to pay- sewers.
ment of assessments, shall not be affected, and as to refunding any excess collected, are hereby made applica-

ble to all assessments for any of the public improvements provided for in this title, relative to the building of sewers.

Fees. § 48. The commissioners provided for in this title shall each receive for his services two dollars a day for each day actually and necessarily spent in the hearing and determination of the matters submitted to them, to be paid in the first instance by the city; and any report and assessment roll provided for in this title, made under the hands of any two of said commissioners, shall be as valid as if signed by all of them.

Two commissioners may act.

TITLE VIII.

PREVENTION AND EXTINGUISHMENT OF FIRES.

Ordinance. § 1. The common council of said city shall have power, by ordinance, to designate such portions or parts of said city as it shall think proper, within which no buildings of wood shall be erected, to require the owners and occupants of all buildings to have scuttles on the roof thereof, with steps leading to the same, and may require the inhabitants of said city to provide fire buckets for each house, and to produce such buckets at any fire.

Ashes, flues &c. § 2. The common council may, by ordinance, regulate and direct the construction of safe deposits for ashes, and may compel the cleaning of chimneys, flues, stovepipes and all other conductors of smoke; and upon the neglect of the owner or occupant of any house, tenement or building of any description having therein any chimney, flues, stove-pipes or other conductors of smoke, to clean the same, as shall have been directed by any ordinance, the common council may cause the same to be cleaned, and may collect the expense thereof, and ten per cent. in addition, from the owner or occupant whose duty it was to have the same cleaned.

Gun-powder. § 3. The common council may, by ordinance, regulate the transporting, keeping and deposit of gunpowder or other dangerous or combustible materials; and may regulate or prevent the carrying on of manufactories dangerous in causing or promoting fires; and may authorize and direct the removal of any hearth, fire-place, stove-pipe, flue, chimney or any other conductor of smoke, or any other apparatus or device in which fire may be used, or to which fire may be applied, that shall be considered dangerous and liable to cause or promote fires, and generally may adopt such other regulations for the prevention and suppression of fires as may be necessary.

§ 4. For the purpose of enforcing such regulations, the common council may authorize any of the officers of said city, at all reasonable hours, to enter into and examine all dwelling houses, buildings and tenements of every description, and all lots, yards or inclosures, and to cause such as are dangerous to be put, in safe condition; and may authorize such officers and persons to inspect all hearths, fire-places, stoves, pipes, flues, chimneys or any other conductor of smoke, or any apparatus or device in which fire may be used or to which fire may be applied, and remove and make the same safe at the expense of the owners or occupants of the buildings in which the same may be; and to ascertain the number and condition of the fire buckets, and the situation of any building in respect to its exposure to fire, and whether scuttles and ladders thereto have been provided, and generally with such other powers and duties as the common council shall deem necessary to guard the city from the calamities of fire.

§ 5. The common council may procure, own, build, erect and keep in repairs such and so many fire engines, with their hose and other apparatus, engine houses, ladders, fire hooks and fire buckets, and other implements and conveniences for the extinguishment of fires, and to prevent injuries by fires; and such and so many public cisterns, wells, reservoirs of water, and engine houses, as they shall from time to time judge necessary, subject, however, to the limitations and restrictions, as to expenditures and creation of debt, contained in title five of this act.

§ 6. The common council may organize and maintain a fire department for the said city, to consist of one chief engineer, two assistant engineers, twice the number of wardens that there are wards in the said city, a proper number of firemen, not exceeding sixty to each engine, such number of hook and ladder men as it may deem necessary; all to have the privileges and exemptions of firemen, and to hold their appointment, when not otherwise provided herein, during the pleasure of the common council.

§ 7. The common council may make rules and regulations for the government of the said engineers, wardens, firemen, and hook and ladder men.; may prescribe their respective duties in case of fire or alarms of fire; may direct the dresses and badges of authority to be worn by them ; may prescribe and regulate the time and manner of their exercise, and may impose reasonable fines for the breach of any such regulations.

§ 8. The engineers and fire wardens, under the direction of the common council, shall have the custody and general superintendence of the fire engines, engine houses, hooks, ladders, hose, public cisterns, and other conveniences for the extinguishment and prevention of fires; and it shall be their duty to see that the same are kept in proper order, and to see that the laws and ordinances relative to the prevention and extinguishment of fires are duly executed ; and to make detailed and particular reports of the state of their department and of the conduct of the firemen, and of the hook and ladder men, to the common council at stated periods, to be prescribed by the said common council, and to make such reports to the mayor whenever required by him ; the certificate of the clerk of the city under its seal that a person is or has been a fireman, shall be evidence of the fact in all courts and places.

§ 9. The common council may, by ordinance, direct the manner in which the bells in the city shall be tolled or rung in cases of fire or alarms of fire, and may impose penalties for ringing or tolling of such bells in such manner at any other time than during a fire or an alarm of fire.

§ 10. The common council may, by ordinance :

1. Prescribe the duties and powers of the engineers and wardens at fires, and in cases of alarms of fire.

2. Prescribe the powers and duties of the mayor and aldermen at fires, and in cases of alarm ; but in no case shall any alderman control or direct the chief engineer or his assistants during any fire.

3. Provide for the removal and keeping away from fires, of all idle, disorderly or suspicious persons, and may confer powers for that purpose on the engineers, fire wardens, or officers of the city.

4. Provide for compelling persons to bring their fire-buckets to any place of fire, and to aid in the extinguish-

Rules therefor.

Custody of engines, &c.

Bells.

Duties and powers of engineers, &c., may be prescribed.

ment thereof, by all proper means, and to aid in the preservation, removal and securing of property exposed to danger by fire.

5. To compel the constables of the city to be present at fires, and to perform such duties as said common council shall prescribe.

§ 11. Whenever any person shall refuse to obey any lawful order of any engineer, fire warden, mayor or aldermen, at any fire, it shall be lawful for the officer giving such order, to arrest, or to direct orally a constable or any citizen, to arrest such person, and confine him temporarily in any safe place, until such fire shall be extinguished; and in the same manner such officers, or any of them, may arrest or direct the arrest and confinement of any person at such fire, who shall be intoxicated or disorderly. *Orders at fires.*

§ 12. Whenever any building in said city shall be on fire, it shall be lawful for any five members of the common council to order and direct such building, or any other building which they may deem hazardous and likely to communicate fire to other buildings, or any part of such building to be pulled down and destroyed, and no action shall be maintained against any person or against the said city therefor; but any person so interested in any such building so destroyed or injured, may, within three months thereafter, apply to the common council to assess and pay the damages he has sustained. At the expiration of the three months, if any such application shall have been made in writing, the common council shall either pay the said claimant such sum as shall be agreed upon by them and the said claimant for such damages, or if no such agreement shall be effected, shall proceed to ascertain the amount of such damages, and shall provide for the appraisal, assessment, collection and payment of the same in the same manner as is provided by this act for the ascertainment, assessment, collection and payment of damages sustained by the taking of lands for purposes of public improvement. *Buildings may be pulled down.*

§ 13. The commissioners appointed to appraise and assess the damages incurred by the said claimant by the pulling down or destruction of such building, by the direction of the said officers of the city as above provided, shall take into account the probability of the same having been destroyed or injured by fire if it had not *Damages therefor.*

been so pulled down or destroyed, and may report that no damages should equitably be allowed to such claimant. Whenever a report shall be made and finally confirmed in the said proceedings for appraising and assessing the said damages, a compliance with the terms thereof by the common council, shall be deemed a full satisfaction of all said damages of the said claimant.

Penalties. § 14 For the violation of any ordinance of the common council authorized in this title, it may impose the penalties provided for in title three of this act.

TITLE IX.

THE POOR AND THEIR SUPPORT.

§ 1. Indigent persons and such others as shall be entitled to relief under the laws of this state, who are or shall become chargeable or likely to become chargeable to said city, being in said city, shall continue to be supported and relieved in the manner provided by law in respect to the county of Schenectady, except as herein otherwise provided.

Overseers of poor. § 2. The overseer of the poor to be appointed under this act, shall possess all the powers and perform all the duties, and be subject to all the provisions of law conferred or imposed upon or applicable to overseers of the poor in the several towns of this state, except in relation to applications for relief by or the granting relief and support, whether permanent or temporary, to indigent persons, and except as may be otherwise inconsistent with the provisions of this act.

Board of magistrates § 3. The board of magistrates shall have and exercise all the powers and discharge all the duties of overseers of the poor of the several towns of this state in relation to all applications of poor persons for relief or support, and as to granting or withholding the same, subject to the direction and control of the common council. The police justice shall be chairman of the board of magistrates, and as such it shall be his duty to take the examination of all persons applying for relief, and shall carry out the decision of the board of magistrates thereon. In the absence of the other members of the board, he shall have power to decide upon such applications, make such order and grant such relief as the circumstances of each case warrant and require. And the common council may, by resolution or ordinance, impose other duties upon said board of magistrates and police justice relative to the poor of said city and the mode and extent of granting relief, and the terms and conditions thereof, as to said common council shall seem proper, with such penalties as shall be consistent with this act; and may declare any order issued for the relief of any poor person, void and uncollectable, if any part of it shall be paid, directly or indirectly, in spirituous or fermented liquor.

§ 4. The money received by the excise commissioners of Schenectady county for licenses granted to persons resident in said city, shall be paid by said commissioners within ten days after the receipt thereof by them, to the treasurer of the city of Schenectady, and shall be applied by said city to the support of its poor, except one-tenth part thereof, which one-tenth shall be paid by said commissioners to the treasurer of the county of Schenectady, and the same shall by him be paid over to the treasurer of the New York State Inebriate Asylum. *Moneys received for licenses to be paid to treasurer of city.*
Exception.

TITLE X.

PUBLIC HEALTH.

§ 1. The board of health appointed under this act shall have all the powers, and perform all the duties, and be subject to all the provisions of law conferred or imposed upon or applicable to boards of health by the laws of this state, except as may be inconsistent with this act, and except that they shall receive no compensation for their services.

§ 2. The city physician shall, by virtue of his office, be the health officer of the board of health, and shall receive no compensation for his services as such health officer, except such as he receives as city physician. *Health officer.*

§ 3. In case of the absence from the city of the city physician, or from sickness, he shall be unable to discharge his duties as health officer, the board of health may appoint a health officer during such disability. *Ibid.*

§ 4. The common council shall have power to take such measures as it shall deem effectual to prevent the entrance of any pestilential or malignant disease into the city; to stop, detain and examine, for that purpose, every person coming from any place infected with such *Powers of common council.*

88

a disease; to establish, maintain and regulate a hospital at some place within the city; to cause any person not being a resident of the city, and who shall be infected with any such disease, to be sent to such hospital; to remove from the city or destroy any furniture, wearing apparel, or other property of any kind, which shall be tainted or infected with any pestilence; to abate all nuisances of every description which are or may be injurious to the public health, in any way and in any manner they may deem expedient; and, from time to time, to do all acts, make all regulations, and pass all ordinances which it shall deem necessary or expedient for the preservation of health and the suppression of disease in the city, and to carry into effect and execute the powers hereby granted.

Punishment of captain of canal boat in certain cases.

§ 5. The captain, master or person in charge of any canal boat, which shall enter the city, having on board thereof any person sick of any malignant fever, or other pestilential or infectious disease, shall be guilty of a misdemeanor, punishable by fine or imprisonment, unless the person so diseased became so on the way and could not be left. It shall be the duty of such captain, master or person in charge, within two hours after his arrival, to report, in writing, to the mayor or some member of the board of health, the fact of such sick persons being on board, and the name, description and location of his craft; and he shall not permit such sick person to land or be landed, until the board of health or some member thereof shall give permission for that purpose; and any neglect or violation of these provisions, or of any or either of them, shall be a misdemeanor, punishable with fine and imprisonment.

The driver, &c., of stages, and the conductors, &c., of railroads, required to give notice in certain cases.

§ 6. The owner, driver, conductor, or person in charge of any stage, railroad car, or other public conveyance, which shall enter the city, having on board any person sick of a malignant fever, or pestilential or infectious disease, shall, within two hours after the arrival of such sick person, report, in writing, the fact, with the name of such person, and the house or place where he was put down in the city, to the mayor or some member of the board of health; and any and every neglect to comply with these provisions, or any of them, shall be a misdemeanor, punishable with fine and imprisonment.

Punishment

§ 7. Any person who shall, knowingly, bring or pro- Tainted property.cure, or cause to be brought into the city, any property of any kind, tainted or infected with any malignant fever, or pestilential or infectious disease, shall be guilty of a misdemeanor, punishable by fine and imprisonment.

§ 8. The board of health shall have power, by an order in writing for that purpose, to be served on the master, captain, or person in charge of any canal boat, or any owner or consignee thereof, if such boat be by them suspected to have on board any person sick with a malignant or pestilential disease, to require such boat not to enter the city, or to remove to some certain distance, not exceeding three miles from the city; and every such master, captain, person in charge, consignee or owner, who shall be served with such order, shall be guilty of a misdemeanor, punishable with fine and imprisonment, if such boat shall enter the city in violation of such order, or shall not be removed according to the tenor of such order within a reasonable time, not exceeding three hours after the service of such notice.

§ 9. Every keeper of an inn, or boarding or lodging Captain of canal boat may be required not to enter the city in certain cases.house in the city, who shall have in his house at any time any traveler, boatman or sailor, sick with any pestilential or malignant disease, shall report the fact and the name of the person in writing, within six hours after he came to the house or was taken sick therein, to the mayor or some officer or member of the board of health; every physician in the city shall report under his hand to one of the officers above named, the name, residence and disease of every patient whom he shall have sick of any malignant or pestilential disease, within six hours after he shall have visited such patient. A violation of either of the provisions of this section, or of any part of either of them, shall be a misdemeanor, punishable by Punishmentfine and imprisonment, the fine not to exceed one hundred dollars, nor the imprisonment six months.

§ 10. All fines imposed under the last five sections Fines.shall belong to the city, and when collected shall be paid into the city treasury, and be devoted to the maintenance and support of the poor of said city.

§ 11. The common council shall have power to pass and Ordinances may be passed for filling up, &c., and draining, &c., certain grounds, &cenact such ordinances as it shall from time to time deem necessary and proper for the filling up, draining, cleansing, cleaning and regulating any grounds, yards, basins, slips or cellars within the said city, that shall be sunken,

damp, foul, incumbered with filth and rubbish or unwholesome, and for filling or altering and amending all
sinks and privies within the city, and for directing the
mode of constructing them in future; and to cause all
such works as may be necessary for the purpose aforesaid, and for the preservation of the public health and
cleanliness of the city, to be executed and done on account of the persons, respectively, upon whom the same
may be assessed : and for that purpose to cause the expenses thereof to be estimated, assessed and collected,
and the lands charged therewith, to be sold in case of
non-payment, in the same manner as is provided by law
with respect to other public improvements within said
city; and in all cases where the said by-laws or ordinances shall require anything to be done in respect to
the property of several persons, the expenses thereof
may be included in one assessment, and the several
houses and lots, in respect to which such expenses shall
have been incurred, shall be briefly described in the
manner required by law in the assessment roll for public
improvements; and the sum of money assessed to each
owner or occupant of any such house or lot, shall be the
amount of money expended in making such improvement upon such premises, together with a ratable proportion of the expenses of assessing and collecting the
moneys expended in making such improvements.

When buildings and fences may be taken down. § 12. Whenever, in the opinion of the common council,
any building, or any part thereof, or any fence or other
erection of any kind, or any part thereof, is liable to
fall down, whereby persons or property may be endangered, it may order any owner or occupant of the premises on which such building, fence or other erection
stands, to take down the same or any part thereof, within
a reasonable time to be fixed by the order, or immediately,
as the case may require; or may immediately, in case
the order is not complied with, cause the same to be
taken down at the expense of the owner of the premises; which expense may be sued for and recovered of
such owner, or occupant, and shall be a lien and charge
until paid on the lot on which such erection stood.
Such order shall be served on the owner or occupant
personally, or by leaving it at his residence, if he resides
in said city; if he do not reside in said city, then in
such manner as the common council shall direct.

TITLE XI.

POLICE.

§ 1. The police justice of said city shall keep his office in some central part of said city, and it shall be his duty to attend at his office at all reasonable hours, and, hear and take cognizance of all complaints of a' criminal nature, or for the violation of any ordinance, and to perform such other duties as are imposed upon him by this act, or shall be so imposed by virtue thereof; but no such police justice shall, during the time he is such, perform any of the duties of a civil magistrate except such as may be authorized by this act.

§ 2. Said police justice shall have and exercise all the powers and discharge all the duties, and be subject to all the provisions of law conferred, or imposed upon, or applicable to justices of the peace in criminal cases in the several towns of this state, and to courts of special sessions therein ; and for all offences or complaints triable before him, he shall have the power to sentence and commit the person convicted to the common jail of the county of Schenectady, at hard labor or not, for a period not exceeding six months, unless otherwise limited herein.

§ 3. For any offence triable before a court of special sessions, and which offence shall have been committed within the city of Schenectady, the said police justice shall, on the accused being brought before him, proceed forthwith to try said accused; or said police justice may, if he deems the ends of justice require it, adjourn such trial for a period not exceeding fifteen days, and may, in his discretion, commit the accused to the county jail until such day, or suffer him to go at large on his executing to said city, and filing with said police justice, a bond to be approved by him, with one or more good and sufficient sureties, in a penalty not exceeding five hundred dollars, conditioned for the personal appearance of the accused before the police justice of said city on the day to which said trial may be adjourned, and that he will not depart the court without leave. In all other respects the said police justice shall try said accused in the manner prescribed by title three, chapter two, part four of the Revised Statutes, and the several acts amendatory thereof.

Bid.

§ 4. Whenever complaint shall be made to said police justice of the violation of any ordinance of said city, it shall be his duty to examine the complainant on oath, and any witness he may produce ; and if it shall appear from such examination that any ordinance of said city has been violated, such police justice shall issue a warrant under his hand, in the name of the city of Schenectady, reciting briefly the accusation, and commanding the officer, to whom it shall be directed, forthwith to take the person accused and bring him before such police justice, to be dealt with according to law ; and such warrant may be executed at any place within the county of Schenectady, and may be executed out of said county on having it duly endorsed.

Ibid.

§ 5. On the person so accused being brought before said police justice, he shall have power to proceed forthwith to hear, try and determine said complaint or prosecution ; or he may, if he deems the ends of justice require it, adjourn the hearing or trial thereof for a period not exceeding fifteen days, and may, in his discretion, commit the accused to the county jail until such day, or suffer him to go at large on his executing to the said city, and filing with said police justice, a bond to be approved by him, with one or more good and sufficient sureties, in a penalty of not more than five hundred dollars, conditioned for the personal appearance of the accused before the police justice of said city, on the day to which said hearing or trial may be adjourned, and that he will not depart court without leave.

Jury.

§ 6. Whenever any person shall have been arrested and brought before the police justice for a violation of any ordinance of said city, he shall be entitled to a trial by jury, if he plead not guilty, and demand such trial, at the time of putting in such plea; and it shall be the duty of the police justice to inform him of his right to such trial at the time he so pleads; such jury shall be summoned, drawn and sworn, and shall hear and determine the matter in the mode prescribed by law for summoning jurors in courts of special sessions in the several towns of this state.

Judgment.

§ 7. If it shall appear upon the trial of any prosecution or offence, triable before said police justice, that the accused was complained of and proceeded against without probable cause, and with intent to injure and harass, the said justice or jury trying the cause may render a verdict for costs against the complainant; and, thereupon, the said police justice shall enter judgment against the complainant for the amount of such costs; and, unless he shall give a bond, with good and sufficient sureties, to the said city, to pay the said costs in thirty days, which bond shall be approved by and filed with said police justice, the said police justice shall issue an execution against the property and person of such complainant, and he to stand committed until he shall satisfy such judgment with the costs of commitment, but such commitment shall in no case exceed a period of sixty days.

§ 8. The common council of said city may enter into an agreement with the supervisors of the county of Albany, or their agent, duly authorized, to receive, imprison and provide for, in the penitentiary of said county; and said common council may, by resolution, adopt such penitentiary as the place of imprisonment, of all persons who may be convicted and sentenced to hard labor in the county jail for a period over thirty days by said police justice for any offence, complaint or prosecution triable before him. And, after such agreement shall have been entered into by the respective parties, it shall be the duty of the sheriff of said county to convey such person so convicted and sentenced, without delay to the said penitentiary and deliver him to the keeper thereof; and it shall be lawful for, and the duty of such keeper, to receive and imprison, subject to the rules, regulations and discipline of said penitentiary, all such persons for the term for which they shall be respectively sentenced. *Agreement relating to confinement of prisoners in penitentiary at Albany.*

§ 9. The said sheriff shall be entitled to receive, and which shall be in full, for all his services and expenses in conveying any such person to said penitentiary, the sum of five dollars, and the farther sum of three dollars for each such additional person he shall convey at the same time; and he shall convey at the same time all persons who shall be in jail under any such sentence. *Fees of sheriff.*

§ 10. The police justice elected under this act, shall furnish to the common council a quarterly statement of all complaints, prosecutions or convictions had before him, the sentence thereon, what fines were imposed, and what fines or other sums of money, with the dates which *Police justice to make quarterly statement.*

have been received by him on account thereof; and shall, at the same time, pay over all such fines or sums of money to the treasurer of said city; which statement shall be sworn to by him, to embrace all such items in full, and to be correct and true, to the best of his knowledge and belief.

§ 11. The salary of the police justice herein provided to be elected, shall not be less than five hundred dollars, nor more than eight hundred dollars a year, and shall be in full compensation for all his services under this act. He shall not receive any fees to his own use or reward for any service. All fees and charges for services performed by said police justice and which are chargeable upon the county of Schenectady, or upon any town therein, shall be audited and allowed by the board of supervisors to and for the benefit of the city of Schenectady.

§ 12. The high constable to be elected under this act, shall have and exercise all the powers and discharge all the duties and be subject to all the provisions of law conferred or imposed upon or applicable to constables in the several towns in this state, except that he shall not as such high constable, serve any process or paper in any civil action or proceeding except such as may be issued by the police justice under an ordinance of said city, nor be required to execute any official bond, unless the common council shall require it; and he shall discharge such other police duties as the said common council may impose upon him by ordinance. The salary of such high constable shall not be less than two hundred dollars, nor more than three hundred dollars a year, in addition to the fees to which he may be entitled by law.

§ 13. No justice of the peace or other magistrate in said city, except the said police justice, shall have or receive any fee for or be bound to render any service in criminal cases other than as an associate justice, except in the absence of the police justice, or his inability to discharge the duties of his office, or when that office shall be vacant; but this restriction shall not apply to any proceeding except such as is by law within the jurisdiction of justices of the peace.

§ 14. Complaints for the violation of any ordinance of said city, shall be instituted and conducted, and actions to recover any penalty or forfeiture for the vio-

Marginal notes:

Salary.

Powers of high constable.

Fees of justices.

Actions.

lation of any such ordinance, shall be brought in the name of the city of Schenectady, and any such action may be commenced by warrant returnable forthwith, without an affidavit showing cause therefor, and without giving security.

§ 15. No person being an inhabitant or tax-payer of Tax payer said city, shall be disqualified for that cause from acting as may act as a judge, justice, juror, referee or commissioner, in the &c. trial or other proceeding upon any complaint made for the violation of or action brought to recover the penalty imposed by any ordinance of said city, or in any other investigation or proceeding in law authorized by this act, nor from serving any process or summoning a jury in such action, proceeding or investigation to which the city is a party; nor shall any judge or justice be disqualified to hear and adjudicate on an appeal in a case of bastardy or other matter originating in said city, because he is an inhabitant or freeholder thereof.

§ 16. If judgment in any action shall be rendered Appeal. against the city by any justice of the peace, or by any court of record, such judgment may be removed by appeal to any court having jurisdiction thereof, in the same manner and with the same effect as if the city were a natural person, except that no undertaking on appeal shall be necessary to be executed by or on behalf of said city.

§ 17. Every execution issued in any action for any Execution. penalty or forfeiture recovered for the violation of any ordinance, may be issued immediately on the rendition of the judgment, and shall command the amount to be made of the property of the defendant, if any such can be found, and if not, then to commit the defendant to the county jail for such time as shall be prescribed in such ordinance unless herein otherwise provided.

§ 18 All persons being habitual drunkards, destitute Vagrants. and without visible means of support; all persons who shall abandon, neglect or refuse to aid in the support of their families; all able bodied beggars who may apply for alms or solicit charity; all persons wandering abroad, lodging in engine houses, out-houses, market places, sheds, stables, or uninhabited dwellings, or in the open air, and not giving a good account of themselves; all common brawlers and disturbers of the public quiet; all persons wandering abroad and begging, or who go about from door to door, or place themselves in the streets or other public places to beg or receive alms within the said city, shall be deemed vagrants, and may be proceeded against before the police justice, and upon conviction, be sentenced to confinement in the common jail of Schenectady county, at hard labor or not, for a period not exceeding sixty days.

Persons who abandon their wives or children, &c. § 19. All persons who shall abandon their wives or children in the city of Schenectady, or who shall refuse or neglect to provide, according to their means, for their wives or children, are hereby declared to be disorderly persons, within the meaning of title five of chapter twenty of part first of the Revised Statutes, and may be proceeded against as such, before the police justice in the manner directed by said title, and upon conviction, may **Punishment** be sentenced to confinement in the common jail of Schenectady county, at hard labor or not, for a period not exceeding six months. And it shall be the duty of the magistrate before whom any such person may be brought for examination, to judge and determine from the facts and circumstances of the case whether the conduct of any such person amounts to such desertion or neglect to provide for his wife and children.

Jurisdiction of police justice. § 20. The police justice of said city shall have jurisdiction in actions brought for a violation of any of the city ordinances, or of the laws concerning the internal policy of the state. He shall not have nor exercise any other civil jurisdiction, but shall have sole and exclusive jurisdiction in preference to any other justice, to hear all complaints, and to conduct all examinations in criminal cases in said city.

Warrants. § 21. Warrants may be issued in criminal cases for the apprehending of offenders by any justice of the peace of said city, but they shall be returnable before the said police justice.

Dockets, &c. § 22. All dockets and other books kept by said police justice shall, at all times, be subject to inspection and examination by the city attorney or any member of the common council, and it shall be the duty of said justice to produce such docket or books whenever and wherever the common council shall direct; and, if he shall neglect or refuse to produce such docket or books as required, the county judge of Schenectady county may, on application to him for that purpose, make an order

requiring the same to be produced, and enforce obedience thereto and punish disobedience thereof, in the
same manner in which obedience to other orders made
by him is enforced, or disobedience thereof punished.

§ 23. It shall be the duty of the police justice, for the *Police jus-
time being, on the first Monday in May and November, tice to ac-
in every year, to deliver an account, verified by his count.*
oath, to the mayor of said city, of all moneys, goods,
wares and merchandize then remaining unclaimed in
the said police office, and immediately thereafter to give
notice for four weeks in one of the public newspapers
printed in the said city to all persons interested or claiming such property, that, unless claimed by the owner
with satisfactory proof of such ownership before a specified day, the same shall be sold at auction to the highest
bidder. On the day and at a place specified in such
notice, all property remaining unclaimed, except money,
shall be sold at auction by said justice, or under his direction. If any goods, wares, merchandize or chattels
of a perishable nature, or which shall be expensive to
keep, shall, at any time, remain unclaimed in said police
office, it shall be lawful for said police justice to sell the
same at public auction, at such time and after such notice as to him and the said mayor shall seem proper.
The said justice shall, immediately after the sale of any
property in accordance herewith, pay to the treasurer of
said city all moneys remaining unclaimed in his hands as
such police justice, and all moneys received by him upon
such sale, after deducting the expenses thereof.

§ 24. It shall be the duty of the police justice afore- *Stolen pro-
said, whenever he shall obtain possession of any stolen perty.*
property, on his receiving satisfactory proof of ownership, to deliver such property to the owner thereof,
on his paying all necessary and reasonable expenses
which may have been incurred for the preservation and
sustenance of such property.

§ 25. No property shall be sold or delivered in pursu- *District at-
ance of the foregoing sections if the district attorney of torney.*
Schenectady county shall direct that it shall remain
unsold or undelivered for the purpose of being used as
evidence in the administration of justice.

§ 26. The high constable and ward constables of said *Orders of
city shall obey the orders of the mayor, and of the police mayor.*
justice, or of any person legally exercising the criminal

jurisdiction of a justice of the peace in said city, in enforcing the laws of this state or the ordinances of said city; and in case of refusal or neglect so to do, he or they shall be subject to a penalty of not less than five dollars, nor more than one hundred dollars, or may be removed from office in the mode specified in this act.

TITLE XII.

MISCELLANEOUS PROVISIONS.

Sufficiency of sureties. § 1. The common council, or the mayor or other officer whose duty it shall be to judge of the sufficiency of the proposed sureties of any officer of whom a bond or instrument in writing may be required under the provisions of this act, shall examine into the sufficiency of such sureties, and shall require them to submit to an examination under oath as to their property; such oath may be administered by the mayor or any alderman of said city. The deposition of the sureties shall be reduced to writing, be signed by him, certified by the person taking the same, and annexed to and filed with the bond or instrument in writing to which it relates.

Oath and affidavit. § 2. The mayor or the chairman of any committee or special committee of the common council shall have power to administer any oath or take any affidavit in respect to any matter pending before the common council or such committee.

Perjury. § 3. Any person who may be required to take any oath or affirmation, or to make any affidavit or statement under oath or affirmation, under or by virtue of any provision of this act, who shall, under such oath or affirmation in any statement or affidavit, or otherwise, wilfully swear falsely as to any material fact or matter, shall be guilty of perjury.

Double costs. § 4. If a suit shall be commenced against any person elected or appointed under this act to any office for any act done or omitted to be done, under such election or appointment, or against any person for having done anything or act, by the command of any such officer, and if final judgment shall be rendered in such suit, whereby any such defendant shall be entitled to costs, he shall recover double costs in the manner defined by law.

Repeal. § 5. From and after the passage of this act, "An act relative to the city of Schenectady," passed April twenty-ninth, eighteen hundred and thirty-three, except Exception. so much of said act as defines the boundaries of said city, and all acts supplementary to and amendatory of that act, and all other acts and parts of acts inconsistent with or repugnant to this act, are hereby repealed so far as concerns said city. But nothing herein contained shall be construed so as to destroy, impair or take away any right or remedy acquired or given by any act hereby repealed; and all proceedings com- Proviso. menced under any such former act shall and may be carried out and completed, and all prosecutions for any offence committed, or penalty or forfeiture incurred, shall be carried out in all respects in the same manner and with the same effect as if this act had not passed.

§ 6. The several persons elected at the last charter Persons already elected. election in said city shall enter upon and discharge the duties of the offices to which they were severally elected, for and during the time they were so elected, the same as though this act had not been passed; and the several persons who have been appointed to any office in said city, or who shall be in office when this act takes effect, whether elected or appointed, shall continue to hold and perform the duties of such offices respectively, for and during the time for which they were so elected or appointed, unless the persons so elected or appointed shall be removed under the provisions of this act or the Statute in such case made and provided; and the provisions of this act shall be applicable to all the officers of said city so elected or appointed.

§ 7. This act is hereby declared to be a public act, and shall take effect immediately.

Chap. 386.

AN ACT to authorize the Canal Commissioners to build a farm bridge over the Genesee Valley canal on the farm of Robert Ramsey, in the town of Belfast, in the county of Allegany.

Passed April 21, 1862; three-fifths being present.

The People of the State of New York, represented in Senate and Assembly, do enact as follows :

SECTION 1. The Canal Commissioners are hereby authorized to build a farm bridge over the Genesee Valley canal on the farm of Robert Ramsey, in the town of Belfast, in the county of Allegany; the expense of said bridge and its approaches shall not exceed the sum of four hundred dollars; provided that after investigation, they shall be of opinion that the state ought equitably to build said bridge, to be paid out of any money appropriated for the construction of the Genesee Valley canal.

§ 2. This act shall take effect immediately.

Chap. 387.

AN ACT providing for the appointment of an additional number of Notaries Public in the city and county of New York.

Passed April 21, 1862.

The People of the State of New York, represented in Senate and Assembly, do enact as follows :

SECTION 1. The Governor is hereby authorized and empowered, and with the advice and consent of the Senate, to appoint in and for the city and county of New York, in addition to the number now prescribed by law, two hundred additional notaries public.

§ 2. This act shall take effect immediately.

Chap. 388.

AN ACT to incorporate the Neversink River Plankroad Company and to authorize the issuing and
holding of certificates of stock therein.

Passed April 21, 1862; three-fifths being present.

*The People of the State of New York, represented in
Senate and Assembly, do enact as follows :*

SECTION 1. Arthur Palen, William M. Hall, Medad T. Corporate name.
Morss, Isaac Grant and their associates, who are entitled
to a deed of conveyance of the plankroad of the Wood-
bourne and Neversink Plankroad Company, are hereby
declared a body corporate by the name of "The Neversink Plankroad Company," possessing all the rights,
powers and privileges conferred on and subject to all the
liabilities imposed on plankroad companies by the laws
providing for the incorporation of companies to construct
plankroads and of companies to construct turnpike roads,
passed May seventh, eighteen hundred and forty-seven,
and the several acts amendatory thereto.

§ 2. The capital stock of said company shall be a sum Capital.
not exceeding six thousand dollars, and the shares of
said stock shall be fifty dollars each, and the officers of
said company are authorized to issue certificates of said
capital stock, to the several persons who have contributed for the purchase of said plankroad in proportion to
the amounts respectively contributed by them.

§ 3. The company hereby intended to be created, shall When articles of
file with the Secretary of State, articles of association of association
said company, within three months after the passage of to be filed.
this act, stating the amount of its capital, the number of
years it shall continue, the number of shares of which
the stock shall consist, and the places to and from which
said road leads. Each shareholder shall subscribe such
articles with his name, residence and number of shares
of stock held by him therein.

§ 4. Arthur Palen, William M. Hall, Isaac Grant, Directors.
Nicholas Wakelee and Medad T. Morss, shall be the first
board of directors of said company, who shall hold their
offices for one year, and until others shall be chosen.

Tolls.   § 5. The company hereby incorporated, may demand
and receive tolls upon said road, at the rate fixed by law
for plankroads in the county of Sullivan.
    § 6. This act shall take effect immediately.

Chap. 389.

AN ACT to amend an act entitled "An act to
    reduce the several acts relating to the district
    courts in the city of New York into one act,
    passed April thirteenth, eighteen hundred and
    fifty-seven."

Passed April 21, 1862 ; three-fifths being present.

*The People of the State of New York, represented in
Senate and Assembly, do enact as follows :*

Jurisdiction.
    SECTION 1. In addition to the jurisdiction now con-
ferred by law upon the district courts of the city of
New York, they shall have jurisdiction of actions in
which the people of this state are a party, where such
actions are brought by the overseers of the poor or the
commissioners of public charities and correction in said
city, upon bastardy or abandonment bonds, and the
amount demanded or recovered does not exceed five
hundred dollars ; the pleadings and proceedings to be
the same as in actions brought on bonds with conditions
other than for the payment of money, and for any
breaches of the condition of such bond given in cases
of bastardy which shall happen after the recovery of
any damages or the commencement of any suit, the district court in which the suit was originally brought shall
have power to issue a new summons, and upon the return thereof, to ascertain the amount of damages arising
from said breach, and to give judgment accordingly ;
and in suits upon bonds given in abandonment cases, the
justice holding such court shall have the same power as
to requiring further security, or committing defendant
in default thereof, as are now conferred by law upon the
judges of courts of record in similar cases.

§ 2. Upon a recovery being had in court in the cases referred to in the preceding section, in addition to the costs now allowed by law therein, the court shall make, and the clerk shall enter in the judgment, an additional allowance of ten per cent on the amount recovered. Ten per cent may be allowed.

Chap. 390.

AN ACT to provide for the election of a police justice in the town of Milton, Saratoga county.

Passed April 21, 1862; three-fifths being present.

The People of the State of New York, represented in Senate and Assembly, do enact as follows:

SECTION 1. There shall be elected in the town of Milton, in the county of Saratoga, an officer to be designated "the police justice of the town of Milton." The first election of such officer shall be held on the third Tuesday of May next, the election to be held at a place to be designated by a majority of the justices of said town, and shall be conducted in the usual manner of the town elections of said town. The person elected by a majority of the persons voting at said election, shall hold his office until the next annual election held in said town. At the annual town election to be held in said town of Milton, in the year eighteen hundred and sixty-three, there shall be elected at the same time, and in the same manner as town officers of the town of Milton, a police justice for said town, who shall hold his office for two years from such election, and until another shall be elected in his place. Election of police justice.

§ 2. The said police justice shall qualify in the same manner, and shall possess the same powers in all criminal cases and proceedings, and be subject to the same duties and liabilities as the justices of the peace of the several towns in this state Oath, &c.

§ 3. It shall be the duty of the said police justice to preside in all courts of special session held in the village of Ballston Spa in said town, and any justice of the peace residing in said village before whom any person shall be charged with any offence cognizable by a court of spe- Duties.

90

cial sessions, shall in all cases when such person shall require to be tried by a court of special sessions, certify the fact, and require the said police justice to try such offender.

Ibid.

§ 4. The said police justice shall attend to all complaints of a criminal nature which may be brought before him, and in case of his removal from the town in which said village is situated, his office shall become vacant, and another shall be appointed to supply his place until the next annual meeting and election in said town.

When justice of the peace, judge &c., to act.

§ 5. No justice of the peace, judge or other magistrate, residing or keeping his office in said village of Ballston Spa, shall be bound to render any services, or entitled to receive any fees in criminal cases, except under the restrictions and circumstances hereinafter provided for :

1st. The complainant before such judge, justice of the peace, or other magistrate, shall prove by his own oath or that of any other person, that the said police justice is sick, absent from the town, or otherwise unable to attend to such application, and if the offence charged be

Felony.

of the degree of felony, the said justice of the peace, judge or other officer to whom the application shall be made, shall be bound to issue a warrant for the apprehension of the person charged with the commission of such offence, and shall be entitled to receive therefor the fees allowed by law to magistrates for like services; but such warrant shall be made returnable before the said police justice, who shall conduct all the subsequent proceedings on the complaint the same as though the warrant had been issued by him.

Offences less than felony.

2nd. If the applicant to any such justice of the peace, judge or other magistrate shall apply for process against any individual charged with the commission of any offence less in grade than felony, such justice of the peace, judge or other magistrate, shall not be bound to render any services in the case, nor shall he receive any compensation for such services, if rendered, unless at the time of making such application the said complainant shall prove by his own oath, or that of some competent witness, that the said police justice has been sick, absent from town, or otherwise unable to perform the duties of his office for the space of two days. The justices of the peace, judge or other magistrates residing in said village, shall receive the fees allowed by law for all services rendered under this section, to be audited by the board of supervisors. And the board of supervisors of the county of Saratoga, at the time of auditing the salary of the said police justice, shall deduct therefrom all fees incurred and allowed to other magistrates for services rendered during the absence of said police justice from the town of Milton, as in this section directed. *Fees.*

§ 6. In all cases of felony, the said police justice shall keep an account of his services rendered, and shall present a bill of the same to the board of supervisors at their annual meeting, which shall be audited by said board, and the amount so audited shall be taxed upon the county, as a county charge, and credited to the town of Milton to assist in paying the salary of said police justice. *Account to be kept.*

§ 7. In all cases when by the determination of the said police justice, or the verdict of a jury assisting the said police justice in the trial of any defendant, the complainant shall be adjudged to pay the costs, the said police justice shall tax for his services in such trial or examination the usual fees of justices of the peace in similar cases, which costs shall be collected in the manner specified in the act entitled "An act to reduce the number of town officers and town and county expenses, and to prevent abuses in auditing town and county accounts," passed May tenth, eighteen hundred and forty-five, and when so collected shall be placed to the credit of the town of Milton, to be appropriated to the payment of the salary of the said police justice. *When costs to be paid, how collected.*

§ 8. The said police justice shall not be entitled to receive any fees for services performed under this act, but in lieu thereof, he shall receive an annual salary of four hundred dollars, which shall be allowed, raised and paid by the town of Milton, as other town charges are allowed and paid. *Salary of police justice.*

§ 9. This act shall take effect immediately.

Chap. 391.

AN ACT to confirm the contract made by the street commissioner of the city of New York with Michael Tracy, for doing certain work in Fifty-sixth street, between Broadway and Sixth avenue.

Passed April 21, 1862; three-fifths being present.

The People of the State of New York, represented in Senate and Assembly, do enact as follows :

SECTION 1. The contract made by the street commissioner of the city of New York, in the name of the corporation of said city with Michael Tracy, for regulating, setting curb and gutter stones and flagging Fifty-sixth street, between Broadway and the Sixth avenue of the city of New York, bearing date April sixth, eighteen hundred and fifty-seven, is hereby declared to be valid so far as to empower the comptroller of said city to settle and adjust and to pay for work done under said contract, at the rates of compensation offered by Terrance Farley, the lowest bidder on the estimates for said work, and to whom the same was awarded by the common council on the twenty-ninth of December, eighteen hundred and fifty-six.

§ 2. It shall be lawful for the mayor, aldermen and commonalty of the city of New York, to cause an assessment for the amount expended and* or to be paid by the said corporation in completing the work named in the first section of this act, to be made among the owners or occupants of all the houses and lots intended to be benefited thereby, in the manner in which assessments are now made for local improvements in said city.

§ 3. This act shall take effect immediately.

*So in original.

· Chap. 392.

AN ACT to release the interest of the state in certain lands of which Paul McCloskey died seized or possessed to Ann McCloskey and others.

Passed April 21, 1862; by a two-third vote.

The People of the State of New York, represented in Senate and Assembly, do enact as follows :

SECTION 1. All the right, title and interest of the people of this state in and to the lands of which Paul McCloskey died seized, acquired by escheat, upon the death of Bridget McCloskey, his wife, or of the child of the said Paul McCloskey, is hereby released to the following described persons, their heirs and assigns forever. The said title of the people acquired as aforesaid in and to the premises known as number one hundred and forty-nine Grand street, in the city of Albany, is released to the brothers and sisters of the said Paul McCloskey, being John McCloskey, James McCloskey, Ann McCloskey and Mary McCloskey, and the said title of the people acquired as aforesaid in and to the premises known as numbers one hundred and forty-one and one hundred and forty-seven Grand street, in the city of Albany, is hereby released to Mary Gannon, of the city of Albany, the mother of the said Bridget McCloskey, deceased.

§ 2. Nothing in this act contained shall affect the rights of any creditors of the said Paul McCloskey, deceased, by way of judgment, mortgage or otherwise.

§ 3. This act shall not take effect until the said John and James McCloskey and Ann and Mary McCloskey shall pay to the Attorney General the costs and disbursements incurred in actions brought to recover said real estate; and the receipt of the Attorney General shall be evidence in all courts of such payment.

Chap. 393.

AN ACT for the collection of taxes in the towns
of Morrisania and West Farms, in the county of
Westchester.

Passed April 21, 1862; three-fifths being present.

*The People of the State of New York, represented in
Senate and Assembly, do enact as follows:*

Tax district SECTION 1. The towns of Morrisania and West Farms,
in the county of Westchester, are hereby constituted and
declared a tax district, to be known by the name of the
" Morrisania and West Farms tax district," and the
office of receiver of taxes for said district is hereby
created and established, and the term of office of the receiver of taxes for said tax district shall be two years,
to commence on the first day of December next succeeding the general election, at which the receiver of taxes
shall be elected.

Receiver of § 2. The receiver of taxes for said tax district shall be
taxes.   elected at each alternate general election, except when
a vacancy in the office shall occur, when he shall be
elected at the general election next succeeding the
occurrence of such vacancy; provided however, that
the supervisors of the towns composing said tax district may appoint a suitable person to discharge the
duties of the office during such vacancy, and until
another person shall be duly elected as above provided
and shall have qualified. Such receiver of taxes shall
be elected by the electors of the towns of Morrisania
and West Farms, and shall be voted for on a separate
ballot in the same manner as a member of assembly is
voted for in said towns; and the inspectors of election
in the several election districts of said towns of Morrisania and West Farms, shall make return of the votes
given for receiver of taxes, one copy of each return to
be placed in the hands of the supervisor of the town in
which the election district is located, the original return
to be filed in the office of the town clerk of said town.
The board of county canvassers shall canvass the vote
given for receiver of taxes and determine the result, and

give the certificate of election to the person who shall have received the greatest number of votes, the same as is given in the case of county officers.

§ 3. The receiver of taxes, after having received his certificate of election and before entering upon the duties of his office, shall take and subscribe the usual oath of office, and give a bond to the people of the State of New York to be executed by himself and at least two freeholders of said tax district, in a penal sum double the amount of all the taxes levied and assessed upon the property and persons of the towns composing said tax district, which said bond shall be conditioned for the faithful performance of the duties of said office; said bond to be approved by the county judge of said county, and be delivered to one of the supervisors in said tax district within twenty-four hours after its approval by said county judge, and shall be filed in the office of the county clerk, and shall be a lien upon the real estate of said tax receiver and his sureties, and all laws and provisions of law relating to the enforcement of penalties against collectors of towns, shall apply to such receiver of taxes and his sureties. *Oath of office and bond.*

§ 4. The said receiver of taxes shall have an office or place for the receipt of taxes, in the town hall in the town of West Farms, or in such other place in said tax district as the supervisors of the towns of Morrisania and West Farms shall designate, and the office of said receiver of taxes shall be kept open on each day of the week (Sundays and public holidays excepted,) from eight o'clock in the morning till three o'clock in the afternoon, for four months succeeding the time of the delivery of the tax rolls of said towns of Morrisania and West Farms to him. *Office of receiver.*

§ 5. It shall be the duty of said receiver of taxes to receive personally all taxes which may be paid at the office, and to keep the assessment rolls delivered to him by the assessors in his office. He shall enter in a suitable book or books the sums of money daily received by him, and shall render a statement of and pay over the same at least once in each week to the treasurer of the county, except such moneys as may be required by law to be paid to town officers of the towns of Morrisania and West Farms, which moneys said receiver of taxes shall pay to the town officers respectively entitled to re- *Receiving taxes.* *Exception.*

ceive the same. Such statement, and all the books in the office of the receiver of taxes, shall be public records, and open at all times to the inspection and examination of the public.

§ 6. Upon all taxes paid after the delivery of said tax rolls to the receiver of taxes, and before the expiration of thirty days thereafter, one per cent shall be added to the same and collected; and upon all taxes paid after that time and before the expiration of the succeeding thirty days, two per cent shall be added and collected; and upon all taxes thereafter paid, five per cent shall be added and collected.

§ 7. After the expiration of ninety days from the delivery of the tax rolls to said receiver of taxes, the taxes remaining unpaid shall be collected from the persons and corporations from whom they are due, and shall be collected in the manner following, to wit: The receiver of taxes shall issue warrants directed to any constable or constables, of either of the towns of said tax district, and the said constable or constables shall thereupon proceed forthwith to collect the same by distress, in the same manner as town collectors of taxes are authorized by law to do; and the taxes so collected shall be paid by said constable or constables to said receiver of taxes immediately after they shall have been collected. Constables in such cases shall be entitled to receive the same fees as are by law allowed them in a levy and sale under execution for the collection of a judgment for debt, such fees to be collected with the taxes.

§ 8. The per centage on taxes paid to and collected by the receiver of taxes, shall be applied to the payment of the salary of said receiver of taxes: and said salary is hereby fixed at the sum of one thousand dollars per annum. The amount of per centage on taxes received by said receiver of taxes, exceeding that sum, shall be paid to the supervisors of Morrisania and West Farms, proportioned according to the corrected valuation of assessments of said towns respectively, to be applied to town purposes in such towns. In case the said per centage shall not amount in the aggregate to the sum of one thousand dollars, then the deficiency shall be assessed upon the taxable property in said towns, and collected with the succeeding year's taxes, and applied on the payment of the deficiency of said salary.

Per cent added.

Collection of taxes.

Salary.

§ 9. The offices of collector of the towns of Morrisania and West Farms, on and after the first election and qualification of a reciver of taxes in said tax district, shall cease to exist and be abolished. All laws and provisions of law applicable to town collectors and not inconsistent with this act are hereby made applicable to the office of receiver of taxes hereby created. *Office of town collector abolished.* *Certain laws applied.*

§ 10. It shall be the duty of the board of supervisors of said county to issue their warrant to the said receiver of taxes in the same manner as warrants are now required by law to be issued to town collectors. The said receiver of taxes is hereby directed aud required, on or before the first day of April in each and every year, to pay over to the treasurer of the county any moneys remaining in his hands and payable to the said treasurer, and to make a just and proper return of all taxes remaining uncollected in said tax district ; and the treasurer of the county, upon receiving the moneys and the making of the return as aforesaid, shall cancel and discharge the bonds of the said receiver of taxes. *Duty of supervisors.*

§ 11. All proper expenses incurred by said receiver of taxes, for office rent, fuel and stationery in the discharge of the duties of said office, shall be audited by the joint board of town auditors of said towns, and be equally assessed upon and paid by said towns respectively. *Expenses of receiver.*

Chap. 394.

AN ACT to amend an act entitled "An act to incorporate the village of Olean, in the county of Cattaraugus, to provide for the election of officers for the same, and to declare the said village a separate road district," passed April first, eighteen hundred and fifty-eight.

Passed April 21, 1862 ; three-fifths being present.

The People of the State of New York, represented in Senate and Assembly, do enact as follows:

SECTION 1. Section one of title six of " An act to amend an act entitled an act to incorporate the village of Olean,

91

in the county of Cattaraugus, to provide for the election
of officers for the same, and to declare the said village
a separate road district," passed April first, eighteen
hundred and fifty-eight, is hereby amended so as to read
as follows, to wit :

The board of trustees of said village shall have
power to raise, levy and collect from all persons owning
property in said village, a sum not exceeding two hundred dollars in any one year, as a contingent fund to defray the necessary expenses of said corporation, and for
such other purposes as they may deem proper not inconsistent with the provisions of act hereby amended ; and
the said board shall also have power to raise such additional sum as the majority of the inhabitants of said
village who pay taxes upon real or personal property
may by vote authorize them to raise.

§ 2. Section two of title six is hereby amended so as
to read as follows :

The said board of trustees shall have power to assess
upon the taxable property and inhabitants of said village annually for highway purposes, a sum not exceeding two hundred dollars, and in addition to said sum of
two hundred dollars, each male inhabitant of the age of
twenty-one years and upwards, not exempt by law, shall
be assessed fifty cents each year, and the tax so raised
for highway purposes shall be appropriated, under the
direction of said board, to the working and improving
of the roads, streets, lanes and alleys of the respective
wards in which said property may be situated.

§ 3. The trustees of said village shall cause the proceedings of each meeting of the board to be published
alternately in each of the newspapers published in said
village, while there is more than one paper published in
said village ; and in case but one paper be at any time
therein published, then in such paper.

§ 4. This act shall take effect immediately.

Chap. 395.

AN ACT to authorize the electors of the town of Covert, in the county of Seneca, to vote a sum of money for the relief of Nathan B. Wheeler, and to raise the same by tax, and to pay the same.

. Passed April 21, 1862; three-fifths being present.

The People of the State of New York, represented in Senate and Assembly, do enact as follows:

SECTION 1. At the next town meeting to be held in the town of Covert, in the county of Seneca, the electors thereof are authorized to consider the claim against said town of Nathan B. Wheeler, for moneys paid by him, as is alleged, for school moneys once in his hands belonging to said town, and held by him as superintendent of common schools of said town, and consumed by fire as is alleged, and may vote to repay him the same, with interest thereon from the time the same was consumed ; and if the said electors shall, by a majority thereof, vote to re-pay the said sum of money and interest thereon, then the said sum shall be raised by a tax upon the personal and real estate of the said town of Covert, in the same manner as other town charges are raised.

Chap. 396.

AN ACT for the relief of Joseph H. Godwin.

Passed April 21, 1862; three-fifths being present.

The People of the State of New York, represented in Senate and Assembly, do enact as follows:

SECTION 1. The Lieutenant-Governor, Comptroller and Attorney-General are hereby appointed referees to hear and determine the alleged claim of Joseph H. Godwin, for fifteen hundred and seventy-seven dollars and nine cents, for money paid in satisfaction of a judgment and in defence of an action brought to recover the value of certain materials specified to, and used in the due performance of his contract for rebuilding the State Arsenal in the city of New York.

§ 2. The said referees shall have full power and authority to compel the attendance of witnesses and to swear and examine the same, and shall by their report find and certify what sum, if any, is equitably due to the said Joseph H. Godwin for damages arising from the payment of said judgment and defence of said action, provided the referees are satisfied that the state is legally and equitably liable therefor.

§ 3. In case such referees shall certify and report any sum to be due to the said Joseph H. Godwin, under the provisions of this act, the amount so reported due, not exceeding fifteen hundred and seventy-seven dollars and nine cents, shall be paid by the Treasurer on the warrant of the Comptroller, out of the funds heretofore appropriated by chapter two hundred and seventy-three of the Laws of eighteen hundred and fifty-nine.

4. This act shall take effect immediately.

Chap. 397.

AN ACT to provide for the payment of certain claims incurred in the organization, equipment and subsistence of troops raised in the State of New York, or received therefrom, for the service of the United States.

Passed April 21, 1862 ; three-fifths being present

The People of the State of New York, represented in Senate and Assembly, do enact as follows :

Board of state officers appointed in 1861, may pay certain claims.

SECTION 1. The board of state officers named in section one, chapter two hundred and seventy-seven of the Laws of eighteen hundred and sixty-one, are hereby authorized and empowered to pay or cause to be paid such sums as may be audited, in the manner hereinafter provided and approved by said board, for claims incurred in the organization, pay, equipment, quartering, subsistence and other proper expenses of troops raised under the authority of said chapter, or under the direction and authority of the commander-in-chief in the State of New York for the service of the United States, or received from this State by the President of the United States before the first of June, eighteen hundred and sixty-one, which are properly chargeable to the several military departments of this state, and which on account of any irregularity either in the mode in which the same were incurred or certified, have not hitherto been allowed and paid.

§ 2. The Inspector General, Judge Advocate General and Quartermaster General, or any two of them, are hereby constituted an auditing board to audit such claims as may be presented under the provisions of this act. *Auditing board.*

§ 3. The board mentioned in the last section shall require all persons presenting claims under the provisions of this act, to furnish good and sufficient vouchers thereof, duly verified or certified, and in all cases of the assignment of any such claim shall require the original vouchers thereof to be produced ; and such board shall have power to examine witnesses upon oath in respect to such claims, and for that purpose each member thereof shall have power to administer oaths and affirmations, and the said board shall report such testimony, together with such vouchers and their opinion upon such claims, to the officers mentioned in the first section of this act. *Vouchers to be furnished.*

§ 4. It shall be the duty of the Governor of this state to cause to be presented to the proper officers of the United States accounts setting forth all payments made under the provisions of this act, with the proper vouchers thereof, and to effect the reimbursement of the same, and to pay into the treasury of this state all sums received in settlement of the same. *Duty of Governor.*

§ 5. The sum of five hundred thousand dollars, or so much thereof as may be necessary, is hereby appropriated out of the general fund for the purposes of this act, payable by the Treasurer upon the warrant of the Comptroller to such persons and for such sums as may be directed by the board of officers named in the first section of this act. *$500,000 appropriated.*

§ 6. The board of officers mentioned in the first section of this act are hereby authorized and empowered, in their discretion, to sell or dispose of any property. *Certain property to be sold.*

hitherto purchased under the provisions of chapters two hundred and seventy-seven and two hundred and ninety-two of the Laws of eighteen hundred and sixty-one, the proceeds thereof to be applied to the purposes of this act.

§ 7. This act shall take effect immediately.

Chap. 398.

AN ACT to amend "An act to incorporate the Harlem Stage and Ferry Company of the city of New York," passed April seventeenth, eighteen hundred and sixty.

Passed April 21, 1862.

The People of the State of New York, represented in Senate and Assembly, do enact as follows:

SECTION 1. The first subdivision of the sixth section of an act entitled "An act to incorporate the Harlem Stage and Ferry Company of the city of New York," passed April seventeenth, eighteen hundred and sixty, is hereby amended so as to read as follows:

1st. Also to run a boat or boats upon the Hudson or North river, from some point near or about the foot of Chambers street in the city of New York, touching at such point or points as may be selected by said directors along the easterly shore of said river, by and with the authority and consent of all such parties as may be interested in those several points, and landing at the foot of One Hundred and Thirtieth street, and to run said boat or boats from said One Hundred and Thirtieth street back to the said point near or about the foot of Chambers street aforesaid, and making the landings aforesaid.

§ 2. The second subdivision of the sixth section of an act entitled "An act to incorporate the Harlem Stage and Ferry Company of the city of New York," passed April seventeenth, eighteen hundred and sixty, is hereby amended so as to read as follows:

2nd. To build, construct and run a line of stages from the said ferry at the foot of One Hundred and Thirtieth street as aforesaid, or the point where said street would be when cut through from the Ninth avenue, to the North or Hudson river, and along the said river up to Manhattan street, and through Manhattan street to One Hundred and Twenty-fifth street, and thence through said One Hundred and Twenty-fifth street to the Third avenue, and thence up the Third avenue as aforesaid to Harlem bridge, and to return by the same route as aforesaid to the said ferry at the foot of One Hundred and Thirtieth street as aforesaid.

§ 3. The third subdivision of the sixth section of the act entitled "An act to incorporate the Harlem Stage and Ferry Company of the city of New York," passed April seventeenth, eighteen hundred and sixty, is hereby amended so as to read as follows:

3rd. To build, construct and erect suitable ferry houses, gates, piers and wharves, as may be necessary for the business and object of the said company or corporation, and to purchase, hold and possess all such horses, omnibuses and all other property necessary for the conducting and management of the stages and ferries aforesaid; and also to buy, build, hold and keep all such real estate as may be purchased for the purposes aforesaid, including stables and depots and all such other property as shall be required in the management and conduct of the said business.

§ 4. Also amend the said sixth section of the above entitled act, by adding a fourth and fifth subdivision to said sixth section, so as to read as follows:

4th. The said company shall have power to establish and charge such prices, fares and rates as to them shall seem fair and reasonable for the conveyance and transportation of stock, produce, property, goods, wares or merchandize, articles and passengers across and upon the said ferry and ferries, or in or upon the said line of stages, which shall be subject to be regulated according to the by-laws of the said company.

5th. Nothing contained in this act or in the act hereby amended, shall be so construed as to take away, destroy or in any way impair any of the rights, privileges or franchises owned, held or enjoyed by the city of New York in their corporate capacity by charter or otherwise.

Chap. 399.

AN ACT for the relief of Leora A. Poole.

Passed April 21, 1862; three-fifths being present.

The People of the State of New York, represented in Senate and Assembly, do enact as follows:

SECTION 1. The Canal Appraisers are hereby authorized and directed to hear and examine the claim of Leora A. Poole, for damages alleged to have been sustained by her in consequence of an appropriation of the fee of about three acres, and the temporary occupancy of about twelve acres more of land in the Onondaga Salt Springs Reservation in Onondaga county, in widening the channel of the outlet of Onondaga lake by the Canal Commissioners and superintendent of the Onondaga salt springs, under chapter ninety-five of the Laws of eighteen hundred and fifty-six; and if upon such examination they find that said Leora A. Poole has from the cause aforesaid sustained any damages for which the state is justly liable, they shall appraise the same and make such award therefor as shall be just and equitable.

§ 2. The Treasurer shall pay upon the warrant of the Comptroller such sum, if any, as shall be awarded under the first section of this act to the said Leora A. Poole, out of any surplus revenues from the salt duties that may be in the treasury.

§ 3. This act shall take effect immediately.

Chap. 400.

AN ACT to provide for laying out and constructing a public highway in the county of Hamilton, and applying the non-resident highway taxes upon certain lands in said county for that purpose.

Passed April 21, 1862; three-fifths being present.

The People of the State of New York, represented in Senate and Assembly, do enact as follows:

SECTION 1. Daniel Underwood, of the county of Washington, Robert G. Ostrander, of the county of Hamilton, and Joseph Fellows, of the city of Albany, are hereby appointed commissioners to lay out a public highway, commencing at a point on the north side of the west branch of the Sacandaga river, at or near the line between township number one and the Oxbow tract, in the county of Hamilton, and running up said river, or as near thereto as practicable, to the saw mill on the outlet of Piseco lake, with two branches from said outlet, one westerly to the Morehouse road, the other southerly to Allen's farm house; and the highway tax on all the following non-resident lands shall be applied to the construction and repair of said highway, viz: all of the lands in the Oxbow tract, and the southwest quarter of township number one, in Totten and Crossfield's purchase, in said county of Hamilton. *Commissioners appointed to lay out road*

§ 2. The damages sustained by any and all owners or occupants of land by reason of laying out said road, shall be caused to be ascertained by the commissioners appointed by this act, and such as may be substituted by the treasurer of Hamilton county in place of such as may die, refuse or neglect to serve, in the manner prescribed by the fifth and sixth sections of the act to reduce the number of town officers and town and county expenses, and to prevent abuses in auditing town and county expenses, passed December fourteenth, eighteen hundred and forty-seven. *Damages.*

§ 3. When said damages are assessed as above provided, it shall be the duty of the commissioners of high- *Road when opened,*

92

ways of the several towns through which said highway runs to cause the same to be opened and worked within three years.

§ 4. The county treasurer of said county of Hamilton shall pay over to the Comptroller, when he makes his annual return of the arrears of taxes, the amount of any highway taxes assessed upon any of said tracts or townships, which may have been paid over to the said treasurer, and the Comptroller shall pay over annually all such moneys so received by him to the said commissioners.

§ 5. If the officers, or any of them, whose duty it shall be to assess the highway tax on said tracts of land mentioned in the first section of this act shall omit to make any assessment of the same, the commissioners appointed by this act shall make such assessment, and the tax so assessed by said commissioners shall be as valid in all respects, and shall be collected in the same manner as other highway taxes on non-resident lands are collected.

§ 6. The said commissioners shall have power to expend the highway tax assessed on the several tracts mentioned in the first section of this act, in laying out, constructing and keeping in repair said road.

§ 7. The said commissioners shall give a bond, with satisfactory sureties, to the treasurer of the county of Hamilton, in the sum of one thousand dollars, for the faithful performance of their duties, before entering upon the discharge thereof.

§ 8. The said commissioners shall render to the treasurer of the county of Hamilton, annually, before the first day of December in each year, an exhibit of their expenditures, with the necessary vouchers for the same.

§ 9. The treasurer of the county of Hamilton shall have power to fill all vacancies that shall occur in the office of said commissioners for any cause.

§ 10. The said commissioners shall be paid and receive for their services one dollar and fifty cents for each day actually employed in the performance of their duties.

§ 11. This act shall take effect immediately, and continue in force three years, and all acts inconsistent with the provisions of this act are hereby rendered of none effect.

Chap. 401.

AN ACT to amend the charter of the village of Dexter.

Passed April 21, 1862; three-fifths being present.

The People of the State of New York, represented in Senate and Assembly, do enact as follows :

SECTION 1. It shall be the duty of the owner or occupant of lands fronting on any of the streets or avenues in the village of Dexter to relay and keep in repair the sidewalks in front of their respective lots, in such manner and of such materials as the said trustees may by a by-law, resolution or ordinance for that purpose legally direct, and if any such owner or occupant shall refuse or neglect to relay or repair the sidewalks opposite to or fronting on the lot or lots owned or occupied by him, after receiving six days notice from the trustees of said village, then it shall be lawful for the trustees to cause such sidewalks to be so relaid or repaired, for or on account of the owner of such lots, and such owner and such lots shall be liable to pay the expenses of such relaying or repairing; and all sums so expended upon sidewalks, after being audited by the trustees, by a vote of the board of trustees of said village, shall thenceforth be an assessment or tax to that amount upon every such lot, and thenceforth it shall be lawful for the said board to issue to the collector of taxes and assessments their warrant, returnable in thirty days, for the collection thereof, out of the goods and chattels of the person legally liable to pay the same; and if such warrant shall be returned unsatisfied in whole or in part, to lease such lot in the manner prescribed in an act entitled "An act to provide for the incorporation of villages," passed December seventh, eighteen hundred and forty-seven, whenever the occupant or lessee of any real estate in said village shall have been required, as above provided, to relay or repair any sidewalks, he may recover the expenses incurred therefor, of the owner of such lot, or set off the amount thereof against the claims for rent or otherwise, of the owner or owners of said premises.

§ 2. This act shall take effect immediately.

Chap. 402.

AN ACT to confirm the acts of Samuel Sizer as commissioner of deeds.

Passed April 21, 1862; three-fifths being present.

The People of the State of New York, represented in Senate and Assembly, do enact as follows:

SECTION 1. All the acts of Samuel Sizer as commissioner of deeds in the city of Buffalo, county of Erie, are hereby declared to be of the same force and validity as though his oath of office as such commissioner had been legally taken and deposited; and all liabilities, penalties and forfeitures incurred by him for having exercised the functions of said office of commissioner of deeds are hereby remitted.

§ 2. This act shall take effect immediately.

Chap. 403.

AN ACT to increase the duties and compensation of the physicians respectively at the Auburn, Sing Sing and Clinton prisons.

Passed April 21, 1862; three-fifths being present.

The People of the State of New York, represented in Senate and Assembly, do enact as follows:

SECTION 1. It shall be the duty of the physicians, respectively, at the Auburn, Sing Sing and Clinton prisons, in addition to the duties now required by law, to attend daily during the proper business hours at the prisons for which they are respectively appointed, and at all times hold themselves in readiness to discharge their duties as such physician, respectively, unless by the direction of an inspector, or of the agent and warden of the prison at which he is employed, he is otherwise engaged in transacting business on account of the prison.

§ 2. From and after the passage of this act, the compensation of the physician at the Sing Sing prison shall be the sum of twelve hundred dollars per annum, and the compensation of the physician at the Auburn prison shall be one thousand dollars per annum, and the compensation of the physician of the Clinton prison shall be eight hundred dollars per annum, each payable monthly.

§ 3. This act shall take effect immediately.

Chap. 404.

AN ACT to authorize Henry Hazard Gillespie, otherwise known as Henry H. Howard, of the city of New York, to change his name to Harry Howard.

Passed April 21, 1862.

The People of the State of New York, represented in Senate and Assembly, do enact as follows:

SECTION 1. It shall be lawful for the person heretofore bearing the name of Henry Hazard Gillespie, otherwise known as Henry H. Howard, of the city of New York, to use and assume the name of Harry Howard, and to be known by that name.

§ 2. This act shall take effect immediately.

Chap. 405.

AN ACT incorporating a permanent Library Association for masonic and kindred works in the city of New York.

Passed April 21, 1862.

The People of the State of New York, represented in Senate and Assembly, do enact as follows:

SECTION 1. The following named persons are hereby constituted a body corporate, under the name and style

of "The Masonic Library Association of the city of
New York," to wit: Finlay M. King, John J. Crane,
Henry C. Banks, Robert D. Holmes, Daniel T. Walden,
James M. Austin, Charles L. Church, John W. Simons,
Robert Macoy, Jotham Post, George F. Woodward,
James Herring, Clinton F. Paige, Stephen H. Johnson,
Godfrey W. Steinbreuner, George A. Hunter, John L.
Lewis, Jr., J. B. Yates Sommers, John P. Jenkins, Wil-
liam H. Robertson, Charles F. Bauer.

§ 2. The incorporators named in the preceding section,
or a majority of them, shall, within one year from the
passage of this act, organize an association pursuant to
the authority hereby given, by the election of a president, vice-president, treasurer, recording secretary, corresponding secretary, librarian, and a board of eleven
directors, who shall ex-officio be the trustees of said
association.

§ 3. The said association shall, in addition to the
general powers now conferred by law upon corporations,
have the right to establish agencies in this state for the
promotion of its objects, whenever and wherever a majority of the trustees may direct, and may adopt such
by-laws, rules and regulations for its government and
management as shall not contravene the laws of this
state, and may amend, change, modify or repeal such
by-laws, rules and regulations at pleasure.

§ 4. The object of said association shall be the collection and establishment in the city of New York of a
permanent reference library of masonic and kindred
works, the establishment of a museum of paintings and
articles of interest, illustrative of the history of mason-
ry, and incidentally, by lectures or otherwise, to advance
the diffusion of masonic and kindred literature and history, under such rules and restrictions as the trustees
may from time to time adopt.

§ 5. Real and personal estate, not to exceed in value
fifty thousand dollars, may be acquired, held or disposed
of by said association for its legitimate uses and purposes, and it may also create a capital stock in shares of
one hundred dollars each, not to exceed ten thousand
dollars, for the advancement of its objects and purposes,
under such general regulations as the trustees may prescribe.

§ 6. The legislature may at any time repeal, modify or amend this act.

§ 7. This act shall take effect immediately.

Chap. 406.

AN ACT to provide for the reconstruction or alteration of the highway leading from Richfield Springs, Otsego county, to the village of Mohawk, in the county of Herkimer.

Passed April 21, 1862; three-fifths being present.

The People of the State of New York, represented in Senate and Assembly, do enact as follows:

SECTION 1. David B. St. John, of the town of Edmes- Commissioners. ton, in the county of Otsego, Cornelius T. E. Van Horne, of the town of Stark, and Ezra D. Beckwith, of the town of Columbia, in the county of Herkimer, are hereby appointed commissioners to alter, reconstruct and improve the public road leading from Richfield Springs, Otsego county, to the village of Mohawk, in the county of Herkimer, which passes through a portion of the towns of Richfield, Warren, Columbia and German Flats, and in case any vacancy by death, or neglect or refusal to serve, of any of the said commissioners, such vacancy shall be filled by the county judge of the county of Herkimer, who shall appoint some suitable freeholder of the town in which the commissioner declining to act resides.

§ 2. The said commissioners are hereby authorized Powers. and required to make a careful survey and examination of the said road, or such parts thereof as in their opinion it shall be necessary or proper to alter, in order to avoid or reduce hills ; also the changes of route and alterations which they shall designate, and in making such changes and alterations they shall not deviate from the present line of the road otherwise than as they shall deem materially conducive to the public benefit and conveni- ence. The said commissioners or a majority of them may, in their discretion, order and direct any part of the road passing over hills to be dug down, specifying the length and depth of the cutting, whenever they shall deem it advisable so to do, instead of changing the route of the road, and that they shall discontinue such parts of the road now in use, as they shall consider necessary for the public use.

Maps, &c., filed and recorded. § 3. The said commissioners shall cause maps and descriptions in writing, signed by them or a majority of them, of the changes and alterations of the route in said road, to be filed in the office of the town clerk of Richfield, Columbia and German Flats, whose duty it shall be to record the same.

Damages to be ascertained. § 4. The damages sustained by any and all owners or occupants of land, by reason of any such alteration or change of route in said road, shall be ascertained by the commissioners appointed by this act, and such as may be substituted by the county judge of Herkimer county in place of such as may die, refuse or neglect to serve, in the manner prescribed by the fifth and sixth sections of the act to reduce the number of town officers and town and county expenses and to prevent abuses in auditing town and county expenses, passed December fourteenth, eighteen hundred and forty-seven.

Road to be opened. § 5. When said damages are assessed as above provided, it shall be the duty of the commissioners of highways of the several towns through which said highway runs, and where alterations have been made by the said commissioners, immediately to cause the same to be opened and worked according to the alterations made.

Fees. § 6. Each of said commissioners shall be entitled to two dollars per day for his services for each day actually and necessarily employed in exploring and altering said road and carrying into effect the provisions of this act, and in addition thereto the expense of the surveys and the expenses of opening, altering and making said road **Damages apportioned** shall be apportioned by the said commissioners named in this act, equally upon the said towns of Richfield, Columbia and German Flats, so that one third of all said expenses shall be apportioned to each of said towns, and the amount so apportioned shall be a claim upon the said several towns, and to be audited and allowed by the board of town auditors in each of said towns.

Proviso. § 7. Nothing in this act shall be construed to require or authorize the said commissioners to lay out a new road for the entire distance, but they may adopt so much of the existing road as part of the highway hereby authorized, as can be done for the public benefit, without essential deviation from the present route ; nor shall this act authorize the said commissioners to alter the route of said road without the consent of the owners or occupants, by running through any lands or grounds that commissioners of highways of towns have not a right by law to lay out a road without the consent of the owner or occupant.

Chap. 407.

AN ACT for the relief of the Brooklyn, Bath and Coney Island Railroad Company.

Passed April 21, 1862.

The People of the State of New York, represented in Senate and Assembly, do enact as follows:

SECTION 1. It shall be lawful for the Brooklyn, and Coney Island Railroad Company, to construct and operate their railroad over the route designated in their certificate of incorporation, and the map thereof to be filed (as required by the general railroad law) upon obtaining the consent of the common council of the city of Brooklyn, or of a majority of the owners of property fronting on said route in said city, and to lay iron rails for the said railroad, of a weight of not less than forty pounds to the lineal yard.

§ 2. This act shall take effect immediately.

Chap. 408.

AN ACT to authorize the issue of bonds by the president and trustees of the American Guano Company, of the city of New York, and the execution by them, as security for the same, of a first mortgage on their property, real and personal, on Jarvis' Island and Baker's Island, in the Pacific Ocean.

Passed April 21, 1862.

The People of the State of New York, represented in Senate and Assembly, do enact as follows:

Bonds may be issued.
SECTION 1. Caleb S. Marshall, president; David R. Stanford, vice-president; and Howard Mather, secretary and treasurer of the American Guano Company, and their successors, are hereby authorized to issue, from time to time as the necessities of the company may require, the bonds of the company, in such sums as may be determined upon by the board of trustees of said company, the proceeds of the sale of which shall be applied to the liquidation of the indebtness first, and after that to the current expenses of said company; but no issue of such bonds or appropriation of proceeds thereof shall *Certain purposes forbidden.* be made for the purpose of giving or working a preference to any creditor being a trustee or other officer of the company, or to any credits transferred by any of them in contemplation of the insolvency of the company, or after actual insolvency, and every such issue or appropriation shall be utterly void.

§ 2. The entire amount of bonds to be issued under this act shall not exceed the sum of three hundred thousand dollars, and the principal of said bonds shall be redeemable in not less than three years from the date of said bonds, which date shall be of a day after the passage of this act, at the office of the company in the city of New York, and at a period of not more than ten years from the date of their issue, and shall not be sold or issued at a rate less than sixty per centum.

Coupons.
§ 3. Said bonds shall be coupon bonds, and shall bear interest at the rate of seven per centum per annum, pay-

able semi-annually, at the office of the company in the city of New York.

§ 4. As a security for the redemption of the principal and interest of said bonds, the president, vice-president and treasurer of said company are hereby empowered to execute a first mortgage on all the property of the company, real and personal, on Jarvis' and Baker's Islands, situated in the Pacific ocean, in favor of three trustees, who shall be neither present nor future officers of said company, or trustees for any purpose other than that herein contemplated; and said mortgage shall embody a declaration of trust, which shall set forth that, in the event of a failure to meet the interest on said bonds, at any time when such principal or interest shall become due, and for six months thereafter, that such failure shall be an immediate judgment under said mortgage, and the trustees under said mortgage shall, thereupon, proceed to take possession of and sell at public auction, at the Merchants' Exchange in the city of New York, after advertising the same in two newspapers in the city of New York, and the state paper in the city of Albany, for eight weeks, once in each week, all or such portions of said property as may be required to meet the principal and interest of said bonds; together with the costs and expenses attending said sale. *Security for redemption*

§ 5. Said mortgage shall set forth and require that, whenever any sale or sales of guano shall hereafter be made by said company, that within a period of ten days after the proceeds of such sale shall be realized, the president and treasurer of said company shall pay over to the trustees under said mortgage a sum equal to fifty cents per ton of the amount of such sales; and said mortgage shall also set forth that, in no case, shall a dividend be declared or paid, nor shall any dividend be declared or paid to the stockholders of said company, unless an amount equal to the entire amount of such dividend, including the amounts realized from the payments of fifty cents per ton as above described, be paid over to the trustees under said mortgage, to be invested in a sinking fund, for the ultimate redemption of the principal and interest of said bonds. *Form of mortgage.*

§ 6. This act shall take effect immediately.

Chap. 409.

AN ACT to confirm and make valid a certain ordinance of the common council of the city of New York, passed November twenty-seventh, eighteen hundred and fifty-five.

Passed April 21, 1862; three-fifths being present.

The People of the State of New York, represented in Senate and Assembly, do enact as follows:

SECTION 1. The ordinance of the mayor, aldermen and commonalty of the city of New York, in common council convened, providing for and authorizing the filling in of the sunken lots on the south side of Fifty-fifth street, between the Tenth and Eleventh avenue, approved November twenty-seven, eighteen hundred and fifty-five, and the contract thereupon for the said filling in, dated May four, eighteen hundred and fifty-six, are hereby respectively legalized, and made valid and effectual; and it shall be lawful for the mayor, aldermen and commonalty of the said city, in their discretion, to cause an assessment to be laid, made and collected upon said ordinance.

§ 2. The comptroller of the city of New York is hereby authorized to audit the account, and ascertain the amount of money equitably due to the contractor or person who executed said work, and to draw his warrant for the payment of the same, after the money for that purpose shall have been assessed and collected, as hereinbefore provided.

§ 3. This act shall take effect immediately.

Chap. 410.

AN ACT to provide for the payment of Francis Crawford, as a soldier in the First Regiment of New York Volunteers in the Mexican war.

Passed April 21, 1862; by a two-third vote.

The People of the State of New York, represented in Senate and Assembly, do enact as follows:

SECTION 1. The Comptroller is hereby authorized to draw his warrant upon the Treasurer for the sum of two hundred and eighty-eight dollars, payable to Francis Crawford, the same being for his services as a soldier in the First Regiment of New York Volunteers, in the Mexican war; and the Treasurer, upon the presentation of such warrant, is authorized to pay the same.

Chap. 411.

AN ACT to incorporate the Blind Mechanics' Association to be located in the city of New York.

Passed April 21, 1862; by a two-third vote.

The People of the State of New York, represented in Senate and Assembly, do enact as follows:

SECTION 1. William F. Havemeyer, Abraham S. Hew- Corporate itt, Robert Ray, Oliver Charlick, George D. Baldwin, John W. Ritch, Sheridan Shook, Robert G. Rankin, Charles White, John W. Edmonds, John N. Haywood, Cyrus Curtis, Aaron Vanderpool and Thomas A. Ledwith, with the mayor and comptroller of the city of New York, who shall be ex-officio members of the board of managers, are hereby created a body corporate by the name, style and title of the "Blind Mechanics' Association."

§ 2. The leading objects of this corporation are hereby Objects. declared to be to promote the welfare of the adult blind by assisting them in procuring work or employment, and thereby aiding them in earning their own livelihood, and it shall not in any sense be considered or conducted as a poor house, asylum or hospital.

Power of managers. § 3. The managers of said association shall have power to purchase or lease suitable work shops and accommodations for the blind mechanics who shall become members of this association, to admit to membership any adult blind mechanic, either male or female, who is a citizen of the State of New York of good moral character, to receive as apprentices such blind persons from all parts of the state as they have means to accommodate, and to regulate the conditions on which such members and apprentices shall be received and to expel any member for improper conduct; the regulations prescribing the admission of members and apprentices to be approved by the Superintendent of Public Instruction; they shall also have power to purchase materials and manufacture and sell such articles as the members of the association are competent to manufacture.

By-laws. § 4. The managers shall have power to make by-laws for the government and regulation of the association not inconsistent with the laws of this state; the time, place and manner of calling and holding all meetings of the members of the association as well as the managers; they shall have power to appoint such persons as may be necessary to regulate, superintend and conduct the business of the association and to regulate the compensation for the same.

Vacancies. § 5. The managers shall have power to fill all vacancies occuring in the board caused by death, resignation or removal from the state. The persons hereinbefore named shall constitute the first board of managers, and they shall as soon after the passage of this act as may **Officers.** be convenient, elect from their number a president, vice-president, a secretary and treasurer.

Report to the legislature, annually. § 6. The managers shall make a report to the Legislature on or before the first day of February in each year, setting forth the value of the assets and amount of liabilities of said corporation, the value of productions and amount of sales effected up to the first day of January next preceding such report, and a statement of its general condition; and such corporation shall be subject to the visitation and inspection of the Superintendent of

Public Instruction in the same manner as is now or may hereafter be provided for the New York Institution for the Blind.

§ 7. The New York Institution for the Blind shall be **To receive $8000.** authorized to pay to the managers of the said association the sum of eight thousand dollars, being the same sum of eight thousand dollars referred to in the second section of an act entitled "An act in relation to the New York Institution for the Blind," passed April thirteenth, eighteen hundred and fifty-nine; and the Comptroller of the state shall draw his warrant in favor of the managers of the said association for the sum of ten thousand dollars; and the Treasurer of the state shall pay, on the warrant of the Comptroller, out of the state treasury, to the said board of managers, the said sum of ten thousand dollars whenever and as soon as the said association shall have raised, by private contribution or otherwise, the like sum of ten thousand dollars.

§ 8. This act is subject to the general provisions contained in the third title of the eighteenth chapter of the first part of the Revised Statutes, and may at any time hereafter be altered, amended, modified or repealed by the Legislature. **Subject to certain provisions of Revised Statutes.**

§ 9 The first section of the act entitled "An act to amend an act entitled 'An act to incorporate the New York Institution for the Blind,' passed April twenty-first, eighteen hundred and thirty-one, and for other purposes," passed April seventh, eighteen hundred and forty-eight, is hereby repealed. **Repeal.**

§ 10 This act shall take effect immediately.

Chap. 412.

AN ACT to facilitate the closing up of insolvent and dissolved mutual insurance companies.

Passed April 21, 1862.

The People of the State of New York, represented in Senate and Assembly, do enact as follows :

SECTION 1. If any controversy or disagreement shall arise between the receiver of an insolvent or dissolved **Referee may be appointed.**

mutual insurance company, in the settlement of any
demand or claim against any member or stockholder of
the company of which he is receiver, or any other person, or if after personal demand for payment of such
demand or claim shall have been made, and the payment
of the sum claimed be neglected or refused, the same
may be referred to a sole referee who may be agreed
upon by the receiver and the person against whom such
demand or claim is made, by a writing to that effect
signed by them, or upon application to any justice of the
supreme court residing in the district where such receiver keeps his office as herein stated, and all controversies relating to such receiver's business may be
referred to one referee in the discretion of the court;
such referee shall be appointed upon ten days' notice to
the adverse party.

Proceed-
ings before
referee.

§ 2. The referee so appointed, shall proceed in a summary manner to hear the proofs and allegations of the
parties upon written or oral pleadings, and shall have
the same powers and be subject to the same duties and
obligations, and shall receive the same compensation as
referees appointed by the supreme court, in personal
actions pending therein, and upon his report a judgment
may be entered in said court and be the judgment of
said court, in the same manner; and the supreme court,
may, on appeal from said judgment to the general term,
set aside the report of the said referee; but no appeal
from such judgment shall suspend or delay the execution
thereon, unless there shall be filed with the notice of
appeal to the clerk of the court, a certificate of a justice
of the supreme court, to the effect that there is probable
error in the said judgment, nor unless security be given
to the satisfaction of said justice for the payment of
said judgment and the costs of the appeal, if said judgment be affirmed.

Notice.

§ 3. All controversies before said referee shall be
brought to a hearing upon notice to the adverse party,
the same as now required by the rules and practice of
the supreme court.

Commis-
sion to ex-
amine wit-
ness.

§ 4. The referee so appointed, at any time after his
appointment and without an issue of fact joined, shall
have the same power and authority to issue a commission to examine witnesses relating to any controversy
before him as a justice of the peace now has.

§ 5. The supreme court shall have power to refer all actions now pending therein, wherein any such receiver is a party, and where any controversy arises as mentioned in the first section of this act, such reference shall in no way prejudice the proceedings already had. Power of supreme court.

§ 6 The prevailing party shall recover the disbursements to the controversy only. This act shall not affect the costs already made in actions pending, and the costs now incurred in actions pending shall abide the event of the action, not to exceed twenty dollars in cases where no judgment has been entered. Costs on appeal may be allowed in the discretion of the court, and may be absolute or directed to abide the event of the action. Disbursements. Saving clause.

§ 7. This act shall take effect immediately.

Chap. 413.

AN ACT to amend chapter two hundred and seventy-seven of the Laws of eighteen hundred and thirty-nine, entitled "An act to amend the charter of the Long Island Railroad Company."

Passed April 21, 1862; three-fifths being present.

The People of the State of New York, represented in Senate and Assembly, do enact as follows:

SECTION 1. The third section of the act entitled "An act to amend the charter of the Long Island Railroad Company," passed April twenty-ninth, eighteen hundred and thirty nine, is hereby amended so as to read as follows:

The said corporation are hereby authorized to construct such branch railroad in any part of Long Island, except the county of Kings, as they may deem expedient and necessary, subject to the provisions of the general railroad law, provided that no such branch railroad be constructed west of the eastern boundary of the village of Jamaica.

§ 2. This act shall take effect immediately.

Chap. 414.

AN ACT for the relief of Hawley, Waldron and Company.

Passed April 22, 1862; three-fifths being present.

The People of the State of New York, represented in Senate and Assembly, do enact as follows:

SECTION 1. The Canal Appraisers are hereby authorized and required to examine the claim of Hawley, Waldron and Company, for damages alleged to have been sustained by them in the flooding of their salt works, in the town of Salina, by the Oswego canal enlargement and by changing the bed of Bloody brook, and award to them such sum, if any, as the state shall be legally and equitably liable for.

§ 2. The Treasurer shall pay, on the warrant of the Auditor of the Canal Department, the sum awarded under the first section of this act, out of any money or moneys appropriated, or to be appropriated, for canal damages.

§ 3. This act shall take effect immediately.

Chap. 415.

AN Act to adapt the canals of this state to the defence of the northern and northwestern lakes.

Passed April 22, 1862; three-fifths being present.

The People of the State of New York, represented in Senate and Assembly, do enact as follows :

SECTION 1. Whenever the government of the United States shall provide the means, either in cash or their six per cent stock or bonds, redeemable within twenty years, for defraying the cost of enlarging a single tier of locks, or building an addition tier in whole or in part upon the Erie and the Oswego canals, including any necessary alteration of said canals, or their structures, to a size sufficient to pass vessels adequate to the defence of northern and northwestern lakes, the Canal Board shall,

When locks to be enlarged, or new ones built.

without delay, put such work under contract, in the manner now required by law, to be constructed and completed 'at the earliest practicable period, without serious interruption to navigation, with power, in the discretion of the Canal Board, to direct the construction of new and independent locks, when found more advantageous. The said Canal Board shall, whenever the government of the United States shall provide the means as aforesaid, construct a canal of the requisite dimensions and capacity, from the Erie canal, at or near the village of Clyde, to some proper point on the Great Sodus Bay or Lake Ontario. *When canal to be built to Great Sodus Bay.*

§ 2. The Canal Board are also hereby authorized, in like manner to enlarge the Champlain canal, and its locks and other structures, to a size sufficient to pass vessels of like capacity, in case the government of the United States shall, in like manner, provide the means required for that purpose.

§ 3. The dimensions and character of all the work herein above mentioned, shall be determined by the Canal Board, subject to the examination and concurrence of the War Department of the government of the United States. Contracts for any of said work may be made payable in the said six per cent stock and bonds of the United States, if the Commissioners of the Canal Fund shall so elect. *Authority of Canal Board.*

§ 4. On completing the said work on either of the said canals, the government of the United States shall have the perpetual right of passage through the canals thus enlarged or built, free from toll or charge, for its vessels of war, boats, gun boats, transports, troops, supplies or munitions of war, subject to the general regulations prescribed by the state from time to time, for the navigation of its canals. *Right of general government.*

§ 5. Any moneys or other means which may be received from the government of the United States, to pay for any of said work, are hereby appropriated to be expended for the purposes herein above mentioned. *Appropriation of moneys.*

§ 6. But nothing in this act contained shall authorize the contracting or incurring of any debt or liability, directly or indirectly, on the part of the state, or the expenditure of any means or money of the State of New York for the purposes specified in this act. *Saving clause.*

Chap. 416.

AN ACT confirming acts of courts of sessions of Cortland county.

Passed April 22, 1862 ; three-fifths being present.

The People of the State of New York, represented in Senate and Assembly, do enact as follows :

SECTION 1. The official acts and proceedings of the courts of sessions of the county of Cortland for the years eighteen hundred and sixty and eighteen hundred and sixty-one, are hereby declared to be of the same force, effect and validity as if the said courts of sessions had been duly designated and appointed.

§ 2. All liabilities and forfeitures incurred by the several persons comprising said courts of sessions are hereby remitted ; and all liabilities and forfeitures incurred by any other person or persons and by any other officer or officers for having done any act founded upon such official act or acts or proceedings, are hereby remitted.

§ 3. This act shall not affect or impair any suit or legal proceedings that may have been had or commenced by reason of the invalidity of any act or proceedings by or before said courts.

§ 4. This act shall take effect immediately.

Chap. 417.

AN ACT to alter the term for which criminals may be sentenced to state prison, and to provide for their earning a commutation of sentence, and an increase of the amount to be paid them on their discharge.

Passed April 22, 1862 ; three-fifths being present.

The People of the State of New York, represented in Senate and Assembly, do enact as follows :

SECTION 1. Section thirteen, of title seven, chapter one, part fourth, of the Revised Statutes, is hereby amended by striking out the words "two years" in the last line of said section, and inserting in the place of the words so stricken out the words "one year."

§ 2. Every convict confined in any state prison in this state, and every convict confined in any penitentiary in this state, under sentence on conviction for a felony, may earn for himself a commutation or diminution of the term of his sentence, subject to the provisions of section four hereof, and in the manner following: *Convicts may earn commutation.*

If he shall diligently work the number of hours prescribed by the rules of the prison or penitentiary, during each day that he is ordered to work, for the space of one month, and if he shall well obey the rules and quietly submit to the discipline of the prison or penitentiary for the space of one month, he shall be entitled, for every period of one month for which he shall so work, obey and submit, to a commutation or deduction from the term for which he has been sentenced of one day. If he shall so work and obey and submit for the space of six or more successive months, he shall be entitled for every one of said six or more successive months to a commutation or deduction from the term for which he was sentenced of two days, which two days shall be in addition to the deduction of one day for each month hereinbefore provided for. The provisions of this section shall, so far as they are applicable, apply to female prisoners confined in any state prison of this state, or in any penitentiary therein, and also to any prisoner confined in any state prison of this state, or in any penitentiary therein, for whom the agent or other officer of said state prison has no work at which to put him under any contract for the labor of convicts; provided, however, that the provisions of this act shall not affect the case of any person who shall be under a sentence of imprisonment for the term of his natural life. *Manner of doing it.* *Female prisoners.* *Proviso.*

§ 3. It shall be the duty of every agent or other officer having charge of a state prison or penitentiary in this state, whenever a convict is delivered to him for confinement in the said state prison or penitentiary, to make known to him the provisions of the second section hereof.

§ 4. It shall be the duty of the keepers and matron of each state prison and penitentiary in this state to keep such record, day by day, of the manner of working of *Keepers and matrons to keep record of work.*

each convict therein to whom the provisions of this act shall be applicable, and of his conduct therein, as shall show what convicts have fulfilled the requirements of the second section thereof, and each of such keepers or

To report same.

matron shall report such record at the end of each month to the agent or principal keeper of the prison or penitentiary, and it shall be the duty of the agent or principal keeper of such state prison or penitentiary to preserve such record; and he shall not, more than thirty days before the term of each convict expires, as diminished by said record, transmit a copy of such record to the Governor, which shall give the name of such convict, the date of his reception, the term of his sentence; and the Governor of the State of New York may thereupon, in his discretion, direct the abatement or deduction of the term of the sentence of said convict of the number of days of commutation or diminution thereof which said convict shall have earned.

Fees received from visitors applied to use of convicts discharged.

§ 5. The funds arising from the fees charged to visitors at the state prisons and penitentiaries may be applied under the direction of the Inspectors of Prisons by the warden to the use and benefit of convicts upon their discharge, provided that no convict shall receive any

Proviso.

greater sum than ten dollars in addition to the amount now allowed by law, and also that the condition of the allowance of such additional sum shall be the good behavior of the convict during his imprisonment.

Repeal.

§ 6. All acts and parts of acts inconsistent herewith, are hereby, so far forth as inconsistent herewith, repealed.

§ 7. This act shall take effect immediately.

Chap. 418.

AN ACT to confirm and legalize certain acts of the common council of the city of New York.

Passed April 22, 1862; three-fifths being present.

The People of the State of New York, represented in Senate and Assembly, do enact as follows:

SECTION 1. The resolution confirming the contract for regulating and grading the Third avenue from Eighty-

sixth to One Hundred and Tenth streets, to John
Pettigrew, approved by the mayor of said city August
thirty-first, eighteen hundred and fifty-eight, is hereby
declared to be valid and in full force and effect:

§ 2. The official acts of the comptroller of the city of
New York, or of the street department, done and performed under said contract, shall be held valid and of
full force and effect; and the said comptroller is hereby
authorized and directed to settle with John Pettigrew
for all the work done or to be done by said Pettigrew in
pursuance of said contract, which is hereby declared
valid.

§ 3. For the purpose of reimbursing the mayor, aldermen and commonalty of the city of New York for the
moneys paid and to be paid under the provisions of this
act, they are hereby authorized and empowered to levy
and collect an assessment upon the property benefited
thereby, in the manner now provided by law.

§ 4. This act shall take effect immediately.

Chap. 419.

AN ACT authorizing the transcribing of certain
registry lists in the town of Whitestown, county
of Oneida.

Passed April 22, 1862; three-fifths being present.

*The People of the State of New York, represented in
Senate and Assembly, do enact as follows:*

SECTION 1. The board of registers of the town of
Whitestown, in the county of Oneida, are hereby authorized to use the lists of registered voters in the hands of
the said board, in making copies for a new registry list,
with the same effect as if such copies had been made
from the lists of such voters filed in the office of the
clerk of said town, which were destroyed by fire on the
seventeenth day of December, eighteen hundred and
sixty-one.

Chap. 420.

AN ACT to incorporate the Union Home and School for the education and maintenance of the children of Volunteers.

Passed April 22, 1862.

The People of the State of New York, represented in Senate and Assembly, do enact as follows:

Corporation   SECTION 1. Mrs. General Robert Anderson, Mrs. Drake Mills, Mrs. Olive M. Devoe, Mrs. David Hoyt, Mrs. Richard Stokes, Mrs. Walter Kidder, Mrs. Sarah Mather, Mrs. J. Bagiola, Miss M. F. Hoyt, Miss H. Sherman, Mrs. John Voorhis and Miss Kate Connell, and such others as shall be associated with them, shall be and they are hereby constituted a body corporate by the name of The Union Home and School, for the education and maintenance of the children of our Volunteers who are left unprovided for.

Managers.   § 2 The management of the affairs and concerns of the home and school, when the society is not in session, shall be conducted by a board of managers to be from time to time appointed by the society. The individuals named in the first section of this act shall be the first managers of the corporation and shall continue in office until a new election is held. Any number of the managers and officers appointed by the said corporation, not less than five, shall constitute a quorum for the transaction of business.

May hold real and personal property.   § 3. For the object designated in the first section of this act generally or for any purpose connected with such object, the said corporation shall have power, from time to time, to purchase, take and hold real and personal estate, and to sell, lease and otherwise dispose of the same; provided the aggregate clear annual value of such estate shall not exceed ten thousand dollars.

Certain part of the Revised Statutes applied.   § 4. The corporation hereby created shall possess the powers and be subject to the restrictions and provisions contained in the fifteenth and eighteenth chapters of the first part of the Revised Statutes, as far as the same are applicable and have not been repealed.

§ 5. This act shall take effect immediately.

Chap. 421.

AN ACT to provide for the reimbursement of certain persons and regiments belonging to the militia of this State for clothing and equipments lost or destroyed in the service of the United States.

Passed April 22, 1862; three-fifths being present.

The People of the State of New York, represented in Senate and Assembly, do enact as follows:

SECTION 1. The Comptroller, State Treasurer, Quartermaster General and Inspector General are hereby constituted a board, who are authorized and required to receive proof, ascertain and determine the sums due to regiments or members of the militia of this State, duly enrolled in the several companies, battalions and regiments thereof, for clothing and equipments, belonging to such persons or regiments, lost or destroyed in the service of the United States since the sixteenth day of April, eighteen hundred and sixty-one. *Board constituted to fix sums due.*

§ 2. No person shall be entitled to receive any compensation under the provisions of this act, who shall not have furnished such uniform and equipments at his own expense, and who is not at the time of presenting his claim a member of the uniformed militia of this state; but any regiment of the uniformed militia of this state that volunteered for three months service, and was mustered into the service of United States, and duly served at the seat of war, shall be entitled to receive and draw in one sum an amount equal to the gross sum which such regiment would receive at the rate of twenty-five dollars for each and every member thereof who actually served at the seat of war; provided the company by-laws of such regiment make the uniforms thereof the common property of the companies of the regiment; and provided also that the gross compensation thus drawn by a regiment shall not exceed in amount the value of the number of uniforms actually filled by such regiment in the service of the United States, at the pro rata valuation provided for in this act, and that the amount thus *No one to have pay who did not furnish uniform at his own expense, &c.* *Pay to uniformed militia.* *Proviso.*

95

drawn by such regiment shall be expended wholly in the purchase of new uniforms under such regulations and restrictions as the board of commissioners named in this act may direct.

Sums deducted. § 3. Any sum received by such person or regiments by way of commutation for clothing from the United States, and the value of any clothing or equipments furnished at the expense of this state, for which such person or regiment shall not have been charged, shall be deducted from the amount which might otherwise become due to persons or regiments applying for compensation under the terms of this act.

Powers of commissioners. § 4. For the purpose of carrying into effect the provisons of this act, the commissioners above named, shall have power to call upon the commandants of the several regiments, battalions, and companies of the uniformed militia of this state to furnish such rolls, rosters and other statements duly verified or certified, as they may deem necessary; and shall have power to administer oaths and affirmations, and to take testimony in regard to such claims.

Claims for compensation. § 5. All claims for compensation, under the provisions of this act, shall be presented to said commissioners in writing duly verified by the person or the field officers of a regiment claiming the same, on or before the first day of July, eighteen hundred and sixty-two, under such regulations as said commissioners shall prescribe.

Warrant upon Treasurer. § 6. The Comptroller, upon the certificate of said commissioners, shall from time to time, draw his warrant upon the Treasurer for such sums as may be required by said commissioners for their necessary and proper expenses, and for such sums as may be awarded by said commissioners to any persons or regiments under the pro-

Proviso. visions of this act; provided, however, that no individual shall be entitled to receive a larger sum than twenty-five dollars for uniform and equipments; and that no regiment shall receive more than the gross amount to which it is entitled at the rate of twenty-five dollars for each and every member thereof who actually served at the seat of war; which sum shall include the value of any clothing furnished by this state for which such person shall not have been charged, and the commutation for clothing mentioned in the third section of this act.

§ 7. The sum of fifty thousand dollars or so much $50,000. thereof as may be necessary, is hereby appropriated for the purposes of this act out of any moneys in the treasury not otherwise appropriated.

§ 8. No regiment or member of the militia of this state, shall be entitled to receive any payment or compensation under the provisions of this act, when such regiment, or the regiment or company to which such member is attached, shall have received payment or compensation from a city or county for the uniforms and equipments worn and used in the service of the United States.

When regiment not to receive pay under this act.

§ 9. It shall be the duty of the Governor of this state to cause to be presented to the proper officers of the United States, accounts to be prepared under the direction of said board, setting forth all payments made under the provisions of this act, with the proper vouchers thereof, and to endeavor to obtain a reimbursement of the same, and to pay into the treasury of this state all sums received in settlement of the same.

Duty of Governor.

§ 10. This act shall take effect immediately.

Chap. 422.

AN ACT to provide for the consolidation of banking associations.

Passed April 22, 1862; three-fifths being present.

The People of the State of New York, represented in Senate and Assembly, do enact as follows:

SECTION 1. Any two or more banking associations, organized under the general banking laws of this state, and located in the same city, village or town, are hereby authorized to consolidate the same into a single association, to be located in the same place in the manner following:

Authority.

§ 2. The directors of the said associations may enter into an agreement under their respective corporate seals, for the union or consolidation of the said associations, prescribing the terms and conditions thereof, the mode of carrying the same into effect, the name and duration

Proceedings to consolidate.

of the new association, the number of directors, the
names of the persons to constitute the first board of
directors, the time and place of holding the first election
of directors, the manner of converting the shares of
each of said associations into the shares of the new
association, with such other details and provisions as
they may deem expedient, not inconsistent with the provisions of the act to authorize the business of banking,
and the acts amendatory thereof.   Notice of the intention to consolidate said associations shall be given
personally or by mail to each stockholder of each of said
associations, at least ten days previous to entering into
said agreement.

Consent of
stockhold-
ers.

§ 3. The written consent of stockholders, owning at
least two-thirds in amount of the capital stock of each
of said associations, shall be requisite to the validity
of said agreement.   Upon the presentation to the Superintendent of the Banking Department, of the said agreement duly proved or acknowledged, together with satisfactory proof, by affidavit or otherwise, of the assent
thereto of stockholders owning two-thirds in amount of
the capital stock of each of said associations so proposing to consolidate, and of the service of notice upon
each stockholder as aforesaid, the said Superintendent
shall, within a reasonable time thereafter, make or cause
to be made an examination of the books, property,
effects, and liabilities of such associations; upon which
examination the officers thereof may be examined on
oath as to the debts, liabilities, property and effects of
such associations respectively.   From the result of such
examination the said Superintendent shall determine the
value, in his judgment, of such property and effects
above and beyond the debts and liabilities aforesaid, and
certify the same in writing, and the amount so determined and certified shall be thereafter the capital stock
of such consolidated banking association.

Superinten-
dent of
Banking
Department

Expense.

§ 4. The expense of the examination herein provided
for by the Superintendent of the Banking Department,
or caused to be made by him, shall be paid by the banking associations for whose benefit the application shall
be made.

Certificate
in writing
to be re-
corded.

§ 5. The determination and certificate in writing, to
be made by the said Superintendent, of the amount at
which the capital stock of any banking association has

been fixed under this act, shall be recorded in the office of the clerk of the county in which such banking association shall be located; and a certified copy thereof filed in the Bank Department of the State of New York; and the same shall be published by the said Superintendent once a week for six weeks successively, in the state paper, and at least one newspaper in the county where such association shall be located, at the expense of the said banking association.

§ 6. Upon the recording of the said agreement and certificate, the said consolidated associations shall be and become a single banking association, in accordance with the said agreement and certificate, with the same franchise, rights, powers and privileges, and subject to the same duties, conditions and limitations, as the several constituent associations; and such consolidated association shall be vested with all the estate, property, credits and effects of the constituent associations, without deed or other transfer, and shall be liable for all their contracts, debts, obligations and liabilities; and the separate existence and operation of such constituent associations shall thereupon cease and determine.

§ 7. No action or other proceeding pending before any court or tribunal, in which either of the constituent associations may be a party, shall be deemed to have abated or been discontinued by reason of their consolidation; but the same may be prosecuted to final judgment and execution in the same manner as if this act had not been passed, or the said new association, by order of the court in which such proceeding may be pending, may be substituted as a party in place of either of the original associations, in any stage of such proceedings.

§ 8. Nothing in this act contained shall in any way change or lessen the liability of the stockholders, of any banking associations consolidating their capital stock under its provisions, to the bill holders or other creditors therefor; or any indebtedness or engagement now existing or that may so exist, either absolutely or contingently, against such association prior to or at the time when such consolidation shall take place; or by which the rights, remedies or security of the then existing creditors shall be weakened or impaired.

Dissent of
any stock-
holder.

§ 9. If any stockholder in either of the associations availing itself of the provisions of this act, who shall not have assented to such consolidation, shall, within twenty days after the agreement and certificate hereinbefore mentioned shall be recorded in the clerk's office of the county in which such associations are located, object in writing to said consolidation, and demand payment for his stock, such consolidated association shall within three months from the filing of such dissent, pay to the dissenting stockholder the value of his stock, as determined in the certificate of the Superintendent of the Banking Department aforesaid ; and upon payment so made by the said association, the interest of said stockholder in the property and effects of said association shall cease, and the said stock may be held and disposed of by the said association for its own benefit.

Chap. 423.

AN ACT to authorize the sale of the property of the Baptist church in the village of New Haven, county of Oswego.

Passed April 22, 1862.

The People of the State of New York, represented in Senate and Assembly, do enact as follows :

Commis-
sioners to
sell build-
ings, &c.

SECTION 1. Abram W. Hewitt, Orin Wilmarth and Avery W. Severance, are hereby appointed commissioners with full powers, and they are hereby authorized to sell the old brick church building and the lot whereon said building stands, and the appurtenances thereunto belonging, situate in the village of New Haven, in the county of Oswego, belonging to the Baptist church and society of said town, and to transfer and convey the same for such price and on such terms as shall in the judgment of said commissioners be most advantageous to the interests of the persons entitled by this act to the avails thereof.

Title of
purchaser.

§ 2. On such sale and conveyance as is prescribed in the first section of this act, the said property shall pass to the purchaser or purchasers thereof, their heirs or assigns, who are hereby authorized to take, hold, use and enjoy the same in the same manner and to the same extent that they would have done if the said Baptist church and society had continued its organization to the present time, and the said property had been duly sold and conveyed by said society in the manner prescribed by law, and the title so conveyed shall be deemed to be a good and valid title for all purposes whatsoever.

§ 3. It shall be the duty of said commissioners to publish in a newspaper printed in said Oswego county, nearest to said village of New Haven, at least once a week for four successive weeks, a notice to the effect that a division is contemplated of the avails of such sale, among the persons who contributed toward the erection of said church building or the purchase of said lot, and · that all such contributors are required to present to said commissioners, at a time and place to be mentioned in. said notice, which shall be at least thirty days subsequent to the first publication of said notice, a statement of the amounts that they so contributed respectively, or they will be debarred from sharing in said proceeds. And it shall be the further duty of said commissioners, to divide the proceeds of such sale, after deducting therefrom all expenses necessarily incurred by them in the discharge of the duties imposed upon them by this act, into parts proportional to the amounts so stated as aforesaid, that they shall determine to have been so contributed, and to pay to each contributor who shall have presented a statement as required by said notice, his proportional part of such proceeds. And the decision of said commissioners, or a majority of them, shall be conclusive of the rights of said contributors. No contributor who shall fail to present such statement as required by said notice, shall be entitled to any part of said proceeds.

§ 4. This act shall take effect immediately.

Chap. 424.

AN ACT to amend an act entitled "An act to revise the charter of the city of Buffalo, and to enlarge its boundaries," passed April thirteenth, eighteen hundred and fifty-three, and the several acts amendatory thereof.

Passed April 22, 1862; three-fifths being present.

The People of the State of New York, represented in Senate and Assembly, do enact as follows:

SECTION 1. Section six of title two of the act entitled "An act to revise the charter of the city of Buffalo, and to enlarge its boundaries," passed April thirteenth, eighteen hundred and fifty-three, and the several acts amendatory thereof, is hereby amended so as to read as follows:

§ 6. The electors of each ward shall elect annually in each ward in the manner now provided by law, one alderman and one constable; and each of said wards, except the thirteenth ward, shall elect two supervisors, and said thirteenth ward shall elect one supervisor; and the electors of each election district in the several wards shall elect three inspectors of elections in the manner prescribed by law. No alderman hereafter elected shall directly or indirectly receive or be allowed a greater sum than one hundred dollars for his services as such alderman in any one year, and in that proportion for any shorter term.

Chap. 425.

AN ACT further to amend the act entitled "An act to provide for the incorporation and regulation of telegraph companies," passed April twelfth, eighteen hundred and forty-eight.

Passed April 22, 1862; three-fifths being present.

The People of the State of New York, represented in Senate and Assembly, do enact as follows:

SECTION 1. Any telegraph company which is duly incorporated under and in pursuance of the act entitled "An act to provide for the incorporation and regulation of telegraph companies," passed April twelfth, eighteen hundred and forty-eight, may construct, own, use and maintain any line or lines of electric telegraph not described in their original certificate of organization, whether wholly within or wholly or partly beyond the limits of this state, and may join with any other corporation or association in constructing, leasing, owning, using or maintaining such line or lines, and may own and hold any interest in any such line or lines, and may become lessees of any such line or lines, upon the terms and conditions and subject to the liabilities prescribed in said act, so far as such provisions are applicable to the construction, using, maintaining, owning or holding of telegraph lines, or any interest therein, pursuant to the provisions of this act. *(Corporate rights of telegraph companies extended.)*

§ 2. In case any company incorporated as before mentioned shall become the owners or lessees of, or engage in the construction, use or maintenance of, any line or lines of electric telegraph, not described in their original certificate of organization, or shall join with any other corporation or association in leasing, constructing, owning, using or maintaining any such line or lines, or shall own or hold any interest in such line or lines, or shall become lessee of any such line or lines, such company, within one year after constructing or becoming such owners or lessees, or after joining with any other corporation or association in such construction, leasing or ownership, or after acquiring any other interest in *(Certificate to be filed with Secretary of State.)*

96

such line or lines, shall file in the office of the Secretary of State of this state a certificate describing the general route of such line or lines, designating the extreme points connected thereby, as provided in section two of the act hereby amended; which certificate shall be executed by at least two-thirds of the directors of such corporation under their hands and seals, and shall be acknowledged by them as prescribed in subdivision five of the second section above mentioned.

Provisions relating to filing certificates of companies already formed. § 3. Any telegraph company incorporated as mentioned in the first section of this act, which before the passing of this act shall have purchased, constructed or leased, or shall have joined with any other corporation or association in the purchase, construction or leasing, or shall have become the owner or holder of any interest in any line or lines of telegraph not described in their original certificate of organization, may, within one year after the passing of this act, make and file in the office of the Secretary of State such certificate as is provided in the second section of this act, and upon the filing of such certificate, their acts, if otherwise within the provisions of this statute, shall be as valid and effectual as if done after the passing of this act, saving all existing rights of other persons.

§ 4. This act shall take effect immediately.

Chap. 426.

AN ACT to amend an act entitled "An act to incorporate the Mount Vernon Savings Bank," passed April seventeenth, eighteen hundred and sixty-one.

Passed April 22, 1862.

The People of the State of New York, represented in Senate and Assembly, do enact as follows:

SECTION 1. Section six of chapter two hundred and eighty-one of the Laws of eighteen hundred and sixty-one, entitled "An act to incorporate the Mount Vernon Savings Bank," is hereby amended so as to read as follows, to wit: The general business and object of the cor-

poration hereby created shall be to receive on deposit
such sums of money as may be from time to time offered
therefor by farmers, tradesmen, clerks, mechanics, laborers, minors, servants and others, and invest the same in
the securities, stocks or bonds of this state or of the
United States, or the stocks or bonds of any city authorized to be issued by the Legislature of this state, or of
the county of Westchester, or loaning the same upon
bonds secured by mortgage on unincumbered, improved,
productive real estate within the county of Westchester,
worth at least double the amount secured thereby, (but
no loan shall exceed the sum of three thousand dollars,)
or in such other manner as is authorized by this act for
the use, interest and advantage of the said depositors
and their legal representatives. And the said corporation shall receive on deposit from persons of the description above mentioned all sums of money which may
be offered for the purpose of being invested as aforesaid, but not to exceed the sum of one thousand dollars
from any individual, which shall, as soon as practicable,
be invested according to the provisions of this act, and
shall be repaid to such depositor when required, at such
times and with such interest, and under such regulations
as the board of trustees shall from time to time prescribe ; which regulations shall be put up in some public
and conspicuous place in the room where the business
of said corporation shall be transacted, but shall not be
altered so as to affect any deposit previously made. No
president, vice-president, trustee, officer or servant of
said corporation shall directly or indirectly borrow the
funds of said corporation, or its deposits, or in any manner use the same or any part thereof, except to pay
necessary current expenses, under the direction of said
board of trustees. All certificates or other evidence of
deposit, made by the proper officers of such corporation,
shall be as binding on such corporation as if they were
made under its common seal. It shall be the duty of
the trustees of the said corporation to regulate the rate
of interest to be allowed the depositors, so that they
may receive, as nearly as may be, a ratable proportion
of all the profits of the said corporation, after deducting all necessary expenses and charges; and all expenses
of searches, examinations and certificates of title and of
drawing, perfecting and recording papers, shall be paid

by such borrower. And it shall be the duty of the trustees of said corporation to invest, as soon as practicable, in public stocks or public securities, or in bonds and mortgages, as provided for in this act, all sums received by them beyond an available fund not exceeding one-third of the total amount of deposits, which said trustees, at their discretion, may keep to meet the current payments of said corporation, and which may by them be kept on deposit or interest or otherwise, in such available form as the trustees may direct. The said corporation is hereby authorized to accumulate an amount not exceeding five per cent. on the amount of deposits therein, to meet any contingency or loss in its business, which amount shall be invested for the security of the depositors of the said corporation; and thereafter at each annual examination of the affairs of said corporation, any surplus over and above said sum shall, in addition to the usual interest, be divided ratably amongst depositors in such manner as the board of trustees may direct.

§ 2. This act shall take effect immediately.

Chap. 427.

AN ACT authorizing the commissioners of highways of the town of Watervliet, in the county of Albany, to lay out and open a certain highway in the said town, of the width of two rods.

Passed April 22, 1862; three-fifths being present.

The People of the State of New York, represented in Senate and Assembly, do enact as follows:

SECTION 1. The commissioners of highways of the town of Watervliet, in the county of Albany, are hereby authorized to lay out and open a highway, two rods wide, in said town, of which the following is a description: Commencing at a point in the Boght road where the division line between John Keeler's land and the land of Samuel Pinchbeck, along said division line to the lands of George Gunnison, thence on and across said Gunnison's land, striking the old road where the track passes on the farm belonging to the heirs of George Haswell, deceased; thence on the lands belonging to said heirs, along the division line between said heirs and Thomas P. Haswell, to a point where the present track passes to the south side of said line on the lands of said Thomas P. Haswell; thence across said Haswell's land to the Witbeck farm : thence on and across said farm to lands of L. and G. Sanders, and turning to the north across said Sanders' farm to the lands of John P. Wiswall; thence across said Wiswall's land to the Boght road, except that the said commissioners are authorized to make slight variations therefrom in their discretion.

§ 2. The said highway shall be laid out, opened and worked by said commissioners of highways in the same manner now provided by law for laying out and opening public highways by commissioners of highways in the several towns in this state, except the same shall be of the width of two rods.

§ 3. This act shall take effect immediately.

Chap. 428.

AN ACT to repeal part of an act passed April fifteenth, eighteen hundred and fifty-eight, entitled "An act to amend an act to establish regulations for the port of New York," passed April sixteenth, eighteen hundred and fifty-seven.

Passed April 22, 1862.

The People of the State of New York, represented in Senate and Assembly, do enact as follows :

SECTION 1. Section nine of the act passed April fifteenth, eighteen hundred and fifty-eight, entitled "An act to amend an act to establish regulations for the port of New York," passed April sixteenth, eighteen hundred and fifty-seven, is hereby repealed.

§ 2. This act shall take effect immediately.

Chap. 429.

AN ACT to incorporate the Fire Department of the Village of Batavia.

Passed April 22, 1862; three-fifths being present.

The People of the State of New York, represented in Senate and Assembly, do enact as follows:

Corporate name. SECTION 1. All such persons as now are or shall hereafter be members of each and every fire company organized and to be organized by the trustees of the village of Batavia, in the county of Genesee, under the charter of said village, shall be and continue a body corporate, by the name of "The Fire Department of the Village of Batavia," and they and their successors by the said name are authorized to purchase, receive by gift, or otherwise hold and convey any real and personal property for the use of said corporation, not exceeding in value the sum of ten thousand dollars.

Trustees. § 2. There shall be a board of trustees, who shall have the management and control of the affairs and property of the said corporation, and such other powers, and subject to such obligations as hereinafter provided. The first trustees shall be David Seaver, Sanford S Clark, Albert R. Warner, William M. Tuttle, Louis M. Cox, Benjamin Goodspeed, William H. Brown, John Passmore, Marsden J. Pierson, William D. W. Pringle, George D. Kenyon, Hollis McCormick, Henry G. Champlin, James Nugent, and Samuel Jennison, of whom the following shall be the first officers, viz: David Seaver, president; Sanford S. Clark, vice president; Albert R. Warner, secretary, and George P. Pringle, treasurer, who shall hold their respective offices until others are chosen in their stead.

Election of officers. § 3. The said several fire companies composing said fire department shall, on the second Tuesday in February next, and on said day in each year thereafter, hold an election, and thereat elect a chief engineer, first assistant engineer, second assistant engineer and treasurer. The said several fire companies shall also, on the first Monday of March next, and on said day in each year thereafter, hold an election, and thereat elect four persons from the

members of said companies respectively, and the persons
so elected, together with the chief and assistant engineers aforesaid, shall thereafter form the said board of
trustees; and the said board shall, on the second Monday
in March next, and on said day in each year thereafter,
chose out of their own body a president, vice president
and secretary, the said secretary to be the secretary of
the department. And the said board shall, by their
president or otherwise, as the board shall direct, make
known to the trustees of the village aforesaid the result
of each election for the offices of chief and assistant
engineers, within three days after such election shall
have been held, and the said trustees shall thereupon
approve or disapprove of the engineers so elected ; and
if said trustees of the village shall disapprove thereof,
or of either thereof for two weeks after being thus
notified of such election, then the board of trustees, by
its secretary, shall call a special election of said fire
department, at which shall be elected persons to fill said
offices, or such of them as are not filled by such prior
election, and appoved by said trustees of the village.
All of the officers aforesaid shall hold their respective
offices until the next election, and until their successors
shall be chosen as aforesaid.

§ 4. The said trustees shall have power to make such Powers of
trustees.
by-laws, rules and regulations, from time to time, as
·they may deem expedient and proper, not inconsistent
with the charter and by-laws of said village, and may
be convened by the president, or as may be provided by
said laws, rules and regulations. The treasurer shall
give security to said board of trustees for the faithful
performance of his duties, and at every annual meeting,
or oftener, if required by the trustees, shall render to
them a true account of the property of the department
and of his action as treasurer. The said trustees shall
have power to remove any of the officers of the board
of trustees, after three days' notice previously given in
writing of the charges preferred, and elect others in
their stead. A majority of the trustees shall constitute
a quorum for the transaction of business, and the acts of
said board herein authorized may be done by such
majority. The board of trustees shall fill, from its members, all vacancies which may occur in the offices of said
board, until the next election after the occurrence of

such vacancies; and may, by its president or otherwise, as said board shall direct, call special elections to fill vacancies in any of the offices in this act mentioned. Notice of the time of all elections under this act shall be given by the secretary at least five days before the time thereof, by publication thereof in at least one of the newspapers of the village.

Application of fines.

§ 5. The board of trustees shall apply the funds of said corporation, which shall arise from chimney fines, certificates of membership, money paid by insurance companies in pursuance of law, and donations, or such parts of said funds or of the income thereof as they shall deem proper, to the relief of the indigent and disabled firemen or their families; and, also, to defray such contingent expenses as may be necessary in the transaction of the business of said board of trustees.

By-laws.

§ 6. Each of said fire companies shall have the right to pass by-laws for its own government, not inconsistent with the by-laws, rules and regulations established by the said board of trustees, or the charter and by-laws of the said village.

Revised Statutes applied.

§ 7. The said fire department shall possess the general powers of a corporation, as defined and limited in title three of the eighteenth chapter of part first of the Revised Statutes of this state, and shall be subject to the provisions of such chapter, so far as they may be applicable to said department and the organization thereof, and so far as the same are not inconsistent with this act; and all such parts of the charter of the said village which are inconsistent with this act are repealed.

Fines, &c.

§ 8. The said board of trustees shall have power to impose reasonable fines and penalties for violation by the members of said corporation of the by-laws, rules and regulations of said board, and to sue in the corporate name for the recovery of such penalties.

Vacancy in office of treasurer.

§ 9. The board of trustees, in case of a vacancy in the office of treasurer, shall immediately appoint a suitable person to hold such office until such vacancy can be filled by an election. Such treasurer shall, on the expiration of his term of office, pay over to his successor in office all moneys and evidences of indebtedness in his hands; and all moneys which by law now are or hereafter may be directed to be paid into the treasury of said village, or otherwise, and which now are or may hereafter by law be directed to be paid by any insurance companies, or other companies or persons, or applied for the purposes of the fire department of said village, shall be payable to the treasurer of the said corporation.

§ 10. This act shall take effect immediately.

Chap. 430.

AN ACT for the appointment of overseers of highways in the town of Schoharie, Schoharie county.

Passed April 22, 1862; three-fifths being present.

The People of the State of New York, represented in Senate and Assembly, do enact as follows:

SECTION 1. The commissioner or commissioners of highways of the town of Schoharie shall annually meet on Tuesday succeeding the annual town meeting in said town, at the place where the last town meeting was held, or as often as vacancies may occur, shall, by warrant under their hands, appoint overseers of highways of the several road districts in said town, and the overseers so appointed shall have the same powers, be subject to the same orders and liable to the same penalties as overseers chosen in town meetings.

§ 2. The commissioner or commissioners making the appointment as in section one, shall cause such warrants to be forthwith filed in the office of the town clerk, who shall immediately give notice to the persons so appointed.

§ 3. This act shall take effect immediately.

Chap. 431.

AN ACT to authorize school district number four
in the town of Greece, to raise money on its
bonds for building a school house.

Passed April 22, 1862; three-fifths being present.

*The People of the State of New York, represented in
Senate and Assembly, do enact as follows:*

SECTION 1. Whenever within one year after the passage of this act, the taxable inhabitants of school district number four of the town of Greece, in the county
of Monroe, shall according to law have determined to
raise by tax upon the taxable property of said district,
a sum exceeding four hundred dollars, for the purpose
of building and furnishing a school house in and for
said district, and shall also in like manner have determined that said sum shall be raised by equal annual installments, if said last mentioned determination shall not
within thirty days thereafter have been reconsidered
and revoked according to law, the trustees of said district may make and subscribe, and it shall be their duty
to make and subscribe, in the name and behalf of said
district, bonds payable to such person or persons as they
shall deem expedient, and conditioned for the payment
to such person or persons of said sum, without interest,
at such times and in such amounts or installments as shall
have been determined as aforesaid. And said trustees
may sell and dispose of, and it shall be their duty to sell
and dispose of the said bonds for ready money, to the best
advantage, as may be needed from time to time, but not
at a discount exceeding the rate of seven per cent on
the amounts thereof respectively. The collector of said
district shall receive, safely keep and disburse on the
order of the trustees, all moneys raised upon said bonds
by the sale and disposal thereof as aforesaid.

§ 2 It shall be the duty of said trustees to apply all
the moneys received by them upon or on account of the
sale or disposal of the said bonds towards the building
and furnishing of said school house.

§ 3. The bonds in the first section of this act mentioned, shall, when sold and disposed of as aforesaid, be binding upon the said school district ; and the trustees of said district shall have power, and it shall be their duty, at least sixty days before any one or more of said bonds shall become due, to levy a tax upon the taxable property of said district sufficient to pay such bond or bonds, and to cause the same to be collected in the same manner as other district taxes, and when collected to pay the said bonds as they shall become due.

§ 4. This act shall take effect immediately.

Chap. 432.

AN ACT to declare the village of Groton, in the county of Tompkins, a separate road district, and to provide for raising money by tax therein for highways, and to compel owners or occupants of property therein to repair sidewalks and for other purposes.

Passed April 22, 1862 ; three-fifths being present.

The People of the State of New York, represented in Senate and Assembly, do enact as follows :

SECTION 1. The said village of Groton shall constitute District. a separate road district in the said town of Groton, and the territory comprised therein shall be exempt from the superintendence and jurisdiction of the commissioners of highways of said town, except the bridges across the Owasco inlet in said village, which shall remain under the supervision of the commissioner of highways of said town, the same as though this act had been passed.* The trustees of said corporation shall have all the powers Power of within said village, and be subject to all the duties and trustees. liabilities of commissioners and overseers of highways of towns, in like cases, and may in their discretion appoint one of their number or any other competent person, to be street commissioner, who shall hold his office until another shall be appointed by the trustees, and whose special duty it shall be to superintend (subject to the con-

* So in the original.

trol of said trustees,) the construction and repairs of all
bridges, (except the bridges above specified,) streets,
roads, sidewalks and crosswalks in said village, and who
shall receive for his services such amount as a majority
of the trustees may deem proper, to be paid out of the
money arising from highway taxes.

Ibid. § 2. The said trustees shall have power to assess upon
all persons owning property in said village, annually,
such amount denominated highway tax as they shall
deem necessary to work and improve the roads, bridges,
crosswalks, streets, lanes and alleys of said village, not
to exceed four hundred dollars. Each male inhabitant
of the age of twenty-one years and upwards shall be assessed fifty cents each year, and the balance of the highway tax shall be assessed upon all persons owning real
and personal estate, banks, and banking associations,
according to the value of their real and personal estate
in said village; and the tax so raised for highway purposes shall be appropriated under the direction of said
trustees to the working and improving of the roads,
streets, bridges, crosswalks, lanes, and alleys of said village.

Sidewalks. § 3. It shall be the duty of every owner or occupant
of real estate in said village, in front of whose premises
a sidewalk has been or shall hereafter be made, to keep
the same at all times in suitable and proper repairs, and
in case of his neglect to do so, he shall be liable for all
damages which shall be sustained by such neglect.

Notice on
owner or
occupant. § 4 In case any owner or occupant shall neglect to
keep his sidewalk in suitable and proper repair, it shall
be the duty of the trustees of said village to cause a
written notice to be served upon such owner or occupant, requiring him or her to repair such sidewalk within thirty days from such service.

Service
thereof. § 5. Such written notice may be served personally or
by leaving the same at his or her place of residence with
some person of suitable age and discretion, between the
hours of eight o'clock in the morning and eight o'clock
in the evening, or in case such owner is a non-resident
of the village, by depositing such notice in the post office
at Groton, in a proper envelope directed to such owner
at his reputed place of residence, and by paying the postage on the same.

§ 6. Such repairs shall correspond in the material used **Repairs.** and in the execution of the work with the walks repaired, unless on application of said owner or occupant the trustees shall consent to the change.

§ 7. In case of neglect of any owner or occupant to **Penalty.** repair his walk within the thirty days specified in such notice, he or she shall forfeit and pay to said village the sum of ten dollars, to be sued for and recovered in the name of said village, in any court having competent jurisdiction.

§ 8. All the provisions of the general act for the incor- **Repeal.** poration of villages, so far as they may conflict with the provisions of this act, are hereby repealed, but this act shall not be construed to deprive the trustees of said **Saving clause.** village of any of their powers conferred upon them by said general act, nor to repeal the provisions therein to compel the inhabitants of any incorporate village to build or repair sidewalks and crosswalks in said village.

§ 9. This act shall take effect immediately.

Chap. 433.

AN ACT to reduce the expenses of criminal proceedings in the town and village of Binghamton.

Passed April 22, 1862; three-fifths being present.

The People of the State of New York, represented in Senate and Assembly, do enact as follows:

SECTION 1. In lieu of the costs, charges and fees now **Compensation of justices of the peace.** allowed by law, for services in criminal proceedings, there shall be paid annually to the justices of the peace residing in the village of Binghamton the sum of eight hundred dollars, to be divided between them in such manner as the board of auditors of town accounts shall determine; and no other or further compensation shall be received by said justices, or any of them, for any services rendered in criminal proceedings had before them.

§ 2. Any justice refusing to hear, examine or try any **Justice refusing to hear.** complaint or criminal charge, shall be liable to an indictment for misdemeanor, punishable by fine and imprisonment.

Accounts to be presented.

§ 3. The said justices of the peace shall present to the board of auditors of town accounts, at their annual meetings, their accounts for the proceedings specified in section one, and made out and verified as now required by law; and the supervisor of the town, acting with said board of auditors, shall determine and certify, from the accounts so presented, what proportion of said sum of eight hundred dollars is chargeable to said town and to said village and to the county of Broome; and also the proportion of said sum each of the said justices shall receive, to be divided according to the amount of services rendered by each, as shall appear by said verified accounts, and the amount so determined shall be allowed to each of said justices, with their other accounts.

Fines, &c.

§ 4. All fines and penalties imposed and received by any of such justices of the peace in criminal proceedings shall, within five days after thus received, be paid over by such justice as follows: So much thereof as shall belong to the said town of Binghamton to the treasurer of the county of Broome, for the benefit of said town; so much thereof as shall belong to said village of Binghamton, to the treasurer of said village, and so much thereof as shall be for the benefit of the poor of said town or of the county of Broome, to one of the superintendents of the poor of said county, for the benefit of such poor, and such justices of the peace shall not be entitled to any portion of such fines and penalties, on any account whatever. The said justices of the peace shall respectively, on the second Tuesday of November in each year, deliver to the supervisor of said town a detailed account or statement in writing of all fines and penalties received and paid over by him for the year directly preceding said time, which shall be verified by his affidavit that the same is true. Any violation of any of the provisions of this section shall be deemed a misdemeanor.

Take effect 1st May, 1862.

§ 5. This act shall take effect on the first day of May, eighteen hundred and sixty-two, and the sum of three hundred dollars shall be allowed the said justices collectively, from said first day of May until the annual meeting of said board of auditors of town accounts in said town, to be apportioned as is provided in the second section of this act.

Chap. 434.

AN ACT in relation to the Susquehanna Seminary at Binghamton.

Passed April 22, 1862; by a two-third vote.

The People of the State of New York, represented in Senate and Assembly, do enact as follows :

SECTION 1. The title to the site and grounds of the Susquehanna Seminary at Binghamton, with the buildings thereon, having been acquired by the state on the foreclosure of a mortgage, given under the provisions of chapter six hundred and seventy-five of the Laws of eighteen hundred and fifty-seven, the same is hereby released by the state to the trustees of the said seminary by its corporate name of the Susquehanna Seminary, on the following conditions : *Release of title to trustees.*

1. The said premises and property so released shall not in any way be aliened, mortgaged, encumbered, or the title thereto impaired or affected by any act or omission of the said trustees, to the end that the same may be preserved in perpetuity for educational purposes. *Conditions of release.*

2. The buildings on the said premises shall be kept insured by the said trustees against loss by fire, for their fair insurable value, and the policy assigned to the Commissioners of the Land Office, and the insurance continued in all respects to the satisfaction of the said commissioners ; the amount of the insurance, in case of total loss, to be paid to the state, and in case of partial loss to be applied to repair the buildings in the discretion of the said commissioners.

3. The said buildings, with the outhouses, fences and grounds shall be kept in good and sufficient repair and condition by the said trustees, to the satisfaction of the said Commissioners of the Land Office.

4. All charges and assessment on said premises for road taxes, streets, sewers and all local improvements, shall be paid by the said trustees.

5. The said trustees shall, within six months from the passage of this act, pay the amount of the costs and

charges attending the foreclosure of the mortgage above referred to, to the satisfaction of the Comptroller.

Power of commissioners of land office.
§ 2. The Commissioners of the Land Office shall have the absolute right to determine whether any breach of the above conditions, or any of them, has occurred ; and if they shall be of opinion at any time that any substantial breach of the said conditions, or any of them, has occurred, they shall have the right and it shall be their duty, unless they deem it proper on satisfactory explanations to excuse such breach, at once and without any process of law to enter into and upon and take possession of the said premises, and the same shall thereupon revert to and again become the property of the people of the state.

Payment of loan.
§ 3. The amount due on the loan made to the said seminary as aforesaid, shall be paid out of the general fund to the common school fund.

§ 4. This act shall take effect immediately.

Chap. 435.

AN ACT making appropriations for the support of Government for the fiscal year commencing on the first day of October, in the year eighteen hundred and sixty-two.

Passed April 22, 1862; by a two-third vote.

The People of the State of New York, represented in Senate and Assembly, do enact as follows :

SECTION 1. The following sums, or such portion of them as shall be authorized by law, are hereby appropriated to the several objects specified in this act, for the fiscal year commencing upon the first day of October, eighteen hundred and sixty-two, namely.

FROM THE REVENUE OF THE GENERAL FUND.

Governor.
For salary of the Governor, pursuant to the provisions of chapter three hundred and seventy-six, of the Laws of eighteen hundred and twenty-nine, four thousand dollars.

Judges court of appeals.
For salaries of the judges of the court of appeals, pursuant to the provisions of chapter two hundred and

seventy-seven of the Laws of eighteen hundred and forty-seven, and of chapter seven hundred and ninety-two of the Laws of eighteen hundred and fifty-seven, thirteen thousand five hundred dollars.

For salaries of the justices of the supreme court, pursuant to the provisions of chapter two hundred and seventy-seven of the Laws of eighteen hundred and forty-seven, and of chapter seven hundred and ninety-two of the Laws of eighteen hundred and fifty-seven, one hundred and thirteen thousand and five hundred dollars **Justices supreme court**

For salary of the Clerk of the Court of Appeals, pursuant to the provisions of chapter two hundred and seventy-seven of the laws of eighteen hundred and forty-seven, two thousand dollars. **Clerk of Appeals.**

For salary of the deputy clerk of the court of appeals, pursuant to the provisions of chapter two hundred and seventy-seven of the Laws of eighteen hundred and forty-seven, one thousand five hundred dollars. **Deputy clerk of appeals.**

For salary of the state reporter, pursuant to the provisions of chapter two hundred and seventy-seven of the Laws of eighteen hundred and forty-seven, two thousand dollars. **State reporter.**

For salary of the Attorney General, pursuant to the provisions of chapter four hundred and ninety-nine of the Laws of eighteen hundred and forty-seven, two thousand dollars. **Attorney General.**

For salary of the deputy attorney general pursuant to the provisions of chapter three hundred and eighty-five of the Laws of eighteen hundred and fifty-five, one thousand five hundred dollars. **Deputy Attorney General.**

For salary of the Secretary of State, pursuant to the provisions of chapter three hundred and ninety-nine of the Laws of eighteen hundred and fifty-four, two thousand five hundred dollars **Secretary of State.**

For salary of the deputy secretary of state, and as clerk of the commissioners of the land office, pursuant to the provisions of part one, chapter nine, title one section three of the Revised Statutes, one thousand five hundred dollars. **Deputy Secretary of State.**

For salary of the State Superintendent of Public Instructions, pursuant to the provisions of chapter ninety-seven of the Laws of eighteen hundred and fifty-four, two thousand five hundred dollars. **Superintendent of Public Instruction.**

98

Comptroller For salary of the Comptroller, pursuant to the provisions of part one, chapter nine, title one, section three of the Revised Statutes, two thousand five hundred dollars.

Deputy Comptroller For salary of the deputy comptroller, pursuant to the provisions of chapter three hundred and eighty-one of the Laws of eighteen hundred and fifty-seven, two thousand dollars.

Accountant and transfer officer Comptroller's office. For salary of the accountant and transfer officer of the Comptroller's department, pursuant to the provisions of chapter four hundred and seven of the Laws of eighteen hundred and fifty-two, one thousand seven hundred and fifty dollars.

Treasurer. For salary of the Treasurer, pursuant to the provisions of chapter three hundred seventy-six of the Laws of eighteen hundred and twenty-nine, one thousand five hundred dollars, and for compensation for countersigning transfers and assignments of securities made in the Banking Department, pursuant to the provisions of chapter one hundred and three of the Laws of eighteen hundred and fifty-seven, one thousand dollars.

Deputy Treasurer. For salary of the deputy treasurer, pursuant to the provisions of chapter two hundred and seventy-four of the Laws of eighteen hundred and forty-one, one thousand five hundred dollars.

Adjutant General. For salary of the Adjutant General, pursuant to the provisions of chapter five hundred and twenty-one of the Laws of eighteen hundred and fifty-five, one thousand five hundred dollars

Deputy Adjutant General. For salary of the deputy adjutant general, pursuant to the provisions of chapter two hundred and sixty-one of the Laws of eighteen hundred and fifty-five, one thousand dollars.

Inspector General. For compensation of the Inspector General and expenses pursuant to the provisions of chapter one hundred and eighty of the Laws of eighteen hundred and fifty-one, two thousand dollars.

Commissary General. For salary of the Commissary General one thousand five hundred dollars.

Governor's private secretary. For salary of the private secretary of the Governor, pursuant to the provisions of chapter sixty-four of the Laws of eighteen hundred and fifty-eight, two thousand dollars.

For compensation of the state assessors and their {State Assessors.} traveling expenses, pursuant to the provisions of chapter three hundred and twelve of the Laws of eighteen hundred and fifty-nine, to each assessor — — — —

For salary of the curator of the State Cabinet of Natu- {Curator Cabinet Natural History.} ral History, one thousand dollars.

For salary of the superintendent of weights and {Superintendent Weights and Measures.} measures, pursuant to the provisions of chapter one hundred and thirty-four of the Laws of eighteen hundred and fifty-one, five huhdred dollars.

For salaries of the Inspectors of State Prisons, pursu- {Inspectors of State Prisons.} ant to the provisions of chapter four hundred and ninety-nine of the Laws of eighteen hundred and forty-seven, four thousand eight hundred dollars ; and for their traveling expenses, one thousand two hundred dollars.

For salary of the deputy state engineer and surveyor, {Deputy State Engineer.} pursuant to the provisions of chapter six hundred and thirty-three of the Laws of eighteen hundred and fifty-seven, two thousand dollars ; and for compensation of clerks to assist him in the preparation of railroad reports, one thousand five hundred dollars ; and for expenses of {Printing railroad reports.} printing and binding said reports three thousand five hundred dollars, which salary, compensation, printing and binding, whether ordered to be printed by the legis- {Railroad companies to pay expense of same.} lature or otherwise, shall be refunded to the treasury by the several railroad companies of this state in proportion to their respective gross receipts pursuant to the provisions of chapter five hundred and twenty-six of the Laws of eighteen hundred and fifty-five

For salary of the inspector of gas metres and contin- {Inspector of gas metres.} gent expenses, pursuant to the provisions of chapter one hundred and sixteen of the Laws of eighteen hundred and sixty, two thousand five hundred dollars ; which amount shall be refunded to the treasury by the several gas-light companies, pursuant to the provisions of chapter three hundred and eleven of the Laws of eighteen hundred and fifty-nine

For compensation of clerks and messengers in the exe- {Clerks in Executive Department} cutive department, pursuant to the provisions of chapter sixty-four of the Laws of eighteen hundred and fifty-eight, two thousand six hundred dollars.

For salaries of clerks in the office of the Secretary of {Clerks in Secretary's office.} State, for indexing the Session Laws, and all other clerical services incident to that office, eight thousand five hundred dollars.

Clerks in Comptroller's office. For salaries of the clerks in the office of the Comptroller. eleven thousand three hundred dollars.

Clerks office of Public Instruction. For salaries of the clerks in the Department of Public Instruction, pursuant to the provisions of chapter ninety-seven of the Laws of eighteen hundred and fifty-four, fifteen hundred dollars, and for salary of deputy superintendent of Public Instruction, fifteen hundred dollars.

Clerks in Treasurer's office. For salaries of the clerks in the office of the Treasurer, two thousand five hundred dollars.

For salaries of the clerk and messenger in the office of the Attorney General, one thousand dollars.

Clerks in State Engineer's office For salaries of the clerks in the office of the State Engineer and Surveyor, two thousand eight hundred and fifty dollars

Clerks in office of Court of Appeals. For salaries of the clerks in the office of the Clerk of the Court of Appeals, three thousand dollars.

Clerks in Adjutant General's office. For salary of the clerk in the office of the Adjutant General, nine hundred dollars.

Members and officers Legislature. For compensation of members and officers of the legislature, ninety-five thousand dollars.

Advances to clerks of Senate and Assembly. For advances to the clerks of the Senate and Assembly for contingent expenses, fourteen thousand dollars; but this appropriation shall not authorize the furnishing of postage stamps to members and officers of the legislature.

Contingent expenses For postage, expenses of committees, pay of witnesses, the Legislative Manual, Croswell's Manual, and other contingent expenses of the legislature, eighteen thousand dollars.

Stationery for public offices. For stationery for the public offices and for the clerks of the Senate and Assembly, pursuant to the provisions of chapter three hundred and thirteen of the Laws of eighteen hundred and forty-eight and chapter five hundred and thirty of the Laws of eighteen hundred and fifty-three, four thousand five hundred dollars.

Fuel for public buildings. For fuel for the Capitol, the State Hall and State Library, two thousand five hundred dollars

Furniture, books, printing, &c., for the public offices. For furniture, books, binding, blanks, printing, and other necessary expenses of the public offices, seven thousand dollars; which amount shall be apportioned as follows: for the office of the Secretary of State, one thousand two hundred dollars; for the office of the Comptroller, one thousand two hundred dollars; for the Department of Public Instruction, one thousand dollars;

for the office of the Clerk of the Court of Appeals, one thousand dollars; for the office of the Treasurer, five hundred dollars; for the office of the Attorney General, five hundred dollars; for the office of the State Engineer and Surveyor, five hundred dollars; for the office of the Adjutant General, one thousand dollars; for the office of the Inspector General, one hundred dollars.

For postage of official letters and documents of the Governor, Secretary of State, Comptroller, Treasurer, Superintendent of Public Instruction, Attorney General, State Engineer and Surveyor, Clerk of the Court of Appeals, Adjutant General and Inspector General, three thousand dollars. Postage for public offices.

For expenses of the capitol and state library, for repairs, cleaning, labor, gas and other necessary purposes, seven thousand dollars. Incidental expenses Capitol and State Library.

For salary of the superintendent of the capital, seven hundred and fifty dollars. Superintendent of Capitol.

For expenses of the state hall, for repairs, cleaning, labor, gas, compensation of the superintendent, and other necessary purposes, four thousand dollars. Expenses State Hall.

To the Regents of the University and the Executive Committee of the State Agricultural Society, for the expenses of the hall for the State Cabinet of Natural History and the Agricultural Museum, which hall is hereby placed under their joint care and control, two thousand and two hundred dollars, which sum shall be applied to superintendence, care, ordinary repairs, cleaning, fuel, gas, and contingent expenses, and all bills for the same shall be audited by the secretary of the said Regents and the secretary of the Agricultural Society, and paid only on their certificate. Regents of the University for expenses of hall for Cabinet of Natural History.

For increase, preservation and so forth of the State Cabinet of Natural History, eight hundred dollars; provided that no part of said sum shall be paid to the curator except to re-imburse him for actual expenses incurred incident to such duties, to be paid on the order of the chancellor of the University. State Cabinet Natural History.

To the trustees of the state library for necessary expenses of that institution, nine thousand eight hundred and fifty dollars, to be apportioned and paid as follows, namely: (for the enlargement of the library, three thousand dollars; for binding, lettering, and marking books, one thousand two hundred dollars;) for expenses in the Trustees of the State Library.

care of the library, transportation of books, and incidental expenses, seven hundred and fifty dollars; for international and state exchanges, four hundred dollars;

Salaries of Librarians. for salaries of the librarian of the law library and of the librarian of the general library, as said librarians shall be henceforth designated, and for compensation of such assistant librarians as said trustees may appoint when necessary, four thousand dollars; for compensation of the janitor, five hundred dollars.

Regents University, printing, &c. For expenses of the Regents of the University, for printing, stationery, postage, clerk hire, and other necessary purposes, one thousand dollars.

Secretary of Regents. For salary of the secretary of the Board of Regents of the University, two thousand dollars.

Incidental expenses of government For incidental expenses of the government, seven hundred and fifty dollars.

Apprehension of fugitives. For apprehension of fugitives from justice, pursuant to the provisions of part four, chapter three, title seven, section forty-five of the Revised Statutes, one thousand dollars

Constables Court of Appeals. For compensation of constables for attendance upon the court of appeals, pursuant to the provisions of chapter four hundred and twenty-nine of the Laws of eighteen hundred and forty-seven, five hundred dollars.

Banking Department For expenses of the Banking Department, for salary of the Superintendent, compensation of clerks, and other necessary purposes, pursuant to chapter one hundred and sixty-four of the Laws of eighteen hundred and fifty-one, and chapter one hundred and three of the Laws of eighteen hundred and fifty-seven, thirty thousand dollars.

Insurance Department For expenses of the Insurance Department, for salary of the Superintendent, compensation of clerks and other necessary purposes, pursuant to the provisions of chapter three hundred and sixty-six of the Laws of eighteen hundred and fifty-nine, ten thousand dollars.

Rent Governor's house For rent and taxes of the house occupied by the Governor, pursuant to the provisions of part one, chapter nine, title one, section thirteen of the Revised Statutes, three thousand three hundred and thirty dollars.

State printing, official canvass, &c For printing for the state, including binding, mapping, engraving, publication of the official canvass in the state paper and in two newspapers in each senate district only, and other official notices pursuant to the provisions of chapter four hundred and twenty-four of the Laws of eighteen hundred and forty-six, and chapter two hundred and forty of the Laws of eighteen hundred and forty-seven, and for printing and binding the report of the commissioners of the Code, one hundred thousand dollars.

For expenditures of the Commissary Department and the compensation of keepers of arsenals, pursuant to the provisions of part one, chapter nine, title one, section twenty-seven of the Revised Statutes, ten thousand dollars. _{Commissary Department.}

For donations to agricultural societies in the several counties, and to the state society for the promotion of agriculture pursuant to the provisions of chapter two hundred and ninety-nine of the Laws of eighteen hundred and forty-eight, ten thousand dollars. And for machinery to test the experiment of manufacturing flax cotton to be expended under the direction of the State Agricultural Society two thousand dollars. _{Agricultural societies}

For salary of the entomologist of the State Agricultural Society, one thousand dollars. _{Salary Entomologist.}

For the support and maintenance of the several state prisons pursuant to the provisions of chapter two hundred and forty of the Laws of eighteen hundred and fifty-four, two hundred and ninety thousand dollars. _{State Prisons.}

For compensation of sheriffs for the transportation of convicts to the prisons, pursuant to the provisions of chapter one hundred and twenty three of the Laws of eighteen hundred and forty-nine, twenty-five thousand dollars. _{Transportation of convicts.}

For purchase of books for the use of convicts in the state prisons, six hundred and fifty dollars, which amount shall be apportioned as follows: To the prison at Sing Sing, three hundred dollars; to the prison at Auburn, two hundred dollars; to the prison at Clinton, one hundred dollars; and to the asylum for insane convicts, fifty dollars. _{Books for convicts.}

For the support and expenses of the asylum for insane convicts, pursuant to the provisions of chapter one hundred and thirty of the Laws of eighteen hundred and fifty-eight, fifteen thousand dollars. _{Asylum Insane Convicts.}

For the maintenance of insane female convicts at the State Lunatic Asylum, six hundred dollars. _{Insane female convicts.}

Agent to examine auctioneer's accounts. For compensation of the agent to examine the accounts of auctioneers, pursuant to the provisions of chapter three hundred and ninety-nine of the Laws of eighteen hundred and forty-nine, eight hundred dollars.

Attorney Seneca Indians. For compensation of the attorney of the Seneca Indians, pursuant to the provisions of chapter one hundred and fifty of the Laws of eighteen hundred and forty-five, one hundred and fifty dollars.

Attorney St. Regis Indians. For compensation of the attorney of the St. Regis Indians, pursuant to the provisions of chapter three hundred and twenty-five of the Laws of eighteen hundred and sixty-one, one hundred and fifty dollars.

Agent Onondaga Indians. For compensation of the agent of the Onondaga Indians, pursuant to the provisions of chapter three hundred and seventy-six of the Laws of eighteen hundred and fifty-one, one hundred dollars.

Agent Onondaga Indians Allegany and Cattaraugus reservations. For compensation of the agent of the Onondaga Indians upon the Allegany and Cattaraugus reservations, pursuant to the provisions of chapter one hundred and seventy-eight of the Laws of eighteen hundred and forty-seven, one hundred and fifty dollars.

Removing intruders on Indian lands. For expenses of removing intruders on Indian lands, pursuant to the provisions of chapter two hundred and four of the Laws of eighteen hundred and twenty-one, two hundred dollars.

Expenses public lands For expenses of public lands including the compensation of the Lieutenant-Governor and of the Speaker of the Assembly for their attendance as commissioners of land office, four thousand dollars.

Fees county clerks. For fees of county clerks, twenty-five dollars.

Fees Surrogates. For fees of surrogates, twenty-five dollars.

Fees sheriffs, &c. For costs of suit, fees of sheriffs, compensation of witnesses, and for expenses and disbursements by the Attorney General, pursuant to the provisions of part three, chapter four, title ten of the Revised Statutes, two thousand five hundred dollars.

Commissioners to examine Treasurer's accounts. For compensation of commissioners to examine the accounts of the Treasurer, and of the Canal and Banking Departments, pursuant to the provisions of chapter five hundred and ninety-two of the Laws of eighteen hundred and fifty-seven, fifteen hundred dollars.

Failure title to lands. For refunding of money in cases of failure to title of lands sold by the state, pursuant to the provisions of part one, chapter nine, title five, section six of the Revised Statutes, three hundred dollars.

For the annuity of James Minor, pursuant to the provisions of chapter two hundred of the Laws of eighteen hundred and fifteen, sixty dollars. *James Minor.*

For compensation of Levi S. Backus for furnishing the Radii to the deaf and dumb persons of this state, pursuant to the provisions of chapter three hundred and twenty-nine of the Laws of eighteen hundred and thirty-nine, three hundred dollars. *Levi S. Backus.*

For furnishing to other states the reports of the court of appeals and the supreme court, pursuant to the provisions of chapter five hundred and thirty-six of the Laws of eighteen hundred and thirty-six, two hundred and fifty dollars. *Law reports to other states.*

For expenses of transportation of the Session Laws, the journals and documents of the legislature, reports, books, packages, and so forth, by express, for the public offices, and for boxes, pursuant to the provisions of chapter two hundred and fifty-four of the Laws of eighteen hundred and forty-seven, three thousand five hundred dollars. *Transportation Session Laws.*

For expenses of the Onondaga salt springs, pursuant to the provisions of chapter two hundred and twenty-nine of the Laws of eighteen hundred and forty-three, twenty-five thousand dollars. *Onondaga Salt Springs.*

For refunding of money paid into the treasury through mistake, pursuant to the provisions of part one, chapter eight, title three, section fifteen of the Revised Statutes, five hundred dollars. *Money paid in treasury through mistake.*

For compensation of the keeper of "Washington's head quarters," at Newburgh, one hundred dollars. *Washington's head quarters.*

For payment of moneys received into the treasury for taxes for opening and improving roads, four thousand dollars. *Opening and improving roads.*

For relief of the Onondaga Indians, pursuant to the provisions of chapter two hundred and six of the Laws of eighteen hundred and fifty-eight, three hundred dollars. *Onondaga Indians, relief of.*

For expenses of books and stationery for the transfer office, at the Manhattan Company, in the city of New York, two hundred dollars *Manhattan Company.*

For interest on the debt created for the benefit of the Stockbridge Indians, pursuant to the provisions of chap- *Stockbridge Indians,* ter two hundred and eight of the Laws of eighteen hundred and forty-eight and chapter thirty-seven of the Laws of eighteen hundred and fifty, two thousand one hundred and sixty dollars.

State stock, Albany basin loan. For interest on the state stock issued on the account of the Albany basin loan, pursuant to the provisions of chapter two hundred of the Laws of eighteen hundred and forty-nine, nine thousand six hundred and twenty-nine dollars and twenty-eight cents.

Interest on canal loan 1849. For interest on the loan of fifty thousand dollars made for extraordinary repairs and improvements of the canals, pursuant to the provisions of chapter three hundred and seventy-four of the Laws of eighteen hundred and forty-nine, three thousand dollars.

Interest on Oswego canal loan. For interest on the loan of two hundred thousand dollars made for the completion of the Oswego canal, pursuant to the provisions of chapter five hundred and one of the Laws of eighteen hundred and fifty-one, twelve thousand dollars.

Interest on canal loan 1858. For interest on the temporary loan of two hundred thousand dollars made in eighteen hundred and fifty-eight, for the enlargement and completion of the canals, ten thousand dollars.

Deficiencies general fund debt Sinking Fund. For estimated deficiencies in the general fund debt Sinking Fund to meet the interest due on that portion of the state debt chargeable to that fund, fifteen thousand six hundred and sixty-seven dollars and fifty-eight cents.

State Lunatic Asylum. For salaries of the officers of the State Lunatic Asylum, pursuant to the provisions of chapter one hundred and thirty-five of the Laws of eighteen hundred and forty-two, seven thousand five hundred dollars.

Mark Jack. For the support of Mark Jack, an insane Indian, at the Lunatic Asylum, two hundred dollars.

Pilot commissioners. To the board of pilot commissioners for their expenses in protecting the harbor of the city of New York and removing obstructions from the same, four thousand five hundred dollars.

N. Y. Ophthalmic Hospital. To the New York Ophthalmic Hospital, one thousand dollars.

Deaf and dumb pupils. For the instruction and maintenance of two hundred and sixty indigent pupils at the Institution for the Instruction of the Deaf and Dumb in the city of New York, provided that that number of indigent pupils shall have been selected by the Superintendent of Public Instruction, and shall have been, for the entire preceding year, instructed and maintained at that institution at its own expense, and pursuant to the provisions of chapter ninety-seven of the Laws of eighteen hundred and fifty-two, thirty-nine thousand dollars, or a proportionate amount for a shorter period of time and a smaller number of pupils, as shall be duly verified by affidavits of the president and secretary of that institution.

For the payment of the interest of the debt owed by the officers of the Institution for the instruction of the Deaf and Dumb in the city of New York, thirteen thousand three hundred and fifty-six dollars. Payment of pupils.

For the instruction and maintenance of one hundred and fifty indigent pupils at the Institution for the Blind in the city of New York, at a rate not exceeding two hundred dollars per year for each pupil, thirty thousand dollars, or a proportionate amount for a shorter period of time and a smaller number of pupils, as shall be duly verified by affidavits of the president and secretary of that institution. Blind pupils

For the Society for the Reformation of Juvenile Delinquents in the city of New York, twenty-four thousand dollars. Juvenile delinquents

For the House of Refuge of Western New York, twenty-five thousand dollars. House of refuge.

For the Thomas Asylum for Orphan and Destitute Indian Children, for the maintenance and instruction of fifty children, one thousand dollars, payable quarterly, provided that that number of Indian children shall have been maintained and instructed at that institution, during the quarter preceding each payment; and a proportionate amount for a shorter period of time or a smaller number of children as shall be duly proven to the Comptroller and Superintendent of Public Instruction. Thomas Asylum, Indian children.

For the Idiot Asylum, eighteen thousand dollars. Idiot asylum.

For the Womens' Hospital in the city of New York, the New York Infirmary for Indigent Women and Children, Buffalo General Hospital, the Buffalo Lying-in-Hospital of the Sisters of Charity, and the several incorporated hospitals in this state, excepting those in the city of New York, to be divided among said institutions in proportion to the number of patients in the same, and Hospitals.

the time that such patients have been under treatment during the year, twenty-five thousand dollars; which proportionate amount shall be paid as directed, upon the presentation of a report duly verified, pursuant to the provisions of chapter four hundred and ten of the Laws of eighteen hundred and fifty-one.

Orphan asylums and other institutions.

For the incorporated orphan asylums in this state, except the Leake and Watts Orphan Asylum of the city of New York, and including the Society for the Relief of Destitute Children of Seamen in the county of Richmond, the Forest Orphan Institute at Maspeth, in the county of Queens, the Five Points House of Industry in the city of New York, the Colored Orphan Asylum in the city of New York, the Female Guardian Society and Home for the Friendless in the city of New York, the Nursery and Child's Hospital in the city of New York, the Poughkeepsie Home for the Friendless, the Albany Guardian Society and Home for the Friendless, the Syracuse Home Association, the Watertown Home for Destitute, Friendless and Orphan Children, and the Rochester Home of the Friendless, forty thousand dollars, which amount shall be apportioned by the Comptroller among the several counties of this state, in the rates of or proportion to their aggregate valuation as established by the board of equalization. The dividend to which the several counties are respectively entitled shall be divided between the several asylums in the said several counties in proportion to the number of indigent and orphan children wholly maintained during the preceding year in each of the said asylums. In the case of counties in which there are no such asylums, the dividend to which said counties shall be entitled shall be paid to the board of supervisors of such counties, to be

Board of Supervisors.

applied by said boards of supervisors to the support and education of orphan and homeless children.

Support of common schools.

From the proceeds of the state tax for the support of schools. For dividends to the common schools of the state one million one hundred thousand dollars or so much of that amount as shall be received from the tax levied for the current fiscal year pursuant to the provisions of chapter one hundred and eighty of the Laws of eighteen hundred and fifty-six.

FROM THE GENERAL FUND DEBT SINKING FUND.

For interest on the general fund state debt of six mil- *Interest general fund state debt.*
lion three hundred and forty-six thousand nine hundred
and fifty-nine dollars and fifty cents, three hundred and
fifty-eight thousand three hundred and five dollars and
ninety-one cents.

For payment of annuities to Indian nations, seven *Annuities to Indian nations.*
thousand three hundred and sixty-one dollars and sixty-
seven cents, to be apportioned as follows :—To the On-
ondagas, two thousand four hundred and thirty dollars ;
to the Cayugas, two thousand three hundred dollars ; to
the Senecas, five hundred dollars, and to the St. Regis
Indians, two thousand one hundred and thirty-one dollars and sixty-seven cents.

FROM THE UNITED STATES DEPOSIT FUND.

For dividends to common schools pursuant to the pro- *Common schools.*
visions of chapter two hundred and thirty seven of the
Laws of eighteen hundred and thirty-eight, including
the salaries of the county school commissioners, pursuant to the provisions of chapter one hundred and seventy-
nine of the Laws of eighteen hundred and fifty-six, one
hundred and sixty-five thousand dollars ; and for dividends to academies under the aforesaid law of eighteen
hundred and thirty-eight, twenty-eight thousand dollars. *Capital common school fund*

For amount to be added to the capital of the Common
School Fund, pursuant to the ninth article of the constitution of the state, twenty-five thousand dollars.

For the instruction of teachers of common schools in *Teachers.*
academies designated for that purpose by the Regents
of the University, pursuant to the provisions of chapter
two hundred and thirty-five of the Laws of eighteen
hundred and fifty-two, eighteen thousand dollars.

For the support of the State Normal School, twelve *State Normal School.*
thousand dollars.

For refunding moneys erroneously paid into the trea- *Erroneous payments.*
sury, five hundred dollars.

FROM THE COMMON SCHOOL FUND.

For dividends to the common schools of this state, one *Common schools.*
hundred and fifty-five thousand dollars.

For maintenance of Indian schools, pursuant to the *Indian schools.*
provisions of chapter seventy-one of the Laws of
eighteen hundred and fifty-six, four thousand dollars.

Teachers' institutes. For maintenance of teachers' institutes in the several counties, pursuant to the provisions of chapter three hundred and sixty-one of the Laws of eighteen hundred and forty-seven, eight thousand dollars.

Refunding moneys. For refunding of money paid into the treasury for the redemption of lands sold for arrears of consideration, pursuant to the provisions of chapter four hundred and thirty-seven of the Laws of eighteen hundred and thirty-six, five hundred dollars.

Refunding moneys. For refunding of surplus moneys received on re-selling of lands, one thousand dollars.

FROM THE LITERATURE FUND.

Academies. For dividends to the academies, pursuant to the provisions of chapter three hundred and twenty-seven of the Laws of eighteen hundred and thirty-eight, twelve thousand dollars

Text books. For purchase of text-books, maps and globes, philosophical and chemical apparatus, specimens of models for the academies, two thousand five hundred dollars.

FROM THE BANK FUND.

Interest on stock. For interest on stock issued on the account of the Bank Fund, pursuant to the provisions of chapter one hundred and fourteen of the Laws of eighteen hundred and forty-five, two thousand five hundred dollars.

Redemption of bills For redemption of bills, twenty dollars.

Contingent expenses. For contingent expenses, pursuant to the provisions of chapter one hundred and sixty-four of the Laws of eighteen hundred and fifty-one, two hundred dollars.

Payments how made. § 2. The several amounts appropriated in this act shall be paid by the Treasurer from the several funds as specified. The Comptroller, before drawing his warrant for such payment, shall require the proper certificates or vouchers to be presented, and except for salaries established by law, a detailed account of the services, duly verified by the affidavit of the party by whom such payment is demanded, and if the demand is for taveling expenses, the aforesaid detailed account must specify the distance traveled, the places of starting and destination, the duty, or business, and the date, together with the items of expense, all duly verified. On all accounts for transportation, stationery and other expenditures where bills can be procured, such bills duly receipted must accompany the accounts. The Treasurer shall report annually to the legislature the details of such expenditures.

Chap. 436.

AN ACT in relation to the draining of certain lands in the town of Ithaca, county of Tompkins.

Passed April 22, 1862; three-fifths being present.

The People of the State of New York, represented in Senate and Assembly, do enact as follows :

SECTION 1. The trustees of the village of Ithaca are hereby empowered to act as commissioners for the purpose of dyking and draining such of the swamp and marsh lands in the village or town of Ithaca, as in their judgment may be necessary to improve the health of the citizens of Ithaca, by erecting suitable dykes or embankments along the several streams in said town and village, and by opening suitable ditches or drains, either upon the surface, beneath the surface, or both, therefrom to the Cayuga lake or other outlets, from and to such points as shall be found, in the judgment of the commissioners hereby appointed or authorized, most available. *Power of trustees of Ithaca.*

§ 2. The said commissioners shall have power to employ a surveyor and engineer, and shall cause accurate surveys and levels to be made of said lands and maps thereof, one of which shall be placed in the county clerk's office, and remain as a matter of record, and shall dig ditches of sufficient capacity, with so many lateral ditches as may be necessary, in the* judgment, to drain said lands, and shall raise suitable dykes or banks along the borders of the streams adjacent to said lands, to prevent the overflow of said streams during periods of high water upon said lands, and shall have power to make temporary loans to carry on the said works, as the same shall from time to time be required. *Survey to be made.* *Loans.*

§ 3. Said commissioners shall assess the expenses of such maps and survey, and the other expenses incurred *Expenses of map and survey and*

*So in the original.

other ex-
penses to
be assessed
on owners
of land. in the performance of their duties, including land damages therefor, on the owners of the land aforesaid, and the citizens of the village of Ithaca at large, in proportion to the benefits received by them respectively, as nearly as may be estimated ; and such assessment on the owners of such drained lands shall be a lien upon the lands benefited to the amount assessed upon each separate parcel or ownership, and the portion assessed upon the citizens at large shall be collected as other village taxes are now provided by law. After the said assessment shall be duly made, the said commissioners shall give the like public notice thereof as is required by law to be given by the assessors of towns of the completion of their rolls, and the same proceedings shall be had upon the application of any person considering himself aggrieved as are had by such assessors. When such assessment shall be completed, a copy thereof shall, with the map and survey mentioned in the second section of this act, be filed in the office of the clerk of Tompkins county, within two months after the work of such drainage shall be completed, and personal notice shall be served on all resident owners, and notice by mail on all non-resident owners of lands then assessed for said drainage, which notice shall describe said lot or parcel of land, and specify the amount assessed thereon, and when and where such assessment is payable ; and said notice shall be thus given at least six weeks before said assessment is payable, and, when so served by mail, by enclosing the same in an envelope directed to the person at his place of residence, and by prepaying the legal postage thereon.

Notice.

Assessment
to be filed
with county
clerk.

Notice.

Assessment
to be pub-
lished. § 4. The said commissioners, on the completion of the assessment, shall cause the same to be published in the Ithaca Journal and Tompkins County Democrat, in the county of Tompkins, for six weeks successively, specifying the time and place in the village of Ithaca where payment of such assessment can be made at least one day in each week to said commissioners, or one of them ; and it shall be the duty of said commissioners to provide for the presence of one of their number at such time and place. The expenses of publication shall be included in such assessment.

When com-
missioners
to sell lands
assessed. § 5. If any of said assessments shall remain unpaid after the expiration of the last day for receiving the

same, pursuant to such notice, the said commissioners shall proceed in the same manner specified in the two preceding sections to give public notice that they will, on a certain day, sell so much and such parcels of said land on which said assessments have not been paid, as may be necessary to pay the amount so remaining unpaid on said assessment, together with the expenses of such sale and notice, and shall on the day and at the place appointed sell the same to the highest bidder. Such notice **Notice.** of sale shall be published six weeks before the day of sale, and such sale shall be made at the village of Ithaca. In case of any surplus remaining from such sale, it shall **Surplus.** be paid by the commissioners to the owner of the land from which the same was realized, if demanded, within thirty days after such sale, on producing a proper evidence of title, and if not demanded, shall be paid to the county treasurer for the use of the party who may be entitled to the same.

§ 6. Such sale may be adjourned for a time not ex- **Adjournment of sale** ceeding one month, if the commissioners shall deem just cause to exist therefor, and the sale shall be made by two of the commissioners. The commissioners mak- **Conveyance of land sold** ing the sale are hereby authorized to execute and deliver to the purchaser or purchasers of said land conveyances of the parcels so sold, setting forth the nature of the sale, the consideration paid, and providing that the owner of the land described in such conveyance, or the person in whose name it was assessed, or his representatives or assigns, may within one year from the date of such **Redemption in one year from sale.** sale pay to the grantee of such conveyance, his heirs, representatives or assigns, or into the office of the treasurer of Tompkins county, for his or their use, the amount of the consideration stated in said conveyance, the fees for recording the same, and ten per cent interest on such consideration, which payment shall render such conveyance void. It shall be the duty of the party receiving such payment, by way of redemption, to acknowledge the same by a written instrument in due form of law, before a commissioner of deeds or other officer, at the expense of the party making such payment; and such instrument may be recorded in the office of the clerk of the county of Tompkins, with the like effect as the satisfaction of a mortgage.

100

§ 7. The said commissioners shall, within one month after the completion of such sale, file a report of their proceedings, duly verified, with the clerk of the county aforesaid.

Commissioners to report.

. § 8. The said commissioners shall have authority to appoint one agent or overseer to superintend and inspect said work, at a compensation of two dollars per day for such time only as he is actually employed on said work; and said commissioners shall be entitled to receive two dollars per day for each day that they are necessarily engaged on the said work.

Agent or overseer may be appointed.

§ 9. Nothing in this act contained shall be construed so as to make the state liable in any case for moneys expended by the said commissioners, or for any services rendered by them in the discharge of their duties under this act.

Saving clause.

§ 10. This act shall take effect when approved by a vote of a majority of the electors of Ithaca at any election held for that purpose pursuant to a notice of the trustees of said village, which notice, when given, shall be for the same time and in the same manner as is now provided by law for a general election.

This act to take effect when approved by a majority of electors of Ithaca.

Chap. 437.

AN ACT to incorporate the Moresville Turnpike Company.

Passed April 22, 1862; three-fifths being present.

The People of the State of New York, represented in Senate and Assembly, do enact as follows:

SECTION 1. Ira S. Birdsall, William W. More, John L. More, with their associates and successors, are hereby created a body corporate, to be known as the Moresville Turnpike Company, and by that name shall have perpetual succession, possess the powers and be liable to the duties and responsibilities which pertain to turnpike companies duly incorporated pursuant to the laws of this state, except so far as the same are affected by the provisions of this act.

§ 2. It shall be lawful for the Moresville Turnpike Company to take, hold and operate for the purposes of a turnpike, all that portion of highway beginning at the eastern terminus of the Delaware Turnpike in the town of Blenheim, in the county of Schoharie, and extending for the space of about ten miles, more or less, to a point within four rods of the western terminus of the Pratts-ville bridge, upon the thoroughfare commonly known as the Windham Turnpike.

§ 3. The capital stock of said turnpike company shall be five thousand dollars.

§ 4. The Moresville Turnpike Company may erect a toll gate upon their road, at a convenient point within one-quarter of a mile east of the village of Moresville, in the town of Roxbury, but shall not demand or receive more than one-half the usual rates of toll from residents of Roxbury passing through the same.

Chap. 438.

AN ACT to provide for the formation of societies for the prevention of horse stealing.

Passed April 22, 1862; three-fifths being present.

The People of the State of New York, represented in Senate and Assembly, do enact as follows :

SECTION 1. Any ten or more persons of full age, citizens of this state and of the United States, who shall desire to associate themselves into a society for the prevention of horse stealing, by the employment of patrolmen, riders and messengers, and the use of all other lawful means to prevent the same, may make, sign and acknowledge before any officer authorized to take the acknowledgement of deeds in this state and file the same in the office of the Secretary of State, and a duplicate thereof in the office of the clerk of the county in which the business of said society is to be conducted, a certificate in writing in which shall be stated the name or title by which such society shall be known in law, the particular business and objects of such society, the number of trustees, directors or managers to manage the same, and the names of the trustees, directors or managers of such society for the first year of its existence ; but such certificate shall not be filed unless by the written consent and approbation of one of the justices of the supreme court of the district in which the place of business of such company or association shall be located, to be endorsed on such certificate.

When a body corporate. § 2. Upon filing a certificate as aforesaid the persons who shall have signed and acknowledged such certificate and their associates and successors, shall thereupon by virtue of this act be a body politic and corporate by the name stated in such certificate, and by that name they and their successors shall and may have succession and **May sue and be sued, &c.** shall be persons in law capable of suing and being sued, and they and their successors may have and use a common seal. And they and their successors by their corporate name shall in law be capable of taking, receiving, purchasing and holding for the purpose of their incorporation and for no other purpose, personal estate to an amount not to exceed one thousand dollars ; to make by-laws for the management of its affairs not inconsistent with the constitution and laws of this state or of the United States ; to elect and appoint the officers and agents of such society for the management of its business and to allow them a suitable compensation.

Revised Statutes applied. § 3. Every corporation formed under this act shall possess the powers and be subject to the provisions and restrictions contained in the third title of the eighteenth chapter of the first part of the Revised Statutes.

§ 4. The legislature may at any time amend, annul or repeal any incorporation formed or created under this act.

§ 5. This act shall take effect immediately.

Chap. 439.

AN ACT to sell and divide the property of the First Congregational Society of Groton, excepting the burying ground.

Passed April 22, 1862.

The People of the State of New York, represented in Senate and Assembly, do enact as follows:

SECTION 1. The trustees of the First Congregational Society of Groton, or a majority of them, are hereby authorized and empowered to sell and convey the property of said society, except the burying ground, at such time or times, on such terms, and in such manner as they or a majority of them shall deem just and equitable, and divide the proceeds thereof.

§ 2. The proceeds of such sale, after deducting the expenses thereof, shall be distributed by said trustees among the proprietors or owners thereof as soon after such sale as the terms thereof will allow, in proportion to the amount each claimant shall be entitled to as determined by said trustees.

§ 3. The said trustees, or a majority of them, shall have power to hear and determine all claims which may be presented to them for any part of said property, and for that purpose shall meet on the first Tuesday of July, at one o'clock P. M., eighteen hundred and sixty-two, at some convenient place in the town of Groton, and may adjourn, from time to time, as may be necessary for the transaction of such business. The said trustees shall cause notices of such meeting to be posted up in at least six public places in the town of Groton at least three months prior to such meeting, and shall cause the same to be published in one or more newspapers, published in the county of Tompkins, for at least sixty days prior to said meeting; and any persons having claims to any of said property, shall present them to said trustees on or before such meeting, or be forever debarred such claims.

§ 4. This act shall take effect immediately.

Chap. 440.

AN ACT to amend an act entitled "An act to incorporate the Society for the Relief of Poor Widows with Small Children," passed April fifth, eighteen hundred and ten.

Passed April 22, 1862.

The People of the State of New York, represented in Senate and Assembly, do enact as follows:

SECTION 1. The first section of an act entitled "An act to incorporate the Society for the Relief of Poor Widows with Small Children," passed April fifth, eighteen hundred and ten, is hereby amended so as to read as follows:

All such persons of the female sex as now are or hereafter shall be annual subscribers to the said corporation, shall be, and hereby are constituted a body corporate by the name of "The Society for the Relief of Poor Widows with Small Children," and by that name shall have perpetual succession, and be in law capable of suing and being sued, defending and being defended in all courts and places whatsoever, and in all manner of actions and causes whatsoever, and may have a common seal and change the same at their pleasure, and shall also, by the same name, be capable in law of purchasing, holding and conveying any estate, real or personal, for the use of the said corporation, provided that such estate shall never exceed in value one hundred thousand dollars, nor be applied to any other purposes than the charitable one for which this incorporation is formed.

§ 2. The second section of the said act is hereby amended so as to read as follows:

The estate and concerns of the said corporation shall be managed and disposed of by a board of direction, to be composed of a first and second directress, a secretary, a treasurer and a board of managers (one-half of whom shall be a quorum) to be elected by plurality of ballots of the members resident in the city of New York, yearly, on the third Thursday of November, at such place in the said city, and after such notice as the board of directors may, from time to time, by ordinance appoint; and if any vacancy shall be occasioned by the death, resignation or removal of a directress, secretary, treasurer or manager, the same shall be filled for the remainder of the year by the board of directors by ballot as aforesaid, to be holden at such time and place in the said city as the board of direction shall appoint.

Chap. 441.

AN ACT to consolidate certain school districts within or adjoining the corporate limits of the village of Sag Harbor, Suffolk county, and to establish a Union School therein.

Passed April 22, 1862; three-fifths being present.

The People of the State of New York, represented in Senate and Assembly, do enact as follows :

SECTION 1. School districts numbers twenty-one and eleven of the town of Southampton, and number nine of the town of East Hampton, all lying within or adjoining the corporate limits of the village of Sag Harbor, are hereby consolidated for the purposes in this act specified, and shall hereafter, for such purposes, form but one school district, to be called the "Union School District of Sag Harbor." <small>Consolidation of districts.</small>

§ 2. The said district shall be under the direction of a board to be styled "the board of education," which board shall consist of six members, four or more of whom shall constitute a quorum for the transaction of business. Cleveland S. Stilwell, Brinley D. Sleight, Oliver R. Wade, William H. Gleason, Stephen B. French and Jonas Winters, shall compose the first board of education, who shall be divided into three classes, each class containing two members, and shall determine by lot their respective terms of office, so that the first class shall serve to the first annual meeting ensuing, the second one year, and the third two years from said meeting. <small>Board of education.</small>

§ 3. At the annual meeting of said district, to be held on the second Tuesday of October in each year, there <small>Election of members of board of education.</small>

shall be ellected by ballot, for three years, two members of said board of education, who shall be residents and taxable inhabitants of said district. The polls of said election shall not be closed within two hours from the time of opening the same.

Powers, duties and liabilities of board.

§ 4. Said board of education shall possess the powers and authority and be subject to the same duties and liabilities in respect to said district as trustees of common schools in this state.

Ibid.

§ 5. Said board of education shall also have the power and it shall be their duty :

1st. To appoint a clerk and librarian, who may be of their number, who shall hold office during the pleasure of the board, and whose compensation shall be fixed by a vote of the taxable inhabitants of said district.

2nd. To divide the said school into primary and higher departments ; to regulate the transfer of scholars from one department to the other ; to provide suitable instructors for each department, and direct what text books shall be used therein.

3d. To fix and regulate the rate of tuition for nonresident scholars in said primary and other higher branches in said school or schools, and sue for and collect, in their corporate name, any sum of money due to said district.

4th. To establish and cause to be kept a school in said village for the instruction of colored children.

5th. To have in all respects the superintendence, supervision, management and control of said school or schools, and to hire, pay and discharge any teacher employed by them in said school.

6th. To purchase fuel and other necessaries for the use of the school or schools in said district ; and all contracts made by them in their official capacity shall be binding upon them and their successors in office, provided that no contract shall be made for a longer period than two years, except contracts relating to the construction of buildings authorized by this act and the loans which may be necessary to effect that purpose.

7th. To make such by-laws as they may deem necessary to secure the prosperity, order and government of said school.

8th. To receive and apply to the uses of said school or schools, or any department thereof, any gift, legacy, bequest, devise or annuities, given, bequeathed or devised to said district for the purposes of said school or schools, and apply the same, or the interest or proceeds thereof, according to the terms or instructions of the donor or testator.

9th. To defray the necessary contingent expenses of the board, including an annual salary to the clerk.

10th. To fill any vacancy which may happen in said board by reason of death, removal or refusal to serve, of any member or officer of said board; and the person so appointed in the place of any member of the board shall hold his office until the next annual meeting of said district.

11th. To prosecute for all forfeitures and penalties under this act, and when recovered to apply the same to the purposes of education in said district.

§ 6. The said board may declare vacant the place of any member thereof who, without satisfactory cause, shall omit to attend the legally called successive meetings of the board. *Vacancies in board.*

§ 7. Every resignation of officers appointed or elected under this act, shall be made in writing, to the president of the board of education, and such resignation shall have no force or effect nor in any degree excuse such officer from the discharge of his duties, until the same be accepted and approved by a resolution of said board. *Resignation of officers.*

§ 8. The several schools under the care of the said boards shall, as to the common school department thereof, be subject to the supervision of the commissioner of common schools in like manner as the other common schools in this state. *Schools to be under care of commissioner of common schools.*

§ 9. The clerk of the said board shall attend all school meetings of the inhabitants of said district, and also all the meetings of the board, and act as secretary thereof. He shall notify all officers elected or appointed, of their election or appointment, within two days thereafter. He shall keep a record of the proceedings of the board, and perform such other duties as they may prescribe. The said record or transcript thereof, certified by the president and clerk, shall be received in all courts as prima facie evidence of the acts of said trustees. *Duties of clerk.*

§ 10. The village collector shall be ex-officio collector of said school district, and shall possess the powers and authority, and be subject to the same duties and *Collector.*

101

obligations, as such officer in the several school districts of this state.

Treasurer
and his
duties.
§ 11. The village treasurer shall be ex-officio treasurer of said school district and all moneys to be raised pursuant to the provisions of this act, and all school moneys or other funds by law appropriated to or provided for the schools of said village, shall be paid to him as such treasurer. He shall be liable to the same penalties for any official misconduct in relation to said moneys as for any similar misconduct in relation to the other moneys of said village. He shall keep the funds authorized by this act to be received by him, separate and distinct from any other fund which he is or may by law be authorized to receive. He shall pay out all school moneys, on the warrant of the board of education, signed by its president and clerk. He shall receive for all moneys that he shall disburse upon said warrant, one-half of one per cent; provided that for all service required of him under this act, he shall not receive an amount exceeding twenty-five dollars in any one year.

Bond of
treasurer
and collec-
tor.
§ 12. Such treasurer and collector shall severally, before entering upon the duties of their offices, execute and deliver to the said board of education a bond, with such sufficient penalty and sureties as the board may require, conditioned for the faithful discharge of the duties of their respective offices. And in case such bond shall not be given, such offices shall thereby become vacant, and said board shall thereupon make other appointments to supply such vacancies.

Notice of
district
meetings.
§ 13. It shall be a sufficient notice of any annual, special or adjourned district meeting, to publish such notice in the papers printed in said village, and by affixing a copy of the same on the outer door of the district school house, (if there be any,) and posting a copy of the same in five other public places in such district; the posting of said notice to be done at least five days before such meeting, and no other notice of any such meeting need be given.

How mo-
neys to be
raised.
§ 14. The legal voters of said district, at any annual, special or adjourned meeting legally held, may by a three-fifths vote raise such sum of money as they shall deem expedient, not exceeding the sum of ten thousand dollars, for the purpose of purchasing a site and building a school house in said district, or for the purpose of pur-

chasing any suitable buildings and site for such purpose : to erect out buildings; to enclose the same with a fence, and for such other improvements as may be considered necessary, and may also direct the board of education to cause the same to be levied by installments, and make out a tax list for the collection of the same as often as such installments shall become due; and the said board of education are hereby authorized to obtain, by loan, the whole or any part of the money legally voted by said district, and secure the payment of the same by their official bond as representatives of said district, as also to collect by tax from said district a sum sufficient to pay interest on said loans.

§ 15. The valuations of taxable property in said district shall be ascertained, as far as possible, from the last assessment roll of the said town, on file in the town clerk's office in said town. *Valuation of taxable property.*

§ 16. The said board of education shall have power to establish and organize a classical department in said school, to be known by the name of the "Sag Harbor Academy," and such academical department shall be under the visitation of the Regents of the University, and shall be subject in its course of education and matters pertaining thereto, (providing said district comply with the provisions of the statutes now in force relating to the organizing and chartering of academies or academical departments,) and to all the regulations made in regard to academies by the said Regents ; and in such department the qualifications for the entrance of any pupil shall be the same as those established by the said Regents for admission into any academy of the state under their supervision. And such academical department shall share in the distribution of the income of the Literature Fund and of the income of the United States Deposit Fund, with academies in the state subject to the visitation of the Regents. *Classical department.*

§ 17. The trustees of said districts numbers twenty-one and eleven, of the town of Southampton, and number nine of the town of East Hampton, holding office at the time of the passing of this act, shall, within three months after the organization and establishment of the union school under this act, sell at public auction or private sale, as they may deem expedient, the district property in their respective districts. *Property of certain districts to be sold.*

§ 18. This act shall take effect immediately.

Chap. 442.

AN ACT to constitute the village of Middleport, in the towns of Royalton and Hartland and county of Niagara, a separate road district.

Passed April 22, 1862; three-fifths being present.

The People of the State of New York, represented in Senate and Assembly, do enact as follows:

SECTION 1. The said village of Middleport shall constitute a separate road district in the towns of Royalton and Hartland, and the territory comprised within the limits of said village shall be exempt from the superintendence and jurisdiction of the commissioners of highways of said towns; and the trustees of said village and their successors shall have all the powers therein, and be subject to all the duties and liabilities of commissioners and overseers of highways of towns in like cases, and may, in their discretion, appoint one of their number or any other competent person, street commissioner, whose special duty it shall be to superintend, subject to the control of said trustees, the construction and repairs of all bridges, streets, roads, crosswalks, public squares and commons, and who shall receive for his services such amount as a majority of the board of trustees may deem proper, to be paid out of the money arising out of highway taxes.

§ 2. The said trustees shall have power to assess upon all persons owning property in said village, annually, such amount denominated highway tax as they shall deem necessary to work and improve the roads, bridges, streets, lanes and alleys of said village. Each male inhabitant of the age of twenty-one years shall be assessed fifty cents each year, and the balance of the highway tax shall be assessed upon all persons owning property and estate, real and personal, incorporated companies, banks and banking associations, according to the value of their said property in said village; and the tax so raised for highway purposes shall be appropriated, under the direction of said trustees, to the working and improving of the roads, streets, lanes and alleys in said corporation. Said tax to be levied and collected as other taxes now are in said village.

§ 3. The trustees of said village shall proceed in the same manner and with the same power, and under the same restrictions as commissioners of highways in towns, in building and repairing bridges in said village, repairing, altering, discontinuing and laying out streets and highways in said village, and assessing damages therefor.

Chap. 443.

AN ACT in relation to boards of health in Orange and Chautauqua counties.

Passed April 22, 1862; three-fifths being present.

The People of the State of New York, represented in Senate and Assembly, do enact as follows:

SECTION 1. From and after the first day of April, eighteen hundred and sixty-two, the expenses of the boards of health of the different towns and corporations of the county of Orange shall be a charge upon the towns where such boards of health are located, and not upon the county; and such charges shall be levied upon the said towns in the same manner as other town taxes are now levied.

§ 2. The provisions of this act shall also apply to the county of Chautauqua.

§ 3. This act shall take effect immediately.

Chap. 444.

AN ACT to extend the time for the completion of
the Lebanon Springs Railroad.

Passed April 22, 1862.

*The People of the State of New York, represented in
Senate and Assembly, do enact as follows:*

SECTION 1. The period allowed for the completion of
the Lebanon Springs Railroad is hereby extended for
the term of five years from the passage of this act.

§ 2. This act shall take effect immediately.

Chap. 445.

AN ACT to incorporate the "American Shipmasters' Association."

Passed April 22, 1862.

*The People of the State of New York, represented in
Senate and Assembly, do enact as follows:*

SECTION I. John D. Jones, Elisha E. Morgan, Charles
H. Marshall, Robert L. Taylor, Ezra Nye, William C.
Thompson, Moses H. Grinnell, Leopold Bierwith, Elwood
Walter, Daniel Drake Smith, Theodore B. Satterthwaite,
Francis S. Lathrop, Richard Lathers, Alfred Edwards,
B. C. Morris, G. Henry Coop, William H. H. Moore and
Isaac H. Upton, and such other persons as they, or a
majority, may associate with them, are hereby constituted a body corporate, by the name of the "American
Shipmasters' Association," for the purpose of collecting
and disseminating information upon the subjects of marine or commercial interest, of encouraging and advancing worthy and well qualified commanders and other
officers of vessels in the merchant service, of ascertaining and certifying the qualifications of such persons as
shall apply to be recommended as such commanders
or officers, and of promoting the security of life and
property on the seas.

§ 2. The said corporation shall have the power to make and adopt a constitution and by-laws, rules and regulations, for the purposes, objects and government thereof, for the admission and regulation of members, for the regulation and payment of fees and dues, and for the management of its funds and property, and from time to time to alter, modify or repeal such constitution, by-laws, rules and regulations.

§ 3. The said corporation may purchase and possess any real estate not yielding an income exceeding five thousand dollars per annum, and may apply its funds and property, from time to time, in bestowing premiums or medals for praiseworthy acts in the merchants' service, and in premiums or donations for charitable and other purposes, and in such other ways as shall seem conducive to the purposes aforesaid.

§ 4. The business, property and affairs of said corporation shall be under the general control and management of a board of managers, and the said corporation shall, in and by their said constitution, prescribe the powers and duties of such board of managers, and of such other officers, as may be deemed necessary, and the rules and regulations for the election, succession and action of such board of managers and other officers. The persons named in the first section of this act shall be the first board of managers, and shall continue in office until others are so elected in their stead respectively.

§ 5. The said corporation may prescribe terms and regulations upon which persons not members thereof may participate in the benefit of said corporation.

§ 6. The said corporation shall possess the general powers and be subject to the general restrictions and liabilities prescribed in the third title of the eighteenth chapter of the first part of the Revised Statutes.

§ 7. Its principal office shall be in the city of New York, but it may establish agencies and connect itself with similar associations elsewhere.

§ 8. The legislature may, at any time, alter or repeal this law.

Chap. 446.

AN ACT to amend an act entitled "An act in relation to the election of superintendents of the poor and coroners in the county. of Kings," passed April seventh, eighteen hundred and fifty-eight.

Passed April 22, 1862 ; three-fifths being present.

The People of the State of New York, represented in Senate and Assembly, do enact as follows:

SECTION 1. Section six of the act entitled "An act in relation to the election of superintendents of the poor and coroners in the county of Kings," passed April seventh, eighteen hundred and fifty-eight, is hereby amended so as to read as follows:

The county of Kings, for the purpose of the election of coroners, is hereby divided into two districts, from each of which a coroner shall hereafter be chosen by the electors of said county at large, who shall be at the time of his election, and continue during the term of his office, a resident of the district from which he is selected, and in case of his removal from such district his office shall be deemed vacant.

§ 2. Section seven of said act is hereby amended so as to read as follows:

The first district shall consist of the first, second, third, fourth, fifth, sixth, seventh, eighth, ninth, tenth, eleventh and twelfth wards of the city of Brooklyn, and of the towns of Flatbush, Flatlands, New Utrecht, and Gravesend ; and the second district shall consist of the thirteenth, fourteenth, fifteenth, sixteenth, seventeenth, eighteenth, and nineteenth wards of the city of Brooklyn, and the town of New Lots.

§ 3. Section nine of said act is hereby amended so as to read as follows:

At the general election in the year eighteen hundred and sixty-two, a coroner from the second district shall be elected by the electors of said county at large, in place of John H. Murphy, whose term of office expires on the first day of January, eighteen hundred and sixty-three, who shall hold his office for three years from said first day of January, eighteen hundred and sixty-three ; and his successor shall be elected in like manner, every third year thereafter, and hold for a similar period.

§ 4. Section ten of said act is hereby amended so as to read as follows :

At the general election in the year eighteen hundred and sixty-four, a coroner from the first district shall be elected by the electors of said county at large, in place of Thomas P. Norris, whose term of office will expire on the first day of January, eighteen hundred and sixty-five, who shall hold his office for the term of three years from the first day of January, eighteen hundred and sixty-five ; and his successor shall be elected in like manner, every third year thereafter, and hold for a similar period.

§ 5. Section eight of said act is hereby repealed.

§ 6 The coroners now elected from the several districts in said county of Kings, as they were laid out and established by said act hereby amended, shall continue to hold their offices, and to exercise their duties within their respective districts, until the expiration of their respective terms for which they were elected.

§ 7. This act shall take effect immediately.

Chap. 447.

AN ACT to amend an act entitled "An act to provide for the erection of a town hall in the town of Flushing, in the county of Queens," passed March nineteenth, eighteen hundred and sixty-one.

Passed April 22, 1862; three-fifths being present.

The People of the State of New York, represented in Senate and Assembly, do enact as follows :

SECTION 1. Section first of the act entitled "An act to provide for the erection of a town hall in the town of Flushing in the county of Queens," passed March nineteenth, eighteen hundred and sixty-one is hereby amended so as to read as follows :

§ 1. It shall be lawful for the supervisor of the town of Flushing and John W. Lawrence, William H. Salt, A. G. Silliman and Charles R. Lincoln of said town, who are hereby appointed commissioners to act in conjunction with said supervisor for the purposes of this act, to borrow on the faith and credit of said town such a sum of money as they may deem necessary for the object hereinafter mentioned, not exceeding twenty thousand dollars, at a rate of interest not exceeding seven per cent per annum, and to execute therefor under their official signatures, bonds with coupons annexed for the payment of the same in ten equal annual installments, with interest payable semi-annually, or ten classes of bonds with the coupons annexed, payable consecutively in ten years with interest payable as aforesaid :

§ 2. Section five of the said act is hereby amended so as to read as follows :

§ 5. The board of supervisors of the said county of Queens shall cause to be levied, collected and paid annually by tax upon the taxable inhabitants and property subject to taxation in said town of Flushing, in the same manner as other taxes in said town are levied, collected and paid, such a sum as over and above the expenses of collecting the same, will equal the interest of said bonds due annually and the principal of the same as said bonds shall become due and payable. The moneys so collected shall be paid by the collector of the town of Flushing to the supervisor of said town, upon his filing security for the same with the town clerk of the town of Flushing in double the amount, and shall be by the said supervisor applied to the payment of the principal and interest on the bonds and coupons issued under this act, as the same shall respectively become due and payable. It shall not be necessary for all of the commissioners to sign the coupons, but the signature of the supervisor of said town, under the direction of said commissioners, shall be deemed sufficient.

Chap. 448.

AN ACT to release the interest of the people of the State of New York in certain lands to Charles G. Gere.

Passed April 22, 1862; by a two-third vote.

The People of the State of New York, represented in Senate and Assembly, do enact as follows:

SECTION 1. The interest of the people of the State of New York, of, in and to certain lands conveyed by David Roach to Charles G. Gere, situated in the county of Cayuga, is hereby released to the said Charles G. Gere, his heirs and assigns. And the said conveyance from the said David Roach shall hereafter be deemed in all courts a valid conveyance notwithstanding the said David Roach was at the time of making said conveyance an alien; and power is given to the said David Roach, to make further conveyance to quiet the title of the said Charles G. Gere.

§ 2. This act shall take effect immediately.

Chap. 449.

AN ACT to amend an act entitled "An act to authorize the formation of Railroad corporations and to regulate the same," passed April second, eighteen hundred and fifty.

Passed April 22, 1862; three-fifths being present.

The People of the State of New York, represented in Senate and Assembly, do enact as follows:

SECTION 1. Section twenty-seven of the act entitled "An act to authorize the formation of railroad corporations and to regulate the same," passed April second, eighteen hundred and fifty, is hereby amended so as to read as follows:

§ 27. No company formed under this act shall lay down or use in the construction of their road, any iron rail of less weight than fifty-six pounds to the lineal yard, except for turnouts, sidings and switches and roads upon which steam power cannot by law be used ; and on the last mentioned roads such weight shall not be less than forty pounds to the lineal yard.

§ 2. This act shall take effect immediately.

Chap. 450.

AN ACT for the establishing academical departments in the different "Union Schools."

Passed April 22, 1862 ; three-fifths being present.

The People of the State of New York, represented in Senate and Assembly, do enact as follows:

SECTION 1. Any union school in this state duly organized according to law, by complying with the requirements of the " Regents of the University " shall be entitled to all the benefits and privileges in the academies in this state.

§ 2. This act shall take effect immediately.

Chap. 451.

AN ACT to establish a tribunal of conciliation in the sixth judicial district.

Passed April 23, 1862 ; three-fifths being present.

The People of the State of New York, represented in Senate and Assembly, do enact as follows:

SECTION 1. A tribunal of conciliation is hereby established in the sixth judicial district of this state.

Judge to be appointed.

§ 2. Such tribunal shall be held by one judge, to be appointed by the Governor, with the advice and consent of the senate, and as often thereafter as may be necessary, who shall hold his office for three years, and until another is appointed in his place.

§ 3. Said tribunal shall, within the sixth judicial district Jurisdiction. of this state, possess like powers and exercise the jurisdiction of the supreme court of this state, and all laws now in force in reference to said supreme court, to special proceedings and the trial of actions in said court, to its orders, judgments and executions, and the enforcement thereof, and of proceedings supplemental to executions and lien of judgments upon real property, to the clerks, attorneys, counsellors and officers thereof and practice therein, and the power to regulate the same by rules or otherwise, and to appeals to the supreme court at general term thereof, shall be applicable to said tribunal, to special proceedings, and the trial of actions in said tribunal, to its orders, judgments and executions, and the enforcement thereof, to proceedings supplemental to executions and the lien of judgments upon real property, to the clerk, attorneys, counsellors and officers thereof, their qualifications, powers and rights, and to the practice of said tribunal, and the power to regulate the same by rules or otherwise, and to appeals to the general term of the supreme court, so far as the same can be applied, except as hereinafter provided ; but said tribunal shall Exception. have no power to render judgment to be obligatory on the parties except they voluntarily submit their matters in difference and agree to abide the judgment or assent thereto, in the presence of such tribunal, and shall have no power to interfere in any matter, action or proceeding pending in the supreme court. But actions pending Transfer of actions. in the supreme court may be transferred to said tribunal by consent of the parties.

§ 4. Any person, whether claiming or resisting a de- Mode of submitting mand of any kind, may cause to be personally served by matters in difference copy upon the other party or parties a written proposal, regulated. subscribed by him or his attorney, briefly stating their matters in difference as he claims them to be, and agreeing on his part to submit the same to and abide the judgment thereon of such tribunal, and requesting such other party or parties to do the same; and such party or parties so served with such proposal may thereupon, within thirty days thereafter, serve upon the party or . his attorney from whom said proposal emanated, either personally or by depositing the same in the post office to his address, a notice signifying his or their acceptance of such proposal, and on filing such proposal and notice

of acceptance, or copies thereof, with the clerk of said
tribunal, said parties shall be deemed to have voluntarily submitted to such tribunal their matters in difference referred to in said proposal, and to have agreed to
abide the judgment; and said tribunal shall have jurisdiction thereof, and to hear, try and render judgment,
which shall be obligatory upon the parties. The issue
or issues, if any, so to be tried upon the matters indicated in said proposal shall, after the filing of said proposal and acceptance, be settled between the parties in
such manner and form as shall be prescribed by the rules
and regulations of such tribunal. Said tribunal shall,
also, without the service of the proposal aforesaid, have
like jurisdiction as aforesaid, when the parties shall
have filed with the clerk thereof a written submission
of their matters in difference, agreeing to abide the
judgment of said tribunal, subscribed by the said parties,
or oral assent thereto given by them in the presence of
such tribunal.

Effect of judgment. § 5. Every judgment rendered by said tribunal and
docketted in the clerk's office thereof, shall become a
lien on the real property of every person against whom
such judgment shall have been rendered, by the filing of
a transcript thereof, certified by the clerk of said tribunal and the docketting thereof in the clerk's office of
the county where such real property may be situated;
and at any time within five years after the docketting of
Execution. said judgment in said tribunal, an execution for the
enforcement thereof may be issued by the clerk of such
county, and such execution, and the issuing, return, and
satisfaction thereof shall be subject to the control of the
supreme court according to the practice of said court on
executions upon judgments therein, except that in said
judicial district the enforcement of judgments by execution or otherwise shall be conducted and controlled by
said tribunal, and executions shall be issued therefrom,
and levied, collected and executed according to the laws
in relation to executions issued upon judgments in said
supreme court.

Tribunal to have a seal. § 6. Said tribunal shall have a seal, and shall be
deemed a court of record, and all laws in relation to
courts of record and their powers and duties as such,
shall be applicable to such tribunal so far as the same
can be applied.

§ 7. Said tribunal may hold sessions and conduct trials before it at such times and places in the county of Delaware as it may from time to time by its rules or by order direct; and such order shall in each case locate the trial in the town where the majority of the witnesses reside and where the interests of the parties may require that such trial shall be held unless in the opinion of the judge there shall be paramount reasons for holding the same in some other town; but at least two regular terms of such tribunal shall be held in each year in the village of Deposit, in said county of Delaware, at such times and places therein as said judge shall direct, or as shall be specified by the rules of said tribunal. The clerk's office of said tribunal and the residence of the judge thereof, after his appointment, shall be in said village, and if his residence shall be elsewhere for six consecutive months he shall be deemed to have vacated his office. *Terms of court and places of holding same.*

§ 8. The board of supervisors of the county of Delaware shall at their next annual meeting after the passage of this act, and every three years thereafter, appoint a clerk of said court, and also two arbitrators, whose duty it shall be, whenever notified by the clerk of said tribunal, to attend the terms thereof, and to assist the judge in the trial of all issues of fact when so requested by either of the parties to such trial, which clerk and arbitrators shall hold their offices for three years, and until their respective successors shall be appointed. Vacancies in said offices or either of them may be filled by said board of supervisors at any meeting thereof. And in case there shall be a vacancy in either of said offices when the board of supervisors is not in session the same may be filled by said judge by his appointment of some suitable person to be such clerk or arbitrator, as the case may be, who shall hold his office until such vacancy shall be filled by said board of supervisors. *Supervisors to appoint clerk of court and two arbitrators to set with the judges.* *Vacancies.*

§ 9. Any party to an issue of fact to be tried in said county of Delaware before such tribunal, may, at least ten days before such trial, notify the clerk thereof, in writing, that he desires the arbitrators to be present at such trial to participate therein. Such clerk shall thereupon notify said arbitrators by personal service of a notice, or by addressing the same to each of them at his place of residence through the post office, stating that their attendance at the time and place of such trial is *Notice for arbitrators to attend.*

desired. And on such trial said arbitrators and judge shall each have an equal voice, and the decision of a

When judge to appoint arbitrator. majority shall be the decision of such tribunal. If, for any cause, either of said arbitrators shall fail to be present at such trial, then said judge may appoint some suitable person to supply his place for the purposes of such trial.

Powers of judge. § 10. The judge of the tribunal established by this act, may make orders and exercise, within said sixth judicial district, the powers of a justice of the supreme court, out of court and at chambers, according to the existing practice, except to stay proceedings in said supreme court after verdict.

Appeals may be had to general term of supreme court § 11. Appeals may be taken to the general term of the supreme court from the orders of said judge, and the judgments of said tribunal upon the law and upon the facts in like cases and conducted and disposed of in like manner, as provided by law for appeals to said general term; and the provisions of sections two hundred and sixty-seven and two hundred and sixty-eight of chapter four of title eight of the amended Code of Procedure, and of chapters three and four of said title, shall be specially applicable to such appeals so far as the same can be ap-

Prohibition plied. But no appeal shall be taken to the court of appeals in any case where the action or proceeding originated in said tribunal.

Costs. § 12. Said tribunal shall, in all actions, matters and proceedings therein, have discretion and control over the amount of costs and questions between the parties in relation thereto, and shall have the right to allow or disallow costs to either party or to any of the parties; but shall have no power to allow or impose more costs than are now allowed by law in the supreme court.

Judge may serve as referee. § 13. Said judge shall serve as sole referee in any action or proceeding in the supreme court, in said sixth judicial district when he shall be appointed pursuant to the provisions of law for the appointment of referees in such court, and such court may appoint him to act as such referee in any county of said district the same as if he were a resident of such county; and in case neither of the parties shall be required to pay him any compensation or fees as such referee, except his expenses.*

* So in the original.

§ 14. Said arbitrators and clerk shall each receive a reasonable salary or compensation for his service as such arbitrator or clerk, to be audited and allowed by the board of supervisors of said county of Delaware, and paid by said county; and all necessary expenses for the organization and maintenance of said tribunal shall be paid by said county. Said judge shall receive an annual salary of fifteen hundred dollars to be paid from the State Treasury in the same manner that the salaries of justices of the supreme court are paid. *Salary of arbitrators and clerk.* *Salary of judge.*

§ 15. All the provisions of this act in reference to arbitrators in the county of Delaware, shall be applicable to every other county in said judicial district, whenever the board of supervisors thereof shall appoint arbitrators for said tribunal in pursuance of the right to do so, which is hereby conferred upon them; and thereafter said tribunal shall hold sessions and conduct trials in every such county in the same manner as in said county of Delaware. Said judge may in his discretion appoint and hold terms and trials by said tribunal without the aid of arbitrators in any county in said district where no arbitrators have been appointed. *When provisions of act may be applied to other counties.*

§ 16. The provisions of this act are extended to Sullivan county. *Extended to Sullivan county.*

§ 17. This act shall take effect immediately and its operations shall cease at the expiration of the first term of office under the same unless the provisions hereof shall be revived by the act of the legislature. *When this act ceases.*

Chap. 452.

AN ACT to enable the board of supervisors of the county of New York to raise money by tax for certain county purposes. Also to regulate the expenditure of certain revenues of said county.

Passed April 23, 1862; three-fifths being present.

The People of the State of New York, represented in Senate and Assembly, do enact as follows:

SECTION 1. In addition to the several amounts of money authorized and required by existing laws to be raised by tax in the city and county of New York for state purposes, and for defraying the contingent and other charges and expenses of said city and county, in and for the year one thousand eight hundred and sixty-two, the board of supervisors of said county are hereby empowered and required, as soon as conveniently may be after the passage of this act, to order and cause to be raised by tax on the estates subject to taxation according to law, within the said county, and to be collected according to law, the following sums of money for the several purposes herein specified, deducting from the aggregate amount thereof the estimated revenues of the county for said year, not otherwise specifically appropriated by law, that is to say : Advertising, fifteen thousand dollars; county contingencies, twenty thousand dollars; county jail, six thousand dollars; election expenses, seventy-two thousand dollars ; new construction of Harlem bridge, one hundred thousand dollars; removal of incumbrances in harbor, two thousand dollars; interest on loans, fifty thousand dollars; lighting and cleaning and supplies for county offices, fifteen thousand dollars; officers' and witnesses' fees, sixty-five thousand dollars; printing, stationery and blank books, fifteen thousand dollars; rents, five thousand dollars ; salaries legislative department, four thousand four hundred dollars ; salaries executive department, fifty-three thousand five hundred dollars ; salaries judiciary, two hundred and twenty-five thousand nine hundred and fifty dollars ; support of prisoners in the county jail, five thousand dollars ; support of detained witnesses, five thousand dollars, and to the interpreter of the Jefferson Market police court, eighth judicial district, the sum of nine hundred and thirty-three dollars and thirty-three cents, being his salary from November first, eighteen hundred and sixty-one, to December thirty-first, eighteen hundred and sixty-two, or so much as may be audited and allowed by the Comptroller of the city of New York.

§ 2. This act shall take effect immediately.

Chap. 453.

AN ACT to exempt St. John's College, in the town of West Farms, county of Westchester, from the school tax.

Passed April 23, 1862; three-fifths being present.

The People of the State of New York, represented in Senate and Assembly, do enact as follows :

SECTION 1. The real estate belonging to the corporation of St. John's College, in its actual occupation or use, at Fordham, in the town of West Farms, in the county of Westchester, with the buildings thereon, are hereby exempted from the payment of any tax hereafter to be assessed or levied in said town or county for the support of schools.

§ 2. This act shall take effect immediately.

Chap. 454.

AN ACT dividing the State into Congressional Districts.

Passed April 23, 1862.

The People of the State of New York, represented in Senate and Assembly, do enact as follows :

SECTION 1. For the election of representatives in congress of the United States, this state shall be and is hereby divided into thirty-one districts, namely :

The counties of Suffolk, Queens and Richmond shall compose the first district.

The sixth, eighth, ninth, tenth, twelfth, fourteenth, sixteenth, seventeenth and eighteenth wards of the city of Brooklyn, and the towns of Flatbush, Flatlands, Gravesend, New Lots and New Utrecht, in the county of Kings, shall compose the second district.

The first, second, third, fourth, fifth, seventh, eleventh, thirteenth, fifteenth and nineteenth wards of the city of

raised by tax in the city and county of New York for
state purposes, and for defraying the contingent and
other charges and expenses of said city and county, in
and for the year one thousand eight hundred and sixty-
two, the board of supervisors of said county are hereby
empowered and required, as soon as conveniently may
be after the passage of this act, to order and cause to be
raised by tax on the estates subject to taxation according
to law, within the said county, and to be collected according to law, the following sums of money for the several
purposes herein specified, deducting from the aggregate
amount thereof the estimated revenues of the county
for said year, not otherwise specifically appropriated by
law, that is to say : Advertising, fifteen thousand dollars; county contingencies, twenty thousand dollars;
county jail, six thousand dollars; election expenses,
seventy-two thousand dollars ; new construction of Harlem bridge, one hundred thousand dollars; removal of
incumbrances in harbor, two thousand dollars; interest
on loans, fifty thousand dollars; lighting and cleaning
and supplies for county offices, fifteen thousand dollars;
officers' and witnesses' fees, sixty-five thousand dollars;
printing, stationery and blank books, fifteen thousand
dollars; rents, five thousand dollars ; salaries legislative
department, four thousand four hundred dollars ; salaries executive department, fifty-three thousand five hundred dollars ; salaries judiciary, two hundred and twenty-
five thousand nine hundred and fifty dollars ; support of
prisoners in the county jail, five thousand dollars ; support of detained witnesses, five thousand dollars, and to
the interpreter of the Jefferson Market police court,
eighth judicial district, the sum of nine hundred and
thirty-three dollars and thirty-three cents, being his salary
from November first, eighteen hundred and sixty-one, to
December thirty-first, eighteen hundred and sixty-two,
or so much as may be audited and allowed by the Comptroller of the city of New York.

§ 2. This act shall take effect immediately.

Chap. 453.

AN ACT to exempt St. John's College, in the town of West Farms, county of Westchester, from the school tax.

Passed April 23, 1862; three-fifths being present.

The People of the State of New York, represented in Senate and Assembly, do enact as follows :

SECTION 1. The real estate belonging to the corporation of St. John's College, in its actual occupation or use, at Fordham, in the town of West Farms, in the county of Westchester, with the buildings thereon, are hereby exempted from the payment of any tax hereafter to be assessed or levied in said town or county for the support of schools.

§ 2. This act shall take effect immediately.

Chap. 454.

AN ACT dividing the State into Congressional Districts.

Passed April 23, 1862.

The People of the State of New York, represented in Senate and Assembly, do enact as follows :

SECTION 1. For the election of representatives in congress of the United States, this state shall be and is hereby divided into thirty-one districts, namely :

The counties of Suffolk, Queens and Richmond shall compose the first district.

The sixth, eighth, ninth, tenth, twelfth, fourteenth, sixteenth, seventeenth and eighteenth wards of the city of Brooklyn, and the towns of Flatbush, Flatlands, Gravesend, New Lots and New Utrecht, in the county of Kings, shall compose the second district.

The first, second, third, fourth, fifth, seventh, eleventh, thirteenth, fifteenth and nineteenth wards of the city of

Brooklyn, in the county of Kings, shall compose the third district.

The first, second, third, fourth, fifth, sixth and eighth wards of the city and county of New York, and Governor's Island, shall compose the fourth district.

The seventh, tenth, thirteenth and fourteenth wards of the city and county of New York, shall compose the fifth district.

The ninth, fifteenth and sixteenth wards of the city and county of New York, shall compose the sixth district.

The eleventh and seventeenth wards of the city and county of New York, shall compose the seventh district.

The eighteenth, twentieth and twenty-first wards of the city and county of New York, shall compose the eighth district.

The twelfth, nineteenth and twenty-second wards of the city and county of New York, and Blackwell's, Ward and Randall's Islands, shall compose the ninth district.

The counties of Westchester, Rockland and Putnam shall compose the tenth district.

The counties of Orange and Sullivan shall compose the eleventh district.

The counties of Dutchess and Columbia shall compose the twelfth district.

The counties of Ulster and Greene shall compose the the thirteenth district.

The counties of Albany and Schoharie shall compose the fourteenth district.

The counties of Rensselaer and Washington shall compose the fifteenth district.

The counties of Warren, Essex and Clinton shall compose the sixteenth district.

The counties of St. Lawrence and Franklin shall compose the seventeenth district.

The counties of Fulton, Hamilton, Montgomery, Saratoga and Schenectady shall compose the eighteenth district.

The counties of Delaware, Otsego and Chenango shall compose the nineteenth district.

The counties of Jefferson, Lewis and Herkimer shall compose the twentieth district.

The county of Onéida shall compose the twenty-first district.

The counties of Madison and Oswego shall compose the twenty-second district.

The counties of Onondaga and Cortland shall compose the twenty-third district.

The counties of Cayuga, Wayne and Seneca shall compose the twenty-fourth district.

The counties of Ontario, Livingston and Yates shall compose the twenty-fifth district.

The counties of Tioga, Tompkins, Broome and Schuyler shall compose the twenty-sixth district.

The counties of Chemung, Steuben and Allegany shall compose the twenty-seventh district.

The counties of Monroe and Orleans shall compose the twenty-eighth district.

The counties of Genesee, Niagara and Wyoming shall compose the twenty-ninth district.

The county of Erie shall compose the thirtieth district.

The counties of Chautauqua and Cattaraugus shall compose the thirty-first district.

Chap. 455.

AN ACT in relation to the disposition of burial plots in the Lutheran cemetery at Middle village, Queens county, Long Island.

Passed April 23, 1862.

The People of the State of New York, represented in Senate and Assembly, do enact as follows:

SECTION 1. The different Lutheran churches in the city of New York, Brooklyn and Williamsburgh which now own, or who may hereafter own in fee, lands purchased of the incorporation of the Lutheran cemetery in their cemetery at Middle village, Queens county, Long Island, are hereby empowered to subdivide the same into burial plots of not more than two hundred square feet each, and to sell and convey the same for

burial purposes in fee; and any conveyance made by
the president of the board of trustees of either of said
churches under their corporate seal shall be sufficient in
law to pass the right, title and interest of such church
therein in fee.

§ 2. This act shall take effect immediately.

Chap. 456.

AN ACT to provide means for the support of
Government, and to pay the sum apportioned to
be paid by this State, of the direct tax levied by
the act of Congress, approved the fifth day of
August, eighteen hundred and sixty-one.

Passed April 23, 1862; three-fifths being present.

*The People of the State of New York, represented in
Senate and Assembly, do enact as follows:*

Tax of one
mill for the
general
fund.

SECTION 1. There shall be imposed, for the fiscal year
commencing on the first day of October, eighteen hundred and sixty-two, a state tax of one mill on each dollar
of the valuation of real and personal property in this
state subject to taxation; which tax shall be assessed,
levied, and collected on and by the annual assessment
and collection of taxes for that year, in the manner prescribed by law, and shall be paid by the several county
treasurers into the treasury of the state, to be held by
the Treasurer for application to the purposes of the
General Fund, and for the payment of those claims and
demands which shall constitute a lawful charge upon
that fund.

Tax of two
mills to pay
tax levied
by congress

§ 2. There shall, also, be imposed, for the fiscal year,
commencing on the first day of October, eighteen hundred and sixty-two, a tax of two mills or so much thereof
as in the judgment of the Comptroller may be necessary,
on each dollar of the valuation of real and personal
property in this state subject to taxation, which tax shall
be assessed, levied and collected in the same manner as
the tax for the General Fund, and shall be paid by the
several county treasurers into the treasury of the state

to be held for the payment to the Government of the United States of the sum of two million six hundred and three thousand nine hundred and eighteen and two-thirds dollars, being the amount apportioned to be paid by this state of the direct tax levied by the act of congress, approved the fifth day of August, eighteen hundred and sixty-one.

Chap. 457.

AN ACT for the relief of Jacob Roth.

Passed April 23, 1862; three-fifths being present.

The People of the State of New York, represented in Senate and Assembly, do enact as follows:

SECTION 1. The Comptroller, Attorney-General and Adjutant General are hereby authorized and required to hear, examine and determine the claim of Jacob Roth, for damages alleged to have been done to the property occupied by him, and known as the arsenal house, in the city of New York, adjoining the arsenal in said city, by reason of the falling of said arsenal in November, eighteen hundred and fifty-eight, and to award to him such sum as they shall determine on account of such damages to his property, but to no greater extent.

§ 2. The Treasurer shall pay, on the warrant of the Comptroller out of the General Fund, such sum as shall be awarded pursuant to the first section of this act.

§ 3. This act shall take effect immediately.

Chap. 458.

AN ACT making appropriations for certain expenses of government.

Passed April 23, 1862 ; by a two-third vote.

The People of the State of New York, represented in Senate and Assembly, do enact as follows :

Treasurer to pay.

SECTION 1. The Treasurer shall pay, on the warrant of the Comptroller, except in those cases in which it is otherwise provided in this act, the several sums named, or so much of them as, in each case, may be necessary for the purposes specified, and to the persons here indicated. But when an appropriation shall have been paid for the same purpose, or to the same person, or shall have been provided by any other enactment or by any section of this act, or by any officer of government, the same here directed to be paid shall not be regarded as an addition to the other appropriation, unless it shall be expressly so declared in this act. In all cases where an appropriation is made by this act for work which is to be performed after the passage of this act, no person being authorized to do the work, the person or persons offering to do it for the lowest compensation, shall be employed to perform such work under the direction of the Comptroller. The Comptroller shall issue his warrant, in no case, for moneys appropriated by this act, except for salaries fixed by law, and for the amounts particularly specified, till he shall receive from the party demanding the same a detailed statement, verified by affidavit, of the amount claimed. Whenever moneys are appropriated for traveling expenses, the statement shall specify the distance, the duty or business, the places visited, the dates, and the several items of expense in traveling ; and when the appropriation is for services, the statement shall specify their nature, the time employed and the rate of compensation. Bills specifying the several items, properly receipted and verified, shall accompany all accounts for transportation, stationery and other expenditures.

Affidavit required in certain cases.

DEFICIENCIES IN APPROPRIATIONS, EXPENDITURES OF STATE
OFFICERS, DEPARTMENTS OF THE GOVERNMENT, AND SO
FORTH.

For deficiency of appropriation for expenses of the executive department, five hundred dollars. *Executive department*

For deficiency in the appropriation for expenses of public lands, for surveys, appraisals, assessments, etc., four thousand five hundred dollars. *Public lands.*

For deficiency in appropriation for postage of official letters of the Governor, Secretary of State, Comptroller, Treasurer, Superintendent of Public Instruction, Attorney-General, State Engineer and Surveyor, Adjutant-General, Inspector-General, and Clerk of the Court of Appeals, five hundred dollars. *Postage.*

For deficiency in appropriation for fuel for the Capitol, State Hall and State Library, five hundred dollars. *Fuel public buildings.*

For deficiency in appropriation for expenses of the hall for the State Cabinet of Natural History and the Agricultural Museum, for repairs, gas, cleaning, labor, fuel, and other necessary expenses, five hundred dollars. *Expenses Cabinet Natural History and Agricultural Museum*

For deficiency in appropriation for refunding of money erroneously paid into the treasury on account of taxes, twelve thousand dollars. *Erroneous payments.*

For deficiency in the appropriation for the refunding of surplus moneys arising from the sale of lands sold by the State Engineer and Surveyor for arrears of interest, five hundred dollars. *Refunding moneys.*

For deficiency in the appropriation for printing for the state, including binding, mapping, engraving and publishing official notices, and for printing the report of the Commissioners of the Code, thirty-five thousand dollars; provided that the Comptroller shall certify to the Treasurer that such binding, mapping and engraving have been actually performed, and that the maps and engravings have been duly included and bound up with the documents which have been published pursuant to law, and that there has been no excess of charge for such printing, mapping, engraving and publication. *Printing, mapping, binding, &c*

For deficiency of appropriation for expenditures in the office of the Adjutant-General, two thousand six hundred and fifty dollars; and to James I. Johnson, W. Wallace Perkins, Charles Evans and John B. Stonehouse, the four principal clerks in the office of the Adjutant- *Adjutant General's office.*

General, to each of them for extra labor, the additional compensation of three hundred dollars.

Charles E. Huxley. To Charles E. Huxley, clerk in the office of the Adjutant-General, for compensation from the first day of April, eighteen hundred and sixty-two, till the thirtieth day of September next, four hundred and fifty dollars; and for additional compensation for extra services rendered during the past year, one hundred dollars.

N. M. Case. To Newell M. Case, for extra services as messenger in the department of the Adjutant-General during the months of April, May, June and July, eighteen hundred and sixty-one, sixty dollars.

Inspector General's office. For compensation of clerks and contingent expenses in the office of the Inspector General, from the first day of February, eighteen hundred and sixty-two, till the first day of April next ensuing, three hundred and sixty dollars.

Quartermaster General's office. For compensation of clerks and other expenses of the Department of the Quartermaster General, actually necessary in the judgment of the Comptroller, two thousand three hundred and sixty dollars.

Surgeon General's office. For compensation of clerks, and for stationery, in the office of the Surgeon General, three hundred and eighty-five dollars.

John N. Parker. To John N. Parker, for services rendered and materials furnished in enclosing and repairing barracks in the city of Albany, and also at the arsenal and military store-house, and for the Departments of the Adjutant General, Inspector General, Surgeon General and Quartermaster General, one thousand seven hundred and fifty-two dollars and eighteen cents.

Geo. F. Nesbit. To George F. Nesbitt and company, for military books, circulars and stationery, furnished to the Department of the Commissary General, three hundred and eighty-six dollars and twenty-six cents.

Frank H. Little. To Frank H. Little, for stationery furnished to the office of the Surgeon General, twenty-one dollars and seventy-seven cents.

Volunteer surgeons. For the personal expenses incurred by volunteer surgeons when called by the Surgeon General into service, one thousand dollars; or so much of that amount as may be necessary.

Postage. To the Surgeon General, for postage of official letters, seventy-five dollars.

To John Sharts for services rendered to the state, John Sharts pursuant to the order of the Comptroller and Secretary of State, one hundred dollars.

For extra traveling expenses of the State Engineer Extra travel of State Engineer. and Surveyor during the year eighteen hundred and sixty-one, to be paid out of the Canal Fund, on the warrant of the Auditor, three hundred dollars.

To George R. Perkins, late deputy state engineer and Geo. R. Perkins. surveyor, for preparing railroad reports for eighteen hundred and sixty-two, and for superintending the printing of the same, the amount to be refunded to the treasury by an equitable assessment on the several railroad companies pursuant to the provisions of chapter five hundred and twenty-six of the Laws of one thousand eight hundred and fifty-five, six hundred dollars.

For compensation of an additional clerk in the office Clerk Canal Appraisers. of the Canal Appraisers, to be paid out of the Canal Fund on the warrant of the Auditor, one thousand dollars.

To Jacob Fonda, to pay an award of the canal con- Jacob Fonda. tracting board, pursuant to the provision of chapter three hundred and thirty of the Laws of eighteen hundred and sixty-one, to be paid out of the Canal Fund on the warrant of the Auditor, two thousand nine hundred and seventy-seven dollars and fifty-one cents.

To Benjamin F. Keals, for work done on the middle Benj. F. Keals. division of the canal, pursuant to contract, thirty-one dollars and twenty-five cents, payable from the Canal Fund.

To Stephen D. Charles, for services as engineer on the Stephen D. Charles. western division of the canals, from the first day of August, eighteen hundred and fifty-nine, till the thirteenth day of September next ensuing, eighty-one dollars, payable from the Canal Fund.

To George Dowd, for extra services in attending a George Dowd. lock on Genesee Valley canal, as by agreement with the Canal Commissioner, fifty dollars, payable from the fund for repairs of the Genesee Valley canal.

To Royal Chamberlain, in full for services rendered as Royal Chamberlain. insurance clerk in the Comptroller's office from the first day of January, eighteen hundred and sixty, till the fifteenth day of that month, one hundred and fifty dollars, or such portion of that amount as the Comptroller shall find to be justly due for such services.

Geological Hall. For painting the Geological Hall, three hundred dollars.

Department Public Instruction. For expenses of the Department of Public Instruction, pursuant to the provisions of the first part, fifteenth chapter, second title, tenth section of the Revised Statutes, three hundred dollars.

New York Teacher. To the Superintendent of Public Instruction for subscriptions to the New York Teacher for gratuitous circulation to school officers and inexperienced teachers, one thousand dollars.

Emerson W. Keyes. To Emerson W. Keyes, late acting Superintendent of Public Instruction, to supply deficiency of salary, seven hundred and eighty-three dollars and thirty-three cents.

Trustees of State Library. To the trustees of the state library, for the completion of the alcoves in the western gallery, and other expenses, two hundred and eighty-three dollars and sixty-three cents ; and for boxes for the arranging of the British patent reports, two hundred and fifty dollars.

James Hall. To James Hall, for salary for the next year, as palæontologist of the state, pursuant to the terms of the contract made with him by the commissioners for completing the Natural History of the state, as authorized by chapter five hundred and thirty-nine of the Laws of eighteen hundred and fifty-five, two thousand dollars ; and for the collection of fossils, under the same contract, for use in the preparation of the fourth volume of the palæontology, one thousand dollars ; and, for the preparation of drawings of said fossils, for the same purpose, one thousand dollars.

Amos Pilsbury. To Amos Pilsbury, for traveling expenses incurred while visiting the several state prisons, pursuant to the direction of the Governor, sixty-four dollars and twenty-seven cents.

Inspectors of State Prisons. To the Inspectors of state prisons, for extra traveling expenses, seven hundred and fifty dollars.

State Prison at Auburn. For repairs of the wing of the state prison at Auburn, eleven thousand dollars ; and for deficiency of appropriation for the completion of the enlargement of the prison, one thousand one hundred dollars.

John S. Laneheart. To John S. Laneheart, in full, for extra services as clerk in the state prison at Auburn during the enlargement of the prison, from September, in the year eighteen hundred and fifty-nine, till March, eighteen hundred and sixty-two, four hundred dollars.

To Franklin W. Whitlock, in full, of all claims against the state, either by reason of the construction given to the contract between him and Thomas Kirkpatrick, agent and warden of the state prison at Auburn, in the year eighteen hundred and fifty-nine, or for the delays caused to him in the performance of the contract, two hundred dollars.

To Richard Low, in full, for extra services in the case of the people of the state of New York against Munson L. Lockwood, two hundred dollars.

To the Inspectors of state prisons, for putting on iron roof upon the forge building at the state prison at Clinton, one thousand five hundred dollars.

For deficiency in the appropriation for the purchase of boilers, pipes, and other apparatus for warming the apartments in the state prison at Clinton, one thousand five hundred dollars.

For pickets for the fences at the state prison at Clinton, five hundred dollars.

For repairs on the plank road leading from the state prison at Clinton to Saranac river, one thousand five hundred dollars.

For maintenance of insane female convicts at the State Lunatic Asylum from the first day of August, in the year eighteen hundred and sixty-one, till the thirtieth day of September, eighteen hundred and sixty-two, seven hundred and fifty dollars, or such portion of that amount as shall be necessary.

To the society for the reformation of juvenile delinquents, to pay the debt incurred in completing their buildings on Randall's Island and to enable them to erect additional dormitories in the boys house, and to render fire-proof those apartments already built, twenty-five thousand dollars.

To Russel F. Hicks, for expenses and costs of suits against William Landon and M. Bradner, one hundred and twenty-two dollars and thirty-nine cents.

To James McGinty, in full, for attendance as constable upon the court of appeals, during the year eighteen hundred and sixty-one, one hundred and fifty dollars, and to John P. Cordell, deputy sheriff, for similar service and attendance at the same time, one hundred and fifty dollars.

Henry Ber-
tholf.

To Henry Bertholf, in full, for service and attendance as constable upon the supreme court in the city of New York, pursuant to the provisions of chapter four hundred and twenty-nine of the Laws of eighteen hundred and forty-seven, one thousand dollars or such portion of that amount as the Comptroller shall find to be due for such service.

Superin-
tendent of
the Capitol.

To the superintendent of the Capitol, for services rendered while the Capitol was occupied for military purposes during the present fiscal year, one hundred and fifty dollars.

Wm. H.
Mink.

To Wm. H. Mink, for services as superintendent of the State Hall for the years eighteen hundred and sixty and eighteen hundred and sixty-one, two hundred dollars.

Weare C.
Little.

To Weare C. Little, in full, for sixty-three copies of the thirty-second, thirty-third, and thirty-fourth volumes of Barbour's Supreme Court Reports, furnished to the Regents of the University for distribution to the governors of the loyal states, one hundred and eighty-nine dollars; and for thirty-three copies of the fourth volume of Parker's Criminal Reports furnished for the same purpose, one hundred and thirty-six dollars and thirteen cents; and in full, for the books furnished by him to the library of the Attorney General for the years eighteen hundred and sixty and eighteen hundred and sixty-one, one hundred and thirty-nine dollars and fifty cents.

Wm. Gould

To William Gould, for books furnished to the library of the Attorney General, fourteen dollars and fifty cents.

Weed, Par-
sons & Co.

To Weed, Parsons and Company, for five hundred and sixty copies of the Legislative Manual of eighteen hundred and sixty-one, furnished to state officers and Regents of the University, pursuant to resolution of the legislature, five hundred and sixty dollars.

Weed, Par-
sons & Co.

To Weed, Parsons and Company, for one hundred and one copies of the civil list, furnished to state officers and Regents of the University, one hundred and fifty-one dollars and fifty cents.

Printing
railroad
reports.

For printing six thousand copies of the report of the State Engineer and Surveyor on railroads, for eighteen hundred and sixty, pursuant to resolution of the Senate and Assembly, passed in January, eighteen hundred and sixty-one, three thousand four hundred and six dollars and thirty-three cents; which amount shall be repaid to the Treasury of the State by the several railroad companies, in proportion to their respective gross receipts, pursuant to the provisions of chapter five hundred and twenty-six of the Laws of eighteen hundred and fifty-five.

To Weed, Parsons and Company for stationery fur- ^{Weed, Parsons & Co.} nished for the index to the Colonial History of the State of New York, for the years eighteen hundred and fifty-eight, eighteen hundred and fifty-nine, eighteen hundred and sixty, and eighteen hundred and sixty-one, sixty-seven dollars.

To E. H. Bender, for stationery, binding, costs, etc., ^{E. H. Bender.} for the departments in the State Hall, and for other expenses, to be in full of all demands against the state for said charges, eight hundred and fifty-eight dollars and sixty-seven cents.

EXPENDITURES OF THE LEGISLATURE.

To the clerk of the Senate, for extra clerical hire and ^{Clerk of the Senate.} engrossing, four hundred dollars; and for properly indexing the journal the documents of the Senate, two hundred and fifty dollars.

To the deputy clerks of the Senate in addition to their ^{Deputy clerks of the Senate.} salary, to each of them, two hundred dollars, to be paid upon the certificate of the clerk of the Senate, that each clerk respectively, has fully and faithfully discharged the duties of his office during the present session; and also the same allowance for mileage which is made to members of the legislature.

To George W. Fay, for compensation as deputy clerk ^{Geo. W. Fay.} of the Senate, six hundred dollars.

To Herman Rulison, librarian of the Senate; William ^{Herman Rulison, Wm. Gamble, Nathaniel Goodwin.} Gamble, assistant postmaster, and Nathaniel Goodwin, superintendent of the Senate chamber, to each of them for every day of actual service, three dollars, and the same allowance for mileage which is provided by law for members of the legislature.

To Robert Campbell, Lieutenant Governor, in behalf ^{Joseph Garlinghouse.} of the legal heirs of Joseph Garlinghouse, deceased, late janitor of the Senate chamber, in full, for fifty days of service, three hundred dollars, and the same allowance for mileage which is provided by law for members of the legislature.

Messengers of the officers of the Senate. To Charles A. Garlinghouse, bank and clerk's messenger of the Senate, two dollars and fifty cents for each day of actual service; to Thomas Fogarty. messenger to the president of the Senate; Bentley P. Murray, post office messenger; Oscar McMurray and William Storey, messengers to the sergeant-at-arms; and Asher P. Cole, messenger to the librarian of the Senate; and to Henry C. Leslie, assistant to superintendent of Senate chamber; to each of them for every day of actual service, two dollars; to be paid on the certificate of the president of of the Senate.

James Terwilliger. To James Terwilliger, to reimburse him for moneys paid for furniture for the Senate chamber and Senate library, upon the production of proper vouchers to the Comptroller, forty-six dollars and fifty cents.

Charles G. Fairman. To Charles G. Fairman, for properly collecting and filing all papers relating to executive business of the Senate from eighteen hundred and thirty-three till eighteen hundred and sixty-two, pursuant to resolution of the Senate, three hundred dollars.

Nathaniel Goodwin. To Nathaniel Goodwin, superintendent of the Senate chamber, one hundred and fifty dollars, in addition to the compensation hereinbefore provided.

Clerk of Senate committee of nine. To the clerk of the Senate select committee of nine, the sum of one hundred and fifty dollars; to be paid on the certificate of the chairman of that committee.

Caleb S. Babcock. To Caleb S. Babcock, for preparation of the annual statistical list of senators and officers of the Senate, twenty dollars.

Senate select committee. For expenses of the select committee of the Senate, appointed to investigate the charges of malfeasance in office made against the harbor masters in the city of New York, including compensation of clerk, sergeant-at-arms, and reporter, one thousand two hundred dollars.

Clergymen officiating as chaplains to the legislature. To the clergymen officiating as chaplains to the Senate and Assembly, during the present session of the legislature, to be paid one-half to James Terwilliger, and one-half to Joseph B. Cushman, for distribution by them to said clergymen, at the rate of three dollars for each day's attendance, six hundred dollars.

Clerks of committees To the clerks of the several committees of the Senate and Assembly, three dollars for each day of actual service, to be certified by the chairman of the respective committees that they have been so employed and engaged.

For compensation of the several women employed in cleaning the Senate and Assembly chambers, and the several rooms connected with them, to each woman for every day of actual service, two dollars. *Women for cleaning Senate and Assembly chambers.*

For compensation of the several pages employed by the Senate and Assembly, for each day of actual service, one dollar and fifty cents. *Pages of the Senate and Assembly.*

To Banks & Brothers, for law books furnished to the libraries of the Senate and Assembly, sixty dollars and thirty-seven cents. *Banks & Brothers.*

To Douglas A. Levien, for services as clerk of the select committee of the Senate appointed in eighteen hundred and sixty-one, to enquire into the irregularity of management and other misconduct by officers of the corporation of the city of New York, seventy-five dollars. *Douglas A. Levien.*

To James C. Clark, sergeant-at-arms of the Senate, during the years eighteen hundred and sixty and eighteen hundred and sixty-one, for mileage, expenses and serving of subpœna upon the district attorney of the county of New York by order of Francis B. Spinola, the chairman of the investigating committee of the Senate, thirty dollars and fifty cents. *James C. Clark.*

To William Hodgins, for the preparation of plans for the improvement of the Senate Chamber, pursuant to a resolution of the Senate, passed in eighteen hundred and sixty, one hundred and thirty-five dollars. *Wm. Hodgins.*

For compensation of the several firemen employed about the Capitol and State Library during the present session of the legislature, to each of them for every day of actual service, three dollars. *Firemen about Capitol and State Library.*

For compensation of the night watchmen employed about the Capitol and State Library during the present session of the legislature, for every day of actual service, three dollars. *Night watchmen about capitol and State Library.*

To Mrs. Gray and Mrs. Moran, the women employed in cleaning the State Library and the several rooms connected with the same, to each of them fifty dollars. *Women for cleaning State Library.*

To the clerk of the Assembly, for extra clerical hire and engrossing, four hundred dollars, and for properly indexing the Assembly journal and documents of the present session, two hundred and fifty dollars. *Extra clerk hire for Assembly.*

Matthew O. Hallenbeck.

To Matthew O. Hallenbeck, for services as assistant to the journal clerk of the Assembly, five hundred dollars.

Elias H. Jenner.

To Elias H. Jenner, for compensation as deputy clerk of the Assembly, six hundred dollars.

Deputy clerks of the Assembly.

To each of the deputy clerks of the Assembly, the sum of two hundred dollars in addition to their salary, to be paid upon the certificate of the clerk of the Assembly, that the duties and labors of each, incident to and consequent upon the session, are fully performed; and also the same allowance for mileage as is made to members of Assembly, to be certified by the speaker.

Certain officers of the Assembly.

To William Carey, postmaster of the Assembly; to James W. Miller, assistant postmaster; to George W. Burger, keeper of the Assembly chamber, and to Henry A. Rodgers, janitor; to each of them for every day of actual service, three dollars, and the same allowance for mileage which is provided for members of the legislature.

Henry C. Wood.

To Henry C. Wood, bank messenger of the Assembly, for each day of actual service, two dollars and fifty cents, to be certified by the speaker of the Assembly.

Messengers of officers of the Assembly.

To Henry S. Williams, speaker's messenger, James Bain, postmaster's messenger, and James O'Sullivan, messenger of the sergeant-at-arms, to each of them, for each day of actual service, to be certified by the speaker of the Assembly, two dollars.

Joseph B. Cushman.

To Joseph B. Cushman, clerk of the Assembly, to reimburse him for moneys paid for gas shades, and for furniture and repairs for furniture of the Assembly chamber, upon the production of proper vouchers to the Comptroller, four hundred dollars.

Hanson A. Risley.

To Hanson A. Risley, late clerk of the Assembly, for services in revising, publishing and mailing the clerk's manual of rules, forms and laws to members elect of the Assembly, one hundred dollars.

Bailey J. Hathaway.

To Bailey J. Hathaway, for compiling and preparing the annual statistical list of members and officers of the Assembly, twenty-five dollars.

Charles D. Easton.

To the legal representatives of Charles D. Easton, late sergeant-at-arms of the Assembly of eighteen hundred and sixty-one, for attendance upon the judiciary committee, serving subpœnas, and so forth, thirty-nine dollars and forty cents; for mileage, expenses, and serving subpœnas, pursuant to order of the select committee appointed to investigate the charges of corruption made against Jay Gibbons, a member of that house, forty-six dollars and sixty cents.

To Sanders Wilson, doorkeeper of the Assembly of eighteen hundred and sixty-one, for ten days' attendance as doorkeeper, pursuant to order of the select committee appointed to investigate charges against Jay Gibbons, thirty dollars. Sanders Wilson.

To Levi M. Guno, sergeant-at-arms of the Assembly, for services, mileage, expenses and subpœnaing witnesses by order of the select committee on the Governor's message, one hundred and forty dollars and twenty-five cents ; for services, mileage, expenses and subpœnaing witnesses by order of the committee of privileges and elections, two hundred and eleven dollars and twenty-five cents, and for clerical and other services made necessary by the long sickness of the assistant sergeant-at-arms, one hundred and fifty dollars. Levi M. Guno.

To Laurin L. Rose, assistant sergeant-at-arms of the Assembly, for mileage, and expenses, and subpœnaing witnesses for the committee of privileges and elections, forty-nine dollars. Laurin L. Rose.

To Francis Kernan, for mileage and expenses while in attendance upon the several sessions of the judiciary committee of the Assembly of eighteen hundred and sixty-one, held during the recess of the legislature, pursuant to resolution of the Assembly, one hundred dollars ; to Nathan Comstock, for the same purpose, one hundred dollars ; to Robert C. Hutchings, for the same, one hundred dollars ; to Daniel Waterbury, for the same, one hundred dollars. Francis Kernan.
Nathan Comstock.
Robert C. Hutchings.
Daniel Waterbury.

For expenses and disbursements of the committee of the Assembly, appointed to consider that portion of the Governor's message relative to the transactions of the state military board, to the chairman, two hundred and twenty dollars ; to the other members of the committee actually attending sessions, eighty dollars each, and for compensation of their stenographer, three hundred and twenty-five dollars Committee for investigating acts of military board.

For expenses of the committee of privileges and elections of the Assembly, when absent from the city of Albany, pursuant to resolutions of the Assembly, three hundred and thirty-seven dollars, and for the hire of stenographer, forty-eight dollars and fifty-three cents. Committee on privileges and elections.

Committee for examining affairs of Institution for the Blind.

For expenses of the select committee of the Assembly, appointed to examine into the affairs of the Institution for the Blind, including mileage, clerk hire, serving of subpœnas, hire of stenographer, three hundred and fifty dollars, or such portion of that amount as the Comptroller shall find to be just and proper.

Jacob Ten Broeck.

To Jacob Ten Broeck, for travelling expenses incurred in visiting the state prisons at Auburn and Sing Sing, as member of the committee on state prisons, authorized and directed by the Assembly to visit those institutions, twenty-five dollars.

Lemuel Stetson.

To Lemuel Stetson, in trust for the expenses of the committee appointed by the Assembly to attend the funeral of Newberry D. Halstead, member of Assembly from the second district of the county of Westchester, twenty-four dollars and fifty cents.

Assembly committee for investigating opening streets in city of N. Y.

For expenses of the select committee of the Assembly of eighteen hundred and sixty-one, appointed to sit during the recess to investigate the subject of opening streets in the city of New York, five hundred dollars, to be paid as follows, namely: to Charles E. Wilbur, stenographer to the committee, for sixty days of service, three hundred dollars; to Joseph J. Camp, sergeant-at-arms to the committee, one hundred dollars; and to Edmund Jones and Company, in full for stationery furnished said committee, one hundred dollars.

Benj. F. Brady.

To Benjamin F. Brady, for engrossing on parchment the Ericsson and Worden resolutions, one hundred and fifty dollars.

Dennis McCabe.

To Dennis McCabe, for fees of counsel and expenses incurred in contesting the seat in the Assembly of eighteen hundred and sixty-one, occupied by Henry Arcularius, one hundred and forty dollars.

Weed, Parsons & Co.

To Weed, Parsons and Company, for copies of the Legislative Manual furnished to the state officers and members of the legislature, pursuant to resolutions of the Senate and Assembly, three thousand and ninety-four dollars; for diagrams of the Senate and Assembly chambers, etc., six hundred and eight dollars and sixty cents, and for fifty census maps furnished to the Senate, pursuant to a resolution of that body, twenty-five dollars.

Printing book of forms.

For printing one thousand five hundred copies of the book of forms, pursuant to a resolution of the Assembly, passed on the twelfth day of April, eighteen hundred and sixty-one, five hundred dollars.

MISCELLANEOUS EXPENDITURES.

The Comptroller is authorized to pay to Weed, Parsons and Company, out of the appropriation of last year for the index to the Colonial History, the sum of one thousand nine hundred and thirty-seven dollars and sixty-eight cents, being for charges, in proof sheets, and for difference in composition between small pica and brevier, if in his judgment the same is equitable and just. Weed, Parsons & Co.

To the treasurer of the county of Genesee, for moneys paid into the treasury of the state for taxes assessed upon Indian lands situated in the towns of Alabama and Pembroke, which were exempt from taxation, pursuant to the provisions of chapter four hundred and ninety-one of the Laws of eighteen hundred and sixty, to be refunded by him to the parties in the town of Alabama, duly authorized to receive the same, three hundred and forty-four dollars; and to the parties in the town of Pembroke, duly authorized to receive the same, two hundred and seventy-two dollars and eighty-seven cents. Treasurer Genesee county.

To Lorenzo H. Olcott, for removing intruders on Indian lands in the county of Genesee, provided, in the judgment of the Comptroller, he is equitably entitled to the same, two hundred and fifty dollars. Lorenzo H. Olcott.

To Benjamin E. Bowen, for reimbursements of legal costs recovered against him by the Bank of Salina, in defending his title to lands purchased at a sale of lands for non-payment of taxes, said sale having been annulled by the supreme court, one hundred and eighty-six dollars and sixteen cents. Benj. E. Bowen.

To Isaac N. Wyckoff, assignee of Anna E. Stannard, in full, of an award made by the commissioners appointed for that purpose, pursuant to the provisions of chapter five hundred and seventeen of the Laws of eighteen hundred and sixty, and for the cancelling of all claims and demands under said act, one thousand five hundred dollars. Isaac N. Wyckoff.

For expenses in full of George W. Patterson, John C. Green and Charles A. Peabody, Quarantine commissioners, three thousand dollars, or such portion of that amount as the Comptroller shall find due for such expenses. Quarantine commissioners.

For expenses of the coroner's inquest upon the body of Augustus T. Wright, a keeper in the state prison at Coroner's inquest at Clinton prison.

Clinton, murdered by. the prisoners, and of the indictment and trial of seven convicts for the murder, to be certified by the supervisors of Clinton county, one thousand five hundred and ten dollars and thirty-seven cents.

Onondaga salt springs
For deficiency of appropriation for expenses of the Onondaga salt springs, eight thousand one hundred dollars; and, in full, for lowering the outlet of Onondaga lake, one thousand nine hundred dollars.

Montezuma salt springs
To the superintendent of the Montezuma salt springs, to be expended upon the new well south of the village of Montezuma, for the development of said springs, three thousand five hundred dollars, or so much thereof as may be necessary, to be expended under the direction of the Comptroller.

Colored school, Flatbush.
To the trustees of the colored school in the town of Flatbush, in the county of Kings, one hundred dollars, to be paid upon the certificate of the Superintendent of Public Instruction, when they shall furnish satisfactory evidence of having incurred legitimate expenses to that amount, and of having maintained said school for at least four months during the present school year, pursuant to the provisions of chapter four hundred and eighty of Laws of eighteen hundred and forty-seven, as modified by subsequent legislation.

Agricultural college at Ovid.
For the commissioners of the land office, twenty-five hundred dollars, or so much of that amount as may be necessary to pay on account of the interest on the first lien of thirty thousand dollars on the Agricultural College at Ovid; and said commissioners shall report to the next legislature the situation and value of the college farm and buildings and the outstanding indebtedness.

Law library at Binghamton.
To Banks and Brothers, for law books furnished on the order of the justices of the supreme court for the sixth judicial district, for the supreme court library at Binghamton, pursuant to the provisions of chapter two hundred and thirty of the Laws of eighteen hundred and fifty-nine, nine hundred and eighty-six dollars and two cents.

Michael Conklin.
To Michael Conklin, for services rendered at Quarantine by the steam propeller Rescue, in the year eighteen hundred and sixty, under order of the health officer, four thousand eight hundred and sixty-five dollars, or so much thereof as the Comptroller shall. upon examination, deem the state justly and legally liable for.

For compensation of the agent employed by the Comptroller to pay the Cayuga Indians residing in western New York, their share of the annuity payable to that nation on the first day of June in each year, fifty dollars. *Agent Cayuga Indians.*

To Harvey Follett, in full, for services as clerk of the commission to examine the claims of the soldiers of the war of eighteen hundred and twelve, one hundred dollars. *Harvey Follett.*

For repairing the pier at the entrance of Cayuga lake, for removing the bars from the inlet so as to give a depth of seven feet of water from Oswego street bridge to the lake, and for the purpose of raising the bridges across the inlet to an altitude sufficient to permit the passage of boats of the largest class, two thousand five hundred dollars, to be expended under direction of the Canal Commissioners. *Pier at entrance of Cayuga lake, removing obstructions, &c.*

To George Jenkins, superintendent of the Capitol, for expenses incurred in the illumination of the Capitol on the occasion of the recent victories actually achieved by our army, forty-two dollars and five cents. *George Jenkins.*

To William H. Mink, superintendent of the State Hall, for expenses incurred in the illumination of the State Hall by order of the Assembly, in honor of victories actually won by our armies, forty-four dollars and eighty-five cents. *William H. Mink.*

To George H. Kitchen, inspector of gas meters, for deficiency in appropriations for his salary in the years eighteen hundred and sixty and eighteen hundred and sixty-one, pursuant to the provisions of chapter one hundred and sixteen of the Laws of eighteen hundred and sixty, two thousand two hundred and fifty dollars, which amount shall be refunded to the treasury by the several gas light companies, pursuant to the provisions of chapter three hundred and eleven of the Laws of eighteen hundred and fifty-nine. *George H. Kitchen.*

For the preservation of Washington's Head Quarters at Newburgh, pursuant to the provisions of chapter two hundred and sixty-five of the Laws of eighteen hundred and fifty, five hundred and ninety-six dollars and four cents. *Washington's head quarters.*

To Lockwood L. Doty, private secretary and military secretary to the Governor, for extra services during the year eighteen hundred and sixty-one, five hundred dollars. *Lockwood L. Doty.*

Chauncey
M. Depew.

To Chauncey M. Depew, for the benefit of the representatives of Newberry D. Halstead, deceased, late a member of the Assembly from the county of Westchester, thirty-six dollars; being his compensation therefor from the fourth to the sixteenth days of April, instant, inclusive.

Charles
Horton.

To Charles Horton, post master of the last Assembly for services rendered after the legislature had adjourned, in returning mail matter to members, twenty-one dollars.

Benjamin
F. Hall.

To Benjamin F. Hall, for services rendered as clerk to the committee on state prisons of the Assembly, of eighteen hundred and fifty-nine, inclusive of ninety-seven dollars paid by him, for expenses, two hundred and fifty dollars.

Republican
Statesman.

To the proprietors of the Republican Statesman, for advertising proclamations, etc., for the Executive Department, to be paid on the certificate of the Governor, that such advertising has been actually performed, two hundred and four dollars and thirty cents.

Engineers,
to consider
defences of
N. Y. harbor.

For compensation and expenses of the board of engineers, seven in number, convened in the month of December, eighteen hundred and sixty-one, to consider and report upon plans for the defence of the harbor of New York, and for other expenses connected with the same, two thousand dollars; or so much of that amount as shall be necessary, to be paid on the certificate of the Governor, with a detailed statement of services and expenses.

James Hay,
estate of
John G.
Lake.

To James Hay, in full for all claims as heir to the estate of John G. Lake, deceased, escheated to the state, two thousand five hundred dollars; to be paid on his full relinquishment of all claims to the said estate on his own part and in behalf of all persons whom he represents in this matter.

Charles Van
Benthuysen

To Charles Van Benthuysen, for printing, binding and delivering one thousand five hundred copies of the catalogue of the State Library, three thousand five hundred and four dollars and eighty-five cents; for engraving on stone, paper and printing in lithography the plates for the fourth volume of the palæontology of the state, one thousand three hundred and thirty two dollars and seventy-five cents; and for printing, binding and delivering two thousand nine hundred and eighty copies of the third volume of the palæontology, four thousand and forty-two dollars and fourteen cents, according to a contract to be found in Assembly documents number nine of eighteen hundred and fifty, page fifty-four.

To Weed, Parsons and Company, in full for printing and binding the second volume of the journal of the legislative council of the colony of New York, together with the index to the work, four thousand seven hundred and seventy-four dollars and fourteen cents. *Weed, Parsons & Co.*

To E. B. O'Callaghan, for six months and a half of services in superintending the printing of the journal of the legislative council of New York and for preparing the index of the same, eight hundred and twelve dollars and fifty cents, and to Thomas McLaughlin, for assisting in preparation of said index, sixty-six dollars and fifty-six cents. *E. B. O'Callaghan.*

For expenses incident to the transportation, care and supplies of hospital for sick and wounded soldiers belonging to this state, in cases in which no provision shall have been made for such purposes by the government of the United States, to be considered a charge against said government; and for the removal of the remains of officers slain in battle or dying while in service, thirty thousand dollars; to be paid on the certificate of the Governor, in each particular case stating that from the attending circumstances it should be a public charge. *Supplies for sick and wounded soldiers.* *Removal of remains of officers.*

To William H. Anthon, Judge Advocate General, to reimburse him for copying and other clerical services, one hundred and fifty-three dollars and sixty-one cents. *Wm. H. Anthon.*

For expenses of courts-martial pursuant to the provisions of sections sixteenth and seventeenth of the seventh title of chapter three hundred and ninety-eight of the Laws of one thousand eight hundred and fifty-four, three thousand five hundred dollars. *Expenses of courts-martial.*

For the purchase of the general regulations and of the United States infantry tactics, one thousand dollars. *Purchase of military books.*

To Charles Roome, colonel of the thirty-seventh regiment of the New York state militia, to reimburse him for money paid for four hundred and eighty sets of accouterments purchased in pursuance of instructions from Major General Charles W. Sandford, eight hundred and thirty-four dollars and forty cents, to be paid on the certificate of the Commissary General. *Charles Roome.*

State arsenal at Brooklyn.

For repairing, grading, paving, fencing and strengthening of the State Ar-enal at Brooklyn, four thousand dollars, or so much of that amount as may be necessary, to be expended under direction of the Commissary General.

Charles Van Benthuysen for claim of R. M. Griffin.

To Charles Van Benthuysen, for the remainder of the assigned claim of R. M. Griffin and Company for job printing done by order of Gideon J. Tucker, Secretary of State, one thousand one hundred and eighty-one dollars and forty cents, or such portion of that amount as the Comptroller, Attorney General and Lieutenant Governor, or a majority of them, on examination of the several items shall find to be justly due.

George H. Moore for manuscript copy of missing legislative journals.

To George H. Moore, for a manuscript copy of the missing journals of the legislature of New York during the colonial period, five hundred dollars or such portion of that amount as the Regents of the University shall deem a fair remuneration; provided that the aforesaid copy shall be properly authenticated and shall supply whatever deficiency is now existing in said history, and that no further appropriation shall be necessary to accomplish the purpose of the one now made.

A. Strong & Co. for advertising.

To A. Strong and Company, proprietors of the Rochester Democrat and American, for the unpaid remainder due for advertising the monthly abstracts of the superintendent of the eleventh section of the Erie canal, in the year eighteen hundred and fifty-nine, according to contract, one hundred and twenty dollars; and for advertising proposals for repairs upon the Champlain and Genesee Valley canals and upon the Genesee Valley canal extension, in the month of June eighteen hundred and sixty, to be paid upon the certificate of the Canal Commissioner authorizing the advertising, two hundred and twenty-four dollars and eighteen cents.

Comstock & Cassidy.

To Comstock and Cassidy, for publication of the Session Laws of eighteen hundred and sixty-one, in the state paper, comprising one thousand six hundred and eight folios, at the rate of thirty cents a folio, four hundred and eighty-two dollars and forty cents.

Meade & Reynolds.

To Meade and Reynolds, for services and expenses incurred at the instance of the Clerk of the court of appeals, in travelling to Bath, to attend sales and for the examination of the titles to mortgaged property, lying in that town, by direction of said clerk, one hundred dollars or such portion of that amount as the Comptroller shall find to be due.

To the Iroquois agricultural society, two hundred and fifty dollars. Iroquois agricultural society.

To the Clerk of the court of appeals, the sum of two hundred and fifty dollars, or so much thereof as may be necessary, to repair the room occupied by the court of appeals, for the purpose of adding to the comfort and quiet of the room. Repair Court of Appeals room.

For repairing the piers and taking care of the canal harbor at the entrance of the Cayuga and Seneca canal into Seneca lake, the sum of five thousand dollars, to be expended, or so much thereof as may be necessary, under the direction of the Canal Commissioners, to be paid from the funds appropriated for ordinary repairs of said canal. Harbor and piers entrance of canal into Seneca lake

To William B. Lewis, State Treasurer, for expenses incurred in defending his claim to his office, contested by Phillip Dorsheimer, one hundred and fifty dollars. Wm. B. Lewis.

To Alexander Ostrander, for rent of rooms to the select committee of the Assembly of eighteen hundred and sixty-one, appointed to investigate the matter of the opening of streets in the city of New York, two hundred dollars. Alexander Ostrander.

To Robert P. Parrott, for shells and other projectiles furnished the state, eight thousand four hundred and seventy-two dollars and fifty cents. Robert P. Parrott, shells and other projectiles.

To Philip Phelps, three thousand dollars, on the recommendation of Azariah C. Flagg, Millard Fillmore, Washington Hunt, John C. Wright, Lorenzo Burrows, Sanford E. Church, James M. Cook and Robert Denniston, who have all respectively held the office of Comptroller of this state, and in recognition of the faithful services of the said Philip Phelps, as deputy in the said Comptroller's office for more than thirty years past, and as compensation for the same in addition to the amount heretofore received by him. Philip Phelps, deputy comptroller

The proviso attached to the grant of one thousand five hundred dollars to the Children's Friend Society in the city of Albany, under chapter two hundred and sixty-six of the Laws of eighteen hundred and sixty-one, is hereby repealed. Children's Friend Society city of Albany.

§ 2. This act shall take effect immediately.

Chap. 459.

AN ACT to prevent animals from running at large in the public highways.

Passed April 23, 1862; three-fifths being present.

The People of the State of New York, represented in Senate and Assembly, do enact as follows:

SECTION 1. It shall not be lawful for any cattle horses, sheep and swine to run at large in any public highway in this state.

§ 2. It shall be lawful for any person to seize and take into his custody and possession any animal which may be in any public highway, and opposite to land owned or occupied by him, contrary to the provisions of the foregoing section. And it shall be lawful for any person to take into his custody and possession any animal which may be trespassing upon premises owned or occupied by him.

§ 3. Whenever any such person shall seize and take into his custody and possession any animal under the authority of the next preceding section, it shall be the duty of such person to give immediate notice thereof to a justice of the peace or a commissioner of highways of the town in which such seizure and possession shall have been taken; and such justice or commissioner shall thereupon give notice by affixing the same in six public and conspicuous places in said town, one of which shall be the district school house nearest the residence of such justice or commissioner, that such animal or animals will be sold at public auction, at some convenient place in said town, not less than fifteen nor more than thirty days from the time of the affixing of such notice, to be specified in such notice, the said justice or commissioner shall proceed to sell the said animal or animals for cash, and out of the proceeds thereof shall, in the first place, retain the following fees and charges for his services in giving said notice and making said sale, viz: For every horse sold, one dollar; for every cow or calf, or other cattle, one half dollar; and for every sheep or swine, fifty cents; and shall then pay to

Animals running at large may be seized.

Proceedings thereon.

the person who shall have seized the said animal or animals the sum following, that is to say : For every horse so seized and sold, one dollar ; for every cow or calf, or other cattle, one half dollar ; and for every sheep or swine, twenty-five cents ; together with a reasonable compensation, to be estimated by such justice or commissioner, for the care and keeping of said animal or animals from the seizure thereof to the time of the sale. If there shall be any surplus moneys arising from said sale, the said justice or commissioner shall retain the same in his hands, and pay the same to the owner or owners of said animal or animals, after a reasonable demand therefor and satisfactory proof of such ownership, provided such owner or owners shall appear and claim such surplus moneys within one year after such sale. And if the owner or owners of such animal or animals shall not appear and demand such surplus moneys within one year after such sale has been made, he shall be forever precluded from recovering any part of such moneys ; and the same shall be paid to the supervisor of the town for the use of the town ; and his receipt therefor shall be a legal discharge to said justice or commissioner.

§ 4. Any owner of any animal which shall have been seized under and pursuant to the foregoing provisions, may, at any time before the sale thereof, demand and shall be entitled to the possession of such animal, upon the payment to him of the several sums hereinbefore required to be paid the said justice or commissioner, and to the person by whom the seizure aforesaid shall have been made, together with a reasonable compensation to the person making such seizure, for the care and keeping such animal, to be estimated and fixed by such justice or commissioner, and upon making, to such justice or commissioner, satisfactory proof of ownership. And if such owner shall make such demand and proof, at least three days before the time appointed for such sale, he shall be entitled to the custody and possession of said animal, upon paying one-half of the several sums above mentioned, together with the whole amount of compensation awarded by the said justice or commissioner. *Right of owner of any animal seized.*

§ 5. In case the animal so seized under the foregoing provisions of this act, shall have been so running at large or trespassing, by the wilful act of any other *Ibid.*

person than the owner, to effect that object, such owner
shall be entitled to the possession of such animal by
making the demand therefor and the proof required in
the next preceding section, and paying to the person
making such seizure the amount of compensation fixed
by such justice or commissioner, for the care and keeping of such animal, and without paying any other
charges. And the person committing such wilful act
shall be liable to a penalty of twenty dollars, to be recovered in an action at law at the suit of the owner of
such animal or the person making such seizure.

Repeal.   § 6. All acts or parts of acts inconsistent herewith are
hereby repealed.

Chap. 460.

AN ACT to amend the Code of Procedure, and to
extend the term of office of the Commissioners
of the Code appointed under the act of April
sixth, eighteen hundred, and fifty-seven, and to
repeal section thirty-seven, article second, title
second, chapter first, part third of the Revised
Statutes.

Passed April 23, 1862; three-fifths being present.

*The People of the State of New York, represented in
Senate and Assembly, do enact as follows :*

SECTION 1. The act known as the Code of Procedure
is hereby amended as follows :

§ 11 amend-
ed as to ap-
peals from
orders.
In the second subdivision of the eleventh section
thereof, after the words " when such order grants," insert the words, " or refuses," so that the first sentence
of said subdivision shall read as follows : " In an order
affecting a substantial right, made in such action, when
such order in effect determines the action, and prevents
a judgment from which an appeal might be taken, and
when such order grants or refuses a new trial."

§ 24 amend-
ed as to ad-
journment
of special
terms.
At the end of the twenty-fourth section of the said
Code of Procedure, add the following words :
And special terms may be adjourned to be held at a
future day at the chambers of any justice of said court

residing within the district, by an entry in the same manner, and then adjourned from time to time, as the justice holding the same shall order and direct.

§ 2. The last sentence of the thirteenth section thereof, is hereby amended so as to read as follows: *§ 13 amended as to calendar in Court of Appeals.*

"On a second, and each subsequent appeal, to the Court of Appeals, or when an appeal has once been dismissed for defect or irregularity, the cause shall be placed on the calendar as of the time of filing the first appeal."

§ 3. The second subdivision of the fifty-third section thereof is hereby amended so as to read as follows: *§ 53 amended.*

An action for damages for injury to rights pertaining to the person, or to personal or real property if the damages claimed do not exceed two hundred dollars. *Justices jurisdiction extended.*

§ 4. Section one hundred and sixteen of the Code of Procedure is hereby amended by adding thereto the following: *§ 116 amended.*

And in actions for the partition of real property, or for the foreclosure of a mortgage or other instrument, when an infant defendant resides out of this state, the plaintiff may apply to the court in which the action is pending, at any special term thereof, and will be entitled to an order, designating some suitable person to be the guardian for the infant defendant, for the purposes of the action, unless the infant defendant, or some one in his behalf, within a number of days after the service of a copy of the order, which number of days shall be in the said order specified, shall procure to be appointed a guardian for the said infant, and the court shall give special directions in the order for the manner of the service thereof, which may be upon the infant himself, or by service upon any relation or person with whom the infant resides, and either by mail or personally upon the person so served. *Guardian for infant defendant in partition and foreclosure cases.*

§ 5. At the end of section one hundred and twenty-one add as follows: *§ 121 amended.*

At any time after the death, marriage or other disability of the party plaintiff, the court in which an action is pending, upon notice to such persons as it may direct, and upon application of any person aggrieved, may in its discretion, order that the action be deemed abated unless the same be continued by the proper parties, within a time to be fixed by the court, not less than six months nor exceeding one year from the granting of the order. *Proceedings in case of death, marriage or other disability of plaintiff.*

§ 132 amended.

§ 6. Section one hundred and thirty-two is hereby amended by adding thereto the following :

Action when deemed pending.

For the purposes of this section an action shall be deemed to be pending from the time of the filing of such notice ; provided, however, that such notice shall be of no avail, unless it shall be followed by the first publication of the summons on an order therefor, or by the personal service thereof on a defendant within sixty days after such filing.

And the court in which the said action is pending may, in its discretion, at any time after the action shall have become abated, as is provided in section number one hundred and twenty-one, on good cause shown, and on application of any party aggrieved, after the action shall have become abated as is provided in section one hundred and twenty-one, direct the notice authorized by this section to be removed from record by the clerk of any county in whose office the same may have been filed.

§ 183 amended.

§ 7. Section one hundred and eighty-three is hereby amended by adding thereto the following :

Notice of order of arrest to be issued.

But said order of arrest shall be of no avail, and shall be vacated or set aside on motion, unless the same is served upon the defendant, as provided by law before the docketing of any judgment in the action, and the defendant shall have twenty days after the service of the order of arrest in which to answer the complaint in the action and to move to vacate the order of arrest, or to reduce the amount of bail.

§ 240 amended.

§ 8. Section two hundred and forty is hereby amended by adding thereto at the end thereof the following words :

Relief from attachment.

And where there is more than one defendant, and several property of either of the defendants has been seized, by virtue of the order of attachment, the defendant whose several property has been seized, may apply to the officer who issued the attachment for relief under this section.

§ 241 amended.

§ 9. Section two hundred and forty-one is hereby amended by adding thereto at the end thereof the following words :

Undertaking relating thereto.

And where there is more than one defendant, and several property of either of the defendants has been seized by virtue of the order of attachment, the defendant whose several property has been seized, may deliver to the court or officer an undertaking in accordance with the provisions of this section, to the effect that he will on demand pay to the plaintiff the amount of judgment that may be recovered against such defendant. And all the provisions of this section applicable to such undertaking shall be applied thereto.

§ 10. Add at the end of subdivision four, section two hundred and forty-four of the Code, as follows:

Receivers of the property within this state, of foreign corporations, shall be allowed the same commissions as are allowed by law to the trustees of the estates of absconding, concealed and non-resident debtors.

§ 11. Section two hundred and seventy-three is hereby amended so as to read as follows:

In all cases of reference the parties, except when an infant may be a party, may agree in writing upon a person or persons, not exceeding three, and a reference shall be ordered to him or them, and no other person or persons, and if the parties do not agree, the court shall appoint one or more referees, not more than three, who shall be free from exception. And no person shall be appointed referee to whom all parties in the action shall object, except in actions for divorce. And no justice or judge of any court, shall sit as referee in any action, pending in the court of which he is a judge, and not already referred Unless the court shall otherwise order, the referee or referees shall make and deliver his report within sixty days from the time the action shall be finally submitted, and on default thereof said referee or referees shall not be entitled to receive any fees, and the action shall proceed as though no reference had been ordered.

§ 12. Section two hundred and seventy-four is hereby amended by adding thereto at the end thereof the following words:

In an action brought by or against a married woman, judgment may be given against her as well for costs as for damages, or both for such costs and for such damages, in the same manner as against other persons, to be levied and collected of her separate estate and not otherwise. And in any proceeding to enforce such judgment, the supreme court shall have jurisdiction, though the amount be less than one hundred dollars.

§ 287
amended.

§ 13. Section two hundred and eighty-seven is hereby amended by adding at the end thereof the following words:

Execution
against
same.

An execution may issue against a married woman, and it shall direct the levy and collection of the amount of the judgment against her from her separate property, and not otherwise.

§ 288
amended.

§ 14. Section two hundred and eighty-eight is hereby amended by adding thereto the following:

Execution
against
person.

But no execution shall issue against the person of a judgment debtor, unless an order of arrest has been served, as in this act provided, or unless the complaint contains a statement of facts showing one or more of the causes of arrest required by section one hundred and seventy-nine.

§ 298
amended.

§ 15. Section two hundred and ninety-eight is hereby amended by adding at the end thereof the following words:

Order ap-
pointing re-
ceiver to be
filed with
clerk.

Whenever the judge shall grant an order for the appointment of a receiver of the property of the judgment debtor, the same shall be filed in the office of the clerk of the county where the judgment roll in the action or transcript from justice's judgment, upon which the proceedings are taken, is filed; and the said clerk shall record the order in a book to be kept for that purpose in his office, to be called "book of orders appointing receivers of judgment debtors," and shall note the time of the filing of said order therein. A certified copy of said order shall be delivered to the receiver named therein, and he shall be vested with the property and effects of the judgment debtor from the time of the filing and recording of the order as aforesaid. The receiver of the judgment debtor shall be subject to the direction and control of the court in which the judgment was obtained, upon which the proceedings are founded; or if the judgment is upon a transcript from justice's court filed in county clerk's office, then he shall be subject to the direction and control of the county court.

§ 16. Section three hundred and four is hereby amended so that the third subdivision thereof shall read as follows:

§ 304, as to
costs,
amended.

"Subdivision three : In the actions of which a court of justice of the peace has no jurisdiction." And also, so that the fourth subdivision thereof shall read as follows: "Subdivision four: In an action for the recovery of money, where the plaintiff shall recover fifty dollars; but in an action for assault, battery, false imprisonment, libel, slander, malicious prosecution, criminal conversation or seduction, if the plaintiff recover less than fifty dollars damages, he shall recover no more costs than damages. And in action to recover the possession of personal property, if the plaintiff recover less than fifty dollars damages, he shall recover no more costs than damages unless he recovers also property the value of which with the damages amounts to fifty dollars, or the possession of property be adjudged to him, the value of which with the damages amounts to fifty dollars; such value must be determined by the jury, court or referee by whom the action is tried. When several actions shall be brought on one bond, recognizance, promissory note, bill of exchange or other instrument in writing, or in any other case, for the same cause of action, against several parties who might have been joined as defendants in the same action, no costs other than disbursements shall be allowed to the plaintiff in more than one of such actions, which shall be at his election, provided that the party or parties proceeded against in such other action or actions shall, at the time of the commencement of the previous action or actions, have been within this state, and not secreted.

§ 17. Section three hundred and seven is hereby amended by adding to subdivision three thereof the following: § 307, as to costs, amended.

To either party for attending upon and taking the deposition of a witness conditionally, or attending to perpetuate his testimony, ten dollars; to either party for drawing interrogatories or cross-interrogatories to annex to a commission for the taking of testimony, ten dollars. And in the seventh line of the fifth subdivision strike out the word "as," and insert the word "or," so that that the clause shall read "or for a new trial on a case made." And subdivision seven thereof is hereby amended by striking out the words "reached or postponed," and inserting the words "tried or is postponed by order of the court."

§ 18. Section three hundred and eight is hereby amended so as to read as follows:

§ 308, as to allowances of per centage, amended.

In addition to these allowances, there shall be allowed to the plaintiff upon the recovery of judgment by him in any action for the partition of real property, or for the foreclosure of a mortgage, or in any action in which a warrant of attachment has been issued, or for an adjudication upon a will or other instrument in writing, and in proceedings to compel the determination of claims to real property, the sum of ten per cent on the recovery, as in the next section prescribed, for any amount not exceeding two hundred dollars; an additional sum of five per cent for any additional amount not exceeding four hundred dollars; and an additional sum of two per cent for any additional amount not exceeding one thousand dollars. And in the actions above named, if the same shall be settled before judgment therein, like allowances upon the amount paid or secured upon such settlement at one-half the rates above specified.

§ 19. The last clause of section three hundred and nine is hereby amended so as to read as follows:

§ 309, ibid.

In difficult and extraordinary cases where a trial has been had, except in any of the actions or proceedings (other than those for the partition of real estate,) specified in section three hundred and eight, and in actions or proceedings for the partition of real estate, the court may also in its discretion, make a further allowance to any party, not exceeding five per cent, upon the amount of the recovery or claim or subject matter involved

§ 311, addition thereto as to judge adjusting costs.

§ 20 Section three hundred and eleven is hereby amended by adding at the end thereof the words:

Whenever it shall be necessary to adjust costs in any interlocutory proceeding in an action or in any special proceedings, the same shall be adjusted by the judge before whom the same may be heard, or the court before which the same may be decided or pending, or in such other manner as the judge or court may direct.

§ 21. Section three hundred and eighteen is hereby amended so as to read as follows:

§ 318 amended so as to include surrogate's courts.

When the decision of a court of inferior jurisdiction in a special proceeding, including appeals from surrogates' courts, shall be brought before the supreme court for review, such proceeding shall for all purposes of costs, be deemed an action at issue on a question of law, from the time the same shall be brought into the supreme court, and costs thereon shall be awarded and collected in such manner as the court shall direct according to the nature of the case.

§ 22. The first clause of section three hundred and forty-nine is hereby amended so as to read as follows : §349 amended as to appeals from orders

An appeal may in like manner, and within the same time, be taken from an order made at a special term by a single judge of the same court, or county, or a special county judge, " or by a recorder, or by any recorder's court of any city," in any stage of the action, including proceedings supplementary to the execution, and may be thereupon reviewed in the following cases :

1. When the order grants or refuses, continues or modifies a provisional remedy.

2. When it grants or refuses a new trial, or when it sustains or overrules a demurrer.

3. When it involves the merits of the action, or some part thereof, or affects a substantial right

4. When the order in effect determines the action and prevents a judgment from which an appeal may be taken.

5. When the order is made upon a summary application in an action after judgment and affects a substantial right.

§ 23. Section three hundred and fifty-two is hereby amended so as to read as follows : §352 amended as to appeals from marine courts and from justices' courts.

When a judgment shall have been rendered by the general term of the marine court of the city of New York, or by a justice of a justices' court of that city, the appeal shall be to the court of common pleas for the city and county of New York.

The appeal from the general term of the marine court prescribed herein shall be from an actual determination at such general term only and shall be taken within twenty days after judgment by such general term. In the city of Buffalo, the appeals from the courts of justices of said city shall be to the superior court of said city. When rendered by any of the other courts enumerated in section three hundred and fifty-one, the appeal shall be to the county court of the county where the judgment was rendered. On such appeal, when the amount of the claim or claims of either party litigated in the court below shall exceed fifty dollars or when in an action to recover the possession of personal property, the value of the property as assessed and the damages recovered shall exceed fifty dollars exclusive of costs, a new trial shall be had in the county court in the following cases:

1. When the judgment was rendered upon an issue of law joined between the parties.

2. When it was rendered upon an issue of fact joined between the parties whether the defendant was present at the trial or not.

§ 24. Section three hundred and sixty is hereby amended so as to read as follows:

§ 360, as to return, amended.

The court below shall thereupon after ten days, and within thirty days after service of the notice of appeal, make a return to the appellate court of the testimony, proceedings and judgment, and file the same in the appellate court. The return may be compelled by attachment. But no justice of the peace shall be bound to make a return unless the fee prescribed by the last section of this chapter be paid on the service of the notice of appeal.

§ 364, as to proceedings on return, amended.

§ 25. Section three hundred and sixty-four is hereby amended so as to read, as follows:

If a return be made, and the appeal is from a judgment where a new trial may not be had, as provided by this chapter, it may be brought to a hearing at a general term of the appellate court, upon notice by either party of not less than eight days It shall be placed upon the calendar, and continue thereon without further notice until finally disposed of. But if neither party bring it to a hearing before the end of the second term, the court shall dismiss the appeal, unless it continue the same by special order for cause shown. If the appeal is from a judgment where a new trial may be had, it may be brought to a hearing or trial at any term of the county court, at which a petit jury shall be summoned to attend upon the same notice, as provided for actions in the supreme court; at least eight days before the court the party desiring to bring on the appeal shall serve a note of issue on the clerk, and the clerk shall thereupon enter the cause on the calendar according to the date of the return.

§ 366, as to hearing and determinations on appeals, amended.

§ 26. Section three hundred and sixty-six is hereby amended so as to read as follows:

Upon the hearing of the appeal, the appellate court shall give judgment according to the justice of the case, without regard to technical errors and defects which do not affect the merits. In giving judgment, the court may affirm or reverse the judgment of the court below, in whole or in part, and as to any or all the parties, and for errors of law or fact. If the appeal is founded on an error in fact in the proceedings, not affecting the merits of the action, and not within the knowledge of the justice, the court may determine the alleged error in fact on affidavits, and may, in its discretion, inquire into and determine the same upon examination of the witnesses. If the defendant failed to appear before the justice, and it is shown by the affidavits served by the appellant or otherwise that manifest injustice has been done, and he satisfactorily excuses his default, the court may, in its discretion, set aside or suspend judgment, and order a new trial before the same or any other justice in the same county at such time and place and on such terms as the court may deem proper. Where a new trial shall be ordered before a justice, the parties must appear before him according to the order of the court, and the same proceedings must thereupon be had in the action as on the return of a summons personally served. If the appeal shall be from a judgment in which a new trial may be had as in this chapter provided, the court shall proceed to the hearing of the cause, if the issue joined before the justice was an issue of law, or to the trial thereof by jury, if such issue was upon a question of fact.

1. If the issue joined before the justice was an issue of law, the court shall render judgment thereon according to the law of the case; and if such judgment be against the pleadings of either party, an amendment of such pleading may be allowed on the same terms and in like case as pleadings in actions in the supreme court; and the court may thereupon require the opposite party to answer such amended pleading or join issue thereon, as the case may require summarily.

2. If upon an appeal in an issue of law the court should adjudge the pleading complained of to be valid, it shall in like manner require the opposite party summarily to answer such pleading or join issue thereon, as the case may require.

3. Upon an issue of fact being so joined, the court shall proceeded to hear the same tried by a jury in the same manner as issues joined in the supreme court.

4. Every issue of fact so joined or brought upon an appeal shall be tried in the same manner as in actions commenced in the supreme court.

5 The court shall have the same power over its own determinations, the verdict of the jury, and shall render judgment thereon in the same manner as the supreme court in actions pending therein.

6. Either party may move for a new trial in said court on a case or exception, or otherwise, and such motion may be made before or after judgment has been entered, and the provisions of this act in relation to the proceedings on receiving the verdict of a jury, exceptions to the decisions of the court, making and settling case and exceptions, motions for new trials, and making up the judgment roll in the supreme court, are hereby made applicable to all appeals brought up for trial as in this chapter provided.

§ 27. Section three hundred and seventy-one is hereby amended so as to read as follows:

Costs shall be allowed to the prevailing party in judgments rendered on appeal in all cases, with the following exceptions and limitations: In the notice of appeal, the appellant shall state in what particular or particulars he claims the judgment should have been more favorable to him. Within fifteen days after the service of the notice of appeal, the respondent may serve upon the appellant and justice an offer, in writing, to allow the judgment to be corrected in any of the particulars mentioned in the notice of appeal. The appellant may, thereupon, and within five days thereafter, file with the justice a written acceptance of such offer, who shall thereupon, make a minute thereof in his docket and correct such judgment accordingly, and the same so corrected shall stand as his judgment and be enforced accordingly, and any execution which has been issued upon the judgment appealed from shall be amended by the justice to correspond with the amended judgment, and no undertaking given to stay execution shall be enforced for more than the amount of the corrected judgment. If such offer be not made, and the judgment in the county court be made favorable to the appellant, then the judgment in the court below, or if such offer be made, and not accepted, and the judgment be more favorable to the appellant than the offer of the respondent, the appellant shall recover costs. The respondent shall be entitled to recover costs where the appellant is not.

§ 28. Whenever costs are awarded to the appellant, he shall be allowed to tax as part thereof the costs and fees paid to the justice on making the appeal as disbursements, in addition to the costs in the appellate court; and when the judgment in the suit before the justice was against such appellant, he shall further be allowed to tax the costs incurred by him, which he would have been entitled to recover in case the judgment below had been rendered in his favor. *Costs, &c., before justice.*

§ 29. If, upon an appeal, a recovery for any debt or damages be had by one party, and costs be awarded to the other party, the court shall set off such costs against such debt or damages, and render judgment for the balance. *When costs may be set off.*

§ 30. The following fees and costs, and no other, except fees of officers, disbursements, and witnesses' fees shall be allowed on appeals to the party entitled to costs as herein provided; when the new trial is in the county court. *Adjustment of costs.*

For proceedings before notice of trial, ten dollars.

For all subsequent proceedings before trial, seven dollars.

For trial of an issue of law, ten dollars.

For every trial of an issue of fact, fifteen dollars.

For argument of a motion for a new trial on a case or bill of exceptions, ten dollars.

In all cases, to either party, for every term not exceeding five, at which the appeal is necessarily on the calendar and is not tried or is not postponed by the court, seven dollars.

In other appeals the costs shall be as follows: To the appellant on reversal, fifteen dollars; to the respondent on the affirmance, twelve dollars. If the judgment appealed from be reversed in part and affirmed as to the residue, the amount of costs allowed to either party shall be such sum as the appellate court may award, not exceeding ten dollars. If the appeal be dismissed for want of prosecution, as provided by section three hundred and sixty-four, no costs shall be allowed to either party. In every appeal, the justice of the peace before whom the judgment appealed from was rendered, shall receive

108

person than the owner, to effect that object, such owner shall be entitled to the possession of such animal by making the demand therefor and the proof required in the next preceding section, and paying to the person making such seizure the amount of compensation fixed by such justice or commissioner, for the care and keeping of such animal, and without paying any other charges. And the person committing such wilful act shall be liable to a penalty of twenty dollars, to be recovered in an action at law at the suit of the owner of such animal or the person making such seizure.

Repeal. § 6. All acts or parts of acts inconsistent herewith are hereby repealed.

Chap. 460.

AN ACT to amend the Code of Procedure, and to extend the term of office of the Commissioners of the Code appointed under the act of April sixth, eighteen hundred, and fifty-seven, and to repeal section thirty-seven, article second, title second, chapter first, part third of the Revised Statutes.

Passed April 23, 1862; three-fifths being present.

The People of the State of New York, represented in Senate and Assembly, do enact as follows:

SECTION 1. The act known as the Code of Procedure is hereby amended as follows:

§ 11 amended as to appeals from orders. In the second subdivision of the eleventh section thereof, after the words "when such order grants," insert the words, "or refuses," so that the first sentence of said subdivision shall read as follows: "In an order affecting a substantial right, made in such action, when such order in effect determines the action, and prevents a judgment from which an appeal might be taken, and when such order grants or refuses a new trial."

§ 24 amended as to adjournment of special terms. At the end of the twenty-fourth section of the said Code of Procedure, add the following words:

And special terms may be adjourned to be held at a future day at the chambers of any justice of said court residing within the district, by an entry in the same manner, and then adjourned from time to time, as the justice holding the same shall order and direct.

§ 2. The last sentence of the thirteenth section thereof, is hereby amended so as to read as follows : *§ 13 amended as to calendar in Court of Appeals.*

"On a second, and each subsequent appeal, to the Court of Appeals, or when an appeal has once been dismissed for defect or irregularity, the cause shall be placed on the calendar as of the time of filing the first appeal."

§ 3. The second subdivision of the fifty-third section thereof is hereby amended so as to read as follows: *§ 53 amended.*

An action for damages for injury to rights pertaining to the person, or to personal or real property if the damages claimed do not exceed two hundred dollars. *Justices jurisdiction extended.*

§ 4. Section one hundred and sixteen of the Code of Procedure is hereby amended by adding thereto the following: *§ 116 amended.*

And in actions for the partition of real property, or for the foreclosure of a mortgage or other instrument, when an infant defendant resides out of this state, the plaintiff may apply to the court in which the action is pending, at any special term thereof, and will be entitled to an order, designating some suitable person to be the guardian for the infant defendant, for the purposes of the action, unless the infant defendant, or some one in his behalf, within a number of days after the service of a copy of the order, which number of days shall be in the said order specified, shall procure to be appointed a guardian for the said infant, and the court shall give special directions in the order for the manner of the service thereof, which may be upon the infant himself, or by service upon any relation or person with whom the infant resides, and either by mail or personally upon the person so served. *Guardian for infant defendant in partition and foreclosure cases.*

§ 5. At the end of section one hundred and twenty-one add as follows : *§ 121 amended.*

At any time after the death, marriage or other disability of the party plaintiff, the court in which an action is pending, upon notice to such persons as it may direct, and upon application of any person aggrieved, may in its discretion, order that the action be deemed abated unless the same be continued by the proper parties, within a time to be fixed by the court, not less than six months nor exceeding one year from the granting of the order. *Proceedings in case of death, marriage or other disability of plaintiff.*

Chap. 461.

AN ACT to enable the supervisors of the county of New York to raise money by tax for the use of the corporation of the city of New York, and to regulate certain expenditures of said corporation.

Passed April 23, 1862; three-fifths being present.

The People of the State of New York, represented in Senate and Assembly, do enact as follows :

Supervisors may raise tax. SECTION 1. The board of supervisors of the county of New York are hereby authorized and required, as soon as conveniently may be after the passage of this act, to order and cause to be raised by tax, upon the estates subject to taxation, according to law, within said county, and to be collected, according to law, for the use of the mayor, aldermen and commonalty of the city of the New York, such sum of money as, with the addition of the estimated amount of income for the current year from the revenues of the General Fund of said corporation not otherwise appropriated by law, will make an aggregate amount of two millions seven hundred and seventy-one thousand five hundred and fifty-eight dollars, which **Application thereof** amount shall be appropriated and applied by the said corporation to the payment of such expenses as are usually estimated and provided for under the heads, and to the amounts respectively hereinafter stated ; that is, to say : abatement of nuisances, two thousand dollars ; advertising for the common council, forty-five thousand dollars ; aqueduct repairs and improvements, thirty-four thousand dollars ; Belgian pavement, seventy-five thousand dollars ; board of health, six thousand dollars ; cleaning streets, two hundred and seventy-nine thousand dollars, which amount shall be assessed only upon the estates aforesaid lying and being south of a line running through the centre of Fifty-seventh street ; cleaning markets, eight thousand five hundred dollars ; city contingencies, sixty-five thousand dollars ; city dispensaries, six thousand dollars ; contingencies, mayor's office, thirteen thousand dollars ; contingencies, comptroller's office, two thousand dollars; contingencies, law department, fifteen thousand dollars; contingencies, street department, ten thousand dollars; contingencies, city inspector's department, twen'y thousand dollars; contingencies, Croton aqueduct board, four thousand dollars; donations, thirty-seven thousand three hundred and eighty-six dollars; election expenses, thirty-five thousand dollars; fire machines and apparatus, one hundred and eight thousand dollars; fire alarm telegraph, three thousand dollars; interest on revenue bonds, fifty thousand dollars; lamps and gas, four hundred thousand dollars; lands and places, twenty thousand dollars; opening new streets, expenses of, sixty-five thousand dollars; printing for the common council, seventy thousand dollars; printing for departments, twenty-five thousand dollars; public buildings, construction and repairs, one hundred and twenty-five thousand dollars; rents, fifty-five thousand dollars; real estate, purchases of, fifty thousand dollars; real estate expenses, thirty thousand dollars; removing night-soil, offal, and dead animals, forty-three thousand dollars; roads and avenues, fifty thousand dollars; salaries, legislative department, for the year one thousand eight hundred and sixty-two, seventy-four thousand five hundred and fifty dollars, including compensation to the members of the common council for their services and expenses at the rate of twelve hundred dollars a year, each which shall be in lieu of and include all charges for carriage hire or other expenses of such members, which compensation the comptroller of the city of New York is hereby authorized and directed to pay; and the said members of the common council are hereby respectively authorized to receive arrears legislative department eighteen hundred and sixty-one, thirty-five hundred dollars. Salaries, mayor's office, thirteen thousand dollars; salaries, department of finance, eighty thousand dollars; salaries, street department, eighty-six thousand four hundred and forty-eight dollars; salaries, Croton aqueduct department, fifty-five thousand eight hundred and fifty-five dollars; salaries, law department, twenty-eight thousand one hundred and eight dollars; salaries, city inspector's department, one hundred and nineteen thousand two hundred and twenty-eight dollars; salaries, commissioners of health, four thousand two hundred and fifty dollars; salaries, fire department, thirty-nine thousand five hundred dollars; salaries, city courts, one hundred and fifteen thousand two hundred and thirty-three dollars; stationery and blank books, thirty thousand dollars; sewers, repairing and cleaning, twenty thousand dollars; street improvements, three thousand dollars; streets, repaving and repairs, sixty-five thousand dollars; society for the reformation of juvenile delinquents, eight thousand dollars; supplies for and cleaning public offices, fifty thousand dollars; tenth precinct station house, twenty-five thousand dollars; water pipes and laying, seventy-five thousand dollars; wharves, piers and slips, one hundred and twenty-five thousand dollars.

Prohibition as to application. § 2. No portion of the said respective sums by this act authorized and required to be appropriated and raised, or of any other sum of money heretofore appropriated by the said corporation, or raised by tax for any specific object or purposes, or which may hereafter be so appropriated, shall be applied to or expended for any other object or purpose than that specially designated in the ordinance making the appropriation, or in the act authorizing the said sum to be so raised; nor shall the said corporation, or any officer, or agent of the same, expend any money, or make, in behalf of the said corporation, any contract involving such expenditure for any other purpose or purposes than those mentioned and provided for in and by this act, or by other laws, or involving the expenditure for such purpose of any greater sum or sums than those duly authorized to be expended for such purpose.

Proviso. Provided, however, that in case any appropriation so made by said corporation shall be found insufficient for the purpose for which it was made, it shall be lawful for the said corporation upon the recommendation of the comptroller, by resolution or ordinance, to direct a transfer to be made to the credit of such deficient appropriation of such amount as may be so recommended, from any other appropriation or amount raised by tax, in which there may be a surplus over and above the estimated expenditures necessary to be made during the then current year, on account of which the said last mentioned appropriation was made or raised by tax, and the amount so transferred may be expended in the same manner as though said amount had been originally embraced in such deficient appropriation.

§ 3. This act shall take effect immediately.

Chap. 462.

AN ACT to amend the act entitled " An act to provide for the payment of interest on certain canal drafts, certificates and awards for damages," passed April seventeenth, eighteen hundred and sixty.

Passed April 23, 1862 ; three-fifths being present.

The People of the State of New York, represented in Senate and Assembly, do enact as follows :

SECTION 1. Section two of the act to provide for the payment of interest on certain canal drafts,.certificates and awards for damages, passed April seventeenth, eighteen hundred and sixty, is hereby amended so as to read as follows :

The Treasurer shall pay, on the warrant of the Auditor of the Canal Department, all sums allowed for interest under this act, and the same shall be paid out of the fund or funds appropriated or to be appropriated to the payment of the drafts, certificates or awards above specified.

§ 2. This act shall take effect immediately.

Chap. 463.

AN ACT for the relief of Samuel Donaldson and Hiram Reynolds.

Passed April 23, 1862; three-fifths being present.

The People of the State of New York, represented in Senate and Assembly, do enact as follows :

SECTION 1. The Treasurer shall pay, on the warrant of the Auditor of the Canal Department, to Samuel Donaldson and Hiram Reynolds, or their legal representatives or assigns, out of any money in the treasury applicable to the payment of Erie canal enlargement drafts, such sum as the Auditor, upon computation, shall find to be the interest on the unpaid balance due said Samuel Donaldson and Hiram Reynolds, or their assigns, for work on sections sixty and sixty-two of the Erie canal enlargement; said interest to be computed at the rate of six per cent per annum, from ninety days after the completion of the work on said sections to the date of the payment of the final estimates to said Donaldson and Reynolds.

§ 2. This act shall take effect immediately.

Chap. 464.

AN ACT for the relief of Murty McCarty and Jeremiah McCarty.

Passed April 23, 1862 ; three-fifths being present.

The People of the State of New York, represented in Senate and Assembly, do enact as follows :

SECTION 1. The Canal Board are hereby authorized and required to examine the contract between the state and Murty McCarty and Jeremiah McCarty, for the completion of sections numbers three hundred and sixteen, three hundred and twenty, three hundred and twenty-one and three hundred and twenty-four on the Erie canal, and adjust their claim for additional compensation on account of extra work not contemplated by them or the state at the time of letting, and done by them under said contract, and to allow them such extra compensation for such extra work, if any, as they shall prove themselves entitled to, and in their judgment and discretion to cancel said contract.

§ 2. The Treasurer shall pay, on the warrant of the Auditor, such sum as shall be awarded under the provisions of the first section of this act.

§ 3. This act shall take effect immediately.

Chap. 465.

AN ACT to amend an act entitled "An act for the removal of obstructions from the outlet of Cayuga lake and the channel of the Seneca river," passed April thirteenth, eighteen hundred and fifty-eight.

Passed April 23, 1862; three-fifths being present.

The People of the State of New York, represented in Senate and Assembly, do enact as follows:

SECTION 1. Section one of the act entitled "An act for removal of obstructions from the outlet of Cayuga lake and the channel of Seneca river," passed April thirteenth, eighteen hundred and fifty-eight, is hereby amended by striking out of the twelfth and thirteenth lines thereof the words, "without obstruction or impediment and."

§ 2. Section two of said act is hereby amended so as to read as follows:

The sum of twenty-five thousand dollars is hereby appropriated, in addition to the money already expended upon said work, for the completion of the same; but no part of said twenty-five thousand dollars shall be expended by said Canal Commissioners except upon a contract that will insure the entire completion of said work within said additional appropriation.

§ 3. This act shall take effect immediately.

109

Chap. 466.

AN ACT to authorize and require the Canal Commissioners to build a bridge over the Cayuga and Seneca canal, at Evans street, in the village of Geneva.

Passed April 23, 1862; three-fifths being present.

The People of the State of New York, represented in Senate and Assembly, do enact as follows:

SECTION 1. The Canal Commissioners are hereby authorized, in their discretion, to build a bridge over the Cayuga and Seneca canal, at Evans street, in the village of Geneva, in the county of Ontario. The expense of said bridge and its approaches shall not exceed the sum of eight hundred dollars, and the expense thereof shall be paid out of any money appropriated for canal repairs.

§ 2. This act shall take effect immediately.

Chap. 467.

AN ACT to prevent the adulteration of milk, and prevent the traffic in impure and unwholesome milk.

Passed April 23, 1862; three-fifths being present.

The People of the State of New York, represented in Senate and Assembly, do enact as follows:

Punishment for selling, &c., impure milk.

SECTION 1. Any person or persons who shall sell or exchange, or expose for sale or exchange, any impure, adulterated or unwholesome milk, shall be deemed guilty of a misdemeanor, and on conviction shall be punished by a fine of not less than fifty dollars, and if the fine is not paid, shall be imprisoned for not less than thirty days in the penitentiary or county jail, or until said fine and cost of suit shall be paid.

Punishment for adulterating milk.

§ 2. Any person who shall adulterate milk with the view of offering the same for sale or exchange, or shall keep cows for the production of milk for market, or for

sale or exchange, in a crowded and unhealthy condition,
or feed the same on food that produces impure, diseased
or unwholesome milk, shall be deemed guilty of a misdemeanor, and on conviction shall be punished by a fine
of not less than fifty dollars, and if the fine is not paid,
shall be imprisoned for not less than thirty days in the
penitentiary or county jail, or until said fine and cost of
suit shall be paid.

§ 3. Any person or persons who shall engage in or
carry on the sale, exchange or any traffic in milk, shall
have the cans in which the milk is exposed for sale or
exchange, and the carriage or vehicle from which the
same is vended, conspicuously marked with his, her or
their names, also, indicating by said mark the locality
from whence said milk is obtained or produced, and for
every neglect of such marking, the person or persons so
neglecting shall be subject to the penalties expressed in
the foregoing section of this act. But for every violation of this act, by so marking said cans, carriage or
vehicle as to convey the idea that said milk is procured
from a different locality than it really is, the person or
persons so offending shall be subject to a fine of one
hundred dollars or imprisonment in the penitentiary or
county jail, or both in the discretion of the court.

§ 4. This act shall take effect immediately.

Chap. 468.

AN ACT to declare the cases in which the office of
county judge of Lewis county shall be vacant.

Passed April 23, 1862; three-fifths being present.

*The People of the State of New York, represented in
Senate and Assembly, do enact as follows :*

SECTION 1. If the county judge of Lewis county, has
accepted or shall accept any military or civil commission, or any military or civil appointment under the
government of the United States, or under the government of this state, and shall from this time absent himself from the county in the discharge of the duties of
such office or appointment, for the space of twenty days

or upwards, his office as such county judge shall be deemed to be vacant.

§ 2. The Governor of this state shall, at once, on the occurrence of such vacancy, appoint some suitable person, a citizen of such county, to fill such vacancy.

§ 3. This act shall take effect immediately.

Chap. 469.

AN ACT making an appropriation to the People's College.

Passed April 24, 1862, (three-fifths being present); without the approval of the Governor.

The People of the State of New York, represented in Senate and Assembly, do enact as follows:

$10,000 appropriated annually for two years on certain conditions.
SECTION 1. Whenever the trustees of the People's College, situated at Havana, in the county of Schuyler, or a majority of them, shall file with the Comptroller of the State a certificate, showing that they, as trustees, own in fee simple a farm of one hundred acres at least, unincumbered, on which their college edifice is built; that the college is prepared and open to receive students, and that seven professors at least, engaged for the purpose, are employed in imparting instruction to students in said college, the sum of ten thousand dollars shall be annually paid by the Treasurer, on the warrant of the Comptroller, from the General Fund for two years to the treasurer of the college, to be by him applied toward the payment of the aforesaid professors and their associates in office, the enlargement of the college library, and for no other purpose.

Duty of trustees.
§ 2. The trustees of the said People's College shall, for the time the aforesaid annuity is granted to them, maintain for the benefit of teachers of common and higher schools of learning, a department for the discipline of youth in the science and art of instruction, and provide for the benefit of the students of the college instruction in the science and art of war, and in the manual of the soldier, and it shall be the duty of the Regents of the University to determine what shall be

the qualifications of youth for admission to this department, and what proportion of the annuity shall be appropriated to support of the same; and whenever the applications for admission to any of the departments of the institution shall exceed its ability to accommodate pupils, the said trustees shall so accept pupils as to afford its advantages as nearly equally as possible to all sections of the state.

§ 3. The amounts which may thus be contributed by the state in aid of the said college, shall be a prior lien on the college grounds, building, furniture and apparatus, to be enforced in such manner as the legislature may hereafter direct, in order to secure in perpetuity, as far as may be, the use of the said college for the purposes for which it was founded.

§ 4. This act shall take effect immediately.

Appropriation by the state a lien on the college property.

Chap. 470.

AN ACT for the relief of the Troy University.

Passed April 24, 1862, (three-fifths being present;) without the approval of the Governor.

The People of the State of New York, represented in Senate and Assembly, do enact as follows:

SECTION 1. There is hereby appropriated from the General Fund, for the use and benefit of the Troy University, the sum of ten thousand dollars.

§ 2. The Treasurer shall pay, on the warrant of the Comptroller, to the trustees of the Troy University, in each of the years eighteen hundred and sixty-two and eighteen hundred and sixty-three, the sum of five thousand dollars, on the first day of May in each of said years, in satisfaction of the sum so as above appropriated. The moneys so advanced, with interest, shall be a lien on the college grounds and property next after the existing liens thereon, to be enforced in such manner as the legislature may hereafter provide.

§ 3. This act shall take effect immediately.

Chap. 471.

AN ACT to facilitate the taking of oaths and affirmations and the acknowledgment or proof of written instruments by persons in the military service of this State or the United States, as Volunteers.

Passed April 23, 1862; three-fifths being present.

The People of the State of New York, represented in Senate and Assembly, do enact as follows :

Who may administer oaths, &c. SECTION 1. Any person holding the rank of colonel or any higher rank in the New York State volunteers in the service of the United States, and any commissioned officer in said service, and who is a counsellor of the supreme court of this state, may administer and certify any oath or affirmation which any person may wish to take or make, who is actually in the said volunteer service, whenever such officer or person shall be out of this state.

Legal effect thereof. § 2. Any oath or affirmation, specified in the previous section of this act when taken and certified according to this act, may be read and used in any place or before any court, officer or tribunal in this state for any purpose with like force and effect as if administered, taken, had, made or done before any civil officer in this state.

Fees. § 3. The persons performing any service under this act shall be entitled to charge and receive the same fees therefor as if performed in this state by any civil officer in this state, authorized to perform a like service.

Copies of act to be distributed. § 4. The Secretary of State of this state shall immediately after the passage of this act, cause ten copies thereof, attested by his hand and official seal to be forwarded at the expense of this state to the commandant of each regiment of the New York State volunteers in the service of the United States.

§ 5. This act shall take effect immediately.

Chap. 472.

AN ACT to amend an act entitled "An act to amend an act entitled 'An act to authorize the formation of corporations for manufacturing, mining, mechanical or chemical purposes,'" passed April thirteenth, eighteen hundred and fifty-four.

Passed April 23, 1862.

The People of the State of New York, represented in Senate and Assembly, do enact as follows:

SECTION 1. Section one of the act entitled "An act to amend an act entitled ' An act to authorize the formation of corporations for manufacturing, mining, mechanical or chemical purposes,' " passed April thirteenth, eighteen hundred and fifty-four, is hereby amended so as to read as follows:

Whenever any person or persons owning five per cent of the capital stock of any company, not exceeding one hundred thousand dollars, or any person or persons owning three per cent of the capital stock of any company exceeding one hundred thousand dollars, formed under the provisions of this act, shall present a written request to the treasurer thereof that they desire a statement of the affairs of such company, it shall be the duty of such treasurer to make a statement of the affairs of said company, under oath, embracing a particular account of all its assets and liabilities, in minute detail, and to deliver such statement to the person who presented the said written request to said treasurer, within twenty days after such presentation, and shall also at the same time place and keep on file in his office, for six months thereafter, a copy of such statement, which shall, at all times during business hours be exhibited to any stockholder of said company demanding an examination thereof; such treasurer, however, shall not be required to deliver such statement in the manner aforesaid, oftener than once in any six months. If such treasurer shall neglect or refuse to comply with any of the provisions of this act, he shall forfeit and pay to the person present-

[marginal note: When treasurer to render statement of assets, &c.]

Forfeiture. ing said written request, the sum of fifty dollars, and the further sum of ten dollars for every twenty-four hours thereafter until such statement shall be furnished, to be sued for and recovered in any court having cognizance thereof.

§ 2. Should not any such written statement as is required by section one of this act, be demanded during the year preceding the annual meeting of the stockholders of any company, formed under the provisions of this act, for the election of directors or trustees, it shall be the duty of the treasurer of every such company to prepare and exhibit to the stockholders then and there assembled, a general statement of the assets and liabilities of such company.

§ 3. This act shall take effect immediately.

Chap. 473.

AN ACT to amend article two of title five of chapter six of part three of the Revised Statutes, entitled "Of executions against property."

Passed April 23, 1862 ; three-fifths being present.

The People of the State of New York, represented in Senate and Assembly, do enact as follows:

Superintendents and overseers of poor may redeem real estate. SECTION 1. The county superintendents and overseers of the poor in the several counties of the state, except the county of New York, shall have the same right to redeem the real estate, which may have been seized by them, pursuant to the provisions of title one of chapter twenty of part one of the Revised Statutes, as is now possessed by judgment creditors, under the said article second of title five of chapter six of part three of the Revised Statutes.

Prohibition § 2. No such redemption shall be made by the said superintendents or overseers, unless at the time of making such redemption the seizure of the real estate sought to be redeemed shall have been confirmed by the court of sessions of the county where such premises may be situated, nor unless such real estate shall, at the time of making such redemption, be held by the said superintendents or overseers, under and by virtue of the seizure made by them, pursuant to the provisions aforesaid.

§ 3. To entitle such superintendents or overseers to acquire the title of the original purchaser, or to be substituted as purchaser from any other creditor, pursuant to the provisions aforesaid, they shall present to and leave with such purchaser or creditor, or the officer who made the sale the following evidence of their right. *Redemption regulated.*

1. A copy of the order of the court of sessions, confirming the warrant and seizure of such real estate, duly certified to by the clerk of the said court of sessions.

2. An affidavit by one of such superintendents or overseers that the real estate sought to be redeemed is held by such superintendents or overseers under such warrant and seizure, and that the same have not been discharged, annulled or reversed, but are then in full force.

§ 4. The said superintendents or overseers shall, for the purpose of making such redemption, have power to use any moneys in their hands belonging to the poor funds of their respective towns or counties.

§ 5. The moneys which may be used by them for the purpose aforesaid, shall be repaid, together with interest thereon, at the rate of seven per cent per annum from the time of such redemption out of the first moneys which may be received by them from the rent or sale of the premises so redeemed.

§ 6. If such redemption shall be made and the person against whom the warrant was issued and seizure made, under the provisions of the said title one of chapter twenty of part one, shall apply to have the said warrant discharged, he shall, before such warrant and seizure shall be discharged, in addition to the security required to be given by section eleven of the said title, pay to such superintendents or overseers the sum so paid by them to redeem the said real estate, together with interest thereon, at the rate of seven per cent per annum from the time of such redemption. *When warrant of seizure may be discharged.*

§ 7. This act shall take effect immediately.

Chap. 474.

AN ACT for the preservation of moose, wild
deer, birds and fresh water fish.

Passed April 23, 1862; three-fifths being present.

*The People of the State of New York, represented in
Senate and Assembly, do enact as follows:*

Kings, Queens and Suffolk, hunting in. SECTION 1. No person shall kill, or pursue with intent to kill, any moose or wild deer, save only during the months of August, September, October, November and December, or shall expose for sale, or have in his or her possession, any green deer skin or fresh venison, save only in the months aforesaid, and also in the month of January and the first fifteen days in the month of February; and no person shall kill, or pursue with intent to kill, any deer in the counties of Kings, Queens and Suffolk, for the term of five years from the passage of this act, and thereafter only in the month of November.

Fawns not to be killed. § 2. No person shall at any time kill any wild fawn during the period when such fawn is in its spotted coat, or expose for sale, or have in his or her possession, any spotted wild fawn skin.

Hunting in other counties. § 3. No person shall hunt or pursue moose or deer with any dog in the counties of Clinton, Franklin, St. Lawrence, Jefferson, Lewis, Herkimer, Hamilton, Essex, Warren, Fulton and Saratoga, save during the month of October; and no person shall in like manner hunt or pursue any moose or deer in any of the other counties of this state, save during the month of November in each year.

Against molesting pigeons in nesting ground. § 4. No person shall kill or catch, or discharge any fire-arm at any wild pigeon while in any nesting ground, or break up or in any manner disturb such nesting ground, or the nests of birds therein, or discharge any fire-arm at any distance within one mile of such nesting place.

Punishment. § 5. Any person violating the foregoing provisions of this act shall be deemed guilty of a misdemeanor, and shall likewise be liable to a penalty of fifty dollars.

§ 6. No person shall at any time, within this state, kill *Against killing, or trap, or expose for sale, or have in his possession, trapping or after the same is killed, any eagle, fish hawk, night hawk, selling birds.* whippoorwill, finch, thrush, lark, sparrow, wren, martin, swallow, tanager, oriole, wood-pecker, bobolink, or any other harmless bird or any song bird ; or kill, trap, or expose for sale any robin or starling, save during the months of October, November and December ; nor destroy or rob the nests of any wild birds whatever, under a penalty of five dollars for each bird so killed, trapped *Penalty.* or exposed for sale, and for each nest destroyed or robbed. This section shall not apply to any person who *Exception.* shall kill or trap any bird for the purpose of studying its habits or history, or having the same stuffed and set up as a specimen.

§ 7. No person shall, at any time within ten years from *Prairie fowl* the passage of this act, kill any pinnated grouse, commonly called the prairie fowl, under a penalty of ten dollars for each bird so killed.

§ 8. No person shall kill, or have in his or her posses- *Partridge and quail.* sion, or expose for sale, any woodcock between the first day of January and the fourth day of July in each year; or any ruffled grouse, commonly called partridge, between the first day of January and the first day of September ; or any quail, sometimes called Virginia partridge, between the first day of January and the twentieth day of October, under a penalty of five dollars for each bird so killed, or had in possession or exposed for sale.

§ 9. No person shall kill any wood duck, dusky duck, *Duck.* (commonly called black duck,) gray duck, (commonly called summer duck,) or teal duck, between the first day of February and the first day of August in each year, under a penalty of five dollars for each bird so killed. But this section shall not apply to the waters of Long *Exception.* Island sound or the Atlantic ocean.

§ 10. No person shall at any time, or in any place *Against trapping within this state, with any trap or snare, take any quail quail or or ruffled grouse, under a penalty of five dollars for each grouse.* quail or grouse so trapped or snared. But on any prosecution under this section, it shall be deemed a defence to prove the said birds to have been taken on land owned by or in possession of the defendant.

§ 11. No person shall place in any fresh water stream, *Against putting lake or pond in which there are fish, any lime or other lime, &c.,*

in stream, lake, &c. deleterous substance with intent to injure fish ; nor any drug or medicated bait with intent thereby to poison or catch fish ; nor place in any pond or lake stocked with or inhabited by trout, pike or pickerel, or sun fish, with intent to destroy such trout. Any person violating the provisions of this section shall be deemed guilty of a misdemeanor, and shall in addition thereto, and in addi-

Penalty. tion to any damage he may have done, be liable to a penalty of one hundred dollars.

Dam upon certain rivers to have a sluice way. § 12. Every person building or maintaining a dam upon the rivers emptying into Lake Ontario, the river St. Lawrence or Lake Champlain, which dam is higher than two feet, shall likewise build and maintain, during the months of March, April, May, September, October and November, for the purpose of the passage of fish, a sluice-way in the mid-channel, at least one foot in depth at the edge of the dam, and of proper width, and placed at an angle of not more than thirty degrees, and extending entirely to the running water below the dam, which sluice-way shall be protected on each side by an apron, at least one foot in height, to confine the water therein.

Catching trout regulated. § 13. No person shall at any time, with intent so to do, catch any speckled brook trout or speckled river trout, with any device save only with a hook and line ; and no person shall catch any such trout, or have any such trout in his or her possession, save only during the months of March, April, May, June, July and August, under a

Penalty. penalty of five dollars for each trout so caught or had in possession. But in any prosecution under this sec-

Defence. tion, it shall be deemed a defence that the trout so taken were taken for the purpose of stocking other waters therewith.

Salmon trout. § 14. No person shall take, or have in possession, any salmon trout between the fifteenth day of November and the first day of February in each year, under a penalty of five dollars for each fish so taken and had in possession.

Black bass, &c. § 15. No person shall take, or have in possession, any black bass or muscalonge between the first day of January and the first day of May, under a penalty of five dollars for each fish so taken or had in possession.

Against taking fish with net, § 16. No person shall take any fish with a net, spear or trap of any description in any of the fresh water lakes, ponds, or bays or outlets thereof or streams of spear or trap in 'certain months this state, or within the jurisdiction of this state, in the waters of Lakes Ontario and Erie, and the St. Lawrence river, during the months of January, February, March, April and May, except in Chaumont bay. Any person violating the provisions of this section shall be deemed guilty of a misdemeanor, and shall, in addition, be liable to a penalty of five dollars for each fish so caught.

§ 17. No person shall at any time fish with spear, or Against fishing with spear, net, &c., in certain waters. set any net, trap, weir or pot, with intent to catch fish in any of the following named streams and lakes, or the outlets thereof, or in the streams emptying therein, at any distance within five miles from such lakes, to wit : Seneca lake ; Na-tan-water or Fish lake, in Oswego county ; Hemlock lake, in the counties of Livingston and Ontario ; Crooked lake, in the counties of Yates and Steuben; Seneca river; Canandaigua lake ; the Canandaigua or Clyde river, and Great Sodus Bay in the county of Wayne; that part of Croton river in Westchester county lying between the Hudson river and the bridge known as Golden's bridge ; Skine lake ; Fish lake and Mud lake, in the town of Freedom in the county of Cattaraugus ; Purcell's pond, in the town of Springwater and county of Livingston ; Black lake in the county of St. Lawrence ; or in any of the lakes in the counties of Fulton, Hamilton or Saratoga, or in the Sacandaga river. But suckers, cat-fish, eels, white-fish, Exception. shad and minnows and frost-fish are exempted from the operation of this and the last two sections, except in Skine or Lime lake in the county of Cattaraugus. Any person violating this section shall be deemed guilty of a Penalty. misdemeanor, and shall in addition be liable to a penalty of twenty-five dollars for each offence.

§ 18. No person shall sell, expose for sale or purchase Against selling. any fish known to have been taken contrary to the three last sections of this act, under a penalty of five dollars for each fish so sold, or exposed for sale or purchased.

§ 19. Any person trespassing on any lands for the Against trespassing on land for purpose of fishing. purpose of taking fish from any private pond, stream or spring, after public notice on the part of the owner or occupant thereof, or of said lands not to so trespass, shall be deemed guilty of trespass, and in addition to any damages recoverable by law, shall be liable to the owner, lessee or occupant in a penalty of twenty-five dollars for each offence.

Against
shooting.

§ 20. Any person who shall at any time enter upon the lawn, garden, orchard or pleasure grounds immediately surrounding a dwelling house, with any fire arm for the purpose of shooting, contrary to the provisions of this act, or shall shoot at any bird or animal thereon, shall be deemed guilty of trespass, and in addition to the damages, shall be liable to a penalty of ten dollars.

Suits for
penalties
regulated.

§ 21. All penalties imposed under the provisions of this act, may be recovered with costs of suit, by any person or persons in his or their own names, before any justice of the peace in the county where the offence was committed or where the defendant resides; or when such suit shall be brought in the city of New York before any justice of any of the district courts, or of the marine court of said city; and any district court judge, justice of the peace, police or other magistrate is authorized upon receiving sufficient security for costs on the part of the complainant, and sufficient proof by affidavit of the violation of the provisions of this act by any person being temporarily within his jurisdiction, but not residing therein, or by any person whose name and residence are unknown, to issue his warrant and have such offender committed or held to bail to answer the charge against him. And any district court judge, justice of the peace, police or other magistrate, may upon proof of probable cause to believe in the concealment of any game or fish mentioned in this act, during any of the prohibited periods, issue his search warrant and cause search to be made in any house, market, boat, car or other building, and for that end may cause any apartment, chest, box, locker or crate to be broken open, and the contents examined. Any penalties when collected, shall be paid by the court before which conviction shall be had, one-half to the overseers of the poor for the use of the poor of the town in which conviction is had, and the remainder to the prosecutor. On the non-payment of the penalty, the defendant shall be committed to the common jail of the county, for a period not less than five days, and at the rate of one day for each dollar of the amount of the judgment, where the sum is over five dollars in amount.

Exemption
from penalties.

§ 22. Any person proving that the birds, fish, skins or animals found is his or her possession during the prohibited periods, were killed prior to such periods, or were killed in any place outside the limits of this state, and that the law of such place did not prohibit such killing, shall be exempted from the penalties of this act.

§ 23. In all prosecutions under this act, it shall be Defence. competent for common carriers or express companies to show that the inhibited article in his or their possession, came into such possession in another state, in which state the law did not prohibit such possession, and such showing shall be deemed a defence to such prosecution.

§ 24. Chapter five hundred and fourteen of the Laws Repeal of of eighteen hundred and fifty-seven; chapter one hun- certain acts dred and sixty-three of the Laws of eighteen hundred and fifty-eight; chapter two hundred and twenty-nine, chapter two hundred and eighty-five, chapter four hundred and sixty-four of the Laws of eighteen hundred and fifty-nine; chapter one hundred and ninety-six, chapter one hundred and nine-nine, chapter one hundred and forty-six, chapter three hundred and two, chapter fifty-four, chapter one hundred and eighty-six, and chapter three hundred and eighty-four of the Laws of eighteen hundred and sixty; chapter one hundred seventy-three; chapter two hundred and fourteen of the Laws of eighteen hundred and sixty-one, and all other acts or parts of acts inconsistent with this act are hereby repealed.

§ 25. This act shall take effect immediately.

Chap. 475.

AN ACT in relation to the boundary line between the town of Geddes and the city of Syracuse.

Passed April 23, 1862.

The People of the State of New York, represented in Senate and Assembly, do enact as follows:

SECTION 1. The west boundary line of the city of Syracuse is extended to the middle of Geddes street, so as to include that portion thereof lying between the easterly line of said street and the centre thereof, and the land covered by this extension of boundary shall be

§ 2. This act shall take effect immediately.

Chap. 476.

AN ACT to amend section thirteen of title one, chapter four of part second of the Revised Statutes.

Passed April 23, 1862 ; three-fifths being present.

The People of the State of New York, represented in Senate and Assembly, do enact as follows :

SECTION 1. Section thirteen of title one, chapter four of part second of the Revised Statutes, is hereby amended so as to read as follows :

Names composing firm. § 13. The business of the partnership shall be conducted under a firm in which the names of all the general partners shall be inserted ; except that where there are more than two general partners the firm name may consist of either two of such partners, with the addition of the words " and company ;" and if the name of any special partner shall be used in such firm, with his privity, he shall be deemed a general partner ; but the said part-

Sign to be put up. nership shall put up upon some conspicuous place on the outside and in front of the building in which it has its chief place of business, some sign on which shall be painted, in legible English characters, all the names in full of all the members of said partnership, and in de-

Pleadings in actions against partners. fault thereof no action shall be abated or dismissed by reason of the proof of plaintiff of the partnership failing to meet the allegations of his pleading as to the names and number of the partnership. But the pleadings may be amended on the trial to conform to the proof in that respect without costs.

Terms of partnership to be published. § 2. Section nine of said title is hereby amended so as to read as follows :

" The partners shall publish the terms of the partnership, when requested, for at least six weeks immediately after such registry in two newspapers, to be designated

by the clerk of the county in which such r(
be made, and to be published in the Senat(
city, or town, in which their business shal
on ; and if such publication be not made, 1
ship shall be deemed general.

Chap. 477.

AN ACT to provide for the enrollm(
militia, the organization and discipl
National Guard of the State of New
for the public defence.

Passed April 23, 1862 ; by a two-tl

*The People of the State of New York, re)
Senate and Assembly, do enact as follows :*

OF THE PERSONS SUBJECT TO MILITARY D

SECTION 1. All able-bodied, white male c
tween the ages of eighteen and forty-five yea
in this state and not exempted by the laws of
States, shall be subject to military duty, exce
1st. All persons in the army or navy o1
forces of the United States.
2d. Ministers and preachers of the gospel.
3d. The Lieutenant Governor, members o
of the legislature, the Secretary of State
General, Comptroller, State Engineer and
State Treasurer, and clerks and employee
offices, judicial officers of this state, including j
the peace, sheriffs, coroners and constables.
4th. Persons being of the people called ĺ
Quakers, professors, teachers and students in a
and professors, teachers and students in t1
academies and common schools.
5th. Persons who have been or hereafte:
regularly and honorably discharged from th
navy of the United States, in consequence o
formance of military duty, in pursuance of a
this state and such firemen as are now exe
law.

111

ing or lodging in such house liable to be enrolled, and all other proper information concerning such persons as such officer may demand.

Penalties for refusal.

§ 7. If any person of whom information is required by any such officer, in order to enable him to comply with the provisions of this act, shall refuse to give such information, or shall give false information, he shall forfeit and pay ten dollars for each item of information demanded of him by any such officer and falsely stated, and the like sum for each individual name that may be refused, concealed or falsely stated; and every person who shall refuse to give his own name and proper information, when applied to by any such officer, or shall give a false name or information, shall forfeit and pay a like sum; such penalties to be recovered in any court of competent jurisdiction, in the name of the people of the State of New York; and it is hereby made the duty of such officer to report the names of all persons who may incur any penalty in this section prescribed, to the commandant of the regimental district in which they reside.

Publication to be made.

§ 8. Whenever an enrollment shall be made as provided in this act, the clerk of the board of supervisors of each county shall cause to be published, once a week for four weeks previous to the first day of August, in a newspaper published in such county, a notice that such rolls have been completed and filed as aforesaid, which notice shall also specify that any person who claims that he is,

Persons claiming to be exempt to file statement.

for any reason, exempt from military duty, shall on or before the fifteenth day of August, then next ensuing, file a written statement of such exemption verified by affidavit in the office of said town or city clerk, or of the county clerk, if there be no such town or city clerk, and the publication of such notice, shall be a sufficient notice of such enrollment to all persons named therein; such roll shall be made in the form prescribed by the Commander-in-Chief, and the Adjutant General shall furnish

Blanks to be furnished.

to all commandants of companies suitable blanks and instructions therefor.

§ 9. Such commandant shall not include in said enrollment the names of any officers nor members of the uni-

Foreman of fire companies to file list of members.

formed militia of this state, nor of the officers or members of any fire company, and the foreman of every fire company in any city, village or town of this state, shall,

shall distinctly specify the names and
persons enrolled, and shall also divide t
classes, the persons between the ages
thirty years to constitute one class, and
tween the ages of thirty and forty-five
cute the other class; four copies of such
be prepared by the officer making the sar
after the same shall have been correcte
provided, shall be retained by him, anot
in the office of the town or city clerk in
pany district is situated, if there be suc
shall be filed in the office of the clerl
where such district is situated, and the
filed in the Adjutant General's office; th
such enrollment may, with the approv
mander-in-Chief, appoint one or more
missioned officers or other proper pers
making said enrollment and copying said
sons making such enrollment shall be con
rate of one dollar and fifty cents per day
necessarily spent in making and copying
number of days to be certified by the
the regiment, and not to exceed ten, and
such compensation to be paid by the Co
production of such certificate, together v
cates of the town clerk, county clerk
General that such rolls have been duly
offices. Such rolls shall be so filed on
first day of July in each year in which s
shall be made.

§ 5. For the purpose of preparing su
the assessors in each city, village, town o
state, shall allow captains or commandant
or other officers appointed for that pur
provided, at all proper times to examine t
rolls and to take copies thereof, and the
towns and cities shall in like manner, at a
allow the said commandant or other offic
and copy the poll lists on file in their offi

§ 6. All tavern keepers, keepers of bo
persons having boarders in their families,
ter and mistress of any dwelling house, sl
application of any officer authorized to ma
ment, give information of the names of all

all other proper information concerning such persons as such officer may demand.

§ 7. If any person of whom information is required by any such officer, in order to enable him to comply with the provisions of this act, shall refuse to give such information, or shall give false information, he shall forfeit and pay ten dollars for each item of information demanded of him by any such officer and falsely stated, and the like sum for each individual name that may be refused, concealed or falsely stated; and every person who shall refuse to give his own name and proper information, when applied to by any such officer, or shall give a false name or information, shall forfeit and pay a like sum; such penalties to be recovered in any court of competent jurisdiction, in the name of the people of the State of New York; and it is hereby made the duty of such officer to report the names of all persons who may incur any penalty in this section prescribed, to the commandant of the regimental district in which they reside.

§ 8. Whenever an enrollment shall be made as provided in this act, the clerk of the board of supervisors of each county shall cause to be published, once a week for four weeks previous to the first day of August, in a newspaper published in such county, a notice that such rolls have been completed and filed as aforesaid, which notice shall also specify that any person who claims that he is,

for any reason, exempt from military duty, shall on or before the fifteenth day of August, then next ensuing, file a written statement of such exemption verified by affidavit in the office of said town or city clerk, or of the county clerk, if there be no such town or city clerk, and the publication of such notice, shall be a sufficient notice of such enrollment to all persons named therein; such roll shall be made in the form prescribed by the Commander-in-Chief, and the Adjutant General shall furnish

to all commandants of companies suitable blanks and instructions therefor.

§ 9. Such commandant shall not include in said enrollment the names of any officers nor members of the uni-

formed militia of this state, nor of the officers or members of any fire company, and the foreman of every fire company in any city, village or town of this state, shall,

before the fifteenth day of May in each
office of the town or city clerk, a lie
names of all persons belonging to their
panies, which list shall show the town
each member of such company resides.

§ 10. All persons claming exemption
ten statement of the same verified by
office of the town or city clerk, or of t
in case there be no such town or city o
the fifteenth day of August, in defaul
person shall lose the benefit of such e:
such as are especially exempt by act of

§ 11. The captain, commandant, or o
ing such enrollment, shall thereupon, if
exempt, according to law, mark the v
opposite the name of each person pre
emption; if such exemption be perman
such person shall not be included in
enrollment. If any person shall swea:
affidavit, he shall be guilty of perjury.

§ 12. The persons thus enrolled shall
militia of the state of New York; th
ages of eighteen and thirty years sha
reserve of the first class, and those betv
thirty and forty-five years shall constit
the second class.

§ 13. The reserve militia of the first a1
except such as shall volunteer, or be dr
of the national guard as hereinafter
assemble in their several company dist
equipped, as provided by law, for parad
on the first Monday of September in ea
hour and place as the captain or co
designate in orders to be posted in thre
in the said company district for ten da
under the orders of the captain or coml
district, and such captain or commands
roster of all such as shall attend at such
and equipped as aforesaid, and shall fil
same on or before the tenth day of Octo
of the Adjutant General and of the cou

§ 14. All persons duly enrolled as afo
neglect to attend said parade, shall be
of one dollar, which, if not paid to the co

in which such company district is situated, and the supervisors of the several counties at their annual meetings are authorized and directed to annex a list of the several delinquents with the fines set opposite their respective names to the assessment rolls of the several towns and wards, and the warrants for the collection of the same shall direct the collectors and receivers of taxes to collect the amount from every person appearing by the said assessment roll liable to pay the same, in the same manner as taxes are collected. The same to be paid to the county treasurer, and when the name of any person, between the ages of eighteen and twenty-one years shall appear on the said roll liable to pay the said fine, the said warrant shall direct the collector to collect the same of the father, master or guardian with whom such person shall reside, or out of any property such minor may have in the city, village, town or ward; and such collector shall proceed and execute such warrant and no property now exempt from execution shall be exempt from the payment of such fine.

§ 15. The county treasurer of each county shall, on or before the fifteenth day of March in each year, pay to the Comptroller, upon his order, the sum of one dollar for each person so enrolled who does not appear from said roster to have attended such parade. And in case he shall not, on the presentation of such draft, have received all or any of the money directed by this act to be collected and paid to him, he is hereby authorized and directed to borrow an amount sufficient to pay said draft upon the credit of the county, and the sum borrowed shall be a county charge, to be assessed by the board of supervisors of said county at their next annual meeting, upon the taxable property of said county, and collected as other county assessments shall be assessed and collected. And it shall be the duty of the county treasurers of the several counties, and the commanding officers of the several regiments, to report and certify under oath to the board of supervisors at their annual meetings the deficiencies arising from the non-collection of military fines within their respective counties and regimental districts.

§ 16. The provisions of article first, title three, chap- Revised Statutes to apply. ter thirteen of part first of the Revised Statutes, shall apply to this act so far as the same are applicable.

§ 17. The bond required to be executed by the col- Bonds of collectors, &c., to apply. lector, receiver of taxes and county treasurer, shall apply to any moneys required to be collected for mili- tary purposes by this act.

§ 18. Any deficiency arising from the non-collection Deficiencies to be a county charge. of said fines shall be a county charge, and shall be raised as aforesaid by the supervisors of said county by taxa- tion, on the real and personal estates therein, in the manner now provided by law.

§ 19. If any collector or receiver of taxes, county Penalties of collectors, &c., in the case of neglect. treasurer, town, county or city clerk, or supervisor, or any other civil or military officer, charged with any duty under the provision of this act, shall refuse or neglect to perform any of the duties required of him by this act, he shall forfeit and pay the sum of not less than twenty- five nor more than one hundred dollars for each and every offence, to be recovered in the name of the people of the State of New York; and if any of such officers shall willfully neglect or refuse to perform such duties as are hereby required, he shall be deemed guilty of a misdemeanor, and it shall be the duty of the district attorney of any county within which such delinquent offender resides, upon the complaint of the commanding officer of the regiment, to prosecute the same. Any penalty incurred and paid or collected under this sec- Penalty to be paid into the county treasury. tion, shall be paid into the treasury of the county, and belong to the military fund of such regiment.

OF THE GENERAL ORGANIZATION OF THE MILITIA, AND THE ORGANIZATION OF THE NATIONAL GUARD OF THE STATE OF NEW YORK.

OF ORGANIZATION.

§ 20. The Commander-in-Chief of the militia of this Commander-in-chief to organise into districts, &c. state shall organize and arrange the same, and the dis- tricts therefor, into divisions, brigades, regiments, bat- talions, squadrons, troops, batteries and companies, and cause the same to be numbered as nearly in conformity to the laws of the United States as local circumstances and the public convenience may permit, and may alter, di- vide, annex or consolidate the same and the districts thrown into any division, brigade, regimental or company district. The present divisions, brigades, regiments, battalions, troops, squadrons, batteries and companies, and the districts thereof, shall remain as now established by law, subject to the power of the Commander-in-Chief, to alter, divide, annex or consolidate the same as above set forth. Regimental districts, except in cities, shall conform, as nearly as convenient, to the assembly districts of this state.

National guard.
§ 21. The organized militia of this state shall be known as "the National Guard of the State of New York," and shall consist of eight divisions, thirty-two brigades, and one hundred and twenty-eight regiments and battalions, and such batteries, troops or squadrons as may be formed in pursuance of the provisions of this act; but nothing herein contained shall be so construed as to interfere with the power of the Commander-in-Chief, in case of war or insurrection, or of imminent danger thereof, to make further drafts of the militia, and to form new regiments, battalions, brigades or divisions, and districts therefor.

Of what composed.
§ 22. The national guard shall include the present uniformed militia of this state, and such volunteers as shall enroll themselves therein in the several districts of this state, and such persons as may be drafted therein, as hereinafter provided, and shall be organized, and shall serve as engineers, artillery, light artillery, cavalry, infantry and rifles, as the Commander-in-Chief shall direct.

Commander-in-chief to appoint and commission.
§ 23. The Commander-in-Chief is hereby authorized and empowered, so soon as may be convenient after the passage of this act, to appoint and commission the brigade, regimental and company officers, in the first instance, necessary to complete the organization of all military districts hereafter to be created, and to fill all vacancies necessary for the complete organization of all military districts now created in this state, but not sufficiently organized for an election. All officers superseded by such appointment shall become supernumerary officers.

Non-commissioned officers.
§ 24. The commandant of each regimental district, for the purpose of organization, is hereby authorized and

required to appoint the non-commissioned officers required by law for each company in his district, and to issue to such non-commissioned officers the proper warrants of their appointment, until the organization of such regiment shall be complete.

§ 25. The organization of the national guard shall conform to the provisions of the laws of the United States, and their system of discipline and exercise shall conform as nearly as may be to that of the army of the United States, as it now is or may hereafter be prescribed by congress. *Organization and discipline.*

§ 26. Company officers shall use their best efforts to obtain sufficient volunteers to raise their respective companies to the number of at least thirty-two non-commissioned officers and privates, which number is hereby fixed as the minimum, and one hundred as the maximum of such company organizations. *Companies.*

§ 27. In case any company of the national guard shall not, on or before the first day of October next, by voluntary enlistments, reach the minimum number of thirty-two non-commissioned officers and privates, or in case such company shall at any time fall below such minimum, or in case a sufficient number of persons shall not volunteer to organize new companies in the unorganized company districts, it shall be lawful for the Commander-in-Chief to order a sufficient number of persons to be drafted from the reserve militia of the first class, in the manner hereinafter provided, to raise such company to and maintain the same at such minimum number. The persons so drafted shall thereupon be enrolled as members of said company, and unless they shall find substitutes as hereinafter provided, shall be subject to the duties herein mentioned, and in case of non-performance of such duties shall be subject to the pains and penalties herein mentioned ; and such persons or their substitutes shall be entitled to all the privileges and exemptions conferred under any of the terms of this act, provided that no new company shall be organized in time of peace, if thereby the entire force shall exceed thirty thousand officers and men. *How filled up.*

§ 28. To every company there shall be one captain, one first, one second lieutenant, four sergeants, four corporals and three musicians, except in companies of artillery and cavalry, which may have one first and two *Officers.*

112

five sergeants and eight corporals.

Districts.

§ 29. Companies shall be formed in separate company districts when practicable, but the Commander-in-Chief may, in his discretion, organize more companies than one in the same district, or parts of a company in different districts.

§ 30. Each division shall consist of not less than two brigades, each brigade not less than two regiments, each regiment of ten battalion companies.

Divisions, brigades and regiments.

§ 31. The Commander-in-Chief shall have power to organize, under the provisions of this act, battalions of infantry and rifles, and battalions, batteries or companies of artillery, or for special services where it is not expedient or convenient to form regimental organizations, or whenever the exigencies of the service may require.

Battalions.

§ 32. No non-commissioned officer, musician or private belonging to any troop of cavalry or company of artillery, light artillery, riflemen or infantry shall leave the troop or company to which he belongs to serve as a fireman in any fire company now raised or hereafter to be raised in any city or county; nor shall he leave such troop or company and enlist in any other, without the written consent of the commandant of the regiment, battalion or battery, and of the squadron, troop or company to which he belongs, except he shall have removed out of the beat of such troop or company. Such exception shall not apply to any troop or company situate in any of the cities of this state.

Men not to leave company to join fire companies.

§ 33. No person under the age of twenty-one years shall hereafter enlist in or join any uniform troop or company without the consent of his parent or guardian, master or mistress, unless drafted in accordance with the provisions of this act.

Enlistments.

§ 34. Every officer of the line and staff, and every officer and private of any uniform company of this state shall provide himself, according to the provisions of this act, with a uniform complete, which shall be such as the Commander-in-Chief shall prescribe, and subject to such restrictions, limitations and alterations as he may order.

Officers. uniforms.

§ 35. Any non-commissioned officer or private may, upon his enlistment or upon being drafted in accordance with the provisions of this act, if he so elect, be furnished at the expense of the state with the proper uniform and equipments of his regiment or corps; in such case an entry to that effect shall be made upon the company roll, and such uniform shall be furnished by the quartermaster general's department upon the requisition of the commandant of the company, countersigned by the commandant of the regiment or battalion; but such uniform and equipments shall in no case be different from those prescribed by the general regulations for the military forces of the State of New York, unless by special authority of the commander-in-chief. *State may furnish uniform forms.*

§ 36. In case such uniform and equipments be furnished in accordance with the last preceding section, the same shall be left at the company armory for safe keeping, and the person applying for the same shall be charged with the value thereof, and shall be entitled to receive half pay only for services, under this act, at drills, parades, encampments and lake and sea coast defence duty, until the sum charged against him therefor shall have been liquidated by such service, when such uniform and equipments shall become the property of such person. *Conditions*

§ 37. Whoever shall presume to sell or dispose of such uniform or equipments, or to secrete or remove the same with intent to sell or dispose thereof, before the same shall become his property by such service as aforesaid, shall be deemed guilty of a misdemeanor, and shall be punished by imprisonment in a county jail for not less than two or more than six months, or by a fine of not more than two hundred and fifty dollars nor less than fifty dollars, or by both such fine and imprisonment. *Penalty for disposing of such uniforms.*

§ 38. The Quartermaster General shall, under the direction and with the approval of the Commander-in-Chief, cause to be manufactured in the several regimental districts of this state, the uniforms and equipments, which may from time to time be required for each regiment for the purposes mentioned in this act. And the Comptroller, upon the order of the Commander-in-Chief, shall draw his warrant upon the Treasurer for such sums as shall, from time to time, be expended for the purchase or manufacture of said uniforms and equipments: Pro- *Uniforms, how furnished.*

vided, always, that the price paid for the same shall, in no case, exceed the prices established by the general regulations for the army of the United States for articles of like description.

Accounts to be audited. § 39. All vouchers and accounts under the last preceding section shall, from time to time, be audited by a committee to consist of the Comptroller, Treasurer, and Secretary of State.

Books of tactics. § 40. The Commander-in-Chief shall, from time to time, direct such books, as to him shall appear expedient, as a guide for the military forces of this state, to be provided, and shall furnish the same to all commissioned officers at the expense of the state.

Companies, &c., to be numbered. § 41. The Commander-in-Chief shall cause each company, squadron, troop, battery, battalion, regiment, brigade, and division to be numbered or lettered in such manner as he shall deem proper and best calculated to secure uniformity. Each company, squadron, troop, battery, battalion, regiment, brigade and division shall be known by its number and designation, which shall be registered at the Adjutant General's office.

Officers, how chosen § 42. Non-commissioned officers shall be chosen from the members of the company to which they belong. All commissioned officers residing in any city or incorporated village in this state shall be deemed to be within the bounds of their respective commands, providing any part of the military district to which they properly belong shall be located within such city or village.

Existing companies. § 43. All existing uniformed companies, in any such regimental district, city or village, shall be deemed to be organized under the provisions of this act; but no such company shall be so constituted, unless at the time of such application it contains thirty-two non-commissioned officers and privates.

When six companies are organized, regimental officers to be chosen. 44. Whenever six uniformed companies shall be organized in any of the regimental districts of this state, the Commander-in-Chief shall order an election to be held for the choice of suitable persons to fill the offices of colonel, lieutenant colonel and major, in such regiment, by directing some suitable officer to give the proper notices of such election, and to preside thereat, unless such officers shall already have been elected or appointed.

§ 45. As soon as the field officers in the regiments in ^Brigade officers.^ any of the brigade districts of this state shall be duly chosen and commissioned, the Commander-in-Chief shall order an election to be held for the choice of a suitable person to fill the office of brigadier general and brigade inspector in such brigade district, by directing some suitable officer to give the pro-notices of such election and preside thereat, unless such brigadier general and brigade inspector shall already have been elected or appointed, as provided by this act.

§ 46. All commissioned officers rendered supernume- ^Supernumerary officers^ rary by the provisions of this act, and every officer rendered supernumerary by any consolidation or alteration of regiments, battalions, squadrons, troops or companies, shall be entitled to all the privileges conferred by any preceding law (except command,) and shall be exempt from the performance of any military duty, except in cases of war and insurrection, provided they shall, within one year after being so rendered supernumerary, have reported themselves to the Adjutant General as such; provided, however, that no officer rendered supernumerary shall be entitled to vote at any election held for the choice of officers, or serve as a member of any court-martial.

§ 47. Volunteers under the provisions of this act may ^Volunteers received in any company.^ be received in any company of the national guard, whether such volunteer reside in the company district or not; but persons liable to military duty shall be drafted only in the district where they may reside.

§ 48. Any officer, non-commissioned officer, musician or uniformed private, who may change his residence ^Change of residence.^ from within the bounds of the first division into any adjacent county, or from within any county adjacent into the said division district, shall not thereby vacate his office or post, but he shall be held to duty in the division, brigade, regiment, troop or company to which he was attached at the time of such change of residence, and he shall be subject to duty therein and shall be entitled to all privileges, immunities and exemptions allowed by law, and shall be liable to fines and penalties, and the collection of them, in the same manner as if such change of residence had not taken place; and process for the collection of such fines and penalties may be executed in either New York or any adjacent county.

vided, always, that the price paid for the same shall, in no case, exceed the prices established by the general regulations for the army of the United States for articles of like description.

Accounts to be audited. § 39. All vouchers and accounts under the last preceding section shall, from time to time, be audited by a committee to consist of the Comptroller, Treasurer, and Secretary of State.

Books of tactics. § 40. The Commander-in-Chief shall, from time to time, direct such books, as to him shall appear expedient, as a guide for the military forces of this state, to be provided, and shall furnish the same to all commissioned officers at the expense of the state.

Companies, &c., to be numbered. § 41. The Commander-in-Chief shall cause each company, squadron, troop, battery, battalion, regiment, brigade, and division to be numbered or lettered in such manner as he shall deem proper and best calculated to secure uniformity. Each company, squadron, troop, battery, battalion, regiment, brigade and division shall be known by its number and designation, which shall be registered at the Adjutant General's office.

Officers, how chosen § 42. Non-commissioned officers shall be chosen from the members of the company to which they belong. All commissioned officers residing in any city or incorporated village in this state shall be deemed to be within the bounds of their respective commands, providing any part of the military district to which they properly belong shall be located within such city or village.

Existing companies. § 43. All existing uniformed companies, in any such regimental district, city or village, shall be deemed to be organized under the provisions of this act; but no such company shall be so constituted, unless at the time of such application it contains thirty-two non-commissioned officers and privates.

When six companies are organized, regimental officers to be chosen. 44. Whenever six uniformed companies shall be organized in any of the regimental districts of this state, the Commander-in-Chief shall order an election to be held for the choice of suitable persons to fill the offices of colonel, lieutenant colonel and major, in such regiment, by directing some suitable officer to give the proper notices of such election, and to preside thereat, unless such officers shall already have been elected or appointed.

§ 45. As soon as the field officers in the regiments in *Brigade offi-cers.* any of the brigade districts of this state shall be duly chosen and commissioned, the Commander-in-Chief shall order an election to be held for the choice of a suitable person to fill the office of brigadier general and brigade inspector in such brigade district, by directing some suitable officer to give the pro-notices of such election and preside thereat, unless such brigadier general and brigade inspector shall already have been elected or appointed, as provided by this act.

§ 46. All commissioned officers rendered supernume- *Supernume-rary officers* rary by the provisions of this act, and every officer rendered supernumerary by any consolidation or alteration of regiments, battalions, squadrons, troops or companies, shall be entitled to all the privileges conferred by any preceding law (except command,) and shall be exempt from the performance of any military duty, except in cases of war and insurrection, provided they shall, within one year after being so rendered supernumerary, have reported themselves to the Adjutant General as such; provided, however, that no officer rendered supernumerary shall be entitled to vote at any election held for the choice of officers, or serve as a member of any court-martial.

§ 47. Volunteers under the provisions of this act may *Volunteers received in any com-pany.* be received in any company of the national guard, whether such volunteer reside in the company district or not; but persons liable to military duty shall be drafted only in the district where they may reside.

§ 48. Any officer, non-commissioned officer, musician or uniformed private, who may change his residence *Change of residence.* from within the bounds of the first division into any adjacent county, or from within any county adjacent into the said division district, shall not thereby vacate his office or post, but he shall be held to duty in the division, brigade, regiment, troop or company to which he was attached at the time of such change of residence, and he shall be subject to duty therein and shall be entitled to all privileges, immunities and exemptions allowed by law, and shall be liable to fines and penalties, and the collection of them, in the same manner as if such change of residence had not taken place; and process for the collection of such fines and penalties may be executed in either New York or any adjacent county.

regulations for the army of the United States for articles of like description.

§ 39. All vouchers and accounts under the last preceding section shall, from time to time, be audited by a committee to consist of the Comptroller, Treasurer, and Secretary of State.

§ 40. The Commander-in-Chief shall, from time to time, direct such books, as to him shall appear expedient, as a guide for the military forces of this state, to be provided, and shall furnish the same to all commissioned officers at the expense of the state.

§ 41. The Commander-in-Chief shall cause each company, squadron, troop, battery, battalion, regiment, brigade, and division to be numbered or lettered in such manner as he shall deem proper and best calculated to secure uniformity. Each company, squadron, troop, battery, battalion, regiment, brigade and division shall be known by its number and designation, which shall be registered at the Adjutant General's office.

§ 42. Non-commissioned officers shall be chosen from the members of the company to which they belong. All commissioned officers residing in any city or incorporated village in this state shall be deemed to be within the bounds of their respective commands, providing any part of the military district to which they properly belong shall be located within such city or village.

§ 43. All existing uniformed companies, in any such regimental district, city or village, shall be deemed to be organized under the provisions of this act; but no such company shall be so constituted, unless at the time of such application it contains thirty-two non-commissioned officers and privates.

44. Whenever six uniformed companies shall be organized in any of the regimental districts of this state, the Commander-in-Chief shall order an election to be held for the choice of suitable persons to fill the offices of colonel, lieutenant colonel and major, in such regiment, by directing some suitable officer to give the proper notices of such election, and to preside thereat, unless such officers shall already have been elected or appointed.

§ 45. As soon as the field officers in the regiments in Brigade officers. any of the brigade districts of this state shall be duly chosen and commissioned, the Commander-in-Chief shall order an election to be held for the choice of a suitable person to fill the office of brigadier general and brigade inspector in such brigade district, by directing some suitable officer to give the pro-notices of such election and preside thereat, unless such brigadier general and brigade inspector shall already have been elected or appointed, as provided by this act.

§ 46. All commissioned officers rendered supernume- Supernumerary officers rary by the provisions of this act, and every officer rendered supernumerary by any consolidation or alteration of regiments, battalions, squadrons, troops or companies, shall be entitled to all the privileges conferred by any preceding law (except command,) and shall be exempt from the performance of any military duty, except in cases of war and insurrection, provided they shall, within one year after being so rendered supernumerary, have reported themselves to the Adjutant General as such ; provided, however, that no officer rendered supernumerary shall be entitled to vote at any election held for the choice of officers, or serve as a member of any court-martial.

§ 47. Volunteers under the provisions of this act may Volunteers received in any company. be received in any company of the national guard, whether such volunteer reside in the company district or not ; but persons liable to military duty shall be drafted only in the district where they may reside.

§ 48. Any officer, non-commissioned officer, musician or uniformed private, who may change his residence Change of residence. from within the bounds of the first division into any adjacent county, or from within any county adjacent into the said division district, shall not thereby vacate his office or post, but he shall be held to duty in the division, brigade, regiment, troop or company to which he was attached at the time of such change of residence, and he shall be subject to duty therein and shall be entitled to all privileges, immunities and exemptions allowed by law, and shall be liable to fines and penalties, and the collection of them, in the same manner as if such change of residence had not taken place ; and process for the collection of such fines and penalties may be executed in either New York or any adjacent county.

§ 49. All major generals and the commissary general shall be nominated by the Governor, and appointed by him, with the consent of the Senate.

§ 50. The resolution of the Senate, concurring in any nomination made by the Governor to a military office, shall be certified by the president and clerk of the Senate, and be transmitted to the Adjutant General, who shall issue the commission and record the same in books to be provided by him.

§ 51. The staff of the Commander-in-Chief shall consist of the adjutant general, an inspector general, engineer-in-chief, judge advocate general, quartermaster general, commissary general of subsistence, paymaster general, surgeon general and three aids, who shall be appointed by the Governor, and whose commission shall expire with the time for which the Governor shall have been elected.

§ 52. The commissary general shall hereafter be known as the commissary general of ordinance, and shall not enter on the duties of his office until he shall have taken the oath of office prescribed in the constitution. Such oath shall be taken before any officer authorized to administer the same oath to the Attorney General within the same period, and subject to the same regulations.

§ 53. Captains, subalterns and non-commissioned officers of organized regiments shall be chosen by the written or printed votes of the members of their respective companies ; field officers of organized regiments and battalions, by the written or printed votes of the commissioned officers of their respective regiments and battalions ; and brigadier generals and brigade inspectors by the written or printed votes of the field officers of their respective brigades, if organized.

§ 54. Major generals, brigadier generals, and commanding officers of regiments or battalions, shall appoint the staff officers of their respective divisions, brigades, regiments or battalions, whose term of office shall expire when the persons appointing them shall retire from office ; but they shall continue to hold such office until their successors shall be appointed and have qualified.

§ 55. The commissioned officers of the militia shall be commissioned by the Governor ; and no commissioned officer can be removed from office unless by the Senate, on the recommendation of the Governor, stating the grounds on which such removal is recommended ; or by the decision of a court martial, or retiring or examining board, pursuant to law.

Removal of commissioned officers.

§ 56. Sergeant majors, quartermaster sergeants, sergeant standard bearers and drum majors shall be appointed by the commanding officer of the regiment or battalion to which they shall belong, by warrant under the hand of such commanding officer, and shall hold their offices during his pleasure.

Subordinate officers how appointed.

§ 57. Whenever the office of a brigadier general is vacant in any organized brigade, the Commander-in-Chief shall issue an order for an election to fill the vacancy, and shall designate a major general or some other proper officer to preside at such election.

Vacancies.

§ 58. The officer so designated shall cause a written or printed notice to be served on each of the field officers of the brigade in which the vacancy exists, at least ten days previous to the election, specifying the time and place of holding such election.

Notice of election.

§ 59. Whenever the office of any field officer in any organized regiment or battalion is vacant, the commanding officer of the brigade to which such regiment or battalion belongs shall cause a written or printed notice to be served on each commissioned officer in such regiment or battalion of an election to fill the vacancy. The notice shall specify the time and place of holding the election, and be served at least five days before such election shall take place.

Vacancy in field office.

§ 60. Whenever the office of a captain or subaltern in any organized company or troop is vacant, the commanding officer of the regiment or battalion to which such company or troop belongs, shall cause a written or printed notice of an election to fill the vacancy, to be served on the members of such company or troop, at least three days before the election shall take place, and shall specify in such notice the time and place of the election.

Vacancy in office of captain or subaltern.

§ 61. All notices for any election shall be served on the persons entitled to vote thereat, in the same manner as non-commissioned officers, musicians and privates are warned to attend a parade, as prescribed in section one hundred and thirty-nine of this act.

Notices, how served.

direct such service; and the person so designated shall

make a return of the persons notified, and of the manner of the services.

§ 63. The return, if made by a commissioned officer, shall be authenticated by his certificate on honor, if by a non-commissioned officer, by the oath of the person making such service. The oath may be administered by any magistrate or by the officer issuing the notice

§ 64. The officer causing the notice to be given for any of the aforesaid elections, shall attend at the time and place of holding such elections; he shall organize the meeting and preside thereat, and may, for sufficient cause, adjourn the same from time to time.

§ 65. If the officer causing the notices to be given shall not attend the meeting for the election, then the officer of the highest rank present, or in case of an equality of rank between two or more, then such of them as the majority of the electors present shall choose, shall preside at such meeting. And the officer issuing such notices, shall cause the proper evidence of service of such notices on all the electors to be delivered to such presiding officer. And at meetings for the election of company officers, the company roll, carefully revised, shall in like manner be delivered with such evidence. And if it shall happen at any election for commissioned officers that legal notice has not been given to all the persons entitled to vote thereat, the presiding officer shall adjourn the meeting, and cause such notice to be given. The presence of a person entitled to vote at any election shall be deemed a waiver of his right to take exception to the want of legal notice.

§ 66. The presiding officer at any election for commissioned officers, shall keep the polls opened at least one hour after the time appointed for holding the same. He shall then publicly canvass the votes received from the electors for the officers to be elected, and shall forthwith declare the result, and give notice to every person elected of his election. If such person shall not, within ten days after being notified of his election, signify to such officer his acceptance, he shall be considered as declining the office to which he shall have been chosen, and an election shall be held for a new choice.

§ 67. Immediately after the person elected shall have signified his acceptance, the officer who shall have presided at the election, shall, in case of the election of a brigadier general, communicate the same to the Commander-in-Chief; and in all other cases, if not himself the commanding officer of the brigade, shall certify to such commanding officer the names of the persons duly elected. *Certificate of election.*

§ 68. If at any election an officer, then in commission, shall be elected to fill a vacancy, and shall accept, the electors present, whether such officer be present or absent, shall proceed to elect a person to fill the place of the officer so promoted, if the officers or persons assembled at such meeting have authority to make the choice. *Vacancy by promotion, how filled.*

§ 69. The commanding officers of brigades shall transmit the names of persons duly elected and approved or appointed to offices in their respective brigades, to the Commander-in-Chief, to the end that commissions may be issued to them. *Names to be sent to Commander-in-chief.*

§ 70. Every person thinking himself aggrieved by the proceedings at any election for a commissioned officer, may appeal, if the election be for a brigadier general, to the Commander-in-Chief, and in other cases to the commanding officer of the brigade to which such person belongs. *Appeal.*

§ 71. The officer appealed to shall have power to administer oaths, and shall hear and determine the appeal; and if in his opinion the proceedings at such election are illegal, he shall declare the election void, and shall order an election to be held without delay for a new choice. *Appeal, how determined.*

§ 72. Any person concerned may appeal from the decision of the commanding officer of the brigade to the Commander-in-Chief, who shall hear and determine such appeal, and in case it shall be necessary, order a new election. *Appeal to Commander-in-chief.*

§ 73. The Commander-in-Chief may make such rules and regulations relative to appeals as he shall deem necessary and proper to give full effect to the provisions of the constitution and of this act. *Conduct of appeals.*

§ 74. The Commander-in-Chief shall issue commissions to all officers duly elected or appointed in pursuance of the provisions of this act; and every officer duly commissioned shall, within ten days after his commission shall be tendered to him, or within ten days *Commissions.*

in readiness for him, by any superior officer, take and subscribe the oath prescribed in the constitution of this state; and in case of neglect or refusal to take such oath within the time mentioned, he shall be deemed to have resigned said office, and a new election shall be forthwith ordered to fill his place. The neglect or refusal of an officer elect to take such oath shall be no excuse for neglect of duty until another shall be duly commissioned in his place.

Oath.

§ 75. Every commissioned officer shall take and subscribe such oath before a judge of some court of record in this state, county clerk, commissioner to take affidavits, justice of the peace, or some general or field officer who has previously taken it himself, and who is hereby authorized to administer the same.

Copy to be filed.

§ 76 A certificate of the oath shall be endorsed by the officer administering the same on the commission, and a copy thereof shall be filed in the Adjutant General's office.

Fees.

§ 77. No fee shall be received for administering any such oath, or endorsing such certificate.

Vacancies in non-commissioned offices.

§ 78. Any organized company or troop may, at any meeting thereof, elect non-commissioned officers to fill any vacancy therein.

Elections, how conducted.

§ 79. Such election shall be directed and conducted by the commanding officer of such company or troop for the time being, who shall certify the names of the persons elected to the commanding officer of the regiment or battalion to which the company or troop belongs, who shall decide upon the legality of the election, and issue warrants to the persons duly elected.

Special meeting of companies.

§ 80. The commandants of companies or troops may, whenever they deem it necessary, call a special meeting of their respective companies or troops for an election of non-commissioned officers.

Votes necessary to a choice.

§ 81. A majority of the votes of all persons present at an election of brigadier general shall be necessary to a choice; in all other cases a plurality shall be sufficient.

Resignations.

§ 82. No officer shall be considered out of the service on the tender of his resignation until it shall have been accepted by the Commander-in-Chief. The commanding officers of brigades shall receive the resignations of such commissioned officers as may resign in their respective brigades, and shall transmit the same to the Adjutant General. Resignations of all other commissioned officers shall be made direct to the Commander-in-Chief.

§ 83. No officer shall be permitted to resign his commission who shall be under arrest, or shall be returned to a court-martial for any deficiency or delinquency; and no resignation shall be accepted unless the officer tendering the same shall furnish to the Adjutant General satisfactory evidence that he has delivered all moneys in his hands as such officer, and all books and other property of the state in his possession to his next superior or inferior officer, or to the officer authorized by law to receive the same, and that his accounts for money or public property are correct. *When not permitted to resign.*

§ 84. In time of war, or when the military forces of this state are in actual service, resignations shall take effect thirty days from the date of the order of acceptance, unless otherwise specially ordered by the Commander-in-Chief. *Regulation in time of war.*

§ 85. On accepting the resignation of any officer, the Commander in Chief shall cause the necessary notices and orders to be given for an election to fill the vacancy so created; provided, however, that when the military forces of this state shall be in the actual service thereof, or in the service of the United States in time of war, insurrection, invasion or imminent danger thereof, the Commander-in-Chief shall fill all vacancies of commissioned officers, by appointment. *Vacancies, how filled.*

§ 86. Every officer who shall move out of the bounds of his command (unless such removal shall not be beyond the bounds of a city in which such command shall lie in whole or in part,) and every officer who shall be absent from his command twelve months without leave of the commanding officer of his brigade, shall be considered as having vacated his office, and a new election shall be held, without delay, to fill the vacancy so created, except as above provided. *Removal from command.*

§ 87. No person shall be allowed to vote at any election for a commissioned or non-commissioned officer of a company unless he is an actual member of such company where he shall offer to vote, and liable to do military duty therein. *Qualification of voters.*

§ 88. If any person offering to vote at any election for a commissioned officer of a company shall be chal- *Challenges.*

so challenged the qualifications of an elector.

Oath.

§ 89. If he shall state himself to be duly qualified, and the challenge shall not be withdrawn, the presiding officer shall then tender him the following oath: "You do swear (or affirm) that you are an actual member of the company commanded by   , and that you are liable to do military duty therein."

Commissions.

§ 90. The commissioned officer who shall receive a commission for any subordinate officer, shall, within thirty days thereafter, give notice thereof to the person entitled to it.

Military commission their powers and duties.

§ 91. The Commander-in-Chief is hereby authorized, so often as he may deem that the good of the service requires, to appoint a military board or commission of not less than three nor more than five officers, to sit at such place as he shall direct, whose duty it shall be to examine into the physical ability, moral character, capacity, attainments, general fitness for the service and efficiency of such commissioned officers as the Commander-in-Chief may order to be examined by said board, or who may be reported for examination to the Adjutant General by colonels of their regiments, or general officers commanding their brigades or divisions, and upon such report may be ordered to be examined by the Commander-in-Chief. If the decision of said board be unfavorable to such officer, and be approved by the Commander-in-Chief, the commission of such officer shall be vacated; provided, always, that no officer shall be eligible to sit on such board or commission whose rank or promotion would in any way be affected by its proceedings, and two members at least, if practicable, shall be of equal rank with the officer to be examined. The officers constituting such board shall receive the same pay and. allowances for traveling expenses as members of courts-martial.

Compensation.

When officers not eligible.

§ 92. No officer whose commission shall have been vacated under the next preceding section shall be eligible for election to any military office for the period of one year, and his election shall be void; and in case the vacancy so created shall not, within thirty days, be filled by the election of some other and proper person, the Commander-in-Chief shall have power to fill such vacancy by appointment.

§ 93. If any commissioned officer sh
or shall hereafter become incapable of
duties of his office, he shall be placed
numerary list, and withdrawn from ad
command.

§ 94. In order to carry out the provis
the Commander-in-Chief shall from tim
casion may require, cause to assemble
less than three nor more than five comm
one of whom at least shall be of the
determine the facts as to the nature and
disability of such officers as appear d
from any cause to perform military serv
being hereby invested with the powers (
quiry and court martial, and their deci-i(
ject to like revision as that of such cou
mander-in-Chief. The board, whenever
cer incapacitated for active service, sh
fact to the Commander-in-Chief, and if h
judgment, the disabled officer shall there
upon the supernumerary list, according to
of this act; provided, always, that the i
board shall in every case be sworn to an
partial performance of their duties, and
shall be placed upon the supernumerary
tion of said board without having had
hearing before the board, if upon due su:
demand it, nor shall any officer be sur
such board unless reported to the Comn
as incapable by a majority of the comm
of his regiment, brigade or division, as th

§ 95. In time of war, insurrection, invi
nent danger thereof, when the military
state shall be in the actual service the
mander-in-Chief shall have power, when
interests may in his opinion so require, t
active service such officer or officers as h
discreet so to suspend and fill the vacancy
appointment; but no such suspension sh
a longer period than thirty days, unless
shall have in the meantime been ordered
such officer or officers.

§ 96. The Commander-in-Chief shall be entitled to three aids, with the rank of colonel, and a military secretary, with the rank of major.

§ 97. Each major-general shall be entitled to two aids, with the rank of major, and each brigadier-general to one aid, with the rank of captain.

§ 98. The Adjutant-General shall have the rank of brigadier-general; and in his department there shall be an assistant adjutant-general, with the rank of colonel; to each division a division inspector, with the rank of colonel; to each brigade, a brigade inspector, to serve also as a brigade major, with the rank of major; and to each regiment or battalion, an adjutant, with the rank of lieutenant.

§ 99. The Inspector-General shall have the rank of brigadier-general, and his duty shall be to attend to the organization of the militia of this state. He shall inspect every branch connected with the military service, attend the military parades and encampments, when other official duties will permit, and report annually to the Commander-in-Chief. In the Inspector-General's department there shall be an assistant inspector-general, with the rank of colonel, who shall also act under the directions of the Inspector-General as inspector of military accounts.

§ 100. The Engineer-in-Chief shall have the rank of brigadier-general; and there shall be in his department, to each division, a division engineer, with the rank of colonel; to each brigade, a brigade engineer, with the rank of major; to each regiment, one engineer, with the rank of captain.

§ 101. In the Quartermaster-General's department there shall be a Quartermaster-General, with the rank of brigadier-general; to each division a division quartermaster, with the rank of lieutenant-colonel; to each brigade a brigade quartermaster, with the rank of captain; and to each regiment or battalion, a quartermaster, with the rank of lieutenant: and the Quartermaster-General may, with the approval of the Commander-in-Chief, appoint so many storekeepers as the exigencies of the service may require, not exceeding one to each storehouse.

§ 102. In the department of the Commissary-General ^{Commissary depart-ment.} of subsistence there shall be a Commissary-General of subsistence, with the rank of colonel ; and in his department there shall be so many assistant commissaries, with the rank of captain, as the exigencies of the service may require ; such assistant commissaries to be appointed by the Commander-in-Chief, and to hold their offices during his pleasure.

§ 103. In the Paymaster-General's department there ^{Paymasters} shall be a Paymaster-General, with the rank of colonel ; to each division a division paymaster, with the rank of major ; and to each brigade a brigade paymaster, with the rank of captain ; but such paymasters may at any time be detached from service in said brigades or divisions.

§ 104. The commissary general shall hereafter be ^{Commissary depart-ment.} known as the commissary general of ordnance, and shall have the rank of brigadier general ; and in his department there shall be an assistant, with the rank of colonel, and so many military storekeepers, for the safe keeping and the preservation of the state arsenals, magazines, fortifications and military stores belonging to this state, as he may find it necessary to appoint, not exceeding one to each arsenal.

§ 105. In the hospital department there shall be a ^{Hospital department.} surgeon general, with the rank of brigadier general ; to each division, a hospital surgeon, with the rank of colonel ; to each brigade, a hospital surgeon, with the rank of major ; to each regiment, a surgeon, with the rank of captain ; and to each regiment or battalion, a surgeon's mate, with the rank of lieutenant, but such rank shall not entitle said officers to promotions in the line, nor regulate their pay or rations in the service ; and all such officers shall be graduates of an incorporated school or college of medicine.

§ 106. To each regiment or battalion there shall be ^{Chaplains.} appointed one chaplain, who shall be a regular ordained minister of a christian denomination.

§ 107. In the judge advocate's department there shall ^{Judge advocate's department.} be a judge advocate general, with the rank of brigadier general ; to each division, a division judge advocate, with the rank of colonel ; and to each brigade, a brigade judge advocate, with the rank of major.

quartermaster sergeant, one commissary sergeant, and one drum major; and to each regiment or battalion of light artillery and cavalry, one trumpet major.

Chief of staff department. § 109. The chief of each staff department shall, under the direction of the Commander-in-Chief, have command over all subordinate officers in his department; and shall, from time to time, issue orders and instructions for their government and practice.

Rules of staff departments. § 110. The Commander-in-Chief is hereby authorized and empowered to organize, in his discretion, the various staff departments, and to prescribe by rules and regulations the duties to be performed by the officers connected therewith, which shall, as far as may be, conform to those which are prescribed for the government of the staff department in the army of the United States.

Blanks to be furnished. § 111. Each chief of such department shall prepare and transmit, at the expense of this state, all blank forms of returns, precepts, warrants and proceedings necessary in his department.

OF THE ORGANIZATION OF BANDS OF MUSICIANS.

Bands. § 112. The commanding officer of each regiment or battalion may, in his discretion, organize a band of musicians, and by warrant, under his hand, may appoint a leader of such band.

To be subject to leader. § 113. Such musicians shall be subject to the orders of such leader, and be under the command of the commanding officer of the regiment or battalion; and the whole or any part of said band may be required by such commanding officer to appear at any meeting of the officers for military purposes, and at the review and inspection or encampment of such regiment or battalion.

Returns of leader. § 114. The leader of each band shall, whenever required by such commanding officer, make returns to him of the warning of the members of his band, and of the delinquents and delinquencies therein; which returns shall be duly authenticated by the oath of such leader, taken before a field officer of such regiment or battalion.

Return to be evidence § 115. Such return, so sworn to, shall be received as evidence in all cases, in the same manner as like returns of non-commissioned officers of infantry companies.

§ 116. Such commanding officer shal
returns of all such delinquents and deli
cases of non-commissioned officers and 1
panies of infantry, and with like effec
martial shall impose the like penalties of
members of said band.

§ 117. The commanding officer of a
battalion shall have authority to dist
whether now or hereafter established, a
warrant of its leader.

§ 118. The provisions of this article i
musicians employed to serve with the m
this state.

OF THE ISSUING AND SAFE KEEPING

§ 119. Whenever any company, orgai
provisions of this act, shall have reache
number of thirty-two non-commissioned
vates, the supervisors of the county in w
pany district is situated shall, upon the
captain or commandant of such company
by the colonel of the regiment, together
cate of the Adjutant General, that such
prises thirty-two non-commissioned office
erect or rent within the bounds of sucl
said company, a suitable and convenier
room and place of deposit for the safe k
arms, uniforms, equipments, accoutreme
equipage as shall be furnished such com
provisions of this act; except in such
public armory shall then exist, the sam
used by several companies, or a regimen
armory to be used by all the companies, a
general shall deem expedient.

§ 120. The expense of erecting or rent
ries shall be a portion of the county cl
county, and shall be levied and raise
manner as other county charges are levi

§ 121. In case such armory shall not
rented by the supervisors for the use of
the commandant of the regiment, in his
the approval of the inspector general, m
or building to be used for the purpose o
and the amount of rent thereof, provided

114

dollars for companies not located in cities shall be a county charge, and shall be paid by such supervisors, and levied and raised as hereinbefore provided.

Armory to be subject to commanding officer. § 122. Such armory, when erected or rented, shall be under the control and charge of the commanding officer of the regiment in whose bounds or district it shall be located; and such commanding officer shall deposit therein all arms and equipments received from time to time for the use of any company in his regiment.

Arms and equipments § 123. The commissary general of the state shall furnish, on the order of the Commander-in-Chief, all necessary arms and equipments, suited to the particular company or corps belonging to each regiment, required for camp and field duty; the same to be furnished at the expense of the state, including transportation. But no arms or equipments shall be furnished to any company or corps, unless such company or corps shall be connected with the regular military organization of the state.

Commanding officer to be responsible. § 124. The commanding officer of each regiment or company shall be responsible for the safe keeping and return of all arms and equipments committed to his charge, and shall execute such bonds as the Commander-in-Chief shall require from time to time; and no company shall be so furnished until bonds for the safe keeping and return shall be made out and approved by the Commander in-Chief, and until a suitable armory or place of deposit shall be assigned, rented or erected in such regiment.

Distribution of arms § 125. The commanding officer of any regiment or company who shall have received, according to the provisions of this act, any arms and equipments from the state for the use of his regiment or company, shall distribute the same to his regiment or company, as he shall deem proper, and require of those to whom they were distributed to return them at such time and place as he shall order and direct; and any officer who shall neglect or refuse to comply, with such order shall forfeit the **Penalty.** sum not to exceed double the price of any arms or equipments he shall have received, to be sued for and collected in the name of the commandant of the regiment, for the use of the military fund of such regiment.

§ 126. The commanding officer of each regiment shall ^{Keeper of armory.} appoint a suitable person to take charge of the armory, armories or place of deposit of his regiment, or of the several companies in his regiment, and all arms, equipments and other property of the state therein deposited, and to discharge all duties connected therewith, as shall be from time to time prescribed by the commanding officer.

§ 127. Such person so appointed shall receive a compensation not to exceed one dollar per day for the time actually employed in cleaning guns, and other duties indispensably necessary for the safe keeping and preservation of such property of the state as shall be committed to his charge. ^{Compensation.}

§ 128. The Commander-in-Chief shall, from time to time, make such orders, rules and regulations as he may deem proper for the observance of all officers having charge of any armory in which arms of the people of this state shall be deposited. ^{Rules.}

§ 129. Whenever the commissioned officers of any uniformed company in this state shall make application to the commanding officer of their regiment for any arms or equipments, suited to the corps to which their company may belong, and who shall, at the same time furnish such commanding officer with sufficient bonds for the safe keeping and return of the same, he may deliver to such officers such arms and equipments belonging to this state as he shall deem proper; but no such arms or equipments, shall be delivered unless the bonds given for the safe keeping and return thereof shall be approved by the sureties who became responsible in the bonds furnished to the Commander-in-Chief for all such arms and equipments ^{Bonds for safe keeping.}

§ 130. Any person who shall willfully injure such armory or its fixtures, or any gun, sword, pistol or other property of the state therein deposited, shall be deemed guilty of a misdemeanor. ^{Penalty.}

§ 131. The Commissary General may, from time to time, require any officer to examine any armory provided as aforesaid, and report to him the condition thereof, and of the arms and camp equipage therein deposited. ^{Examination of armory.}

§ 132. All officers applying for the issue of camp equipage shall set forth in their application the number ^{Camp equipage.}

of tents which they will require, the time when their
respective regiments or companies go into camp, and the
number of days which such encampment will continue;
and the commanding officer of each camp shall, immediately after the breaking up of the encampment, cause
the equipage to be returned to such of the state arsenals,
or turned over to such officer as may be directed by the
Adjutant-General; provided, however, that such tents
and camp equipage shall be deposited in some one of the
state arsenals on or before the first day of November
in each year.

OF THE DRILLS, PARADES AND RENDEZVOUS OF THE NATION-AL GUARD, AND OF COMPENSATION FOR MILITARY SERVICES.

Annual parade.

§ 133. Whenever any company or companies shall be
organized, uniformed and equipped in any regimental district of this state, such company or companies shall parade
annually thereafter by regiment, battalion or company, at
such time and place, between the first day of May and
the first day of November, as the commanding officers of
their respective brigades shall order and direct, for the
purpose of discipline, inspection and review. At any
such parade, all the commissioned and non-commissioned
officers, musicians and privates shall appear and discharge any and all the duties required to be performed
by the commanding officer. No person shall be permitted in the ranks on any parade who does not appear in
full uniform, and armed and equipped suited to the
company to which he belongs; and no person shall be
permitted in the ranks who is not fully armed and
equipped according to the provisions of this act and
the laws of the United States; and all members who
shall appear without such arms and equipments, or without a uniform, at any parade, shall be returned as absent
from parade, and fined accordingly.

Six drills or parades an-nually.

§ 134. In addition to the annual inspection herein
specified, there shall be six drills or parades of the
national guard in each year, not less than three of which
shall be by regiment or battalion, and at such times and
places as the Commander-in-Chief, commandant of division, brigade, regiment or battalion, shall direct

Power of command-ing officer.

§ 135. The commanding officer, at any parade, may
cause those under his command to perform any field or

camp duty he shall require; and also to ᵖ
for the day or time of continuing such
cer, musician or private who shall disob
his superior officer, or in any way interrⁱ
of the day; also, all'other persons who ᵗ
the parade ground, or in any way or ᵐ
or molest the orderly discharge of duty
arms; and also may prohibit and preveⁱ
spirituous liquors within one mile of suⁱ
campment; and also, in his discretion, ᵗ
auction sales or gambling may be abated

§ 136. In addition to the drills and
specified, the commanding officers of coⁱ
quire the officers, non-commissioned off
and privates of their companies to meⁱ
drill and parade once in each month froⁱ
May, and so much oftener as a majority ⁽
of such company shall prescribe in and
for the government of the same.

§ 137 No parade or rendezvous of the
shall be ordered on any day during whiⁱ
special election shall be held, nor withiⁱ
vious to such election, except in cases o
or insurrection, or of imminent danger ᵗ
any officer shall order any such parade
he shall forfeit and pay to the people of
sum of five hundred dollars.

§ 138. For the purpose of warning tᵇ
sioned officers, musicians and privates
encampment or place of rendezvous, the ⁽
each company shall issue his orders, und
his non-commissioned officers, or to such
may deem proper, requiring them respeⁱ
all the non-commissioned officers, musiciaⁱ
of his company to appear at such parad
or place of rendezvous, armed and equip
to law and regulation.

§ 139. Each non-commissioned officer
order shall be directed, shall warn everⁱ
he shall be therein required to warn, ⁱ
orders, or stating the substance thereof
of such person; or in case of his absenⁱ
notice thereof at his usual place of abo
with some person of suitable age and dⁱ

sending the same to him by mail, directed to him at the postoffice nearest his place of residence.

§ 140. Such non-commissioned officer shall make a return to his commandant, in which he shall state the names of all persons by him warned, and the manner of warning them respectively, and shall make oath to the truth of such return; which oath shall be administered by the commandant, and certified by him on the warrant or return.

§ 141. Such commandant shall deliver the return, together with his own return of all delinquencies, to the president of the proper court martial

§ 142. The return of such non-commissioned officer, so sworn to and certified, shall be as good evidence, on the trial of any person returned as a delinquent, of the facts therein stated, as if such officer had testified to the same before the court martial on such trial.

§ 143. Every commandant of a company shall make the like return, upon honor, and with like effect, of every delinquency and neglect of duty of his non-commissioned officers, either in not attending on any parade or encampment, or not executing or returning a warrant to them directed, or not obeying the orders of their commanding officers; and also the names of every non-commissioned officer, musician or private who shall refuse or neglect to obey the orders of his superior officer, or to perform such military duty or exercise as may be required, or depart from his colors, post or guard, or leave the ranks without permission from his superior officer.

§ 144 Any commissioned officer of a company may, without a warrant, warn any or all of the members of his company to appear at any parade, encampment or place of rendezvous Such warning may be given by him, either personally or by leaving or affixing a notice, in the same manner as if given by a non-commissioned officer; and his certificate, upon honor, shall be received by any court martial as legal evidence of such warning.

§ 145. Nothing in the provisions of this act shall be so construed as to preclude, in the absence of a proper return, the giving in evidence, at any court martial upon trial for delinquencies, neglects of duty or offence whatsoever, matters of fact which go to substantiate the charge or offence; but all such proof shall be received under the usual rules of evidence in courts of justice.

§ 146. Every non-commissioned offic
private of any uniform corps of this stat
to duty therein for the term of sever
enlistment, unless disability after enlist
pacitate him to perform such duty,
regularly discharged by the command
ment; all general and staff officers, all fi
all commissioned and non-commissione
cians and privates of the military forc
shall be exempt from jury duty during
shall perform military duty, and from
highway taxes, not exceeding six days in
and every such person not assessed for
shall be entitled to a deduction, in the a
real and personal property, to the amout
dred dollars; and every person who sh
seven years, and shall have been honorat
as required by this section, shall forever
as he remains a citizen of this state, b
two days' highway taxes in each year; ai
of any city of this state, he shall forever
a deduction in the assessment of his rea
property, to the amount of five hundre
year; the exemption and deduction herei
to be allowed only on the production, to
assessors of the town or ward in which l
certificate from the commanding officer of
in which he last served.

§ 147. All notices, warrants or summo
non-commissioned officers, musicians ar
any company or troop to attend a drill
meeting or court martial, may be served ei
or by leaving a written or printed notice,
substance of such notice, warrant or su
dwelling house, store, counting house or
business of the person to be notified, v
moned, with some person of suitable age
and any officer, non-commissioned offic€
private may also be warned to attend ι
campment or drill by enclosing a notice,
at his place of residence, by mail, direct€
nearest post office, at least five days befc
required of him.

. § 148. The officers and non-commissioned staff officers of each regiment shall be warned to attend any parade or drill in the same manner as is prescribed by law for the warning of the privates of any company, and the commanding officer of each regiment may designate and order any or all of the non-commissioned staff officers of the regiment to perform that duty, who shall make return thereof to the commanding officer or the adjutant of the regiment, in the same manner and under the same penalties for delinquencies as are by law imposed on non-commissioned officers of companies for similar delinquencies.

§ 149. All orders for encampment, inspection and review shall be published at least twenty days previous to such parade, in such manner as the commandant of the brigade shall direct, and notice thereof shall at the same time be given to the Inspector General; and all commanding officers of regiments, battalions or companies, may, on any parade, read brigade, regimental or battalion orders, and notify their several commands to appear as specified in said brigade or regimental order for the purposes therein contained, which notice shall be a sufficient warning to all persons present.

§ 150. Every officer, non-commissioned officer, musician and private of any uniformed company, who shall unnecessarily neglect to appear on the days at the time and place appointed for such duty, agreeably to the provisions of this act, shall be subject to such fines and penalties as are hereinafter provided.

§ 151. The commanding officer of any brigade, regiment or battalion, in addition to the rendezvous above prescribed, may require the commissioned officers and non-commissioned officers to meet for exercise and improvement, at such times and places as he shall appoint; and he may require them to appear with such arms and accoutrements as he may prescribe; said officers shall thereupon be formed into a corps of instruction, without regard to rank, and shall be thoroughly instructed in the manual of arms, the school of the soldier and company, and in such other theoretical and practical details of duty as the said commanding officer shall deem proper.

§ 152 Each commandant of division may review either one of the brigades in his division in each year; and he

shall require the officers of the division a
equipped as the law and regulation direc
him.

§ 153. The commandant of each briga
with the officers of the brigade staff, arme
as the law and regulation direct, the an
and review of the several regiments and t
brigade.

§ 154. It shall be the duty of comma
panies, at the annual inspection, to furni
inspector with a return which shall show

1. The number of commissioned, non
officers, musicians and privates of his con
present on parade, designating the numb

2. The number of such company absen

3. The uniforms, arms and equipments

4. The number of uniforms belonging t
or troop.

. 5. The arms and equipments in the pos
company or troop.

§ 155. It shall be the duty of each con
regiment or battalion, within twenty d
annual inspection, to furnish the brigade
a return of the field and staff officers, non
staff officers, musicians of said regiment
present and absent, armed and equipped a
according to law and regulation.

§ 156. At all encampments, the bigade i
attend on the first day thereof, to superint
cises and manoeuvres, and to introduce t
discipline which is or shall be prescribed
on such day he shall take the command a
so far as shall be necessary to the execu
duties ; and he shall also make an annual
such times as the commanding officer o.
shall order and direct.

§ 157. It shall be the duty of the brigad
transmit a copy of the inspection return,
the Adjutant General, and a duplicate of t
division inspector, within thirty days afte
tion shall be made.

§ 158. It shall be the duty of the briga
within thirty days after the annual review
to transmit to the Adjutant General a stat

115

reviews and inspection of the several regiments or battalions in his brigade, attended by the commanding officer of division, accompanied by division staff, armed and equipped and uniformed according to law and regulation, and also the commanding officer of brigade, with the brigade staff, armed and equipped according to law and regulation.

Excuse for neglect to attend. § 159. In case any general officer or any member of his staff shall neglect to attend such inspection and review, it shall be the duty of the Adjutant General to require such officer to render an excuse in writing, to the Commander-in-Chief for his delinquency. If the Commander-in-Chief shall deem such excuse insufficient, he shall order a court martial to try the delinquency.

By-laws of uniform companies. § 160. Each uniform company may form by-laws, rules and regulations, not inconsistent with this act for the government and improvement of its members in military science, and when approved of by two-thirds of all the members belonging to any such company, shall be binding; but may be altered from time to time as may become necessary.

Violations of rules, how punished. § 161. For violations of the by-laws of any uniformed company, the non-commissioned officer, musician or private offending, by a vote of the company, three-fifths being present, may be expelled from the company; and upon the action of the company being confirmed in orders by the commandant of the regiment, the name of such person or persons shall be stricken from the roll of such company, his certificate of membership shall be surrendered and cancelled, and he or they shall cease to be a member or members of such company, and his or their term of service in said company shall not be allowed under the provisions of this act.

Enlisting orders. § 162. The Adjutant General shall prescribe the form of enlisting orders to be furnished and used by each company or troop in recruiting or filling up such company or troop with its required number.

Division commanders. § 163. The commandants of division shall discharge the duties, possess the powers, and be liable to the penalties pertaining to their office, as granted by law or military custom, provided that no division parades, except of the first division, or in case of invasion, insurrection, or to aid the civil authorities, shall be ordered without the consent of the Commander-in-Chief.

§ 164. The Commander-in-Chief may order such parades or drills of the uniformed troops, or any part of them, as he shall deem proper. *Commander-in-chief may order parades.*

§ 165. There shall be a camp of instruction once in each year after the present year, in each of the division districts of this state, if the Commander-in-Chief shall so order, to be held at such time and in such manner as he shall direct; and the Commander-in-Chief is hereby authorized and empowered to order such companies and regiments from such division districts, respectively, to attend such camps as he may deem proper, but in such manner that all the companies and regiments therein shall be ordered to attend such camp from year to year in rotation; provided, always, that not more than ten thousand men in any one year shall be ordered to attend said camps; and in case suitable ground cannot be found in any district for said camp, the same may be held in the adjoining district. *Camps of instruction*

§ 166. Such camps shall continue for a period not exceeding ten days, and shall be governed by the rules and regulations of the army of the United States. *Time limited.*

§ 167. The Commander-in-Chief is hereby authorized and empowered, at his discretion, to order such regiments, battalions, batteries or companies as he shall deem proper, and without regard to arm, not, however, exceeding one thousand men in any one year, to be stationed at such forts or other places as may be furnished by the United States government, or as may be convenient for that purpose within the State of New York for a period not exceeding ten days in any one year, for instruction in the management of heavy artillery for sea and lake coast defence under such instructors as he shall assign for that purpose. *Artillery practice, and instruction in United States forts.*

§ 168. The Commander-in-Chief shall designate commissioned officers of proper rank, without regard to military districts, to command such camps, forts or other places, and shall assign such other officers, also without regard to military districts, to duty as field and staff officers and instructors, as may be required to fully officer such camps and forts. *Officers to be assigned commands.*

§ 169. The Commissary General of ordnance shall furnish, upon the requisition of the Commander-in-Chief, such arms, ordnance and ammunition as may be necessary for the use of the military forces so encamped or stationed. *Ordnance to be furnished.*

Camp equipage. § 170. The Quartermaster General shall, upon the requisition of the Commander-in-Chief, furnish such tents, camp equipage, or other state property as may be required for the use of the military forces so encamped or stationed, and shall also furnish the transportation necessary for conveying said forces to and from such camps or stations.

Subsistence. § 171. The Commissary General of subsistence shall, upon the requisition of the Commander-in-Chief, provide the subsistence necessary for said forces, such subsistence to conform in price and quantity to the ration prescribed by the general regulations for the army of the United States, and to be issued in kind.

Expenses to be paid. § 172. The Commander-in-Chief is hereby authorized and empowered to draw his warrant upon the state treasury for such sum as shall be required by the engineer and quartermaster of said camps, forts or stations, in laying out and preparing the ground designated for such purpose, and in furnishing quarters for said forces and for the services of the officers, instructors and privates ordered to attend the same, also for all necessary expenses of said forces, including transportation and subsistence; such expenses to be audited by a board to consist of the Commander-in-Chief, Comptroller, State Treasurer and Inspector General.

OF COMPENSATION FOR MILITARY SERVICES.

Compensation. § 173. The military forces of this state, when in the actual service of the state in time of war, insurrection, invasion, or imminent danger thereof, shall, during their time of service, be entitled to the same pay, rations and allowances for clothing as are or may hereafter be established by law for the army of the United States.

§ 174. There shall be paid to such officers, non-commissioned officers and privates as shall be specially ordered to attend encampments, and sea and lake coast defence duty in pursuance of the provisions of this act, not to exceed the following sum each, for every day actually on duty:

1. To all non-commissioned officers, musicians and privates, one dollar.

2. To all commissioned officers of the line below the rank of captain, two dollars.

3. To all commanding officers of companies, three dollars.

4. To all field officers, below the rank of colonel, four dollars.

5. To all commanding officers of regiments, five dollars.

6. To all regimental staff officers, two dollars and fifty cents, and to all non-commissioned staff offiers, one dollar and fifty cents.

7. To all brigadier generals, six dollars.

8. To all brigade staff officers, four dollars.

9. To all major generals, eight dollars.

10. To all division staff officers, five dollars.

11. All mounted officers, and all members of any company of cavalry or artillery, mounted or equipped, shall receive one dollar per day for each horse actually used by them.

12. To each military stŏre-keeper, such sum, not exceeding twenty-five dollars per annum, as the Commander-in-Chief shall think proper to allow.

§ 175. The staff of the Commander-in-Chief and the assistants in the several departments, in lieu of all compensation and allowances now provided by law in time of peace, when upon actual duty under the provisions of this act, either at drills, parades, encampments, lake and sea coast defence duty or otherwise, shall receive such compensation as is provided in this act for officers of the same rank, with their necessary and proper expenses, and those of their departments, to be paid by the state, upon the certificate of the Commander-in-Chief.

§ 176. In case of war, insurrection, rebellion or invasion, or imminent danger thereof, when the military forces of the State of New York, or any part thereof, shall be in the actual service of the state, or in the service of the United States, the staff of the Commander-in-Chief, while on duty, the assistants and clerks in the several staff departments, and such other officers as may be detailed by the Commander-in-Chief for the performance of any duties connected with the recruiting, mustering, enrolling, equipping, arming, providing and administering of justice for such forces, shall, in lieu of all other allowances under this act, receive such reasonable and proper compensation, not exceeding the pay and allowances of officers of the same rank in the service of the United States, as the Commander-in-Chief shall deem proper together with their necessary expenses, and those of their departments, to be paid by the state upon the certificate of the Commander-in-Chief, showing a detailed statement of such services and expenses.

Clerks to be employed.

§ 177. Such clerks shall be employed in the several departments of the general staff of this state as shall be actually necessary for the public service, in the opinion of the Commander-in-Chief, and they shall receive, for the time they may be actually necessarily employed, such compensation as the Commander-in-Chief shall prescribe, not exceeding, however, in any case, the rate of twelve hundred dollars per annum.

Captain to make out list of company.

§ 178. The commanding officer of every uniformed company which shall have been ordered into camp, or to perform sea and lake coast defence duty, in accordance with the provisions of this act, shall, at the close of the term for which such company shall have been ordered to such camp or duty, make out an alphabetical list of the members of his company who shall have appeared and performed such duty, uniformed, armed and equipped as the law and regulations direct, and shall set opposite to each name the number of days each shall have performed duty, and the amount of pay each is entitled to receive for such service, and deliver the same, certified on oath to be correct and true, to the commanding officer of the camp or post, who shall immediately cause the same to be transcribed in a book or books to be kept by him for that purpose; such company commandant shall also set forth, opposite to the name of each member of his company, whether such member is indebted to the state in any and what amount on account of his uniform and equipments.

List of officers to be made.

§ 179. The commanding officer of the camp or post shall, also, at the close of the time for which each company, battery, battalion or regiment shall have been ordered to attend for duty thereat, make or cause to be made a complete roster or list of all commissioned officers and non-commissioned staff officers who shall have appeared and performed duty at such parade or encampment, uniformed, armed and equipped, as the law and regulations direct, and shall set opposite to each name the number of days each shall have performed duty at such encampment or post, and the amount of pay

each is entitled to receive for such serv
mediately cause the said list to be trans
or books to be bept by him for that pur

§ 180. The Commander-in-Chief shal
rant upon the Comptroller for the am
become due to officers, non-commissic
privates, for services rendered at the dr
ments for which payment is allowed by

§ 181. The Paymaster General, or a
gade paymaster under his directions, sh
year, visit the different regimental distr
and shall pay to the officers, non-comm
and privates, such sums as they may b
ceive therefor under this act.

§ 182. The Commander-in-Chief shal
prescribe such further rules and regula
for the more convenient payment of all
become due to officers, non-commissio
privates, under the provisions of this ac
master-General, under the direction of t
in-Chief, shall prepare the necessary
rolls, and cause the same to be transmit
mandants of such regiments, camps and

OF THE REGIMENTAL FUND AND REGIMEN AUDITORS.

§ 183. The Comptroller shall annuall
rant upon the Treasurer in favor of the
of each county, for the sum of five hun
each regiment or battalion, certified b
General to be organized according to tl
this act, within his county, which sum, to
fines collected from delinquent officer
sioned officers, musicians and privates,
the military fund of such regiment.

§ 184. There shall be a board of office
ment, which shall consist of the comma
the brigade, who shall be president ther
field officers of the regiment and the
therein, any three of whom shall form
business, the commanding officer of the
one.

§ 185. The commandant of each brig
time to time as he shall deem necessar
board of officers of each regiment create

§ 186. Such board, when so convened, shall audit all just claims on the military fund of such regiment for contingent expenses of the regiment, and shall make their order on the proper county treasurer, which shall require him to pay such order out of any money in his hands belonging to the military fund of such regiment.

§ 187. Such board may also direct such printing and publishing to be performed and executed as shall be necessary for the best interest of the regiment and service; the members of such board shall be entitled to receive for each day's service, as such members, the sum of two dollars, for not more than three days in any one year; such sum to be certified and paid in the same manner. Such board shall enter their proceedings from time to time in a book to be kept for that purpose by each regiment.

§ 188. All county and city treasurers shall report to the brigadier-general, within the bounds of whose brigades he may reside, the amount of all moneys received by them, respectively, by the first days of April and December, annually, and the balance then remaining in their hands, and the number of the regiment to which the same belongs.

OF THE COURTS OF INQUIRY AND COURTS MARTIAL.

OF THE COURTS OF INQUIRY AND COURTS MARTIAL FOR THE TRIAL OF OFFICERS.

§ 189. Courts of inquiry may be instituted by the Commander-in-Chief, or the commanding officer of division or brigade, in relation to those officers for whose trial they are authorized to appoint courts martial for the purpose of investigating the conduct of any officer, either by his own solicitation or on a complaint or charge of improper conduct degrading to the character of an officer, or for the purpose of settling rank; but no such court shall consist of more than one officer, who may, if approved of by the officer ordering the court, require a judge-advocate to attend such court in taking testimony, and in investigating any complaint that may come before such court.

§ 190. Such court shall, without delay, report the evidence adduced, a statement of facts, and an opinion thereon, when required, to the officer instituting such

court, who may in his discretion ther
court martial for the trial of the office
shall have been inquired into.

§ 191. Every court martial for the
general shall be ordered by the Con
and shall consist of five officers, any
shall constitute a quorum.

§ 192. Every court martial for the tr
general shall be ordered by the Con
and shall consist of five officers, any
shall constitute a quorum.

§ 193. All other courts martial for 1
missioned officers shall consist of three
be ordered, if for the trial of officers at
tain, by the commanding officer of div
other officers, by the commanding office

§ 194. No officer arrested shall be
unless a copy of the charges and specifi
by the officer ordering the arrest, shall
him, or left at his usual place of abo
days after his arrest; nor unless the
such court martial shall have ordered
thirty days after receiving notice of t
copy of the charges and specifications
days after a copy of a list of the name
detailed to form the court shall have b
the officer arrested, or left at his usual p

§ 195. The officer ordering the court n
supply any vacancy that, from any cau
therein.

§ 196. If the officer accused shall ha
challenge to any member of such court,
a reasonable time after receiving a copy
and a list of the members, deliver his car
in writing, to the officer ordering such o
thereupon determine as to the validity
lenge; and if, in his opinion, the cause
he shall appoint another member of such

§ 197. After the court shall be assem
all challenges, if any are made, shall he
mined, the judge advocate, whether c
special, shall administer to each membe
oath: "You,   , do swe
faithfully discharge the duties of a mer

martial now assembled, according to the best of your ability."

Sentence to be kept secret. § 198. Every judge advocate, whether commissioned or special, and every member of a court martial, shall keep secret the sentence of the court, until the same shall be approved or disapproved according to law; and shall keep secret the vote or opinion of any particular member of the court, unless required to give evidence thereof by a court of justice.

Effect of sentence. § 199. The sentence of any such court martial shall be according to the nature and degree of the offence, and according to military usage ; but shall not extend farther, in time of peace, than cashiering the officer convicted, and disqualifying him from holding any office in the militia of this state, and imposing a fine not exceeding one hundred dollars.

§ 200. The proceedings and sentence of every court martial shall, without delay, be delivered to the officer ordering the court, who shall approve or disapprove thereof within fifteen days thereafter, and shall give notice of his approval or disapproval to the president of such court martial and to the arresting officer, and he may, at his discretion, publish the sentence, as approved When to be executed. or disapproved, in orders ; but no part of such sentence shall be executed until after the time allowed for appeal has expired.

Full proceedings to be sent to Adjutant General. § 201. He also shall transmit such proceedings and sentence, and his approval or disapproval thereof, to the Adjutant General, to be kept in his office.

§ 202. The right of appeal to the Commander-in-Chief, as it now exists by military usage, is reserved ; but no Appeal. appeal shall be received, unless made within twenty days after the decision appealed from is made known to the person appealing.

Compensation. § 203. There shall be allowed and paid out of the treasury, to each division and brigade judge advocate, and to each president and member of any court of inquiry or court martial for the trial of officers, two dollars for each day actually employed on duty ; and the like compensation to every marshal appointed by any such court, for every day employed in the execution of the duties required of him.

Accounts to be audited. § 204. The accounts of all persons who under this article are entitled to be paid out of the treasury, shall

be audited by the Comptroller, who she
cation of the Gorvernor, draw his warra |
surer for such sums of money as may be
execution of the provisions of this act ; |
the chief of each staff department to ac :
for all money received by him for the pu |
with his department.

OF REGIMENTAL AND BATTALION COU :

§ 205. The commandant of each brig |
time appoint a regimental or battalion (|
any regiment or battalion in his brigad |
practicable of a field officer or captain.

§ 206. The appointment of said court :
ed in orders at least three weeks previou |
ing of the court ; and the officer appoir |
shall fix the day on which it shall con '
convened the court may adjourn from t .
shall become necessary for the transact (
but the whole session of the court, fr .
which it shall convene until its dissoluti :
ceed three weeks.

§ 207. In case any vacancy shall happ :
or a new court shall be required, the offi :
court, or his successor in command, may :
or order a new court.

§ 208. The officer constituting such (|
shall enter on his duties as such, shall ta |
oath : " I,   , do swear that
truly try and determine, according to evi
ters between the people of the State of |
any person or persons which shall come '
mental (or battalion) court martial to wh :
appointed."

§ 209. Such oath shall be taken by th(
or before the day on which the court sha |
fore a justice of the county in which he |
field officer of his regiment or battalion :
the duty of such justice or field officer to
oath without fee or reward.

§ 210. Such court shall direct a noi
officer, or other fit person or persons.
designated to summon all delinquents and
to appear before the court, at a time and

him appointed, which service shall be personal or by leaving such summons at the residence of such parties.

Return.

§ 211. Such non-commissioned officer, or other person or persons so designated, shall make the like return, and with like effect as commissioned and non-commissioned officers are authorized and required to make, in cases of warning to a company or regimental parade, and shall be subject to the like penalties for neglect of duty.

Jurisdiction.

§ 212 The court, when organized, shall have the trial of all offences, delinquencies and deficiencies in the regiment or battalion for which it shall have been called, and shall have power to impose and direct to be levied all the fines to which non-commissioned officers, musicians or privates are declared to be subject by the provisions of this act.

Appeal.

§ 213. From the sentence of any such court, imposing a fine for any offence, delinquency or deficiency, an appeal if made within twenty days, shall be allowed to the officer instituting the court, or to his successor in command, who may remit or mitigate such penalty or fine.

Compensation.

§ 214. There shall be allowed and paid out of the military fund of said regiment :

1. To the officer constituting said court, a sum equal to one day's pay for field duty, for each day he may be actually employed in holding the court or engaged in the business thereof, or in traveling to or from the court, allowing thirty miles for a day's travel.

2. To the non-commissioned officer or other person who shall have summoned delinquents to appear before the court, one dollar and twenty-five cents for each day he may have been necessarily so employed, and the same sum for each day of his attendance on the court.

3. Each officer to whom a warrant for the collection of fines may be directed, shall be entitled to the same fees and be subject to the same penalties for any neglect, as are allowed and provided for on executions issued out of justices' courts.

4. For all other services and commitments under this act, the sheriff, jailor and constables executing the same shall be entitled to the like fees as for similar services in other cases.

Fines to whom paid.

§ 215. All fines and penalties imposed by any regimental or battalion court martial shall be paid, by the officer collecting the same, to the treasurer of the county

within which the officer instituting the c
and shall belong to the military fund of

OF THE IMPOSITION OF PENALTIES AND FINE
THE PROVISIONS OF THIS AC'

§ 216. In time of peace, every comm
for disobedience of orders, neglect or ig
unofficer like conduct or disrespect to a
or for neglecting to furnish himself wit
equipments within six months after rec
mission, shall be arrested and brought
court martial, who may, on conviction, ε
be cashiered, incapacitated from holdi
commission, or fined to an amount no
hundred dollars, or to be reprimanded, (
him to all or either of such penalties, in

§ 217. Every commissioned officer r
over moneys in his hands, as is direct
visions of this act, shall be liable to
cashiered, or otherwise punished there
martial.

§ 218. Every commissioned officer, ε
commissioned officer, musician and priva
conviction, be subject for the following
fines thereto annexed :

1. Every non-commissioned officer, m
vate, for non-appearance, when duly w
moned at a company parade, a fine of tv
regimental or battalion parade or encam
than three nor more than six dollars ; a
rendezvous, when called into actual serv.
exceeding twelve month's pay, nor less tl
pay.

2. Every commissioned officer, for no
any parade or encampment, and every su
commissioned officer, musician and priva
refusing to obey the orders of his sup
any day of parade or encampment, or to
military duty or exercise as may be requ
ing from his colors, post or guard, or lea
or ranks without permission, a fine not
hundred nor less than five dollars.

3. For neglecting or refusing to obe
warrant to him lawfully given or directe

proper return thereof, if such return be necessary, or making a false return, or neglecting or refusing, when required, to summon a delinquent before a court martial, or duly to return such summons, a fine not more than one hundred nor less than five dollars.

Refusal to act when elected. § 219. Every commissioned officer, for neglecting or refusing to act as such when duly elected and commissioned, may be sentenced to pay a fine not less than ten dollars; every non-commissioned officer, for neglecting or refusing to act as such when duly appointed and warranted, may be sentenced to pay a fine not less than five dollars; and every non-commissioned officer for neglect of duty or disorderly or unofficer like conduct, in addition to other penalties, may be reduced to the ranks by the commandant of the company, with the approbation of the commandant of the regiment or battalion.

Discharge. of fire-arms. § 220. Every non-commissioned officer, musician or private, who shall unlawfully discharge any fire-arms within two miles of any parade, on the day thereof, shall be sentenced to pay a fine of one dollar.

Retaining commission § 221. Any commissioned officer who shall retain a commission received by him for any subaltern for more than thirty days, without giving notice by mail or otherwise to the person entitled to it, shall be liable to pay a fine not exceeding twenty-five dollars to be imposed by the proper court matial on the complaint of any officer interested. In addition to the penalties imposed by any of the provisions of this act, every commissioned and non-commissioned officer, musician and private of a company or troop, or any other person who shall appear at any parade or encampment wearing any personal **Appearing in ludicrous dress.** disguise or other unusual or ludicrous article of dress, or any arms, weapons or other implements not required by law, and calculated to excite ridicule or to interrupt the orderly and peaceable discharge of duty by those under arms, shall be liable to a fine of not more than twenty-five and not less than five dollars, to be imposed by the proper court martial.

Excuse for delinquency § 222. The court martial by which any delinquent is tried, may excuse such delinquent, if it shall be made satisfactorily to appear to the court that he has a reasonable excuse for such delinquency.

§ 223. No action shall be maintained ε
ber of a court martial, or officer or agε
its authority, on account of the imposi
the execution of a sentence on any per
son shall have been returned as a deli:
summoned, and shall have neglected to
der his excuse for such delinquency, or
tion before such court.

§ 224. When a suit or proceeding sha
in any court by any person against an
state for any act done by such officε
capacity, in the discharge of any duty
or against any person acting under auth
any such officer, or by virtue of any wε
him pursuant to law, or against any coll
of taxes, the defendant may require the
suit to file security for the payment of th
be incurred by the defendant in such su:
and the defendant, in all cases, may pl
issue, and give the special matter in ε
case the plaintiff shall be non-prossed o
have a verdict or judgment against hin
shall recover treble costs.

OF THE COLLECTION OF FINES AND F

§ 225. For the purpose of collecting sι
be imposed by any court martial authori
the president of the court shall, within t
the fines have been imposed, make a lis·
sons fined, designating the company :
respectively belong, and the sums impι
each person, and shall draw his warrant
and seal, directed to any marshal, sheriff
any city or county (as the case may be
manding him to levy such fine or fines, to
costs, of the goods and chattels of suc
and if any such delinquent shall be undε
with his father or mother, master or m
levy such fine or fines with the costs of
chattels of such father or mother, master
the case may be ; no property now ε
shall be exempt from the payment of su
case the goods and chattels of any del:
goods and chattels of the father or mot

mistress, of any delinquent under age, cannot be found,
Body to be taken. wherewith to satisfy the same, then to take the body of
such delinquent and convey him to the jail of the city or
county where he shall reside.

Confined in jail.   § 226. It shall be the duty of the jailor to whom such
delinquent may be delivered, to keep him closely confined,
without bail or mainprize, for two days, for any fine not
exceeding two dollars, and two additional days for every
dollar above that sum, unless the fine, together with the
costs and the jailor's fees, shall sooner be paid.

Officer to make returns.   § 227. Every such martial, sheriff or constable to whom
any such list and warrant shall be directed and delivered,
may execute the same by levying and collecting the
fines, or by taking the body of the delinquent in any
city, town or county in this state, and shall make return
thereof, within forty days from the receipt of such warrant, to the officers who issue the same.

§ 228. If the marshal, sheriff or constable shall not be
able to collect the fines or take the bodies within the
forty days aforesaid, then the officers issuing the warrant may, at any time thereafter within two years from
New warrant may be issued. the time of imposing the fines, issue a new warrant
against any delinquent, or renew the former warrant,
from time to time, as may become necessary.

Warrants renewed.   § 229. Any warrant for the collection of fines, issued
by virtue of this chapter, shall and may be renewed in
the same manner that executions issued from justices'
courts may by law be renewed.

Fines to be paid into the county treasury.   § 230. The amount of any fines so collected shall be
paid by the officer collecting the same into the county
treasury, and shall form a portion of and be credited to
the regimental fund of the regiment to which the person so fined belonged.

Additional bond required.   § 231. In addition to the bond now required by law
to be given by the marshal, sheriff, constable or other
officer for the faithful discharge of his duties, such
named officers shall execute a bond for the payment of
all moneys by them collected, under the provisions of
this act; and the sureties of such officers, hereby authorized to collect fines and penalties, shall be liable for
any official delinquency under this act. Such bonds to
be approved by the county judge of each county.

GENERAL PROVISIONS APPLICABLE TO ALL C(
AND COURTS OF INQUIRY.

§ 232. The president of every court n
every court of inquiry, both before and
have been sworn, and also the judge a(
quired, shall issue subpœnas for all witne
tendance at such court may, in his opinion
in behalf of the people of this state, and
cation for all witnesses in behalf of any o
or accused, or persons returned as delinqu
direct the commandant of any company t
subpœna to be served on any witness or n
company.

§ 233. The president of such court m
court of inquiry shall have power to a(
usual oath to witnesses, and shall have the
to compel attending witnesses to be swor
and to preserve order, as courts of comm
diction, and all sheriffs, jailors and constabl
required to execute any precept issued b
dent or court for that purpose.

§ 234. Every witness not appearing in
such subpœna when duly served, personally
of the same, and not having a sufficient c
excuse, shall forfeit to the people of this sta
less than ten nor more than fifty dollars; a
dent of such court shall, from time to tin
the district attorney the names of all such
witnesses, together with the names and pl
dence of the persons serving such subpœn
to enable him to prosecute for such forfeitu

§ 235. Whenever it shall appear to the sa
any court martial or court of inquiry, by
before such court, that any person duly su
appear as a witness before said court, shall l
or neglected without just cause to attend as i
in conformity to such subpœna, and the par
behalf such witness shall have have subp(
make oath that the testimony of such witnes
such court, or the president thereof, shall l
to issue an attachment to compel the attend
witness.

§ 236. Every such attachment shall be exe
same manner as a warrant, and by any officer

117

to execute warrants, and the fees of the officers serving the same shall be paid by the person against whom the same shall have been issued, unless he shall show reasonable cause, to the satisfaction of such court, for his omission to attend ; such costs shall be ascertained by the court, who may thereupon issue an execution for the collection against the person liable to pay the same, and which may be collected as other executions are collected, and by any officer authorized to collect executions issued from courts of justice.

Disorderly conduct. § 237. Any person or persons who shall be guilty of disorderly, contemptuous or insolent behavior in, or use any insulting or contemptuous or indecorous language or expressions to or before any court-martial or court of inquiry, or any member of either of such courts, in open court, intending to intercept the proceedings or to impair the respect, the authority of such courts, may be committed to the jail of the county in which said courts shall sit, by warrant under the hand and seal of the president of such court.

Warrant how served. § 238. Such warrant shall be directed to the sheriff or any or either of the constables and marshals of any such county, or any officer attending the court, and shall set forth the particular circumstances of the offence adjudged to have been committed ; and shall command the officer to whom it is directed to take the body of such person and commit him to the jail of the county, there to remain without bail or mainprize, in close confinement, for a time to be limited, not exceeding three days, and until the officer's fees for committing and the jailor's fees be paid.

Duty of sheriff. § 239. Such sheriff shall receive the body of any person who shall be brought to him by virtue of such warrant, and keep him until the expiration of the time mentioned in the warrant, and until the officer's and jailor's fees shall be paid, or until the offender shall be discharged by due course of law, unless sooner discharged by any judge of a court of record, in the same manner and under the same rules as in cases of imprisonment under process for contempt from a court at law.

Senior officer to preside in absence of president. § 240. In the absence of the president of any court martial, the senior officer present may preside, with all the powers of the president ; and all the members of such courts shall, when on duty, be in full uniform.

§ 241. The president of any court martial or any court of inquiry may appoint, by warrant under his hand and seal, one or more marshals. *Marshals.*

§ 242. The marshals so appointed may not only perform the usual duties of such marshals, but may also execute all process lawfully issued by such president or court, and perform all acts and duties in this act imposed on and authorized to be performed by any sheriff, marshal or constable. *Their powers.*

§ 243. Whenever the sentence of any court martial shall be appealed from, the officer hearing the appeal shall require the court, or the president thereof, to furnish him forthwith with a statement of the case, and of the evidence touching the same; which statement and evidence shall, in case of an appeal to the commanding officer of the brigade, be forthwith, on notice of such appeal, transmitted to him. *Appeal papers.*

§ 244. Such statement being furnished, the officer hearing the appeal may hear such further evidence, by affidavit or otherwise, as the nature of the case may require, and for that purpose he shall have power to administer the usual oaths to witnesses produced before him, except in cases where trials may have been had upon charges preferred. *May receive further testimony.*

§ 245. The last two sections shall extend to appeals made from the order of an officer approving the sentence of a court martial.

§ 246. If any officer having a warrant for the collection of any fine, shall not be able to collect the fine within the time specified therein, then the officers issuing the warrant may, at any time thereafter, within two years from the time of imposing the fines, issue a new warrant against any delinquent, or renew the former warrant, from time to time, as may become necessary. *Renewal of warrants.*

§ 247. Any warrant for the collection of fines, issued by virtue of this act, shall and may be renewed in the same manner that executions issued from justice's courts may by law be renewed.

§ 248. It shall be the duty of the respective presidents of courts martial to prosecute, in the name of the people of the state of New York, any marshal or constable, sheriff and their sureties, who shall incur any penalty for neglect in the execution or return of any warrant, or in paying over moneys collected by him. *Marshals, sheriffs and constables to be prosecuted for neglect.*

§ 249. Whenever any court martial shall consist of one person, he shall be deemed the president thereof within the meaning of this act. •

Chiefs of staff to make returns of delinquents.

§ 250. The chiefs of the staff in each division, regiment or battalion, shall, on or before the first day of November in each year, return to the commandants of division and brigade, respectively, the names of all commissioned officers absent from any parade, encampment or drill which they shall be required by law to attend. Within ten days after the receipt of such returns, the respective commandants of division or brigade, as the case may be, shall order a court martial, to consist of three commissioned officers, without regard to rank, to pass upon such delinquency. It shall not be necessary to cause the arrest of such absentee, nor to serve any charges, unless, in the discretion of the officer ordering the court, it may be proper ; but the delinquent may be fined, pursuant to the provisions of this act, provided notice of the return and of the time appointed for holding the court martial shall have been delivered to him or left at his usual place of abode at least ten days before the assembling of said court.

Delinquents to be court martialed.

§ 251. The court may excuse any delinquent for good cause shown.

Offences against by-laws.

§ 252. Any fine for offences against the by-laws of any company of the national guards or of regimental boards, not exceeding the sum of twenty-five dollars, a certified copy of the proceedings relating to the infliction of which has been returned to any regimental court martial or court of appeals, may be enforced by such court in the manner hereinbefore provided, due notice being given to the delinquent, and further provided that a certified copy of said by-laws be filed with the commandant of the regiment.

Regulations of United States army to govern.

§ 253. Whenever any portion of the military forces of this state shall be ordered to assemble for purposes of military instruction, under the authority of the Commander-in-Chief, or whenever any part of the state forces shall be ordered to assemble, under his authority, in time of war, insurrection, invasion or public danger, the rules and articles of war, and general regulations for the government of the army of the United States, so far as they are applicable, and with such modifications as the Commander-in-Chief may prescribe, shall be considered in force and regarded as a part of this act, during the continuance of such instruction, and to the close of such state of war, invasion, insurrection or public danger ; but no punishment under such rules and articles which shall extend to the taking of life shall, in any case, be inflicted, except in time of actual war, invasion or insurrection, declared by proclamation of the Governor to exist.

OF THE DUTIES OF CERTAIN STAFF OFFICERS, AND OF VARIOUS MATTERS CONNECTED WITH THEIR VARIOUS RESPECTIVE DEPARTMENTS.

OF THE ADJUTANT GENERAL.

§ 254. The Adjutant General shall keep a roster of all the officers of the military forces of this state, containing the date of their commissions, their ranks, the corps to which they belong, the division, brigade and regiment of such corps, and the places of their residence, as accurately as can be ascertained, which roster shall be revised and corrected every year. *Roster of officers.*

§ 255. He shall also enter in a book, to be kept for that purpose, a local description of the several company, regimental, brigade and division district. *Description of districts.*

§ 256. It shall be the duty of the commandants of divisions and brigades, to furnish the Adjutant General with a roster of their officers, containing the facts requisite to enable him to comply with the provisions of this act. *Roster of divisions and brigades.*

§ 257. The books required by the Adjutant General to comply with this act, shall be furnished him at the expense of this state, and shall go to his successors in office. *Books.*

§ 258. The seal now used in the office of the Adjutant General shall continue to be the seal of his office, and shall from time to time be delivered to his successor in office ; and all copies of records or papers in his office, duly certified and authenticated under the said seal, shall be evidence in all cases, in like manner as if the originals were produced. *Seal.*

§ 259. It shall be the duty of the Adjutant General to cause so much of the militia laws as shall at any time be in force to be printed in proper form, from time to *Printing and distribution of militia laws* time, and to distribute one copy to each commissioned officer, and to each town clerk, supervisors' clerk and county treasurer in this state ; and also, to prepare and

To furnish blank books, forms, &c. cause all necessary blank books, forms and notices to be transmitted at the expense of this state, to carry into full effect the provisions of this act; and the Comptroller is hereby directed to draw his warrant on the Treasurer of this state for the expenses incurred under this section.

Assistant. § 260. The Adjutant General is hereby authorized to appoint an assistant, who shall have the rank of colonel, and be commissioned by the Commander-in-Chief, and who shall hold such office during the pleasure of the Adjutant General. In the absence of the Adjutant General from the city of Albany, or in case of his inability to perform his duties, his assistant shall have full power to perform all the duties appertaining to the office of Adjutant General. But nothing in this section shall be so construed as to give any validity to the acts of said assistant in case of the disapproval of the Adjutant General.

OF THE COMMISSARY GENERAL.

Care of arsenals and magazines. § 261. The Commissary General shall keep in good repair the arsenals and magazines of the state, and attend to the due preservation and safe keeping, cleaning and repairing of the ordnance, arms, accoutrements, ammunition, munitions of war and implements of every description, the property of this state; and he shall at all times have the control and disposition of the same for that purpose.

Damaged munitions. § 262. He shall, under the direction of the Commander-in-Chief, dispose to the best advantage of all damaged powder, and of all ordnance, arms, ammunition, accoutrements, tools, implements and warlike stores of every kind whatsoever, that shall be deemed unsuitable for the use of the state.

Account of sales. § 263. He shall from time to time render a just and true account of all sales made by him, with all convenient speed, to the Governor, and shall pay the proceeds of such sale into the treasury of the state for military purposes, or expend the same in the purchase of suitable arms, ammunition and camp or other equipage, as the Commander-in-Chief may direct.

§ 264. Whenever the commanding officer of a brigade shall certify that a stand of colors or any drums, fifes or bugles, are necessary for any company, battalion or regiment in his brigade, the commissary general, with the approbation of the Commander-in-Chief, shall furnish such company, battalion or regiment with a stand of colors, and a sufficiency of drums, fifes and bugles at the expense of the state. *Drums, colors, &c., to be furnished.*

§ 265. The Commissary General shall issue the proper allowance of powder and balls to artillery companies for practice; and the several commandants of artillery companies shall annually report to the Commissary General the situation and state of the pieces of ordnance, arms, implements and accoutrements, the property of the state, entrusted to their charge respectively. *Powder and ball for practice.*

§ 266. The Commissary General shall issue all ammunition suited to the several arms of the service, upon the requisition of any commandant of brigade, regiment or battalion ; and shall, on a like requisition, replace such articles or implements for ordnance as may be by use rendered unfit for service. *Requisition.*

§ 267. The Commissary General shall report annually to the Commander-in-Chief, whose duty it shall be to transmit the same to the legislature, a true and particular statement, showing the actual situation and disposition of all the ordnance, arms, ammunition and other munitions of war, property or things, which in anywise appertain to or respect the department confided to his keeping. *Annual report.*

§ 268. He shall keep a just and true account of all the expenses necessarily incurred in and about his department, which shall include all expenses for transportation, to and from the arsenals, all ordnance, arms, ammunition and camp equipage, and deliver the same to the Comptroller, who shall thereupon examine and audit the same, and shall draw his warrant on the Treasurer for such sum as he shall audit and certify to be due. *Account of expenses.*

§ 269. It shall be the duty of the Judge Advocate General to prosecute any bond, the condition of which is violated by a neglect or refusal of any officer to report the condition of any arms or equipage, or to return the same to any of the arsenals of this state as required by law. *Judge advocate general to prosecute bond.*

Assistant commissary

§ 270. The Commissary General is authorized to appoint an assistant with the rank of colonel, and who shall be commissioned by the Commander-in-Chief and hold his office during the pleasure of the Commissary General, and shall perform the duties now required by law to be performed by the military store keeper at the New York arsenal, and shall be compensated in the same manner as such military store keeper has been compensated. In the absence of the Commissary General from the city of New York, or in case of his inability to perform his duties, his assistant shall have full power to perform all the duties appertaining to the office of the Commissary General; but nothing in this section shall be so construed as to give any validity to the acts of such assistant in case of the disapproval of the Commissary General.

OF THE INSPECTOR GENERAL.

To visit and inspect.

§ 271. It shall be the duty of the Inspector General to visit, at least once in every two years, each regimental district in the state. He shall critically inspect, as often as he may deem necessary, every branch connected with the military service, including armories, arsenals and military store-houses; and he shall also attend to the organization of the militia, and report to general headquarters the improvement in discipline and tactical instruction of the uniformed forces.

Commandants to furnish information.

§ 272. Commandants of regiments and companies shall furnish to the Inspector General such information, as he may require, as to the number and kinds of arms, equipments and military property of the state issued to their respective regiments and companies; and, at the conclusion of the inspection of any armory, arsenal or military storehouse, if he find the property which ought to be kept therein, or any part of it, missing, injured, unfit for use, or deficient in any respect, he shall forthwith report the facts, in respect thereto, to the Commander-in-Chief.

To inspect tents, &c.

§ 273. It shall be his duty, after the first day in November in each year, to inspect the tents and camp equipage belonging to the state, and report any deficiency therein to the Commander-in-Chief, on or before the first day of January thereafter.

§ 274. In his annual report he shall state what general and field officers have been in command of parades and encampments, what changes of general or field officers have been made, and what degree of improvement has been attained by both officers and men, and whether the general regulations have been observed, together with such suggestions as he may see fit to make. Annual report.

§ 275. To the Inspector General will be referred, by order of the Commander-in-Chief, such matters as require an examination at a distance from the general headquarters, for the information of the Commander-in-Chief, and it shall be the duty of Inspector General, upon such reference, to report upon the qualifications of persons named to the Commander-in-Chief, for appointment to military office, and also upon the possession of the necessary requsites by the applicants for the organization of companies. Matters referred to him.

§ 276. The division and brigade inspectors, whenever required by the Inspector General, shall report to him the condition of their respective divisions or brigades, and shall also, upon his request, report to him upon any matter properly belonging to his department, which may require examination within their respective division or brigade districts. Reports to be made to him when required.

§ 277. The Inspector General shall visit the several encampments which shall be ordered by the Commander-in-Chief, and to ascertain whether the troops have been properly instructed in the exercises and evolutions of the field; he will cause them to be exercised in the manoeuvers required to be practiced during the year, as prescribed by the regulations; and he will give his instructions, as to the exercises, to the commanding officer, who will issue all necessary orders and directions to the troops for their execution. To visit encampments To give instructions.

§ 278. The Inspector General shall, at least once in every two years, examine the book of proceedings of the board of auditors of each regiment, and the accounts filed with the secretary of such board during the two years previous, or since the last examination made by the Inspector General, and he shall carefully compare the book of proceedings with accounts; he shall also examine the warrants drawn by the board of auditors, in the possession of the county treasurer; and he shall specially report to the Commander-in-Chief whether the To examine books and accounts of boards of auditors.

proceedings of the board of auditors are regularly and properly entered, and whether the warrants are in due form ; and whether any military funds have been drawn from the county treasurer for improper purposes, or by persons not entitled thereto.

Assistant. § 279. The Inspector General is hereby authorized to appoint an assistant, who shall have the rank of colonel, and be commissioned by the Commander-in-Chief, and who shall hold such office, during the pleasure of the Inspector General, and shall receive the same compensation as the assistant adjutant general. In the absence of the Inspector General from the city of Albany, or in case of his inability to perform his duties, his assistant shall have full power to perform all duties appertaining to the office of the Inspector General. But nothing in this section shall be so construed as to give any validity to the acts of said assistant in case of the disapproval of the Inspector General.

OF THE JUDGE-ADVOCATE GENERAL.

§ 280. The Judge-Advocate General, as chief of his department, is charged with the supervision, care and management of all things relating to the administration of justice among the military forces of this state. He **To examine all cases that have been appealed.** shall diligently scrutinize and examine the proceedings of all courts martial where an appeal has been taken and report thereon for the information of the Commander-in-Chief; he shall also, in like manner, report in all cases of disputed elections where an appeal has been taken. Under the orders of the Commander-in-Chief, the Judge-Advocate General shall act as judge-advocate at any court-martial where the public interests shall require his attendance.

Legal adviser of staff departments. § 281. The Judge-Advocate General is the legal adviser of the several staff departments, upon all legal questions which may arise therein, and to him may be referred for supervision all contracts, agreements or other instruments to be drawn or executed in the course of the business of such department.

§ 282. The officers of the Judge-Advocate General's department, when not engaged in the special duties of the same, may be detailed for such other staff duty as the commandants of their respective brigades or divisions shall direct.

OF INVASION, INSURRECTION, BREACHES OF THE PEACE, AND DRAFTS OF THE MILITIA.

OF INVASION AND INSURRECTION.

§ 283. In cases of insurrection or invasion, or imminent danger thereof, the Commander-in-Chief may, by proclamation or otherwise, order and direct the commandants of such company districts as he shall designate to accept sufficient volunteers, should the same offer, to raise said company and maintain the same at the maximum number provided by law, and if sufficient volunteers should not offer, then a sufficient number shall be drafted from the reserve militia of said districts in the manner hereinafter provided, who shall thereupon be enrolled as national guards in said company, and shall be liable to duty in case the military forces of the state should be called into service. Volunteers to be accepted. Drafting.

§ 284. The Commander-in-Chief shall have power, in case of insurrection or invasion, or imminent danger thereof, to order into the service of the state such number and description of companies or regiments of the national guard, or of other militia of the state as he shall deem proper, and under the command of such officers as he shall direct; and in such case the forces so called into service shall receive the same pay and rations as troops in the service of the United States. And all the acts, proclamations and orders of the Governor of this state, since the sixteenth day of April, eighteen hundred and sixty-one, relating to the calling out of the militia or volunteers from this state for the service of the United States, are hereby approved, and in all respects legalized and made valid, to the same intent and with the same effect as if they had been issued and done with the previous express authority and direction of the legislature of this state, and all commissions issued or hereafter to be issued to the officers of such volunteer forces by the Governor of this state, in accordance with the act of congress in such cases made and provided, are hereby confirmed. Acts of Governor confirmed.

§ 285. In case of any invasion, or of imminent danger thereof, within the limits of any division, brigade, regiment or battalion, it shall be the duty of the commandant of such division, brigade, regiment or battalion to Invasion.

order out, for the defence of the state, the militia or any part thereof, under his command, and immediately report what he has done to the Commander-in-Chief, through the Adjutant-General.

§ 286. It shall also be his duty to give immediate notice of such invasion, and of the circumstances attending the same, to his immediate commanding officer, by whom such information shall be transmitted, with the utmost expedition, to the Commander-in-Chief.

§ 287. The commandant of every regiment or battalion, within the limits of which an insurrection may happen, shall immediately assemble his regiment or battalion, under arms, and with the utmost expedition shall transmit information of such insurrection to the commandant of his brigade and to the Commander-in-Chief.

§ 288. He shall also give immediate notice of such insurrection to any judge of the county in which it shall happen, and shall take such measures for its suppression as to such judge shall appear most proper and effectual.

§ 289. If the said judge shall deem a greater force requisite to quell the insurrection, he shall require such additional force as he may deem necessary from the commandant of the division, or of any brigade therein whose duty it shall be to obey his requisition.

§ 290. Every person who, whilst in the actual service of this state, shall be wounded or disabled in opposing or suppressing any invasion or insurrection, shall be taken care of and provided for at the expense of the state

OF RIOTS, TUMULTS, BREACHES OF THE PEACE AND RESISTANCE TO PROCESS.

§ 291. In case of any breach of the peace, tumult, riot or resistance to process of this state, or apprehension of imminent danger of the same, it shall be lawful for the sheriff of any county, or the mayor of any city, to call for aid from any division, brigade, regiment, battalion or company; and it shall be the duty of the commanding officer of such division, brigade, regiment, battalion or company, to whom such order is given, to order out, in aid of the civil authorities, the military force or any part thereof under his command.

§ 292. In such case it shall not be necessary for commandants of companies to issue written orders or notices

Side notes:
Notice to be given.
Regiments to be assembled.
Notice to judge.
Judge may order additional force.
Wounded or disabled men.
Suppression of riots, &c.
Verbal orders.

for calling out their men, but verbal orders and notices shall be sufficient.

§ 293. In shall be the duty of the commanding officer of any division, brigade, regiment, battalion or company, in all cases when so called into service, to provide **Militia how to be armed** the men of his command, so ordered out, with at least twenty-four rounds of ball cartridge, and arms in complete order for actual service.

§ 294. Such officer shall be subject, as provided by **Officer to be subject to sheriff.** law, to the sheriff or public officer who shall so require his aid; and for refusing or neglecting to obey the order of such sheriff or public officer so requiring service, or for interfering or in any way hindering or preventing the men of his command from performing such duty, or in any manner, by neglect or delay, preventing the due execution of law, every such commanding officer, and every commissioned officer under his command so offending, shall be liable to a fine of not less than one hundred nor more than five hundred dollars, and imprisonment in the county jail for a period not exceeding six months.

§ 295. It shall be the duty of the district attorney of **Disobedience, how punished.** any county where such offence shall be committed to prosecute the same; and in addition thereto, such officer shall be liable to be tried by court martial and sentenced to be cashiered and incapacitated forever after for holding military commission in this state.

§ 296. Any non-commissioned officer, musician or pri- **Penalty.** vate who shall neglect or refuse to obey the orders of his commanding officer in the case above provided for, shall be liable to a fine of not less than twenty-five nor more than one hundred dollars, and imprisonment in the county jail for a period not to exceed three months, to be prosecuted and recovered in the manner hereinbefore provided in the case of commissioned officers.

§ 297. All officers, non-commissioned officers and pri- **Compensation.** vates, in cases of riot, tumult, breach of the peace, resistance to process, or whenever called upon in aid of the civil authorities, shall receive the compensation provided by an act entitled "An act to enforce the laws and preserve order," passed April fifteenth, eighteen hundred and forty-five, which continues in force, and shall be published with this act; and every person who shall be wounded or disabled in such service, shall be taken care of and provided for at the expense of the county where such service shall be rendered.

OF DRAFTS OF THE MILITIA.

§ 298. Whenever the Commander-in-Chief shall order a draft from the reserved militia of any company district, to raise the company of the national guard therein to and maintain the same at either the minimum or maximum number provided by this act, or whenever a general draft of the militia shall be made by order of the Commander-in-Chief, or of the President of the **Lots to be drawn.** United States, such draft shall be determined by lot, to be drawn by the clerk of the county in which such roll has been filed, in the presence of the county judge and the mayor of any city, or the supervisor of any town or ward, upon the requisition of the commanding officer of the regiment within whose bounds such person may reside.

Exemption. § 299. Any person so drafted may, within five days after receiving notice of the same, present to the county judge of such county his certificate of exemption, or other proof of his non-liability to military duty, which shall be duly verified, and if such county judge shall decide that such person is exempt or not liable, he shall be discharged and another person shall be drafted in his stead, in accordance with the provisions of this act.

§ 300. Any person so drafted, in accordance with the **Substitutes.** above provisions, may offer a substitute at the time of the rendezvous of the drafted military force and militia, and such substitute, if he shall be an able bodied man, of the age of twenty-one years and upwards, and shall consent in writing to subject himself to all the duties, fines, forfeitures and punishments to which his principal would have been subject had he personally served, shall be accepted by the commandant of the company of drafted militia to which his principal may belong.

§ 301. Whenever the President of the United States or the Commander-in-Chief shall order a draft from the **Draft, how made.** militia for public service, such draft shall be made in the following manner:

1. When the draft required to be made shall be a number equal to one or more companies to each brigade, such draft shall be made by company, to be determined by lot, to be drawn by the commandant of brigade in the

presence of the commanding officers of the regiments composing said brigade from the military forces of the state in his brigade, organized, uniformed, armed and equipped according to the provisions of this act.

2. In case such draft shall require a number equal to one regiment, such shall be determined by lot in the manner above prescribed.

3. In case such draft shall require a larger number than the whole number of men composing the military force of said brigade, such additional draft shall be made of the requisite number to supply such deficiency from the military roll of the reserve militia of each town or ward, filed in the office of the city, village or town clerk, as hereinbefore provided.

§ 302. The Commander-in-Chief shall prescribe such **Distribu-tion of arms** rules, orders and regulations, relative to the distribution of arms, ammunition and military stores, to the militia when called into actual service as he may deem proper.

§ 303. The command of any military force, called into **Senior officer to command.** service under the provisions of this title, shall devolve upon the senior officer of such force, unless otherwise specially ordered by the Commander-in-Chief.

OF THE MILITARY FUND OF THE STATE AND APPROPRIATIONS FOR MILITARY PURPOSES.

§ 304. The moneys received from the several county **Moneys to be kept separate.** treasurers, under the provisions of this act, shall be kept separate and apart from the current and ordinary finances of this state, and shall be applied to the purposes mentioned in this act and to no other.

§ 305. For the purchase of uniforms and equipments, **Appropriation.** pay of officers and privates and other expenditures authorized by this act, the sum of three hundred thousand dollars is hereby appropriated from the moneys mentioned in the last preceeding section, and from any other moneys in the treasury not otherwise appropriated.

MISCELLANEOUS PROVISIONS.

§ 306. The Commander-in-Chief is hereby authorized **Rules and regulations.** to establish and prescribe such rules, regulations, forms and precedents as he shall deem proper for the use and government of the military forces of the state, and to carry into full effect the provisions of this act. Such rules, regulations, forms and precedents shall be pub-

lished in orders by the Adjutant General, and, from time
to time, distributed to the commissioned officers of the
state.

Certificate
of seven
years ser-
vice.

§ 307. Whenever any non-commissioned officers, musicians or privates of any uniformed company or troop,
shall have performed service in any such company or
troop for the space of seven years from the time of his
enlistment therein, properly uniformed according to the
provisions of law, he shall be furnished, on application,
by the commanding officer of such company or troop,
with a certificate, duly setting forth such facts, which
shall, for all purposes, be deemed prima facie evidence
thereof.

Certificate
of member-
ship.

§ 308. The commanding officer of every uniform company or troop, shall, on the application of any commissioned, non-commissioned officer, musician or private of his company, deliver to him a certificate,
stating that such person is a member of his company,
and whether he is uniformed according to law, and
how recently he may have performed duty in said
company. Such certificate, when dated within six
months, shall be deemed for all purposes prima facie
evidence of the matters therein stated.

Arms, &c.,
exempt
from sale or
execution.

§ 309. Every officer, non-commissioned officer, musician and private of the uniform militia of this state,
who shall have provided himself with a uniform, arms
or accoutrements required by law or regulations, shall
hold the same exempt from all suits, distresses, executions or sales for debts, or for the payment of taxes;
and every mounted officer, and every member of a troop
of cavalry or light artillery, who shall own a suitable
horse necessary for his use as such officer or member,
shall hold the same with the like exemption.

Rules and
regulations.

§ 310. The rules and regulations, prepared by a board
of officers under section one of title nine of the militia
law, passed April seventeen, eighteen hundred and fifty-four, with such changes and modifications as are provided
in this act, having received the approval of the Commander-in-Chief, are hereby ratified and confirmed, and
the Commander-in-Chief is hereby authorized to make
such changes and alterations in said regulations, from
time to time, as he may deem expedient.

Ordnance
sergeants.

§ 311. The commandants of regiments may appoint
ordnance sergeants as keepers of armories, not exceeding

one to each armory, who shall be under the authority and hold offi e during the pleasure of the commandant; such ordnance sergeants shall be paid as now provided for keepers of armories.

§ 312. No person belonging to the military forces shall be arrested on any civil process while going to, remaining at, or returning from any place at which he may be required to attend for military duty. *Exemption from civil process.*

§ 313 Any person who shall purchase, retain, or have in custody or possession without right any military property belonging to this state marked as or known to him to be such, and shall, after proper demand, refuse to deliver the same to any officer entitled to the possession thereof, shall be liable to an action for the recovery of the possession of such military property, and of a penalty of not less than ten nor more than one hundred dollars. *Military property belonging to the state.*

§ 314. Any person belonging to the military forces who shall, contrary to the lawful order of the proper officer, retain in his possession or control any military property of this state, shall be liable to an action to recover the possession thereof and to pay a fine of not less than ten nor more than one hundred dollars, and shall also be deemed guilty of a misdemeanor; and any commanding officer may take possession thereof or of such military property mentioned in the preceding section wherever the same may be found. *Penalty.*

§ 315 Actions to recover the possession of military property and the amount of any fine or penalty under the two preceding sections may be brought, by any officer entitled to the possession of such property, in any court of competent jurisdiction, and such fine or penalty together with all other fines and penalties prescribed by this act, and by chapter three hundred and ninety-eight of the Session Laws of eighteen hundred and fifty-four shall be paid to the treasurer of the county where the offender may reside, for the benefit of the military fund of the regiment located therein. The possession of any military property, or the amount of a fine or penalty may be recovered in the same action Proceedings at law shall not preclude the punishment of any military person in the military courts. *Actions to recover.*

§ 316. Any person belonging to the military forces of this state, going to or returning from any parade, en- *Toll gates, &c., to be free.*

119

campment, drill or meeting, which he may be required by law to attend, shall, together with his conveyance and the military property of the state, be allowed to pass free through all toll-gates, over toll-bridges and ferries.

Honorary brevet. § 317. Whenever any officer shall have served or shall hereafter serve continuously and honorably as commandant of any military company, under a military commission, issued under the laws of this state, for the period of twenty years, the Commander-in-Chief shall have power to confer upon such officer the brevet or honorary rank of colonel, but such brevet shall not confer additional pay or emoluments for services under this act.

Compensation in case of riot, &c. § 318. All officers, non-commissioned officers, musicians and privates of the national guard, while on duty or assembled therefor, pursuant to the order of the sheriff of any county, or the mayor of any city, in cases of riot, tumult, breach of peace, resistance to process, or whenever called upon in aid of the civil authorities, shall receive the compensation provided by the twenty-first section of the act entitled "An act to enforce the laws and preserve order," passed April fifteen, eighteen hundred and forty-five, and such compensation shall be Supervisors to pay. audited, allowed and paid by the supervisors of the county where such service is rendered, and shall be a portion of the county charges of said county, to be levied and raised as other county charges are levied and raised.

Acts repealed. § 319. Chapter three hundred and ninety-eight of the laws of eighteen hundred and fifty-four, except such parts of the same as are referred to in sections five and ten of this title, chapters two hundred and sixty-one and five hundred and thirty-six of the laws of eighteen hundred and fifty-five, chapters one hundred and twenty-nine and three hundred and forty-three of the laws of eighteen hundred and fifty-eight, and all other acts and parts of acts conflicting with this act, are hereby repealed ; but such repeal shall not affect any legal proceedings commenced under them.

§ 320. This act shall take effect immediately.

Chap. 478.

AN ACT for the better security of mechanics, laborers and others who perform labor or furnish materials for buildings and other improvements on land in the counties of Kings and Queens.

Passed April 24, 1862; three-fifths being present.

The People of the State of New York, represented in Senate and Assembly, do enact as follows:

SECTION 1. Any person who shall hereafter perform any labor or furnish any materials in building, altering or repairing any house, building or other improvement upon lands or appurtenances to such house or other building, by virtue of any contract with the owner thereof, or his agent, or with any contractor or sub-contractor, or any person permitted by the owner of such lands to build, repair, alter or improve as aforesaid, within the counties of Kings or Queens, shall, upon filing the notice prescribed in the third section of this act, have a lien for the value of such labor and materials upon such house, building and appurtenances, and upon the lot of land upon which the same stand, to the extent of the right, title and interest at that time existing, of such owner, in the manner and to the extent hereinafter provided ; but such owner shall not be obliged to pay for or on account of such house, other building or appurtenances, in consideration of all the liens authorized by this act to be created, any greater sum or amount than the price stipulated and agreed to be paid therefor in and by such contract, except in the case hereinafter provided. But if any such owner contractor, or sub-contractor, or agent for either of them shall pay any person any money on any contract for building or repairing any building by collusion, for the purpose of avoiding the provisions of this act, or in advance of the terms of any contract, and the amount still due the contractor or his assigns after such payment has been made, shall be insufficient to satisfy the demands made in conformity to the provisions of this act, the owner shall be liable to

[margin note: Lien for labor and materials.]

[margin note: Exception and proviso]

the amount that would have been due and owing to said contractor or his assignee at the time of the filing of the notice made in the third section of this act, in the same manner as if no such payment had been made. In cases in which the owner has made an agreement to sell and convey the premises to the contractor or other person, such owner shall be deemed to be the owner within the meaning and intent of this act, until a deed shall have been actually delivered so as to pass the fee simple of said promise.

How lien enforced. § 2. Any claimant, under or by virtue of any such lien or any such notice, may, after such labor has been performed or materials furnished, and after the filing of the notice mentioned in the third section of this act, enforce or bring to a close such lien, by a civil action in a court of record in the city or county in which such lands or any portion of them may be situated ; subject, however, to the following provisions and restrictions, namely :

Restrictions. First The manner and form of instituting and prosecuting any such action to judgment, including the personal service of process therein shall be the same as in other civil actions in the court in which the same may be brought except as herein otherwise provided.

Summons. Second. The summons shall be in the form and manner and as required by the second subdivision of section one hundred and twenty-nine of the civil Code of Procedure.

Complaint. Third. The claimant under said lien, who shall be the plaintiff in the action, shall annex to his complaint, or set forth therein, a copy of the notice mentioned in the third section of this act, and demand an accounting and settlement in such court of the amount due or claimed to be due for the labor performed or materials furnished as aforesaid, and such complaint shall contain such other matter and allegations as may be material and proper to establish the claim and cause of action of the claimant and plaintiff.

Pleadings. Fourth. The pleadings shall be in manner, form and substance the same as required by law in civil actions and in accordance with the rules and practice of the court in which the action may be brought, and such action shall be brought to an issue and to trial, put upon the calendar, tried, judgment had and entered, and appeal be **Appeal, &c.** taken therefrom, and costs taxed and recovered pursuant to such law, rules and practice in such civil actions in which the summons is, as mentioned in subdivision two of this section, and such action shall be governed and the judgment thereon enforced in the same manner as *Judgment.* upon issues joined and judgments rendered in all other such civil actions aforesaid.

§ 3. Within three months after the performance of *Notice of claim to be* such labor, or the furnishing of such materials, the con- *served* tractor, sub-contractor, laborer, person furnishing mate- *on county clerk.* rials, or other claimant, shall serve a notice in writing upon the county clerk of the county or counties aforesaid, in which the land and premises, or any portion thereof, may be situated, specifying the amount of the claim and the person against whom the claim is made, the name of the owner of the building, and the situation of the building by its street and number, if the number be known. The said county clerk shall enter the particulars of such notice in a book to be kept in his office, *Lien docket to be kept.* to be called "the lien docket," which shall be suitably ruled in columns, headed "claimants," "against whom *Contents.* claimed," "owners," "building," "amount claimed," "date of notice, hour and minute," and "what proceedings have been had." The names of owners and persons against whom the claim is made shall be inserted in alphabetic order. A fee of ten cents shall be paid to the county clerk on filing such lien. A copy of said *Notice to be served on* notice shall be served on said owner by delivering the *owner of building.* same when personally, or if he be out of this state by delivering the same to his agent personally ; and after such service such owner shall not be protected in any payments made by him to such contractor or other claimant in this section specified.

§ 4. In case the defendant or defendants shall not *Proceedings when no* answer the plaintiff's complaint within the time, and as *answer is served.* required by law, the plaintiff may apply to the court on proof of the service of the summons and complaint, and that no answer has been served, as required by the summons, for a writ of inquiry, and the same may be issued to the sheriff of the county in which the action may be brought to assess the amount of such claim, or the amount of such claim may be assessed by the court, and upon the return of the writ of inquiry or the assessment by the court, judgment shall be entered upon the same and execution shall issue for the enforcement of said claim, so adjudicated and established in the same manner as in analogous cases upon other judgments in such court.

§ 5. A transcript of every judgment rendered, headed "lien docket," shall be furnished by the clerk of the court to the successful party, who may file the same with the county clerk, whose duty it shall be to enter the name of the court and the amount of the judgment, or when the judgment is against the claimant, after the expiration of thirty days if no appeal has been taken the word discharged under the last head in his docket.

§ 6. Costs shall be allowed upon the same principles and by the same rules in the action as they are now allowed by statute in civil actions aforesaid, and shall form a part of the judgment except in cases where the amount of the recovery is less than fifty dollars, no more costs than damages shall be allowed to the party recovering such judgment.

§ 7. The lien may be discharged as follows :

1st. By filing a certificate of the claimant or his successor in interest, acknowledged or proved in the same manner as the satisfaction of a mortgage, stating that the lien is discharged.

2d. By the deposit with the clerk, if before suit, of a sum of money equal to the amount claimed, or, after suit, equal to such amount and the amount of costs incurred, which money shall thereupon be held subject to the lien.

3d. By an entry of the clerk made in the book of liens, after one year has elapsed since the filing of the claim, stating that no notice has been given to him of legal steps to enforce the lien.

4th. By an affidavit of service of a notice from the owner to the claimant, requiring him to commence an action for the enforcement of his lien, on or before a certain hour, a day specified in said notice, and the lapse of thirty days thereafter without any affidavit from the claimant being filed of the issuing or service of the summons and complaint in an action for an enforcement of such lien.

5th. By the satisfaction of the lien, or a final judgment in an action for the enforcement thereof.

§ 8. Every lien created under this act shall continue until the expiration of one year from the creation thereof, and until judgment rendered in any proceedings for the enforcement thereof.

§ 9. Whenever judgment shall be rendered in favor of the claimant in any proceeding commenced under this act, such judgment shall direct the sale of the interest of the owner in the land and premises upon which the lien exists, to the extent of the right of such owner at the time of the filing of the notice of lien in pursuance of this act, and that the proceeds of such sale shall be applied to the payment of the costs of the action and proceeding, and of the amount found to be due to such claimant or plaintiff, and that the residue of such proceeds be paid to the clerk of the court in which such action or proceeding may have been instituted, to abide the further order of the court. *Entries in judgment,*

§ 10. The owner may apply to the court for an order directing the clerk to pay him the surplus proceeds of such sale so paid to the said clerk, upon producing the certificate of the county clerk of the county or counties in which any portion of said land and premises may be situated that there are no liens docketed in his office against or affecting the said premises which have been filed under this act, and which remain unsatisfied. *Order for surplus.*

§ 11. If it shall appear that there are other liens on file with the clerk of either of said counties affecting the said premises, notice of such application shall be given to the claimants respectively filing the notices creating such liens, and thereupon the said court shall distribute such surplus proceeds among the parties entitled thereto, according to their respective rights and priorities, and may order a reference to take proofs in relation to such rights and priorities. *Notice of other liens to be served* *When surplus distributed.*

§ 12. In all sales under judgments to be rendered in these proceedings, the interest of the owner shall be sold subject to all prior liens existing thereon, unless the claimants under such liens shall be made parties to the proceedings, in which case the court shall settle the rights of the respective claimants, and the payment of the owner of any valid lien, or of any judgment recovered in pursuance of this act, shall enure to him as a payment to the amount thereof to the contractor or sub-contractor, as the case shall be. *Sales to be made subject to prior liens.*

§ 13. When the action or proceedings are commenced by a person having a claim against a contractor, with the owner, or against a sub-contractor with the contractor or other sub-contractor, such contractor or sub- *Who may be made parties.*

contractor may be made a defendant with such owner, and judgment may be rendered against the contractor or sub-contractor for the amount which shall be found owing by him, in addition to the judgment hereinbefore provided for against such owner, and the court may award costs against such of the parties as shall be just.

Certain acts repealed.

§ 14. Chapter three hundred and thirty-five of the Laws of eighteen hundred and fifty-three, entitled "An act for the better security of mechanics and others erecting buildings, performing work or furnishing materials, in the county of Kings," passed June eighth, eighteen hundred and fifty-three, and chapter two hundred and four of the Laws of eighteen hundred and fifty-eight, passed April fourteenth, eighteen hundred and fifty-eight so far as the same applies to the counties of Kings and Queens, aforesaid, are hereby repealed.

§ 15 This act shall take effect immediately.

Chap. 479.

AN ACT to amend an act entitled "An act in relation to the rates of wharfage, and to regulate piers, wharves, bulkheads and slips in the cities of New York and Brooklyn," passed April tenth, eighteen hundred and sixty.

Passed April 24, 1862; three-fifths being present.

The People of the State of New York, represented in Senate and Assembly, do enact as follows :

SECTION 1. The seventh section of the act entitled "An act in relation to the rates of wharfage, and to regulate piers, wharves, bulkheads and slips in the cities of New York and Brooklyn," passed April tenth, eighteen hundred and sixty, being chapter two hundred and fifty-four of the Session Laws of eighteen hundred and sixty, is hereby amended by striking out the words "two hundred and seventh," and inserting the words "two hundred and seventeenth."

§ 2. This act shall take effect immediately.

Chap. 480. •

AN ACT to authorize William Beard and others
to erect, construct, build and maintain sea walls
or break-water piers, docks, wharves, bulkheads,
piers and warehouses, and a basin for commercial uses, in front of their lands in the twelfth
ward of the city of Brooklyn.

Passed April 24, 1862.

Whereas, William Beard, Jeremiah P. Robinson and
others, owners of land adjoining the eas erly portion of
that part of Gowanus bay laid down as basin number
one on sheet twenty-four of the atlas of the harbor commissioners as altered, have, in their memorial to the
legislature set forth that they are constructing wharves
and excavating slips for the accommodation of shipping
on and adjoining their said lands, and are willing to
build sea walls and breakwater piers in front of their
said lands in a good and substantial manner. And,
whereas, as a protection from the westerly winds to vessels that may come within the basin to be formed by
said sea walls and breakwater piers, it is advisable to
have stores or other structures built on said sea walls
and breakwater piers : Now, therefore,

*The People of the State of New York, represented in
Senate and Assembly, do enact as follows :*

SECTION 1. It shall be lawful for William Beard and
others, owners of real estate fronting on the water, in
the twelfth ward of the city of Brooklyn, and their heirs
and assigns to erect, construct, build and maintain sea
walls or breakwater piers, docks, wharves, bulkheads,
piers and warehouses, and a basin for commercial purposes on the land under water in front of their lands
in the city of Brooklyn, in manner following, that is to
say : To erect a sea wall or breakwater pier, the outer
line of which shall commence at the bulkhead line as laid
down on the map record, in the office of the Secretary of
State, entitled sheet number twenty-four of the atlas of
the harbor commissioners, at a point where the said line

120

intersects the middle of Van Brunt street as extended ;
running thence southerly six hundred and sixty-six feet
to the outer sea wall line as recently established ; thence
to a point in a line which is parallel to and two hundred
feet easterly from the easterly side of Van Brunt street,
which point in said line is five hundred and seventy-five
feet from the bulkhead line as established ; thence from
the last mentioned point along the said line to the said
bulkhead line : on the southerly and easterly sides of the
said sea wall or breakwater pier, there shall be a street
of thirty feet in width ; and, also, to erect another sea
wall or breakwater pier to be three hundred feet in
width, the outer line of which shall commence at a point
in the outer sea wall line of basin number one of the
Gowanus bay basins, as recently established ; one hundred and seventy-five feet southerly from where the said
outer line intersects the middle line of Van Brunt street,
as extended ; running thence southerly and easterly
along the said outer sea wall line to a point at which the
said sea wall line would intersect the westerly side of
Otsego street, as extended ; the northerly end of the
said sea wall last mentioned to be parallel to and one
hundred and fifty feet from the southerly boundary of
the sea wall or breakwater pier first herein described,
and to have streets fifty feet in width on the outer and
inner edges, and at the end thereof ; and, also, to erect
another sea wall or breakwater pier, commencing at a
point where the said outer sea wall line intersects the
westerly side of Otsego street, as extended ; running
thence along the said westerly side of Otsego street to
the bulkhead line, as established , and to extend to a
line two hundred and fifty feet easterly from and parallel to the said westerly line of Otsego street, and from
the said outer sea wall line to the said bulkhead line ; on
the southerly and westerly sides of the sea wall or
breakwater pier last mentioned shall be streets fifty feet
in width.   All such sea walls and breakwater piers shall
be constructed with solid filling.

§ 2. The space within the sea walls or breakwater
piers and the bulkhead line, in the last section mentioned, shall consitute a basin, to be used for commercial
purposes, to be called the Erie basin.   It shall be lawful
for the said William Beard, and said other owners and
their assigns, to erect warehouses and other buildings

for commercial uses, on all such parts of the said sea walls or breakwater piers as are not to be used for streets, as hereinbefore provided for; and it shall be lawful for them to build bulkheads on the line by law established therefor within said basin, and such piers within said basin as may by them be deemed necessary, provided that the said piers be built on piles and blocks at the ends in a substantial manner, and to charge and receive reasonable storage, dockage and wharfage from all persons using the said sea walls or breakwater piers, and the said warehouses, piers, docks or the basin that may be constructed pursuant to this act.

§ 3. This act shall take effect immediately.

. Chap. 481.

AN ACT to amend an act entitled "An act to establish bulkhead and pier lines for the port of New York," passed April seventeenth, eighteen hundred and fifty-seven.

Passed April 24, 1862; three-fifths being present.

Whereas, Owners of land adjoining basin number one of the Gowanus Bay basins, as established by law, are constructing wharves and excavating slips for the accommodation of shipping of a large class; and

Whereas, It appears that on the exterior side of the sea wall or break-water pier of said basin, as established by law, there is not sufficient depth of water to give access to the said basin for the class of vessels which it is intended to accommodate, and which the increasing commerce of the port of New York requires: Now, therefore,

The People of the State of New York, represented in Senate and Assembly, do enact as follows :

SECTION 1. The outer sea wall line of basin number one of Gowanus Bay basin shall be altered as follows: The said outer line shall begin at the point of its commencement, as now established, namely : At a point in the line of the westerly side of Ferris street, as extended southerly five hundred and fifty-four feet from the westerly side of Coast Wharf; running thence in a straight line to a point in the middle line of Van Brunt street, as extended southerly eleven hundred and fifty-five feet from the southerly side of Reid street; running thence in a straight line to a point one hundred feet westerly-from the sea wall line, as heretofore established, which point is ten hundred and sixty-one feet distant from and perpendicular to the westerly side of Otsego street, as extended southerly at a point distant seventeen hundred and nineteen feet from the southerly side of Cuba street; and running thence six hundred and sixteen feet six inches in an arc, which arc has a radius of six hundred and ninety-six feet, the centre of said arc being at a point four hundred and fifty-three feet distant from and perpendicular to the westerly side of Otsego street, as extended southerly at a point fourteen hundred and eighty-seven feet distant from the southerly side of Cuba street to a point in the said sea wall line, as now established. The new line hereby established being marked in red ink on a map entitled "sheet number twenty-four of the atlas of the harbor commissioners, as altered to show the extension of the sea wall of Gowanus Bay basin number one, drawn by A. Kurth, city surveyor, thirteenth of March, eighteen hundred and sixty-two," which shall be verified by the signature of the Secretary of State and filed in his office, there to remain of record.

§ 2. This act shall take effect immediately.

Chap. 482.

AN ACT to provide for the collection of demands against ships and vessels.

Passed April 24, 1862; three-fifths being present.

The People of the State of New York, represented in Senate and Assembly, do enact as follows:

When debt a lien on vessel, tackle, &c.

SECTION 1. Whenever a debt, amounting to fifty dollars or upwards, as to a sea going or ocean bound vessel, or amounting to fifteen dollars or upwards, as to any

other vessel, shall be contracted by the master, owner,
charterer, builder or consignee, of any ship or vessel or
the agent of either of them within this state, for either
of the following purposes:

1st On account of work done or materials or other
articles furnished in this state for or towards the building. repairing, fitting, furnishing or equipping such ship
or vessel.

2d. For such provisions and stores furnished within
this state as may be fit and proper for the use of such
vessel, at the time when the same were furnished.

3d. On account of the wharfage and expenses of
keeping such vessel in port, including the expense incurred in employing persons to watch her.

4th. On account of loading or unloading, or for advances made for the purpose of procuring necessaries
for such ship or vessel, or for the insurance thereof.

5th. Or whenever a debt amounting to twenty-five
dollars or upwards shall be contracted as aforesaid,
within this state, on account of the towing or piloting
such vessel, or on account of the insurance or premiums
of insurance of or on such vessel, or her freight. Such
debt shall be a lien upon such vessel, her tackle, apparel
and furniture, and shall be preferred to all other liens
thereon, except mariners' wages.

§ 2. Such debt shall cease to be a lien at the expiration of six months after the said debt was contracted,
unless at the time when said six months shall expire
such ship or vessel shall be absent from the port at
which such debt was contracted, in which case the said
lien shall continue, until the expiration of ten days
after such ship or vessel shall next return to said port;
and, in all cases, such debt shall cease to be a lien upon
such ship or vessel, whenever such ship or vessel shall
leave the port at which such debt was contracted, unless
the person having such lien shall, within twelve days
after such departure, cause to be drawn up and filed
specifications of such lien, which may consist either of
a bill of particulars of the demand or a copy of any
written contract under which the work may be done,
with a statement of the amount claimed to be due from
such vessel, the correctness of which shall be sworn to
by such person, his legal representative, agent or assigns.

Specifica-
tion of lien
to be filed
in county
clerk's of-
fice.

§ 3. Such specification shall be filed in the office of the clerk of the county in which such debt shall have been contracted, except that when such debt shall have been contracted in either of the counties of New York, Kings or Queens such specification shall be filed in the office of the clerk of the city and county of New York.

When war-
rant may
issue to en-
force lien.

§ 4. Any person having a lien upon any ship or vessel for any debt contracted for any of the purposes hereinbefore specified, may make application to any officer authorized by law to perform the duties of a justice of the supreme court at chambers in the county within which such ship or vessel shall then be, for a warrant to enforce the said lien, and to collect the amount thereof.

Application
for warrant.

§ 5. Such application shall be in writing, and shall exhibit and specify:

1st. By whom and when such debt was contracted, and for what ship or vessel; 2d. The items composing such debt; 3d. The amount claimed, and that the same is justly due to the person in whose behalf the application is made, over and above all payments and just deductions; 4th. Any assignment or transfer of such debt, if any such has taken place since the same was contracted; 5th. When and where the specification of such debt was filed. Such application shall be verified by the affidavit of the creditor, or of the person making the application, or of his or their agent in that behalf.

Warrant.

§ 6. The officer to whom such application shall be made shall thereupon issue a warrant to the sheriff specifying the amount of the claim, and the names of the persons making such claim, and commanding him to attach, seize and safely keep said ship or vessel, her tackle, apparel and furniture, to satisfy such claim, if established, to be a lien upon such vessel, according to law, and to make return of his proceedings under such warrant to the officer who issued the same within ten days after such seizure. Such sheriff shall also, in his return, state whether he has seized said ship or vessel by virtue of any other warrant or warrants, and specify in whose behalf, and for what sums such other warrants have been issued, respectively, and the time of his reception thereof.

Underta-
king.

§ 7. Such warrant shall not be issued unless the person applying therefor shall deliver to the officer to whom the application is made to be filed by him, an undertaking to the effect that if the said applicant do not within the time hereafter specified in section eleventh of this act prosecute any bond which may be given upon the discharge of such warrant, or if the said applicant in any action brought upon such bond be finally adjudged not to have been entitled to such warrant, the parties giving such undertaking will pay all costs that may be awarded against such applicant, not exceeding the sum specified in the undertaking, which shall be at least one hundred dollars, and any damages that may be sustained by reason of the seizure of such vessel under such warrant, not exceeding the sum of fifty dollars. The undertaking required by this section shall be executed by the applicants or one of them, or their agent, and at least one surety, who shall be a resident and householder within this state. Such undertaking shall be approved by the said officer.

§ 8. Any sheriff to whom such warrant shall have been directed and delivered shall forthwith execute the same, and shall keep the said vessel, her tackle, apparel and furniture to be disposed of as is herein directed. *Duty of sheriff.*

§ 9. The person applying for such warrant shall, within three days after the issuing thereof, cause a notice to be published once in each week for four successive weeks in some newspaper published in the county in which such vessel may then be, or, if no newspaper be so published in such county, then in the nearest county in which a newspaper shall be so published, setting forth that such warrant has been issued, the amount of the claim specified therein, the day when such warrant was issued, and that such vessel will be sold for the payment of the claims against her, unless the master, owner or consignee thereof, or some person interested therein, appear and discharge such warrant according to law, within thirty days from the first publication of such notice *Notice of issuing warrant to be published.*

§ 10. The owner, consignee, agent or commander of any vessel seized by virtue of any warrant issued pursuant to the provisions of this title, or any person interested in such vessel, may at any time before such vessel be sold, as hereinafter provided, apply in person or by attorney to the officer who issued such warrant, on one day's notice, to the said attaching creditor or his attorney, for an order to discharge the same. Said no- *Application to discharge warrant.*

tice shall specify the names, places of residence and places of business of the proposed sureties.

Bond. § 11. Such person shall execute and deliver to the officer to whom such application is made a bond to the creditors prosecuting such warrant in a penalty at least double the amount specified in the warrant, conditioned that the obligors therein will pay the amount of any and all claims and demands which shall be established to be due to the person or persons in whose behalf such warrant was issued, and to have been a subsisting lien upon such vessel pursuant to the provisions of this act at the time of exhibiting the same. In all such cases the attaching **Sureties.** creditors shall have the right to examine the sureties as to their sufficiency, at such time and place as shall be fixed by the judge to whom application is made.

When warrant to be discharged. § 12. Upon such bond being executed and delivered to such attaching creditor or his attorney, and the taxed fees of the sheriff paid, the said officer shall thereupon grant his order discharging the warrant that may have been issued by him in favor of such creditor, and no further proceedings against the said vessel so seized shall be had under the provisions of this title founded upon any demand secured by such bond. Such bond may be prosecuted in any court having jurisdiction thereof at any time within three months after such delivery, but not afterwards.

Action in bond. § 13. If in any action brought upon such bond it be found that any sum be due the plaintiff, which was a subsisting lien upon such ship or vessel at the time of exhibiting the same as herein provided, judgment shall be rendered that the plaintiff recover the same with the costs and allowances of the action and the costs of the attachment, as herein provided, and he have execution therefor. But if in such action it be found that no subsisting lien existed in favor of the plaintiff at the time of exhibiting his claim, then judgment shall be rendered against such plaintiff for the costs and allowances of such action and the costs of the attachment as herein provided, including the amount of the sheriff's fees due and paid on releasing such vessel from the warrant.

Costs on attachment. § 14. The costs of the attachment shall be in addition to the disbursements; for filing specification of a lien, two dollars; for exhibiting a lien and procuring a warrant therefor, when the amount of the lien is under fifty dollars, ten dollars; when the amount of the lien exceeds fifty dollars and is under two hundred and fifty dollars, twenty dollars; when the amount of the lien exceeds two hundred and fifty dollars and is under one thousand dollars, thirty dollars; and when the amount of the lien exceeds one thousand dollars, fifty dollars; for attending to the discharge of any warrant upon a bond, ten dollars. The sheriff shall be entitled Sheriff's fees in proceedings under this act to the following fees and expenses: For serving warrant, one dollar; for returning the same, one dollar; for the expenses of keeping such vessel in custody, the necessary sums paid by him therefor, not exceeding, however, the sum of two dollars and fifty cents for each day the vessel shall have been held by him in custody. Such sheriff shall not be entitled to receive any other or greater sums than those above specified, for any service rendered by him in any proceeding under this act, nor shall he be allowed expenses of custody upon more than one warrant at the same time. All costs, disbursements and fees shall be verified by affidavit and adjusted by the officer who issued the warrant.

§ 15. If the creditor who shall have exhibited his When property to be claim shall not have been satisfied, and if such vessel sold. shall not have been discharged within thirty days after the first publication of the notice required by the ninth section of this act, upon due proof of the publication of such notice, the officer who issued such warrant shall issue his order to the sheriff holding the vessel under such warrant, directing such sheriff to proceed and sell the vessel so seized by him, her tackle, apparel and furniture, and such order shall state the amount deemed necessary to be raised to satisfy all unsatisfied liens which have been exhibited against such vessel. Upon proof of personal service of the notice required by the ninth section of this act, and of notice of the application for sale upon the owners of the vessel, and upon all other unpaid creditors who have filed specifications of their liens pursuant to the provisions of this act, such order of sale may in the discretion of the officer be issued at any time after the seizure of such vessel.

§ 16. Within ten days after the service of such order Notice of the sheriff shall, unless such order be sooner vacated, sale. proceed to sell the vessel so seized by him, her tackle, apparel and furniture, upon the same notice, in the same manner, and in all respects subject to the provisions of law in case of the sale of personal property upon execution.

Proceeds of sale. § 17. The sheriff shall return to the officer granting such order his proceedings under the same, and the proceeds of such sale, after deducting his fees and expenses in seizing, preserving, watching and selling such vessel when duly taxed, shall be retained by such sheriff in his hands, to be distributed and paid as hereinafter directed.

Notice of distribution of proceeds. § 18. At the time of issuing any such order of sale, the officer granting the same shall order a notice to be published in the same newspaper in which the notice of seizure is required hereby to be published once a week for three weeks, requiring all persons who have any liens upon such vessel by virtue of the provisions of this act, and the master, owner, agent or consignee and all other persons interested in such vessel to appear before him at a day to be therein specified, not less than thirty and not more than forty days from the first publication of such notice, to attend a distribution of the proceeds arising from the sale of such vessel, her tackle, apparel and furniture. The officer may in his discretion direct such distribution to be made before a referee to be appointed by him on notice.

Liens against proceeds of sale. § 19. Such proceeds of any sale under the provisions of this act shall, until distributed as herein provided, stand in place of the vessel, and until such distribution any person entitled under this act to enforce a lien against such vessel may enforce the same against such proceeds, in the same manner as is herein provided for enforcing a lien against the vessel herself, and with like effect. Upon the distribution of such proceeds, the various claims exhibited, which are found to be subsisting liens upon such vessel, or the proceeds thereof according to the provisions of this act, shall, with their respective costs, expenses and allowances, be ordered to be paid out of such proceeds in the order of the delivery **Costs of distribution** of the respective warrants to the sheriff. The costs, disbursements and allowances upon such distribution shall be the same as those allowed in civil actions upon a trial.

Who may contest claims. § 20. At any time before the final distribution of such proceeds the master, owner, agent, consignee or any

person having any interest whatever in such proceeds
may contest any claim which shall have been exhibited
against such vessel or the proceeds thereof.

§ 21. In case of such contest the party making objec- Statement to be filed with officer,
tion to any such claims shall file with the officer a written
statement or answer designating the claims he desires
to contest, and controverting such of the allegations of
the petition exhibiting such claim as he may be able to
controvert, and likewise setting up any other matter of
defence thereto. Such statement or answer shall be
verified by the party presenting the same, to the effect
that the same is true to the best of his knowledge or
belief. A copy thereof shall within five days from the Copy served
filing thereof be served upon the person whose claim it
is intended to contest or his attorney, otherwise it shall
be deemed abandoned.

§ 22. If such answer do not contain matter of defence When state-ment strick-en out.
to such claim, it may be stricken out on motion of any
person who has exhibited any claim against said vessel
or the proceeds thereof.

§ 23. The issue between such contestants shall be tried Trial of issues thereon.
before a judge in like manner as other issues which are
authorized by law to be tried before a judge, and at
some early day to be fixed by the officer who issued the
warrant, or the same may be referred by such officer to
some competent referee, to hear and determine the same
in like manner as in civil actions.

§ 24. Either party may have the same right to except Appeal.
to and appeal from the report of such referee or the decision of such judge as in civil actions, and on such
appeal the finding of such referee or court, both of law
and of fact, shall be examined and may be reversed or
modified, or a new trial may be ordered. Judgment for
costs shall be rendered in favor of the successful party
as in personal actions, and the successful party shall be
entitled to recover the costs and allowances provided for
in the Code of Procedure in civil actions.

§ 25. When the amount of all the claims which shall Distribu-tion regu-lated.
have been exhibited, and which are found to have been
subsisting liens upon such vessel at the time of exhibiting the same, shall have been finally determined, the
said proceeds shall be distributed by the court as provided in section eighteen of this act, on motion of any
person interested therein or otherwise. Any uncon-

tested claims entitled by this act to be paid out of such proceeds prior to the claims which may be contested, shall, on motion of the parties interested, be paid in the order of their respective priorities, notwithstanding such contest with costs ; and if at any time it be made to appear that after payment of all prior uncontested claims and their respective costs, and after deducting an amount sufficient to pay all prior contested claims and costs, there will remain a surplus of such proceeds applicable to the payment of any subsequent uncontested claims. Such claims may, on notice to the owner or agent of the vessel, or other parties interested, be ordered to be paid out of such surplus, with costs.

Proceeds subject to direction of court. § 26. The proceeds of any sale of any vessel under the provisions of this act shall be subject to the direction of the court, and may at any time be invested by such court, according to the practice thereof.

Lien may be assigned § 27. Whenever any person having a lien against any ship or vessel shall have filed specifications thereof as provided by this act, such lien may be assigned and transferred by an instrument in writing, duly acknowledged and filed in the same place where the original specifications of such liens were filed ; such assignment shall describe the debt intended to be transferred, and specify the date of the filing the specification thereof, and shall state to whom it is intended to transfer it. Such transfer, and the name of the person or persons to whom such lien has been transferred, shall be noted by the clerk opposite the original entry of such lien, and after the filing of such assignment and transfer, but not otherwise, the person to whom such lien has been transferred shall be entitled to enforce the same in like manner as the person who transferred the same could have done.

Further provisions as to discharge of lien, § 28. Whenever any specifications of any lien upon any ship or vessel shall have been filed pursuant to the provisions of this act, and no warrant has been issued to enforce the same, any person owning or interested in such ship or vessel may apply to any justice of the supreme court for leave to discharge such lien upon giving bonds therefor. Such application shall be. in writing, and shall set forth the amount of the lien claimed to be subsisting and the grounds of defence thereto ; it shall also set forth the names of two persons, proposed sureties for such lien, with their respective residences and places of business, which sureties shall, if leave to bond be granted, justify on notice to the person having the lien before the officer granting such leave. Upon presenting such application, with proof that a copy thereof, with at least five days' notice of the time and place of presenting the same, has been served upon the person having such lien, such officer may, if no just cause be shown in opposition thereto, grant leave to bond the said claim.

§ 29. When such leave be given, and upon the execu- *Discharge of lien.* tion and delivery to the person having such lien of the bond prescribed in section seven of this act approved by the officer, such officer shall direct that the said lien be marked by the clerk as discharged, and the same shall cease to be a lien upon such vessel.

§ 30. If after payment of all claims which have been *Distribution of surplus.* exhibited and been found to be payable out of the proceeds of the sale of any vessel under this act, a surplus thereof remain, such surplus may be distributed by the court to the persons entitled thereto, but such distribution shall not be made until a notice shall have been published specifying the amount of such surplus, proceeds, the names of the persons applying therefor, together with the name of the ship or vessel from which the same arose, and the date of the sale of such vessel. Such notice shall be published in the same manner and for the same time as prescribed in section nine of this act.

§ 31. Whenever any proceeding under this act shall *Absence or inability of judge.* have been commenced before any judge, the same and every part thereof may, in the absence or inability of such judge, or by his order to that effect, be continued before any other judge of the same court.

§ 32. Every sheriff to whom a warrant may have been *Sheriff may be compelled to return warrant.* delivered, may be compelled by any officer having jurisdiction over the proceedings thereon, to return such warrant, with his proceedings thereon, and to pay over moneys in his hands, and to take any steps necessary for the safety of said vessel pursuant to any order for that purpose, by an order of such officer, and by process of attachment for disobedience thereof, on the application of any person interested therein.

Lien on vessel causing damage.

§ 33. Whenever any ship or vessel shall have been run down or afoul of by any other ship or vessel, through the negligence or willful misconduct of those navigating such other ship or vessel, and shall thereby have sustained damage to the extent of fifty dollars, the owner of the ship or vessel so sustaining damage shall have a lien upon the ship or vessel causing such damage in manner aforesaid, her tackle, apparel and furniture, to the extent of such damage. The master, owner, agent or consignee of the ship or vessel so receiving damage, may enforce the said lien in like manner and with the same effect as in case of other liens created by this act, but such proceedings must be commenced within ten days after the damage shall be done, otherwise such damage shall cease to be a lien upon such ship or vessel.

Repeal.

§ 34. Title eight, article one of chapter eight, of part third of the Revised Statutes, entitled of proceedings for the collection of demands against ships and vessels, and all acts amendatory thereof, and also an act entitled an act to extend the provisions of the law relative to proceedings for the collection of demands against ships and vessels, passed eighteen hundred and thirty-one, chapter three hundred and eighteen, are hereby repealed.

§ 35. This act shall not apply to debts contracted before this act shall take effect.

Chap. 483.

AN ACT to prevent fraud in the opening and laying out of streets and avenues in the city of New York.

Passed April 24, 1862; three-fifths being present.

The People [of the State of New York, represented in Senate and Assembly, do enact as follows:

Fees of commissioners.

SECTION 1. The compensation to the commissioners in any proceeding hereafter to be commenced, lot opening or altering any street or avenue in the city of New York, north of Fourteenth street, shall not exceed in the aggregate exclusive of necessary disbursements

hereinafter mentioned, the sum of thirty cents a foot
for the lineal extent of the street or avenue, or the
portion thereof so to be opened or altered. The said Limit of appoint-ment.
commissioners shall complete said proceeding on their
part, within four months from the time of their appointment, unless further time shall be allowed by the supreme
court.

§ 2. It shall not be necessary for the said commis- Surveys.
sioners to cause any survey to be made of the lands or
any part thereof, to be affected by such proceeding,
unless such survey shall be specially directed by said
court. For the purpose of ascertaining and defining
the extent and boundaries of the respective tracts or
parcels of land to be taken or to be assessed in such
proceeding, it shall be sufficient for said commissioners,
and they are hereby authorized to take or procure such
copies as they may require, of any maps or profiles
deposited or filed in any of the public offices of said
city, showing the boundaries or profiles of said lands or
any part thereof. From the copies thus procured and
such other information as the said commissioners shall
possess or obtain, they shall cause diagrams to be pre- Diagrams to be prepared
pared which shall distinctly indicate by separate num-
bers, the names of the owners of or claimants to the
respective tracts or parcels of land to be taken or
assessed in such proceeding, and which shall also specify
in figures, with sufficient accuracy, the dimensions,
metes and bounds of each of said tracts or parcels.
Whenever the said commissioners shall be unable to
ascertain with sufficient certainty the name of any
owner of any parcel of said lands, they shall indicate
such parcel upon the diagram embracing it and in their
report as belonging to unknown owners.

§ 3. The said commissioners shall deposit with the Abstract of estimate, &c., to be deposited with street commis-sioner.
street commissioners of said city an abstract of their
estimate and assessment at least forty days before their
report shall be presented to said court for confirmation,
which abstract shall be accompanied by copies of the said
diagrams and which shall refer to the numbers thereby
indicated, and state the several sums respectively estimated for or assessed upon each of said parcels, with
the name or names, claimant or claimants, so far as ascertained by said commissioners. They shall also pub- Publication of notice.
lish a notice for thirty days in two of the daily news-

LAWS OF NEW YORK.

papers pu'lished in said city, stating their intention to present their report for confirmation to the said court at a time and place to be specified in said notice, and that all persons interested in such proceeding or in any of the lands affected thereby having objections thereto shall file the same, in writing, with said commissioners, within thirty days after the first publication of said notice, and that the said commissioners will hear such objections within the ten week days next after the expiration of said thirty days.

Report to be made to the court. § 4. After considering said objections, if any, and making any correction or alteration of their estimate or assessment which said commissioners, or any two of them, shall find to be just and proper, the said commissioners, or any two of them, shall present their report to the court at the time and place specified in said notice. The said report shall consist of said diagrams, duly corrected, when necessary, with a tabular abstract of said estimate and assessment, with any corrections or alterations thereof by said commissioners, and shall **Of what the report shall consist.** refer to the numbers of the tracts and parcels indicated by said diagrams and state the several sums respectively estimated for or assessed upon each of said tracts or parcels, with the name or names of the owners or claimants of each, if ascertained by said commissioners. It shall not be necessary in said report to describe any of the said tracts or parcels by metes and bounds, but only by reference to the said diagrams. Duplicate copies of **Report to be filed.** said report, signed by the said commissioners, or any two of them, shall be filed by the counsel to the corporation of said city, one in the office of the street commissioner thereof and the other in the office of the clerk of the city and county of New York.

Limit of expenditures. § 5. No costs, charges or expenses of any description shall be allowed in such proceeding or charged on any lands affected thereby, except the compensation of the commissioners as above limited, and their necessary disbursements for clerical services in copying, comparing or correcting said maps or profiles, extracting boundary lines from title papers preparing the said diagrams and abstracts, and keeping proper minutes of the said proceeding; and also for surveys and maps thereof, when specially directed by said court; and also for room rent actually paid, but in no case to exceed one dollar per day ; for advertising, printing or posting any notices required by law, and for any other necessary incidental expense not exceeding one hundred dollars.

§ 6. A bill of said costs, charges and expenses shall be filed with the street commissioners of said city at least ten days before the same shall be presented for taxation, and a notice of at least ten days shall be published in two of the daily newspapers published in the said city, of the time and place of taxing said costs, charges and expenses, which shall be thereupon taxed by a judge of the supreme court, or a referee under his special order and before the report of said commissioners shall be presented for confirmation. *Bill of costs to be filed.* *Notice to be published.*

§ 7. The counsel to the corporation of said city, shall perform without charge, beyond the salary now paid that officer, all the legal services necessary to enable the said commissioners to conduct and complete their duties in said proceeding, and shall prepare all notices and orders of court thereto pertaining. *Duty of corporation counsel.*

§ 8. Any notice now required or hereafter to be required by law to be published in any proceeding for the opening, excluding, widening or altering any street, avenue, public place, square or park in said city, shall hereafter be published in not more than two daily newspapers to be selected from those designated at the time by the common council of said city for publishing its corporated ordinances, and if from any cause the publication of such notice shall not be completed, the same may be published in any two other daily newspapers printed in said city, and whenever hand-bills now are or hereafter may be required by law to be posted in any such proceeding, they shall be posted and affixed with paste or other adhesive substance in three conspicuous places upon or near the lands to be taken in such proceeding, and proof of such posting shall be sufficient evidence without further proof of said notice having remained posted during the whole of the period required by law. *Publications, how made.*

§ 9. Whenever in any proceeding to take lands for extending, altering or opening any street, avenue, public place, square or park in said city, the rights or interests of the mayor, aldermen and commonalty of the said city shall in the judgment of the comptroller thereof be injuriously affected, he may in his discretion, employ *When comptroller may employ counsel.*

122

counsel to protect the rights or interests of the said mayor, aldermen and commonalty of the city of New York in said proceeding, against any commissioners or other authority prosecuting the same, if said rights and interests in his judgment, cannot be fully protected by the counsel to the corporation.

§ 10. Such parts of the act of the ninth of April in the year one thousand eight hundred and thirteen, and of the act of the twentieth of April, in the year one thousand eight hundred and thirty-nine, or of any other act inconsistent with the provisions of the present act, are hereby repealed.

*Acts re-
pealed.*

Chap. 484.

AN ACT in relation to the courts in the city and county of New York.

Passed April 24, 1862 ; three-fifths being present.

The People of the State of New York, represented in Senate and Assembly, do enact as follows:

*Prohibition
as to attor-
neys.*

SECTION 1. No person shall ask, demand or receive, directly or indirectly, any compensation for appearing as attorney in any of the courts in the city and county of New York, nor be permitted to make it a business to practice as an attorney in any of said courts unless he shall have been regularly admitted by the supreme court of the State of New York, to practice as an attorney and counsellor in all the courts of this state.

*Punish-
ment for
violations
of this act.*

§ 2. Any person violating the provisions of this act, shall be guilty of a misdemeanor, punishable by not less than one month's imprisonment in the county prison, or by a fine of not less than one hundred dollars, or more than two hundred and fifty dollars, or by both such fine and imprisonment ; and any judge of said courts, who knowingly allows or permits any person not regularly admitted to practice in the said courts, shall be guilty of a misdemeanor, punishable in the same manner as herein provided ; but this act shall not prohibit any person from appearing in his own behalf, in any of said courts.

§ 3. The rules and regulations of the supreme court of this state, shall apply to the marine and district courts, as far as the same can be made applicable, and such changes; alterations and additions as will be from time to time made, in and to said rules and regulations by said supreme court, shall affect the said marine and district courts, in the same manner as the said supreme court is affected by them; and such alterations, changes and additions shall be as binding upon said courts as they will be upon the said supreme court. *Rules, &c., of supreme court applied to marine and district courts.*

§ 4. The constables of the city of New York, elected or appointed after the passage of this act, shall be denominated the marshals of the city of New York, and they shall have the same power and perform all the duties that have heretofore appertained to the office; and each of said marshals shall be a resident of the district wherein the court for, or to which he is or shall be appointed is located. *Constables to act as marshals.*

§ 5. Any marshal hereafter appointed or elected shall not be permitted to enter upon the duties of the office until he shall execute a bond, with two sufficient sureties, who shall be residents of and shall own real estate in the county of New York to the amount of double the penalty of the bond, to the mayor, aldermen and commonalty of the city of New York, in the penal sum of one thousand dollars, jointly and severally, to answer the said mayor, aldermen and commonalty of the city of New York, and any parties that may complain, conditioned that such marshal shall well and faithfully execute the duties of said office of marshal without fraud, deceit or oppression, such sureties to justify in double the amount of such bond. The said bond shall be delivered to the mayor of said city for approval, who shall judge of and determine the competency of the sureties; and should he approve of the same, he shall note his approval thereon, and shall cause such bond to be filed in the office of the clerk of the court of common pleas in and for the city and county of New York, within ten days after the same shall have been approved of by him, and he shall either approve of or reject such bond within five days after the same shall have been presented to him for that purpose. *Bond.* *Approval of sureties.* *Bond to be filed.*

§ 6. Any person who shall be aggrieved by any official misconduct on the part of any marshal, and who may *Prosecution of bond.*

desire to prosecute his official bond, and who shall have first obtained judgment against such marshal for official misconduct, may move before a justice of the court of common pleas in and for the city and county of New York, at the chambers thereof, after giving such marshal and his sureties eight days' previous notice of intention so to do by personal service of said notice on them, stating when such motion will be made, and of the papers to be used on such motion, for leave to prosecute such official bond in his own name, and such leave shall be granted upon it appearing satisfactorily to such court :

1st. That a judgment has been obtained in his favor against such marshal for official misconduct, specifying the time when and the court whereby such judgment was rendered, and the amount thereof.

2d. That a transcript of such judgment has been filed in the office of the clerk of the city and county of New York, specifying the time when such transcript was filed and execution issued, and that said sheriff has returned said execution wholly or partly unsatisfied, after having demanded payment thereof of such marshal ; and his neglect or refusal to pay the same, and if any payments have been made on such execution, specifying the amount thereof, but where such marshal shall have died or removed from the county, a demand for the payment of the amount of such execution shall not be necessary.

3d. That such judgment is wholly or partly unpaid, specifying the amount uncollected or unpaid, and that the sureties have been served with the notice and papers hereinbefore mentioned.

Where a bond may be prosecuted. § 7. Such justice may order such bond to be prosecuted in any of the district courts in the city of New York or in the marine court of the city of New York, and either of said courts shall have jurisdiction in actions brought on such bond, upon such leave being granted, and the said justice upon said motion may award the aggrieved party his reasonable costs on such motion, not exceeding the sum of ten dollars, which shall be included in the judgment obtained upon such bond.

Transcript of judgment § 8. Whenever any judgment shall be rendered against any marshal or his sureties in the marine court of the city of New York, or in any of the district courts of said city, a transcript thereof shall be filed in the office of the clerk of the court of common pleas in and for the city and county of New York, and from the filing of such transcript such judgment shall be deemed to be a judgment of such court, and shall be enforced in the same manner as other judgments of said court. And no execution on such judgment shall issue to any other officer than the sheriff of the city and county of New York, and all such executions must be made returnable to the clerk of said court.

§ 9. The clerk of said court shall make a memorandum on the official bond of every marshal, upon the filing of every transcript of a judgment obtained against him and his sureties, and of the time when and the court whereby such judgment was rendered, and the amount thereof, and shall be entitled to a fee of fifty cents therefor, which the court rendering judgment shall have power to include in such judgment, together with whatever other disbursements are or may be necessarily incurred in said action, and the said bond shall be cancelled to the amount of such judgment

§ 10. Whenever any action shall be commenced against the sureties of any marshal, and such sureties shall pay the amount for which such suit is brought, and the costs and disbursements incurred therein, or any part thereof, the party or parties so paying shall be entitled to have such sum so paid, credited upon such bond, upon presenting the certificate of the plaintiff or his attorney in such action, acknowledging such payments to such clerk aforesaid, and upon such clerk endorsing such payment on such bond, it shall be cancelled to the amount so paid.

§ 11. Whenever any complaint shall be made by any person against any marshal aforesaid, for official or disorderly misconduct, or for fraudulent practices in and about said courts, to any of the justices of the court of common pleas aforesaid, or to the mayor of the city of New York, and it shall satisfactorily appear to such justice, or to said mayor, after hearing said marshal in regard to such complaint, that such marshal is guilty of the offence charged by such person against him, such marshal may be suspended by such justice or mayor from performing the duties of the office for such time as the said mayor or justice shall direct; or such mayor

Margin notes:
To whom execution to issue.
Entry to be made on bond.
Amount collected to be credited on bond.
When marshal may be suspended or removed.

or justice, in their discretion, may remove such marshal, and forbid and prevent him from further performing any'duties as marshal aforesaid, and upon such removal being made some fit and proper person shall be elected or appointed in his place.

When bond to be renewed.

§ 12. Whenever judgment shall be rendered against the official bond of any marshal sufficient to cancel the same, the clerk of the court of common pleas aforesaid shall report to the mayor of the city of New York that fact, and it shall be the duty of the mayor of the city of New York to compel such marshal to renew his official bond, and should such marshal neglect or refuse to renew such bond within ten days after being notified so to do, he shall be removed by the mayor aforesaid, or suspended from performing the duties of the office until such time as he shall renew the same, and such bond shall be renewed in the same manner as often as the same shall be canceled.

When appointment or election of marshal waived.

§ 13. Every marshal elected or appointed under the provisions of this act, shall, within thirty days after his appointment, enter into a bond in the manner aforesaid, or he shall be deemed to have waived his appointment or election as such marshal, and some other suitable and proper person shall be appointed in his place and stead to discharge the duties appertaining to such office of marshal.

Who to serve process.

§ 14. Every summons, attachment or warrant issued by any of said district courts must be served by a marshal of the city of New York, except that the justice of the court wherein the action is commenced, upon the application of the plaintiff or his attorney in such action, may designate some competent person to serve the summons and complaint in such action.

Fees of marshal.

§ 15. The marshals aforesaid shall be entitled to the following fees: For serving every summons or warrant on one defendant, sixty-three cents; for every additional defendant served, thirty-seven cents; for going with the plaintiff or defendant to procure security where security shall be ordered by the court, one dollar; for taking the defendant into custody on a warrant, execution or commitment, seventy-five cents; for serving every attachment, one dollar; for serving every subpœna, twenty-five cents; for every juryman served, thirteen cents; for drawing any bond, undertaking or other paper to be used in any action, one dollar.

§ 16. Any justice of any of the district courts in the city of New York may, upon motion made before him, open and set aside any default made in any action tried before or by him, and may award such costs, not exceeding ten dollars, as a condition for opening such default against the party in default, as in his discretion shall be just and proper. He may, likewise, as a condition of opening such default, order such party, in default, to give an undertaking with sufficient sureties, to the effect that such defendant will not sell, assign or transfer any of his property with intent to hinder, delay or defraud the plaintiff in the collection of his claim or demand, if he shall prevail on the trial of such action, and that he or his sureties will pay the amount of any judgment recovered against such defendant in such action. *When default may be opened.* *Terms may be imposed.*

§ 17. Sections two hundred and six to two hundred and seventeen inclusive, of the Code of Procedure, shall apply to the marine court of the city of New York and to the district courts in the city of New York, except that in actions commenced in the district courts all papers or other processes in such actions shall be served by one of the marshals of the city of New York, and except that the marine court of the city of New York and the district courts of the city of New York shall have jurisdiction where the value of the property claimed does not exceed two hundred and fifty dollars. *Certain sections of the Code applied to marine and district courts.* *Exception as to value of property claimed.*

§ 18. All laws relating to the election of constables in the city of New York are hereby repealed, and hereafter the marshals of the city of New York shall be appointed by the mayor of the city of New York, by and with the advice and consent of the board of supervisors of the county of New York, and such marshals shall not exceed thirty ; and such marshals so appointed shall hold their office for the term of three years. *Laws relating to election of constables repealed, and marshals to be appointed.*

§ 19 The clerks of the district courts in the city of New York shall hereafter be appointed by the board of supervisors of the county of New York. *Clerks to be appointed.*

§ 20. Section thirteen, subdivision one of an act to reduce the several acts relating to the district courts into one act, passed April thirteenth, eighteen hundred and fifty-seven, shall read as follows:

Where the defendants or either of several defendants is not a resident of the city, the summons shall be re- *Return day of summons* turnable in not less than two nor more than four days from its date. Such summons. shall be served at least two days before the day for appearance mentioned therein. (When the plaintiff or either of several plaintiffs is not a resident of the city, the summons may be returnable as above provided, and if so returnable, it shall be governed by the above rule of service.)

§ 21. Section twenty-three of the same act is hereby amended so as to read as follows:

When undertaking to be filed. When the plaintiff does not reside in the city of New York and has no place of business or of stated employment therein, or when the above is true of all the plaintiffs, before the issuing of the short summons as provided in subdivision one of section thirteen of this act, there shall be filed with the clerk of the court a written undertaking, executed by one or more sureties, to the effect that if the defendant recover judgment such surety or sureties will pay all costs and extra costs that may be awarded to defendant, not exceeding one hundred dollars; if the defendant shall recover judgment in such case and the execution thereon be returned unsatisfied, in whole or in part, the clerk shall deliver to the defendant such undertaking to be prosecuted according to law.

§ 22. Section four of the same act is hereby amended by adding thereto the following subdivision:

Where action may be brought. 3. By plaintiffs not residing in the city and county of New York, in the district in which the defendant or one of the defendants reside, and against a defendant or defendants not residing in said city and county, in the district in which the plaintiff or one of the plaintiffs resides; but where all the parties reside out of said city and county the action may be brought in any district.

§ 23. No person who shall have a place of business in the city of New York shall be deemed to be a non-resident under the provisions of this act.

Chap. 485.

AN ACT to amend section thirty-six, of title first, chapter fifth, part third of the Revised Statutes.

Passed May 10, 1862; three-fifths being present.

The People of the State of New York, represented in Senate and Assembly, do enact as follows:

SECTION 1. Section thirty-six, of title first, chapter fifth, of part third of the Revised Statutes is hereby amended so as to read as follows:

§ 36. Every judgment in the action of ejectment rendered upon a verdict of a jury, or a report of a referee upon the facts, or upon a decision of a single judge upon the facts, shall be conclusive as to the title established in such action, upon the party against whom the same is rendered, and against all persons claiming from, through or under such party, by title accruing after the commencement of such action, subject to the exceptions hereinafter contained.

§ 2. Chapter two hundred and twenty-one of the Laws of eighteen and sixty-one is hereby repealed.

§ 3. This act shall take effect immediately.

Chap. 486.

AN ACT to amend an act to provide for the rebuilding the locks on the Oneida Lake canal.

Passed May 21, 1862; three-fifths being present.

The People of the State of New York, represented in Senate and Assembly, do enact as follows:

SECTION 1. The first section of an act entitled "An act to provide for the rebuilding of the locks on the Oneida Lake canal," passed March first, eighteen hundred and sixty, is hereby amended by striking out the words following, to-wit: "and defray the expense thereof out of any moneys in their hands not otherwise appropriated," and insert in lieu thereof the following, to-wit: "and for the purpose of ascertaining the increase of expense beyond the cost of reconstructing the locks on the old plan, the Canal Commissioners shall cause accurate estimates to be made of the cost of rebuilding the locks of the present dimensions, and also the cost of constructing the enlarged locks, and such addition shall be paid by the Treasurer, on the warrant of the Comptroller, out of any unappropriated moneys belonging to the General Fund, but said locks are not to be rebuilt so long as ordinary repairs above high water mark in the canal will keep them in good navigable condition.

§ 2. To pay the difference in the cost of rebuilding the locks on this canal, of wood, of enlarged dimensions, over the cost of rebuilding them of the same material of the present dimensions, the sum of twenty-five thousand dollars is hereby appropriated from the General Fund, or so much thereof as may be necessary for that purpose. But said moneys are not to be paid out therefor so long as the present locks may be kept in repair, as provided in the first section.

§ 3. This act shall take effect immediately.

Chap. 487.

AN ACT defining and regulating the powers duties and compensation of the captain of the port and harbor masters of the port of New York.

Passed May 22, 1862; three-fifths being present.

The People of the State of New York, represented in Senate and Assembly, do enact as follows:

SECTION 1. The Governor shall appoint by and with the consent of the Senate, an officer to be called captain of the port of New York, and to assist him, subordinate to his directions, eleven harbor masters. All of said harbor masters shall reside, after their appointment and

(margin note: Captain of port and harbor masters to be appointed.)

during their term of office in the city of New York or
in the city of Brooklyn. Said captain of the port or
any of the harbor masters shall not be directly or indirectly interested as owners or agents in any steam
tow boat, tug boat, ship, vessel, canal boat, barge or
lighter, navigating the port of New York. Said harbor Term of
masters shall hold their office two years, and said captain office.
of the port shall hold his office three years, and until
others are appointed, unless sooner removed for cause.
Before entering on his duties, said captain of the port
shall execute a bond to the people of this state in the Bond.
penal sum of ten thousand dollars, with at least two
sufficient sureties, to be approved by a justice of the
supreme court, conditioned for the faithful performance
of the duties of his office, and the proper application of
all fees and moneys that may come into his hands as such
officer; and each of said harbor masters shall execute a
like bond in the penal sum of two thousand five hundred
dollars, conditioned for the faithful performance of the
duties of his office, said bonds shall be filed in the office
of the clerk of the county of New York.

§ 2. It shall be the duty of and the captain of the Port to be
port shall have power to divide the port of New York divided into
into eleven districts, specifying the limits and boundaries 11 districts.
thereof, and he may, whenever the exigencies of business
demand, re-district the said port, or alter any such districts. To each of such districts he shall have power
to assign a harbor master to perform the duties thereof,
(and may change such harbor master from one district
to another,) or put two or more districts under the care
of one harbor master, as the exigencies of business may
require.

§ 3. The said captain of the port shall set apart, keep, Duties of
and reserve all that part of the water adjacent to the captain of
wharves of the city of New York, from the east side of port.
pier number two to and including the east side of pier
number nine East river, from the twentieth day of March
to the first day of January in each year, for the exclusive use and accommodation of canal boats and barges,
engaged in the business of transporting property on the
Hudson river or coming to tide water from the canals
of the state, or arriving in said port from Albany or any
place north or west thereof, and he shall assign such
other accommodations for said canal boats and barges

in other parts of the port of New York as may from time to time be necessary in receiving or discharging their cargoes.

Regulations as to the port. § 4. No vessel, other than canal boats, barges, or lighters receiving or delivering property from or to said canal boats or barges, shall use or enter into for the purpose of using any part of the port of New York set apart for the use of canal boats and barges, without the written consent of the captain of the port first had and obtained therefor, and then only between the first day of January and twentieth day of March in each year, and when not occupied by canal boats, under a penalty of one hundred dollars for every day that such vessel shall remain in said part of said port so set apart, after being notified to leave by the captain of the port or a harbor master, and said penalty shall be a lien upon any such vessel, and be enforced by proceedings against, instituted by and in the name of the captain of said port according to the provisions of the laws of this state concerning attachments against vessels.

Captain of port to receive fees for services of harbor masters. § 5. It shall be the duty of the captain of said port to collect and receive all fees hereafter provided for the services of harbor masters, and on the first Monday of each month to make out an account and duly verify the same on oath, of all moneys which have become due for fees, and have been collected and uncollected, and such account shall be open to the inspection of said harbor masters at all times, and the money received shall be divided equally between each of said harbor masters and himself, share and share alike, after deducting such office and legal expenses as may have been necessarily expended in the discharge of his duties as captain of **Proviso.** the port; provided, however, that such office and legal expenses shall not exceed, in any one month, the sum of one hundred and fifty dollars.

Fees. § 6. The following fees shall be collected under this act, and no others: All ships or vessels of the United States of more than one hundred and fifty tons burthen, except canal boats, lighters, tugs, barges, sound and river steamboats, employed on regular lines, and all ships or vessels of any foreign nation that are permitted by the by-laws of the United States to enter on the same terms as vessels of the United States, which shall enter the said port of New York, or load or unload, or make fast to any wharf therein, shall pay one and one-half of one cent per ton, to be computed from the tonnage expressed in the registers of enrollments of such ships or vessels respectively. All other foreign ships or vessels which shall arrive at and enter the said port, and load or unload, or make fast to any wharf therein, shall pay three cents per ton, to be computed on the tonnage expressed in the registers or the documents on board, except that all coastwise sloops and schooners over one hundred and fifty tons shall pay two dollars fee, and no more. And where difficulties arise between vessels of less than one hundred and fifty tons burthen, and the captain of the port or a harbor master is called upon to settle the same, the vessel, canal boat or barge in fault shall pay five dollars. Such fees shall be paid by the masters, owners or consignees of such ships or vessels at the office of the captain of the port, or to persons authorized by him to collect the same, within forty-eight hours after the arrival of such ship or vessel, and in default thereof, if the same shall have been first duly demanded, such master, owner or consignee, on whom such demand shall have been previously made, shall pay double the amount of such fees, to be sued for and recovered in the name of the captain of said port, in any court having cognizance thereof. All fees under this act shall be paid to the captain of the port, or upon his written order, and he shall have power to employ the necessary assistance in making collections thereof, at an expense of not more than five per cent upon the amount collected, which expense shall not be considered office expense.

§ 7. Each harbor master shall have power, within the *Powers of* district assigned to him, to provide and assign suitable *harbor masters.* accommodations for all ships and vessels, and regulate them in the stations they are to occupy at the wharves or in the stream, and to remove from time to time such vessels as are not employed in receiving or discharging their cargoes, to make room for such others as require to be more immediately accommodated for the purpose of receiving or discharging their cargoes, and shall have power to determine as to the fact of their being fairly and in good faith employed in receiving or discharging their cargoes, and shall have authority to determine how far and in what instance it is the duty of the master and others having charge of ships and vessels to accommodate each other in their respective situations. And if any master or any person having charge of any vessel, canal boat, barge or lighter, shall refuse or neglect to move his vessel, canal boat, barge or lighter, when ordered to do so by the captain of the port, or by a harbor master, or shall resist or forcibly oppose said officers in the discharge of their duties, such master or person so refusing, neglecting, resisting or opposing shall, for every such offence, forfeit and pay the sum of fifty dollars, to be recovered with costs of suit by and in the name of the captain of the port, before any court having cognizance thereof.

Duties of harbor masters.
§ 8. Each of said harbor masters shall remain in and perform the duties of the district or districts assigned to him by the captain of the port, and shall not absent himself from the cities of New York or Brooklyn without the written permission of the captain of the port. He shall not appoint any deputy or assistant, or delegate the powers of his office to any person or persons whatsoever. He shall not collect any fees under this act, unless authorized to do so by the captain of the port; he shall not take or receive directly or indirectly any money or valuable thing or compensation for his services, or on account of the exercise of his powers of office, except as provided by this act. Any harbor master violating any of the provisions of this section shall, upon conviction thereof in any court of record, be punished by a fine of five hundred dollars, and in addition thereto may, in the discretion of the court, be imprisoned in the county jail for a term not exceeding thirty days.

False representations prohibited.
§ 9. Any person who shall falsely represent himself to be a harbor master, or wrongfully perform the duties of harbor master, shall be deemed guilty of a misdemeanor, and, upon conviction thereof, shall be imprisoned in the county jail for a term not exceeding sixty days, and fined, in the discretion of the court, a sum not exceeding twenty-five dollars

Complaints against harbor masters
§ 10. It shall be the duty of the captain of the port to hear any complaint against any harbor master for improperly attending to or discharging the duties of his office, and his defence thereto. He shall examine into such complaint and defence, and have authority to ad-

minister oaths upon such examinations, and if, after such examinations, there shall, in his judgment, be sufficient ground therefor, he shall send said complaint, with the evidence in the matter, to the Governor of the state, within ten days from the receipt of such complaint by the captain of the port, and until the decision of the matter by the Governor, he may suspend such harbor master from the exercise of the duties of his office, and during the period of such suspension such harbor master shall not receive or be entitled to any pay, if he be adjudged guilty of the offence charged.

§ 11. If the captain of the port shall charge, or receive, or bargain to take or receive, directly or indirectly, any fees greater than those allowed by this act, or shall receive or agree to receive any money or valuable thing, or compensation whatever, as a present or gratuity for the exercise of his official judgment or discretion, or shall refuse to divide with the harbor masters the moneys received by him as aforesaid for each and every refusal, he shall be deemed guilty of a misdemeanor, and, upon conviction thereof, shall be fined five hundred dollars and imprisoned for the term of one month in the county jail. *Punishment for violation of this statute.*

§ 12. All fines and penalties collected under this act, shall be for and applied* the use of the New York hospital.

§ 13. The captain of the port shall report to the Governor of the state, under oath, the whole amount of fees received under this act, each year, to the thirty-first of December, and such report shall be made within ten days from such thirty-first of December. *Report of fees.*

§ 14. The terms of office of the present captain of the port and harbor masters shall continue during the terms for which they were appointed, unless they shall be removed for cause, according to the provisions of this act, and the present captain of the port and harbor masters shall be governed by and be subject to this act. *Terms of office of present captain of port and harbor masters.*

§ 15. It shall be the duty of the captain of the port or a harbor master whenever required by the captain, owner, or consignee of any vessel, or any person having charge of any vessel, to show a copy of this act to such captain, owner, or consignee, and no person shall be fined for a violation of this act until that has been done. *Copy of act to be shown.*

* So in the original.

Removal of captain of port and harbor masters. § 16. The Governor shall have power to remove the said captain of the port, or any of said harbor masters, from office for any malfeasance of office or wilful neglect of the duties thereof.

Repeal of certain statutes. § 17. All acts heretofore existing relating to the captain of the port, or to harbor masters of the port of New York, are hereby repealed, but nothing contained in this act shall be construed to change, alter or repeal, or in any way interfere with an act passed April fifteenth, eighteen hundred and fifty-eight, entitled "An act to regulate the use of wharves and slips in the city of New York, which shall be leased to certain steamboat lines." Nor shall steamboats, employed in river or sound navigation, or steamboats occupying their own wharves, or wharves and slips leased under said act be liable to the payment of fees under section six or any other section of this act.

§ 18. This act shall take effect immediately.

Chap. 488.

AN ACT to incorporate the New York Warehouse and Security Company.

Passed June 7th, 1862.

The People of the State of New York, represented in Senate and Assembly, do enact as follows:

SECTION 1. James Harper, Josiah Oakes, George J. Forrest, N. W. Burtis, D. B. Britton, Henry S. Wilson, James M. Post, John Butler, Jr., Benjamin P. Fairchild, Names of corporators. D. W. Lee, F. Saunders, Jr., William J. Peck, John Roach, Anthony J. McCarty, and such other persons as may hereafter be associated with them, and their successors, are hereby constituted a body corporate, under the name of the New York Warehouse and Security Company, to be located in the city of New York, and by that name shall have perpetual succession, and may sue and be sued in any court whatever, with powers and privileges as are hereinafter provided.

Capital stock. § 2. The capital stock of said company shall not exceed one million of dollars, in shares of one hundred dollars each, but when one hundred thousand dollars shall have been actually subscribed, and fifty thousand dollars paid in in cash, the said company may organize and proceed to business under this charter.

§ 3. The said company shall have power to guarranty the payment, punctual performance and collection of promissory notes, bill of exchange, contracts, bonds, accounts, claims, rents, annuities, mortgages, choses in action, evidences of debt, and certificates of property or value at such rates of interest, and upon such terms as may be established by the board of directors of said company ; such rate of interest not to exceed seven per cent per annum ; to receive upon storage, deposit or otherwise, merchandize, bullion, specie, plate, stocks, bonds, promissory notes, certificates and evidences of debt, contracts or other property, and to take the management, custody and charge of real and personal estate and property, and to advance moneys, securities and credits upon any property, real or personal, on such terms and at such rates of interest as may be established by the directors of said company, such rate of interest not to exceed seven per cent per annum. `

§ 4. The business and the corporate powers of said company shall be exercised by a board of seven directors, to be chosen as hereinafter provided, who shall elect from their number a president, five of which directors shall constitute a quorum for the transaction of business.

§ 5. James Harper, George J. Forrest, D. B. Britton and Henry S. Wilson shall be and they are hereby appointed commissioners to open books for subscription to the capital stock of said company, at such time and place as they or a majority of them shall deem proper, and for such amounts as in their judgment the business of the company may require, but for no less amount of subscription than one hundred thousand dollars, as hereinbefore provided. The said commissioners are hereby appointed members of the board of directors of said company for one year after the passage of this act, and until others shall be elected in their stead. The remaining directors for the same period shall be elected by a majority in interest of the stockholders, voting at an election to be held under the inspection of said commissioners within twenty days from the closing of the

Powers of company.

Directors.

Commissioners.

Manner of choosing directors.

subscription, called for by them, and all the directors must be stockholders in said company.

Further powers of company. § 6. It shall be lawful for said company to lease, purchase, hold and convey all such real or personal estate as may be necessary to carry on their business, as well as such real or personal estate as they may deem it necessary to acquire in the enforcement or settlement of any claim or demand arising out of their business transactions, and to sell or exchange the same for other property, as they may determine that the interests of the company require; and the said company are hereby authorized to make, execute and issue in the transaction of their business all necessary receipts, certificates and contracts, which receipts, certificates and contracts shall bear the impress or stamp of the seal of the company, and shall be signed by the president and countersigned by the secretary or treasurer thereof.

Ibid. § 7. It shall be lawful for said company to sell at public auction or private sale, as may be specified in the contract between the parties, all property of what kind soever mentioned in or affected by said contract, after two months shall have elapsed from the time of the maturity of any obligation under said contract, or immediately upon the discovery of any fraud, misrepresentation or concealment in regard to the ownership, character or any other matter relating to the property mentioned in or affected by said contract, and to reimburse themselves out of the avails of such sale for the moneys due them, with the interest, costs and charges, and to indemnify themselves for any loss they may have sustained by the non-fulfillment of said contract.

In regard to property deposited with them. § 8. It shall be the duty of said company to use all reasonable care and diligence in the keeping of all property deposited with them, but they shall not be deemed insurers thereof, or responsible for any loss or damage not specially provided for in the contract; and, in case any property deposited with the said company, upon which any advances shall have been made by them, shall, before the maturity of the contract, from any cause, decrease in value from the price originally fixed, said company may give notice to the owner of such property or his agent to perform the conditions of the contract, or make good the deficiency caused by such decrease in value, within ten days, and in default thereof, may sell and dispose of such property at public sale, and out of the proceeds thereof, may retain the amount due them under the contract, together with the costs, charges and expenses.

§ 9. The stock of said company shall be transferable only on the books of the company. Stock.

§ 10. This act shall take effect immediately.

Chap. 489.

AN ACT to enable the Harmony Fire and Marine Insurance Company to increase their capital and otherwise to amend their charter.

Passed June 7th, 1862; three-fifths being present.

The People of the State of New York, represented in Senate and Assembly, do enact as follows:

SECTION 1. The Harmony Fire and Marine Insurance Company are hereby authorized to receive subscriptions payable in cash, and to issue therefor receipts Manner of increasing bearing interest, which receipts shall set forth that they stock. are given in advance of premiums of insurance, and that the amounts for which they are issued, and every part thereof, are liable for the losses and expenses of the said company; and said receipts shall be received by the said company only in payment of premiums of insurance or on account thereof; as soon as the whole amount of said subscriptions so paid in shall reach the sum of two hundred thousand dollars, the said company may, with the written consent of three-fourths of their stockholders, call in and pay off the outstanding stock of the said company, at such valuation as may be determined on by the commissioners to be appointed as hereinafter set forth, and as soon as the said stock shall have been so paid off, the said company may carry on business on the mutual plan, under the name and style of the "Mutual Fire Insurance Company," but nothing in this act contained shall in any way affect or impair any right or liability of the said Harmony Fire and Marine Insurance Company, and they shall sue and be sued in their new corporate name.

Commis-
sioners to
appraise
stock.

§ 2. The Superintendent of the Insurance Department shall appoint three commissioners to determine the value of the said stock, who shall appraise the same with reference to the worth of the securities, and the liabilities of the company.

§ 3. The board of directors shall ascertain annually the balance of interest and profits remaining after the payment of losses and expenses, and scrip may be issued for the whole or any part thereof, to those persons to whom said company shall, within the preceding year, have issued any policy or policies which shall then have expired, in proportion to the amount of premium paid by each; such scrip may be issued in such form and for such amounts, and bear such rate of interest, and be redeemable and transferable, and be subject to be reduced to pay losses and expenses, in such manner as the by-laws of the company may determine; provided, nevertheless, that the scrip herein mentioned shall not be redeemed until it exceeds the sum of three hundred thousand dollars, and then to the extent of such excess only.

Scrip may
be issued.

Directors.

§ 4. The said company may increase the number of their directors and provide for the election in classes instead of in a body as at present, by the holders of their receipts, and by the scrip holders, in such manner and at such time as their by-laws may direct; but no person shall be qualified to hold office as such director unless he shall own scrip or receipts or both, amounting to five hundred dollars at its or their par value.

Persons not
individually
liable.

§ 5. The dealers of the said company and persons holding their certificates of profits, shall not, by reason thereof, become individually liable for the debts or engagements of the said company.

§ 6. This act shall take effect immediately.

NEW TOWNS ERECTED OR BOUNDARIES ALTERED BY THE BOARDS OF SUPERVISORS, &C.

Chap. 490.

AN ACT to alter the boundary line between the towns of Springwater and Sparta, in the county of Livingston, by the board of Supervisors of said county.

Passed November 19, 1861 ; two-thirds of all the members elected to such board voting in favor thereof.

SECTION 1. Be it enacted by the board of supervisors of the county of Livingston, that instead of the present line between the towns of Springwater and Sparta, it be altered as follows:

Beginning at the north east corner of lot number sixty-five (65) in the town of Sparta, in the county of Livingston and State of New York, at a point in the centre of the highway in the south line of the town of Conesus, and running from thence southerly on a line of lots and in the centre of the highway called the "Story road," to the north line of the town of Wayland, in the county of Steuben, thereby adding to and including within the bounds of the town of Springwater, all lands lying east of the aforesaid highway or Story road, heretofore included within the bounds of the town of Sparta ; and also adding to and including within the bounds of the town of Sparta, all lands lying west of the aforesaid highway or Story road, heretofore included within the bounds of the town of Springwater.

§ 2. The line so described hereafter to be the line between the aforesaid towns of Springwater and Sparta.

§ 3. This act shall take effect immediately.

SUPERVISORS' CLERK'S OFFICE, ⎱
     Livingston County.   ⎰ *ss*.

I, James B. Adams, clerk of the board of supervisors of said county, do hereby certify that I have compared the foregoing with the original act passed by the board of supervisors of said county, and that the same is a correct transcript therefrom, and of the whole of the said original; and I further certify that the map hereto annexed is a correct copy of the map presented to said board, with the petition and application for an alteration of said boundary line.

In witness whereof, I have hereunto set my hand this 28th day of December, 1861.

JAMES B. ADAMS, Clerk.

Chap. 491.

AN ACT to change the boundary lines between the towns of Arrietta, Long Lake, and Morehouse, in the county of Hamilton.

Passed November 15, 1861; two-thirds of all the members elected to said board voting in favor of the same

Whereas : An application has been made to this board subscribed by at least twelve freeholders of the town of Arrietta, and also subscribed by at least twelve freeholders of the town of Long Lake, and also subscribed by at least twelve freeholders of the town of Morehouse, and this board having been furnished with a map and survey of the said towns to be effected thereby showing the proposed alteration, and

Whereas, It appears by evidence furnished to this board that a notice of said intended application subscribed by at least twelve freeholders of the towns thereby effected, was duly published in the Hamilton County Sentinel of said county, at least once in each week, for six weeks successively, immediately preceding said application, and that the like notice was posted in at least five of the most public places in each of the towns thereby effected for four weeks preceding said application.

Therefore the board of supervisors of the county of Hamilton, do enact as follows :

SECTION 1. The town line between the towns of Long Lake and Morehouse in said county, is hereby altered by commencing on the county line at a point where said county line intersects the division line between township number eight, John Brown tract, and township number forty-one, Totten and Crossfield's purchase, and runs thence southerly on the division line between said John Brown tract and township number forty-one to the south-west corner of township forty-one, and the south-east corner of number eight, John Brown tract. Thence northerly on the division line of township number five, and forty-one of Totten and Crossfield's purchase until it strikes township forty of said last mentioned purchase. Thence southerly between townships five and forty until it reaches the old or former town line between the towns of Arrietta and Morehouse as the same existed previous to an act of the legislature of this state, Laws of eighteen hundred and sixty, chapter two hundred, passed April seventh, eighteen hundred and sixty, thence south to the southerly line of said township five, annexing part of township five, Totten and Crossfield's purchase, part of township number three, Moose river tract, and a part of township number eight, John Brown tract, to the town of Morehouse.

§ 2. The north line of the town of Arrietta, shall commence at a point on the easterly line of township number forty, Totten and Crossfield's purchase, where the old or former town line of Arrietta, and Morehouse intersected said township line and running thence southerly to the south-west corner of township number forty and the north-west corner of township number six, of said purchase; thence northerly on the township line between townships six and forty, until said line intersects or strikes township number thirty-five; thence southerly until it strikes the old or former town line, between the towns of Arrietta and Lake Pleasant; thence south on said former town line to the south line of said township six annexing to the town of Arrietta, parts of townships five and six of Totten and Crossfield's purchase.

§ 3. The south line of the town of Long Lake shall correspond with the north line of the towns of Arrietta and Morehouse, so far as the same is described in section one and two of this act.

§ 4. Nothing herein contained, shall in any manner affect the authority of the collectors of the towns of Arrietta, Long Lake or Morehouse, as the same have heretofore existed for the current year.

§ 5. This act shall take effect immediately.

The Chair put the question thereon, and the clerk called the roll of the members who voted as follows: to wit:—in the affirmative Messrs. Daniel Rudes, Edmund Anibal, James H. Brownell, Joseph W. Fish, G. G. Porter, Havilla Winchell, Rose Whitman

In the negative, Messrs. Asa F. Kellogg.

We, the chairman and clerk of the board of supervisors of the county of Hamilton, do hereby certify that the foregoing is a true copy of an act, passed by the said board at their annual session, held at Sageville.

November 15, 1861.

JOSEPH W. FISH, *Chairman.*

CYRUS H. BROWNELL, *Clerk of the board of supervisors.*

Chap. 492.

AN ACT to annex a part of the town of Schroon to the town of Ticonderoga, both in the county of Essex, State of New York.

Passed the 10th day of December, 1861.

Whereas: An application has been made to this board, subscribed by at least twelve freeholders of the town of Ticonderoga, and also subscribed by at least twelve freeholders of the town of Schroon, and this board having been furnished with a map and survey of the said towns to be affected thereby, showing the proposed alterations:

And whereas, It appears by evidence furnished to this board that notice of said intended application, subscribed by at least twelve freeholders of the towns thereby affected, was duly published in two of the newspapers

published in said county at least once in each week for
six successive weeks immediately preceding said application, and that the like notices were posted in at least
five of the most public places in each of said towns
thereby affected, to wit: the said towns of Ticonderoga and Schroon, for four weeks next preceding said
application; therefore,

The Board of Supervisors do enact as follows:

SECTION 1. All that part of and territory of the
said town of Schroon lying within the following described boundaries, to wit: beginning at the north
west corner of lot number fifty-two, in the Paradox
tract, which point is also the southwest corner of
the new line of the town of Crown Point (as established in the year eighteen hundred and sixty,) thence
south along the west line of said lot number (52)
fifty-two until it strikes the north line of lot number
fifty-four; thence west along the north line of said lot
fifty-four to the northwest corner of the same; thence
south along the west line of said lot number fifty-four,
the west line of lots number eight, number nine, number
twelve, number thirteen, number sixteen, number seventeen, number twenty, number twenty-one, (a lot marked
Location,) lot number twenty-six, number twenty-seven,
twenty-eight, (said last lots, from number eight to
twenty-eight, belong to the Hague tract,) to the south
line of Essex county; thence easterly along the line of
said county to the present southeast corner of Schroon
and southwest corner of Ticonderoga; thence northerly
along the present west line of Ticonderoga until it intersects the west line of the town of Crown Point, being at the southeast corner of lot number three in the
Paradox tract; thence westerly along the south line of
the town of Crown Point to the place of beginning, is
hereby taken from the said town of Schroon, and
annexed to the said town of Ticonderoga, and shall hereafter form and be a part of said town of Ticonderoga.

§ 2. This act shall take effect on the first day of
March, A. D., eighteen hundred and sixty-two.

§ 3. Nothing in this act shall affect the validity of any
tax or assessment imposed previous to the passage of
this act, nor the rights, powers and duties of any collector of such taxes or assessments in the said town of

125

Schroon, nor in any manner affect or impair the power or authority of any town officer of said town of Schroon within the territory hereby annexed to said town of Ticonderoga, until this act takes effect.

Given under our hands this 10th day of December, 1861.

JAMES H. PIERCE,

Chairman of the Board of Supervisors

of the county of Essex.

GEO. S. NICHOLSON, *Clerk.*

BOARD OF SUPERVISORS, } ss.
  County of Essex. }

I certify that I have compared the above with the original act passed by the board of supervisors of said county, and that the same is a correct transcript there- . of, and of the whole of said original.

GEO. S. NICHOLSON,

Clerk of the Board of

Supervisors of Essex county.

CONCURRENT RESOLUTIONS

OF THE

SENATE AND ASSEMBLY.

CONCURRENT RESOLUTION RELATIVE TO THE ABOLISHMENT OF FRANKING POWER.

Resolved (if the Senate concur), That our senators in Congress be instructed, and that our respresentatives in Congress be requested, to vote for the bill now before that body for the abolition of the franking power, believing that this system has for years been a great source of expense to the people, and an unjust and unnecessary burthen which ought not longer to be borne.

STATE OF NEW YORK, }
IN ASSEMBLY, *January* 14th, 1862. }

The foregoing resolution was duly passed.

By order of the Assembly,

J. B. CUSHMAN, *Clerk.*

STATE OF NEW YORK, }
IN SENATE, *January* 17, 1862. }

The foregoing resolution was duly passed.

By order of the Senate.

JAS. TERWILLIGER, *Clerk.*

CONCURRENT RESOLUTION REQUESTING SENATORS AND REPRESENTATIVES IN CONGRESS TO VOTE FOR MODIFICATION OF ACTS FOR PURPOSES OF REVENUE THAT EACH STATE MAY ASSUME AND PAY IN ACCORDANCE WITH ITS OWN LAWS.

Resolved (if the Assembly concur), That our senators and representatives in Congress be requested to procure, if possible, such a modification of the acts already passed, and such provisions in acts hereafter to be passed for the purpose of raising revenue, as that the entire amount to be raised in any state, by any mode of taxation, except by duties upon imports, may be ascertained by some reasonable method of estimating the same, and that each state be allowed to assume the payment of such amount, and to assess and collect the same in accordance with its own laws and through its own officers.

STATE OF NEW YORK,
IN SENATE, *January* 23, 1862.

The foregoing resolution was duly passed.

By order of the Senate,

JAS. TERWILLIGER, *Clerk.*

STATE OF NEW YORK,
IN ASSEMBLY, *January* 25, 1862.

Resolved, that the Assembly concur in the foregoing.

By order of the Assembly.

J. B. CUSHMAN, *Clerk.*

CONCURRENT RESOLUTION DIRECTING THE GOVERNOR TO NOTIFY THE SECRETARY OF THE UNITED STATES TREASURY THAT THIS STATE WILL ASSUME AND PAY ITS QUOTA OF THE TAX LEVIED BY CONGRESS, AUGUST FIFTH, EIGHTEEN HUNDRED AND SIXTY-ONE.

Whereas, By the act of Congress entitled "An act to provide for increased revenue from imports, to pay interest on the public debt, and for other purposes, passed August fifth, eighteen hundred and sixty-one," a direct tax of twenty millions of dollars is annually to be levied upon the taxable property of the United States;

And, whereas, Said act provides a mode of commutation by which any state, upon giving notice through its proper officer to the Secretary of the Treasury of the United States, on or before the second Tuesday of February in each year, of its intention to assume and pay, or to assess, collect and pay into the Treasury of the United States the direct tax imposed by said act, may in its own way and through its own officers, assess and collect the same, and any state assuming to assess, collect and pay, shall be entitled to a deduction of fifteen per cent on the quota of direct tax apportioned to such state; provided said tax be so paid on or before the last day of June, or of ten per cent if paid before the last day of September;

And, whereas, The quota of said direct tax to be assessed, collected and paid by the State of New York is two million six hundred three thousand nine hundred and eighteen dollars, which if assumed as above provided, would reduce the sum three hundred and ninety thousand five hundred and eighty-six dollars, leaving the sum of two million two hundred thirteen thousand three hundred and thirty-two dollars to be paid by said state; therefore,

Resolved (If the Assembly concur), That his excellency the Governor of the State of New York be, and is hereby authorized to forthwith notify the Secretary of the Treasury of the United States, that this state will assume and pay its quota of said direct tax on or before the last day of June next.

STATE OF NEW YORK, }
IN SENATE, *January* 17, 1862. }

The foregoing preamble and resolution were duly passed.

By order of the Senate,
JAS. TERWILLIGER, *Clerk.*

STATE OF NEW YORK, }
IN ASSEMBLY, *January* 25, 1862. }

Resolved, That the Assembly concur in the foregoing.

By order of the Assembly,
J. B. CUSHMAN, *Clerk.*

CONCURRENT RESOLUTIONS RELATIVE TO THE RECENT VICTORIES ACHIEVED BY THE NATIONAL ARMY AND NAVY.

Resolved (If the Senate concur) That we hail the news of the recent victories of the national arms at Fort Henry, Roanoke Island, Fort Donelson and Savannah and other points along the lines of the Grand Army of the Union, with lively emotions of patriotic rejoicing, and hereby express the heartfelt thanks of a grateful state to the brave officers and soldiers who have covered themselves with glory by their heroic achievements, and to the War Department for the renewed evidence of vigor displayed in the conduct of the war, and pledge to the government of the United States the undivided support of the people of the State of New York in the gigantic work of suppressing this monstrous and unnatural rebellion, and restoring the supremacy of the Constitution and laws of the Federal Government over every rood of our national territory.

Resolved, That the keepers of the capitol and state house be instructed to illuminate these buildings tonight in honor of the victories gained by our Army and Navy.

STATE OF NEW YORK,
IN ASSEMBLY, *February 17th*, 1862.

The foregoing resolution was duly passed.

By order of the Assembly,

J. B. CUSHMAN, *Clerk.*

STATE OF NEW YORK,
IN SENATE, *February 17*, 1862.

The foregoing resolution was duly passed.

By order of the Senate,

JAS. TERWILLIGER, *Clerk.*

RESOLUTION FROM THE CANAL BOARD, IN RELATION TO THE REDUCTION OF TOLLS ON CERTAIN ARTICLES NAMED THEREIN.

Resolved, (if the legislature concur,) That the rates of toll on buffalo, moose and deer skins be reduced from five mills a thousand pounds a mile to three mills ; that the rates of toll on furs and skins of animals producing furs be reduced from one cent a thousand pounds a mile to three mills ; that the rate of toll on mahogany, except veneering reduced to inch measure, be reduced from one cent and five mills per thousand feet a mile to five mills and six-tenths of a mill ; that the rates of toll on furniture for stoves, not cast iron, and on stove pipe, be reduced from six mills a thousand pounds a mile to three mills ; that the rate of toll on foreign salt be reduced from five mills a thousand pounds a mile to two and a half mills, and that the rate of toll on gypsum, foreign and the product of other states, be reduced from three mills a thousand pounds a mile to two mills.

STATE OF NEW YORK, }
IN SENATE, *March* 19, 1862. }

The foregoing resolution was duly passed:

By order of the Senate.

JAS. TERWILLIGER, *Clerk.*

STATE OF NEW YORK, }
IN ASSEMBLY, *March* 26, 1862. }

The foregoing resolution was duly passed.

By order of the Assembly.

J. B. CUSHMAN, *Clerk.*

RESOLUTION FROM THE CANAL BOARD, IN RELATION TO THE REDUCTION OF TOLLS ON CERTAIN ARTICLES NAMED THEREIN.

Resolved, That if the honorable legislature concur, the rates of toll on the following named articles per thousand pounds per mile be reduced as follows : On cabinet ware and chairs, from four to three mills ; on carts, carriages, wagons, sleighs, drill barrows, fanning mills, plows, harrows, mowing, reaping and thrashing machines, looking glasses, willow ware, mattrasses, piano fortes, and tile for roofing, from four to two mills.

STATE OF NEW YORK,   }
In ASSEMBLY, *March* 26, 1862. }

The foregoing resolution was duly passed.

By order of the Assembly.

J. B. CUSHMAN, *Clerk.*

STATE OF NEW YORK,   }
In SENATE, *March* 28, 1862. }

The foregoing resolution was duly passed.

By order of the Senate.

JAS. TERWILLIGER, *Clerk.*

CONCURRENT RESOLUTION RELATIVE TO PRINTING THE TRANSACTIONS OF THE STATE AGRICULTURAL SOCIETY.

Reso'ved, (if the Senate concur,) That one thousand copies of the transactions of the agricultural society, be printed for the State Agricultural Society ; twenty-five copies for each member and officer of the legislature ; fifteen copies for each reporter of the legislature ; twenty copies for each county agricultural society in counties electing one member of Assembly, and a proportionate additional number in counties electing more than one member of Assembly ; ten copies for each town agricultural society ; fifteen copies for each union agricultural society, and fifty copies for the Regents of the University ; and that said report be printed and bound in the same manner as last year, and be distributed in accordance with the foregoing resolution without delay.

STATE OF NEW YORK,
IN ASSEMBLY, *April* 5, 1862.

The foregoing resolution was duly passed.

By order of the Assembly.
J. B. CUSHMAN, *Clerk.*

STATE OF NEW YORK,
IN SENATE, *April* 15, 1862.

The foregoing resolution was duly concurred in.

By order of the Senate.
JAS. TERWILLIGER, *Clerk.*

CONCURRENT RESOLUTION RELATIVE TO THE STATE DAM AT PHŒNIX, AND THE STATE DAM ACROSS THE SENECA RIVER AT WATERLOO.

Resolved, (if the Senate concur,) That the Canal Board be requested so to regulate and maintain the heighth of the state dam at Phœnix, so as to cause the depth of water in the canal to be seven feet and no more, and that no repairs shall be made or flush boards used on said dam, which shall raise the water in said canals above the heighth of seven feet, and to prescribe penalties and the manner of enforcing the same against persons violating such regulation, the same penalties and manner of enforcing the same, shall apply to the state dam across the Seneca river at Waterloo.

STATE OF NEW YORK,
IN ASSEMBLY, *March* 31, 1862.

The foregoing resolution was duly passed.

By order of the Assembly.
J. B. CUSHMAN, *Clerk.*

STATE OF NEW YORK,
IN SENATE, *April* 18, 1862.

The foregoing resolution was duly passed.

By order of the Senate.
JAS. TERWILLIGER, *Clerk.*

126

CONCURRENT RESOLUTION RELATIVE TO THE SURVEY OF THE ALLEGANY RIVER.

Resolved, (if the Senate concur,) That the State Engineer and Surveyor, be and he is hereby directed to make an examination and survey of the Allegany river from the termination of, and junction with the said river and the Genesee Valley canal, to the mouth of the Great Valley creek, past and near the crossing of the Buffalo and Bradford railroad, and to report to the next legislature the practibility of making slack water navigation, on said river between the two points named, and the probable cost of the same.

STATE OF NEW YORK, }
IN ASSEMBLY, *April* 19, 1862. }

The foregoing resolution was duly passed.

By order of the Assembly,

J. B CUSHMAN, *Clerk.*

STATE OF NEW YORK, }
IN SENATE *April* 22, 1862. }

The foregoing resolution was duly passed.

By order of the Senate,

JAS. TERWILLIGAR, *Clerk.*

CONCURRENT RESOLUTION RELATIVE TO PRINTING THE TRANSACTIONS OF THE AMERICAN INSTITUTE.

Resolved, (if the Senate concur,) That there be printed of the Transactions of the American Institute, for the year eighteen sixty-one, twenty-five copies for each member, officer and reporter of the legislature ; seven hundred and fifty copies for said Institute ; twenty copies for each county agricultural society, in counties electing one member of Assembly, and a proportionate number in counties electing more than one member of Assembly ; ten copies for each town agricultural society, and fifty copies for the Regents of the University for exchange ; and that they be printed and bound in the same manner as last year, in accordance with the foregoing resolution immediately.

STATE OF NEW YORK, }
IN ASSEMBLY *April* 5, 1862 }

The foregoing resolution was duly passed.

By order of Assembly,
J. B. CUSHMAN, *Clerk,*

STATE OF NEW YORK, }
IN SENATE *April* 22d, 1862 }

The foregoing resolution was duly passed.

By order of the Senate,
JAS. TERWILLIGER, *Clerk.*

CONCURRENT RESOLUTION DIRECTING THE GOVERNOR TO TRANSMIT A COPY OF THE BILL ENTITLED "AN ACT TO ADAPT THE CANALS OF THIS STATE TO THE DEFENCE OF THE NORTHERN AND NORTH WESTERN LAKES." TO THE PRESIDENT OF THE UNITED STATES.

Resolved, (if the Assembly concur,) That his Excellency the Governor be and hereby is requested to transmit to the President of the United States, a copy of the act passed by the present legislature, entitled "An act to adapt the canals of this state to the defence of the Northern and North-Western lakes," and to take such measures as he may find necessary and proper for inviting the attention of the general government, to the measures therein proposed, and their great importance to the national interest.

STATE OF NEW YORK, }
IN SENATE *April* 22, 1862. }

The foregoing resolution was duly passed.

By order of the Senate.
JAS. TERWILLIGER, *Clerk.*

STATE OF NEW YORK, }
IN ASSEMBLY *April* 22, 1862. }

The foregoing resolution was duly passed.

By order of the Assembly,
J. B. CUSHMAN, *Clerk.*

NAMES CHANGED

UNDER AND IN PURSUANCE OF CHAPTER 80, OF THE LAWS OF 1860.

———•◆•———

NEW YORK COMMON PLEAS.

CLERK'S OFFICE, No. 13 CITY HALL, }
New York, Dec. 31, 1861. }

Pursuant to chapter eighty of the Laws of the State of New York, passed March 17, 1860, I hereby report that the names of the following persons have been changed by the Court of Common Pleas for the city and county of New York, viz:

James Ward to James W. Hamblet.

            Order entered March 11, 1861.

James Ferguson to James Robert Ferguson.

            Order entered April 24, 1861.

Thaddeus V. Shemanski to Thaddeus Victor Taber.

            Order entered 23d Nov., 1861.

NATH'L JARVIS, JR.,
Clerk of the Court of Common Pleas
for the city and county of New York.

KINGS COUNTY, CLERK'S OFFICE, }
Dec. 31, 1861. }

I, Charles W. Thomas, clerk of the county of Kings, do hereby certify that the following changes of names have been made by the county court of this county during the year 1861, to-wit:

ORIGINAL NAME.	NAME AS CHANGED.
Theodore Honeywell McCoy.	Theodore Honeywell.
Annie Matilda McCoy.	Annie Matilda Honeywell.
Elizabeth Ann McCoy.	Elizabeth Ann Honeywell.
Mayo Vale Smith.	Sidney Vale Lowell.

The names of the following persons were changed by the county court during the year 1860, but were omitted to be returned :

ORIGINAL NAME.	NAME AS CHANGED.
William Lee Solomon.	William Lee.
Catharine Solomon.	Catharine Lee.
Emma Louisa Solomon.	Emma Louisa Lee.
John F. Solomon, Jr.	John Francis Lee, Junior.
Charles Edwin Solomon.	Charles Edwin Lee.
Kate Henrietta Solomon.	Kate Henritta Lee.
Henry Alpheus Solomon.	Henry Alpheus Lee.
John F. Solomon.	John Francis Lee.
Sarah Gertrude Solomon.	Sarah Gertrude Lee.
Sarah Elizabeth Solomon.	Sarah Elizabeth Lee.

(L. S.)   .

C. W. THOMAS,
Clerk, Kings Co.

INDEX.

Arbitrators, Appointment of.

Arms—Armories.

Arnold, Augusta Theresa, and Mary Ulrich.

Arrietta, Long Lake, and Morehouse.

129

Claims.

Clapp, Benjamin B.

131

Cortland County.

County Clerks.

County Judge.

Courts.

Court of Appeals.

Courts Martial.

Crawford, Francis.

Criminal Laws.

Crooked Lake.

134

PAGE.

Kings county.

Kingston.

Kitchen, George H.

Knickerbocker Fire Engine Company.

Knickerbocker Life Insurance Company.

Krutina, Frederick.

Labels.

Lands.

Landlord and Tenant.

Lake Navigation Companies.

Laneheart, John S.

Larceny.

Laville, Catharine.

Law Library, Binghamton.

Law Reports.

Nanuet Fire Engine Company.

Narrows, Obstructions Across.

Navigation Companies, on Lakes and Rivers.

Niagara County.

Niagara Falls, Village of.

Niagara River.

Nesbit, Geo. F.

Neversink River Plank Road Company.

State Officers.

State Printing.

State Prisons.

State Reporter.

139

Town Insurance Companies.

Trade Marks.

Tracy, Michael.

Treasurer.

Treasurer and other State officers.

Treasurers, County.

Lightning Source UK Ltd.
Milton Keynes UK
UKHW021146051118
331794UK00009B/449/P